Lecture Notes in Artificial Intelligence   8764

Subseries of Lecture Notes in Computer Science

LNAI Series Editors

Randy Goebel
  University of Alberta, Edmonton, Canada
Yuzuru Tanaka
  Hokkaido University, Sapporo, Japan
Wolfgang Wahlster
  DFKI and Saarland University, Saarbrücken, Germany

LNAI Founding Series Editor

Joerg Siekmann
  DFKI and Saarland University, Saarbrücken, Germany

Fabio Cuzzolin (Ed.)

Belief Functions: Theory and Applications

Third International Conference, BELIEF 2014
Oxford, UK, September 26-28, 2014
Proceedings

 Springer

Volume Editor

Fabio Cuzzolin
Oxford Brookes University
Department of Computing and Communication Technologies
Wheatley Campus
Oxford OX33 1HX, UK
E-mail: fabio.cuzzolin@brookes.ac.uk

ISSN 0302-9743   e-ISSN 1611-3349
ISBN 978-3-319-11190-2   e-ISBN 978-3-319-11191-9
DOI 10.1007/978-3-319-11191-9
Springer Cham Heidelberg New York Dordrecht London

Library of Congress Control Number: 2014948940

LNCS Sublibrary: SL 7 – Artificial Intelligence

© Springer International Publishing Switzerland 2014

Typesetting: Camera-ready by author, data conversion by Scientific Publishing Services, Chennai, India

Printed on acid-free paper

Springer is part of Springer Science+Business Media (www.springer.com)

Preface

The theory of belief functions, also referred to as evidence theory or Dempster–Shafer theory, is a well-established general framework for reasoning with uncertainty, with well-understood connections to other frameworks such as probability, possibility, and imprecise probability theories. First introduced by Arthur P. Dempster in the context of statistical inference, the theory was later developed by Glenn Shafer into a general framework for modelling epistemic uncertainty. These early contributions have been the starting points of many important developments, including the transferable belief model and the theory of hints.

The series of biennial BELIEF conferences is dedicated to the confrontation of ideas, the reporting of recent achievements, and the presentation of the wide range of applications of this theory. This conference series started in Brest, France, in 2010, while the second edition was held in Compiègne, France, in May 2012. The conference series is organized by the Belief Functions and Applications Society (BFAS).

The Third International Conference on Belief Functions, BELIEF 2014, was held during September 26–28 at St. Hugh's College, Oxford, UK. Oxford is a world-famous university city, home of two major universities, Oxford University and the younger but very active Brookes University. It is conveniently located 60 miles north-west of London, and enjoys direct coach links with all major London airports such as Heathrow, Gatwick, Luton, and Stansted.

The aim of the conference was to provide opportunities to exchange ideas and present new results on the theory of belief functions and related areas such as random sets, imprecise probability, and possibility theory. Original contributions were solicited on theoretical aspects (including mathematical foundations, decision making, combination rules, continuous belief functions, independence and graphical models, statistical estimation, etc.), as well as on applications to all areas of computer science, business, and engineering, including data fusion, pattern recognition and machine learning, tracking, data mining, signal and image processing, computer vision, medical diagnosis, business decision, risk analysis, climatic change, and many others.

Authors of selected papers from the BELIEF 2014 conference were invited to submit extended versions of their papers for inclusion in a dedicated special issue of Elsevier's *International Journal of Approximate Reasoning*. We received 56 submissions, of which 47 were accepted (83%). This edited volume is a collection of all the accepted papers in their final, camera-ready form. There were two invited talks by major researchers in AI. Nando de Freitas, Professor of Computer Science at Oxford University, gave a talk on the challenges facing the wider field of AI in the near future. Thomas Lukasiewicz, also Professor of Computer Science at Oxford University, spoke about "Uncertainty in the Semantic Web," outlining how uncertainty is dealt with in semantic web applications, and illustrating in more detail some of his most recent published work.

The Program Committee (PC) consisted of 45 academics with diverse research interests and expertise, ranging from experts in the theory and application of belief functions to scientists active in imprecise probabilities and random sets, mainstream statisticians, computer scientists, and engineers. Papers were reviewed in blind mode, with each paper assigned to at least three reviewers, sometimes four or five. While 35 papers were accepted after the first round of reviews (62%), 14 others underwent a rebuttal stage in which authors were asked to revise their paper in accordance to the reviews, and prepare an extensive response addressing the reviewers' concerns. The final decision was made by the program chair, sometimes with the assistance of the reviewers. As a result, 12 additional papers were accepted for publication in the proceedings, and the quality of the manuscripts saw a significant improvement.

We ensured that all papers received a fair and objective evaluation by experts, with particular attention paid to highlighting strengths and weaknesses of papers. The 162 submitted reviews were, on average, of a high-quality standard when compared with other well-established international conferences, providing a detailed list of suggestions and criticisms that in the end contributed greatly to the quality of the material published in this volume. The rebuttal stage, introduced for the first time in this edition of BELIEF, was a clear success and we recommend its adoption for the future editions of the conference as well.

For the first time we introduced a best paper and a best student paper award, to give recognition to the authors of substantial contributions to the theory of belief functions. We hope this will be a long-standing practice. We had a discussion panel on the status and future of the theory of belief functions, which we believe helped bring our community together and set clear targets for its future development and further growth.

The Third International Conference on Belief Functions enjoyed the support of several sponsors, including Onera - The French Aerospace Lab - and Oxford Brookes University, Faculty of Technology, Design and Environment. Elsevier - "the leading provider of science information" - provided a 1,000-euro prize to go to the authors of the best paper, selected by the BFAS board of directors from a shortlist based on the reviewers' scores. ISIF, International Society of Information Fusion, was the main contributor and asked to fund a best student paper award, whose lead author received a free student registration for the FUSION 2015 international conference. We would like to thank Onera's Alain Appriou, ISIF's Anne-Laure Jousselme, Oxford Brookes' Ray Ogden, and Thierry Denœux, Editor-in-Chief of IJAR, for their assistance in securing these sponsorships.

We would like to sincerely thank authors of all submissions – those whose papers made it into the program and those whose papers did not. We, and the PC as a whole, were impressed by the quality of submissions contributed from all around the world, from the USA to France, Tunisia, China, and Thailand, among others.

We would like to extend our sincere gratitude to the PC. We were very fortunate that so many talented people put such an inordinate amount of time to write reviews and actively participate in discussions for nearly three weeks. They quickly responded to our requests for extra reviews, opinions, comments, comparisons, and inputs. We also would like to thank the external reviewers, some contacted by us directly and some through PC members, who significantly contributed to the comprehensive evaluation of papers. A list of PC members and external reviewers appears after this note.

Finally, we would like to thank Arnaud Martin for his help with managing registration and accounts, HG3 in the person of Nicola Peel for their help with providing accommodation at discounted rates in a difficult area like Oxford's, Anne-Laure Jousselme for her valuable help in building a mailing list of authors of belief functions papers, and Alfred Hofmann, Anna Kramer, and their colleagues at Springer for providing a meticulous service for the timely production of this volume.

July 2014   Fabio Cuzzolin

BELIEF 2014

Third International Conference on Belief Functions

Oxford, UK

September 26–28, 2014

General Chair

Fabio Cuzzolin   Oxford Brookes University, UK

Honorary Chairs

Arthur P. Dempster   Harvard University, USA
Glenn Shafer   Rutgers University, USA

Program Committee

Alessandro Antonucci   IDSIA, Switzerland
Alain Appriou   Onera, France
Boutheina Ben Yaghlane   IHEC Carthage, Tunisia
Malcolm Beynon   Cardiff Business School, UK
Yaxin Bi   University of Ulster, UK
Isabelle Bloch   ENST - CNRS, France
Mohamed Boudaren   Ecole Militaire Polytechnique, Algeria
Thomas Burger   CNRS, France
Veronique Cherfaoui   UTC – CNRS, France
Olivier Colot   Université Lille 1, France
Frank Coolen   Durham University, UK
Milan Daniel   Institute of Computer Science, Czech Republic
Yong Deng   Southwest University, China
Thierry Denoeux   Université de Technologie de Compiègne,
                                   France
Sebastien Destercke   Université de Technologie de Compiègne,
                                   France
Jean Dezert   Onera, France
Didier Dubois   IRIT/RPDMP, France
Zied Elouedi   LARODEC, ISG de Tunis, Tunisia
Scott Ferson   RAMAS, USA
Michel Grabisch   Université Paris 1, France
Van Nam Huyn   JAIST, Japan

Sponsors

Silver Sponsors

International Society of Information Fusion

Oxford Brookes University – Faculty of
Technology, Design and the Environment

Bronze sponsors

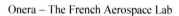

Onera – The French Aerospace Lab

Elsevier – the leading provider of science and
health information

Table of Contents

Applications 1

Theory 1

Applications 2

Networks

Theory 2

Information Fusion

Data Association

Geometry

α-Junctions of Categorical Mass Functions

John Klein, Mehena Loudahi, Jean-Marc Vannobel, and Olivier Colot

Lille1 University, LAGIS UMR CNRS 8219,
avenue Carl Gauss, cité scientifique, 59650 Villeneuve d'Ascq, France
{john.klein,mehena.loudahi,jean-marc.vannobel,
olivier.colot}@univ-lille1.fr
http://www.lagis.cnrs.fr

Abstract. The set of α-junctions is the set of linear associative and commutative combination operators for belief functions. Consequently, the properties of α-junctive rules make them particularly attractive on a theoretic point of view. However, they are rarely used in practice except for the α = 1 case which corresponds to the widely used and well understood conjunctive and disjunctive rules. The lack of success of α-junctions when α < 1 is mainly explained by two reasons. First, they require a greater computation load due to a more complex mathematical definition. Second, the mass function obtained after combination is hard to interpret and sometimes counter-intuitive. Pichon and Denœux [4] brought a significant contribution to circumvent both of these two limitations. In this article, it is intended to pursue these efforts toward a better understanding of α-junctions. To that end, this study is focused on the behavior of α-junctions when categorical mass functions are used as entries of an α-junctive combination rule. It is shown that there exists a conjunctive and a disjunctive canonical decomposition of the mass function obtained after combination.

Keywords: evidence theory, Dempster-Shafer theory, combination rules, α-junctions, categorical mass functions.

1 Introduction

The belief function theory (BFT) is an appealing framework for reasoning under uncertainty when imperfect data need to be aggregated through an information fusion process. Indeed, imprecise and uncertain pieces of evidence can be efficiently represented and aggregated as part of the BFT. Combination rules are well-defined mathematical operators designed for such a purpose.

In [9], Smets introduced a family of combination rules known as α-junctions. This family is the union of two sub-families: the α-conjunctive rules and the α-disjunctive rules. These rules possess interesting properties, each of them being clearly justified in an information fusion context. When the parameter α is set to 1, two classical rules are retrieved: the conjunctive and disjunctive rules. However, for other values of α, performing the combination requires an increased computation time and the results are sometimes hard to interpret.

F. Cuzzolin (Ed.): BELIEF 2014, LNAI 8764, pp. 1–10, 2014.

Pichon and Denœux [4] alleviated these drawbacks. First, they explained that combination results are far better understood if α is viewed as a parameter related to the truthfulness of information sources. In addition, they provided means to fasten α-junction computations.

Besides, it is known that the BFT restricted to categorical mass functions equipped with the conjunctive and disjunctive rules boils down to Cantor's set theory. In this article, it is intended to analyze the same matter when the conjunctive and disjunctive rules are replaced with α-junctions for a given $\alpha < 1$. Pichon already briefly discussed this matter in [6]. Some additional results or analyses are given for the direct computation of combined categorical mass functions as well as for other set-functions representing combined evidence (commonality, implicability, conjunctive and disjunctive weight functions). In addition, a conjunctive and a disjunctive canonical decomposition of these mass functions are also introduced. In section 2 some mathematical notations are given and some definitions are re-called. Section 3 and 4 present the obtained results for α-conjunctive and α-disjunctive rules respectively. Section 5 concludes the paper.

2   Belief Function Framework: Notations and Definitions

In this section, mathematical notations for classical belief function concepts are given. The reader is expected to be familiar with belief function basics and consequently some definitions are not recalled. More material on belief functions basics is found for instance in [1]. A greater stress is given to a reminder on α-junctions.

2.1   Belief Function Basics

Suppose one has collected several bodies of evidence $\{Ev_i\}_{i=1}^{M}$. For a given body of evidence Ev_i, the corresponding **mass function** representing this piece of evidence is denoted by m_i. Mass functions are set-functions with respect to a **frame of discernment** denoted by Ω. The power set 2^{Ω} is the set of all subsets of Ω and it is the domain of mass functions. For any $A \in 2^{\Omega}$, the **cardinality** of this set is denoted by $|A|$ and $|\Omega| = n$. The cardinality of 2^{Ω} is denoted by $N = 2^n$. Mass functions have $[0, 1]$ as codomain and they sum to one. A **focal element** of a mass function m_i is a set $A \subseteq \Omega$ such that $m_i(A) > 0$. A mass function having only one focal element A is called a **categorical mass** function and it is denoted by m_A.

Several alternatives for evidence representation are commonly used in the BFT. The **belief** and **commonality** functions bel_i and q_i are respectively the inverse Möbius and inverse co-Möbius transforms of the mass function m_i. The **plausibility** function pl_i is the conjugate of bel_i and the **implicability** function b_i is such that $\forall X \subseteq \Omega$, $b_i(X) = bel_i(X) + m_i(\emptyset)$. There is a one-to-one correspondence between a mass function m_i and any of these four functions.

If the reliability of the evidence encoded in a mass function can be evaluated through a coefficient $\alpha \in [0,1]$, then a so-called **discounting** operation on m can be performed. A discounted mass function is denoted by m^α and we have :

$$m^\alpha = (1 - \alpha)m + \alpha m_\Omega. \tag{1}$$

α is called the **discounting rate**. Since m_Ω represents a state of ignorance, this categorical mass function is called the **vacuous** mass function. Consequently, setting $\alpha = 1$ turns a mass function into the neutral element of the conjunctive rule and its corresponding evidence is discarded from further processing.

Another useful concept is the **negation** $\overline{m}$ of a mass function m. The function $\overline{m}$ is such that $\forall A \subseteq \Omega,\ \overline{m}(A) = m(\overline{A})$ with $\overline{A} = \Omega \setminus A$.

2.2   Mass Function Combination Using α-Junctions

In this subsection, a brief presentation of α-junctions is proposed. A thorough presentation is provided in [4]. Suppose f is a combination operator for mass functions, *i.e.*, $m_{12} = f(m_1, m_2)$ with m_{12} a mass function depending only on two initial mass functions m_1 and m_2. Such an operator is an **α-junction** if it possesses the following properties [9]:

- Linearity[1]: $\forall \lambda \in [0,1]$ and for any other mass function m we have
  $f(m, \lambda m_1 + (1 - \lambda)m_2) = \lambda f(m, m_1) + (1 - \lambda) f(m, m_2)$,
- Commutativity: $f(m_1, m_2) = f(m_2, m_1)$,
- Associativity: $f(f(m_1, m_2), m_3) = f(m_1, f(m_2, m_3))$,
- Neutral element: $\exists m_e \mid \forall m,\ f(m, m_e) = m$,
- Anonymity: for any σ extending by set-union on 2^Ω a permutation on Ω,
  $f(m_1 \circ \sigma, m_2 \circ \sigma) = m_{12} \circ \sigma$,
- Context preservation: $pl_1(X) = 0$ and $pl_2(X) = 0 \implies pl_{12}(X) = 0$.

The justifications behind these properties are given in [9]. In the same article, Smets also proves that the neutral element can be either $m_\emptyset$ or m_Ω. Depending on this, two sub-families arise: the α-disjunctive rules denoted by $\unicode{x24CE}^\alpha$ and the α-conjunctive rules denoted by $\unicode{x24C4}^\alpha$. For the sake of clarity, the following notations will be used: $m_{1 \cup \alpha 2} = m_1 \unicode{x24CE}^\alpha m_2$ and $m_{1 \cap \alpha 2} = m_1 \unicode{x24C4}^\alpha m_2$. Pichon and Denœux [4] provided the following computation formulae: $\forall X \subseteq \Omega, \forall \alpha \in [0,1]$

$$m_{1 \cap \alpha 2}(X) = \sum_{(A \cap B) \cup (\overline{A} \cap \overline{B} \cap C) = X} m_1(A)\, m_2(B)\, \alpha^{|\overline{C}|} \overline{\alpha}^{|C|}, \tag{2}$$

$$m_{1 \cup \alpha 2}(X) = \sum_{(A \cap \overline{B}) \cup (\overline{A} \cap B) \cup (A \cap B \cap C) = X} m_1(A)\, m_2(B)\, \alpha^{|C|} \overline{\alpha}^{|\overline{C}|}, \tag{3}$$

with $\overline{\alpha} = 1 - \alpha$. Note that they also provide faster means to compute the combined mass function using matrix calculus. It is also noteworthy that, if

---

[1] The operator is linear on the vector space spanned by categorical mass functions but the output of the operator remains a mass function only in case of convex combination.

$\alpha = 1$, the classical conjunctive and disjunctive rules are retrieved. We denote these rules by $\textcircled{\cap} = \textcircled{\cap}^1$ and by $\textcircled{\cup} = \textcircled{\cup}^1$.

Concerning the interpretation of α-junctions, Pichon and Denœux [4] state that for any $\omega \in \Omega$:

- for α-conjunctions, α is understood as the belief that at least one of the sources tells the truth, given that the event $\{\omega\}$ is true,
- for α-disjunctions, α is understood as the plausibility that both sources tell the truth, given that the event $\{\omega\}$ is true.

In [6], Pichon gives further explanations and justifications of this interpretation. He shows that α-conjunctions are understood as a particular case of a combination process introduced in [7] where meta-knowledge on the truthfulness of information sources is formalized.

3 α-Conjunctive Combination of Categorical Mass Functions

In this section, several results related to the combination of categorical mass functions using an α-conjunctive rule are given. A straightforward formula for the computation of α-conjunction of categorical mass functions is evoked in [6]. We state this result in a slightly more formal way:

Proposition 1. *Let A and $B \subseteq \Omega$. $\forall X \subseteq \Omega$, one has:*

$$m_{A \cap'' B}(X) = \begin{cases} \alpha^{|\overline{A \Delta B}| - |X|} \overline{\alpha}^{|X| - |A \cap B|} & \text{if } A \cap B \subseteq X \subseteq \overline{A \Delta B} \\ 0 & \text{otherwise} \end{cases}, \qquad (4)$$

with Δ the set symmetric difference.

Proof. A sketch of proof is already given in [6]. We provide a few more details in here. Applying equation (2) with categorical mass functions gives:

$$m_{A \cap'' B}(X) = \sum_{\substack{C \subseteq \Omega \\ (A \cap B) \cup (\overline{A} \cap \overline{B} \cap C) = X}} \alpha^{|\overline{C}|} \overline{\alpha}^{|C|}$$

Observing that no subset C can satisfy $(A \cap B) \cup (\overline{A} \cap \overline{B} \cap C) = X$ unless $A \cap B \subseteq X \subseteq \overline{A \Delta B}$ accounts for the two seperate cases in equation (4) depending on the condition $A \cap B \subseteq X \subseteq \overline{A \Delta B}$.

Suppose $A \cap B \subseteq X \subseteq \overline{A \Delta B}$ is true. Let $C_1 = C \cap (A \cup B)$ and $C_2 = C \cap (\overline{A \cup B})$. Since $A \cup B$ together with $\overline{A \cup B}$ is a partition of Ω, one has $C_1 \cup C_2 = C$ and $C_1 \cap C_2 = \emptyset$. Observing that $(A \cap B) \cup (\overline{A} \cap \overline{B} \cap C) = (A \cap B) \cup C_2 = X \implies C_2 = X \setminus (A \cap B)$, we deduce that choosing C is tantamount to choosing C_1 which lives in $2^{A \cup B}$. This gives:

$$m_{A\cap^{\prime\prime}B}(X) = \sum_{C_1 \subseteq A\cup B} \alpha^{|\overline{C_1 \cup X \setminus (A\cap B)}|}\overline{\alpha}^{|C_1 \cup X \setminus (A\cap B)|}$$

$$= \alpha^{n-|X|+|A\cap B|}\overline{\alpha}^{|X|-|A\cap B|} \sum_{C_1 \subseteq A\cup B} \left(\overline{\alpha}/\alpha\right)^{|C_1|}$$

$$= \alpha^{n-|X|+|A\cap B|}\overline{\alpha}^{|X|-|A\cap B|} \left(\overline{\alpha}/\alpha + 1\right)^{|A\cup B|}$$

$$= \alpha^{|\overline{A\Delta B}|-|X|}\overline{\alpha}^{|X|-|A\cap B|}. \qquad \square$$

Figure 1 illustrates the variety of potential focal sets of mass function $m_{A\cap^{\prime\prime}B}$. First It can be noted that according to proposition 1:

$$A\cup B = \Omega \implies m_{A\cap^{\prime\prime}B} = m_{A\cap B}.$$

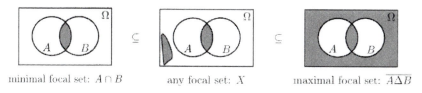

minimal focal set: $A\cap B$ any focal set: X maximal focal set: $\overline{A\Delta B}$

Fig. 1. Example of focal sets of mass function $m_{A\cap^{\prime\prime}B}$

When $A\cup B \neq \Omega$, proposition 1 also sheds light on the fact that the α-conjunction of two deterministic sets yields a random set[2] [3]. This means that some latent uncertainty has been unveiled by the combination process and that this uncertainty is not encoded in the initial mass functions. Following the interpretation of Pichon and Denœux, the uncertainty observed in $m_{A\cap^{\prime\prime}B}$ comes from the uncertainty on the truthfulness of the sources. This uncertainty is expressed on another frame of discernment Θ and $m_{A\cap^{\prime\prime}B}$ is the marginal of a broader mass function on $\Omega \times \Theta$.

Let us now introduce some results on the commonality function $q_{A\cap^{\prime\prime}B}$ and a canonical conjunctive decomposition of $m_{A\cap^{\prime\prime}B}$.

Proposition 2. *Let A and $B \subseteq \Omega$. $\forall X \subseteq \Omega$, one has:*

$$q_{A\cap^{\prime\prime}B}(X) = \begin{cases} \overline{\alpha}^{|X\setminus(A\cap B)|} & \text{if } X \subseteq \overline{A\Delta B} \\ 0 & \text{otherwise} \end{cases}. \qquad (5)$$

Proof. By definition of commonality function and using proposition 1, one has:

$$q_{A\cap^{\prime\prime}B}(X) = \sum_{\substack{Y \supseteq X \\ A\cap B \subseteq Y \subseteq \overline{A\Delta B}}} \alpha^{|\overline{A\Delta B}|-|Y|}\overline{\alpha}^{|Y|-|A\cap B|},$$

$$= \sum_{(A\cap B)\cup X \subseteq Y \subseteq \overline{A\Delta B}} \alpha^{|\overline{A\Delta B}|-|Y|}\overline{\alpha}^{|Y|-|A\cap B|}.$$

---

[2] Mass functions can also be viewed as random set distributions.

Observing that no subset Y can satisfy $(A \cap B) \cup X \subseteq Y \subseteq \overline{A \Delta B}$ unless $X \subseteq \overline{A \Delta B}$ accounts for the two separate cases in equation (5) depending on the condition $X \subseteq \overline{A \Delta B}$. Now if $X \subseteq \overline{A \Delta B}$, one has:

$$q_{A \cap^{\alpha} B}(X) = \alpha^{|\overline{A \Delta B}|} \overline{\alpha}^{-|A \cap B|} \sum_{W \subseteq \overline{A \Delta B} \setminus ((A \cap B) \cup X)} (\overline{\alpha}/\alpha)^{|W \cup ((A \cap B) \cup X)|},$$

$$= \alpha^{|\overline{A \Delta B}|} \overline{\alpha}^{-|A \cap B|} \sum_{W \subseteq \overline{A \cup B} \setminus X} (\overline{\alpha}/\alpha)^{|W| + |(A \cap B) \cup X|},$$

$$= \alpha^{|\overline{A \Delta B}| - |(A \cap B) \cup X|} \overline{\alpha}^{-|A \cap B| + |(A \cap B) \cup X|} \sum_{W \subseteq \overline{A \cup B} \setminus X} (\overline{\alpha}/\alpha)^{|W|},$$

$$= \alpha^{|\overline{A \cup B}| - |X \setminus (A \cap B)|} \overline{\alpha}^{|X \setminus (A \cap B)|} (\overline{\alpha}/\alpha + 1)^{|\overline{A \cup B} \setminus X|},$$

$$= \overline{\alpha}^{|X \setminus (A \cap B)|}. \qquad \square$$

Proposition 3. *Let A and $B \subseteq \Omega$. $\forall X \subseteq \Omega$, one has:*

$$m_{A \cap^{\alpha} B} = m_{\overline{A \Delta B}} \bigcirc \left(\bigcap_{y \in \overline{A \cup B}} m_{\overline{A \Delta B} \setminus \{y\}}^{\overline{\alpha}} \right). \qquad (6)$$

Proof. Proving equation (6) is equivalent to proving that $q_{A \cap^{\alpha} B} = g$ with g a set function such that $\forall X \subseteq \Omega$:

$$g(X) = q_{\overline{A \Delta B}}(X) \prod_{y \in \overline{A \cup B}} q_{\overline{A \Delta B} \setminus \{y\}}^{\overline{\alpha}}(X).$$

$q_{\overline{A \Delta B} \setminus \{y\}}^{\overline{\alpha}}$ is the commonality function corresponding to $m_{\overline{A \Delta B} \setminus \{y\}}^{\overline{\alpha}}$:

$$q_{\overline{A \Delta B} \setminus \{y\}}^{\overline{\alpha}}(X) = \begin{cases} 1 & \text{if } X \subseteq \overline{A \Delta B} \setminus \{y\} \\ \overline{\alpha} & \text{otherwise} \end{cases}.$$

$q_{\overline{A \Delta B}}$ is the commonality function corresponding to $m_{\overline{A \Delta B}}$:

$$q_{\overline{A \Delta B}}(X) = \begin{cases} 1 & \text{if } X \subseteq \overline{A \Delta B} \\ 0 & \text{otherwise} \end{cases}.$$

If $X \not\subseteq \overline{A \Delta B}$, then $q_{\overline{A \Delta B}}(X) = 0 \implies g(X) = 0$ and consequently, given proposition 2, $q_{A \cap^{\alpha} B}$ and g coincide on these sets.

All other remaining sets X in 2^{Ω} are such that $X \subseteq \overline{A \Delta B}$. Under this assumption and given the definition of $q_{\overline{A \Delta B} \setminus \{y\}}^{\overline{\alpha}}$, one can thus write $g(X) = \overline{\alpha}^{|C|}$ with $C = \{y \in \overline{A \cup B} \mid X \not\subseteq \overline{A \Delta B} \setminus \{y\}\} \subset \Omega$. It can be proved that $C = X \setminus (A \cap B)$ thereby proving that $q_{A \cap^{\alpha} B}$ and g also coincide when $X \subseteq \overline{A \Delta B}$. $\qquad \square$

Let us first provide a toy example to better grasp the gist of proposition 3:

Example 1. *Suppose that* $\Omega = \{a, b, c\}$, $A = \{a\}$ *and* $B = \{a, b\}$. *Consequently, we have* $\overline{A \Delta B} = \{a, c\}$ *and* $\overline{A \cup B} = \{c\}$. *The mass functions before combination, those involved in the conjunctive decomposition in equation (6) as well as the output mass function* $m_{A \cap^\alpha B}$ *are as follows:*

subsets:	$\emptyset$	$\{a\}$	$\{b\}$	$\{a, b\}$	$\{c\}$	$\{a, c\}$	$\{b, c\}$	Ω
$m_A = m_{\{a\}}$		1						
$m_B = m_{\{a,b\}}$				1				
$m_{\overline{A\Delta B}} = m_{\{a,c\}}$						1		
$m^{\overline{\alpha}}_{\overline{A\Delta B}\setminus\{c\}} = m^{\overline{\alpha}}_{\{a\}}$	α							$\overline{\alpha}$
$m_{A \cap^\alpha B}$	α					$\overline{\alpha}$		

Proposition 3 could not have been anticipated by Smets' work [8] on canonical decomposition because $m_{A \cap^\alpha B}$ is dogmatic, *i.e.* $m_{A \cap^\alpha B}(\Omega) = 0$. For the same reason, the decomposition of $m_{A \cap^\alpha B}$ is not unique in Smet's sense. Nonetheless, provided that a restriction from 2^Ω to $2^{\overline{A\Delta B}}$ is performed, then uniqueness result applies. Indeed, the restriction of $m_{A \cap^\alpha B}$ to $2^{\overline{A\Delta B}}$ is a non-dogmatic mass function on the frame $\overline{A\Delta B}$ and therefore the decomposition is unique. Since there is no restriction to a greater set than $\overline{A\Delta B}$ that remains non-dogmatic, we say that this decomposition is still canonical by abuse of language. This phenomenon is also illustrated in example 1 in which $m_{A \cap^\alpha B}$ happens to be a simple mass function if defined on $2^{\overline{A\Delta B}}$.

Following notations and definitions given in [1], we define the conjunctive weight function of an α-conjunction of two categorical mass functions $w_{A \cap^\alpha B}$ as follows:

$$\forall X \subseteq \Omega, \; w_{A \cap^\alpha B}(X) = \begin{cases} 0 & \text{if } X = \overline{A\Delta B}, \\ \overline{\alpha} & \text{if } X \subsetneq \overline{A\Delta B} \text{ and } |X| = |\overline{A\Delta B}| - 1, \\ 1 & \text{otherwise .} \end{cases}$$

Conjunctive weights are interesting in the sense that they represent the elementary pieces of evidence that lead to the current state of knowledge. These weights also induce an information content related partial order for mass functions. They can also be used to define other combination rules [1,5].

Besides, the proposed conjunctive decomposition allows the following interpretation of α-conjunctions of categorical mass functions: given $\overline{A\Delta B}$, there are $|\overline{A \cup B}|$ sources supporting with strength α respectively that any element $y \in \overline{A \cup B}$ may be discarded and all of these sources are truthful.

4 α-Disjunctive Combination of Categorical Mass Functions

In this section, the dual results of those of section 3 are given for the combination of categorical mass functions using an α-disjunctive rule. Proofs are not given because they are obtained by applying the De Morgan laws [10] to results of section 3. The De Morgan laws state that for any mass functions m_1 and m_2 on a frame Ω, one has:

$$\overline{m_1 \textcircled{$\cap$}^\alpha m_2} = \overline{m}_1 \textcircled{$\cup$}^\alpha \overline{m}_2, \tag{7}$$

$$\overline{m_1 \textcircled{$\cup$}^\alpha m_2} = \overline{m}_1 \textcircled{$\cap$}^\alpha \overline{m}_2. \tag{8}$$

Proposition 4. *Let A and $B \subseteq \Omega$. $\forall X \subseteq \Omega$, one has:*

$$m_{A \cup^\cap B}(X) = \begin{cases} \alpha^{|X| - |A \Delta B|} \overline{\alpha}^{|A \cup B| - |X|} & \text{if } A \Delta B \subseteq X \subseteq A \cup B \\ 0 & \text{otherwise} \end{cases}. \tag{9}$$

Figure 2 illustrates the variety of potential focal sets of mass function $m_{A \cup^\cap B}$. It can be noted that according to proposition 4:

$$A \cap B = \emptyset \implies m_{A \cup^\cap B} = m_{A \cup B}. \tag{10}$$

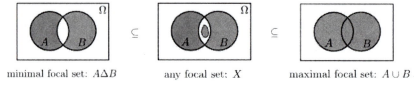

minimal focal set: $A \Delta B$ any focal set: X maximal focal set: $A \cup B$

Fig. 2. Example of focal sets of mass function $m_{A \cup^\cap B}$

Proposition 5. *Let A and $B \subseteq \Omega$. $\forall X \subseteq \Omega$, one has:*

$$b_{A \cup^\cap B}(X) = \begin{cases} \overline{\alpha}^{|(A \cup B) \setminus X|} & \text{if } A \Delta B \subseteq X \\ 0 & \text{otherwise} \end{cases}. \tag{11}$$

Proposition 6. *Let A and $B \subseteq \Omega$. $\forall X \subseteq \Omega$, one has:*

$$m_{A \cup^\cap B} = m_{A \Delta B} \textcircled{$\cup$} \left(\underset{y \in A \cap B}{\textcircled{$\cup$}} \underline{m}^{\overline{\alpha}}_{(A \Delta B) \cup \{y\}} \right), \tag{12}$$

with $\underline{m}^{\overline{\alpha}}_{(A \Delta B) \cup \{y\}}$ denoting a negative simple mass function which is such that $\underline{m}^{\overline{\alpha}}_{(A \Delta B) \cup \{y\}} = \overline{\alpha} m_\emptyset + \alpha m_{(A \Delta B) \cup \{y\}}$.

Example 2. *(Example 1 continued). Suppose that $\Omega = \{a, b, c\}$, $A = \{a\}$ and $B = \{a, b\}$. Consequently, we have $A \Delta B = \{b\}$ and $A \cap B = \{a\}$. The mass functions before combination, those involved in the conjunctive decomposition in equation (12) as well as the output mass function $m_{A \cup^\cap B}$ are as follows:*

subsets:	$\emptyset$	$\{a\}$	$\{b\}$	$\{a,b\}$	$\{c\}$	$\{a,c\}$	$\{b,c\}$	Ω
$m_A = m_{\{a\}}$		1						
$m_B = m_{\{a,b\}}$				1				
$m_{A\Delta B} = m_{\{b\}}$			1					
$m_{A\Delta B \cup \{a\}}^{\overline{\alpha}} = m_{\{a,b\}}^{\overline{\alpha}}$	$\overline{\alpha}$			α				
$m_{A \cup^{\alpha} B}$			$\overline{\alpha}$	α				

The existence of the proposed disjunctive decomposition, like in the conjunctive case, could not have been anticipated using existing theorems. From section 3, the conjunctive decomposition of $m_{\overline{A} \cap^{\alpha} \overline{B}}$ is unique in some sense, therefore the disjunctive decomposition of $m_{A \cup^{\alpha} B}$ is unique to the same regard. We say that it is canonical by abuse of language. In compliance with [1], we define the disjunctive weight function of an α-disjunction of two categorical mass functions $v_{A \cup^{\alpha} B}$ as follows:

$$\forall X \subseteq \Omega,\ v_{A \cup^{\alpha} B}(X) = \begin{cases} 0 & \text{if } X = A\Delta B, \\ \overline{\alpha} & \text{if } A\Delta B \subsetneq X \text{ and } |X| = |\overline{A\Delta B}| + 1, \\ 1 & \text{otherwise}. \end{cases}$$

Besides, the proposed disjunctive decomposition allows the following interpretation of α-disjunctions of categorical mass functions: there are $|A \cap B|$ sources supporting $A\Delta B$ with strength $\overline{\alpha}$ and $A\Delta B$ plus any element $y \in A \cap B$ with strength α and at least one of these sources is truthful.

Furthermore, it can be noted that any combination of categorical mass functions using an α-junction can be decomposed both conjunctively and disjunctively. Indeed, any mass function $m_{A \cap^{\alpha} B}$ can be decomposed conjunctively using proposition 3. Now let $C = \overline{A \cup B} \cup X$ and $D = \overline{A \cup B} \cup Y$ with $\{X, Y\}$ a partition of $A \cap B$. We thus have :

$$C \cap D = \overline{A \cup B},$$
$$C \Delta D = A \cap B,$$
$$C \cup B = \overline{A\Delta B}.$$

Using propositions 1 and 4, it is immediate that $m_{C \cup^{\overline{\alpha}} D} = m_{A \cap^{\alpha} B}$. By using proposition 6 on $m_{C \cup^{\overline{\alpha}} D}$, a disjunctive decomposition of $m_{A \cap^{\alpha} B}$ is also obtained.

5 Conclusion

In this article, α-junctions of categorical mass functions have been investigated. We provided straightforward equations for the computation of several set functions pertaining to evidence theory in both the conjunctive and disjunctive cases. In particular, a canonical conjunctive (respectively disjunctive) decomposition of the α-conjunction (respectively α-disjunction) of categorical mass functions have been obtained. In this particular situation, an α-conjunction (respectively an α-disjunction) is thus a series of purely conjunctive (respectively disjunctive) combinations. This leads to new complementary interpretations of α-junctions of deterministic pieces of information that are compliant with Pichon and Denœux's interpretation [4].

Concerning the generalization of these results for the α-junctions of any mass functions, it can only be concluded that an α-conjunction (respectively an α-disjunction) is a convex combination of series of purely conjunctive (respectively disjunctive) combinations. Pichon and Denœux actually already proposed decompositions of α-junctions of any mass functions, but these decompositions are obtained using a cross product of two frames of discernment. In future works, we hope to provide results on α-junction decompositions on a single frame.

It would be also interesting to investigate the ties between the conjunctive and disjunctive weights obtained in this article with the α-conjunctive and α-disjunctive weights introduced in chap. 7 of [5]. These other weights are defined using signed belief functions and consequently take their values in $(-\infty, +\infty) \setminus \{0\}$.

Finally, we also hope to apply α-junctions in information fusion problems involving partially truthful pieces of evidence. Truthfulness issues in information fusion arise in the presence of an unreliable or malicious information source. An unreliable source is accidentally untruthful whereas a malicious source is purposely untruthful (see [2] for an example of a such an application). α-junctions are appealing combination tools for the latter case. Indeed, if the value of α can be inferred using contextual information, an α-junction is likely to efficiently circumvent erroneous pieces of evidence.

References

1. Denoeux, T.: Conjunctive and disjunctive combination of belief functions induced by non-distinct bodies of evidence. Artificial Intelligence 172(2-3), 234–264 (2008)
2. El Zoghby, N., Cherfaoui, V., Ducourthial, B., Denoeux, T.: Distributed Data fusion for detecting Sybil attacks in VANETs. In: Denoeux, T., Masson, M.-H. (eds.) Belief Functions: Theory and Applications. AISC, vol. 164, pp. 351–358. Springer, Heidelberg (2012)
3. Nguyen, H.T.: On random sets and belief functions. Journal of Mathematical Analysis and Applications 65(3), 531–542 (1978)
4. Pichon, F., Denoeux, T.: Interpretation and computation of α-junctions for combining belief functions. In: 6th Int. Symposium on Imprecise Probability: Theories and Applications (ISIPTA 2009), Durham, U.K. (2009)
5. Pichon, F.: Belief functions: canonical decompositions and combination rules. Ph.D. thesis, Université de Technologie de Compiègne – UTC (march (2009)
6. Pichon, F.: On the α-conjunctions for combining belief functions. In: Denoeux, T., Masson, M.H. (eds.) Belief Functions: Theory and Applications. AISC, vol. 164, pp. 285–292. Springer, Heidelberg (2012)
7. Pichon, F., Dubois, D., Denoeux, T.: Relevance and truthfulness in information correction and fusion. International Journal of Approximate Reasoning 53(2), 159–175 (2012); Theory of Belief Functions (BELIEF 2010)
8. Smets, P.: The canonical decomposition of weighted belief. In: Int. Joint. Conf. on Artificial Intelligence. pp. 1896–1901 (1995)
9. Smets, P.: The alpha-junctions: Combination operators applicable to belief functions. In: Nonnengart, A., Kruse, R., Ohlbach, H.J., Gabbay, D.M. (eds.) FAPR 1997 and ECSQARU 1997. LNCS, vol. 1244, pp. 131–153. Springer, Heidelberg (1997)
10. Smets, P.: The application of the matrix calculus to belief functions. International Journal of Approximate Reasoning 31(1-2), 1–30 (2002)

Truthfulness in Contextual Information Correction

Frédéric Pichon, David Mercier, François Delmotte, and Éric Lefèvre

Univ. Lille Nord de France, F-59000 Lille, France
UArtois, LGI2A, F-62400 Béthune, France
{frederic.pichon,david.mercier,
francois.delmotte,eric.lefevre}@univ-artois.fr

Abstract. Recently, a dual reinforcement process to contextual discounting was introduced. However, it lacked a clear interpretation. In this paper, we propose a new perspective on contextual discounting: it can be seen as successive corrections corresponding to simple contextual lies. Most interestingly, a similar interpretation is provided for the reinforcement process. Two new contextual correction mechanisms, which are similar yet complementary to the two existing ones, are also introduced.

Keywords: Dempster-Shafer theory, Belief functions, Information correction, Discounting.

1 Introduction

Information correction has received quite a lot of attention in recent years in belief function theory (see, *e.g.*, [9,11]). It is an important question that deals with how an agent should interpret a piece of information received from a source about a parameter $\mathbf{x}$ defined on a finite domain $\mathcal{X} = \{x_1, \ldots, x_K\}$. Classically, the agent has some knowledge regarding the reliability of the source and, using the discounting operation [12], he is able to take into account that knowledge and to modify, or *correct*, the initial piece of information accordingly.

Since its inception, the discounting operation has been extended in different ways. Notably, Mercier *et al.* [10,9] consider the case where one has some knowledge about the reliability of the source, conditionally on different subsets (contexts) A of $\mathcal{X}$, leading to the so-called contextual discounting operation. One may also refine the discounting operation in order to take into account knowledge about the source truthfulness [11]. Of particular interest for the present work is the dual reinforcement operation to contextual discounting introduced in [9]. Mercier *et al.* [9] show that this correction mechanism amounts to the negation [6] of the contextual discounting of the negation of the initial information, but unfortunately they do not go further in providing a clear interpretation for this interesting operation.

In this paper, we study further contextual correction mechanisms. We present (Section 3) a new framework for handling detailed meta-knowledge about source

F. Cuzzolin (Ed.): BELIEF 2014, LNAI 8764, pp. 11–20, 2014.

truthfulness. Using this framework, we then derive the contextual discounting operation (Section 4.1) and its dual (Section 4.2), leading to a new perspective on the former and an interpretation for the latter. We proceed (Section 4.3) with the introduction of two new contextual correction mechanisms, whose interpretations are similar yet complementary to the two existing ones. Background material on belief function theory is first recalled in Section 2.

2   Belief Function Theory: Necessary Notions

In this section, we first recall basic concepts of belief function theory. Then, we present existing correction mechanisms that are of interest for this paper.

2.1   Basic Concepts

In this paper, we adopt Smets' Transferable Belief Model (TBM) [14], where the beliefs held by an agent Ag regarding the actual value taken by $\mathbf{x}$ are modeled using a belief function [12] and represented using an associated mass function. A mass function (MF) on $\mathcal{X}$ is defined as a mapping $m : 2^{\mathcal{X}} \to [0,1]$ verifying $\sum_{A \subseteq \mathcal{X}} m(A) = 1$. Subsets A of $\mathcal{X}$ such that $m(A) > 0$ are called *focal sets* of m. A MF having focal sets $\mathcal{X}$ and $A \subset \mathcal{X}$, with respective masses w and $1 - w$, $w \in [0,1]$, may be denoted by A^w. A MF having focal sets $\emptyset$ and $A \neq \emptyset$, with respective masses v and $1 - v$, $v \in [0,1]$, may be denoted by A_v. The negation $\overline{m}$ of a MF m is defined as $\overline{m}(A) = m(\overline{A})$, $\forall A \subseteq \mathcal{X}$, where $\overline{A}$ denotes the complement of A [6].

Beliefs can be aggregated using so-called combination rules. In particular, the conjunctive rule, which is the unnormalized version of Dempster's rule [5], is defined as follows. Let m_1 and m_2 be two MFs, and let $m_{1 \bigcirc\!\!\!\cap 2}$ be the MF resulting from their combination by the conjunctive rule denoted by $\bigcirc\!\!\!\cap$. We have:

$$m_{1 \bigcirc\!\!\!\cap 2}(A) = \sum_{B \cap C = A} m_1(B) \, m_2(C), \quad \forall A \subseteq \mathcal{X}. \tag{1}$$

Other combination rules of interest for this paper are the disjunctive rule $\bigcirc\!\!\!\cup$ [6], the exclusive disjunctive rule $\bigcirc\!\!\!\underline{\cup}$ and the equivalence rule $\bigcirc\!\!\!\underline{\cap}$ [13]. Their definitions are similar to that of the conjunctive rule: one merely needs to replace $\cap$ in (1) by, respectively, $\cup$, $\underline{\cup}$ and $\underline{\cap}$, where $\underline{\cup}$ (exclusive OR) and $\underline{\cap}$ (logical equality) are defined respectively by $B \underline{\cup} C = (B \cap \overline{C}) \cup (\overline{B} \cap C)$ and $B \underline{\cap} C = (B \cap C) \cup (\overline{B} \cap \overline{C})$ for all $B, C \subseteq \mathcal{X}$. The interpretations of these four rules are discussed in detail in [11].

2.2   Correction Mechanisms

Knowledge about a source reliability is classically taken into account in the TBM through the *discounting* operation. Suppose a source S providing a piece of information represented by a MF m_S. Let β, with $\beta \in [0,1]$, be Ag's degree of belief that the source is reliable. Ag's belief m on $\mathcal{X}$ is then defined by [12]:

$$m(\mathcal{X}) = \beta \, m_S(\mathcal{X}) + (1 - \beta), \; m(A) = \beta \, m_S(A), \forall A \subset \mathcal{X}. \tag{2}$$

Mercier *et al.* [9] consider the case where Ag has some knowledge about the source reliability, conditionally on different subsets A of $\mathcal{X}$. Precisely, let β_A, with $\beta_A \in [0,1]$, be Ag's degree of belief that the source is reliable in context $A \subseteq \mathcal{X}$ and let $\mathcal{A}$ be the set of contexts for which Ag possesses such contextual meta-knowledge. Ag's belief m on $\mathcal{X}$ is then defined by the following equation known as *contextual discounting* that subsumes discounting (recovered for $\mathcal{A} = \{\mathcal{X}\}$):

$$m = m_S \bigcup\nolimits_{A \in \mathcal{A}} A_{\beta_A}. \tag{3}$$

In addition, a dual reinforcement process to contextual discounting, called contextual reinforcement hereafter, is introduced in [9]. Let m_S be a MF provided by a source S. The contextual reinforcement of m_S is the MF m defined by:

$$m = m_S \bigcap\nolimits_{A \in \mathcal{A}} A^{\beta_A}, \tag{4}$$

with $\beta_A \in [0,1]$, $A \in \mathcal{A}$. Mercier *et al.* [9] show that this correction amounts to the negation of the contextual discounting of the negation of m_S. However, they do not go further in providing a clear explanation as to what meta-knowledge on the source this correction of m_S corresponds. One of the main results of this paper is to provide such an interpretation.

3   A Refined Model of Source Truthfulness

In the correction schemes recalled in Section 2.2, the reliability of a source is assimilated to its relevance as explained in [11]. In [11], Pichon *et al.* assume that the reliability of a source involves in addition another dimension: its truthfulness. Pichon *et al.* [11] note that there exists various forms of lack of truthfulness for a source. For instance, for a sensor, it may take the form of a systematic bias. However, Pichon *et al.* [11] study only the crudest description of the lack of truthfulness, where a non truthful source is a source that declares the contrary of what it knows. According to this definition, from a piece of information of the form $\mathbf{x} \in B$ for some $B \subseteq \mathcal{X}$ provided by a relevant source S, one must conclude that $\mathbf{x} \in B$ or $\mathbf{x} \in \overline{B}$, depending on whether the source S is assumed to be truthful or not.

In this section, we propose a new and refined model of source truthfulness that allows the integration of more detailed meta-knowledge about the lack of truthfulness of an information source.

3.1   Elementary Truthfulness

Assume that a relevant source provides a piece of information on the value taken by $\mathbf{x}$ of the form $\mathbf{x} \in B$, for some $B \subseteq \mathcal{X}$. Let us now consider a particular value

$x \in \mathcal{X}$. Either $x \in B$ or $x \notin B$, that is, the source may tell that x is possibly the actual value of $\mathbf{x}$ or it may tell that x is not a possibility for the actual value of $\mathbf{x}$. Furthermore, for each of those two possible declarations by the source about the value x, one may have some knowledge on whether the source is truthful or not. For instance, one may believe that the source is truthful when it tells that x is a possibility – in which case one must conclude that x is possibly the actual value of $\mathbf{x}$ if the source does tell that x is a possibility for $\mathbf{x}$ – and that it lies when it tells that x is not a possibility – in which case one must conclude that x is possibly the actual value of $\mathbf{x}$ if the source does tell that x is not a possibility for $\mathbf{x}$.

To account for such detailed knowledge about the behavior of the source, let us introduce two binary variables $\mathbf{p}_x$ and $\mathbf{n}_x$, with respective frames $\mathcal{P}_x = \{p_x, \neg p_x\}$ and $\mathcal{N}_x = \{n_x, \neg n_x\}$: p_x (resp. $\neg p_x$) corresponds to the state where the source is truthful (resp. not truthful) when it tells that x is possibly the actual value for $\mathbf{x}$; n_x (resp. $\neg n_x$) corresponds to the state where the source is truthful (resp. not truthful) when it tells that x is not a possibility for the actual value of $\mathbf{x}$.

Now, we can define a variable $\mathbf{t}_x$ with associated frame $\mathcal{T}_x = \mathcal{P}_x \times \mathcal{N}_x$, which contains four states $t_x = (p_x, n_x)$, $\neg t_x^n = (p_x, \neg n_x)$, $\neg t_x^p = (\neg p_x, n_x)$ and $\neg t_x = (\neg p_x, \neg n_x)$ allowing us to model the global truthfulness of the source with respect to the value x: t_x corresponds to the case where the source tells the truth whatever it says about the value x, in short the source is said to be truthful for x; $\neg t_x^n$ corresponds to the case of a source that lies only when it tells that x is not a possibility for $\mathbf{x}$, which will be called a negative liar for x; $\neg t_x^p$ corresponds to the case of a source that lies only when it says that x is a possibility for $\mathbf{x}$, which will be called a positive liar for x; $\neg t_x$ corresponds to the case where the source lies whatever it says about the value x, in short the source is said to be non truthful for x.

There are thus four possible cases:

1. Suppose the source tells x is possibly the actual value of $\mathbf{x}$, *i.e.*, the information $\mathbf{x} \in B$ provided by the source is such that $x \in B$.

    (a) If the source is assumed to be truthful (t_x) or a negative liar ($\neg t_x^n$), then one must conclude that x is possibly the actual value of $\mathbf{x}$;

    (b) If the source is assumed to be a positive liar ($\neg t_x^p$) or non truthful ($\neg t_x$), then one must conclude that x is not a possibility for the actual value of $\mathbf{x}$;

2. Suppose the source tells x is not a possibility for the actual value of $\mathbf{x}$, *i.e.*, $x \notin B$.

    (a) If the source is assumed to be in state t_x or in state $\neg t_x^p$, then one must conclude that x is not a possibility for the actual value of $\mathbf{x}$;

    (b) If the source is assumed to be in state $\neg t_x^n$ or in state $\neg t_x$, then one must conclude that x is possibly the actual value of $\mathbf{x}$;

3.2   Contextual Truthfulness

Let $\mathcal{T}$ denote the possible states of S with respect to its truthfulness for all $x \in X$. By definition, $\mathcal{T} = \times_{x \in \mathcal{X}} \mathcal{T}_x$. $\mathcal{T}$ is clearly a big space, however we will be interested in this paper only by a smaller subspace of $\mathcal{T}$, which we define below.

Let $h_A^{t_1,t_2} \in \mathcal{T}$, $A \subseteq \mathcal{X}$, $t_1, t_2 \in \mathcal{T}_x$, denote the state where the source is in state t_1 for all $x \in A$, and in state t_2 for all $x \notin A$. For instance, let $\mathcal{X} = \{x_1, x_2, x_3, x_4\}$, $A = \{x_3, x_4\}$, $t_1 = \neg t_x^p$ and $t_2 = t_x$, then $h_A^{t_1,t_2} = h_{\{x_3,x_4\}}^{\neg t_x^p, t_x} = \left(t_{x_1}, t_{x_2}, \neg t_{x_3}^p, \neg t_{x_4}^p\right)$, i.e., the source is a positive liar for x_3 and x_4, and is truthful for x_1 and x_2.

Consider now the following question: what must one conclude about $\mathbf{x}$ when the source tells $\mathbf{x} \in B$ and is assumed to be in some state $h_A^{t_1,t_2}$? To answer this question, one merely needs to look in turn at each $x \in \mathcal{X}$ and to consider 4 cases for each of those $x \in \mathcal{X}$: 1) $x \notin B$ and $x \notin A$; 2) $x \notin B$ and $x \in A$; 3) $x \in B$ and $x \notin A$; 4) $x \in B$ and $x \in A$. Table 1 lists, for each of the 4 cases and for all states $h_A^{t_1,t_2}$, $t_1, t_2 \in \mathcal{T}_x$, whether one should deduce that a given value $x \in \mathcal{X}$ is possibly the actual value of $\mathbf{x}$ or not – the former is indicated by a 1 and the latter by a 0 in columns $h_A^{t_1,t_2}, t_1, t_2 \in \mathcal{T}_x$.

Table 1. Interpretations of the source testimony according to its contextual truthfulness

$x\in B$	$x\in A$																
0	0	0	0	0	0	0	0	0	0	1	1	1	1	1	1	1	1
0	1	0	0	0	0	1	1	1	1	0	0	0	0	1	1	1	1
1	0	0	0	1	1	0	0	1	1	0	0	1	1	0	0	1	1
1	1	0	1	0	1	0	1	0	1	0	1	0	1	0	1	0	1

According to Table 1, when the source is assumed to be in, e.g., state $h_A^{t_x, \neg t_x^p}$, i.e., the source is truthful for all $x \in A$ and a positive liar for all $x \in \overline{A}$, then one should deduce that $x \in \mathcal{X}$ is a possible value for $\mathbf{x}$ iff $x \in B$ and $x \in A$, and therefore, since this holds for all $x \in \mathcal{X}$, one should deduce that $\mathbf{x} \in B \cap A$. For instance, consider state $h_{\{x_3,x_4\}}^{t_x, \neg t_x^p}$ and testimony $\mathbf{x} \in \{x_1, x_3\}$, then one should deduce $\{x_1, x_3\} \bigcap \{x_3, x_4\} = \{x_3\}$.

Another interesting state is $h_A^{\neg t_x^n, t_x}$, i.e., the source is a negative liar for all $x \in A$ and truthful for all $x \in \overline{A}$, in which case $x \in \mathcal{X}$ is a possible value for $\mathbf{x}$ iff $x \in B$ or $x \in A$, and thus one should conclude that $\mathbf{x} \in B \cup A$. More generally, as can be seen from Table 1, the couples $(t_1, t_2) \in \mathcal{T}_x^2$ yields all possible binary Boolean connectives.

Of particular interest in this paper are the states $h_A^{t_x, \neg t_x^p}$ and $h_A^{\neg t_x^n, t_x}$, which have already been discussed, and the states $h_A^{t_x, \neg t_x}$ (the source is truthful for all $x \in A$ and non truthful for all $x \in \overline{A}$) and $h_A^{\neg t_x, t_x}$ (the source is non truthful for all $x \in A$ and truthful for all $x \in \overline{A}$), which yield respectively $\mathbf{x} \in B \bar{\cap} A$ and $\mathbf{x} \in B \bar{\cup} A$. Accordingly, we will consider in the sequel only the following subspace $\mathcal{H} \subseteq \mathcal{T}$: $\mathcal{H} = \left\{ h_A^{t_1,t_2} | A \subseteq \mathcal{X}, (t_1, t_2) \in \{(t_x, \neg t_x^p), (\neg t_x^n, t_x), (t_x, \neg t_x), (\neg t_x, t_x)\} \right\}$.

Following [11], we can encode the above reasoning by a multivalued mapping $\Gamma_B : \mathcal{H} \to \mathcal{X}$ indicating how to interpret the information $\mathbf{x} \in B$ in each state $h \in \mathcal{H}$; we have for all $A \subseteq \mathcal{X}$:

$$\Gamma_B(h_A^{t_x, \neg t_x''}) = B \cap A, \Gamma_B(h_A^{\neg t_x'', t_x}) = B \cup A, \Gamma_B(h_A^{t_x, \neg t_x}) = B \cap A, \Gamma_B(h_A^{\neg t_x, t_x}) = B \cup A.$$

If the knowledge about the source state is imprecise and given by $H \subseteq \mathcal{H}$, then one should deduce the image $\Gamma_B(H) := \bigcup_{h \in H} \Gamma_B(h)$ of H by Γ_B.

3.3 Uncertain Testimony and Meta-knowledge

More generally, both the testimony provided by the source and the knowledge of Ag about the source truthfulness may be uncertain. Let m_S be the uncertain testimony and $m^{\mathcal{H}}$ the uncertain meta-knowledge. In such case, the *Behavior-Based Correction* (BBC) procedure introduced by Pichon *et al.* [11], can be used to derive Ag knowledge on $\mathcal{X}$. It is represented by the MF m defined by [11]:

$$m(C) = \sum_{H \subseteq \mathcal{H}} m^{\mathcal{H}}(H) \sum_{B : \Gamma_B(H) = C} m_S(B), \quad \forall C \subseteq \mathcal{X}. \tag{5}$$

For convenience, we may denote by $f_{m^{\mathcal{H}}}(m_S)$ the BBC of m_S according to meta-knowledge $m^{\mathcal{H}}$, i.e., we have $m = f_{m^{\mathcal{H}}}(m_S)$ with m defined by (5).

4   Interpretation of Contextual Corrections

In this section, we propose a new perspective on contextual discounting by recovering it using the framework introduced in Section 3. Then, using a similar reasoning, we provide an interpretation for contextual reinforcement. Finally, we introduce two new contextual correction schemes that are complementary to the two existing ones.

4.1 Contextual Discounting in Terms of BBCs

Let us consider a particular contextual lie among those introduced in Section 3.2: the states $h_A^{\neg t_x'', t_x}$, $A \subseteq \mathcal{X}$, corresponding to the assumptions that the source is a negative liar for all $x \in A$ and truthful for all $x \in \overline{A}$. Among these states, $h_\emptyset^{\neg t_x'', t_x}$ admits a simpler interpretation: it corresponds to assuming that the source is truthful $\forall x \in \mathcal{X}$.

Theorem 1. *Let m_S be a MF. We have, $\forall \mathcal{A}$ and with $\beta_A \in [0, 1]$, $\forall A \in \mathcal{A}$:*

$$m_S \bigcirc_{A \in \mathcal{A}} A_{\beta_A} = (\circ_{A \in \mathcal{A}} f_{m_{A, \cup}^{\mathcal{H}}})(m_S), \tag{6}$$

where $\circ$ denotes function composition (i.e., $(g \circ f)(x) = g(f(x))$) and where $m_{A, \cup}^{\mathcal{H}}$ is defined by $m_{A, \cup}^{\mathcal{H}}(\{h_\emptyset^{\neg t_x'', t_x}\}) = \beta_A$, $m_{A, \cup}^{\mathcal{H}}(\{h_A^{\neg t_x'', t_x}\}) = 1 - \beta_A$, $\forall A \in \mathcal{A}$.

Proof. This theorem can be shown by applying for each $A \in \mathcal{A}$, $\mathcal{A}$ being finite, the following property:

$$f_{m^{\mathcal{H}}_{A,\cup}}(m_S) = m_S \copyright A_{\beta_A}, \quad \forall A \in \mathcal{A}, \tag{7}$$

which is shown as follows.

From (5) and the definition of $m^{\mathcal{H}}_{A,\cup}$, $\forall C \subseteq \mathcal{X}$:

$$f_{m^{\mathcal{H}}_{A,\cup}}(m_S)(C) = \beta_A \sum_{B:B=C} m_S(B) + (1 - \beta_A) \sum_{B:B\cup A=C} m_S(B) . \tag{8}$$

Which means:

$$f_{m^{\mathcal{H}}_{A,\cup}}(m_S) = \beta_A m_S + (1 - \beta_A)(m_S \copyright m_A) , \tag{9}$$

with m_A a MF defined by $m_A(A) = 1$.

On the other hand, $\forall A \in \mathcal{A}$:

$$m_S \copyright A_{\beta_A} = m_S \copyright \begin{cases} A \mapsto 1 - \beta_A \\ \emptyset \mapsto \beta_A \end{cases} = \beta_A m_S + (1 - \beta_A)(m_S \copyright m_A) . \tag{10}$$

$\square$

In other words, contextual discounting, which appears on the left side of (6), corresponds to successive behavior-based corrections – one for each context $A \in \mathcal{A}$ – where for each context A, we have the following meta-knowledge: with mass β_A the source is truthful for all $x \in \mathcal{X}$, and with mass $1 - \beta_A$ the source is a negative liar for all $x \in A$ and truthful for all $x \in \overline{A}$.

Successive corrections of an initial piece of information is a process that may be encountered when considering a chain of sources, where the information provided by an initial source may be iteratively corrected by the sources down the chain according to the knowledge each source has on the behavior of the preceding source. The chain of sources problem is an important and complex one, which has received different treatments in logic [4], possibility theory [1] and belief function theory [2,3]: in particular a solution involving successive corrections, precisely successive discountings, was proposed in [1]. The fact that contextual discounting may be relevant for this problem had not been remarked yet.

4.2 Contextual Reinforcement in Terms of BBCs

Let us consider another kind of contextual lie: the states $h_A^{t_x, \neg t''_x}$, $A \subseteq \mathcal{X}$, corresponding to the assumptions that the source is truthful for all $x \in A$ and a positive liar for all $x \in \overline{A}$. Among these states, $h_{\mathcal{X}}^{t_x, \neg t''_x}$ has the same simple interpretation as $h_{\emptyset}^{\neg t''_x, t_x}$.

Theorem 2. *Let m_S be a MF. We have, $\forall A$ and with $\beta_A \in [0,1]$, $\forall A \in \mathcal{A}$:*

$$m_S \cap_{A \in \mathcal{A}} A^{\beta_A} = (\circ_{A \in \mathcal{A}} f_{m^{\mathcal{H}}_{A,\cap}})(m_S), \tag{11}$$

where $m^{\mathcal{H}}_{A,\cap}$ is defined by $m^{\mathcal{H}}_{A,\cap}(\{h_{\mathcal{X}}^{t_x, \neg t''_x}\}) = \beta_A$, $m^{\mathcal{H}}_{A,\cap}(\{h_A^{t_x, \neg t''_x}\}) = 1 - \beta_A$, $\forall A \in \mathcal{A}$.

Proof. The proof is similar to that of Theorem 1.   □

Theorem 2 is important as it constitutes the first known interpretation for contextual reinforcement. It shows that, similarly to contextual discounting, contextual reinforcement (left side of (11)) corresponds to successive behavior-based corrections – one for each context. The only difference between the two correction mechanisms is what is assumed with mass $1 - \beta_A$: with the former that the source is a negative liar for all $x \in A$ and truthful for all $x \in \overline{A}$, whereas with the latter that the source is truthful for all $x \in A$ and a positive liar for all $x \in \overline{A}$.

Example 1. Let us consider a series of three agents: agent 1 reports to agent 2, who reports in turn to agent 3. Let m_i denote the beliefs of agent i on $\mathcal{X} = \{x_1, x_2, x_3\}$ and let $m_i^{\mathcal{H}}$, $i > 1$, denote the meta-knowledge of agent i about agent $i - 1$. Furthermore, assume that $m_2^{\mathcal{H}}(\{h_{\mathcal{X}}^{t_x, \neg t_x'}\}) = 0.6$ and $m_2^{\mathcal{H}}(\{h_{\{x_1, x_2\}}^{t_x, \neg t_x'}\}) = 0.4$, that is, agent 2 believes with mass 0.6 that agent 1 is truthful for all $x \in \mathcal{X}$, and with mass 0.4 that agent 1 is truthful for x_1 and x_2 and a positive liar for x_3. Suppose further that $m_3^{\mathcal{H}}(\{h_{\mathcal{X}}^{t_x, t_{\neg x}}\}) = 0.8$ and $m_3^{\mathcal{H}}(\{h_{\{x_2, x_3\}}^{t_x, t_{\neg x}}\}) = 0.2$. From Theorem 2, we have

$$m_2 = m_1 \oslash \{x_1, x_2\}^{0.6},$$
$$m_3 = m_2 \oslash \{x_2, x_3\}^{0.8},$$
$$m_3 = m_1 \oslash \{x_1, x_2\}^{0.6} \oslash \{x_2, x_3\}^{0.8}.$$

4.3   Two New Contextual Correction Mechanisms

Contextual discounting and contextual reinforcement are based on corrections induced by simple pieces of meta-knowledge $m_{A,\cup}^{\mathcal{H}}$ and $m_{A,\cap}^{\mathcal{H}}$ respectively. In practice, those pieces of meta-knowledge transform a testimony $\mathbf{x} \in B$ as follows: they both allocate mass β_A to B, and mass $1 - \beta_A$ to $B \cup A$ and to $B \cap A$, respectively.

Now, as we have seen in Section 3.2, there exist states $h_A^{t_1, t_2} \in \mathcal{T}$ that lead to other binary Boolean connectives than the disjunction and the conjunction. This suggests a way to extend contextual discounting and contextual reinforcement. Of particular interest are states $h_A^{t_x, \neg t_x}$ (the source is truthful for all $x \in A$ and non truthful for all $x \in \overline{A}$) and $h_A^{\neg t_x, t_x}$ (the source is non truthful for all $x \in A$ and truthful for all $x \in \overline{A}$), which yield respectively $\mathbf{x} \in B \underline{\cap} A$ and $\mathbf{x} \in B \underline{\cup} A$. Indeed, the properties satisfied by connectives $\underline{\cap}$ and $\underline{\cup}$ allow us to obtain similar relations as those obtained for contextual discounting and contextual reinforcement:

Theorem 3. *Let m_S be a MF. We have, $\forall \mathcal{A}$ and with $\beta_A \in [0, 1]$, $\forall A \in \mathcal{A}$:*

$$m_S \underline{\bigcap}_{A \in \mathcal{A}} A^{\beta_A} = (\circ_{A \in \mathcal{A}} f_{m_{A,\cap}^{\mathcal{H}}})(m_S), \tag{12}$$

$$m_S \underline{\bigcup}_{A \in \mathcal{A}} A_{\beta_A} = (\circ_{A \in \mathcal{A}} f_{m_{A,\cup}^{\mathcal{H}}})(m_S), \tag{13}$$

where $m_{A,\cap}^{\mathcal{H}}$ and $m_{A,\cup}^{\mathcal{H}}$ are defined by $m_{A,\cap}^{\mathcal{H}}(\{h_{\mathcal{X}}^{t_x, \neg t_x}\}) = m_{A,\cup}^{\mathcal{H}}(\{h_{\emptyset}^{\neg t_x, t_x}\}) = \beta_A$, and $m_{A,\cap}^{\mathcal{H}}(\{h_A^{t_x, \neg t_x}\}) = m_{A,\cup}^{\mathcal{H}}(\{h_A^{\neg t_x, t_x}\}) = 1 - \beta_A$, $\forall A \in \mathcal{A}$.

Proof. The proof is similar to that of Theorem 1.   □

Eqs. (12) and (13) are the $\sqcap$ and $\sqcup$ counterparts to Eqs. (6) and (11), which are based on connectives $\cup$ and $\cap$. Hence, if contextual discounting and contextual reinforcement are renamed as $\cup$-contextual correction and $\cap$-contextual correction, then Eqs. (12) and (13) may be called $\sqcap$-contextual correction and $\sqcup$-contextual correction. Let us also stress that although the $\sqcap$ and $\sqcup$-contextual correction mechanisms are based on less classical combination rules than contextual discounting and contextual reinforcement, these two new contextual correction schemes seem to be as reasonable from the point of view of the meta-knowledge that they correspond to. Actually, their interpretations are even simpler since they rely on the classical assumptions of truthfulness and non truthfulness, whereas contextual discounting and contextual reinforcement involve negative and positive lies, which are less conventional. Finally, we note that the computational complexity of the $\sqcap$ and $\sqcup$-contextual correction mechanisms is similar to that of $\cup$ and $\cap$-contextual correction mechanisms: it merely corresponds to the complexity of applying $|\mathcal{A}|$ combinations by the rules $\textcircled{\cap}$ and $\textcircled{\cup}$, respectively, where $|\mathcal{A}|$ denotes the cardinality of $\mathcal{A}$.

5   Conclusion

Using a new framework for handling detailed meta-knowledge about source truthfulness, a new view on contextual discounting and an interpretation for contextual reinforcement were proposed. In addition, two similar yet complementary contextual correction mechanisms were introduced.

Future work will be dedicated to the application of contextual correction mechanisms. Similarly as contextual discounting [7,10], their parameters β_A, $A \in \mathcal{A}$, could be obtained from a confusion matrix or learnt from training data, and then they could be used in classification problems. Other potential applications include those involving chain of sources communicating pieces of information between themselves, as is the case in vehicular ad-hoc networks [8].

References

1. Baerecke, T., Delavallade, T., Lesot, M.-J., Pichon, F., Akdag, H., Bouchon-Meunier, B., Capet, P., Cholvy, L.: Un modèle de cotation pour la veille informationnelle en source ouverte. 6éme colloque Veille Stratégique Scientifique et Technologique, Toulouse, France (2010)
2. Cholvy, L.: Evaluation of information reported: A model in the theory of evidence. In: Hüllermeier, E., Kruse, R., Hoffmann, F. (eds.) Proc. of the Int. Conf. on Information Processing and Management of Uncertainty in Knowledge-Based Systems. CCIS, vol. 80, pp. 258–267. Springer, Heidelberg (2010)
3. Cholvy, L.: Collecting information reported by imperfect information sources. In: Greco, S., Bouchon-Meunier, B., Coletti, G., Fedrizzi, M., Matarazzo, B., Yager, R.R. (eds.) Proc. of the Int. Conf. on Information Processing and Management of Uncertainty in Knowledge-Based Systems. CCIS, vol. 299, pp. 501–510. Springer, Heidelberg (2012)

4. Cholvy, L.: Un modèle de cotation pour la veille informationnelle en source ouverte. In: European Workshop on Multi-agent Systems, Toulouse, France (2013)

5. Dempster, A.P.: Upper and lower probabilities induced by a multivalued mapping. Annals of Mathematical Statistics 38, 325–339 (1967)

6. Dubois, D., Prade, H.: A set-theoretic view of belief functions: logical operations and approximations by fuzzy sets. International Journal of General Systems 12(3), 193–226 (1986)

7. Elouedi, Z., Lefevre, E., Mercier, D.: Discountings of a belief function using a confusion matrix. In: Int. Conf. on Tools with Artificial Intelligence, vol. 1, pp. 287–294 (2010)

8. Bou Farah, M., Mercier, D., Lefévre, E., Delmotte, F.: A high-level application using belief functions for exchanging and managing uncertain events on the road in vehicular ad hoc networks. Annals of Telecommunications 69(3-4), 185–199 (2014)

9. Mercier, D., Lefèvre, E., Delmotte, F.: Belief functions contextual discounting and canonical decompositions. International Journal of Approximate Reasoning 53(2), 146 (2012)

10. Mercier, D., Quost, B., Denœux, T.: Refined modeling of sensor reliability in the belief function framework using contextual discounting. Information Fusion 9(2), 246 (2008)

11. Pichon, F., Dubois, D., Denœux, T.: Relevance and truthfulness in information correction and fusion. International Journal of Approximate Reasoning 53(2), 159–175 (2012)

12. Shafer, G.: A mathematical theory of evidence. Princeton University Press, Princeton, N.J. (1976)

13. Smets, P.: The α-junctions: combination operators applicable to belief functions. In: Nonnengart, A., Kruse, R., Ohlbach, H.J., Gabbay, D.M. (eds.) FAPR 1997 and ECSQARU 1997. LNCS, vol. 1244, pp. 131–153. Springer, Heidelberg (1997)

14. Smets, P., Kennes, R.: The Transferable Belief Model. Artificial Intelligence 66, 191–243 (1994)

The Choice of Generalized Dempster-Shafer Rules for Aggregating Belief Functions Based on Imprecision Indices

Andrey G. Bronevich[1,*] and Igor N. Rozenberg[2]

[1] National Research University Higher School of Economics, Pokrovskiy Boulevard, 11, 109028 Moscow, Russia
brone@mail.ru
[2] JSC "Research, Development and Planning Institute for Railway Information Technology, Automation and Telecommunication", Orlikov per.5, building 1 107996 Moscow, Russia
I.Rozenberg@gismps.ru

Abstract. In the paper we investigate the criteria of choosing generalized Dempster-Shafer rules for aggregating sources of information presented by belief functions. The approach is based on measuring various types of uncertainty in information and we use for this linear imprecision indices. Some results concerning properties of such rules are also presented.

Keywords: Generalized Dempster-Shafer rules, belief functions, imprecision indices.

1 Introduction

In the literature there are many generalizations of Dempster-Shafer (D-S) rule, see for instance [14]. Many of them [16,10,12] were the answer on the critique of this combination rule by Zadeh [17]. In this paper we support the idea of Smets [15], in which the whole family of rules of combination is divided on various types like conjunctive and disjunctive rules, and the use of them should be chosen in each application. Many critiques [12,13] of D-S rule is also concerned the case when sources of information are conflicting (or contradictory) and the measure of conflict of two sources of information based on D-S rule is not adequate. There are also works, see for example [1], where you can find argumentation that the classical D-S rule is not justified in probability theory. In this paper we investigate the generalized Dempster-Shafer (GD-S) rules that was firstly introduced by Dubois and Yager [11], where each GD-S rule is defined as follows. In the D-S theory each source of information can be described by a random set. If we assume that two sources of information are independent, then we get the D-S rule by taking the intersection of these two sets. In the GD-S rule the joint probability distribution of random sets is not known and the choice of

* This study (research grant No 14-01-0015) was supported by The National Research University Higher School of Economics Academic Fund Program in 2014/2015.

F. Cuzzolin (Ed.): BELIEF 2014, LNAI 8764, pp. 21–28, 2014.

the rule can be based on the least commitment principle [7], the principle of the minimum conflict between sources of information [3] and others [8,4]. In the paper we thoroughly investigate and generalize well-known approaches of choosing GD-S rules and find probabilistic interpretation of them. We come to the conclusion that any GD-S rule can be conceived as an approximation from above of two belief functions by using the partial order on belief functions usually called specialization. Using this order we propose several approaches to find such approximations that generalize well-known ones.

2   Evidence Theory and Generalized Dempster-Shafer Rules

Let X be a finite set and let 2^X be the powerset of X. One can say that the *body of evidence* is given on 2^X if a non-negative set function $m : 2^X \to [0, 1]$ is defined with $\sum\limits_{A \in 2^X} m(A) = 1$. Through the body of evidence the following functions are also introduced $Bel(B) = \sum\limits_{A \subseteq B} m(A)$, $Pl(B) = \sum\limits_{A \cap B \neq \emptyset} m(A)$, which are called *belief function* and *plausibility function* respectively. The function m is usually called the *basic belief assignment* (bba). We accept here the *transferable belief model* [15], where $m(\emptyset) = Bel(\emptyset)$ shows the degree of contradiction (or conflict) in the information. If the contradiction in information is equal to zero, then the corresponding belief function is called *normalized*. In the next we will use the following notations and definitions.

1. A set $A \in 2^X$ is called *focal* if $m(A) > 0$.
2. A belief function is called *categorical* if the body of evidence contains only one focal element $B \in 2^X$. This belief function is denoted $\eta_{\langle B \rangle}$ and obviously
$$\eta_{\langle B \rangle}(A) = \begin{cases} 1, & B \subseteq A, \\ 0, & otherwise. \end{cases}$$. Using categorical belief functions, we can express any belief function by the formula $Bel = \sum\limits_{B \in 2^X} m(B)\eta_{\langle B \rangle}$.
3. A belief measure is called a *probability measure* if $m(A) = 0$ for $|A| > 1$.
4. We denote correspondingly by $\bar{M}_{bel}$ and $\bar{M}_{pr}$ the families of all belief functions and probability measures on 2^X, and if these families are normalized we denote them by M_{bel} and M_{pr}.
5. For any set functions μ_1, μ_2 on 2^X we write $\mu_1 \leqslant \mu_2$ if $\mu_1(A) \leqslant \mu_2(A)$ for all $A \in 2^X$.

Let us consider the probabilistic interpretation of the transferable belief model based on random sets. A random set ξ is a random value taking its values in 2^X. Any such random value can be defined by probabilities $P(\xi = A)$ being identified with values $m(A)$ in the theory of evidence. Given two random sets ξ_1 and ξ_2 with values in 2^X. If we assume that these random sets are independent, then
$$P(\xi_1 = A, \xi_2 = B) = P(\xi_1 = A)P(\xi_2 = B).$$

Dempster proposes to aggregate these sources of information by a new random set ξ defined by

$$P(\xi = C) = \sum_{A \cap B = C} P(\xi_1 = A, \xi_2 = B).$$

Let us notice that if we assume that the sources of information are independent, then we get the original D-S rule defined by:

$$P(\xi = C) = \sum_{A \cap B = C} P(\xi_1 = A)P(\xi_2 = B).$$

If we denote $m(C) = P(\xi = C)$, $m_1(A) = P(\xi_1 = A)$ and $m_2(B) = P(\xi_2 = B)$. Then we get the D-S rule (or conjunctive rule) in usual notations

$$m(C) = \sum_{A \cap B = C} m_1(A)m_2(B) \tag{1}$$

The value

$$r_{DS} = m(\emptyset) = \sum_{A \cap B = \emptyset} m_1(A)m_2(B),$$

is called the measure of conflict between two sources of information, described by functions m_1 and m_2. Because in the original evidence theory there are considered normalized belief functions, the D-S rule is used in the form:

$$m(C) = \frac{1}{1 - r_{DS}} \sum_{A \cap B = C} m_1(A)m_2(B),$$

where $C \neq \emptyset$ and $m(\emptyset) = 0$. In the following we will use the D-S rule in the conjunctive form, i.e. based on formula (1). Analogously, the generalized D-S rule in conjunctive form is represented as

$$m(C) = \sum_{A \cap B = C} m(A, B),$$

where the function $m(A, B)$ obeys the following conditions:

$$\begin{cases} \sum_{B \in 2^X} m(A, B) = m_1(A), \\ \sum_{A \in 2^X} m(A, B) = m_2(B). \end{cases} \tag{2}$$

In the next we will also use the following representation of D-S rule: let us assume that $Bel_1 = \sum_{A \in 2^X} m_1(A)\eta_{\langle A \rangle}$ and $Bel_2 = \sum_{B \in 2^X} m_2(B)\eta_{\langle B \rangle}$ are belief functions, then

$$Bel = \sum_{A, B \in 2^X} m(A, B)\eta_{\langle A \cap B \rangle}.$$

3   Imprecision Indices

As you see above, in evidence theory we describe uncertainty with the help of set functions that are called belief measures. The generalization of such a model can be based on the notion of monotone measure. By definition [6], a set function $\mu : 2^X \to [0,1]$ is called a *monotone measure* if the following conditions hold: 1) $\mu(\emptyset) = 0$, $\mu(X) = 1$ (norming); 2) $\mu(A) \leqslant \mu(B)$ (monotonicity).

Let us notice that probability measures are special kinds of monotone measures. A monotone measure is a probability measure if it satisfies the additivity property:

$$\mu(A) + \mu(B) = \mu(A \cup B) \text{ for all } A, B \in 2^X \text{ such that } A \cap B = \emptyset.$$

We can check whether a monotone measure is a belief function using the Möbius transform [5]:

$$m(A) = \sum_{B \subseteq A} (-1)^{|A \setminus B|} \mu(B),$$

that should be non-negative for belief functions. Certainly, the formula

$$\mu = \sum_{B \in 2^X} m(B) \eta_{\langle B \rangle},$$

is also valid, but values of m is not non-negative for the general case.

The model of uncertainty based on monotone measures uses set functions that can be interpreted as lower or upper estimates of probabilities. A monotone measure μ is called an *lower probability* if there is a $P \in M_{pr}$ with $\mu \leqslant P$. For the sake of convenience, we will use the following notations: M_{mon} is the set of all monotone measures on 2^X; M_{low} is the set of all monotone measures on 2^X.

In the model of uncertainty based on lower probabilities we can describe uncertainty also by a convex set of probability measures $\mathbf{P}(\mu) = \{P \in M_{pr} | P \geqslant \mu\}$, called the *credal set*. In this model the conflict is associated with probability measures and non-specificity is caused by the choice of unknown probability measure from $\mathbf{P}(\mu)$.

In [2] the notion of imprecision index was proposed that generalizes the generalized Hartley measure. By definition, a functional $\nu : M_{low} \to [0,1]$ is an *imprecision index* if
1) $\nu(\mu) = 0$ for any $\mu \in M_{pr}$;
2) $\nu(\eta_{\langle X \rangle}) = 1$ (norming condition) ;
3) $\nu(\mu_1) \leqslant \nu(\mu_2)$ if $\mu_1 \geqslant \mu_2$.

In addition, an imprecision index is called *linear* if $\nu(a\mu_1 + (1 - a)\mu_2) = a\nu(\mu_1) + (1 - a)\nu(\mu_2)$ for any $a \in [0,1]$ and $\mu_1, \mu_2 \in M_{low}$.

The theoretical description of linear imprecision indices can be found in [2]. As examples of linear imprecision indices one can use the following functionals:

1) $\nu_c(\mu) = \sum\limits_{A \in 2^X \setminus \{\emptyset, X\}} c(A)(1 - \mu(A) - \mu(\bar{A}))$, where non-negative coefficients $c(A)$ should be chosen such that $\sum\limits_{A \in 2^X \setminus \{\emptyset, X\}} c(A) = 1$. In particular, if $c(A)$ takes the same value for all $A \in 2^X \setminus \{\emptyset, X\}$, we get the following index

$$\nu_1(\mu) = \frac{1}{2^n - 2} \sum\limits_{A \in 2^X \setminus \{\emptyset, X\}} (1 - \mu(A) - \mu(\bar{A})).$$

2) The generalized Hartley measure: $GH(\mu) = \frac{1}{\ln |X|} \sum\limits_{A \in 2^X} m(A) \ln |A|$, where m is the Möbius transform of μ.

By definition, an imprecision index ν is called *strict* if $\nu(\mu_1) < \nu(\mu_2)$ for $\mu_1 > \mu_2$ ($\mu_1 > \mu_2$ means that $\mu_1 \geqslant \mu_2$ and $\mu_1 \neq \mu_2$).

Remark 1. In the sequel we will apply imprecision indices to measures in $\bar{M}_{bel}$. In this case any $Bel \in \bar{M}_{bel}$ is represented as

$$Bel = (1 - m(\emptyset))Bel' + m(\emptyset)\eta_{\langle \emptyset \rangle},$$

where $Bel' \in M_{bel}$ is the non-contradictory part of Bel, and $\eta_{\langle \emptyset \rangle}$ is its contradictory part. Let us notice that $\eta_{\langle \emptyset \rangle}(A) = 1$ for all $A \in 2^X$. We assume that $\nu(\eta_{\langle \emptyset \rangle}) = 0$, and for any imprecision index

$$\nu(Bel) = (1 - m(\emptyset))\nu(Bel').$$

4   Generalized Dempster-Shafer Rules and the Partial Order of Specialization

Given a belief function Bel_1 and m_1 is its bba. In the next we will consider set functions $\Phi : 2^X \times 2^X \to [0, 1]$ with the following property: $\sum\limits_{B \in 2^X} \Phi(A, B) = 1$ for any $B \in 2^X$. Then a belief function Bel_2 with the bba $m_2(B) = \sum\limits_{A \in 2^X} \Phi(A, B)m_1(A)$ is the linear transform of Bel_1 produced by the linear operator Φ. One can distinguish contraction and expansive linear transforms. A linear transform Φ is called the *contraction transform* if $\Phi(A, B) = 0$ for $A \supset B$, and it is called *expansive* if $\Phi(A, B) = 0$ for $A \subset B$. We will write $Bel_1 \preccurlyeq Bel_2$ if Bel_2 can be obtained from Bel_1 using some contraction transform, or equivalently, if Bel_1 can be obtained from Bel_2 using an expansive transform. In evidence theory such partial order is called *specialization* [9]. It is easy to show [9] that $Bel_1 \preccurlyeq Bel_2$ implies $Bel_1 \leqslant Bel_2$, but the opposite is not true in general.

Lemma 1. $Bel_1 \preccurlyeq Bel_2$ *iff* Bel_1 *and* Bel_2 *can be represented as* $Bel_1 = \sum\limits_{i=1}^{N} a_i \eta_{\langle A_i \rangle}$, $Bel_2 = \sum\limits_{i=1}^{N} a_i \eta_{\langle B_i \rangle}$, *where* $A_i \supseteq B_i$, $a_i > 0$, $i = 1, ..., N$, $\sum\limits_{i=1}^{N} a_i = 1$.

Let us show that the GD-S rule can be considered as the contraction linear transform. Let $Bel_1, Bel_2 \in M_{bel}$ with corresponding bbas m_1 and m_2. Then the

GD-S rule is computed with the help of m, satisfying (2), by formula:

$$Bel = \sum_{A,B \in 2^X} m(A,B)\eta_{\langle A \cap B \rangle}.$$

Since $Bel = \sum_{B \in 2^X} m(A,B)\eta_{\langle A \rangle}$, $Bel_2 = \sum_{A \in 2^X} m(A,B)\eta_{\langle B \rangle}$ and $\eta_{\langle A \cap B \rangle} \geqslant \eta_{\langle A \rangle}$, $\eta_{\langle A \cap B \rangle} \geqslant \eta_{\langle B \rangle}$, with the help of Lemma 1 we find that $Bel_1 \preccurlyeq Bel$ and $Bel_2 \preccurlyeq Bel$.

5 The Choice of Generalized Dempster-Shafer Rules Based on Imprecision Indices

It is well-known that the classical D-S rule leads to strange results if it is applied to conflicting sources of information or to sources that contradict to each other. For example, if we apply the D-S rule to sources of information that are described by the same probability measure P on 2^X, where $X = \{x_1, ..., x_n\}$. Then we get the probability measure P' with

$$P'(\{x_i\}) = P^2(\{x_i\})/\sum_{k=1}^{n} P^2(\{x_k\}).$$

Thus, the analysis of applicability of D-S rule can be based on measuring uncertainty in the sources of information and the results of its application. For example, it may be assumed that the D-S rule is applicable if the value r_{DS} is close to 1. On the other hand, we can use the GD-S rule, in which values $m(A,B)$ are unknown. In this case the results of such rules are characterized by the contradiction in resulting belief measure and by the measure of its non-specificity or imprecision. Based on the maximum uncertainty principle, we can formulate the optimization problem of choosing the optimal GD-S rule as follows.

1. The GD-S rule is applicable if the contradiction in the obtained result is not less than a chosen value r_0.

2. Among all applicable rules one can choose the rule with the most imprecise result.

3. If we get the non-unique solution on the step 2, then we take the rule giving less contradiction.

Thus, the choice of the optimal GD-S rule is a linear programming problem if for measuring uncertainty we take linear imprecision indices. In this case the linear programming problem is formulated as follows.

Find a non-negative function $m(A,B)$, satisfying

$$\begin{cases} \sum_{B \in 2^X} m(A,B) = m_1(A), A \in 2^X, \\ \sum_{A \in 2^X} m(A,B) = m_2(B), B \in 2^X, \\ \sum_{A \cap B = \emptyset} m(A,B) \leqslant r_0, \end{cases}$$

and giving the maximum of $\nu(Bel)$, where ν is a strict imprecision index, and the belief measure Bel corresponds to bba $m(C) = \sum_{A \cap B = C} m(A, B)$. If this optimization problem has a non-unique solution, then we choose m with the minimal contradiction $r = \sum_{A \cap B = \emptyset} m(A, B)$.

Theorem 1. *The choice of optimal GD-S rule is equivalent to the following optimization problem.*

Find $Bel \in \bar{M}_{bel}$ for given $Bel_1, Bel_2 \in M_{bel}$ such that

1) $Bel = \arg \sup \{\nu(Bel) | Bel_1 \preccurlyeq Bel, Bel_2 \preccurlyeq Bel, Bel(\emptyset) \leqslant r_0\}$;

2) If we have non-unique solution in 1) then we choose Bel with less $Bel(\emptyset)$.

Remark 2. Let us notice that $\bar{M}_{bel}$ is a partially ordered set w.r.t. $\preccurlyeq$, and Theorem 1 shows that minimal elements of $\{Bel \in \bar{M}_{bel} | Bel_1 \preccurlyeq Bel, Bel_2 \preccurlyeq Bel\}$ for fixed $Bel_1, Bel_2 \in M_{bel}$ can be constructed by the GD-S rules.

Remark 3. In [3] Cattaneo proposes to seek for an optimal GD-S rule among rules with the less contradiction and with the minimum of non-specificity measured by the generalized Hartley measure.

Example 1. Consider two belief functions $Bel_1 = 0.5\eta_{\langle \{x_1, x_2\} \rangle} + 0.5\eta_{\langle \{x_1\} \rangle}$, $Bel_2 = 0.5\eta_{\langle \{x_1, x_2\} \rangle} + 0.5\eta_{\langle \{x_2\} \rangle}$ on 2^X, where $X = \{x_1, x_2\}$. Then applying the classical D-S rule gives the following result:

$$DS(Bel_1, Bel_2) = 0.25\eta_{\langle \{x_1, x_2\} \rangle} + 0.25\eta_{\langle \{x_1\} \rangle} + 0.25\eta_{\langle \{x_2\} \rangle} + 0.25\eta_{\langle \emptyset \rangle}.$$

If we choose a GD-S rule by any strict imprecision index with $r_0 \in [0, 0.5]$ we get the following result:

$$GDS(Bel_1, Bel_2) = r_0\eta_{\langle \{x_1, x_2\} \rangle} + (0.5 - r_0)\eta_{\langle \{x_1\} \rangle} + (0.5 - r_0)\eta_{\langle \{x_2\} \rangle} + r_0\eta_{\langle \emptyset \rangle}$$

Let us notice that if $r_0 = 0$ then the result of GD-S rule is a probability measure, taking $r_0 = 0.25$ we get the classical D-S rule and the value $r_0 = 0.5$ implies the most imprecise result.

6   Conclusion

In this investigation we propose new ways of choosing optimal GD-S rules for aggregating sources of information based on imprecision indices. These optimal GD-S rules have desirable properties, in particular, it is possible to extract consonant and non-consonant in bodies of evidence of combining belief functions. The presented Theorem 1 allows us to make the conclusion that the choice of the optimal rule should be based on the solution of approximation problem, in which we approximate from above the maximum of aggregating belief functions.

Many interesting problems remain outside of this article. For instance, it is also very important to find additional criteria, when GD-S rules are not applicable or when the application of different GD-S rules can lead to the opposite results. In this case it is possible to choose a decision based on all possible optimal rules and this may be a field of future research.

References

1. Brodzik, A.K., Enders, R.H.: A case of combination of evidence in the Dempster-Shafer theory inconsistent with evaluation of probabilities. CoRR abs/1107.0082 (2011)
2. Bronevich, A.G., Lepskiy, A.E.: Measuring uncertainty with imprecision indices. In: Proc. of the Fifth International Symposium on imprecise probability: Theory and Applications, Prague, Czech Republic, pp. 47–56 (2007)
3. Cattaneo, M.: Combining belief functions issued from dependent sources. In: Bernard, J.-M., Seidenfeld, T., Zaffalon, M. (eds.) ISIPTA 2003, Proceedings in Informatics, vol. 18, pp. 133–147. Carleton Scientific, Waterloo (2003)
4. Cattaneo, M.: Belief functions combination without the assumption of independence of the information sources. International Journal of Approximate Reasoning 52, 299–315 (2011)
5. Chateauneuf, A., Jaffray, J.Y.: Some characterizations of lower probabilities and other monotone capacities through the use of Möbius inversion. Mathematical Social Sciences 52, 263–283 (1989)
6. Denneberg, D.: Non-additive measure and integral. Kluwer, Dordrecht (1997)
7. Destercke, S., Dubois, D., Chojnacki, E.: Cautious conjunctive merging of belief functions. In: Mellouli, K. (ed.) ECSQARU 2007. LNCS (LNAI), vol. 4724, pp. 332–343. Springer, Heidelberg (2007)
8. Destercke, S., Dubois, D.: Can the minimum rule of possibility theory be extended to belief functions? In: Sossai, C., Chemello, G. (eds.) ECSQARU 2009. LNCS, vol. 5590, pp. 299–310. Springer, Heidelberg (2009)
9. Dubois, D., Prade, H.: A set-theoretic view of belief functions: logical operations and approximations by fuzzy sets. International Journal of General Systems 12, 193–226 (1986)
10. Dubois, D., Prade, H.: Representation and combination of uncertainty with belief functions and possibility measures. Comput. Intell. 4, 244–264 (1988)
11. Dubois, D., Yager, R.: Fuzzy set connectives as combination of belief structures. Information Sciences 66, 245–275 (1992)
12. Lefevre, E., Colot, O., Vannoorenberghe, P.: Belief function combination and conflict management. Information Fusion 3, 149–162 (2002)
13. Liu, W.: Analyzing the degree of conflict among belief functions. Artificial Intelligence 170, 909–924 (2006)
14. Martin, A., Osswald, C., Dezert, J.: General combination rules for qualitative and quantitative beliefs. Journal of advances in information fusion 3, 67–89 (2008)
15. Smets, P.: Analyzing the combination of conflicting belief functions. Information Fusion 8, 387–412 (2007)
16. Yager, R.: On the Dempster-Shafer framework and new combination rules. Information Sciences 41, 93–137 (1987)
17. Zadeh, L.A.: Review of Shafer's "A Mathematical Theory of Evidence". AI Magazine 5, 81–83 (1984)

General Schemes of Combining Rules
and the Quality Characteristics of Combining

Alexander Lepskiy*

Higher School of Economics, 20 Myasnitskaya Ulitsa, Moscow, 101000, Russia
alex.lepskiy@gmail.com

Abstract. Some general schemes and examples of aggregation of two belief functions into a single belief function are considered in this paper. We find some sufficient conditions of change of ignorance when evidences are combined with the help of various rules. It is shown that combining rules can be regarded as pessimistic or optimistic depending on the sign of the change of ignorance after applying.

Keywords: combining rules, change of ignorance.

1 Introduction

The study of combining rules of evidence is one of the central directions of research in the belief function theory. The combining rule can be considered as an operator which aggregates the information obtained from different sources. The review of some popular combining rules can be found in [14].

This paper has two purposes. The first purpose is research of general schemes of combining of evidences. We can consider the combining rule as a special type of aggregation function [9] $\varphi : Bel^2(X) \to Bel(X)$, where $Bel(X)$ be a set of all belief functions on finite set X. The different axioms of aggregation of information obtained from different sources are considered (see, for example, [16], [4], [11], [10]). Some general schemes and examples of aggregation of two belief functions into a single belief function are given in Section 4.

The second purpose is research of quality characteristics of combining. These characteristics can be divided into a priori characteristics that estimate the quality of information sources and a posteriori characteristics which estimate the result of combining. The following characteristics are relevant to the first group: a) the reliability of sources in discount rule [15]; b) the conflict measure of evidence [12] in Dempster's rule, Yage's rule [17] etc.; c) the degree of independence of evidence. The amount of change of ignorance after the use of combining rule is the most important a posteriori characteristic. The amount of ignorance that contained in evidence can be estimated with the help of imprecision indices [3]. The generalized Hartley measure is an example of such index [6]. Some sufficient

---

* The study was implemented in the framework of The Basic Research Program of the Higher School of Economics. This work was supported by the grant 14-07-00189 of RFBR (Russian Foundation for Basic Research).

F. Cuzzolin (Ed.): BELIEF 2014, LNAI 8764, pp. 29–38, 2014.

conditions of change of ignorance when evidences are combined with the help of various rules are described in Section 5.

We have to take into account not only aggregated evidences but also who combines this evidence. For example, let we have information from two sources about prognosticated share price. Let the first source predicted that share price will be in an interval A_1 and the second source predicted share price in an interval A_2. If a pessimist aggregates the information from two sources then he will predict the share price in the set $A_1 \cup A_2$. But if an optimist aggregates the information then he will predict the share price in the set $A_1 \cap A_2$. In other words, decision maker applies the different combining rules in depending on the price of a wrong decision, an own caution and other factors. It is known that some combining rules (for example, Dubois and Prade's disjunctive consensus rule [8]) have a pessimistic character in the sense that amount of ignorance does not decrease after their applying. The other rules are optimistic because the amount of ignorance is decreased after their applying. The majority of rules have the mixed type because their character depends on a posteriori characteristics of information sources. In Section 6 it is shown that level of optimism or pessimism in combining rule can be estimated numerically with the help of imprecision indices.

2   Basic Definitions and Notation

The notion of belief function is the main notion of Dempster-Shafer theory (evidence theory). Let X be a finite universal set, 2^X is a set of all subsets of X. We will consider the belief function (or belief measure) [15] $g : 2^X \to [0,1]$. The value $g(A)$, $A \in 2^X$, is interpreted as a degree of confidence that the true alternative of X belongs to set A. A belief function g is defined with the help of set function $m_g(A)$ called the basic probability assignment (bpa). This function should satisfy the following conditions [15]: $m_g : 2^X \to [0,1]$, $m_g(\emptyset) = 0$, $\sum_{A \subseteq X} m_g(A) = 1$. Then

$$g(A) = \sum_{B:\, B \subseteq A} m_g(B).$$

Let the set of all belief measures on 2^X be denoted by $Bel(X)$ and the set of all set functions on 2^X be denoted by $M(X)$.

The belief function $g \in Bel(X)$ can be represented with the help of so called categorical belief functions $\eta_{\langle B \rangle}(A) = \begin{cases} 1, B \subseteq A, \\ 0, B \not\subseteq A, \end{cases}$ $A \subseteq X$ $B \neq \emptyset$. Then $g = \sum_{B \in 2^X \setminus \{\emptyset\}} m_g(B)\eta_{\langle B \rangle}$. The subset $A \in 2^X$ is called a focal element if $m_g(A) > 0$. Let $\mathcal{A}(g)$ be the set of all focal elements related to the belief function g. The pair $F(g) = (\mathcal{A}(g), m_g)$ is called a body of evidence. Let $\mathcal{F}(X)$ be the set of all bodies of evidence on X.

3   Combining Rules

We consider below only a few basic combining rules.

a) Dempster's rule. This rule was introduced in [5] and generalized in [15] for combining arbitrary independent evidence. This rule is defined as

$$m_D(A) = \frac{1}{1-K} \sum_{A_1 \cap A_2 = A} m_{g_1}(A_1) m_{g_2}(A_2), \ \ A \neq \emptyset, \ \ m_D(\emptyset) = 0, \qquad (1)$$

$$K = K(g_1, g_2) = \sum_{A_1 \cap A_2 = \emptyset} m_{g_1}(A_1) m_{g_2}(A_2). \qquad (2)$$

The value $K(g_1, g_2)$ characterizes the amount of conflict in two information sources which defined with the help of bodies of evidence $F(g_1)$ and $F(g_2)$. If $K(g_1, g_2) = 1$ then it means that information sources are absolutely conflicting and Dempster's rule cannot be applied.

The discount of bpa was introduced by Shafer [15] for accounting of reliability of information:

$$m^\alpha(A) = (1-\alpha)m(A), \ \ A \neq X, \ \ m^\alpha(X) = \alpha + (1-\alpha)m(X). \qquad (3)$$

The coefficient $\alpha \in [0, 1]$ characterizes the degree of reliability of information. If $\alpha = 0$ then it means that information source is absolutely reliable. If $\alpha = 1$ then it means that information source is absolutely non-reliable. The Dempster's rule (2) applies after discounting of bpa of two evidences. This modification often called the discount rule.

b) Yager's modified Dempster's rule. This rule was introduced in [17] and it is defined as

$$q(A) = \sum_{A_1 \cap A_2 = A} m_{g_1}(A_1) m_{g_2}(A_2), \ \ A \in 2^X, \qquad (4)$$

$$m_Y(A) = q(A), \ \ A \neq \emptyset, X, \ \ m_Y(\emptyset) = q(\emptyset) = K, \ \ m_Y(X) = m_Y(\emptyset) + q(X). \quad (5)$$

c) Zhang's center combination rule. This rule was introduced in [18] and it is defined as

$$m_Z(A) = \sum_{A_1 \cap A_2 = A} r(A_1, A_2) m_{g_1}(A_1) m_{g_2}(A_2), \ \ A \in 2^X,$$

where $r(A_1, A_2)$ is a measure of intersection of sets A_1 and A_2.

d) Dubois and Prade's disjunctive consensus rule [8]:

$$m_{DP}(A) = \sum_{A_1 \cup A_2 = A} m_{g_1}(A_1) m_{g_2}(A_2), \ \ A \in 2^X. \qquad (6)$$

Any combining rule of two bodies of evidence induces aggregation of two belief functions which correspond to these bodies.

4   Combining Rule Both the Aggregation of Evidence

We will consider an operator $\varphi : Bel^2(X) \to Bel(X)$ that is called the aggregation of two belief functions $g_1, g_2 \in Bel(X)$ in one belief function $g = \varphi(g_1, g_2) \in Bel(X)$. The vector of bpa $(m_g(B))_{B \subseteq X}$ corresponds bijective (with the help of Möbius transform) to belief function $g \in Bel(X)$ if we define some ordering of all subsets of the universal set X: $g \leftrightarrow \mathbf{m}_g = (m_g(B))_{B \subseteq X}$. Therefore there is an aggregation of bpa $\mathbf{m}_g = \Phi(\mathbf{m}_{g_1}, \mathbf{m}_{g_2})$ for any aggregation of belief functions $g = \varphi(g_1, g_2)$ and vice versa. We consider some special cases of aggregation of belief functions.

1. Pointwise Aggregation of Belief Functions. The new value of belief function $g(A) = \varphi(g_1(A), g_2(A))$ is associated with every pair $(g_1(A), g_2(A))$ of belief functions on the same set $A \in 2^X$. In this case the aggregation operator φ is a function $\varphi : [0, 1]^2 \to [0, 1]$ which must satisfy the special conditions for preserving total monotonicity of resulting set function. These conditions can be formulated in terms of finite differences, defined with the help of the following constructions: if $\Delta \mathbf{x}_1, ..., \Delta \mathbf{x}_s \in [0, 1]^2$ $(\mathbf{x} + \Delta \mathbf{x}_1 + ... + \Delta \mathbf{x}_k \in [0, 1]^2$ for all $k = 1, ..., s)$ then $\Delta^s \varphi(\mathbf{x}; \Delta \mathbf{x}_1, ..., \Delta \mathbf{x}_s) = \sum_{k=0}^{s} (-1)^{s-k} \sum_{1 \leq i_1 < ... < i_k \leq s} \varphi(\mathbf{x} + \Delta \mathbf{x}_{i_1} + ... + \Delta \mathbf{x}_{i_k})$ (if $k = 0$ then appropriate summand is equal $(-1)^s \varphi(\mathbf{x})$).

Theorem 1. *[1], [2]. The function $\varphi : [0, 1]^2 \to [0, 1]$ defines the aggregation operator of belief functions by the rule $g(A) = \varphi(g_1(A), g_2(A))$, $A \in 2^X$, $g_1, g_2 \in Bel(X)$ iff it satisfies the conditions:*

1. $\varphi(\mathbf{0}) = 0$, $\varphi(\mathbf{1}) = 1$;
2. $\Delta^k \varphi(\mathbf{x}; \Delta \mathbf{x}_1, ..., \Delta \mathbf{x}_k) \geq 0$, $k = 1, 2, ...$ *for all* $\mathbf{x}, \Delta \mathbf{x}_1, ..., \Delta \mathbf{x}_k \in [0; 1]^2$, $\mathbf{x} + \Delta \mathbf{x}_1 + ... + \Delta \mathbf{x}_k \in [0, 1]^2$.

2. Pointwise Aggregation of BPA. The new bpa $m_g(A) = \Phi(m_{g_1}(A), m_{g_2}(A))$ is associated with every pair $(m_{g_1}(A), m_{g_2}(A))$ of bpa for all $A \in 2^X$. Note that this aggregation was considered in [13] in the case of probability measures and it was called Strong Stepwise Function Property.

Theorem 2. *The continuous function $\Phi : [0, 1]^2 \to [0, 1]$ defines the aggregation operator of bpa by the rule $m_g(A) = \Phi(m_{g_1}(A), m_{g_2}(A))$, $A \in 2^X$, $g_1, g_2 \in Bel(X)$ iff it satisfies the condition $\Phi(s, t) = \lambda s + (1 - \lambda)t$, $\lambda \in [0, 1]$.*

Proof. We prove this result for $X = \{x_1, x_2\}$ without loss of generality. Let $S = \{\mathbf{x} = (x_i) : \sum_i x_i = 1, x_i \in [0, 1] \; \forall i\}$. Then function $\Phi : [0, 1]^2 \to [0, 1]$ defines the above operator of aggregation satisfying the condition: if $\mathbf{x} = (x_i)$, $\mathbf{y} = (y_i) \in S$ and $\Phi(x_i, y_i) = z_i$, then $\mathbf{z} = (z_i) \in S$. We have for $\mathbf{x} = (\alpha, r - \alpha, 1 - r)$, $\mathbf{y} = (p, p, 1 - 2p) \in S$

$$\Phi(\alpha, p) + \Phi(r - \alpha, p) + \Phi(1 - r, 1 - 2p) = 1, \tag{7}$$

where $\alpha, r, r - \alpha \in [0, 1]$, $p \in [0, \frac{1}{2}]$. On the other side the following equality

$$\Phi(r, p) + \Phi(1 - r, 1 - p) = 1 \tag{8}$$

is true for $\mathbf{x} = (r, p, 0)$, $\mathbf{y} = (1 - r, 1 - p, 0) \in S$. Then we have from (7) and (8)

$$\Phi(\alpha, p) + \Phi(r - \alpha, p) = \Phi(r, p) + \Phi(1 - r, 1 - p) - \Phi(1 - r, 1 - 2p).$$

If we take $p = 0$ in last equality then the following equation is true $\Phi(\alpha, 0) + \Phi(r - \alpha, 0) = \Phi(r, 0)$. If $r - \alpha = \beta$ then last equality can be rewritten as $\Phi(\alpha, 0) + \Phi(\beta, 0) = \Phi(\alpha + \beta, 0)$. In other words, the function $\Phi(s, 0)$ satisfies Cauchy's functional equation on $[0, 1]$. It is known that if a continious function satisfies Cauchy's functional equation then it is an additive function: $\Phi(s, 0) = k_1 s$, $s \in [0, 1]$ and $k_1 \in [0, 1]$ because $\Phi(s, 0) \in [0, 1]$ for all $s \in [0, 1]$. By analogy $\Phi(0, t) = k_2 t$, $t \in [0, 1]$, $k_2 \in [0, 1]$. Now we get from (7) for $r = 1$, $p = 0$

$$\Phi(1, 0) + \Phi(0, 1) = k_1 + k_2 = 1. \tag{9}$$

If $\mathbf{x} = (1 - \alpha, 0, \alpha)$, $\mathbf{y} = (0, 1 - \beta, \beta) \in S$, $\alpha, \beta \in [0, 1]$ then we have $\Phi(1 - \alpha, 0) + \Phi(0, 1 - \beta) + \Phi(\alpha, \beta) = 1$. Thus $\Phi(\alpha, \beta) = 1 - \Phi(1 - \alpha, 0) - \Phi(0, 1 - \beta) = 1 - k_1(1 - \alpha) - k_2(1 - \beta) = k_1 \alpha + k_2 \beta$, with account of (9).

This result is a generalization of the corresponding result for probability measures [13].

3. Bilinear Aggregation of Belief Functions. In this case the aggregation function φ should be linear for each argument so

$$\varphi(\alpha g_1 + (1 - \alpha) g_2, g_3) = \alpha \varphi(g_1, g_3) + (1 - \alpha) \varphi(g_2, g_3), \quad \alpha \in [0, 1]. \tag{10}$$

Since we have $g_i = \sum_{B \in 2^X \setminus \{\emptyset\}} m_{g_i}(B) \eta_{\langle B \rangle} \in Bel(X)$, $i = 1, 2$, then every bilinear function on $Bel^2(X)$ has the form

$$\varphi(g_1, g_2) = \sum_{A, B \in 2^X \setminus \{\emptyset\}} m_{g_1}(A) m_{g_2}(B) \gamma_{A,B}, \tag{11}$$

where $\gamma_{A,B} = \varphi(\eta_{\langle A \rangle}, \eta_{\langle B \rangle})$ is some set function on 2^X.

We consider the non-empty set $\mathcal{B}(X) \subseteq Bel^2(X)$ which satisfies the condition: if $(g_1, g_2) \in \mathcal{B}(X)$ then $(\eta_{\langle A \rangle}, \eta_{\langle B \rangle}) \in \mathcal{B}(X)$ for all $A \in \mathcal{A}(g_1)$, $B \in \mathcal{A}(g_2)$.

Theorem 3. *The bilinear set function $\varphi : \mathcal{B}(X) \to M(X)$ of the form (11) determines the belief function iff $\gamma_{A,B} = \varphi(\eta_{\langle A \rangle}, \eta_{\langle B \rangle}) \in Bel(X)$ for all $(\eta_{\langle A \rangle}, \eta_{\langle B \rangle}) \in \mathcal{B}(X)$.*

The Dubois and Prade's disjunctive consensus rule and Dempster's rule (Yager's rule) for non conflicting evidences are the examples of bilinear aggregation functions of the form (11).

4. Bilinear Normalized Aggregation of Belief Functions. We consider the aggregation function of belief measures of the form

$$\varphi_0(g_1, g_2) = \frac{\varphi(g_1, g_2)}{\varphi(g_1, g_2)(X)}, \tag{12}$$

where $\varphi(g_1, g_2)$ is a bilinear aggregation function which satisfies the condition (10). We will consider that $\gamma_{A,B}(C) \geq 0$ for all $A, B, C \in 2^X \setminus \{\emptyset\}$. It is obvious that aggregation function φ_0 cannot be determined on the whole set $Bel^2(X)$. The function φ_0 will be determined on the set

$$\mathcal{B}_\varphi(X) = \left\{ (g_1, g_2) \in Bel^2(X) \mid \exists\, A_i \in \mathcal{A}(g_i),\ i = 1, 2:\ \varphi\left(\eta_{\langle A_1\rangle}, \eta_{\langle A_2\rangle}\right)(X) \neq 0 \right\}$$

that follows from (11).

Theorem 4. *Let φ be a bilinear aggregation function which satisfies the condition (10). The function $\varphi_0 : \mathcal{B}_\varphi(X) \to M(X)$ of the form (12) determines the belief function iff $\gamma_{A,B}/\gamma_{A,B}(X) \in Bel(X)$, $\gamma_{A,B} = \varphi\left(\eta_{\langle A\rangle}, \eta_{\langle B\rangle}\right)$ for all $\left(\eta_{\langle A\rangle}, \eta_{\langle B\rangle}\right) \in \mathcal{B}_\varphi(X)$.*

The Dempster's rule and Zhang's center combination rule are the examples of bilinear normalized aggregation functions of the form (12):

5   Change of Ignorance When Evidences Are Combined

Let we have two sources of information, and this information is described by belief functions $g_1, g_2 \in Bel(X)$ respectively. Let some rule φ be used for combining of these belief functions. We will get the new belief function $g = \varphi(g_1, g_2) \in Bel(X)$. The different information characteristics of aggregation of belief functions were studied in a number of works (see [7]). Below we consider only one aspect associated with change of information uncertainty. The measure of information uncertainty associated to the each belief function. Then we have a question about change of this measure after combining of evidence. There are some approaches for defining uncertainty measures in evidence theory. We will follow the approach which was considered in [3]. This approach is based on the notion of imprecision index.

Let we know only that true alternative belongs to the non-empty set $B \subseteq X$. This situation can be described with the help of primitive belief measure $\eta_{\langle B\rangle}(A)$, $A \subseteq X$, which gives the lower probability of an event $x \in A$. The degree of uncertainty of such measure is described by the well-known Hartley's measure $H(\eta_{\langle B\rangle}) = \log_2 |B|$. There is the generalization of Hartley's measure. Let g be a belief function that can be represented by $g = \sum_{B \in 2^X \setminus \{\emptyset\}} m_g(B)\eta_{\langle B\rangle} \in Bel(X)$. Then the generalized Hartley's measure is defined by [6] $GH(g) = \sum_{B \in 2^X \setminus \{\emptyset\}} m_g(B)\log_2 |B|$.

Definition 1. *[3]. A functional $f : Bel(X) \to [0, 1]$ is called an imprecision index if the following conditions are fulfilled:*

1. *if g is a probability measure then $f(g) = 0$;*
2. *$f(g_1) \geq f(g_2)$ for all $g_1, g_2 \in Bel(X)$ where $g_1 \leq g_2$ (i.e. $g_1(A) \leq g_2(A)$ for all $A \in 2^X$);*
3. *$f\left(\eta_{\langle X\rangle}\right) = 1$.*

We call the imprecision index strict if $f(g) = 0 \Leftrightarrow g$ is a probability measure. The imprecision index f on $Bel(X)$ is called linear (lii) if for any linear combination $\sum_{j=1}^{k} \alpha_j g_j \in Bel(X)$, $\alpha_j \in \mathbb{R}$, $g_j \in Bel(X)$, $j = 1, ..., k$, we have $f\left(\sum_{j=1}^{k} \alpha_j g_j\right) = \sum_{j=1}^{k} \alpha_j f(g_j)$.

Since any linear functional f on $Bel(X)$ is defined uniquely by its values on a set of primitive measures $\{\eta_{\langle B \rangle}\}_{B \in 2^X \setminus \{\emptyset\}}$, then it allows us to define f with the help of set function $\mu_f : 2^X \to \mathbb{R}$ by the rule $\mu_f(B) = f\left(\eta_{\langle B \rangle}\right)$, $B \in 2^X \setminus \{\emptyset\}$. We set by definition that $\mu_f(\emptyset) = 0$ for every imprecision index f.

Proposition 1. *[3]. A functional $f : Bel(X) \to [0,1]$ is a lii on $Bel(X)$ iff $f(g) = \sum_{B \in 2^X \setminus \{\emptyset\}} m_g(B) \mu_f(B)$, where set function μ_f satisfies the conditions:*

1. *$\mu_f(\{x\}) = 0$ for all $x \in X$;*
2. *$\mu_f(X) = f\left(\eta_{\langle X \rangle}\right) = 1$;*
3. *$\sum_{B: A \subseteq B} (-1)^{|B \setminus A|} \mu_f(B) \leq 0$ for all $A \neq \emptyset, X$.*

Now we are going to give some sufficient conditions for the different rules under which the amount of ignorance decreases or increases after combining. The first result is well known [7].

Proposition 2. *If $g = \varphi_{DP}(g_1, g_2)$, $g_1, g_2 \in Bel(X)$, where φ_{DP} is the Dubois and Prade's disjunctive consensus rule (6), then inequalities $f(g) \geq f(g_i)$, $i = 1, 2$ are true for any lii f.*

Proposition 3. *Let g_1, g_2 be such belief measures that their conflict measure $K(g_1, g_2) = 0$ and $g = \varphi_{\alpha, \beta}(g_1, g_2)$, where $\varphi_{\alpha, \beta}$ is a Dempster's rule (1) after applied of discount rule (3) to the g_1, g_2 with coefficients $\alpha, \beta \in [0, 1]$ correspondingly. If the inequality $\alpha\beta + (1 - \alpha)\beta m_{g_1}(X) + \alpha(1 - \beta)m_{g_2}(X) \leq (\alpha + \beta - \alpha\beta)f(g_i)$, is true for lii f then $f(g) \leq f(g_i)$, $i = 1, 2$.*

The last Proposition shows that the amount of ignorance is decreased obviously after combining of evidence with the help of discount rule if ignorance of initial evidence were largish.

Proposition 4. *Let g_1, g_2 be such belief measures that their conflict measure (see formula (2)) $K = K(g_1, g_2)$ satisfies the condition $K + m_{g_1}(X)m_{g_2}(X) \leq m_{g_i}(X)$, $i = 1, 2$, $g = \varphi_Y(g_1, g_2)$, where φ_Y is a Yager's rule (4)-(5). Then the inequalities $f(g) \leq f(g_i)$, $i = 1, 2$ are true for any lii f.*

The value $m_{g_1}(X)$ characterizes the imprecision of information given by function g_1. Therefore the condition $K + m_{g_1}(X)m_{g_2}(X) \leq m_{g_1}(X) \Leftrightarrow K \leq m_{g_1}(X) (1 - m_{g_2}(X))$ in Proposition 4 means that the amount of ignorance can be decreased with the help of Yager's rule if the conflict between the evidences is not very large with respect to amount of ignorance.

Corollary 1. *Let g_1, g_2 be such belief measures that their conflict measure (see formula (2)) $K(g_1, g_2) = 0$, $g = \varphi(g_1, g_2)$, where φ is Dempster's rule (1). Then the inequalities $f(g) \leq f(g_i)$, $i = 1, 2$ are true for any lii f.*

This corollary shows that the imprecision of information is not increased if we aggregate information from many non-conflict sources with the help of Dempster's rule (Yager's rule). If we have conflicting information sources ($K > 0$) then resulting evidence can have a larger imprecision than the imprecision of sources (see [12]). But we can formulate the following sufficient condition of decreasing of ignorance for Dempster's rule and conflicting ($K > 0$) information sources.

Let C be the smallest number satisfying the inequality $\mu_f(A_1 \cap A_2) \leq C\mu_f(A_1)$ $\mu_f(A_2)$ for all $A_i \in \mathcal{A}(g_i)$, $i = 1, 2$. Note that $\min\limits_{A:\mu_f(A)>0} \mu_f(A) \leq \frac{1}{C}$. Moreover $C \geq 1$ if belief functions g_1, g_2 are not probability measures and f is a strict lii.

Proposition 5. *Let g_1, g_2 are such belief measures that their conflict measure $K = K(g_1, g_2) \neq 1$ satisfies the condition $K \leq 1 - Cf(g_2)$ ($K \leq 1 - Cf(g_1)$), $g = \varphi_D(g_1, g_2)$, where φ_D is a Dempster's rule (1). Then inequality $f(g) \leq f(g_1)$ ($f(g) \leq f(g_2)$) is true for any strict lii f.*

6   Pessimistic and Optimistic Combining Rules

Let we have two sources of information, and this information is described by primitive belief functions $\eta_{\langle A \rangle}$ and $\eta_{\langle B \rangle}$ respectively, where $A, B \in 2^X \setminus \{\emptyset\}$. The first source states that true alternative is contained in set A, but second source states that true alternative is contained in set B.

If we apply the Dubois and Prade's disjunctive consensus rule for these primitive belief functions then we will get $\varphi_{DP}(\eta_{\langle A \rangle}, \eta_{\langle B \rangle}) = \eta_{\langle A \cup B \rangle}$. By other words we got the statement that a true alternative is contained in set $A \cup B$. This statement can be considered as more pessimistic than an initial statement because uncertainty does not decreased after combining. For example, if lii of initial measures was equal to $f(\eta_{\langle A \rangle}) = \mu_f(A)$ and $f(\eta_{\langle B \rangle}) = \mu_f(B)$ respectively, then this index is equal to $f(\eta_{\langle A \cup B \rangle}) = \mu_f(A \cup B) \geq f(\eta_{\langle A \rangle})$ for resulting measure.

If we apply the Dempster's rule for these primitive belief functions then we will get $\varphi_D(\eta_{\langle A \rangle}, \eta_{\langle B \rangle}) = \eta_{\langle A \cap B \rangle}$ for $A \cap B \neq \emptyset$. We got the statement after combining that a true alternative is contained in set $A \cap B$. This statement can be considered to be more optimistic than the initial statement because uncertainty does not increased after combining: $f(\eta_{\langle A \cap B \rangle}) = \mu_f(A \cap B) \leq f(\eta_{\langle A \rangle})$.

If we apply the discount rule for these two primitive belief functions with parameters $\alpha, \beta \in [0, 1]$ respectively, then we will get new measures after discounting $\eta_{\langle A \rangle}^{(\alpha)} = (1 - \alpha)\eta_{\langle A \rangle} + \alpha\eta_{\langle X \rangle}$, $\eta_{\langle B \rangle}^{(\beta)} = (1 - \beta)\eta_{\langle B \rangle} + \beta\eta_{\langle X \rangle}$. Let $A \cap B \neq \emptyset$. Then the conflict $K = 0$ and we get resultant measure after application of Dempster's rule to new discounting measures:

$$g_{\alpha, \beta} = \varphi_D\left(\eta_{\langle A \rangle}^{(\alpha)}, \eta_{\langle B \rangle}^{(\beta)}\right) =$$

$$(1 - \alpha)(1 - \beta)\eta_{\langle A \cap B \rangle} + (1 - \alpha)\beta\eta_{\langle A \rangle} + \alpha(1 - \beta)\eta_{\langle B \rangle} + \alpha\beta\eta_{\langle X \rangle}. \tag{13}$$

We will suppose that the information sources are sufficiently reliable. Then $\alpha, \beta \approx 0$. In this case we will get the following resulting measure instead of (13) if we neglect members of second order of α and β

$$g_{\alpha,\beta} = \varphi_D \left(\eta_{\langle A \rangle}^{(\alpha)}, \eta_{\langle B \rangle}^{(\beta)} \right) = (1 - \alpha - \beta)\eta_{\langle A \cap B \rangle} + \beta\eta_{\langle A \rangle} + \alpha\eta_{\langle B \rangle}.$$

The linear imprecision index of this measure is equal to $f(g_{\alpha,\beta}) = (1 - \alpha - \beta)\mu_f(A \cap B) + \beta\mu_f(A) + \alpha\mu_f(B)$. It is easy to see that in this case we can get different relations between the indices $f(g_{\alpha,\beta})$ and $f(\eta_{\langle A \rangle}) = \mu_f(A)$, $f(\eta_{\langle B \rangle}) = \mu_f(B)$ depending on the choice α and β. In particular, we have

$$\begin{cases} f(g_{\alpha,\beta}) \le f(\eta_{\langle A \rangle}), \\ f(g_{\alpha,\beta}) \le f(\eta_{\langle B \rangle}) \end{cases} \Leftrightarrow \alpha\Delta(B, A) + \beta\Delta(A, B) \le \min\{\Delta(A, B), \Delta(B, A)\},$$

where $\Delta(A, B) = \mu_f(A) - \mu_f(A \cap B)$.

From last estimations we can make the following conclusion. If the degree of reliability of information sources is large (i.e. $\alpha \approx 0$, $\beta \approx 0$) then discount rule will act as optimistic rule. Otherwise, when the information sources are non reliable (α and β are large) then discount rule will be act as pessimistic rule.

7   Conclusion

In this paper we consider some general schemes and examples of aggregation of two belief functions into one belief function. The well-known combining rules are obtained from these general schemes in particular cases. Furthermore, an important a posteriori characteristic of quality of combining like a change of ignorance after the use of combining rule is considered. This value is estimated in this paper with the help of linear imprecision indices.

Some sufficient conditions of change of ignorance after applying of different combining rules are found. In particular we show that amount of ignorance do not decrease after using of Dubois and Prade's disjunctive consensus rule. In contrast the amount of ignorance does not increase after using of Dempster's rule for two non-conflict evidences.

In this sense these rules can be considered as a pessimistic rule and optimistic rule correspondingly. At the same time, the discount rule can be the pessimistic rule or the optimistic rule depending of values of reliability coefficients of information sources. The sufficient conditions on reliability coefficients of this rule to be pessimistic or optimistic were found.

References

1. Bronevich, A.G.: On the closure of families of fuzzy measures under eventwise aggregations. Fuzzy sets and systems 153, 45–70 (2005)
2. Bronevich, A., Lepskiy, A.: Operators for convolution of fuzzy measures. In: Grzegorzewski, P., et al. (eds.) Soft Methods in Probability, Statistics and Data Analysis, pp. 84–91. Physical-Verl., Heidelberg (2002)
3. Bronevich, A., Lepskiy, A.: Measuring uncertainty with imprecision indices. In: Proc. of the Fifth International Symposium on Imprecise Probabilities and Their Applications (ISIPTA 2007), Prague, Czech Republic, pp. 47–56 (2007)

4. Cheng, Y., Kashyap, R.L.: An axiomatic approach for combining evidence from a variety of sources. Journal of Intelligent and Robotic Systems 1(1), 17–33 (1988)
5. Dempster, A.P.: Upper and Lower Probabilities Induced by a Multivalued Mapping. The Annals of Mathematical Statistics 38(2), 325–339 (1967)
6. Dubois, D., Prade, H.: A note on measures of specificity for fuzzy sets. Int. J. of General Systems 10, 279–283 (1985)
7. Dubois, D., Prade, H.: A set-theoretic view of belief functions — Logical operations and approximation by fuzzy sets. Int. J. of General Systems 12(3), 193–226 (1986)
8. Dubois, D., Prade, H.: On the combination of evidence in various mathematical frameworks. In: Flamm, J., Luisi, T. (eds.) Reliability Data Collection and Analysis, pp. 213-241. Brussels, ECSC, EEC, EAFC (1992)
9. Grabisch, M., Marichal, J.L., Mesiar, R., Pap, E.: Aggregation Functions. Cambridge University Press (2009)
10. Jiao, L., Pan, Q., Liang, Y., Feng, X., Yang, F.: Combining sources of evidence with reliability and importance for decision making. Central European Journal of Operations Research, 1–20 (December 2013)
11. Johnson, N.L., Kotz, S.: Axiomatic approaches to formulas for combining likelihoods or evidence. Journal of Statistical Computation and Simulation 31(1), 49–54 (1989)
12. Lepskiy, A.: About Relation between the Measure of Conflict and Decreasing of Ignorance in Theory of Evidence. In: Proc. of the 8th Conf. of the European Society for Fuzzy Logic and Technology, pp. 355–362. Atlantis Press, Amsterdam (2013)
13. McConway, K.J.: Marginalization and Linear Opinion Pools. Journal of the American Statistical Association 76(374), 410–414 (1981)
14. Sentz, K., Ferson, S.: Combination of evidence in Dempster-Shafer theory. Report SAND 2002-0835, Sandia National Laboratories (2002)
15. Shafer, G.: A Mathematical Theory of Evidence. Princeton University Press (1976)
16. Smets, P.: The Combination of Evidence in the Transferable Belief Model. IEEE Trans. PAMI 12, 447–458 (1990)
17. Yager, R.: On the Dempster-Shafer Framework and New Combination Rules. Information Sciences 41, 93–137 (1987)
18. Zhang, L.: Representation, independence, and combination of evidence in the Dempster-Shafer theory. In: Yager, R.R., Kacprzyk, J., Fedrizzi, M. (eds.) Advances in the Dempster-Shafer Theory of Evidence, pp. 51–69. John Wiley & Sons, New York (1994)

An Optimal Unified Combination Rule

Yanyan He[1] and M. Yousuff Hussaini[2]

[1] Scientific Computing and Imaging Institute, Salt Lake City, Utah, USA
[2] Department of Mathematics, Florida State University, Tallahassee, FL, USA
`yhe@sci.utah.edu, yousuff@fsu.edu`

Abstract. This paper presents an optimal unified combination rule within the framework of the Dempster-Shafer theory of evidence to combine multiple bodies of evidence. It is optimal in the sense that the resulting combined m-function has the least dissimilarity with the individual m-functions and therefore represents the greatest amount of information similar to that represented by the original m-functions. Examples are provided to illustrate the proposed combination rule.

Keywords: Dempster-Shafer theory of evidence, Basic belief assignments, Inagaki's rule, Distance measure, Total distance, Optimal unified combination rule.

1 Introduction

Data fusion techniques combine/integrate data from multiple sources (such as models, sensors, institutes, etc.), to achieve more specific and more accurate inference than that obtained from individual sources. Belief functions in the framework of the Dempster-Shafer (DS) theory of evidence have been widely used to represent the uncertainty in each single source of information. Combining information from different sources to obtain a single belief function by implementing proper combination rules on multiple belief functions is our objective. Dempster's rule of combination evolved from the earlier works of Dempster in the 1960s [5], [6] as formalized by Shafer [18]. However, it may produce counterintuitive results when its requirements that the sources are independent, fully reliable, and that the belief functions are correctly constructed are not satisfied.

Numerous alternative combination rules have been proposed over the last few decades [17], [25], [21], [23], [24], [12], [19], [8], [9], [3], [4], [20]. For example, Smets' unnormalized conjunctive rule [21] is based on the open-world assumption and assigns the conflict to the empty set while Yager's rule [23], [24] assigns the conflict to the universal set, which however increases uncertainty; Inagaki [12] introduces a unified rule – a continuous parametrized class of combination rules assigning partial conflict to focal elements proportionally, including Dempster's rule and Yager's rule as special cases.

In the present work, we assume all the pre-processing work (estimating the reliability of sources, discounting the basic belief assignments (BBAs)) has been done and we propose an optimal unified combination rule to combine the processed BBAs. Specifically, we adopt the unified rule due to Inagaki and propose

F. Cuzzolin (Ed.): BELIEF 2014, LNAI 8764, pp. 39–48, 2014.

an optimization problem to determine the values of the parameters (weighting factors). The chosen values are optimal in the sense that the resulting combined BBA represents the greatest amount of information similar to that represented by the individual BBAs.

The paper is organized as follows. The basic concepts of Dempster-Shafer theory including measures, and combination rules are briefly introduced in Section 2. The optimal unified combination rule is proposed in Section 3, where an optimization problem is constructed for the unified rule and the optimal values of the parameters are obtained. Finally, we illustrate the proposed combination rule in a simple example.

2   Background of DS Theory

We recall here the basic notions of Dempster-Shafer theory. Let X be the quantity of interest with the collection of possible values $\mathbf{X} = \{X_1, X_2, ..., X_n\}$, where $\mathbf{X}$ is called the universal set or the frame of discernment. Let A, B be any subsets of $\mathbf{X}$. In Dempster-Shafer theory, there are two important measures: belief (Bel) and plausibility (Pl).

$$Bel(A) = \sum_{B \subseteq A} m(B); \quad Pl(A) = \sum_{B \cap A \neq \emptyset} m(B),$$

where the m-function, also called the basic belief assignment (BBA), assigns a number (called mass or belief mass) in $[0, 1]$ to an element in the power set $2^{\mathbf{X}}$, which satisfies

$$m(\emptyset) = 0, \quad \sum_{A \subseteq \mathbf{X}} m(A) = 1.$$

There are different interpretations of these measures [10], [15]. In this work, we adopt the interpretation due to Shafer [18]: the belief function $Bel(A)$ measures the strength of evidence supporting the proposition A while the plausibility function $Pl(A)$ quantifies the maximum possible support from the evidence to the proposition A.

In DS theory, m-functions are used to encode distinct bodies of evidence and combination rules are implemented to combine the m-functions. Suppose N_S ($N_S \geq 2$) distinct bodies of evidence are associated with the N_S number of m-functions: m_1 with focal elements A_i^1 ($1 \leq i \leq n_1$), m_2 with focal elements A_j^2 ($1 \leq j \leq n_2$), and so on. The conjunctive sum of m_1, m_2,..., m_{N_S} is defined as

$$m_{\cap}(C) = \sum_{A_i^1 \cap A_j^2 \cap ... \cap A_k^{N_S} = C} m_1(A_i^1) m_2(A_j^2)...m_{N_S}(A_k^{N_S}), \qquad (1)$$

$$m_{\cap}(\emptyset) = \sum_{A_i^1 \cap A_j^2 \cap ... \cap A_k^{N_S} = \emptyset} m_1(A_i^1) m_2(A_j^2)...m_{N_S}(A_k^{N_S}), \qquad (2)$$

where $C \subseteq \mathbf{X}$, $C \neq \emptyset$.

(Dempster's rule) Dempster's rule of combination of multiple m-functions is defined as an orthogonal sum [18]:

$$m_1 \oplus m_2... \oplus m_{N_S}(C) = \frac{m_\cap(C)}{1 - m_\cap(\emptyset)}, \ m_\cap(\emptyset) \neq 1,$$

$$m_1 \oplus m_2... \oplus m_{N_S}(\emptyset) = 0.$$

(Yager's rule) Yager proposes an alternative combination rule (Yager's rule) with a quasi-associative operation [23], [24]:

$$m_{Yager}(C) = m_\cap(C), \ C \subset \mathbf{X},$$

$$m_{Yager}(\mathbf{X}) = m_\cap(\mathbf{X}) + m_\cap(\emptyset); \ m_{Yager}(\emptyset) = 0.$$

(Unified rule) Inagaki defines a continuous parametrized class of combination operations (the unified rule) which assigns fractions of $m_\cap(\emptyset)$ to the focal elements proportionally [12]:

$$m_{uni}(C) = (1 + \beta m_\cap(\emptyset))m_\cap(C), \ C \subset \mathbf{X}, C \neq \emptyset, C \neq \mathbf{X}, \tag{3}$$

$$m_{uni}(\mathbf{X}) = (1 + \beta m_\cap(\emptyset))m_\cap(\mathbf{X}) + (1 + \beta m_\cap(\emptyset) - \beta)m_\cap(\emptyset), \tag{4}$$

$$m_{uni}(\emptyset) = 0, \tag{5}$$

with $0 \leq \beta \leq \frac{1}{1-m_\cap(\emptyset)-m_\cap(\mathbf{X})}$.

With the unified rule, for any subsets $C, D \neq \mathbf{X}, \emptyset$, $m_{uni}(C)/m_\cap(C) = m_{uni}(D)/m_\cap(D)$. The parameter β controls the portion of $m_\cap(\emptyset)$ reassigned to the universal set, which directly affects the value of the combined m-function. For $\beta = 0$, the unified rule reduces to Yager's rule, while for $\beta = \frac{1}{1-m_\cap(\emptyset)}$, it becomes Dempster's rule. However, how to choose the optimal value for β is the crux of the problem [12].

Note: Inagaki also proposes a more general combination rule without the constraint $m_{uni}(C)/m_\cap(C) = m_{uni}(D)/m_\cap(D)$, which involves $2^{|\mathbf{X}|} - 1$ ($|\mathbf{X}|$ is the cardinality of $\mathbf{X}$) unknown parameters (weighting factors). Lefevre et al. [16] propose an automatic learning of weighting factors by minimizing the mean square deviation between the pignistic probability and the membership indicator. However, the approach is not applicable if the required training set with membership is not available. In addition, the parameters learned from the training set might not be optimal for the further combinations. In the current work, the unified rule with a single parameter β is considered and an approach is proposed to find the optimal value for the parameter. The proposed optimization problem can be solved analytically, therefore it is not computationally expensive.

3   The Optimal Unified Combination Rule

In this section, we propose an optimization problem to obtain the optimal value for the unknown parameter β in Inagaki's unified rule. We name the rule with the optimal parameter as the optimal unified combination rule.

Intuitively, the optimal value for β should be chosen in such a manner that the combined m-function (representing the fused information) remains similar to the original m-functions (representing the original sources of information) as much as possible, i.e., the combined m-function should represent the greatest amount of information similar to that represented by the individual m-functions. In other words, the dissimilarity between the combined m-function and the individual m_is ($1 \leq i \leq N_S$, where N_S is the number of bodies of evidence) should be minimized, assuming that the less dissimilarity the two m-functions have, the greater amount of similar information the two m-functions represent. There are a number of formulas in the literature to measure the dissimilarity between two m-functions [13], [22], [2], [7]. In the present work, Jousselme's distance [13] is adopted as a measure of dissimilarity. It possesses the desirable properties of nonnegativity, symmetry, definiteness, and triangle inequality [14].

Definition 1. *Let m_1 and m_2 be two m-functions on the same universal set* **X**, *containing N mutually exclusive and exhaustive hypotheses. The distance between m_1 and m_2 is [13]*

$$d_{Jou}(m_1, m_2) = \sqrt{\frac{1}{2}(\boldsymbol{m}_1 - \boldsymbol{m}_2)^T \underline{D}(\boldsymbol{m}_1 - \boldsymbol{m}_2)}, \tag{6}$$

where $\boldsymbol{m}_1$ and $\boldsymbol{m}_2$ are the vector forms of the m-functions m_1 and m_2; $\underline{D}$ is an $2^N \times 2^N$ matrix whose elements are

$$\underline{D}(A, B) = \frac{|A \bigcap B|}{|A \bigcup B|}, \ \emptyset \neq A, B \subseteq \mathbf{X};$$

$$\underline{D}(A, B) = 0, \ A, B = \emptyset.$$

For example, with $m(\{\theta_1\}) = 0.6$, $m(\{\theta_2\}) = 0.1$, $m(\{\theta_1, \theta_3\}) = 0.3$, the vector form of m is $\boldsymbol{m} = [0; \ 0.6; \ 0.1; \ 0; \ 0; \ 0.3; \ 0; \ 0]$.

Definition 2. *The total distance is defined as the root mean square of Jousselme's distances between the combined m-function and the individual m-functions (m_1, m_2 ... m_{N_S}):*

$$Dis = \sqrt{\frac{1}{N_S}\left(d_{Jou}(m, m_1)^2 + d_{Jou}(m, m_2)^2 + ... + d_{Jou}(m, m_{N_S})^2\right)}. \tag{7}$$

The total distance is an implicit function of the unknown parameter β since the combined m-function using Inagaki's unified rule depends on β (i.e., $m = m_{uni}(\beta)$). We want to minimize the total distance with respect to β. The total distance can explicitly be rewritten as the objective function [11]:

$$J(\beta) = \left(\frac{1}{2N_S}\left((\boldsymbol{m}_{uni}(\beta) - \boldsymbol{m}_1)^T \underline{D}(\boldsymbol{m}_{uni}(\beta) - \boldsymbol{m}_1) + ...\right.\right.$$

$$\left.\left. + (\boldsymbol{m}_{uni}(\beta) - \boldsymbol{m}_{N_S})^T \underline{D}(\boldsymbol{m}_{uni}(\beta) - \boldsymbol{m}_{N_S}))\right)^{1/2}, \right. \tag{8}$$

subject to

$$0 \le \beta \le \frac{1}{1 - m_\cap(\emptyset) - m_\cap(\mathbf{X})}, \tag{9}$$

and the optimal value of the parameter β satisfies $J(\beta^*) = \min_\beta J(\beta)$.

Note: While the optimal unified combination rule seeks the combined m-function to represent maximum similar information gleaned from the constituent m-functions, it does not concern itself with its precision or consistency although the similarity between/among m-functions is related to consistency. We would like to explore the proper definitions of precision of a belief function and consistency between different belief functions, and try to develop improved combination rules with more desirable properties in future.

3.1 Solution of the Minimization Problem

The optimization problem with objective function (8) can be solved analytically as follows. Rewrite $m_{uni}(\beta)$ ($m(\beta)$ or m for short) defined as Eqs. (3)-(5) in the vector form with length 2^N:

$$\boldsymbol{m}(\beta) = \begin{pmatrix} 0 \\ (1 + \beta * m_\cap(\emptyset)) * \boldsymbol{m}_\cap(2) \\ \vdots \\ (1 + \beta * m_\cap(\emptyset)) * \boldsymbol{m}_\cap(2^N - 1) \\ (1 + \beta * m_\cap(\emptyset)) * m_\cap(\mathbf{X}) + (1 + \beta * m_\cap(\emptyset) - \beta) * m_\cap(\emptyset) \end{pmatrix}.$$

where $\boldsymbol{m}_\cap = [m_\cap(\emptyset); ...; m_\cap(\mathbf{X})]$ is the vector form of the conjunctive sum $m_\cap$.

Let $\hat{\beta} = 1 + \beta * m_\cap(\emptyset)$, then $\boldsymbol{m}$ can be written as a linear form of $\hat{\beta}$:

$$\boldsymbol{m} = \hat{\beta} * \boldsymbol{m}_{m\cap} + \boldsymbol{m}_c, \tag{10}$$

where $\boldsymbol{m}_{m\cap}$ and $\boldsymbol{m}_c$ are constant vectors independent of the unknown parameter β:

$$\boldsymbol{m}_{m\cap} = [0; \boldsymbol{m}_\cap(2); \ldots; \boldsymbol{m}_\cap(2^N - 1); m_\cap(\emptyset) + m_\cap(\mathbf{X}) - 1];$$
$$\boldsymbol{m}_c = [0; 0; \ldots; 0; 1].$$

As a result, the objective function (without the square root operator and the constant factor $1/(2N_S)$) can be written as a second order polynomial in $\hat{\beta}$:

$$2 * N_S * (J(\beta))^2 = C_1 * (\hat{\beta})^2 + C_2 * \hat{\beta} + C_3$$

with the following coefficients:

$$C_1 = N_S * \boldsymbol{m}_{m\cap}^T \underline{D} \boldsymbol{m}_{m\cap},$$
$$C_2 = -2 * (\boldsymbol{m}_{m\cap}^T \underline{D} \hat{\boldsymbol{m}}_1 + \boldsymbol{m}_{m\cap}^T \underline{D} \hat{\boldsymbol{m}}_2 + \ldots + \boldsymbol{m}_{m\cap}^T \underline{D} \hat{\boldsymbol{m}}_{N_S}),$$
$$C_3 = \hat{\boldsymbol{m}}_1^T \hat{\boldsymbol{m}}_1 + \hat{\boldsymbol{m}}_2^T \hat{\boldsymbol{m}}_2 + \ldots + \hat{\boldsymbol{m}}_{N_S}^T \hat{\boldsymbol{m}}_{N_S},$$

where $\hat{\boldsymbol{m}}_i = \boldsymbol{m_i} - \boldsymbol{m_c}$ $(i = 1, 2, ..., N_S)$.

The objective function $J(\beta)$ is minimized when $\hat{\beta} = -C_2/(2C_1)$. Taking into account the domain of β, β^* (the optimal choice of β) should be:

$$\beta^* = \begin{cases} 0 & \text{if } \hat{\beta} < 1 \\ \frac{\hat{\beta}-1}{m_\cap(\emptyset)} & \text{if } 1 \leq \hat{\beta} \leq \frac{m_\cap(\emptyset)}{1-m_\cap(\emptyset)-m_\cap(\mathbf{X})} \\ \frac{1}{1-m_\cap(\emptyset)-m_\cap(\mathbf{X})} & \text{if } \hat{\beta} > \frac{m_\cap(\emptyset)}{1-m_\cap(\emptyset)-m_\cap(\mathbf{X})} \end{cases}$$

3.2   Implementation

The commutative and associative properties of the conjunctive sum make it easy to implement the optimal unified combination rule. We first calculate the conjunctive sum of the N_S m-functions $(\boldsymbol{m}_1,...,\boldsymbol{m}_{N_S})$ using the associativity. The optimal value of β can then be obtained using the formulas in Section 3.1. Finally we obtain the combined m-function using Eqs. (3)-(5) with $\beta = \beta^*$.

Data: $\boldsymbol{m}_1,...,\boldsymbol{m}_{N_S}$
Result: $\boldsymbol{m}$
Let $\boldsymbol{m}_\cap = \boldsymbol{m}_1$;
Let $i = 2$;
while $i \leq N_S$ **do**
$\quad\big|\quad$ Calculate the conjunctive sum between $\boldsymbol{m}_\cap$ and $\boldsymbol{m}_i$ using Eqs. (1)-(2);
$\quad\big|\quad$ Update $\boldsymbol{m}_\cap$ with the conjunctive sum;
end
Calculate C_1, C_2, C_3 from $\boldsymbol{m}_\cap$, and obtain the the optimal value β^*;
Get the combined m-function m using Eqs. (3)-(5) with β^*.

4   Illustrative Examples

In this section, the proposed optimal unified combination rule is illustrated with a few special examples and is then applied to radiotherapy data analysis.

4.1   Special Examples

Example 1. Two m-functions m_1 and m_2 are constructed on the universal set: $\mathbf{X} = \{\theta_1, \theta_2\}$ to represent two bodies of evidence from two independent sources respectively:

$$m_1 : m_1(\{\theta_1\}) = 1; m_1(\{\theta_2\}) = 0; m_1(\mathbf{X}) = 0,$$
$$m_2 : m_2(\{\theta_1\}) = 0; m_2(\{\theta_2\}) = 1; m_2(\mathbf{X}) = 0.$$

The combined m-function obtained from the optimal unified combination rule is compared to those obtained from Dempster's rule of combination and Yager's rule in Table. 1.

Table 1. The combined m-functions for Example 1

Belief mass	$m(\{\theta_1\})$	$m(\{\theta_2\})$	$m(\mathbf{X})$
Dempster's rule	-	-	-
Yager's rule	0	0	1
Optimal unified rule	0	0	1

As we have seen in the definition, Dempster's rule of combination is not applicable here since $m_\cap(\emptyset) = 1$. Yager's rule assigns the whole belief to the universal set, indicating the full uncertainty. The optimal unified combination rule is applicable, specifically, it becomes Yager's rule when $m_\cap(\emptyset) = 1$.

Example 2. Two m-functions m_1 and m_2 are constructed on the universal set: $\mathbf{X} = \{\theta_1, \theta_2, \theta_3\}$ to represent two bodies of evidence from two independent sources respectively:

$$m_1 : m_1(\{\theta_1\}) = 0.0; m_1(\{\theta_2\}) = 0.0; m_1(\{\theta_1, \theta_2\}) = 1.0; m_1(\{\theta_3\}) = 0.0,$$
$$m_2 : m_2(\{\theta_1\}) = 0.3; m_2(\{\theta_2\}) = 0.2; m_2(\{\theta_1, \theta_2\}) = 0.3; m_2(\{\theta_3\}) = 0.2.$$

The combined m-function obtained from the optimal unified combination rule is compared to those obtained from Dempster's rule of combination and Yager's rule in Table. 2.

Table 2. The combined m-functions for Example 2

Belief mass	$m(\{\theta_1\})$	$m(\{\theta_2\})$	$m(\{\theta_1, \theta_2\})$	$m(\mathbf{X})$	Dis
Dempster's rule	0.375	0.25	0.375	0	0.2580
Yager's rule	0.3	0.2	0.3	0.2	0.2466
Optimal unified rule	0.32126	0.21417	0.32126	0.14331	0.2445

In Example 2, Dempster's rule of combination becomes Dempster's rule of conditioning, which considers m_1 as fully correct and the proposition $\{\theta_1, \theta_2\}$ as the truth. Neither Yager's rule nor the optimal unified combination rule takes the proposition $\{\theta_1, \theta_2\}$ as truth. The optimal unified combination rule produces the result which is the most similar to the original two m-functions as expected.

4.2 Radiotherapy Data Analysis

The proposed optimal unified combination rule can be applied to fuse the information from three different institutes – Memorial Sloan-Kettering Cancer Center (MSKCC), Duke University Medical Center (Duke) and MD Anderson Cancer center (MD Anderson) – regarding radiotherapy dose/volume/outcome data. Radiation therapy causes normal tissue complications to cancer patients, such as radiation pneumonitis to patients with lung cancer. Therefore it is important to estimate the complication risk. Let $\mathbf{X} = \{RP, non\text{-}RP\}$ be a universal set where RP represents having radiation pneumonitis and non-RP represents not having radiation pneumonitis. Regarding the incidence of radiation pneumonitis at a specific mean lung dose (MLD), such as $MLD = 20Gy$, three bodies of evidence from MSKCC, Duke and MD Anderson are represented by the three m-functions [1]:

$$m_1 : m_1(\{RP\}) = 0.15; m_1(\{non\text{-}RP\}) = 0.65; m_1(\mathbf{X}) = 0.20,$$
$$m_2 : m_2(\{RP\}) = 0.1082; m_2(\{non\text{-}RP\}) = 0.7882; m_2(\mathbf{X}) = 0.1036.$$
$$m_3 : m_3(\{RP\}) = 0.23; m_3(\{non\text{-}RP\}) = 0.61; m_3(\mathbf{X}) = 0.16.$$

The belief and plausibility ranges of radiation pneumonitis (i.e., $Bel(\{RP\}) - Pl(\{RP\})$) are $m_1 : 15\% - 35\%; \quad m_2 : 10.82\% - 21.18\%; \quad m_3 : 23\% - 39\%$.

The combined m-function, the belief and plausibility ranges after combination using Dempster's rule, Yager's rule and the optimal unified combination rule are shown as in Table 3.

Table 3. The combined m-function, belief and plausibility range and Dis from three different combination rules)

Combination rules	$m(\{RP\})$	$m(\{non\text{-}RP\})$	$Bel(\{RP\})$-$Pl(\{RP\})$	Dis
Dempster's rule	0.0420	0.9525	0.0420 -0.0475	0.2188
Yager's	0.0256	0.5804	0.0256 -0.4196	0.1372
Optimal unified rule	0.0304	0.6886	0.0304 - 0.3114	0.1139

Dempster's rule of combination has produced counterintuitive results because all the belief-plausibility ranges from three institutions are outside the range of belief and plausibility after combination; the maximum strength of the combined evidence supporting pneumonitis is even smaller than the strength of each body of original evidence supporting pneumonitis. It is obviously due to the renormalization, which reinforces the proposition (focal element) with larger degree of belief. Yager's rule yields relatively better results but the belief-plausibility ranges are rather wide, which implies increased uncertainty. The reason is that the belief mass associated with the empty set is added to the belief mass assigned to the universal set. Compared to Yagers rule, the optimal unified rule produces result with smaller belief-plausibility range, indicating thereby less uncertainty. The comparison of the results from the three different combination rules regarding the total distance (defined as (7)) indicates that the combined m-function from the optimal unified rule has the least dissimilarity with the individual m-functions (m_1, m_2 and m_3) and therefore represents the greatest amount of information similar to that represented by m_1, m_2 and m_3.

5   Summary and Conclusion

An optimal unified combination rule is proposed to combine multiple bodies of evidence. To obtain the optimal value for the single parameter in Inagaki's unified rule, which controls the uncertainty content, we construct an optimization problem. The optimization step satisfies the principle that the combined/aggregated data should contain as much similar information from each body of evidence as possible. The proposed optimal unified combination rule is illustrated in examples.

References

1. Chen, W., Cui, Y., He, Y., Yu, Y., Galvin, J., Hussaini, M.Y., Xiao, Y.: Application of Dempster-Shafer theory in dose response outcome analysis. Phys. Med. Biol. 57(2), 5575–5585 (2012)
2. Cuzzolin, F.: Two new bayesian approximations of belief functions based on convex geometry. IEEE Transactions on Systems, Man, and Cybernetics Part B: Cybernetics 37(4), 993–1008 (2007)
3. Daniel, M.: Distribution of contradictive belief masses in combination of belief functions. In: Bouchon-Meunier, B., Yager, R., Zadeh, L. (eds.) Information, Uncertainty and Fusion, pp. 431–446. Kluwer Academic Publishers, Boston (2000)
4. Daniel, M.: Comparison between dsm and minc combination rules. In: Smarandache, F., Dezert, J. (eds.) Advances and Applications of DSmT for Information Fusion, pp. 223–240. American Research Press, Rehoboth (2004)
5. Dempster, A.: New methods for reasoning towards posterior distributions based on sample data. Ann. Math. Statist. 37, 355–374 (1966)
6. Dempster, A.: Upper and lower probabilities induced by a multivalued mapping. Ann. Math. Statist. 38, 325–339 (1967)
7. Denoeux, T.: Inner and outer approximation of belief structures using a hierarchical clustering approach. Int. J. Uncertain. Fuzz. 9(4), 437–460 (2001)
8. Dubois, D., Prade, H.: A set-theoretic view of belief functions: logical operations and approximations by fuzzy sets. Int. J. Gen. Syst. 12, 193–226 (1986)
9. Florea, M., Jousselme, A., Bossé, É., Grenier, D.: Robust combination rules for evidence theory. Information Fusion 10(2), 183–197 (2009)
10. Halpern, J., Fagin, R.: Two views of belief: Belief as generalized probability and belief as evidence. Artificial Intelligence 54, 275–318 (1992)
11. He, Y.: Uncertainty Quantification and Data Fusion Baesd on Dempster-Shafer Theory. Ph.D. thesis, Florida State University, Florida, US (December 2013)
12. Inagaki, T.: Interdependence between safety-control policy and multiple-sensor schemes via Dempster-Shafer theory. IEEE Trans. Rel. 40(2), 182–188 (1991)
13. Jousselme, A., Grenier, D., Bossé, É.: A new distance between two bodies of evidence. Information Fusion 2(2), 91–101 (2001)
14. Jousselme, A., Maupin, P.: Distances in evidence theory: Comprehensive survey and generalizations. Int. J. Approx. Reason. 53, 118–145 (2012)
15. Kohlas, J., Monney, P.: A Mathematical Theory of Hints: An Approach to Dempster-Shafer Theory of Evidence. Springer, Berlin (1995)
16. Lefevre, E., Colot, O., Vannoorenberghe, P.: Belief function combination and conflict management. Information Fusion 3(2), 149–162 (2002)
17. Sentz, K., Ferson, S.: Combination of evidence in Dempster-Shafer theory. Tech. Rep. SAND 2002-0835, Sandia National Laboratory (2002)
18. Shafer, G.: A Mathematical Theory of Evidence. Princeton University Press, NJ (1976)

19. Smarandache, F., Dezert, J.: Proportional conflict redistribution rules for information fusion. In: Smarandache, F., Dezert, J. (eds.) Advances and Applications of DSmT for Information Fusion, pp. 3–66. American Research Press, Rehoboth (2006)
20. Smets, P.: Data fusion in the transferable belief model. In: Proceeding of the Third International Conference on Information Fusion, Paris, France, PS21–PS33 (July 2000)
21. Smets, P.: Analyzing the combination of conflicting belief functions. Information Fusion 8(4), 387–412 (2007)
22. Tessem, B.: Approximations for efficient computation in the theory of evidence. Artificial Intelligence 61(2), 315–329 (1993)
23. Yager, R.: On the Dempster-Shafer framework and new combination rules. Information Sciences 41(2), 93–137 (1987)
24. Yager, R.: Quasi-associative operations in the combination of evidence. Kybernetes 16, 37–41 (1987)
25. Zhang, L.: Representation, independence, and combination of evidence in the Dempster-Shafer theory. In: Yager, R., Fedrizzi, M., Kacprzyk, J. (eds.) Advances in the Dempster-Shafer Theory of Evidence, pp. 51–69. John Wiley & Sons, Inc., New York (1994)

Evidential Logistic Regression for Binary SVM Classifier Calibration

Philippe Xu[1], Franck Davoine[1,2], and Thierry Denœux[1]

[1] UMR CNRS 7253, Heudiasyc, Université de Technologie de Compiègne, France
{philippe.xu,franck.davoine,thierry.denoeux}@hds.utc.fr
https://www.hds.utc.fr/~xuphilip
[2] CNRS, LIAMA, Beijing, P. R. China

Abstract. The theory of belief functions has been successfully used in many classification tasks. It is especially useful when combining multiple classifiers and when dealing with high uncertainty. Many classification approaches such as k-nearest neighbors, neural network or decision trees have been formulated with belief functions. In this paper, we propose an evidential calibration method that transforms the output of a classifier into a belief function. The calibration, which is based on logistic regression, is computed from a likelihood-based belief function. The uncertainty of the calibration step depends on the number of training samples and is encoded within a belief function. We apply our method to the calibration and combination of several SVM classifiers trained with different amounts of data.

Keywords: Classifier calibration, theory of belief functions, Dempster-Shafer theory, support vector machines, logistic regression.

1 Introduction

The combination of pattern classifiers is an important issue in machine learning. In many practical situations, different kinds of classifiers have to be combined. If the outputs of the classifiers are of the same nature, such as probability measures or belief functions, they can be combined directly. Evidential versions of several classification methods such as the k-nearest neighbor rule [2], neural network [3] or decision trees [11] can be found in the literature. Otherwise, if their outputs are of different type, they have to be made comparable.

The transformation of the score returned by a classifier into a posterior class probability is called calibration. Several methods can be found in the literature [8,13,14]. The quality of the calibration highly depends on the amount of training data available. The use of belief functions is often more appropriate when dealing with few training data. It becomes especially critical when the classifiers to combine are trained with different amounts of training data. In this paper, we introduce an evidential calibration method that transforms the outputs of a binary classifier into belief functions. It is then applied to the calibration of SVM classifiers.

F. Cuzzolin (Ed.): BELIEF 2014, LNAI 8764, pp. 49–57, 2014.

The rest of this paper is organized as follows. In Section 2, we present likelihood-based belief functions for both statistical inference and forecasting. In particular, the case of a Bernoulli distribution is detailed. Its application to a logistic regression based calibration method is then introduced in Section 3. Experimental results on the calibration and combination of SVM classifiers are then presented in Section 4.

2   Likelihood-Based Belief Function

In this section, we present the formulation of likelihood-based belief functions. Our presentation follows the work of Denœux [4] for statistical inference and the work of Kanjanatarakul et al. for its application to forecasting [6].

2.1   Statistical Inference

Let $X \in \mathbb{X}$ be some observable data and $\theta \in \Theta$ the unknown parameter of the density function $f_\theta(x)$ generating the data. Information about θ can be inferred given the outcome x of a random experiment. Shafer [10] proposed to build a belief function Bel_x^Θ on Θ from the likelihood function. Denœux further justified this approach in [4]. After observing $X = x$, the likelihood function $L_x : \theta \mapsto f_\theta(x)$ is normalized to yield the following contour function:

$$pl_x^\Theta(\theta) = \frac{L_x(\theta)}{\sup_{\theta' \in \Theta} L_x(\theta')}, \quad \forall \theta \in \Theta, \tag{1}$$

where sup denotes the supremum operator. The consonant plausibility function associated to this contour function is

$$Pl_x^\Theta(A) = \sup_{\theta \in A} pl_x^\Theta(\theta), \quad \forall A \subseteq \Omega. \tag{2}$$

The focal sets of Bel_x^Θ are defined as

$$\Gamma_x(\gamma) = \{\theta \in \Theta \mid pl_x^\Theta(\theta) \geq \gamma\}, \quad \forall \gamma \in [0, 1]. \tag{3}$$

The random set formalism can be used to represent the belief and plausibility functions on Θ. Given the Lebesgue measure λ on $[0, 1]$ and the multi-valued mapping $\Gamma_x : [0, 1] \to 2^\Theta$, we have

$$\begin{array}{c} Bel_x^\Theta(A) = \lambda(\{\gamma \in [0, 1] \mid \Gamma_x(\gamma) \subseteq A\}) \\ Pl_x^\Theta(A) = \lambda(\{\gamma \in [0, 1] \mid \Gamma_x(\gamma) \cap A \neq \emptyset\}) \end{array}, \quad \forall A \subseteq \Theta. \tag{4}$$

2.2   Forecasting

Suppose that we now have some knowledge about θ after observing some training data x. The *forecasting* problem consists in making some predictions about some random quantity $Y \in \mathbb{Y}$ whose conditional distribution $g_{x,\theta}(y)$ given $X = x$

depends on θ. A belief function on $\mathbb{Y}$ can be derived from the sampling model proposed by Dempster [1]. For some unobserved auxiliary variable $Z \in \mathbb{Z}$ with known probability distribution μ independent of θ, we define a function φ so that

$$Y = \varphi(\theta, Z). \tag{5}$$

A multi-valued mapping $\Gamma'_x : [0,1] \times \mathbb{Z} \to 2^{\mathbb{Y}}$ is defined by composing Γ_x with φ

$$\Gamma'_x : \begin{array}{rcl} [0,1] \times \mathbb{Z} & \to & 2^{\mathbb{Y}} \\ (\gamma, z) & \mapsto & \varphi(\Gamma_x(\gamma), z). \end{array} \tag{6}$$

A belief function on $\mathbb{Y}$ can then be derived from the product measure $\lambda \otimes \mu$ on $[0,1] \times \mathbb{Z}$ and the multi-valued mapping Γ'_x

$$\begin{array}{l} Bel_x^{\mathbb{Y}}(A) = (\lambda \otimes \mu)\left(\{(\gamma, z) \mid \varphi\left(\Gamma_x(\gamma), z\right) \subseteq A\}\right) \\ Pl_x^{\mathbb{Y}}(A) = (\lambda \otimes \mu)\left(\{(\gamma, z) \mid \varphi\left(\Gamma_x(\gamma), z\right) \cap A \neq \emptyset\}\right) \end{array}, \quad \forall A \subseteq \Omega. \tag{7}$$

2.3 Binary Case Example

In the particular case where Y is a random variable with a Bernoulli distribution $\mathcal{B}(\omega)$, it can be generated by a function φ defined as

$$Y = \varphi(\omega, Z) = \begin{cases} 1 \text{ if } Z \leq \omega, \\ 0 \text{ otherwise,} \end{cases} \tag{8}$$

where Z has a uniform distribution on $[0,1]$. Assume that the belief function Bel_x^{Ω} on Ω is induced by a random closed interval $\Gamma_x(\gamma) = [U(\gamma), V(\gamma)]$. In particular, it is the case if it is the consonant belief function associated to a unimodal contour function. We get

$$\Gamma'_x(\gamma, z) = \varphi\left([U(\gamma), V(\gamma)], z\right) = \begin{cases} 1 & \text{if } Z \leq U(\gamma), \\ 0 & \text{if } Z > V(\gamma), \\ \{0,1\} & \text{otherwise.} \end{cases} \tag{9}$$

The *predictive* belief function $Bel_x^{\mathbb{Y}}$ can then be computed as

$$Bel_x^{\mathbb{Y}}(\{1\}) = (\lambda \otimes \mu)(\{(\gamma, z) \mid Z \leq U(\gamma)\}) \tag{10a}$$

$$= \int_0^1 \mu(\{z \mid z \leq U(\gamma)\}) f(\gamma) d\gamma \tag{10b}$$

$$= \int_0^1 U(\gamma) f(\gamma) d\gamma = \mathbb{E}(U) \tag{10c}$$

and

$$Bel_x^{\mathbb{Y}}(\{0\}) = (\lambda \otimes \mu)(\{(\gamma, z) \mid Z > V(\gamma)\}) \tag{11a}$$

$$= 1 - (\lambda \otimes \mu)(\{(\gamma, z) \mid Z \leq V(\gamma)\}) \tag{11b}$$

$$= 1 - \mathbb{E}(V). \tag{11c}$$

As U and V take only non-negative values, these quantities have the following expressions:

$$Bel_x^{\mathbb{Y}}(\{1\}) = \int_0^{+\infty}(1 - F_U(u))du = \int_0^{\hat{\omega}}(1 - pl_x^{\Omega}(u))du \tag{12a}$$

$$= \hat{\omega} - \int_0^{\hat{\omega}} pl_x^{\Omega}(u)du \tag{12b}$$

and

$$Pl_x^{\mathbb{Y}}(\{1\}) = 1 - Bel_x^{\mathbb{Y}}(\{0\}) = \int_0^{+\infty}(1 - F_V(v))dv \tag{13a}$$

$$= \hat{\omega} + \int_{\hat{\omega}}^1 pl_x^{\Omega}(v)dv, \tag{13b}$$

where $\hat{\omega}$ is the value maximizing pl_x^{Ω}. In many practical situations, the belief function $Bel_x^{\mathbb{Y}}$ cannot be expressed analytically. However, they can be approximated either by Monte Carlo simulation using Equations (10) and (11) or by numerically estimating the integrals of Equations (12) and (13).

3   Classifier Calibration

Let us consider a binary classification problem. Let $x = \{(x_1, y_1), \ldots, (x_n, y_n)\}$ be some training data, where $x_i \in \mathbb{R}$ is the score returned by a pre-trained classifier for the i-th training sample which label is $y_i \in \{0, 1\}$. Given a test sample of score $s \in \mathbb{R}$ and unknown label $y \in \{0, 1\}$, the aim of calibration is to estimate the posterior class probability $P(y = 1|s)$. Several calibration methods can be found in the literature. Binning [13], isotonic regression [14] and logistic regression [8] are the most commonly used ones. Niculescu-Mizil and Caruana [7] showed that logistic regression is well-adapted for calibrating maximum margin methods like SVM. Moreover, it is less prone to over-fitting as compared to binning and isotonic regression, especially when relatively few training data are available. Thus, logistic regression will be considered in this paper.

3.1   Logistic Regression-Based Calibration

Platt [8] proposed to use a logistic regression approach to transform the scores of an SVM classifier into posterior class probabilities. He proposed to fit a sigmoid function

$$P(y = 1|s) \approx h_s(\theta) = \frac{1}{1 + \exp(a + bs)}. \tag{14}$$

The parameter $\theta = (a, b) \in \mathbb{R}^2$ of the sigmoid function is determined by maximizing the likelihood function on the training data,

$$L_x(\theta) = \prod_{k=1}^n p_k^{y_k}(1 - p_k)^{1-y_k} \quad \text{with} \quad p_k = \frac{1}{1 + \exp(a + bx_k)}. \tag{15}$$

To reduce over-fitting and prevent a from becoming infinite when the training examples are perfectly separable, Platt proposed to use an out-of-sample data model by replacing y_k and $1 - y_k$ by t_+ and t_- defined as

$$t_+ = \frac{n_+ + 1}{n_+ + 2} \quad \text{and} \quad t_- = \frac{1}{n_- + 2}, \tag{16}$$

where n_+ and n_- are respectively the number of positive and negative training samples. This ensures L_x to have a unique supremum $\hat{\theta} = (\hat{a}, \hat{b})$.

3.2 Evidential Extension

After observing the score s of a test sample, its label $y \in \{0, 1\}$ can be seen a the realisation of a random variable Y with a Bernoulli distribution $\mathcal{B}(\omega)$, where $\omega = h_s(\theta) \in [0, 1]$. A belief function $Bel_{x,s}^{\mathbb{Y}}$ can thus be derived from the contour function $pl_{x,s}^{\Omega}$ as described in Section 2.3. Function $pl_{x,s}^{\Omega}$ can be computed from Pl_x^{Θ} as

$$pl_{x,s}^{\Omega}(\omega) = \begin{cases} 0 & \text{if } \omega \in \{0, 1\} \\ Pl_x^{\Theta}\left(h_s^{-1}(\omega)\right) & \text{otherwise,} \end{cases} \tag{17}$$

where

$$h_s^{-1}(\omega) = \left\{ (a, b) \in \Theta \;\middle|\; \frac{1}{1 + \exp(a + bs)} = \omega \right\} \tag{18}$$

$$= \left\{ (a, b) \in \Theta \;\middle|\; a = \ln\left(\omega^{-1} - 1\right) - bs \right\}, \tag{19}$$

which finally yields

$$pl_{x,s}^{\Omega}(\omega) = \sup_{b \in \mathbb{R}} pl_x^{\Theta}\left(\ln\left(\omega^{-1} - 1\right) - bs, b\right), \quad \forall \omega \in (0, 1). \tag{20}$$

Figure 1 illustrates the computation of the predictive belief function $Bel_{x,s}^{\mathbb{Y}}$. Fig. 1 (a) shows level sets of the contour function pl_x^{Θ} computed from the scores of an SVM classifier trained on the UCI[1] Australian dataset. The value of $pl_{x,s}^{\Omega}(\omega)$ is defined as the maximum value of pl_x^{Θ} along the line $a = \ln(\gamma^{-1} - 1) - bs$ represented by the doted lines. It can be approximated by a gradient descent algorithm. Fig. 1 (b) shows the contour function $pl_{x,s}^{\mathbb{Y}}$ from which $Bel_{x,s}^{\mathbb{Y}}$ can be computed using Equations (12) and (13). Fig. 1 (c-d) displays the calibration results for $n = 20$ and $n = 200$, respectively.

4   Experimental Evaluation

Experiments were conducted using three binary classification problems from the UCI dataset: Adult, Australian and Diabetes. For each dataset, 10 non-linear

---

[1] http://archive.ics.uci.edu/ml

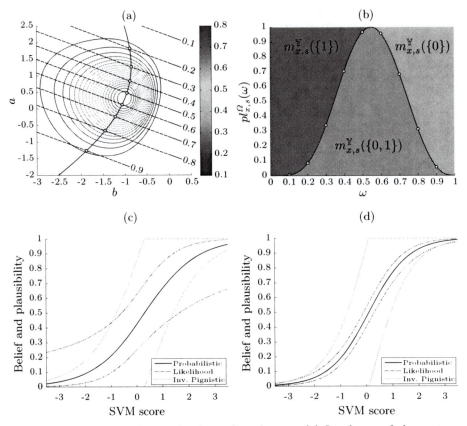

Fig. 1. Calibration results on the Australian dataset. (a) Level sets of the contour function pl_x^{Θ}. (b) Contour function $pl_{x,s}^{\Omega}$ with $s = 0.5$. The three coloured areas correspond to the predictive mass function $m_{x,s}^{\mathbb{Y}}$. (c) Calibration results with $n = 20$. (d) Calibration results with $n = 200$.

SVM classifiers with RBF kernel were trained using non-overlapping training sets of different sizes. Three scenarios were considered, as illustrated in Fig. 2. In the first scenario (a), all 10 classifiers were trained using the same amount of training data. In the second one (b), one half of the classifiers were trained with five times more data than the other half. Finally, in (c), one classifier was trained with 2/3rd of the data, a second one used 1/5th and the eight other ones shared the rest uniformly. The total amounts of training and testing data are detailed in Table 1.

The LibSVM[2] library was used to train the classifiers. For each experiment, 5-fold cross validation was conducted on the training data to get both the SVM parameters and the scores for calibration. As each classifier was trained with different training data, they were assumed to be independent. After calibration, the classifier outputs were thus combined with Dempster's rule. The class with

---

[2] http://www.csie.ntu.edu.tw/~cjlin/libsvm/

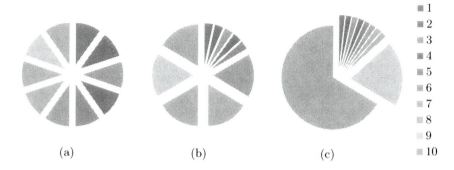

Fig. 2. Proportions of data used to train each of the 10 classifier. (a) All classifiers use 10% of the training data. (b) One half the classifiers use $1/6^{\text{th}}$ of the data and the other half the rest. (c) One classifier uses $2/3^{\text{rd}}$ of the data, a second one uses $1/5^{\text{th}}$ and the eight other classifiers use the rest.

Table 1. Classification accuracy for several datasets and different scenarios. The best results are underlined and those that are not significantly different are in bold.

Scenario	Adult #train=600, #test=16,281			Australian #train=300, #test=390		
	(a)	(b)	(c)	(a)	(b)	(c)
Probabilistic	83.24%	82.70%	80.90%	**85.13%**	**85.90%**	85.90%
Inv. Pign.	**83.32%**	82.79%	81.02%	**85.13%**	**85.90%**	86.41%
Likelihood	**83.29%**	**83.03%**	**81.65%**	**85.13%**	**86.67%**	**88.46%**

Scenario	Diabetes #train=300, #test=468		
	(a)	(b)	(c)
Probabilistic	**78.42%**	**77.14%**	53.42%
Inv. Pign.	**78.63%**	**77.14%**	54.70%
Likelihood	**79.06%**	**77.35%**	**68.16%**

maximum plausibility was selected for decision. The probabilistic calibration served as baseline. We compared it the likelihood-based evidential approach and the inverse pignistic transformation. The classification accuracies on the testing data are shown in Table 1.

To compare the performances of the different calibration approaches, the significance of the results was evaluated from a McNemar test [5] at the 5% level. The best results were always obtained by the likelihood-based approach except for Adult (a). In particular, expect for the inverse pignistic transformation on the Australian dataset, the results were always significantly better for scenario (c). For the Adult dataset, the likelihood-based calibration always gave significantly better results than the probabilistic approach. We can see that the likelihood-based approach is more robust when the training sets have highly unbalanced sizes.

5   Conclusion

In this paper, we showed how to extend logistic regression-based calibration methods using belief functions. Belief functions can better represent the uncertainty of the calibration procedure, especially when very few training data are available. The method was used to calibrate the scores from SVM classifiers but it may also be used for other classification algorithms. Evidential formulations of other calibration methods such as binning [13] and isotonic regression [14] will be considered in future work. Extension to multi-class problem is also possible through the use of one-vs-one or one-vs-all binary decompositions. Comparison of probabilistic approaches [12] and evidential ones [9] will be considered in future work.

Acknowledgments. This research was carried out in the framework of the Labex MS2T, which was funded by the French Government, through the program "Investments for the future" managed by the National Agency for Research (Reference ANR-11-IDEX-0004-02). It was supported by the ANR-NSFC Sino-French PRETIV project (Reference ANR-11-IS03-0001).

References

1. Dempster, A.: The Dempster-Shafer calculus for statisticians. International Journal of Approximate Reasoning 48(2), 365–377 (2008)
2. Denœux, T.: A k-nearest neighbor classification rule based on dempster-shafer theory. IEEE Transactions on Systems, Man and Cybernetics 25(5), 804–813 (1995)
3. Denœux, T.: A neural network classifier based on dempster-shafer theory. IEEE Transactions on Systems, Man and Cybernetics 30(2), 131–150 (2000)
4. Denœux, T.: Likelihood-based belief function: justification and some extensions to low-quality data. International Journal of Approximate Reasoning (in Press, 2014), http://dx.doi.org/10.1016/j.ijar.2013.06.007, doi:10.1016/j.ijar.2013.06.007
5. Dietterich, T.G.: Approximate statistical tests for comparing supervised classification algorithms. Neural Computation 10(7), 1895–1923 (1998)
6. Kanjanatarakul, O., Sriboonchitta, S., Denœux, T.: Forecasting using belief functions: an application to marketing econometrics. International Journal of Approximate Reasoning 55(5), 1113–1128 (2014)
7. Niculescu-Mizil, A., Caruana, R.: Predicting good probabilities with supervised learning. In: Proceedings of the 22nd International Conference on Machine Learning, Bonn, Germany, pp. 625–632 (2005)
8. Platt, J.C.: Probabilistic outputs for support vector machines and comparisons to regularized likelihood methods. In: Smola, A.J., Bartlett, P., Schölkopf, B., Schuurmans, D. (eds.) Advances in Large-Margin Classifiers, pp. 61–74. MIT Press (1999)
9. Quost, B., Denœux, T., Masson, M.H.: Pairwise classifier combination using belief functions. Pattern Recognition Letters 28(5), 644–653 (2007)
10. Shafer, G.: A mathematical theory of evidence. Princeton University Press, Princeton (1976)

11. Sutton-Charani, N., Destercke, S., Denœux, T.: Classification trees based on belief functions. In: Denoeux, T., Masson, M.H. (eds.) Belief Functions: Theory and Applications. AISC, vol. 164, pp. 77–84. Springer, Heidelberg (2012)
12. Wu, T.F., Lin, C.J., Weng, R.C.: Probability estimates for multi-class classification by pairwise coupling. Journal of Machine Learning Research 5, 975–1005 (2004)
13. Zadrozny, B., Elkan, C.: Obtaining calibrated probability estimates from decision trees and naive Bayesian classifiers. In: Proceedings of the 18th International Conference on Machine Learning, Williamstown, USA, pp. 609–616 (2001)
14. Zadrozny, B., Elkan, C.: Transforming classifier scores into accurate multiclass probability estimates. In: Proceedings of the 8th ACM SIGKDD International Conference on Knowledge Discovery and Data Mining, New York, USA, pp. 694–699 (2002)

The Evidence-Theoretic k-NN Rule for Rank-Ordered Data: Application to Predict an Individual's Source of Loan

Supanika Leurcharusmee[1], Peerapat Jatukannyaprateep[1],
Songsak Sriboonchitta[1], and Thierry Denoeux[2]

[1] Faculty of Economics, Chiang Mai University,
Chiang Mai 50200, Thailand
[2] Université de Technologie de Compiègne
CNRS, UNR 7253 Heudiasyc, France

Abstract. We adapted the nonparametric evidence-theoretic k-Nearest Neighbor (k-NN) rule, which was originally designed for multinomial choice data, to rank-ordered choice data. The contribution of this model is its ability to extract information from all the observed rankings to improve the prediction power for each individual's primary choice. The evidence-theoretic k-NN rule for heterogeneous rank-ordered data method can be consistently applied to complete and partial rank-ordered choice data. This model was used to predict an individual's source of loan given his or her characteristics and also identify individual characteristics that help the prediction. The results show that the prediction from the rank-ordered choice model outperforms that of the traditional multinomial choice model with only one observed choice.

Keywords: Rank-ordered Choice Data, k-Nearest Neighbor, Belief Functions, Classifier, Household Debt.

1 Introduction

For the purpose of understanding the objective and the contribution of this study, let us first clarify the distinction between the traditional *multinomial choice data* and the *rank-ordered choice data* that is of the concern here. Suppose there are M available objects. In traditional multinomial choice data, there is only one choice for each individual. In contrast, the rank-ordered choice data contains more information regarding each individual's preference as they capture each individual's ranking of the objects. If the ranks of all M objects can be observed, the data are said to be *completely* rank-ordered. If only $L < M$ ranks are observed, the data are *partially* rank-ordered. Moreover, if the number L_i of observed ranks for each individual i is different across i, then the data are called *heterogenous* rank-ordered. From these definitions, the rank-ordered choice data is reduced to the multinomial choice data when $L_i = 1$, for all i.

The main purpose of the model is to predict each individual's most preferred choice out of M available alternatives using heterogenous rank-ordered data. In

F. Cuzzolin (Ed.): BELIEF 2014, LNAI 8764, pp. 58–67, 2014.
© Springer International Publishing Switzerland 2014

particular, we modify the Evidence-theoretic k-Nearest Neighbor (k-NN) Rule, which was originally designed for traditional multinomial choice data [14] to take advantage of the additional information provided by rank-ordered choice data. The main idea is that the secondary or other choices also provide valuable information for the primary choice prediction.

Two main problems can be considered in relation with rank-ordered data. The first problem is to predict an individual's choices given information on choice attributes. Suppose we have a new alternative with a set of attributes, this problem is to predict the chance that this alternative will be chosen. The traditional methods to tackle this problem in economics are the rank-ordered logit model and the rank-ordered probit model. These models were later extended into the rank-ordered mixed logit model [3] [13]. The second problem is to predict an individual's choices given information on individual characteristics. Suppose we have an individual with a set of characteristics, we may wish to predict the alternative that he or she is most likely to choose. There is no logit/probit-based model designed to solve this problem. The closest methods are those developed to explain how each individual chooses a bundle of products. As discussed in Bhat, Srinivasan and Sen (2006) [5], commonly used models are the traditional multinomial probit/logit models with composite alternatives and the multivariate probit/logit models [2] [4]. Although both models allow each individual to choose more than one alternative, all the choices are equally weighted. Moreover, none of these models is appropriate for problems with a large choice set. Since there is no standard methodology for the second problem, a contribution of this study is to develop a methodology to fill this gap.

Traditional methods to analyze multiple choice problems in economics are mostly of the logit/probit types and based on maximum likelihood (ML) method. In contrast, the k-NN method is intuitively simple and requires fewer assumptions. Formally, k-NN is a classification method that can be used to predict an individual's choice based on information from the observed choices of the k neighbors with the closest characteristics. An advantage of the k-NN model being nonparametric is that it does not require distributional assumptions like the ML method. Moreover, since the method only uses the k nearest neighbors for prediction, it is robust to outliers. It is also flexible in the sense that it can be applied consistently for complete, partially and heterogeneous rank-ordered data. With a set of restrictions, the method boils down to the traditional evidence-theoretic k-NN rule.

The Application of the evidence-theoretic k-NN rule model relies on the availability of ranking data. The most obvious applications concern consumer choice models, in which each customer buys more than one product or one brand. For the empirical application considered in this study, the model was used to analyze each individual's choices of loan sources. The main objective of this exercise is to predict where each individual borrows from, given his or her characteristics.

This paper is organized as follows. Section 2 recalls the original evidence-theoretic k-NN rule for multinomial choice data. Section 3 introduces the evidence-theoretic k-NN rule for heterogeneous rank-ordered data and discusses how the method can be applied to completely and partially rank-ordered data. Section 4 provides an empirical example by applying the method to predict an individual's primary source of borrowing. Finally, Section 5 presents our conclusions and remarks.

2   The Evidence-Theoretic k-NN Rule

The original Evidence-theoretic k-NN Rule is a method to classify each individual into M classes based on his attributes [14] [7]. The model can thus be applied for the multiple choice problem using multinomial choice data. Let the set of alternatives be $\Omega = \{\omega_1, \omega_2, ..., \omega_M\}$. For each individual i, we observe information $(x^{(i)}, \omega^{(i)})$, where $x^{(i)}$ is the vector for individual i's attributes and $\omega^{(i)}$ is the alternative that individual i has chosen. That is, $(x^{(i)}, \omega^{(i)})$ constitutes an evidence for the class membership of x. The mass function for each individual i is

$$
\begin{aligned}
m^{(i)}(\omega^{(i)}) &= \alpha\phi(d^{(i)}) \\
m^{(i)}(\Omega) &= 1 - \alpha\phi(d^{(i)}),
\end{aligned}
\tag{1}
$$

where $d^{(i)}$ is the distance between x and $x^{(i)}$, ϕ is the inverse distance-normalization function that maps the distance $d^{(i)}$ from $[0, +\infty)$ to $[0, 1]$ and α is a parameter in $[0, 1]$.

Information from each individual is considered as evidence. For independent and identically distributed (iid) data, we can combine all the pieces of evidence from k nearest neighbors using Dempster's rule. The combined mass function for each choice $\{\omega_q\}$ is

$$
\begin{aligned}
m(\{\omega_q\}) &= \frac{1}{K}(1 - \prod_{i \in I_{k,q}} (1 - \alpha\phi(d^{(i)}))) \prod_{r \neq q} \prod_{i \in I_{k,r}} (1 - \alpha\phi(d^{(i)})) \\
m(\Omega) &= \frac{1}{K} \prod_{r=1}^{M} \prod_{i \in I_{k,r}} (1 - \alpha\phi(d^{(i)})),
\end{aligned}
\tag{2}
$$

where $I_{k,q}$ is the set of the k nearest neighbors that chose alternative q and K is the normalizing factor.

3   The Evidence-Theoretic k-NN Rule for Heterogeneous Rank-Ordered Data

Consider a general model for heterogenous rank-ordered choice data with M available alternatives, $L_i \leq M$ of which are ranked for each individual i. The objective of this model is to predict the choice of an individual given his or her T characteristics x. Therefore, we construct a model using the data $(\omega^{(i)}, x^{(i)})$ from k individual i whose characteristics $x^{(i)}$ are the closest to x. Each of the

k individuals ranks L_i objects, providing L_i pieces of evidence for his or her preferences through the mass functions. For each individual i, we can observe the L_i most preferred choices $\omega^{(i)} = \{\omega^{(i1)}, ..., \omega^{(iL_i)}\}$, where $\omega^{(i1)}$ is the most preferred choice $\omega^{(iL_i)}$ is the L_i^{th} choice. The mass function for individual i can be defined as

$$
\begin{aligned}
m^{(i)}(\{\omega^{(i1)}\}) &= \alpha_1 \phi(d^{(i)}) \\
m^{(i)}(\{\omega^{(ij)}\}) &= \begin{cases} \alpha_j \phi(d^{(i)}), & \text{if } j \leq L_i \\ 0, & \text{otherwise} \end{cases} \\
m^{(i)}(\Omega) &= 1 - \sum_{j=1}^{L_i} \alpha_j \phi(d^{(i)}).
\end{aligned}
\tag{3}
$$

where $d^{(i)} = (x - x^{(i)})' \Sigma (x - x^{(i)})$ is the weighted squared Euclidean distance between x and $x^{(i)}$ with a $T \times T$ diagonal matrix $\Sigma = diag(\sigma_1, ..., \sigma_Y)$ with and $\phi(d^{(i)}) = \exp(-\gamma d^{(i)^2})$ is the inverse distance-normalization function.

The mass function (3) satisfies the basic probability assignment (BPA) properties, which are $m(\emptyset) = 0$ and $\sum_{A \in 2^\Omega} m(A) = 1$. That is, the mass $m^{(i)}(\{\omega_q\})$ captures the proportion of all relevant and available evidence from individual i that supports the claim that an individual with characteristics x will choose alternative q. From Equations (3), each mass depends on two factors, which are 1) the distance between $x^{(i)}$ and x and 2) the rank of the alternative.

The parameters to be estimated are $\theta = \{\alpha_1, ..., \alpha_M, \sigma_1, ..., \sigma_T, \gamma\}$. Parameters $0 \leq \alpha_j \leq 1, j = 1, ..., M$ capture different weights for the mass functions of objects with different ranks. Since the higher ranked objects should have higher weights, $\alpha_1 \geq \alpha_2 \geq ... \geq \alpha_L$. Parameters $0 \leq \sigma_t \leq 1, t = 1, ..., T$ capture different weights for each characteristic of individual i in the vector $x^{(i)}$. A characteristic that is more important as a determinant of the choice selection should have a higher weight. Lastly, the parameter γ is a positive scale parameter for the inverse distance-normalization function.

In the belief function framework, the belief on a claim can be represented as a belief-plausibility interval. The belief function measures the extent to which the evidence implies the claim and is defined as $Bel(A) = \sum_{B \in A} m(B)$. The plausibility function measures to what extent the evidence does not contradict the claim; it is defined as $Pl(A) = \sum_{B \cap A \neq \phi} m(B)$. Here, the belief and plausibility of each alternative q from individual i are $Bel^{(i)}(\{\omega_q\}) = m^{(i)}(\{\omega_q\})$ and $Pl^{(i)}(\{\omega_q\}) = m^{(i)}(\{\omega_q\}) + m^{(i)}(\Omega)$, respectively.

The plausibility of each alternative q for individual i can thus be written as

$$
Pl^{(i)}(\{\omega_q\}) = 1 - \sum_{j=1}^{L_i} (\alpha_j \phi(d^{(i)}))^{(1-y_{jq}^{(i)})}, \quad \forall q = 1, ..., M,
\tag{4}
$$

where $y_{jq}^{(i)} = \begin{cases} 1 & \text{if } j^{th} \text{ choice of individual } i \text{ is } \omega_q \\ 0 & \text{otherwise} \end{cases}$.

When all observations are independent and identically distributed (iid), all pieces of evidence from the k nearest neighbors can be combined using Dempster's rule. Cobb and Shenoy (2006) proposed the plausibility transformation method to convert Dempster-Shafer belief function models to Bayesian probability models that are consistent with Dempster's rule. The *plausibility probability function* is the normalized form of the combined plausibility function $Pl(\{\omega_q\})$ [6]. Furthermore, the plausibility of each singleton after combination by Dempster's rule is the product of the plausibilities from each piece of evidence. Therefore, the plausibility probability function is

$$Pl\_P_m(\{\omega_q\}) = K^{-1}Pl(\{\omega_q\}) = K^{-1}\prod_{i=1}^{k}\left[1 - \sum_{j=1}^{L_i}(\alpha_j\phi(d^{(i)}))^{(1-y_{jq}^{(i)})}\right], \quad (5)$$

where $K = \sum_{r=1}^{M} Pl(\{\omega_r\})$ is the normalization constant.

Estimation: The vector of parameters $\theta = \{\alpha_1, ..., \alpha_M, \sigma_1, ..., \sigma_T, \gamma\}$ can be estimated by minimizing the mean squared error (MSE)[1]. To compute the MSE, we estimate $Pl\_P_M^{(i)}$ for each observation i given its characteristics $x^{(i)}$. Let $t_q^{(i)}$ be a vector representing the observed choice of individual i where the chosen element q equals to 1 and other elements equal to 0. The MSE is

$$MSE = \frac{1}{NM}\sum_{i=1}^{N}\sum_{q=1}^{M}(Pl\_P_m^{(i)}(\{\omega_q\}) - t_q^{(i)})^2. \quad (6)$$

The procedure is repeated for all possible k to find the optimal value of k that minimizes the MSE. For the prediction rule, the predicted choice of individual i is the choice with the highest plausibility probability $Pl\_P_M^{(i)}(\{\omega_q\})$.

Special Cases: The evidence-theoretic k-NN model for heterogenous rank-ordered data can be consistently applied to partial and complete rank-ordered data. In particular, when $L_i = L < M$ for all i, the partial rank-ordered model is recovered. When $L_i = M$ for all i, we have the complete rank-ordered model. Moreover, the model is consistent with the original k-NN model for the traditional multinomial choice data. That is, when $L = 1$, we get the traditional multinomial choice model with only one observed choice.

Variations in Model Specification: The k-NN method for the rank-ordered choice data can be modified to capture several aspects of heterogeneity in the data. In particular, each parameter in $\theta = \{\alpha_1, ..., \alpha_M, \sigma_1, ..., \sigma_T, \gamma\}$ can be modified to be alternative-specific. For instance, the scale parameter γ can be generalized to γ_q in order to capture the different chance of occurring of each alternative. The σ_t can also be generalized to σ_{qt} to capture the different contribution of each

---

[1] We used the fmincon procedure in Matlab, with the active set algorithm.

characteristic t in predicting each alternative q. It should be noted that adding more parameters allows the model to capture more characteristics of the data. However, it also causes inefficiency especially for studies with a small number of observations.

4   Predicting an Individual's Source of Loan

In this section, we report on the application of the above method to predict an individual's primary source of loan given his set of characteristics x.

The data used in this study are the 2010 cross-sectional data from the Panel Household Socio-Economic Survey (SES) conducted by the National Statistical Office of Thailand. The dependent variable is the source of loan. In the SES, each individual was provided with eight choices of loan sources and asked whether he had borrowed any money in the past year. If the individual had borrowed, the survey asked for his or her two largest sources of loan in order.

In this study, we performed and compared four types of Evidence-theoretic k-NN rule models including the multinomial model with equal weights (MEW), the rank-ordered model with equal weights (REW), the multinomial model with optimized weights (MOW) and the rank-ordered model with optimized weights (ROW).

Multinomial models use the information only from the primary choice to estimate the vector of parameters θ. Rank-ordered choice models use the information from both primary and secondary choices. Formally, multinomial choice models are rank-ordered models with $\alpha_2 = 0$. The equal weight assumption restricts all the weight $\sigma_t = 1$, for all t. This restriction implies that all characteristics in x have an equal contribution to the loan choice prediction. Optimizing the weights allows the weights to vary across characteristics. Therefore, the prediction using the optimized weight models relies more on the characteristics with higher weights. That is, equal weight models are optimized weight models with $\sigma_t = 1$, for all t. It should be noted each characteristic in x was normalized so that the weights σ_t can be compared across t. In addition, in this study, we allowed the scale parameter γ in the inverse distance-normalization function $\phi(\cdot)$ to vary with each individual's primary choice. Specifically, γ_q is the scale parameter for each individual with $\omega^{(i1)} = q$. The estimated parameters for each of the four models are reported in Table 1.

In Table 1, consider the models REW and ROW. The parameter $\alpha_2 \neq 0$ indicates that including the information from the secondary loan choice helps the model to predict the primary choice more accurately. Consider the models MOW and ROW. The parameters $\sigma_t \neq 1$, for all t show that characteristics in x are not equally important for the loan source prediction. The characteristics with highest contribution to the prediction accuracy include *total saving, college, total income* and *urban*.

To ensure that the parameters in Table 1 minimize the MSE, it is necessary to check that the MSE function is smooth and convex with respect to all parameters. Fig. 1 shows the MSE contour plot for parameters α_1 and α_2 for the ROW model.

Table 1. Comparison of the four models

	MEW	REW	MOW	ROW
Alphas - α_j				
Primary choice	0.12	0.11	0.12	0.11
Secondary choice	0.00	0.03	0.00	0.04
Gammas - γ_q				
Commercial bank	0.01	0.02	0.00	0.00
BAAC	0.00	0.00	0.00	0.00
GHB	0.00	0.00	0.01	0.01
Village Fund	0.04	0.04	0.35	0.67
Co-ops/Credit Union	0.00	0.00	0.01	0.01
Other financial inst.	0.04	0.04	0.25	0.25
Friend/relative	0.03	0.02	0.50	0.54
Other source	0.81	1.00	1.00	1.00
Weights - σ_t				
Age	1.00	1.00	0.01	0.12
Total income	1.00	1.00	0.52	0.43
Total saving	1.00	1.00	1.00	1.00
Female	1.00	1.00	0.01	0.00
Urban	1.00	1.00	0.32	0.22
College	1.00	1.00	0.97	0.86
Employed	1.00	1.00	0.00	0.00
Agricultural household	1.00	1.00	0.21	0.02
House owner	1.00	1.00	0.00	0.00

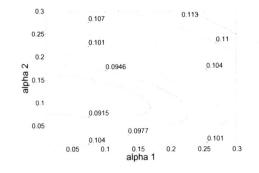

Fig. 1. MSE contour plot for parameter α_1 and α_2 for the ROW model

The optimal number of neighbour $k = 37$ for all k-NN models. It should be noted that k was endogenously determined in the model and the number needs not to be the same across models. However, changes of the MSE with respect to k have the same pattern across the four models in this study as shown in Fig. 2.

Table 2 compares the performances of the four k-NN models with the multinomial logit (MLogit) model, which is commonly used for choice prediction. The performance comparison statistics used in this study are the out-sample MSE

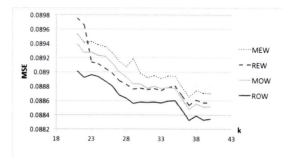

Fig. 2. MSE of the MEW, REW, MOW and ROW models for different values of k

Table 2. 5-fold cross validation results

	MLogit	MEW	REW	MOW	ROW
MSE	0.0958	0.0918	0.0918	0.0916	0.0916
	(0.0022)	(0.0022)	(0.0022)	(0.0022)	(0.0022)
Classification error	0.6263	0.6168	0.6078	0.6134	0.6048
	(0.0232)	(0.0232)	(0.0232)	(0.0232)	(0.0232)
McNemar's χ^2 stat	10.26	2.57	2.12	1.30	-
	(0.0013)	(0.1089)	(0.1454)	(0.2542)	

*For MSE and classification error, standard deviations in parentheses.
**For McNemar's test, p-values in parentheses.

and classification errors estimated using 5-fold cross validation [11]. The rank-ordered models have smaller MSE than the multinomial models and the optimized weight models have smaller MSE than the equal weight models. Moreover, the results also show that models with a smaller MSE also yield a lower classification error. Using the McNemar's test [1] to compare all models with the ROW model, we can see that the ROW model has significantly higher prediction power than the multinomial logit model. However, the McNemar's test did not give significant results for other cases. In this dataset, only 20.68% of the data borrowed from the second source, which can explain why the performance improvement from using the rank-ordered model was rather small. It can be expected that more information on the non-primary ranks would increase the performance improvement.

5   Conclusions

The evidence-theoretic k-NN rank-ordered choice model was shown to outperform the traditional multinomial choice model, which shows the benefit of including the additional information from each individual's non-primary choices. The weight matrix contributes significantly to the prediction accuracy, indicating that all the characteristics are not equally informative.

Despite the non-parametric nature of the model, a number of assumptions were made. It is important to discuss a few alternatives for the model specification as it may improve the model performance for different studies. The first assumption of this model is related to the distance function $d(\cdot)$. The second assumption is on the confidence measure. This study uses the plausibility probability function $Pl\_P_m(\cdot)$. Alternatives are the belief, the plausibility and the pignistic functions [6]. The last assumption is on the optimization rule. The optimization rule used in this study is the mean squared error (MSE) minimization. Alternative criteria are entropy or the modified MSE as suggested in Denoeux and Zouhal (2001) [9].

The evidence-theoretic k-NN model has been extended in several aspects, many of which can be applied to this rank-ordered choice model. An advantage of using the evidence-theoretic method is that it can be modified to cope with uncertain and imprecise data in which a set of alternatives is observed for each rank. For example, if we can only observe that individual i dislikes choice ω_q, then we know that all other available choices are preferred to ω_q but we do not know the ranking of those choices. In this case, the first rank would contain more than one alternative and the model can take advantage of the evidence theoretic method more fully.

Moreover, the belief function approach makes it possible to combine pieces of evidence from several different sources. Therefore, the output from the belief function classifier can conveniently be combined with evidence from other classifiers or with other information such as expert opinions.

References

1. Alpaydin, E.: Introduction to Machine Learning. MIT Press (2004)
2. Baltas, G.: A Model for Multiple Brand Choice. European Journal of Operational Research 154(1), 144–149 (2004)
3. Beggs, S., Cardell, S., Hausman, J.: Assessing the Potential Demand for Electric Cars. Journal of Econometrics 17(1), 1–19 (1981)
4. Bhat, C.R., Srinivasan, S.: A Multidimensional Mixed Ordered-response Model for Analyzing Weekend Activity Participation. Transportation Research Part B: Methodological 39(3), 255–278 (2005)
5. Bhat, C.R., Srinivasan, S., Sen, S.: A Joint Model for the Perfect and Imperfect Substitute Goods Case: Application to Activity Time-use Decisions. Transportation Research Part B: Methodological 40(10), 827–850 (2006)
6. Cobb, B.R., Shenoy, P.P.: On the Plausibility Transformation Method for Translating Belief Function Models to Probability Models. International Journal of Approximate Reasoning 41(3), 314–330 (2006)
7. Denoeux, T.: A k-nearest neighbor classification rule based on Dempster-Shafer theory. IEEE Transactions on Systems, Man and Cybernetics 25(5), 804–813 (1995)
8. Denoeux, T.: Analysis of Evidence-Theoretic Decision Rules for Pattern Classification. Pattern recognition 30(7), 1095–1107 (1997)
9. Denoeux, T., Zouhal, L.M.: Handling Possibilistic Labels in Pattern Classification Using Evidential Reasoning. Fuzzy Sets and Systems 122(3), 409–424 (2001)
10. Maddala, G.S.: Limited-dependent and Qualitative Variables in Econometrics. Cambridge University Press (1986)

11. Mosteller, F., Tukey, J.W.: Data Analysis, Including Statistics. The Collected Works of John W. Tukey: Graphics 123(5), 1965–1985 (1988)
12. The Mathworks, Optimization Toolbox: User's Guide (R2014b). The MathWorks, Inc. (2014)
13. Train, K.: Data analysis, Including Statistics Discrete Choice Methods with Simulation. Cambridge University Press (2009)
14. Zouhal, L.M., Denoeux, T.: An Evidence-theoretic k-NN Rule with Parameter Optimization. Systems, Man, and Cybernetics, Part C: Applications and Reviews, 28(2), 263-271 (1998)

Belief Hierarchical Clustering

Wiem Maalel, Kuang Zhou, Arnaud Martin, and Zied Elouedi

LARODEC, ISG.41 rue de la Liberté, 2000 Le Bardo, Tunisia
IRISA, Université de Rennes 1. IUT de Lannion. Rue Edouard Branly BP 30219,
22302 Lannion cedex. France
Wiem.Maalel@gmail.com, kzhoumath@163.com,
Arnaud.Martin@univ-rennes1.fr, Zied.Elouedi@gmx.fr

Abstract. In the data mining field many clustering methods have been proposed, yet standard versions do not take into account uncertain databases. This paper deals with a new approach to cluster uncertain data by using a hierarchical clustering defined within the belief function framework. The main objective of the belief hierarchical clustering is to allow an object to belong to one or several clusters. To each belonging, a degree of belief is associated, and clusters are combined based on the pignistic properties. Experiments with real uncertain data show that our proposed method can be considered as a propitious tool.

Keywords: Clustering, Hierarchical clustering, Belief function, Belief clustering.

1 Introduction

Due to the increase of imperfect data, the process of decision making is becoming harder. In order to face this, the data analysis is being applied in various fields.

Clustering is mostly used in data mining and aims at grouping a set of similar objects into clusters. In this context, many clustering algorithms exist and are categorized into two main families:

The first family involves the partitioning methods based on density such as k-means algorithm [6] that is widely used thanks to its convergence speed. It partitions the data into k clusters represented by their centers. The second family includes the hierarchical clustering methods such as the top-down and the Hierarchical Ascendant Clustering (HAC) [5]. This latter consists on constructing clusters recursively by partitioning the objects in a bottom-up way. This process leads to good result visualizations. Nevertheless, it has a non-linear complexity.

All these standard methods deal with certain and precise data. Thus, in order to facilitate the decision making, it would be more appropriate to handle uncertain data. Here, we need a soft clustering process that will take into account the possibility that objects belong to more than one cluster.

In such a case, several methods have been established. Among them, the Fuzzy C-Means [1] which consists in assigning a membership to each data point corresponding to the cluster center, and the weights minimizing the total weighted

F. Cuzzolin (Ed.): BELIEF 2014, LNAI 8764, pp. 68–76, 2014.

mean-square error. This method constantly converges. Patently, Evidential c-Means (ECM) [3], [7] is deemed to be a very fateful method. It enhances the FCM and generates a credal partition from attribute data. This method deals with the clustering of object data. Accordingly, the belief k-Modes method [4] is a popular method, which builds K groups characterized by uncertain attribute values and provides a classification of new instances. Schubert has also found a clustering algorithm [8] which uses the mass on the empty set to build a classifier.

Our objective in this paper is to develop a belief hierarchical clustering method, in order to ensure the membership of objects in several clusters, and to handle the uncertainty in data under the belief function framework.

This remainder is organized as follows: in the next section we review the ascendant hierarchical clustering, its concepts and its characteristics. In section 3, we recall some of the basic concepts of belief function theory. Our method is described in section 4 and we evaluate its performance on a real data set in section 5. Finally, Section 6 is a conclusion for the whole paper.

2   Ascendant Hierarchical Clustering

This method consists on agglomerating the close clusters in order to have finally one cluster containing all the objects x_j (where $j = 1, .., N$).

Let's consider $\mathcal{P}^K = \{C_1, ..., C_K\}$ the set of clusters. If $K = N$, $C_1 = x_1, ...,$ $C_N = x_N$. Thereafter, throughout all the steps of clustering, we will move from a partition $\mathcal{P}^K$ to a partition $\mathcal{P}^{K-1}$. The result generated is described by a hierarchical clustering tree (dendrogram), where the nodes represent the successive fusions and the height of the nodes represents the value of the distance between two objects which gives a concrete meaning to the level of nodes conscripted as "indexed hierarchy". This latter is usually indexed by the values of the distances (or dissimilarity) for each aggregation step. The indexed hierarchy can be seen as a set with an ultrametric distance d which satisfies these properties:
i) $x = y \Longleftrightarrow d(x, y) = 0$.
ii) $d(x, y) = d(y, x)$.
iii) $d(x, y) \leq d(x, z) + d(y, z), \forall x, y, z \in \mathbb{R}$.

The algorithm is as follows:

− Initialisation: the initial clusters are the N-singletons. We compute their dissimilarity matrix.
− Iterate these two steps until the aggregation turns into a single cluster:
  • Combine the two most similar (closest) elements (clusters) from the selected groups according to some distance rules.
  • Update the matrix distance by replacing the two grouped elements by the new one and calculate its distance from each of the other classes.

Once all these steps completed, we do not recover a partition of K clusters, but a partition of $K − 1$ clusters. Hence, we had to point out the aggregation criterion (distance rules) between two points and between two clusters. We can use the Euclidian distance between N objects x defined in a space $\mathbb{R}$. Different distances can be considered between two clusters: we can consider the minimum as follows:

$$\mathbf{d}(C_j^i, C_{j'}^i) = \min_{x_k \in C_j^i, x_{k'} \in C_{j'}^i} d(x_k, x_{k'}) \tag{1}$$

with $j, j' = 1, ..., i$. The maximum can also be considered, however, the minimum and maximum distances create compact clusters but sensitive to "outliers". The average can also be used, but the most used method is Ward's method, using Huygens formula to compute this:

$$\Delta I_{inter(C_j^i, C_{j'}^i)} = \frac{m_{C_j} m_{C_{j'}}}{m_{C_j} + m_{C_{j'}}} d^2(\mathbf{C_j^i}, \mathbf{C_{j'}^i}) \tag{2}$$

where m_{C_j} and $m_{C_{j'}}$ are numbers of elements of C_j and $C_{j'}$ respectively and $\mathbf{C_j^i}, \mathbf{C_{j'}^i}$ the centers. Then, we had to find the couple of clusters minimizing the distance:

$$(C_l^k, C_{l'}^k) = d(C_l^i, C_{l'}^i) = \min_{C_j^i, C_{l'}^i \in \mathcal{C}^i} \mathbf{d}(C_j^i, C_{j'}^i) \tag{3}$$

3   Basis on The Theory of Belief Functions

In this Section, we briefly review the main concepts that will be used in our method that underlies the theory of belief functions [9] as interpreted in the Transferable Belief Model (TBM) [10]. Let's suppose that the frame of discernment is $\Omega = \{\omega_1, \omega_2, ..., \omega_3\}$. Ω is a finite set that reflects a state of partial knowledge that can be represented by a basis belief assignment defined as:

$$m : 2^\Omega \to [0, 1]$$
$$\sum_{A \subseteq \Omega} m(A) = 1 \tag{4}$$

The value $m(A)$ is named a basic belief mass (bbm) of A. The subset $A \in 2^\Omega$ is called focal element if $m(A) > 0$. One of the important rules in the belief theory is the conjunctive rule which consists on combining two basic belief assignments m_1 and m_2 induced from two distinct and reliable information sources defined as:

$$m_1 \text{\textcircled{$\cap$}} m_2(C) = \sum_{A \cap B = C} m_1(A) \cdot m_2(B), \quad \forall C \subseteq \Omega \tag{5}$$

The Dempster rule is the normalized conjunctive rule:

$$m_1 \oplus m_2(C) = \frac{m_1 \text{\textcircled{$\cap$}} m_2(C)}{1 - m_1 \text{\textcircled{$\cap$}} m_2(\emptyset)}, \quad \forall C \subseteq \Omega \tag{6}$$

In order to ensure the decision making, beliefs are transformed into probability measures recorded BetP, and defined as follows [10]:

$$\text{BetP}(A) = \sum_{B \subseteq \Omega} \frac{|A \cap B|}{|B|} \frac{m(B)}{(1 - m(\emptyset))}, \forall A \in \Omega \tag{7}$$

4   Belief Hierarchical Clustering

In order to set down a way to develop a belief hierarchical clustering, we choose to work on different levels: on one hand, the object level, on the other hand, the cluster level. At the beginning, for N objects we have, the frame of discernment is $\Omega = \{x_1, ..., x_N\}$ and for each object belonging to one cluster, a degree of belief is assigned. Let $\mathcal{P}^N$ be the partition of N objects. Hence, we define a mass function for each object x_i, inspired from the k-nearest neighbors [2] method which is defined as follows:

$$m_i^{\Omega_i}(x_j) = \alpha e^{-\gamma d^2(x_i, x_j)}$$
$$m_i^{\Omega_i}(\Omega_i) = 1 - \sum m_i^{\Omega_i}(x_j) \tag{8}$$

where $i \neq j$, α and γ are two parameters we can optimize [11], d can be considered as the Euclidean distance, and the frame of discernment is given by $\Omega_i = \{x_1, ..., x_N\} \setminus \{x_i\}$.

In order to move from the partition of N objects to a partition of $N-1$ objects we have to find both nearest objects (x_i, x_j) to form a cluster. Eventually, the partition of $N-1$ clusters will be given by $\mathcal{P}^{N-1} = \{(x_i, x_j), x_k\}$ where $k = 1, ..., N \setminus \{i, j\}$. The nearest objects are found considering the pignistic probability, defined on the frame Ω_i, of each object x_i, where we proceed the comparison by pairs, by computing firstly the pignistic for each object, and then we continue the process using $arg\,max$. The nearest objects are chosen using the maximum of the pignistic values between pairs of objects, and we will compute the product pair one by one.

$$(x_i, x_j) = arg\,max_{x_i, x_j \in \mathcal{P}^N} \mathrm{BetP}_i^{\Omega_i}(x_j) * \mathrm{BetP}_j^{\Omega_j}(x_i) \tag{9}$$

Then, this first couple of objects is a cluster. Now consider that we have a partition $\mathcal{P}^K$ of K clusters $\{C_1, ..., C_K\}$. In order to find the best partition $\mathcal{P}^{K-1}$ of $K-1$ clusters, we have to find the best couple of clusters to be merged. First, if we consider one of the classical distances $\mathbf{d}$ (single link, complete link, average, etc), presented in section 2, between the clusters, we delineate a mass function, defined within the frame Ω_i for each cluster $C_i \in \mathcal{P}^K$ with $C_i \neq C_j$ by:

$$m_i^{\Omega_i}(C_j) = \alpha e^{-\gamma d^2(C_i, C_j)} \tag{10}$$

$$m_i^{\Omega_i}(\Omega_i) = 1 - \sum m_i^{\Omega_i}(C_j) \tag{11}$$

where $\Omega_i = \{C_1, ..., C_K\} \setminus \{C_i\}$. Then, both clusters to merge are given by:

$$(C_i, C_j) = arg\,max_{C_i, C_j \in \mathcal{P}^K} \mathrm{BetP}^{\Omega_i}(C_j) * \mathrm{BetP}^{\Omega_j}(C_i) \tag{12}$$

and the partition $\mathcal{P}^{K-1}$ is made from the new cluster (C_i, C_j) and all the other clusters of $\mathcal{P}^K$. The point by doing so is to prove that if we maximize the degree of probability we will have the couple of clusters to combine. Of course, this approach will give exactly the same partitions than the classical ascendant hierarchical clustering, but the dendrogram can be built from BetP and the best partition (*i.e.* the number of clusters) can be preferred to find. The indexed hierarchy will be indexed by the sum of BetP which will lead to more precise and specific results according to the dissimilarity between objects and therefore will facilitate our process.

Hereafter, we define another way to build the partition $\mathcal{P}^{K-1}$. For each initial object x_i to classify, it exists a cluster of $\mathcal{P}^K$ such as $x_i \in C_k$. We consider the frame of discernment $\Omega_i = \{C_1, \dots, C_K\} \setminus \{C_k\}$, m, which describes the degree that the two clusters could be merged, can be noted m^Ω and we define the mass function:

$$m_i^{\Omega_i}(C_{k_j}) = \prod_{x_j \in C_{k_j}} \alpha e^{-\gamma d^2(x_i, x_j)} \tag{13}$$

$$m_i^{\Omega_i}(\Omega_i) = 1 - \sum_{x_j \in C_{k_j}} m_i^{\Omega_i}(C_{k_j}) \tag{14}$$

In order to find a mass function for each cluster C_i of $\mathcal{P}^K$, we combine all the mass functions given by all objects of C_i by a combination rule such as the Dempster rule of combination given by equation (6). Then, to merge both clusters we use the equation (12) as before. The sum of the pignisitic probabilities will be the index of the dendrogram, called BetP index.

5   Experimentations

Experiments were first applied on diamond data set composed of twelve objects as describe in Figure 1.a and analyzed in [7]. The dendrograms for both classical and Belief Hierarchical Clustering (BHC) are represented by Figures 1.b and 1.c. The object 12 is well considered as an outlier with both approaches. With the belief hierarchical clustering, this object is clearly different, thanks to the pignistic probability. For HAC, the distance between object 12 and other objects is small, however, for BHC, there is a big gap between object 12 and others. This points out that our method is better for detecting outliers. If the objects 5 and 6 are associated to 1, 2, 3 and 4 with the classical hierarchical clustering, with BHC these points are more identified as different. This synthetic data set is special because of the equidistance of the points and there is no uncertainty.

We continue our experiments with a well-known data set, Iris data set, which is composed of flowers from four types of species of Iris described by sepal length, sepal width, petal length, and petal width. The data set contains three clusters known to have a significant overlap.

In order to reduce the complexity and present distinctly the dendrogram, we first used the k-means method to get initial few clusters for our algorithm. It is not necessary to apply this method if the number of objects is not high.

Several experiments have been used with several number of clusters. We present in Figure 2 the obtained dendrograms for 10 and 13 clusters. We notice different combinations between the nearest clusters for both classical and

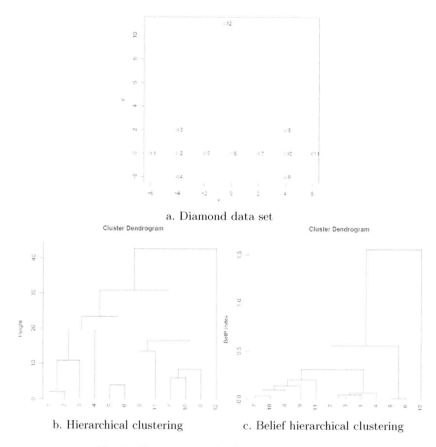

a. Diamond data set

b. Hierarchical clustering   c. Belief hierarchical clustering

Fig. 1. Clustering results for Diamond data set

belief hierarchical clustering. The best situation for BHC is obtained with the pignistic equal to 0.5 because it indicates that the data set is composed of three significant clusters which reflects the real situation. For the classical hierarchical clustering the results are not so obvious. Indeed, for HAC, it is difficult to decide for the optimum cluster number because of the use of the euclidean distance and as seen in Figure 2.c it indistinguishable in terms of the y-value. However, for BHC, it is more easy to do this due to the use of the pignistic probability.

In order to evaluate the performance of our method, we use some of the most popular measures: precision, recall and Rand Index (RI). The results for both BHC and HAC are summarized in Table 1. The first three columns are for BHC, while the others are for HAC. In fact, we suppose that F_c represents the final number of clusters and we start with $F_c = 2$ until $F_c = 6$. We fixed the value of k_{init} at 13. We note that for $F_c = 2$ the precision is low while the recall is of high value, and that when we have a high cluster number ($F_c = 5$ or 6), the precision will be high but the recall will be relatively low. Thus, we note that for the same number of final clusters (*e.g.* $F_c = 4$), our method is better in terms of precision, recall and RI.

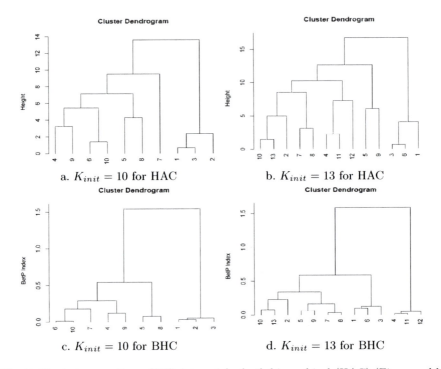

a. $K_{init} = 10$ for HAC   b. $K_{init} = 13$ for HAC

c. $K_{init} = 10$ for BHC   d. $K_{init} = 13$ for BHC

Fig. 2. Clustering results on IRIS data set for both hierarchical (HAC) (Fig. a and b) and belief hierarchical (BHC) (Fig. c and d) clustering (K_{init} is the cluster number by k-means first).

Table 1. Evaluation results

	BHC			HAC		
	Precision	Recall	RI	Precision	Recall	RI
$F_c = 2$	0.5951	1.0000	0.7763	0.5951	1.0000	0.7763
$F_c = 3$	0.8011	0.8438	0.8797	0.6079	0.9282	0.7795
$F_c = 4$	0.9506	0.8275	0.9291	0.8183	0.7230	0.8561
$F_c = 5$	0.8523	0.6063	0.8360	0.8523	0.6063	0.8360
$F_c = 6$	0.9433	0.5524	0.8419	0.8916	0.5818	0.8392

Tests are also performed to a third data base, Congressional Voting Records Data Set. The results presented in Figure 3 show that the pignistic probability value increased at each level, having thereby, a more homogeneous partition. We notice different combinations, between the nearest clusters, that are not the same within the two methods compared. For example, cluster 9 is associated to cluster 10 and then to 6 with HAC, but, with BHC it is associated to cluster 4 and then to 10. Although, throughout the BHC dendrograms shown in Figure 3.c and Figure 3.d, the best situation indicating the optimum number of clusters can be clearly obtained. This easy way is due to the use of the pignistic probability. For this data set, we notice that for $F_c = 2$ and 3, the precision is low while the

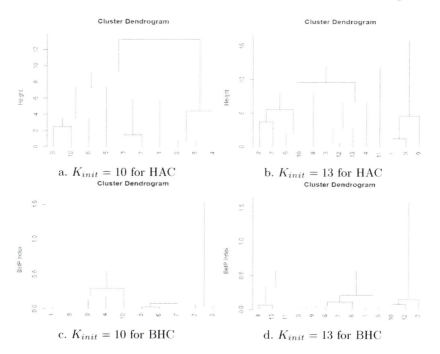

a. $K_{init} = 10$ for HAC

b. $K_{init} = 13$ for HAC

c. $K_{init} = 10$ for BHC

d. $K_{init} = 13$ for BHC

Fig. 3. Clustering results on Congressional Voting Records Data Set for both hierarchical and belief hierarchical clustering

Table 2. Evaluation results for Congressional Voting Records Data Set

	BHC			HAC		
	Precision	Recall	RI	Precision	Recall	RI
$F_c = 2$	0.3873	0.8177	0.5146	0.5951	1.0000	0.7763
$F_c = 3$	0.7313	0.8190	0.8415	0.6288	0.8759	0.7892
$F_c = 4$	0.8701	0.6833	0.8623	0.7887	0.7091	0.8419
$F_c = 5$	0.8670	0.6103	0.8411	0.7551	0.6729	0.8207
$F_c = 6$	0.9731	0.6005	0.8632	0.8526	0.6014	0.8347

recall is high. However, with the increasing of our cluster number, we notice that BHC provides a better results. In fact, for $F_c = 3, 4, 5$ and 6 the precision and RI values relative to BHC are higher then the precision and RI values relative to HAC, which confirmed the efficiency of our approach which is better in terms of precision and RI.

6   Conclusion

Ultimately, we have introduced a new clustering method using the hierarchical paradigm in order to implement uncertainty in the belief function framework. This method puts the emphasis on the fact that one object may belong to several clusters. It seeks to merge clusters based on its pignistic probability. Our method was proved on data sets and the corresponding results have clearly shown its efficiency. The algorithm complexity has revealed itself as the usual problem of the belief function theory. Our future work will be devoted to focus on this peculiar problem.

References

1. Bezdek, J.C., Ehrlich, R., Fulls, W.: Fcm: The fuzzy c-means clustering algorithm. Computers and Geosciences 10(2-3), 191–203 (1984)
2. Denœux, T.: A k-Nearest Neighbor Classification Rule Based on Dempster-Shafer Theory. IEEE Transactions on Systems, Man, and Cybernetics - Part A: Systems and Humans 25(5), 804–813 (1995)
3. Denœux, T., Masson, M.: EVCLUS: Evidential Clustering of Proximity Data. IEEE Transactions on Systems, Man, and Cybernetics - Part B: Cybernetics 34(1), 95–109 (2004)
4. Ben Hariz, S., Elouedi, Z., Mellouli, K.: Clustering approach using belief function theory. In: AIMSA, pp. 162–171 (2006)
5. Hastie, T., Tibshirani, R., Friedman, J., Franklin, J.: The elements of statistical learning; data mining, inference and prediction. Springer, New York (2001)
6. MacQueen, J.: Some methods for classification and analysis of multivariate observations. In: Proceedings of the 5th Berkeley Symposium on Mathematical Statistics and Probability, vol. 11 (1967)
7. Masson, M., Denœux, T.: Clustering interval-valued proximity data using belief functions. Pattern Recognition Letters 25, 163–171 (2004)
8. Schubert, J.: Clustering belief functions based on attracting and conflicting metalevel evidence. In: Bouchon-Meunier, B., Foulloy, L., Yager, R.R. (eds.) Intelligent Systems for Information Processing: From Representation to Applications, Elsevier, Amsterdam (2003)
9. Shafer, G.: Mathematical Theory of evidence. Princeton Univ. (1976)
10. Smets, P., Kennes, R.: The Transferable Belief Model. Artificial Intelligent 66, 191–234 (1994)
11. Zouhal, L.M., Denœux, T.: An Evidence-Theoric k-NN Rule with Parameter Optimization. IEEE Transactions on Systems, Man, and Cybernetics - Part C: Applications and Reviews 28(2), 263–271 (1998)

Logistic Regression of Soft Labeled Instances via the Evidential EM Algorithm

Benjamin Quost

Université de Technologie de Compiègne
Laboratoire Heudiasyc, UMR UTC-CNRS 7253
benjamin.quost@utc.fr

Abstract. We address the issue of fitting a logistic regression model to soft labeled data, when the soft labels take the form of plausibility degrees for the classes. We propose to use the E2M algorithm to take this partial information into account. The resulting procedure iterates two steps: first, expected class memberships are computed using the soft labels and the current parameter estimates; then, new parameter estimates are obtained using these expected memberships. Experimental results show the interest of our approach when the data labels are corrupted with noise.

Keywords: Statistical inference from incomplete data, Semi-supervised learning, Partially-supervised learning.

1 Introduction

In this paper, we address the problem of multiclass classification. In particular, we are interested in learning a parametric model for the posterior probabilities $\Pr(\omega_k|\mathbf{x}, \mathbf{w})$ of the classes $\omega_k \in \Omega = \{\omega_1, \ldots, \omega_K\}$. Classically, such a model is learnt by estimating the parameter $\mathbf{w}$ from a training set of labeled instances $\{(\mathbf{x}_1, y_1), \ldots, (\mathbf{x}_n, y_n)\}$, where y_i indicates the class of the instance $\mathbf{x}_i$. The problem of training a classifier from data with incomplete or partial labels has recently received much attention. In semi-supervised learning [4], some instances are precisely labeled, and other unlabeled; partially supervised learning [1,8,10] considers a set of plausible classes for each training instance. More generally, a soft label may be used to indicate to which extent a training instance may belong to the classes considered. In [6], a new version of the EM algorithm for uncertain data, known as the Evidential EM (E2M) algorithm, was successfully applied to clustering when the uncertainty on both instances and labels is represented using belief functions.

We consider in this work the logistic model [3], which has been studied in the semi-supervised [2,7,9] and partially supervised [8,10] settings. Very recently, the case of probabilistic labels has been addressed using ranking techniques [13] and self-training [12]. In [11], the problem of learning from fuzzy information (instances or labels) using generalized loss functions has been addressed. The approach was applied to logistic regression on a simple classification problem.

F. Cuzzolin (Ed.): BELIEF 2014, LNAI 8764, pp. 77–86, 2014.
© Springer International Publishing Switzerland 2014

Here, we propose to represent the class information of an instance $\mathbf{x}_i$ by a set of plausibility degrees $\pi_{i1}, \ldots, \pi_{iK}$ over the classes. We interpret π_{ik} as the plausibility that $\mathbf{x}_i \in \omega_k$. Obviously, the classical approach to fitting the model cannot be used any more: now, the class information of an instance is only known up to these plausibility degrees. Here, we show that the E2M algorithm mentioned above may be used to fit the model to such partially labeled data. Essentially, the algorithm iteratively alternates estimating the expected class memberships of the training instances knowing the plausibilistic labels and a current fit for the model parameters, and computing a new fit for the model parameters by maximizing the corresponding expected log-likelihood.

The paper is organized as follows. Section 2 presents basic knowledge about the classical logistic model and reminds how the model parameters may be determined in the binomial case ($K = 2$). In Section 3, we describe our approach for fitting a logistic model to data with plausibilistic labels. Section 4 presents some experiments realized over classical real datasets, for which the labels have been corrupted. The results clearly show the interest to take into account the information of uncertainty of the class labels when it is available. Eventually, we conclude in Section 5.

2   Logistic Regression from Hard-Labeled Instances

2.1   Model

As mentioned above, assume that we want to compute the posterior probabilities of the classes $\omega_1, \ldots, \omega_K$ for a given instance $\mathbf{x} = (x_1, \ldots, x_p) \in \mathcal{X}$. The logistic model postulates that the posterior probabilities $p_k = \Pr(\omega_k | \mathbf{x}, \mathbf{w})$ are obtained by

$$p_k = \Pr(\omega_k | \mathbf{x}, \mathbf{w}) = \frac{\exp(\mathbf{w}_k{}^t \mathbf{x})}{1 + \sum_{\ell=1}^{K-1} \exp(\mathbf{w}_\ell{}^t \mathbf{x})}, \quad \text{for } k = 1, \ldots, K - 1; \quad (1a)$$

$$p_K = \Pr(\omega_K | \mathbf{x}, \mathbf{w}) = \frac{1}{1 + \sum_{\ell=1}^{K-1} \exp(\mathbf{w}_\ell{}^t \mathbf{x})}. \quad (1b)$$

Note that an intercept may be included in the model. In this case, a constant term is included in the feature vector: $\mathbf{x} = (1, x_1, \ldots, x_p)$.

The parameter vector $\mathbf{w} = (\mathbf{w}_1, \ldots, \mathbf{w}_{K-1})$ is obviously unknown and can be estimated from a set of labeled training instances $\mathcal{T} = \{(\mathbf{x}_1, y_1), \ldots, (\mathbf{x}_n, y_n)\}$, $\mathbf{x}_i \in \mathcal{X}$, $y_i \in \Omega$. The maximum likelihood approach is commonly used for this purpose. Let

$$Z_{ik} = \begin{cases} 1 \text{ if } Y_i = \omega_k, \\ 0 \text{ otherwise.} \end{cases} \quad (2)$$

Since the indicator variable Z_{ik} follows a Bernoulli distribution $\mathcal{B}(p_{ik})$ with $p_{ik} = \Pr(\omega_k | \mathbf{x}_i, \mathbf{w})$, we may compute the likelihood function of the model parameters $\mathbf{w}$ given the training labels $\mathbf{z}_1, \ldots, \mathbf{z}_n$:

$$L(\mathbf{w}; \mathbf{z}_1, \ldots, \mathbf{z}_n) = \prod_{i=1}^{n} \prod_{k=1}^{K} \Pr(Z_{ik} = z_{ik}) \propto \prod_{i=1}^{n} \prod_{k=1}^{K} p_{ik}^{z_{ik}}, \quad (3a)$$

where $\mathbf{z}_i = (z_{i1}, \ldots, z_{iK})$ is the vector indicating the class membership of the training instance $\mathbf{x}_i$ determined from y_i. The log-likelihood function is thus

$$\log L(\mathbf{w}) \propto \sum_{i=1}^{n} \sum_{k=1}^{K} z_{ik} \log p_{ik}; \tag{3b}$$

it has to be maximized jointly with respect to the vectors $\mathbf{w}_k$ ($k = 1, \ldots, K-1$).

2.2 Parameter Estimation (Binomial Case)

In the case of two classes, the log-likelihood can be written as:

$$\log L(\mathbf{w}; z_1, \ldots, z_n) = \sum_{i=1}^{n} \left[z_i \mathbf{w}^{\mathrm{t}} \mathbf{x}_i - \log(1 + \exp(\mathbf{w}^{\mathrm{t}} \mathbf{x}_i)) \right], \tag{4}$$

where $z_i = 1$ if $y_i = \omega_1$, and 0 otherwise. Then, $\mathbf{w}$ is estimated so as to maximize $\log L$. For this purpose, let us compute the vector $\nabla \log L$ of first order derivatives:

$$\nabla \log L = \frac{\partial \log L(\mathbf{w})}{\partial \mathbf{w}} = \sum_{i=1}^{n} \mathbf{x}_i \left(z_i - \frac{\exp(\mathbf{w}^{\mathrm{t}} \mathbf{x}_i)}{1 + \exp(\mathbf{w}^{\mathrm{t}} \mathbf{x}_i)} \right) = X^{\mathrm{t}}(\mathbf{z} - \mathbf{p}), \tag{5a}$$

where X is the $n \times p$ instance matrix (or $n \times (p+1)$ matrix if an intercept is used), $\mathbf{z} = (z_1, \ldots, z_n)^{\mathrm{t}}$ is the vector of class indicators, and $\mathbf{p} = (p_1, \ldots, p_n)^{\mathrm{t}}$ of probabilities. Note that the Hessian matrix (of second-order derivatives) is definite negative:

$$H = \frac{\partial^2 \log L(\mathbf{w})}{\partial \mathbf{w} \partial \mathbf{w}^{\mathrm{t}}} = \sum_{i=1}^{n} \mathbf{x}_i \left(-\frac{\partial}{\partial \mathbf{w}^{\mathrm{t}}} \left(\frac{\exp(\mathbf{w}^{\mathrm{t}} \mathbf{x}_i)}{1 + \exp(\mathbf{w}^{\mathrm{t}} \mathbf{x}_i)} \right) \right) = -X^{\mathrm{t}} W X, \tag{5b}$$

where W is the diagonal matrix with general term $w_{ii} = p_i(1 - p_i)$. Thus, setting $\nabla \log L$ to zero yields a maximum for the log-likelihood. In spirit, it aims at updating the parameter vector $\mathbf{w}$ so that the posterior probabilities p_i become closer to the labels z_i, $i = 1, \ldots, n$.

Unfortunately, Eq. (5a) is non-linear in $\mathbf{w}$, and one has to resort to iterative techniques to find a local maximum for Eq. (4). Classically, $\nabla \log L$ and H are used in the Newton-Raphson maximization procedure. This algorithm starts from an initial value $\mathbf{w}^{(0)}$ of the parameter vector, and iterates then until convergence:

$$\mathbf{w}^{(q+1)} = w^{(q)} - \left(H^{(q)} \right)^{-1} \nabla^{(q)} \log L = w^{(q)} + \left(X^{\mathrm{t}} W^{(q)} X \right)^{-1} X^{\mathrm{t}}(\mathbf{z} - \mathbf{p}^{(q)}), \tag{5c}$$

where $\nabla^{(q)} \log L$, $H^{(q)}$, $\mathbf{p}^{(q)}$ and $W^{(q)}$ are computed at iteration q using the current fit $\mathbf{w}^{(q)}$ of $\mathbf{w}$.

3   Logistic Regression from Soft-Labeled Instances

In this section, we remind basic material on belief functions, and we show how they can be used to represent partial knowledge of the class information of an instance. The ML estimate of $\mathbf{w}$ cannot be straightforwardly estimated as before when such imprecise information is available: therefore, we briefly remind the principle of the Evidential EM (E2M) algorithm [6], which can be used for this purpose. Finally, we detail how it may be applied to estimate a multinomial logistic model.

3.1   Belief Functions

Let Y be a variable of interest, representing for example the actual class of an instance $\mathbf{x}$. Partial knowledge of Y can be quantified by a *mass function* $m : 2^\Omega \to [0,1]$, such that $\sum_{A \subseteq \Omega} m(A) = 1$. Here, 2^Ω denotes the power set of Ω. In the following, we will assume that m is normal: then, $m(\emptyset) = 0$. Subsets $A \subseteq \Omega$ such that $m(A) > 0$ are called focal elements of m.

If m has a unique focal element, that is $m(A) = 1$ for only one $A \subseteq \Omega$, then it is said to be categorical. Bayesian mass functions are such that $m(A) = 0$ for any A such that $|A| \neq 1$: they are equivalent to a probability distribution over Ω. If a mass function m is both Bayesian and certain, that is $m(\{\omega\}) = 1$ for some $\omega \in \Omega$, then the actual value of Y is precisely known to be ω.

The mass function m is in one-to-one correspondence with its associated *plausibility function* $Pl : 2^\Omega \to [0;1]$, defined for all $A \subseteq \Omega$ by:

$$Pl(A) = \sum_{B \cap A \neq \emptyset} m(B).$$

The degree $Pl(A)$ can be interpreted as the maximal amount of belief mass that could be assigned to A if further information justifying such a transfer became available [15]. Finally, the function $pl : \Omega \to [0;1]$ such that $pl(\omega) = Pl(\{\omega\})$ is called the *contour function* [14] associated with m.

In this article, we are interested in the case where the labeling information of the instances $\mathbf{x}_i$, $i = 1, \ldots, n$ is incomplete. More precisely, we assume that the partial knowledge of each label is represented by a contour function, or equivalently by a set of degrees of plausibility over the classes. For each instance $\mathbf{x}_i$, we thus have a vector $\Pi_i = (\pi_{i1}, \ldots, \pi_{iK})$, where π_{ik} is the plausibility $Pl(Z_{ik} = 1)$ that the actual class of $\mathbf{x}_i$ is ω_k, for $k = 1, \ldots, K$. Note that this kind of labeling encompasses a broad set of situations:

- precise labeling, whenever $\pi_{ik} = 1$ for some k and $\pi_{i\ell} = 0$, for all $\ell \neq k$;
- when $\pi_{ik} = 1$ for all $\omega_k \in A$, the labeling is partial: all the classes in the set A are equally and totally plausible, the other ones being impossible; note that if $A = \Omega$, the actual label of $\mathbf{x}_i$ is unknown.
- Finally, the labeling is probabilistic when the degrees π_{ik} are such that $\sum_{k=1,\ldots,K} \pi_{ik} = 1$.

3.2   Evidential EM Algorithm

When the likelihood function depends on unknown variables (here, the indicator variables Z_{ik}, $i = 1, \ldots, n$, $k = 1, \ldots, K$), the log-likelihood function cannot be directly maximized. The E2M algorithm makes it possible to overcome this problem when partial information regarding the missing values is available. It proceeds iteratively with the *expected* log-likelihood: in a nutshell, it consists in replacing the unknown variables by their mathematical expectations, computed using both the available imprecise class labels and a current estimate of the model parameters $\mathbf{w}$.

The expected log-likelihood is thus maximized by iterating two alternative steps. At iteration q, the E-step consists in computing the expectation of the complete log-likelihood with respect to the imprecise information available: here,

$$Q(\mathbf{w}; \mathbf{w}^{(q)}) = \mathbf{E}[\log L(\mathbf{w}; \mathbf{z}) | \mathbf{w}^{(q)}, \Pi], \tag{6}$$

with $\mathbf{w}^{(q)}$ the current estimate of the parameter vector $\mathbf{w}$, and $\Pi = (\Pi_1, \ldots, \Pi_n)$ the set of imprecise class labels of all the instances. The M-step then requires the maximization of $Q(\mathbf{w}; \mathbf{w}^{(q)})$ with respect to $\mathbf{w}$. The E2M algorithm alternatively repeats the E- and M- steps until a convergence condition is met. In [6], it is shown that it converges towards a local maximum of the log-likelihood.

3.3   Model Estimation

E-Step. In our case, the expectation of the log-likelihood defined by Eq. (3b) writes

$$Q(\mathbf{w}; \mathbf{w}^{(q)}) = \mathbf{E}[\log L(\mathbf{w}; \mathbf{z}) | \mathbf{w}^{(q)}, \Pi] \propto \sum_{i=1}^{n} t_{ik}^{(q)} \log p_{ik}, \tag{7}$$

where $t_{ik}^{(q)} = \mathbf{E}[Z_{ik} | \mathbf{w}^{(q)}, \Pi_i]$. Note that this expression is identical to Eq. (4), except for the indicator variables z_{ik} that are now unknown and thus replaced by their expectations. As before, each indicator variable Z_{ik} follows a Bernoulli distribution $\mathcal{B}(p_{ik})$. Thus, following [6], its expectation $t_{ik}^{(q)}$ may be computed as:

$$t_{ik}^{(q)} = \mathbf{E}[Z_{ik} | \mathbf{w}^{(q)}, \Pi_i] = \Pr(Z_{ik} = 1 | \mathbf{x}_i, \mathbf{w}^{(q)}, \Pi_i)$$

$$= \frac{\Pr(Z_{ik} = 1 | \mathbf{x}_i, \mathbf{w}^{(q)}) \, pl(Z_{ik} = 1)}{\sum_{z_{i\ell}} \Pr(Z_{i\ell} = z_{i\ell} | \mathbf{x}_i, \mathbf{w}^{(q)}) \, pl(z_{i\ell} = 1)} = \frac{p_{ik}^{(q)} \pi_{ik}}{\sum_{\ell=1}^{K} p_{i\ell}^{(q)} \pi_{i\ell}}.$$

Replacing the current estimates $p_{ik}^{(q)}$ of the probabilities with their expressions (Eq. (1a-1b)), we finally obtain:

$$t_{ik}^{(q)} = \frac{\pi_{ik} \exp(\mathbf{w}_k^{(q)\mathsf{t}} \mathbf{x}_i)}{\sum_{\ell=1}^{K-1} \pi_{i\ell} \exp(\mathbf{w}_\ell^{(q)\mathsf{t}} \mathbf{x}_i) + \pi_{iK}}, \quad \text{for } k = 1, \ldots, K-1; \tag{8a}$$

$$t_{iK}^{(q)} = \frac{\pi_{iK}}{\sum_{\ell=1}^{K-1} \pi_{i\ell} \exp(\mathbf{w}_\ell^{(q)\mathsf{t}} \mathbf{x}_i) + \pi_{iK}}. \tag{8b}$$

M-Step. Once these expected class labels have been obtained in the E-step, the M-step consists in maximizing Eq. (7) with respect to $\mathbf{w}$, in order to obtain a new estimate $\mathbf{w}^{(q+1)}$ of the model parameters. This is trivial once the similarity between Eq. (7) and Eq. (3b) has been noticed. Indeed, any procedure for estimating a logistic model from data with precise labels can be used for this purpose, by replacing each precise (and now missing) class label z_{ik} with its expected value $t_{ik}^{(q)}$ computed in the E-step via Eq. (8a-8b).

3.4   Algorithm, Convergence, and Computational Complexity

Algorithm 1 summarizes our procedure for estimating a multinomial logistic model from data with imprecise labels. We propose to check for convergence by comparing the square norm between two successive parameter vectors $\mathbf{w}^{(q)}$ and $\mathbf{w}^{(q+1)}$ to some predefinite threshold ε.

Algorithm 1. Fitting a Logistic Model to Soft Labeled Instances

---

Inputs: training set $\{(\mathbf{x}_1, \Pi_1), \ldots, (\mathbf{x}_n, \Pi_n)\}$, with $\mathbf{x}_i \in \mathcal{X}$, $\Pi_i \in [0,1]^K$, $i = 1, \ldots, n$; initial parameter vector $\mathbf{w}^{(0)}$; threshold ε

repeat

  1. E-step: compute the expected class labels $t_{ik}^{(q)}$ ($i = 1, \ldots, n$, $k = 1, \ldots, K$), using the current parameter vector $\mathbf{w}^{(q)} = (\mathbf{w}_1^{(q)}, \ldots, \mathbf{w}_{K-1}^{(q)})$, via Eq. (8a-8b),

  2. M-step: compute a new parameter vector $\mathbf{w}^{(q+1)}$ by maximizing Eq. (7) with respect to $\mathbf{w}$, using ay classical procedure for logistic regression.

until the algorithm converges: $\|\mathbf{w}^{(q+1)} - \mathbf{w}^{(q)}\|^2 \leq \varepsilon$

Outputs: Maximum likelihood estimate $\widehat{\mathbf{w}}$ of the parameter vector, and corresponding observed log-likelihood $\log L(\widehat{\mathbf{w}})$.

The convergence of the EM algorithm is classically based on the relative increase of the expected log-likelihood Q. However, this function can be very flat in some regions of the parameter space, leading to erroneously detect convergence. Thus, we rather propose to check for convergence by comparing the square norm between two successive model parameters $\mathbf{w}^{(q)}$ and $\mathbf{w}^{(q+1)}$ to some pre-definite threshold ε.

We may remark that this estimation strategy requires using an iterative optimization procedure to maximize $Q(\mathbf{w}; \mathbf{w}^{(q)})$ *at each iteration of the E2M algorithm*. Note, however, that two successive estimates of the class labels $t_{ik}^{(q)}$ and $t_{ik}^{(q+1)}$ are generally close to each other; thus, this is likely to be the same for two successive parameter estimates $\mathbf{w}^{(q)}$ and $\mathbf{w}^{(q+1)}$, particularly after a few iterations of the E2M algorithm. Therefore, $\mathbf{w}^{(q)}$ is a good choice for the starting value of the optimization procedure deployed in the M-step at iteration $q + 1$.

4   Experiments

In this section, we report results obtained by fitting a logistic model to several classical datasets, which are described in Table 1. These datasets may be downloaded from the UCI Machine Learning Repository at the following URL: http://archive.ics.uci.edu/ml/.

Table 1. Dataset description

dataset	amount of instances	number of classes	dimension
Ecoli	336	8	7
Glass	214	6	9
Ionosphere	350	2	34
Iris	150	3	4
Optdigits	5620	10	64
Pageblocks	5473	5	10
Satimage	6435	6	36
Segment	2310	7	19
Sonar	208	2	60
Spambase	4601	2	57
Vehicles	4230	4	18
Vowel	528+462	11	10
Waveform	5000	3	21
Yeast	1484	10	8

For each dataset, we repeated the following procedure. First, the constant features were removed from the data. Then, we randomly selected 66% of the data for the training set, and kept the remaining ones apart for testing. Note that the Vowel dataset is already split into training and test sets, which shall not be mixed together.

We introduced noise in the labels as follows. With probability $\rho = 0.2$, a training label y_i was replaced by one of the labels in presence, chosen at random according to a uniform distribution. We thus considered three different labelings: one defined by the actual labels $\mathbf{z}_1, \ldots, \mathbf{z}_n$, another with the corrupted labels $\tilde{\mathbf{z}}_1, \ldots, \tilde{\mathbf{z}}_n$, and eventually a soft labeling where the plausibilistic label Π_i associated with an instance $\mathbf{x}_i$ is defined as follows:

$$\pi_{ik} = \begin{cases} 1 \text{ if } \tilde{z}_{ik} = 1, \\ \rho \text{ otherwise.} \end{cases} \tag{9}$$

Thus, when the degree of noise ρ is known to be zero, a plausibilistic label boils down to a precise one; on the contrary, if $\rho = 1$, all the classes are equally and completely plausible: no information regarding the actual label of the instance is then available.

We trained two precise logistic models: one on the training instances with actual labels, another on those associated with corrupted labels; and we trained an "imprecise" logistic model on the data with plausibilistic labels using our method. The remaining test instances were then classified using these three models. This procedure was repeated 25 times, to provide average error rates and 95% confidence intervals in order to compare the accuracy of the different models. The results are provided in Table 2.

Table 2. Average test error rates and associated 95% confidence intervals

dataset	actual labels	corrupted labels	soft labels
Ecoli	0.128 +/- 0.011	0.161 +/- 0.012	0.158 +/- 0.011
Glass	0.374 +/- 0.019	0.422 +/- 0.026	0.432 +/- 0.027
Ionosphere	0.139 +/- 0.010	0.195 +/- 0.017	0.203 +/- 0.019
Iris	0.051 +/- 0.014	0.182 +/- 0.025	0.117 +/- 0.025
Optdigits	0.057 +/- 0.005	0.072 +/- 0.003	0.085 +/- 0.003
Pageblocks	0.039 +/- 0.002	0.057 +/- 0.003	0.039 +/- 0.002
Satimage	0.142 +/- 0.003	0.183 +/- 0.004	0.146 +/- 0.003
Segment	0.057 +/- 0.006	0.158 +/- 0.008	0.057 +/- 0.003
Sonar	0.274 +/- 0.017	0.366 +/- 0.020	0.359 +/- 0.023
Spambase	0.075 +/- 0.003	0.115 +/- 0.005	0.091 +/- 0.004
Vehicles	0.179 +/- 0.003	0.206 +/- 0.004	0.173 +/- 0.003
Vowel	0.513	0.624 +/- 0.012	0.529 +/- 0.015
Waveform	0.131 +/- 0.003	0.148 +/- 0.003	0.137 +/- 0.003
Yeast	0.447 +/- 0.009	0.463 +/- 0.014	0.428 +/- 0.008

These results clearly show the interest of taking into account the label uncertainty. Indeed, over the 14 datasets processed, it improves the accuracy of the model estimated in 11 cases (significantly in 9 cases), and degrades it in three cases (significantly in one case, although the difference in accuracy remains reasonable). Surprisingly, fitting a model from soft corrupted labels seems to give slightly better results than using the actual labels for two datasets (Vehicles and Yeast). A possible explanation would be the presence of atypical instances in the original data.

5 Conclusions

In this paper, we presented a method for fitting a logistic model to soft labeled data. When the class membership are crisp, the logistic model is fit by maximizing the likelihood with respect to the model parameters. When the membership information is available in the form of degrees of plausibility over the classes, we propose to fit the model by applying the Evidential EM algorithm.

In this case, the model is estimated via an iterative procedure that alternates between two steps. At each iteration, the E-step consists in computing the expected class memberships of the training instances, given the plausibilistic labels and the current fit for the model parameters. Then, the M-step consists in computing a new fit for the model parameters, by maximizing the log-likelihood obtained with these new estimates of the class memberships. This may be carried out by applying any classical procedure for training a logistic model from precisely labeled data, the only difference being that the expected memberships computed in the E-step are used instead of classical crisp labels.

Although a logistic model needs to be estimated at each step of the EM algorithm (each time the expected memberships are recomputed), two successive fits for the model parameters are likely to be close to each other. For this reason, the parameter vector estimated at a given iteration of the E2M algorithm may be used as a starting value for the optimization procedure deployed in the M-step of the next one.

We conducted experiments on some classical real datasets. In these experiments, we introduced noise in the training labels. Then, we compared the results obtained by fitting a logistic model to the data with (precise) actual labels, with corrupted precise labels, and with corrupted plausibilistic labels designed so as to model labeling uncertainty. The results obtained clearly show the interest of taking into account the labeling uncertainty into account.

In further work, we plan to investigate fitting the logistic model when the feature vectors describing the instances are also uncertain. Note, however, that the log-likelihood function depends non-linearly on these feature vectors. For this reason, this will probably require using Monte-Carlo estimation techniques to compute the conditional expectations in the E-step of the E2M algorithm. We also plan to compare our procedure to similar approaches, such as the ones described in [11,13].

Acknowledgements. The author is indebted to Yves Grandvalet for fruitful discussions about logistic regression from precise and imprecise labels, as well as for providing the code for precise multiclass logistic regression.

References

1. Ambroise, C., Govaert, G.: EM algorithm for partially known labels. In: 7th Conference of the International Federation of Classification Societies (IFCS 2000), pp. 161–166 (2000)
2. Amini, M.R., Gallinari, P.: Semi-supervised logistic regression. In: 15th European Conference on Artificial Intelligence (ECAI 2002), pp. 390–394 (2002)
3. Bishop, C.M.: Pattern Recognition and Machine Learning. Springer (2006)
4. Chapelle, O., Schślkopf, B., Zien, A.: Semi-supervised learning. The MIT Press, Cambridge (2006)

5. Cour, T., Sapp, B., Taskar, B.: Learning from Partial Labels. Journal of Machine Learning Research 12, 1501–1536 (2011)
6. Denœux, T.: Maximum likelihood estimation from Uncertain Data in the Belief Function Framework. IEEE Transactions on Knowledge and Data Engineering 25(1), 119–130 (2013)
7. Erkan, A.N., Altun, Y.: Semi-Supervised Learning via Generalized Maximum Entropy. In: 13th International Conference on Artificial Intelligence and Statistics (AISTATS 2010), pp. 209–216 (2010)
8. Grandvalet, Y.: Logistic regression for partial labels. In: 9th International Conference on Information Processing and Management of Uncertainty in Knowlege-based Systems (IPMU 2002), vol. III, pp. 1935–1941 (2002)
9. Grandvalet, Y., Bengio, Y.: Semi-supervised learning by entropy minimization. In: Neural Information Processing Systems 17 (NIPS 2004), pp. 529–536. The MIT Press (2005)
10. Hüllermeier, E., Beringer, J.: Learning from ambiguously labeled examples. In: Famili, A.F., Kok, J.N., Peña, J.M., Siebes, A., Feelders, A. (eds.) IDA 2005. LNCS, vol. 3646, pp. 168–179. Springer, Heidelberg (2005)
11. Hüllermeier, E.: Learning from imprecise and fuzzy observations: Data disambiguation through generalized loss minimization. International Journal of Approximate Reasoning, DOI: 10.1016/j.ijar.2013.09.003 (2013) (in Press)
12. Li, J., Bioucas-Dias, J.: Semisupervised Hyperspectral Image Classification using Soft Sparse Multinomial Logistic Regression. IEEE Geoscience and Remote Sensing Letters, 318–322 (2013)
13. Nguyen, Q., Valizadegan, H., Hauskrecht, M.: Learning classification models with soft-label information. J. Am. Med. Inform. Assoc. (2014), doi:10.1136/amiajnl-2013-001964
14. Shafer, G.: A mathematical theory of evidence. Princeton University Press (1976)
15. Smets, P., Kennes, R.: The Transferable Belief Model. Artificial Intelligence 66, 191–243 (1994)

Training and Evaluating Classifiers from Evidential Data: Application to E^2M Decision Tree Pruning

Nicolas Sutton-Charani, Sébastien Destercke, and Thierry Denœux

Université Technologie de Compiègne UMR 7253 Heudiasyc
60203 COMPIEGNE Cedex France
{nicolas.sutton-charani,sebastien.destercke,
t.denoeux}@hds.utc.fr
http://www.hds.utc.fr/

Abstract. In many application data are imperfect, imprecise or more generally uncertain. Many classification methods have been presented that can handle data in some parts of the learning or the inference process, yet seldom in the whole process. Also, most of the proposed approach still evaluate their results on precisely known data. However, there are no reason to assume the existence of such data in applications, hence the need for assessment method working for uncertain data. We propose such an approach here, and apply it to the pruning of E^2M decision trees. This results in an approach that can handle data uncertainty wherever it is, be it in input or output variables, in training or in test samples.

Keywords: classification, uncertain data, E^2M algorithm, error rate, belief functions, E^2M decision trees, pruning.

1 Introduction

Data uncertainty can have many origins: measurements approximations, sensor failures, subjective expert assessments, etc. Taking into account this uncertainty to learn a classifier is challenging because of the analytical and computational difficulties to extend standard statistical learning methodologies to uncertain data. However, in the past years, several approaches [6,3] have been proposed to learn model from uncertain data.

Once a classifier is built from a learning (uncertain) samples, it is usually evaluated by a *misclassification* or *error* rate which is computed from test samples. This error rate corresponds to the probability of misclassification and is estimated by the frequency of misclassified test samples. However, even in methods dealing with uncertain data, this misclassification rate is usually computed using precise test samples. This can be explained by the absence of genuine uncertain benchmark datasets, that remain to be built.

Yet, there is no reason to separate the training and the learning data by making only the former uncertain. In practice, one should be able to tackle uncertainty in all the data sets, without distinction. This is the main issue tackled in this paper, in which we propose a means to evaluate classifiers and models from uncertain test data. The uncertain data, from now on called *evidential data*, will be modelled by the means of belief functions, that offer a flexible framework to model epistemic uncertainty.

F. Cuzzolin (Ed.): BELIEF 2014, LNAI 8764, pp. 87–94, 2014.

We will use the evidential likelihood [3] as a generic tool to learn and to assess probabilistic models from such evidential data.

In addition, we will apply our proposition to the E^2M decision trees classification model [8], which is a decision tree methodology adapted to uncertain learning data modelled by belief functions. It is learned using the E^2M algorithm [3] which is an extension of the well known EM algorithm to evidential data. Our proposal will be applied in two different manners: to prune E^2M decision trees, and to evaluate the resulting classifiers. Indeed, pruning requires to evaluate the pruned trees performances, hence to potentially evaluate them on evidential data in the case of E^2M decision trees.

Section 2 introduces the problem of learning under evidential data, and recalls the evidential likelihood approach, together with the E^2M decision tree approach. In Section 3 we give the details of the evidential error rate estimations and in Section 4 a E^2M pruning procedure is proposed and some experiments are presented. Apart from solving the evaluation problem with evidential data, it will also provides us with a classification technique able to handle uncertain data at all levels, both in training and in test phases.

2   Background

This section briefly reminds required elements to understand the paper. Further details can be found in complementary papers [3,8]

2.1   Classification under Evidential Data

The goal of a classification technique is to learn a mapping $\mathscr{C}$ from J attributes $X = \{X_1,\ldots,X_J\} \in \Omega_1 \times \cdots \times \Omega_J = \Omega_X$ to a class $Y \in \Omega_Y = \{C_1,\ldots,C_K\}$. Classically, this is done using a set of n learning precise data (x,y). In this paper, we consider evidential data, meaning that each datum is modelled by a mass function on Ω_X (for the input uncertainty) and Ω_Y (for the class uncertainty). Recall that a mass function on a space Ω is a positive mass $m : 2^\Omega \to [0,1]$ defined on Ω power set such that $\sum_{E \subseteq \Omega, E \neq \emptyset} m(E) = 1$. The contour function[1] $pl : \Omega \to [0,1]$ induced by it is $pl(\omega) = \sum_{\omega \in E} m(E)$.

We consider that this classifier $\mathscr{C}$ is learned from an evidential learning set of n samples

$$(m_\ell^x, m_\ell^y) = \begin{pmatrix} m_{1,\ell}^x & m_{1,\ell}^y \\ \vdots & \vdots \\ m_{n,\ell}^x & m_{n,\ell}^y \end{pmatrix}$$

and is evaluated using an evidential test sample of n' samples

$$(m_t^x, m_t^y) = \begin{pmatrix} m_{1,t}^x & m_{1,t}^y \\ \vdots & \vdots \\ m_{n',t}^x & m_{n',t}^y \end{pmatrix}.$$

While data are assumed to be evidential, we want to learn a probabilistic parametric classifier with parameters θ providing for an (evidential) entry m^x a probability $P_\theta(Y|m^x)$, the decided class then corresponding to $\mathscr{C}(m^x) = \arg\max_{C_i \in \Omega_Y} P_\theta(C_i|m^x)$.

---

[1] No other notions will be needed in this paper.

2.2   Evidential Likelihood and E^2M Algorithm

In standard probability theory, the likelihood $L(\theta;w)$ of a parameter θ given a sample w corresponds to the probability $P_\theta(W = w)$ of observing this sample given that parameter. Maximising this likelihood provides good estimators of the parameter value. Denoeux [3] has extended this concept to evidential data.

When $w \in A$ is imprecisely observed, then an imprecise likelihood corresponding to the probability to pick a sample *inside* A in the population can be computed as

$$L(\theta;A) = \sum_{w \in A} L(\theta;w) = P_\theta(W \in A)$$

If our knowledge about w is not only imprecise but also uncertain and modelled by a mass function m^w having $A_1,\ldots,A_z$ as focal elements, the evidential likelihood of the parameter becomes

$$L(\theta;m^w) = \sum_{i=1}^{z} m^w(A_i)L(\theta;A_i). \tag{1}$$

In general, finding the (global) value θ maximizing Eq. (1) is difficult, as the function is non-convex and complex. However, the E^2M algorithm provides a means to obtain a local maximum of (1). It is an iterative algorithm very similar to the EM algorithm [2], the main difference is the measure used to compute expectations at the E step. In order to take into account both the available knowledge (represented by m^w) and the model aleatory uncertainty, the E step uses the conjunctive combination $P(. \mid \theta, m^w) := P_\theta \bigcirc m^w$, which is a probability measure, to compute the expectation. Algorithm 1 summarizes the E^2M algorithm.

Algorithm 1. Estimation with the E^2M algorithm

   Input: $\theta^{(0)}, \gamma$
   Output: final θ
1 $r = 1$;
2 **repeat**
3   E-step: $Q(\theta, \theta^{(r)}) = E[log(L(\theta;W)) \mid \theta^{(r)}, m^W]$;
4   M-step: $\theta^{(r+1)} = \arg\max_{\theta \in \Theta} Q(\theta, \theta^{(r)})$;
5      $r = r + 1$;
6 **until** $\dfrac{L(\theta^{(r)};m^w) - L(\theta^{(r-1)};m^w)}{L(\theta^{(r-1)};m^w)} < \gamma$.
7 $\theta = \theta^{(r)}$;

2.3 E^2M Decision Trees

Decision trees or more precisely classification trees are famous classifiers that provide interpretable outputs [1]. They recursively partition the space Ω_X into leaves that contains probabilities over the classes Ω_Y.

The purity of a leaf t_h (defining a subset of Ω_X) is usually evaluated by some impurity measure such as Shanon entropy $i(t_h) = -\sum_{k=1}^{K} \alpha_h^k \log(\alpha_h^k)$ where $\alpha_h^k = P(Y = C_k | t_h)$. The purity gain obtained by splitting t_h into t_L and t_R is computed as $\delta i = i(t_h) - \pi_L i(t_L) - \pi_R i(t_R)$ where $\pi_L = P(t_L | t_h)$ and $\pi_R = P(t_R | t_h)$ are the probabilities of being in each children leaves. In usual approaches the leaves probabilities π_h and the class probabilities inside leaves α_h^k are estimated by frequencies of learning samples in leaves and of their different class labels inside the leaves:

$$\tilde{\pi}_h = \frac{n(t_h)}{n} \qquad \tilde{\alpha}_h^k = \frac{n_k(t_h)}{n(t_h)}$$

where n is the number of learning samples, $n(t_h)$ is the number of learning sample in the leaf t_h and $n_k(t_h)$ is the number of learning samples of class C_k inside the leaf t_h.

E^2M decision trees [8] are an extension of classical decision trees to evidential data. The main idea is to see the tree as a mixture (the leaves weights π_h) of multinomial distributions (the class probabilities α_h^k), and to learn this probabilistic model using the E^2M. We proposed to estimate the probabilities of leaves and of class in leaves by maximising their likelihood in regard to the uncertain learning sample (m_ℓ^x, m_ℓ^y). We have:

$$\{\hat{\pi}_h, \hat{\alpha}_h^k\}_{h,k} = \hat{\theta} = \arg\max_{\theta \in \Theta} L(\theta; (m_\ell^x, m_\ell^y))$$

Within decision trees techniques, *pruning* is a classical way to avoid over-fitting and that are usually based on a compromise between interpretability and accuracy [1,4]. Most of them consider possible sub-trees of the initial learned tree, and pick one satisfying an evaluation criteria always based (at least partially) on classification accuracy. Yet, evidential data do not allow a straightforward computation of accuracy, hence a need of new evaluation techniques to be able to prune.

3   Uncertain Classifiers Evaluation with the E^2M Algorithm: Evidential Error Rates Estimation

While techniques introduced in the previous sections allow to learn from evidential data (see also [5]), the problem of evaluating classifiers with an evidential test data set (m_t^x, m_t^y) remains. This section proposes a solution also exploiting the evidential likelihood and E^2M algorithm.

Let $E \in \{0,1\}$ be an aleatory *Bernoulli* variable representing the *misclassification* of $\mathscr{C}$, equal to 1 in case of misclassification, 0 in case of good classification. We have $E \sim Ber(\varepsilon)$ where ε is the *misclassification* rate, i.e., $P(Y \neq \mathscr{C}(x)|x)$.

With precise data, ε, whose estimation $\tilde{\varepsilon}$ is the frequency of misclassified examples in the learning test and corresponds to maximising its likelihood $L(\theta; e = \{e_1, \ldots, e_{n'}\})$ with $e_i = 0$ if $\mathscr{C}(x_{i,t}) \neq y_{i,t}$, 1 otherwise. We therefore get $\tilde{\varepsilon} = n_1/n'$ where n_1 is and the number of 1 in e.

In practice, when one has evidential data, the E^2M model still provides a unique prediction $\mathscr{C}(m_{i,t}^{y})$, which has to be compared to an evidential output $m_{i,t}^{y}$. In practice, each $m_{i,t}^{y}$ can be mapped to a mass function m_i^e over $\{0,1\}$ such that

$$m_i^e(\{0\}) = m_{i,t}^{y}(\mathscr{C}(m_{i,t}^{y})) \tag{2}$$

$$m_i^e(\{1\}) = \sum_{E \subseteq \Omega_y : \mathscr{C}(m_{i,t}^{y}) \notin E} m_{i,t}^{y}(E) \tag{3}$$

$$m_i^e(\{0,1\}) = \sum_{E \subseteq \Omega_y : \mathscr{C}(m_{i,t}^{y}) \in E, |E| > 1} m_{i,t}^{y}(E) \tag{4}$$

Given this sample, the evidential accuracy can be computed as follows:

$$L(\varepsilon; m^e) = \prod_{i=1}^{n}[(1-\varepsilon)pl_i(0) + \varepsilon pl_i(1)] \tag{5}$$

$$Q(\varepsilon; \hat{\varepsilon}^{(q)}) = n log(1-\varepsilon) + log(\frac{\varepsilon}{1-\varepsilon})\sum_{i=1}^{n}\xi_i^{(q)} \tag{6}$$

$$\hat{\varepsilon}^{(r+1)} = \underset{\varepsilon \in [0.1]}{\operatorname{argmax}}\, Q(\varepsilon; \hat{\varepsilon}^{(q)}) = \frac{1}{N}\sum_{i=1}^{N}\xi_i^{(q)} \tag{7}$$

where

$$\xi_i^{(q)} = E[E_i \mid \hat{\varepsilon}^{(q)}; m_i^e] = \frac{\hat{\varepsilon}^{(q)}pl_i(1)}{(1-\hat{\varepsilon}^{(q)})pl_i(0) + \hat{\varepsilon}^{(q)}pl_i(1)}$$

with $pl_i(0) = Pl(\{e_i = 0\}) = m_i^e(\{0\}) + m_i^e(\{1,0\})$ and $pl_i(1) = Pl(\{e_i = 1\}) = m_i^e(\{1\}) + m_i^e(\{1,0\})$

$\hat{\varepsilon} = 0.4$ $\hat{\varepsilon} = 0.6$

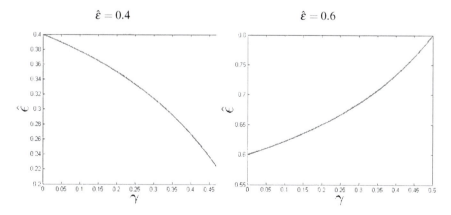

Fig. 1. Variations of the evidential error rate $\hat{\varepsilon}$ with the uncertainty level γ when $\tilde{\varepsilon} = 0.4$ and 0.6

As an illustration, Figure 1 represents the variation of the evidential error rate in function of $m_i^e(\{0,1\}) = \gamma$ for $n' = 100$ samples, and where the proportion of samples where $m_i^e(\{1\}) = 1 - \gamma$ versus samples where $m_i^e(\{0\}) = 1 - \gamma$ is given by the precise error rates $\hat{\varepsilon}$ 0.4 and 0.6. Interestingly we can see that the estimation, by privileging the most present observation, tends to accentuate either the quality of accurate models ($\hat{\varepsilon} < 0.5$) or the unreliability of inaccurate ones. We can therefore expect this evidential accuracy to provide reliable choices.

4 Application: Pruning of E^2M Decision Trees

This section illustrates the evidential error rate to the pruning of E^2M decision trees. Considering the sequence of sub-trees induced by successive splits, we simply pick the one that obtains the smallest evidential error rate on a pruning sample (different from the initial learning sample). Indeed, our goal is not to define optimal pruning criterion, but simply to illustrate the use of evidential error rates.

Our experiments concern five precise benchmark datasets (coming from UCI) in which we artificially injected uncertainty. For each observation w_i (attribute and class) of the precise datasets, a noise level γ_i was uniformly sampled in $[0, 1]$. A number u was then uniformly sampled on $[0, 1]$, if $u < \gamma_i$ then the (noised) value w_i is replaced by another value w_i^* drawn uniformly from Ω_W (either attribute or class spaces), otherwise $w_i^* = w_i$. Obtained evidential data are $m(w_i^*) = 1 - \gamma_i$ and $m(\Omega_W) = \gamma_i$.

We learnt simultaneously standard $CART$ decision trees and E^2M ones and compared their error rates. For each test we learnt the trees on one third of the datasets, pruned them on another third and test them on the left third by computing standard error rates and evidential ones. All computations are achieved on noised data (considering crisp replacements for CART and evidential ones for E^2M) The stopping criteria were composed of a maximum of 10 leaves and a relative minimum purity gain of 5%.

Table 1. Comparison of $CART$ and E^2M decision trees efficiency before and after pruning

data set	naive	classical error rate				naive	evidential error rate			
		CART		E^2M			CART		E^2M	
		unpruned	pruned	unpruned	pruned		unpruned	pruned	unpruned	pruned
iris	0.67	0.60	0.60	0.57	0.58	0.79	0.65	0.66	0.59	0.60
balance scale	0.60	0.60	0.60	0.58	0.58	0.63	0.62	0.62	0.51	0.51
wine	0.65	0.61	0.62	0.60	0.60	0.75	0.64	0.67	0.64	0.64
glass	0.68	0.69	0.68	0.68	0.67	0.74	0.73	0.73	0.67	0.67
e.coli	0.72	0.73	0.72	0.74	0.73	0.75	0.74	0.74	0.71	0.70

Table 1 summarizes the means of error rates obtained for 100 tests for each dataset. For each methodology the error rate are compared before the learning (the *naive* error rate is obtained by predicting systematicaly the class the most frequent in the learning sample), once the trees are learnt but before pruning and after pruning. The high error rates are due to noise both in the learning and in the testing phases.

Both evidential and classical error rates are slightly smaller for E^2M trees than for $CART$ ones. If this is not surprising for the evidential error rate after pruning (as it is the minimized criterion), the other better scores confirm the interest of using evidential approaches. The pruning strategy also increases accuracy for the *balance* and *glass* datasets, despite the small size of the learnt trees. E^2M trees appear to be naturally smaller than $CART$ ones but can still be pruned thank to the evidential error rates computations.

Table 2. Comparison of $CART$ and E^2M decision trees sizes before and after pruning

data set	CART				E^2M			
	before pruning		after pruning		before pruning		after pruning	
	# failures	# leaves	# failures	# leaves	# failures	# leaves	# failures	# leaves
iris	3	9.57	13	4.57	0	4.36	6	3.39
balance scale	99	1.01	99	1.01	0	7.01	0	5.21
wine	0	10	15	4.79	0	4.05	10	3.06
glass	52	5.26	70	2.08	0	6.92	14	4.46
e.coli	52	5.26	70	2.08	0	6.92	14	4.46

Table 2 compares the size of the $CART$ and E^2M trees before and after pruning. A learning failure occurs when the *noised* dataset does not enable any first split in regards to the stopping criteria. $CART$ trees appears to be bigger than E^2M ones before and after pruning. We can interpret this as an impact of the data uncertainty on the complexity of the learnt model. In deed, it is not necessary to have a complex model with partially unreliable data.

5   Conclusions

We have introduced a way, through the notion of evidential likelihood, to evaluate classifier in presence of uncertain (evidential) data. Such a technique appears as essential and necessary if we want to fully tackle the problem of uncertain data, as assuming uncertain learning data and certain test data (at least in the output), if valid on benchmark data sets, seems unrealistic in practical applications. We have also tested our approach on the E^2M decision trees, and doing so have proposed, to our knowledge, the first method that is able to handle data uncertainty in attributes and classes, both in learning and testing.

As perspective, it would be interesting to compare our study to other approaches, both from a theoretical and practical standpoint. For example, we could compare ourselves to the strategy consisting of transforming evidential data into probabilistic one through the pignistic transform [7].

References

1. Breiman, L., Friedman, J., Stone, C.J., Olshen, R.A.: Classification and Regression Trees (1984)
2. Dempster, A.P., Laird, N.M., Rubin, D.B.: Maximum likelihood from incomplete data via the em algorithm. Journal of the royal statistial society, series B 39(1), 1–38 (1977)
3. Denœux, T.: Maximum likelihood estimation from uncertain data in the belief function framework. IEEE Trans. on Know. and Data Eng. (2011)
4. Esposito, F., Malerba, D., Semeraro, G., Kay, J.: A comparative analysis of methods for pruning decision trees. IEEE Transactions on Pattern Analysis and Machine Intelligence 19(5), 476–491 (1997)
5. Masson, M.H., Denoeux, T.: Ecm: An evidential version of the fuzzy c-means algorithm. Pattern Recognition 41(4), 1384–1397 (2008)
6. Périnel, E.: Construire un arbre de discrimination binaire à partir de données imprécises. Revue de statistique appliquée 4747, 5–30 (1999)
7. Smets, P.: Belief induced by the partial knowledge of the probabilities. In: Proceedings of the Tenth International Conference on Uncertainty in Artificial Intelligence, UAI 1994, pp. 523–530. Morgan Kaufmann Publishers Inc., San Francisco (1994)
8. Sutton-Charani, N., Destercke, S., Denœux, T.: Learning decision trees from uncertain data with an evidential em approach. In: 12th International Conference on Machine Learning and Applications, ICMLA (2013)

Reflections on DS/AHP: Lessons to Be Learnt

Malcolm J. Beynon

Cardiff Business School, Cardiff University,
Colum Drive, Cardiff, CF10 3EU, Wales, UK
BeynonMJ@cardiff.ac.uk

Abstract. DS/AHP is a technique for multi-criteria decision making (MCDM), based on the Dempster-Shafer Theory of evidence (DST) and the Analytic Hierarchy Process (AHP). Since its introduction it has been developed and applied by a number of authors, as well as form the foundation for other DST related MCDM techniques. This paper reviews the evolution and impact of DS/AHP, culminating in a critical perspective, over relevant criteria, namely i) Ease of understanding, ii) A champion, iii) Software development and iv) Its pertinent development, for its position in the area of MCDM. The critical perspective will include the impacting role DST has had in the evolution of DS/AHP. The lessons learnt, or not learnt, will be of interest to any reader undertaking research with strong influence from DST-based methodologies.

Keywords: AHP, Dempster-Shafer Theory, DS/AHP, Reflections.

1   Introduction

This paper considers the DS/AHP technique for multi-criteria decision making (MCDM) [1, 6]. The rudiments of DS/AHP are based on the Dempster-Shafer theory (DST) of evidence ([9, 23] - DS part of name) and the Analytic Hierarchy Process ([22] - AHP part of name). The remit of DS/AHP is the preference ranking of decision alternatives (DAs) based over a number of different criteria. From its introduction it has been technically developed [2, 3, 4, 5, 7] and applied in real world problems [17, 27, 28], as well as contributed to the definition of derivative techniques [10, 11, 13, 14].

This paper attempts to put into perspective the evolution of the DS/AHP technique, including emphasis on the impact of using DST in its methodology. In the relative short time since its introduction, academic researching/publishing has changed, with other issues beyond just the concomitant publications (associated with the introduction and development of a novel analysis technique) required to be considered. For example, one of these issues is research impact, how the research being undertaken has had impact in a wider context. With this in mind, thoughts on how the evolution of DS/AHP has progressed, from one of its main developers, may resonate similar thoughts with academics using DST in the introduction and development of other novel analysis techniques.

F. Cuzzolin (Ed.): BELIEF 2014, LNAI 8764, pp. 95–104, 2014.
© Springer International Publishing Switzerland 2014

A critical perspective will develop on the evolution of DS/AHP, rounding on four pertinent criteria to consider, namely, i) Ease of understanding, ii) A champion, iii) Software development and iv) Its pertinent development. For the reader, interested in DST, lessons may be learnt from what to keep in perspective when undertaking technique based research with DST.

2   The DS/AHP

In this section we briefly describe the DS/AHP technique for MCDM, through an example problem (only basic features of DS/AHP are shown - for a full description see [1, 6] and later references). The example concerns the ability of a decision maker (DM) to preference rank eight decision alternatives (DAs), A, B, C, D, E, F, G and H (making up the frame of discernment Θ), considered over three criteria, c_1, c_2 and c_3. The intended goal of the DM is to identify 'Best DA(s)', where DA(s) denotes that more than one DA may be wanted to be identified as best.

With the intention of employing DS/AHP, the DM makes judgements on the preference of identified groups of DAs over the different criteria (preferences relative to Θ), see Fig. 1.

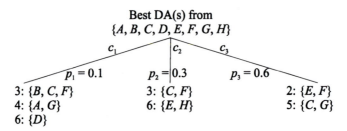

Fig. 1. Preference judgements made on 'Best DAs' MCDM problem

In Fig. 1, three, two and two groups of DAs have been identified for preference on the criteria, c_1, c_2 and c_3, respectively. Each identified group of DAs have a respective scale value assigned to them, here, a '2 to 6' scale was adopted, with inference on the identified group of DAs relative to Θ ranging from moderately preferred (2) to extremely preferred (6), see [2]. Also shown in Fig. 1 are the criterion importance values (CIVs) for the different criteria, c_1: $p_1 = 0.1$, c_2: $p_2 = 0.3$ and c_3: $p_3 = 0.6$ (found through a weight assignment approach - see [4] for example). From Fig. 1, for the c_2 criterion, the associated comparison matrix is of the form:

$$
\begin{array}{c c c c}
 & \{C,F\} & \{E,H\} & \Theta \\
\{C,F\} & \begin{pmatrix} 1 \\ 0 \\ 1/(3p_2) \end{pmatrix} & \begin{matrix} 0 \\ 1 \\ 1/(6p_2) \end{matrix} & \begin{matrix} 3p_2 \\ 6p_2 \\ 1 \end{matrix} \end{pmatrix},
\end{array}
$$

which gives the respective mass values and focal elements (using general CIV p_2), forming a *criterion* BOE (body of evidence - made up of the mass values

$$m_h(s_i) = a_i p \bigg/ \left(\sum_{j=1}^{d} a_j p + \sqrt{d} \right), \ i = 1, 2, \ldots d \ \text{and} \ m_h(\Theta) = \sqrt{d} \bigg/ \left(\sum_{j=1}^{d} a_j p + \sqrt{d} \right) \ \text{- see}$$

[1]), defined $m_2(\cdot)$, in this case given as:

$$m_2(\{C, F\}) = \frac{3p_2}{9p_2 + \sqrt{2}}, \ m_2(\{E, H\}) = \frac{6p_2}{9p_2 + \sqrt{2}} \ \text{and} \ m_2(\Theta) = \frac{\sqrt{2}}{9p_2 + \sqrt{2}}.$$

These general expressions for the mass values in the criterion BOE $m_2(\cdot)$, and the other criterion BOEs $m_1(\cdot)$ and $m_3(\cdot)$ associated with the c_1 and c_3 criteria, are graphically illustrated in Fig. 2.

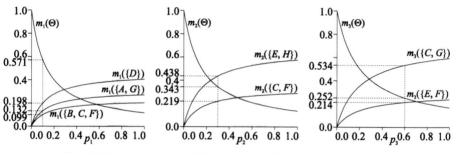

Fig. 2. Mass value graphs of the criterion BOEs, $m_1(\cdot)$, $m_2(\cdot)$ and $m_3(\cdot)$

In Fig. 2, the effect of a CIV (p_i value), on the formulisation of mass values in the criterion BOEs is clearly exposited (as $p_i \to 0$ the majority of the exact belief is assigned to local ignorance ($m_i(\Theta) \to 1$) and as $p_i \to 1$ more exact belief is assigned to the identified groups of DAs). Also shown for each criterion are the specific mass values (associated with focal elements) based on their respective CIVs of; $p_1 = 0.1$, $p_2 = 0.3$ and $p_3 = 0.6$. For the case of the c_2 criterion, the criterion BOE $m_2(\cdot)$ is of the form (with $p_1 = 0.3$):

$$m_2(\{C, F\}) = 0.219, \ m_2(\{E, H\}) = 0.438 \ \text{and} \ m_2(\Theta) = 0.343.$$

Similar results can be found for the other two criteria ($m_1(\cdot)$ for c_1 and $m_3(\cdot)$ for c_3). Dempster's combination rule can then be used to combine the evidence from the individual criterion BOEs, resulting in the *final* BOE, defined $m(\cdot)$, and is of the form:

$$m(\{C\}) = 0.177, \ m(\{D\}) = 0.031, \ m(\{E\}) = 0.098, \ m(\{F\}) = 0.071,$$
$$m(\{G\}) = 0.044, \ m(\{A, G\}) = 0.021, \ m(\{C, F\}) = 0.068, \ m(\{C, G\}) = 0.192,$$
$$m(\{E, F\}) = 0.077, \ m(\{E, H\}) = 0.115, \ m(\{B, C, F\}) = 0.016, \ m(\Theta) = 0.091.$$

This final BOE contains all the evidence from the judgements made by a DM over the three criteria. How this evidence is used to identify the most preferred DA or groups of DAs (Best DA(s)) is dependent on how the presence of ignorance is accommodated for. For example, from this final BOE, most preferred groups of DAs can be evaluated, based on the Belief ($\text{Bel}(s_i) = \sum_{s_j \subseteq s_i} m(s_j)$ for all $s_i \subseteq \Theta$) and Plausibility ($\text{Pls}(s_i) = \sum_{s_j \cap s_i \neq \varnothing} m(s_j)$ for all $s_i \subseteq \Theta$) functions, see Table 1.

Table 1. Groups of DAs of with largest belief and plausibility values

Size	Belief - Bel($\cdot$)	Plausibility - Pls($\cdot$)
1	$\{C\}$, 0.177	$\{C\}$, 0.543
2	$\{C, G\}$, 0.413	$\{C, E\}$, 0.833
3	$\{C, F, G\}$, 0.517	$\{C, E, F\}$, 0.903
4	$\{C, E, F, G\}$, 0.726	$\{C, E, F, G\}$, 0.969

In Table 1, each row identifies the group of DAs, of a certain size, with the largest belief and plausibility values from all other possible groups of DAs of that size. To demonstrate, for a group of DAs of size two, the groups, $\{C, G\}$ and $\{C, E\}$, respectively, were identified as most preferred, based on the belief and plausibility values, respectively.

3   The Development and Application of DS/AHP

Beyond the introductory research on DS/AHP, presented in [1, 6], around the year 2000, its early development followed similar developments/issues considered across other MCDM techniques, in particular the AHP, understandably. The impact of the employed preference scale values used and their effect on the results from the employment of DS/AHP was considered in [2], which also looked at possible bounds on the level of ignorance from preference judgements made. There was early effort to present DS/AHP in a software tool, as in [7], which enabled a relatively simple user-friendly utilization of an early version of DS/AHP. [3] incorporated more existing DST formulation, notably involving the non-specificity measure to describe the judgements made and results found using DS/AHP.

Two further developments considered DS/AHP within the group decision making environment, importantly showing the DS/AHP can be used in a multi-level hierarchy in MCDM. [4] considered group decision making, using DS/AHP when there is non-equal importance of the decision makers in the group – using a discount rate formulation developed in DST. [5] considered inter-group alliances and majority rule in group decision making using DS/AHP, using a DST based distance measure to iteratively aggregate the judgements from different members of the decision making group.

Developments away from the original author(s) work on DS/AHP, commenced in 2004 (we believe). [19] developed the DS/AHP approach to handle three types of ambiguous evaluations, termed, missing, interval-valued, and ambiguous lottery evaluations, then applying it to a real estate investment problem. They further suggest future research could conduct psychological experiments to refine and validate models, as well as considering DS/AHP in a fuzzy environment. [20] also developed DS/AHP in creating preference relations of groups of DAs based on their belief intervals, suggesting DS/AHP may not satisfy the transitive property. [21] considered the sensitivity of DS/AHP when using different combination rules (and adding DAs beyond the original DAs included).

[24] furthered the DS/AHP method to collect and aggregate the preferences of multiple DMs, and how this information can then be encoded as weight interval constraints in stochastic multi-criteria acceptability analysis. It should be noted, as

suggested in [25], that the main excellent idea underlying the DS/AHP method is in the applying of DST to the AHP, moreover [1, 6] proposing to compare groups of DAs by means of their comparisons with the set of all DAs. [29] examined DS/AHP in a majority rule group decision making context (similar investigation to that in [5]). [26] extended DS/AHP, for when there are several hierarchical levels of criteria, they also reduced the computation procedure for the processing and aggregating the incomplete information about criteria and DAs down to solving a finite set of linear programming problems. [15] utilised DS/AHP when comparing results from different combination axioms.

[10] considered DS/AHP in the context of Dezert-Smarandache theory, formulating DSmT/AHP, which included the use of the PCR5 combination rule. In [13], developing DS/AHP, with derivative named technique Belief AHP, took the ability to group DAs together to the criteria level of an MCDM problem, allowing preference judgements to be made also on groups of criteria. Calling it TIN-DS/AHP, [17] developed DS/AHP using the notion of Three-point Interval Number, suggesting it is more inclusive of the complexity of decision problem and fuzziness of human thought.

In terms of applications, [4] applied DS/AHP in a textbook selection problem, using judgements from fellow academics. Incorporating with TOPSIS, [16] applied DS/AHP in deciding on emergency alternatives. The problem of fire extinguishing systems evaluation was considered using DS/AHP in [17]. [27] applied the DS/AHP for decision-making in urban power system planning (they suggest DS/AHP compared with AHP is clear, more tangible, convenient and easy to calculate). [28] applied DS/AHP to enable uncertainty information fusion for flood risk assessment. In a financial context, and part of a bigger research problem, [12] employed DS/AHP to determine the relative importance weights of supply chain performance measures. DS/AHP was applied in [18] to identify attacker type in a game-theoretic approach for preventing threats in intelligent surveillance systems.

It is worthy to note [8] included DS/AHP in their description of the five existing techniques employing evidence theory (DST) in MCDM, suggesting it needed to be tested on large complex problems.

4   DS/AHP Lessons to Be Learnt?

This section offers insights into the evolution of DS/AHP. In a general context, it offers evidence of how a technique, heavily based on DST, can find its place amongst other techniques, each potentially offering the same opportunities for analysis, in this case in the area of MCDM. A number of subsections will elaborate on some of the key issues I believe have impacted on its evolution (or not).

4.1   Ease of Understanding

The DS/AHP technique, while advocating a clearer or more simplistic approach to MCDM than AHP (as suggested in [20]), or offering a more practical MCDM technique, did have an issue of ease of understanding. During its introduction, while what it could do sounded all very positive, how it actually did it was not as easy to exposit, because of the use of DST possibly, and its own newness.

For the DST literate, I surmise, there was not a problem with understanding the technical rudiments of the technique, whether it made sense in the realm of MCDM was perhaps less assured. However, perhaps where the problem lay was in the MCDM relevant researchers and their ability, or perhaps desire, to work through the various relevant technical issues of DST, including bodies of evidence, mass values and combining evidence etc.

In the early years of its evolution, being an academic in a business school, the early authors' platforms for talking about DS/AHP were mostly through MCDM seminar tracks in Management or Operations Research conferences, where much of the time in seminar presentations was taken up expositing small examples of how DST worked, before then going onto the technique specifically. Clearly, this early exposition meant one cohort of 'potentially interested' researchers got to experience the DS/AHP technique, perhaps a number of them got more benefit from seeing DST in action, possibly for the first time, both initially through small general examples as well as through DS/AHP. However, the DST based academics were never really brought on board in the early years of its introduction, and importantly its development.

This pertinently brings me on to the next issue, namely the championing of the DS/AHP technique.

4.2   A Champion

From the first introduction of the DS/AHP technique its early evolution was steered by one researcher, a champion so to speak, myself I have to admit, as a person who had helped teach Dempster-Shafer theory in my home university I was keen to use it in some research field. Having an initial 'loose' interest in MCDM I endeavored to see how DST could be employed in some way in MCDM.

Considering AHP from the start, it took a while, but it was possible to construct a development on AHP which was based on DST, and importantly, could bring some advantages over the original AHP (see literature). From the early concomitant research, and spurred on by the success of the first publications [1, 6], in regard to DS/AHP I considered its technical development. This followed two directions, firstly, what did AHP have that could be mimicked with DS/AHP, but also what did DST have that could be positively brought into the DS/AHP, bringing further advantages over the original AHP.

While this sounds all very positive, with other commitments and interests the time spent on DS/AHP may not have been enough for its potential to be fully brought out. Further, there were never other full-on champions of the DS/AHP technique, instead the early work on it has been piecemeal by other academics, possibly as part of their PhDs etc. Over the years, the notion of a champion has never been full-on, only 'now and again' exposited at conferences. Whether a champion may still materialize we shall wait and see, of a champion of a later derivative of the technique may be what happens.

4.3   Software Development

One issue relating to the DS/AHP has been the availability of pertinent software that can undertake the relevant MCDM analysis. In [7], some rudimentary software was created, through a summer-employment-scheme of an undergraduate computer science student (one of the co-authors in [7]). The creation of this software was not with the emphasis of getting software out there to be used by other potential users (back then there wasn't the motivation to push this), instead, it was more of an academic exercise in seeing what could be done in terms of how software could bring out the characteristics of DS/AHP, and in-particular the novel features DST brings with it, as well as checking on its usability, if my memory serves me right (in the potential real world).

This I perceive was a missed opportunity in the evolution of DS/AHP, with even rudimentary software 'freely' available to potential users; it would have itself contributed to the championing of the technique. By the nature of the nascence of DS/AHP, it would have been tested in many different applications, with its usability, as well as technical efficiencies/inefficiencies brought to the fore. Moreover, it would have been tested by individuals who may not have had the full working knowledge of the technique (a form of robustness checking). It is a shame that I do not have a running version of this software created early in the evolution of DS/AHP. With other academics working on DS/AHP, I am not aware of freely available DS/AHP software, something that would be of great benefit to its evolution.

Today's increasingly technical world is far different from what was even back in the 2000s, perhaps a smart-phone/ipad app based software approach may be the way forward, something to seriously think about, need to find the time though.

4.4   Its Pertinent Development

Evidenced from section 3, DS/AHP has been developed from its original introduction (in [6]), both from work by the original author of the technique, but also from academics taking independent perspectives on its pertinence/development. It is understandable that any technique, from its initial introduction, will quite possibly be developed in someway, improving its ability to undertake what it is intended for, as well as accessorizing it with the characteristics necessary for other domains it can potentially operate successfully in.

The point here is that how this succession of developments happens is itself a crucial series of moments in the future impact of a technique. That is, especially in the case of academics who work on a technique like DS/AHP, who didn't originally introduce it, they want to put their stamp on it, very often in the form of assigning a derivative name to the resultant development, in this case for example DSmT-AHP ([23]), Belief AHP ([26, 27]) and TIN-DS/AHP ([24]). There is nothing wrong in doing this, but for the technique in question, or the general methodology underlying the technique, its future impact is fractured into many bits, depending on how many derivative names of derivative versions of the technique have been advocated in the research papers produced.

It may well be that the future impact of DS/AHP will not be ultimately considered/defined under its original name (which only came into being in the second publication on the technique in [1] it has to be said), but under a derivative name, which may have appropriately developed the technique to a successful level of usability, as well as possibly being successful in the other three points outlined in this section of the paper (its championing etc.). Perhaps the accompanying question here is when it is appropriate and advantageous to all concerned to simply add-on developments to a known technique or to attribute a derivative name to the development of the technique. A question that stems from this section, perhaps itself one to consider carefully is, how important, and impacting, is the actual name of a technique to its future impact (survivability) in a problem area.

5   Conclusions

This paper has pondered the evolution of the DS/AHP technique for MCDM. Having written the document in the order it is presented, perhaps the first conclusion I have is to not know, or ask the question, on what is success/failure in terms of the evolution/impact of an MCDM based or other technique (based on DST or otherwise). As the early champion of the technique, including being a co-author and single author of the early research publications on DS/AHP, this paper has made me look back and wonder if it has become, or is it where, I hoped it would be. I suppose not, but as mentioned earlier, what is the timeframe to make such judgments in the evolution/impact of a technique.

How to nurture the DS/AHP technique as a viable/popular technique for MCDM is perhaps what we would all like to know. For any technique, especially using DST in line with this conference, are there shackles of tech-ignorance of the DST methodology that shackles any DST-based technique. Further, are the rudiments of DST themselves still evolving, and so there maintains uncertainty in what are the best technical rudiments to employ in DS/AHP?

It may well be that DS/AHP will be known, or its contribution at least, may be that a future technique, with evolved name, will find the optimum position as a popular and versatile technique in the area of MCDM. My final words in this paper are that I may just be missing something on what to do with DS/AHP, I may also be missing the time to put into its championing (or it may not be good enough as a technique for MCDM in its current evolution – who knows).

References

1. Beynon, M.: DS/AHP Method: A Mathematical Analysis, including an Understanding of Uncertainty. European Journal of Operational Research 140(1), 149–165 (2002)
2. Beynon, M.J.: An Investigation of the Role of Scale Values in the DS/AHP Method of Multi-Criteria Decision Making. Journal of Multi-Criteria Decision Analysis 11(6), 327–343 (2002)

3. Beynon, M.J.: Understanding Local Ignorance and Non-specificity in the DS/AHP Method of Multi-criteria Decision Making. European Journal of Operational Research 163, 403–417 (2005)
4. Beynon, M.J.: A Method of Aggregation in DS/AHP for Group Decision-Making with the Non-Equivalent Importance of Individuals in the Group. Computers & Operations Research 32(7), 1881–1896 (2005)
5. Beynon, M.J.: The Role of the DS/AHP in Identifying Inter-Group Alliances and Majority Rule within Group Decision Making. Group Decision and Negotiation 15(1), 21–42 (2006)
6. Beynon, M., Curry, B., Morgan, P.: The Dempster-Shafer Theory of Evidence: An Alternative Approach to Multicriteria Decision Modelling. OMEGA - International Journal of Management Science 28(1), 37–50 (2000)
7. Beynon, M., Cosker, D., Marshall, D.: An Expert System for Multi-Criteria Decision Making using Dempster Shafer Theory. Expert Systems with Applications 20(4), 357–367 (2001)
8. Boujelben, M.A., De Smet, Y.: About the application of evidence theory in multicriteria decision aid. In: Doumpos, M., Grigoroudis, E. (eds.) Multicriteria Decision Aid and Artificial Intelligence: Links, Theory and Applications (Google eBook), pp. 161–183 (2013)
9. Dempster, A.P.: Upper and lower probabilities induced by a multiple valued mapping. Ann. Math. Statistics 38, 325–339 (1967)
10. Dezert, J., Tacnet, J.-M., Batton-Hubert, M., Smarandache, F.: Multi-criteria decision making based on DSmT-AHP. In: BELIEF 2010: Workshop on the Theory of Belief Functions, Brest, France (2010)
11. Du, Y., Han, C., Jing, Y., Liu, J.: TIN-DS/AHP: An Intelligent Method for Group Multiple Attribute Decision Making. Applied Mathematics & Information Sciences 8(2), 857–868 (2014)
12. Elgazzar, S.: Enhancing the Company's Financial Performance through Managing the Performance of Supply Chain Operations: A Case Study of an Egyptian Manufacturing Company, Doctoral Thesis, University of Huddersfield (2013)
13. Ennaceur, A., Elouedi, Z., Lefevre, E.: Handling Partial Preferences in the Belief AHP Method: Application to Life Cycle Assessment. In: Pirrone, R., Sorbello, F. (eds.) AI*IA 2011. LNCS, vol. 6934, pp. 395–400. Springer, Heidelberg (2011)
14. Ennaceur, A., Elouedi, Z., Lefevre, E.: Reasoning under uncertainty in the AHP Method Using the Belief Function Theory. In: Greco, S., et al. (eds.) IPMU, pp. 373–382 (2012)
15. Jiao, L., Liang, Y., Feng, X., Yang, F.: Combining sources of evidence with reliability and importance for decision making. Central European Journal of Operational Research (2013)
16. Ju, Y., Wang, A.: Emergency alternative evaluation under group decision makers: A method of incorporating DS/AHP with extended TOPSIS. Expert Systems with Applications 39(1), 1315–1323 (2012)
17. Liu, B., Tian, Y., Qiu, J.: Fire Extinguishing Systems' State Evaluation Basing on Analytic Hierarchy Process and Dempster-Shafer. In: The 2nd International Conference on Computer Application and System Modeling (2012)
18. Ma, W., Liu, W., Miller, P., Luo, X.: A Game-Theoretic Approach for Preventing Threats in Intelligent Surveillance Systems. In: Lomuscio, A., et al. (eds.) Proceedings of the 13th International Conference on Autonomous Agents and Multiagent Systems, Paris, France (2014)
19. Ma, W., Xiong, W., Luo, X.: A Model for Decision Making with Missing, Imprecise, and Uncertain Evaluations of Multiple Criteria. International Journal of Intelligent Systems 28, 152–184 (2013)

20. Nedashkovskaya, N.I.: Multi-Criteria Decision Making with Incomplete Expert Information when the AHP is Used. In: 21st International CODATA Conference (2008)
21. Pankratova, N., Nedashkovskaya, N.: Estimation of Sensitivity of the DS/AHP Method While Solving Foresight Problems with Incomplete Data. Intelligent Control and Automation 4, 80–86 (2013)
22. Saaty, T.L.: The Analytic Hierarchy Process. McGraw-Hill, New York (1980)
23. Shafer, G.: A Mathematical Theory of Evidence. Princeton University Press, Princeton (1976)
24. Tervonen, T., Lahdelma, R., Salminen, P.: A Method for Elicitating and Combining Group Preferences for Stochastic Multicriteria Acceptability Analysis, TUCS Technical Report (No 638) (November 2004)
25. Utkin, L.V., Simanova, N.V.: Multi-criteria Decision Making by Incomplete Preferences. Journal of Uncertain Systems 2(4), 255–266 (2008)
26. Utkin, L.V., Simanova, N.V.: The DS/AHP Method under Partial Information about Criteria and Alternatives by Several levels of Criteria. International Journal of Information Technology & Decision Making 11(2), 307–326 (2012)
27. Wei, G., Liu, J.: A DS/AHP Method for Comprehensive Decision-making in Urban Power System Planning. In: CICED 2008 (2008)
28. Xie, Y., Yi, S., Cao, Y., Lu, Y.: Uncertainty Information Fusion for Flood Risk Assessment Based on DS-AHP Method. IEEE (2011)
29. Yao, S., Guo, Y.-J., Huang, W.-Q.: An improved method of aggregation in DSAHP for multi-criteria group decision-making based on distance measure. Control and Decision 25(6), 894–898 (2010)

Evidential Database: A New Generalization of Databases?

Ahmed Samet[1,2], Éric Lefèvre[2], and Sadok Ben Yahia[1]

[1] Université Tunis El Manar, LIPAH, Faculty of Sciences of Tunis, Tunisia
{ahmed.samet,sadok.benyahia}@fst.rnu.tn
[2] Univ. Lille Nord de France UArtois, EA 3926 LGI2A, F-62400, Béthune, France
eric.lefevre@univ-artois.fr

Abstract. In this paper, we tackle the problem of data representation in several types of databases. A detailed survey of the different support measures in the major existing databases is described. The reminder of the paper aims to prove the importance of using evidential databases in case of handling imperfect information. The evidential database generalizes several ones by the use of specific Basic Belief Assignments. In addition, we show that the precise support, initially introduced on evidential database, generalizes several support measures.

Keywords: Evidential database, Binary database, Probabilistic database, Fuzzy database, Support.

1 Introduction

Data mining is a technique that uses a variety of data analysis tools to discover, hidden but interesting patterns and relationships in data that may be used to make valid predictions. Thanks to its simple formulas, it associates performance and quality in its retrieved results. For this reason, it is used in various fields and attracted interest in different applications [9].

The first studies on data mining relies on a data model under which transactions captured doubtless facts about the items that are contained in each transaction. These *binary databases* have only two scenarios : 1 if an element exists, 0 otherwise. However, in many applications, the existence of an item in a transaction is better captured by likelihood measures. The obvious limits of the binary databases in handling such types of data led the data mining community to adopt imprecise frameworks in order to mine more pertinent knowledge.

In this paper, we present a non exhaustive review of existing data mining databases. The characteristics of binary, probabilistic, fuzzy and evidential databases are detailed. The support measures in the databases are presented. The aim of this paper is to demonstrate the pivotal role of the evidential database, which relies on the evidence theory [5,12], in representing imprecision and uncertainty. The importance of using an evidential database rather than the other ones is justified. Indeed, we prove that the precise support measure [10] in evidential databases is a generalization of that of the classical ones.

F. Cuzzolin (Ed.): BELIEF 2014, LNAI 8764, pp. 105–114, 2014.

The remainder of the paper is organized as follows: in section 2, the key basic settings of the evidential database are recalled. In section 3, the binary database is studied and its relationship with the evidential database is highlighted. In section 4, probabilistic databases are scrutinized and the correlation between the precise support and the probabilistic support is highlighted. Section 5 stresses on the snugness connection between fuzzy databases with the evidential ones. Finally, we conclude and we describe issues for future work.

2   Evidential Database and Precise Support

In this section, we detail the main concepts of evidential databases as well as as the notion of precise support.

2.1   Evidential Database Concept

Introduced by Lee [8], the evidential database was aimed at modelling imperfect information. This type of database is supposed to handle imprecise and uncertain data. An evidential database is a triplet $\mathcal{EDB} = (\mathcal{A}_{\mathcal{EDB}}, \mathcal{O}, R_{\mathcal{EDB}})$. $\mathcal{A}_{\mathcal{EDB}}$ is a set of attributes and $\mathcal{O}$ is a set of d transactions (i.e., lines). Each column A_i $(1 \leq i \leq n)$ has a domain θ_{A_i} of discrete values. $R_{\mathcal{EDB}}$ expresses the relation between the jth line (i.e., transaction T_j) and the ith column (i.e., attribute A_i) by a normalized BBA as follows:

$$m_{ij} : 2^{\theta_{A_i}} \rightarrow [0,1] \quad with$$

$$\begin{cases} m_{ij}(\emptyset) = 0 \\ \sum_{\omega \subseteq \theta_{A_i}} m_{ij}(\omega) = 1. \end{cases} \quad (1)$$

Table 1. Evidential transaction database $\mathcal{EDB}$

Transaction	Attribute A	Attribute B
T1	$m(A_1) = 0.7$	$m(B_1) = 0.4$
	$m(\theta_A) = 0.3$	$m(B_2) = 0.2$
		$m(\theta_B) = 0.4$
T2	$m(A_2) = 0.3$	$m(B_1) = 1$
	$m(\theta_A) = 0.7$	

Table 1 illustrates an example of an evidential database. An item corresponds to a focal element. An itemset corresponds to a conjunction of focal elements having different domains. The inclusion operator is defined in [3] such that for two itemsets X and Y, we have:

$$X \subseteq Y \iff \forall x_i \in X, x_i \subseteq y_i.$$

where x_i and y_i are the ith element of X and Y. For the same evidential itemsets X and Y, the intersection operator is defined as follows:

$$X \cap Y = Z \iff \forall z_i \in Z, z_i \subseteq x_i \text{ and } z_i \subseteq y_i.$$

An *evidential associative rule* R is a causal relationship between two itemsets that can be written in the following form $R : X \to Y$ such that $X \cap Y = \emptyset$.

Example 1. In Table 1, A_1 is an item and $\theta_A \times B_1$ is an itemset such that $A_1 \subset \theta_A \times B_1$ and $A_1 \cap \theta_A \times B_1 = A_1$. $A_1 \to B_1$ is an evidential associative rule.

In the following subsection, we consider the precise support and confidence measures.

2.2 Support and Confidence in Evidential Database

Several definitions for the support's estimation have been proposed for the evidential itemsets such as [3,6]. Those definitions assess the support based on the belief function $Bel()$. The based belief support is constructed from the Cartesian product applied to the evidential database. Interested readers may refer to [6]. The support is computed as follows:

$$Support_{\mathcal{EDB}}(X) = Bel_{\mathcal{EDB}}(X) \tag{2}$$

such that:

$$Bel : 2^\theta \to [0, 1] \tag{3}$$

$$Bel(A) = \sum_{\emptyset \neq B \subseteq A} m(B). \tag{4}$$

In a previous work [10], we introduced a new metric for support estimation. The latter has been shown to provide more accuracy and to overcome several drawbacks of using the belief function. This measure is called Precise support Pr and it is defined by:

$$Pr : 2^{\theta_i} \to [0, 1] \tag{5}$$

$$Pr(x_i) = \sum_{x \subseteq \theta_i} \frac{|x_i \cap x|}{|x|} \times m_{ij}(x) \qquad \forall x_i \in 2^{\theta_i}. \tag{6}$$

The evidential support of an itemset $X = \prod_{i \in [1...n]} x_i$ in the transaction T_j (i.e., Pr_{T_j}) is then equal to:

$$Pr_{T_j}(X) = \prod_{x_i \in \theta_i, i \in [1...n]} Pr(x_i). \tag{7}$$

Thus, the evidential support $Support_{\mathcal{EDB}}$ of the itemset X becomes:

$$Support_{\mathcal{EDB}}(X) = \frac{1}{d} \sum_{j=1}^{d} Pr_{T_j}(X). \tag{8}$$

Additionally, in [11], we introduced a new measure of confidence for evidential associative rules that we called the *precise confidence measure*. Let us assume an evidential association rule such as $R : R_a \rightarrow R_c$, where R_c and R_a respectively, denote the conclusion and the antecedent (premise) part of the rule R. The precise confidence measure can be written as follows:

$$Confidence(R : R_a \rightarrow R_c) = \frac{\sum_{j=1}^{d} Pr_{T_j}(R_a) \times Pr_{T_j}(R_c)}{\sum_{j=1}^{d} Pr_{T_j}(R_a)}. \tag{9}$$

In the following sections, we highlight the relationships between evidential databases and the main other ones. The link between existing measures and the evidential precise one is also demonstrated.

3   Binary Data Mining

The first database variants studied from a data mining view are the binary ones. A binary database can be represented by a triplet $\mathcal{BDB} = (\mathcal{A}, \mathcal{O}, R_{\mathcal{BDB}})$. $\mathcal{A}$ represents the set of n binary attributes (i.e., columns). $R_{\mathcal{BDB}}$ is the relation that reflects the existence of an item in a transaction by only the values 0 and 1. $R_{\mathcal{BDB}}(A_i, T_j) = 1$ means that the item A_i exists in the transaction T_j and $R_{\mathcal{BDB}}(A_i, T_j)$ is set equal to 0 otherwise.

Since the inception of the Apriori algorithm [2], several other approaches have been introduced to reduce the computational complexity of mining these "frequent" binary itemsets. The support of an item A_i in a transaction T_j is defined as follows:

$$Support_{T_j}(A_i) = R_{\mathcal{BDB}}(A_i, T_j). \tag{10}$$

The support of an item A_i in those binary databases is still computed with the same manner:

$$Support(A_i) = \sum_{j=1}^{d} R_{\mathcal{BDB}}(A_i, T_j) = count(A_i). \tag{11}$$

The same goes for an itemset $A \cup B$ (or $A \times B$ if we keep the product notation):

$$Support(A \times B) = count(A \cup B). \tag{12}$$

Thus, the support is computed by counting the number of transactions having both A and B. From the support, the confidence measure of a rule $R : R_a \rightarrow R_c$ is computed as follows:

$$confidence(R : R_a \rightarrow R_c) = \frac{count(R_a \cup R_c)}{count(R_a)}. \tag{13}$$

A binary database can be constructed by redefining the $R_{\mathcal{EDB}}$ as a precise BBA. Indeed, each item $A_i \in \mathcal{A}$ can be redefined as an evidential item having the following frame of discernment $\theta_{A_i} = \{\exists, \not\exists\}$. $\exists$ and $\not\exists$ denote respectively the existence and absence of the attribute A_i in the considered transaction. Such a BBA can be written as follows:

$$\begin{cases} m_{ij}(\{\exists\}) = R_{\mathcal{BDB}}(A_i, T_j) \\ m_{ij}(\{\not\exists\}) = 1 - R_{\mathcal{BDB}}(A_i, T_j) \end{cases} \tag{14}$$

where m_{ij} is equivalent to a certain BBA. In that case, the support measure proposed in [10] is equivalent to the binary support equation defined in Equation (10). To demonstrate that equivalence, let us consider a binary database $\mathcal{D}$ and the evidential database $\mathcal{EDB}$ constructed as in the described procedure. Suppose that $R_{\mathcal{BDB}}(A_i, T_j) = 1$ such that $A_i \in \mathcal{A}$, then the corresponding evidential attribute is an $A_i \in \mathcal{A}_{\mathcal{EDB}}$ with $\theta_{A_i} = \{\exists, \not\exists\}$:

$$Pr_{T_j}(\exists) = \frac{|\exists \cap \exists|}{|\exists|} m_{ij}(\{\exists\}) + \frac{|\not\exists \cap \exists|}{|\not\exists|} m_{ij}(\{\not\exists\}) = m_{ij}(\{\exists\}) = R_{\mathcal{BDB}}(A_i, T_j). \tag{15}$$

From this point, we deduce that the evidential precise support is a generalization of the binary one. The same goes for the precise confidence given in Equation (9) that generalizes binary confidence since they both rely on the same support fraction.

Example 2. In this example, Table 2 shows how to create an evidential database from a binary one.

Table 2. The evidential transformation of $\mathcal{BDB}$ (Table (a)) to $\mathcal{EDB}$ (Table (b))

	A B C
T_1	X X
T_2	X X
T_3	X X
(a)	

	A	B	C
T_1	$m_{11}(\{\exists\}) = 0$	$m_{21}(\{\exists\}) = 1$	$m_{31}(\{\exists\}) = 1$
	$m_{11}(\{\not\exists\}) = 1$	$m_{21}(\{\not\exists\}) = 0$	$m_{31}(\{\not\exists\}) = 0$
T_2	$m_{12}(\{\exists\}) = 1$	$m_{22}(\{\exists\}) = 1$	$m_{32}(\{\exists\}) = 0$
	$m_{12}(\{\not\exists\}) = 0$	$m_{22}(\{\not\exists\}) = 0$	$m_{32}(\{\not\exists\}) = 1$
T_3	$m_{13}(\{\exists\}) = 0$	$m_{23}(\{\exists\}) = 1$	$m_{33}(\{\exists\}) = 1$
	$m_{13}(\{\not\exists\}) = 1$	$m_{23}(\{\not\exists\}) = 0$	$m_{33}(\{\not\exists\}) = 0$
	(b)		

The equivalency of the support measure is shown for the itemset $B \times C$.

The support of the itemset $B \times C$ from the transactions of Table 2.a is $Support(B \times C) = \frac{2}{3}$. In the evidential database, it is computed as follows:

$$Support_{\mathcal{EDB}}(B \times C) = \frac{1}{3} \sum_{j=1}^{3} Pr_{T_j}(A) \times Pr_{T_j}(B)$$

$Support_{\mathcal{EDB}}(B \times C) = \frac{1}{3}(m_{21}(\{\exists\}) \times m_{31}(\{\exists\}) + m_{22}(\{\exists\}) \times m_{32}(\{\exists\}) + m_{23}(\{\exists\}) \times m_{33}(\{\exists\})) = \frac{2}{3}$

Thus, the support retrieved from the binary database is the same as the precise support computed from the evidential database.

In the following section, we review the basics of the probabilistic support. A transformation method from a probabilitic database to evidential one is introduced. The equivalency between the probabilistic support and the precise one is studied.

4   Probabilistic Data Mining

Probabilistic data mining [1] was introduced to represent imperfect information thanks to the probability support. It can be represented by a triplet $\mathcal{PDB} = (\mathcal{A}_{\mathcal{PDB}}, \mathcal{O}, R_{\mathcal{PDB}})$. The degree of existence of the item A_i in the transaction T_j is measured through the probability function $p(A_i, T_j) \in [0, 1]$. The support of an itemset $X \in \mathcal{A}_{\mathcal{PDB}}$ in such type of database is defined as follows [4]:

$$p(X, T_j) = \prod_{i \in X} p(i, T_j). \tag{16}$$

Thus, the support of an itemset X in a database is the sum of its expected probability in the transaction:

$$Support_{\mathcal{PDB}}(X) = \sum_{j=1}^{d} p(X, T_j). \tag{17}$$

An equivalent evidential database can be constructed through using Bayesian BBA[1]. The BBA can be modeled on a two-member-based frame of discernment $\theta_i = \{\exists, \not\exists\}$ where $\exists$ indicates that A_i belongs to the considered transaction, whereas $\not\exists$ performs the opposite. Such a BBA can be constructed as follows:

$$\begin{cases} m_{ij}(\{\exists\}) = p(i, T_j) \\ m_{ij}(\{\not\exists\}) = 1 - p(i, T_j). \end{cases} \tag{18}$$

With this construction, the probabilistic support defined in Equation (17) is equivalent to the proposed precise support. Indeed, the assertion can be verified i.e.:

$$Pr_{T_j}(\exists) = \frac{|\exists \cap \exists|}{|\exists|} m_{ij}(\{\exists\}) + \frac{|\not\exists \cap \exists|}{\not\exists} m_{ij}(\{\not\exists\}) = m_{ij}(\{\exists\}) = p(i, T_j). \tag{19}$$

As is the case for a binary database, the Evidential Data mining Algorithm (EDMA) generalizes the probabilistic version of Apriori: i.e., U-Apriori [4].

Example 3. Table 3 shows how to create an evidential database from a probabilistic one.

---

[1] A BBA is called Bayesian only if all its focal sets are singletons.

Table 3. The evidential transformation of $\mathcal{PDB}$ (Table (a)) to $\mathcal{EDB}$ (Table (b))

	A	B	C
T_1	$m_{11}(\{\exists\}) = 0$	$m_{21}(\{\exists\}) = 0.7$	$m_{31}(\{\exists\}) = 0.8$
	$m_{11}(\{\nexists\}) = 1$	$m_{21}(\{\nexists\}) = 0.3$	$m_{31}(\{\nexists\}) = 0.2$
T_2	$m_{12}(\{\exists\}) = 0.9$	$m_{22}(\{\exists\}) = 0.7$	$m_{32}(\{\exists\}) = 0.1$
	$m_{12}(\{\nexists\}) = 0.1$	$m_{22}(\{\nexists\}) = 0.3$	$m_{32}(\{\nexists\}) = 0.9$
T_3	$m_{13}(\{\exists\}) = 0$	$m_{23}(\{\exists\}) = 0.8$	$m_{33}(\{\exists\}) = 0.7$
	$m_{13}(\{\nexists\}) = 1$	$m_{23}(\{\nexists\}) = 0.2$	$m_{33}(\{\nexists\}) = 0.3$

(b)

	A	B	C
T_1	0.0	0.7	0.8
T_2	0.9	0.7	0.1
T_3	0	0.8	0.7

(a)

The equivalency of the support measure is shown for the itemset $B \times C$. The support of the itemset $B \times C$ from the transactions of the Table 3.a is $Support(B \times C) = \frac{(0.7 \times 0.8) + (0.7 \times 0.1) + (0.8 \times 0.7)}{3} = 0.4$. In the evidential database, it is computed as follows:

$$Support_{\mathcal{EDB}}(B \times C) = \frac{1}{3} \sum_{j=1}^{3} Pr_{T_j}(A) \times Pr_{T_j}(B)$$

$Support_{\mathcal{EDB}}(B \times C) = \frac{1}{3}(m_{21}(\{\exists\}) \times m_{31}(\{\exists\}) + m_{22}(\{\exists\}) \times m_{32}(\{\exists\}) + m_{23}(\{\exists\}) \times m_{33}(\{\exists\})) = \frac{1.2}{3} = 0.4$

Thus, the support retrieved from the probabilistic database is the same as the precise support computed from the evidential database.

In the following section, we review the basics of fuzzy data mining and we study its relation with the evidential one.

5 Fuzzy Data Mining

Let us assume the triplet $\mathcal{FDB} = (\mathcal{A}_{\mathcal{FDB}}, \mathcal{O}, R_{\mathcal{FDB}})$ that denotes a fuzzy database. $R_{\mathcal{FDB}}$ denotes the fuzzy relationship between an item and a transaction expressed through a membership function. The membership function $\mu_{T_j}(i) = \alpha$ ($\alpha \in [0,1]$) rates the degree of membership of the considered item to the transaction T_j. The support computation in such databases is done by the use of the $count()$ function in the following manner [7]:

$$count(i) = \sum_{j=1}^{d} \mu_{T_j}(i). \tag{20}$$

The support of item i in the fuzzy database is found as follows:

$$Support(i) = \frac{count(i)}{d}. \tag{21}$$

Thus, for an itemset X of size q such that $x_i \in X$ and $i \in [1, q]$, the support becomes:

$$support(X) = \frac{\sum_{j=1}^{d} min\{\mu_{T_j}(x_i), i = 1 \ldots q\}}{d}. \tag{22}$$

The numerator of the support could be seen as the Gödel t-norm (minimum t-norm).

Assuming a fuzzy database is available, it is possible to construct an evidential database. In addition, the precise support sustains fuzzy support in its formulation. Indeed, as can be seen in Equation (8), the precise support is also equal to the sum of the transactional support divided by the database size.

In the following, we show how to obtain analogous evidential support of the fuzzy support. Assuming an attribute $A_i \in \mathcal{A}_{\mathcal{EDB}}$ having a frame of discernment θ_{A_i} such that $\omega_1 \subset \cdots \subset \omega_n \subseteq \theta_{A_i}$, the corresponding BBA for a fuzzy relation $R_{\mathcal{FDB}}(\omega_1, T_j) = \mu_{T_j}(\omega_1)$ is constructed in this form:

$$\begin{cases} m_{ij}(\omega_1) = \mu_{T_j}(\omega_1) \\ \sum m(\cup_k \omega_k) = 1 - \mu_{T_j}(\omega_1). \end{cases} \tag{23}$$

We can obviously remark that:

$$T(\mu(A_i), \mu(A_j)) = min(Bel(A_i), Bel(A_j)) \tag{24}$$

where T is a minimum t-norm. Thus, the fuzzy support can be retrieved in an evidential database as follows:

$$Support_{\mathcal{FDB}}(X) = \frac{\sum_{T_j \in \mathcal{O}} min\{Bel(x_i), x_i \in X\}}{d}. \tag{25}$$

Interestingly enough, an equivalent to fuzzy database support in evidential database does exists.

Example 4. Table 4 shows how to create an evidential database from a fuzzy one.

Table 4. The evidential transformation of $\mathcal{FDB}$ (Table (a)) to $\mathcal{EDB}$ (Table (b))

	A		B	
	ω_1	ω_2	ω_1	ω_2
T_1	0.3	0.7	0.1	0.8
T_2	0.5	0.2	0.3	0.8
T_3	0.8	0.1	1.0	0.2

(a)

	A		B	
	ω_1	ω_2	ω_1	ω_2
T_1	$m_{11}(\omega_1) = 0.3$	$m_{21}(\omega_2) = 0.7$	$m_{31}(\omega_1) = 0.1$	$m_{41}(\omega_2) = 0.8$
	$m_{11}(\Omega) = 0.7$	$m_{21}(\Omega) = 0.3$	$m_{31}(\Omega) = 0.9$	$m_{41}(\Omega) = 0.2$
T_2	$m_{12}(\omega_1) = 0.5$	$m_{22}(\omega_2) = 0.2$	$m_{32}(\omega_1) = 0.3$	$m_{42}(\omega_2) = 0.8$
	$m_{12}(\Omega) = 0.5$	$m_{22}(\Omega) = 0.8$	$m_{32}(\Omega) = 0.7$	$m_{42}(\Omega) = 0.2$
T_3	$m_{11}(\omega_1) = 0.8$	$m_{21}(\omega_2) = 0.1$	$m_{31}(\omega_1) = 1.0$	$m_{41}(\omega_2) = 0.2$
	$m_{11}(\Omega) = 0.2$	$m_{21}(\Omega) = 0.9$	$m_{31}(\Omega) = 0$	$m_{41}(\Omega) = 0.8$

(b)

The equivalency of the support measure is shown for the itemset $B \times C$. The support of the itemset $A_{\omega_1} \times B_{\omega_2}$ from the Table 4.a is $Support(A_{\omega_1} \times B_{\omega_2}) = \frac{0.3+0.5+0.2}{3} = 1.0$. In the evidential database, Table 4.b, it is computed as follows:

$$Support_{\mathcal{EDB}}(A_{\omega_1} \times B_{\omega_2}) = \frac{1}{3} \sum_{j=1}^{3} min(Bel(A_{\omega_1}), Bel(A_{\omega_2}))$$
$$Support_{\mathcal{EDB}}(A_{\omega_1} \times B_{\omega_2}) = \frac{1}{3}(Bel_{T_1}(A_{\omega_1}) + Bel_{T_2}(A_{\omega_1}) + Bel_{T_2}(B_{\omega_2}))$$
$$Support_{\mathcal{EDB}}(A_{\omega_1} \times B_{\omega_2}) = 1.0$$

Despite the fact that the precise support is not equivalent to the fuzzy support, it is still possible to recover the same value with the use of the Equation (25).

6 Conclusion

In this paper, we detailed the data mining measures such as the support and the confidence on the several databases such as binary, probabilistic, fuzzy databases. We have proven the generalization relation between precise measures in evidential databases and measures used in other databases. In future works, we aim to study the evidential transformation of other imperfect databases such as fuzzy-possibilistic database [13].

References

1. Aggarwal, C.C.: Managing and Mining Uncertain Data. Springer Publishing Company, Incorporated (2009)
2. Agrawal, R., Srikant, R.: Fast algorithm for mining association rules. In: Proceedings of international conference on Very Large Data Bases, Santiago de Chile, Chile, pp. 487–499 (1994)
3. Bach Tobji, M.A., Ben Yaghlane, B., Mellouli, K.: Incremental maintenance of frequent itemsets in evidential databases. In: Proceedings of the 10th European Conference on Symbolic and Quantitative Approaches to Reasoning with Uncertainty, Verona, Italy, pp. 457–468 (2009)
4. Chui, C.-K., Kao, B., Hung, E.: Mining frequent itemsets from uncertain data. In: Zhou, Z.-H., Li, H., Yang, Q. (eds.) PAKDD 2007. LNCS (LNAI), vol. 4426, pp. 47–58. Springer, Heidelberg (2007)
5. Dempster, A.: Upper and lower probabilities induced by multivalued mapping. AMS-38 (1967)
6. Hewawasam, K.K.R., Premaratne, K., Shyu, M.L.: Rule mining and classification in a situation assessment application: A belief-theoretic approach for handling data imperfections. Trans. Sys. Man Cyber. Part B 37(6), 1446–1459 (2007)
7. Hong, T.P., Kuo, C.S., Wang, S.L.: A fuzzy AprioriTid mining algorithm with reduced computational time. Applied Soft Computing 5(1), 1–10 (2004)
8. Lee, S.: Imprecise and uncertain information in databases: an evidential approach. In: Proceedings of Eighth International Conference on Data Engineering, Tempe, AZ, pp. 614–621 (1992)
9. Liao, S.H., Chu, P.H., Hsiao, P.Y.: Data mining techniques and applications – a decade review from 2000 to 2011. Expert Systems with Applications 39(12), 11303–11311 (2012)

10. Samet, A., Lefevre, E., Ben Yahia, S.: Mining frequent itemsets in evidential database. In: Proceedings of the Fifth International Conference on Knowledge and Systems Engeneering, Hanoi, Vietnam, pp. 377–388 (2013)
11. Samet, A., Lefèvre, E., Ben Yahia, S.: Classification with evidential associative rules. In: Proccedings of 15th International Conference on Information Processing and Management of Uncertainty in Knowledge-Based Systems, IPMU, Montpellier, France (to appear, 2014)
12. Shafer, G.: A Mathematical Theory of Evidence. Princeton University Press (1976)
13. Weng, C., Chen, Y.: Mining fuzzy association rules from uncertain data, springer-verlag new york, inc. new york, ny, usa issn: 0219-1377 doi. knowledge and information systems 23, 129–152 (2010)

Belief Approach for Social Networks

Salma Ben Dhaou, Mouloud Kharoune, Arnaud Martin,
and Boutheina Ben Yaghlane

LARODEC, IHEC.41 rue de la Liberté, 2000 Le Bardo, Tunisia
IRISA, Université de Rennes 1, IUT de Lannion, Rue Edouard Branly BP 30219,
22302 Lannion cedex, France
salma.bendhaou@hotmail.fr,
{Mouloud.Kharoune,Arnaud.Martin}@univ-rennes1.fr,
boutheina.yaghlane@ihec.rnu.tn

Abstract. Nowadays, social networks became essential in information exchange between individuals. Indeed, as users of these networks, we can send messages to other people according to the links connecting us. Moreover, given the large volume of exchanged messages, detecting the true nature of the received message becomes a challenge. For this purpose, it is interesting to consider this new tendency with reasoning under uncertainty by using the theory of belief functions. In this paper, we tried to model a social network as being a network of fusion of information and determine the true nature of the received message in a well-defined node by proposing a new model: the belief social network.

Keywords: Social Networks, Belief Network, Information Fusion, Belief functions.

1 Introduction

Social networks appeared long before the birth of Internet. A social network can be defined as a group of persons or organizations connected between them by relations and social exchanges which they maintain. However, with the evolution of connection rates and collaborative technologies which are continuously changing, Internet provides access to new networks that are wider, and more playful social but also less easily recognizable.

Furthermore, an important volume of incomplete and imperfect information are spreading on the network. Therefore, the management of the uncertainty is fundamental in several domains, especially in social networks. In fact, belief functions theory allows, not only the representation of the partial knowledge, but also the fusion of information. In the case of social networks, this theory allows to attribute mass functions to the nodes which represent, for example, persons, associations, companies and places as well as links that can be friendly, family and professional and on messages that can be of type for example: personal commercial, personal not commercial, impersonal commercial and impersonal not commercial. Therefore, we will have a global view on exchanges made on the network and this will lead us to make a better decision.

F. Cuzzolin (Ed.): BELIEF 2014, LNAI 8764, pp. 115–123, 2014.
© Springer International Publishing Switzerland 2014

In addition, by using uncertainty, we can better monitor the behaviour of the social network. Thus, extending the work on the real plane, we can predict such a terrorist act or assess the quality of a product or follow a buzz. . .

In this context, previous works have focused on models and methods devoted to the analysis of social network data [12] [2] while others have interested in information fusion in order to have a global information about the network [13].

The aim of this paper is to propose a new model, a belief social network which is a network supplied by the masses. In fact, we attribute a mass function to the nodes, edges and messages.

This paper is structured as follows. In section 2, we briefly recall some concepts related to the theory of belief functions. We propose in section 3 our model: the belief social network. In section 4, we present the fusion of the masses on belief social network. Finally, section 5 is devoted to illustrate the belief social network and section 6 concludes the paper.

2   Basic Concepts of Belief Function

In this section, we will remind the basic concepts of the theory of belief functions used to instrument our model, the belief social network. Let Ω be a finite and exhaustive set whose elements are mutually exclusive, Ω is called a frame of discernment. A mass function is a mapping $m : 2^{\Omega} \to [0, 1]$ such that $\sum_{X \in 2^{\Omega}} m(X) = 1$ and $m(\emptyset) = 0$. The mass $m(X)$ expresses the amount of belief that is allocated to the subset X. In order to deal with the case of the open world where decisions are not exhaustive, Smets [10] proposed the conjunctive combination rule. This rule assumes that all sources are reliable and consistent. Considering two mass functions m_1 and m_2 for all $A \in 2^{\Omega}$, this rule is defined by:

$$m_{\bigcirc}(A) = \sum_{B \cap C = A} m_1(B) * m_2(C) \tag{1}$$

We will also consider the normalized conjunctive rule, the Dempster rule, given for two mass functions m_1 and m_2 for all $x \in 2^{\Omega}$ by:

$$m_{\oplus}(A) = \frac{m_{\bigcirc}(A)}{1 - m_{\bigcirc}(\emptyset)} \tag{2}$$

The coarsening corresponds to a grouping together the events of a frame of discernment Θ to another frame compatible but which is more larger Ω [10,11]. Let Ω and Θ be two finite sets. The refinement allows the obtaining of one frame of discernment Ω from the set Θ by splitting some or all of its events [8].

In order to make a decision, we try to select the most likely hypothesis which may be difficult to realize directly with the basics of the theory of belief functions where mass functions are given not only to singletons but also to subsets of hypothesis. Some solutions exist to ensure the decision making within the theory of belief functions. The best known is the pignistic probability proposed by the

Transferable Belief Model (TBM). Other criteria exists like the maximum of credibility and the maximum of plausibility [1].

The TBM is based on two level mental models: The "credal level" where beliefs are entertained and represented by belief function and the "pignistic level" where beliefs are used to make decision and represented by probability functions called the pignistic probabilities. When a decision must be made, beliefs held at the credal level induce a probability measure at the pignistic measure denoted BetP [9]. The link between these two functions is achieved by:

$$\text{BetP}(A) = \sum_{B \subseteq \Theta} \frac{|A \cap B|}{|B|} \frac{m(B)}{1 - m(\emptyset)}, \forall A \subseteq \Theta \tag{3}$$

To focus on the type of relationship between two different frames of discernment, we may use the multi-valued mapping introduced by Hyun Lee [5]:

$$m_\Gamma(B_j) = \sum_{\Gamma(e_i) = B_j} m(e_i) \tag{4}$$

with $e_i \in \Omega$ and $B_j \subseteq \Theta$. Therefore the function Γ is defined as follow $\Gamma : \Omega \to 2^\Theta$.

The vacuous extension, being a particular case of multi-valued mapping has the objective to transfer the basic belief assignment of a frame of discernment Ω towards the Cartesian product of frames of discernment $\Omega \times \Theta$. The operation of vacuous extension, noted $\uparrow$, is defined by:

$$m^{\Omega \uparrow \Omega \times \Theta}(B) = \begin{cases} m^\Omega(A) & \text{if } B = A \times \Theta \\ 0 & \text{otherwise} \end{cases} \tag{5}$$

The marginalization allows, from a basic belief assignment defined on a space produced to find the basic belief assignment on one of the frames of discernment of the produced space. This operation, noted $\downarrow$ is defined by:

$$m^{\Omega \times \Theta \downarrow \Omega}(A) = \sum_{B \subseteq \Omega \times \Theta} m^{\Omega \times \Theta}(B) \quad \forall A \subseteq \Omega \tag{6}$$

where A is the result of the projection of B on Ω.

3   Belief Social Network

Several works have focused on the representation of networks with graphs. A classical graph is represented by $G = \{V; E\}$ with: V a set of nodes and E a set of edges. This representation does not take into account the uncertainty of the nodes and edges.

In fact, graphical models combine the graph theory with any theory dealing with uncertainty like probability [6], [3] or possibility or theory of belief functions to provide a general framework for an intuitive and a clear graphical representation of real-world problems [4]. The propagation of messages in networks has been modelled using the theory of belief functions combined with other theories such as hidden Markov chains [7].

In this context, we introduce our model: the belief social network which has the role of representing a social network using the theory of belief functions. Indeed, we will associate to each node, link and message an a priori mass and observe the interaction in the network to determine the mass of the message obtained in a well-defined node. To do this, we consider an evidential graph $G = \{V^b; E^b\}$ with: V^b a set of nodes and E^b a set of edges. We attribute to every node i of V^b a mass $m_i^{\Omega_N}$ defined on the frame of discernment Ω_N of the nodes. Moreover, we attribute also to every edge (i, j) of E^b a mass $m_{ij}^{\Omega_L}$ defined on the frame of discernment Ω_L of the edges. Therefore, we have:

$$V^b = \{V_i, m_i^{\Omega_N}\} \tag{7}$$

and

$$E^b = \{(V_i^b, V_j^b), m_{ij}^{\Omega_L}\} \tag{8}$$

This evidential graph structure is given by Fig 1. In social network, we can have for example the frame of the nodes given by the classes Person, Company, Association and Place. The frame of discernment of the edges can be Friendly, Professional or Family. Moreover we note: $\Omega_N = \{\omega_{n_1}, \ldots, \omega_{n_N}\}$ and $\Omega_L = \{\omega_{l_1}, \ldots, \omega_{n_L}\}$.

In social network, many messages can transit in the network. They can be categorized as commercial, personal, and so on. The class of the message is also full of uncertainty. Therefore to each message, we add a mass function in the considered frame of discernment $\Omega_{\text{Mess}} = \{\omega_{M_1}, \ldots, \omega_{M_k}\}$.

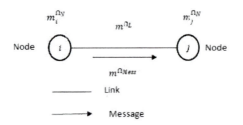

Fig. 1. Evidential graph structure for social network

4   Fusion of Masses on Belief Social Network

In social network, we can receive the same information from different users. But, can we have the confidence to this information? Moreover, the information can be contradictory. We propose here to take into account the structure of belief social network presented in the previous section to analyse the messages received by one node.

In order to integrate the belief on the nodes and on the edges, we first make a vacuous extension on $\Omega_N \times \Omega_L$ for each mass for the nodes of V^b and on each mass for the edge of E^b. Therefore, we obtain on each node V_i^b a mass: $m_i^{\Omega_N \times \Omega_L}$ and on each edge $E_{ij} = (V_i^b, V_j^b)$ between the nodes V_i^b and V_j^b a mass: $m_{ij}^{\Omega_N \times \Omega_L}$. If we consider a coming message from the node V_i^b to the node V_j^b through the edge E_{ij}, the belief of the network $m_R^{\Omega_N \times \Omega_L}$ is given by the mass function on the node V_i and the edge E_{ij}:

$$m_R^{\Omega_N \times \Omega_L} = m_{V_i}^{\Omega_N \uparrow \Omega_N \times \Omega_L} \oplus m_{E_{ij}}^{\Omega_L \uparrow \Omega_N \times \Omega_L} \tag{9}$$

Here, the index R denotes the resulted belief network from the nodes and the link between them regardless of the message.

We use the multi-valued operation to combine mass functions on different frames of discernment. In fact, a multi-valued mapping Γ describes a mapping function:

$$\Gamma : \Omega_N \times \Omega_L \to \Omega_{\text{Mess}} \tag{10}$$

We can calculate these equations by using the formula (4):

$$\Gamma : m_\Gamma^{\Omega_{\text{Mess}}}(B_j) = \sum_{\Gamma(e_i) = B_j} m^{\Omega_N \times \Omega_L}(e_i) \tag{11}$$

with $e_i \in \Omega_N \times \Omega_L$ and $B_j \subseteq \Omega_{\text{Mess}}$. From the function Γ, we can combine the mass given by the network $m_\Gamma^{\Omega_{\text{Mess}}}$ and the mass of the message to obtain the mass of the message considering the network:

$$m_R^{\Omega_{\text{Mess}}} = m^{\Omega_{\text{Mess}}} \copyright m_\Gamma^{\Omega_{\text{Mess}}} \tag{12}$$

Now, if we consider n messages coming from n different nodes $V_{i_1}^b, \ldots, V_{i_n}^b$ to the same node V_j^b. We can merge the obtained results from the equation (12) for the n nodes. The goal is to obtain a more precise information on an event describe by the n messages. We then take into account the local network $m_{R_i}^{\Omega_{\text{Mess}}}$ of the node V_j^b. A local network is defined as a branch of the global network composed of many nodes linked to a same node, the connecting links and the received messages. For example, we can have two nodes which send two messages simultaneously to a third node. We obtain the mass of the global network $m_{G_R}^{\Omega_{\text{Mess}}}$:

$$m_{G_R}^{\Omega_{\text{Mess}}} = m_{R_1}^{\Omega_{\text{Mess}}} \copyright m_{R_2}^{\Omega_{\text{Mess}}} \copyright \ldots \copyright m_{R_n}^{\Omega_{\text{Mess}}} \tag{13}$$

Then, we will be able to take a decision on the nature of the resulting message with the pignistic probability using equation (3).

5   Illustrations

In this section, we will present various experiments conducted to validate our model. We consider three frames of discernment of the nodes, the links and the messages:
$\Omega_N = \{Person, Company, Association, Place\}$, $\Omega_L = \{Friendly, Family, Prof.\}$, ($Prof.$ for professional), $\Omega_{\text{Mess}} = \{PC, PNC, IC, INC\}$, with PC for Personal Commercial, PNC for Personal Not Commercial, IC for Impersonal Commercial and INC for Impersonal Not Commercial. We used the passage function Γ given in Table 1 which allows.

Table 1. Definition of the function Γ given the correspondences between $\Omega_N \times \Omega_L$ and Ω_{Mess}

Γ	Person	Association	Company	Place
Friendly	PNC	$PNC \cup INC$	$PC \cup IC$	$INC \cup IC$
Family	$PNC \cup INC$	$PNC \cup INC$	$PC \cup IC$	$INC \cup IC$
Professional	$PNC \cup IC$	IC	IC	IC

For the purposes of our model, we will evaluate three cases. For the first one, we consider a mass function associated to:

- a node with: $m^{\Omega_N}(Person) = 0.75$ and $m^{\Omega_N}(\Omega_N) = 0.25$
- a link with: $m^{\Omega_L}(Friendly) = 0.75$ and $m^{\Omega_L}(\Omega_L) = 0.25$
- a message with: $m_1^{\Omega_{\text{Mess}}}(PNC) = 0.6$ and $m_1^{\Omega_{\text{Mess}}}(\Omega_{\text{Mess}}) = 0.4$

Following our proposed procedure, first, we calculate the vacuous extension of m^{Ω_N} and m^{Ω_L} on $\Omega_N \times \Omega_L$ and we combine both mass functions. We obtain:

$$m_R^{\Omega_N \times \Omega_L}(\{Person, Friendly\}) = 0.5625$$
$$m_R^{\Omega_N \times \Omega_L}(\{Person, Friendly\}, \{Person, Family\}, \{Person, Prof.\}) = 0.1875$$
$$m_R^{\Omega_N \times \Omega_L}(\{Person, Friendly\}, \{Association, Friendly\}, \quad\quad (14)$$
$$\{Company, Friendly\}, \{Place, Friendly\}) = 0.1875$$
$$m_R^{\Omega_N \times \Omega_L}(\Omega_N \times \Omega_L) = 0.0625$$

Then, we use the Γ function to calculate the passage from $\Omega_N \times \Omega_L$ to Ω_{Mess}. We obtain:

$$m_\Gamma^{\Omega_{\text{Mess}}}(PNC) = 0.5625$$
$$m_\Gamma^{\Omega_{\text{Mess}}}(\Omega_{\text{Mess}}) = 0.4375 \quad\quad (15)$$

Then, we make the conjunctive combination of $m_\Gamma^{\Omega_{\text{Mess}}}$ and m_{Mess}^{Ω}:

$$m_R^{\Omega_{\text{Mess}}}(PNC) = 0.8250$$
$$m_R^{\Omega_{\text{Mess}}}(\Omega_{\text{Mess}}) = 0.1750 \qu\quad (16)$$

Finally, to make a decision, we calculate the pignistic probability:

$$BetP(PC) = 0.0438$$
$$BetP(IC) = 0.0438$$
$$BetP(PNC) = 0.8687$$
$$BetP(INC) = 0.0438$$
(17)

If we consider the results, we note that the pignistic probability on Personal Not Commercial is 0.8687. This pignistic probability was equal to 0.7 before considered the network. Hence, we show that considering the network we can reinforce our belief for a given message.

In the second case, we consider the same network, with the same masses m^{Ω_N} and m^{Ω_L}, but we consider a mass function associated to a message with:

$$m_2^{\Omega_{\text{Mess}}}(PC) = 0.6 \text{ and } m_2^{\Omega_{\text{Mess}}}(\Omega_{\text{Mess}}) = 0.4$$

In this case the mass is on the Personal Commercial instead of Personal Not Commercial. As the network is the same we obtain the same mass $m_R^{\Omega_N \times \Omega_L}$ given by equation (14) as before and also using the Γ function the same mass given by the equation (15).

However the result of the conjunctive combination $m_\Gamma^{\Omega_{\text{Mess}}}$ and $m^{\Omega_{\text{Mess}}}$ is now:

$$m_R^{\Omega_{\text{Mess}}}(\emptyset) = 0.3375$$
$$m_R^{\Omega_{\text{Mess}}}(PC) = 0.2625$$
$$m_R^{\Omega_{\text{Mess}}}(PNC) = 0.2250$$
$$m_R^{\Omega_{\text{Mess}}}(\Omega_{\text{Mess}}) = 0.1750$$
(18)

In this case there is a conflict between the information of the network and the message, therefore a mass come out the empty set. The pignistic probability gives:

$$BetP(PC) = 0.4623$$
$$BetP(IC) = 0.0660$$
$$BetP(PNC) = 0.4057$$
$$BetP(INC) = 0.0660$$
(19)

We note that in the first example, the highest pignistic probability is associated with the Personal Not Commercial message that had the larger mass function at the beginning. While in the second example, we find ourselves faced with almost equal probability of Personal Not Commercial and Personal Commercial types where the need for a second decision on the type of message received.

Now we consider the fusion of the two examples cited above that come on the same node. We obtain the results given in Table 2. We note that by combining the two examples, we get the message Personal Not Commercial that has the highest pignistic probability.

Working on real data, we can assign the mass functions to the nodes, edges and messages by evaluating certain parameters, for example, the type of contacts that are related to the profile in question as well as the type of publications produced (case of facebook).

Table 2. Fusion of the two examples: the mass function and the pignistic probability

Focal	Mass
∅	0.5541
PNC	0.3694
PC	0.0459
Ω_{Mess}	0.0306

Message	BetP
PC	0.1202
IC	0.0172
PNC	0.8455
INC	0.0172

6   Conclusion

In this work we presented in the first section a general introduction in which we reviewed the notion of social networks and the interest of the proposed method to respond to the expectations for reasoning under uncertainty. In the second section, we briefly introduced the basic concepts used in the theory of belief functions. Then we focused on the introduction of our model and the different notation used. Indeed, we treated step by step development of the construction of the graph. Finally, we detailed the process of merging the information flowing through the network. We also showed how the process is carried out of the fusion and explained how we can make a decision on the nature of the messages received by using the pignistic probability. In fact, in many cases, we can take a new decision on the nature of the message received by a well-defined node. This idea was explained in the second example in the illustration part. In future work, we aim to represent the update of the elements composing the network as well as to scale.

References

1. Janez, F.: Fusion de sources d'information définies sur des référentiels non exhaustifs différents. Ph.D. thesis, Université d'Angers (November 1996)
2. Kempe, D., Kleinberg, J., Tardos, E.: Maximizing the spread of influence through a social network. In: KDD 2003 Proceedings of the Ninth ACM SIGKDD International Conference on Knowledge Discovery and Data Mining, pp. 137–146. ACM Press (2003)
3. Khan, A., Bonchi, F., Gionis, A., Gullo, F.: Fast reliability search in uncertain graphs. In: International Conference on Extending Database Technology (EDBT) (2014)
4. Laamari, W., ben Yaghlane, B., Simon, C.: Dynamic directed evidential networks with conditional belief functions:application to system reliability. IPMU (1), 481–490 (2012)
5. Lee, H.: Context reasoning under uncertainty based on evidential fusion networks in home based care. Tech. rep., Faculty of the Graduate School of The University of Texas (2010)
6. Parchas, P., Gullo, F., Papadias, D., Bonchi, F.: The pursuit of a good possibe world: Extracting representative instances of uncertain graphs. In: SIGMOD 2014. ACM Press, Snowbird (2014)
7. Ramasso, E.: Contribution of belief functions to hidden markov models with an application to fault diagnosis. IEEE (1), 1–6 (2009)

8. Shafer, G.: A mathematical theory of evidence. Princeton University Press (1976)
9. Smets, P.: Constructing the pignistic probability function in a context of uncertainty. Uncertainty in Artificial Intelligence 5, 29–39 (1990)
10. Smets, P.: Belief Functions: the Disjunctive Rule of Combination and the Generalized Bayesian Theorem. International Journal of Approximate Reasoning 9, 1–35 (1993)
11. Smets, P.: Imperfect information: Imprecision - Uncertainty. In: Motro, A., Smets, P. (eds.) Uncertainty Management in Information Systems, pp. 225–254. Kluwer Academic Publishers (1997)
12. Wasserman, S., Faust, K.: Social Network Analysis, Methods and Application. The Press Syndicate of the University of Cambridge (1994)
13. el Zoghby, N., Cherfaoui, V., Ducourthial, B., Denoeux, T.: Fusion distribuée évidentielle pour la détection d'attaque sybil dans un réseau de véhicules (1), 1–8

Methods Handling Accident and Traffic Jam Information with Belief Functions in VANETs

Mira Bou Farah[1], David Mercier[1], François Delmotte[1], Éric Lefèvre[1], and Sylvain Lagrue[2]

[1] Univ. Lille Nord de France, F-59000 Lille, France, UArtois, LGI2A, F-62400, Béthune, France
mira_boufarah@ens.univ-artois.fr, firstname.lastname@univ-artois.fr
[2] Univ. Lille Nord de France, F-59000 Lille, France, UArtois, CRIL, F-62300, Lens, France, CNRS, UMR 8188, F-62300 Lens, France
lagrue@cril.fr

Abstract. In this paper, different methods using belief functions are proposed to share and manage information about local and spatial events on the road in V2V communications. In order to take into account messages ageing, a reinforcement mechanism considering that events disappear over the time is compared to the discounting mechanism. Two strategies for messages management are also emphasized: a first one where each message is stored and sent when possible and a second one where only fused messages are considered. Presented work shows how results can be upgraded when considering the world update, especially for dynamic events. Finally, an influence mechanism is introduced for traffic jam events to smooth and improve results when vehicles receive information about only some parts of the road.

Keywords: Vehicular Ad-hoc Network (VANET), events on the road, imperfect information exchange, belief functions, information fusion.

1 Introduction

The car is currently by far the most used transportation mean. Many studies have been conducted in order to improve car safety and increase comfort standard using Vehicular Ad-Hoc Networks VANET [1,2], which are wireless networks formed of highly dynamic nodes capable of being organized without infrastructure. Present work concerns Vehicle to Vehicle (V2V) communication where vehicles do not use any centralized access point to build their own information assembly. Environment is very proactive. Vehicles receive a large amount of information which is most of the time uncertain.

Different methods [3,5,4,6] have been introduced in previous works to share and manage local events such as accidents in V2V communication using the theory of belief functions [7,8] which constitutes a rich and flexible framework for representing and manipulating imprecise and uncertain information. This paper completes the work on local events presented in [6], by introducing new

F. Cuzzolin (Ed.): BELIEF 2014, LNAI 8764, pp. 124–133, 2014.

methods based on the notion of *update* [9], fixing the ageing coefficient and finalizing experiments. Concerning spatial events such as traffic jam, different methods have been proposed in [10,3,11]. We clarify in this paper first ideas given in [11], and develop and experiment a method for handling traffic jams.

2   Credal Methods for Handling Accident Events

2.1   Methods Descriptions

Vehicles exchange information about events on the road. Each created message M gives information about one event, it is represented as a 5-tuple (S, t, d, ℓ, m) :

- S is the source which has perceived the event;
- t is the type of the event;
- d indicates the date when the source S has created the message to inform about the event presence;
- ℓ is the location of the event;
- m is a mass function (MF) held by the source S and expressed on the frame $\Omega = \{\exists, \nexists\}$ where: $\exists$ stands for *the event which is of type M.t, is present at time M.d at location M.ℓ*; and $\nexists$ stands for *the event which is of type M.t, is not present at time M.d at location M.ℓ*.

An example of a message sent and then transferred is illustrated in Figure 1.

Vehicle v_1 (v_1, t, d, ℓ, m) sent   Vehicle v_2 (v_1, t, d, ℓ, m) transferred   Vehicle v_3

Fig. 1. Example of a message sent and transferred

In order to represent and manage information about events, traffic lanes are divided into small rectangular areas named **cells**. Their length depends on the event type. An event e is a couple (t, c) where t represents the event type and c is the cell where the event is located.

Obsolete messages in databases are deleted using a threshold, denoted Del_t depending on the type t of the event: each message M such that $\Delta(now, M.d) > Del_t$ with Δ a distance measure, is suppressed. In order to fix Del_t for the event type "accident", the proposed solution assumes that we have learned from a historical knowledge of accidents in a city that the duration of accidents D follows a normal distribution $D \sim \mathcal{N}(\mu, \sigma^2)$. Threshold Del_t is chosen such that $P(D \leq Del_t) = 99\%$, i.e. $Del_t = \mu + u_{.99} * \sigma$.

Descriptions of the six proposed methods using belief functions and a simple one are then given below. Methods are summarized in Table 1. Note that method n°1 to method n°4 have been introduced in [6].

Table 1. Methods summary dealing with local events

Method	Kept messages	Update?	Ageing	Combination
1	original	no	discounting	conjunctive
2	original	no	reinforcement	conjunctive
3	fusion only	no	discounting	conjunctive / cautious
4	fusion only	no	reinforcement	conjunctive / cautious
5	original	yes	discounting	conjunctive
6	original	yes	reinforcement	conjunctive
7	last message only (yes/no)	yes	no	no

Method n°1 – Keep Original Messages, Discount. Each vehicle has an internal database regrouping created and received messages, where all messages $M_{e,i}$ concerning the same event e are grouped into the same table M_e. All messages are kept in vehicle database and considered in fusion process.

In order to consider the messages ageing, the discounting operation [7, page 252] is used. It is defined by:

$$^{\alpha}m = (1 - \alpha)\, m + \alpha\, m_{\Omega} \,, \tag{1}$$

where $\alpha \in [0,1]$ is called the discount rate; coefficient $\beta = (1 - \alpha)$ represents the degree of reliability regarding the information provided.

Each message $M_{e,i}$ is discounted with a rate $\alpha_{e,i} = \frac{\Delta(now, M_{c,i}.d)}{Del_t}$, with this operation, over time $^{\alpha_{c,i}} M_{e,i}.m$ tends to the total ignorance m_{Ω}.

For each event in vehicle database, discounted MFs are then combined using the conjunctive rule of combination [8].

Finally, the pignistic probability [8] regarding the event presence is computed for each event.

In this method, the fusion result is not communicated to neighboring vehicles.

Method n°2 – Keep Original Messages, Reinforce. This method differs from the first method only by the ageing mechanism. The reinforcement mechanism [12] is used, it is defined by:

$$^{\nu}m = (1 - \nu)\, m + \nu\, m_A \,, \tag{2}$$

where $\nu \in [0,1]$ is the reinforcement rate, m_A is a categorical MF, and A is the element expected by the agent when the MF m is totally reinforced.

In this method, each message $M_{e,i}$ is reinforced with a rate $\nu_{e,i} = \frac{\Delta(now, M_{c,i}.d)}{Del_t}$, over time $^{\nu_{c,i}} M_{e,i}.m$ tends to $m_{\overline{\jmath}}$ meaning that event e has disappeared.

Method n°3 – Keep Only Fusion Result, Discount. Only the fusion results are kept in databases and exchanged between vehicles in this method.

A received message Mr concerning an event e already identified is fused with message M_e such that the new MF of M_e is obtained as follows:

- First the MF of the message having the oldest date among M_e and Mr is discounted to take into consideration its aging (rate equal to $\frac{|\Delta(Mr.d, M_c.d)|}{Del_t}$).
- Then if $Mr.S \cap M_e.S = \emptyset$, the new MF $M_e.m$ is obtained from the conjunctive combination of the corrected MF (among $M_e.m$ and $Mr.m$) and the non-corrected MF, otherwise the cautious rule [13] is used.
- The new set of sources $M_e.S$ is equal to $M_e.S \cup Mr.S$.
- The date of M_e becomes the most recent date among $M_e.d$ and $Mr.d$.
- To give an overview of the situation to the driver, for each event e, the MF $M_e.m$ is discounted with a rate $\alpha_e = \frac{\Delta(now, M_c.d)}{Del_t}$, and the pignistic probability is computed.

If the event e is not already identified in the vehicle database, message M_e is created with the attributes of Mr: $M_e.S = \{Mr.S\}$, $M_e.t = Mr.t$, $M_e.d = Mr.d$, $M_e.\ell = Mr.\ell$ and $M_e.m = Mr.m$.

The Algorithm 1 is used for the management of a received message.

Algorithm 1. Methods n°3 and n°4: management of a received message not already considered in vehicle database.

Require: A received message Mr.
Require: $Cell_t(\ell)$ returns the cell number for the type t on which ℓ is located.
Ensure: Message Mr processing, when Mr is not already considered in vehicle database.
  begin
  if $\exists M_e \in M$ t.q. $Mr.t = M_e.t$ and $Cell_{M_c.t}(M_e.\ell) = Cell_{Mr.t}(Mr.\ell)$ **then**
    $\{Mr$ corresponds to an event e already identified in $M.\}$
    if $Mr.d > M_e.d$ **then**
      $M_e.m \leftarrow \overset{\frac{|\Delta(M_e.d, Mr.d)|}{Del_{M_c.t}}}{} M_e.m$
      $M_e.d \leftarrow Mr.d$
    end if
    if $M_e.d > Mr.d$ **then**
      $Mr.m \leftarrow \overset{\frac{|\Delta(M_e.d, Mr.d)|}{Del_{Mr.t}}}{} Mr.m$
    end if
    if $M_e.S \cap Mr.S = \emptyset$ **then**
      $\{$The sources are independant.$\}$
      $M_e.m \leftarrow M_e.m \textcircled{\cap} Mr.m$
    else
      $\{$The sources are not independent.$\}$
      $M_e.m \leftarrow M_e.m \textcircled{\wedge} Mr.m$
    end if
    $M_e.S \leftarrow M_e.S \cup Mr.S$
    $M_e.\ell \leftarrow M_e.\ell \cup Mr.\ell$
  else
    $\{$A new event is detected.$\}$
    Create a new event e, and add Mr in the table Me.
  end if
  end

Note that the main difference between this method and the method proposed by Cherfaoui et al. in [3] is that in the latter, only one source is kept for each event, which does not allow to decide finely of the dependence between messages before fusing them.

Method n°4 – Keep Only Fusion Result, Reinforce. This method is a variant of the third method. The difference is the using of the reinforcement mechanism instead of the discounting mechanism, over time MF tends to $m_{\overline{\exists}}$.

Method n°5 – Keep Original Messages, Consider World Update, Discount. This method differs from the first method by considering the world update [9]. When a received message contradicts (in term of pignistic probabilities) the acquired knowledge in the vehicle database, the latter is updated instead of being rectified if the date of the received message is greater than the last update considered in the vehicle database. Messages before an update are considered as no more relevant and are suppressed. This suppression is processed before the fusion of messages, it is defined by Algorithm 2.

Algorithm 2. Methods n°5 and n°6: suppression of messages which dates are earlier than the last world update.

Require: Event (t, c) with t the type of the event and c the cell where the event is located.
Ensure: Suppression of messages to consider world update for the event (t, c).
  begin
  {Get the date of the earlier message informing that the event (t, c) is present.}
  $d_{\exists} \leftarrow maximum(M_{(t,c),i}.d)$ where $M_{(t,c),i}.m(\{\exists\}) > 0$.
  {Get the date of the earlier message informing that the event (t, c) is not present.}
  $d_{\overline{\exists}} \leftarrow maximum(M_{(t,c),i}.d)$ where $M_{(t,c),i}.m(\{\overline{\exists}\}) > 0$.
  Suppress all messages $M_{(t,c),i}$ having a date $M_{(t,c),i}.d \leq minimum(d_{\exists}, d_{\overline{\exists}})$.
  end

Method n°6 – Keep Original Messages, Consider World Update, Reinforce. This method differs from the previous method only by the use of the reinforcement mechanism instead of the discounting mechanism.

Method n°7 – Keep Only the Last Message yes/no. Messages inform if "yes" or "no" an event is present (confidence degree is equal to 100%), and only the last message is considered, it is given as a result to the driver. The aim is to compare the proposed methods using belief functions to this simple method in Section 2.2.

2.2   Experiments

Performance rates of models are measured for each type t of event and for each vehicle v by the adequacy to the reality of the information given to the driver. Formally, at each time step τ, the set equal to the union of the events present in the vehicle database and the existing events in the reality is considered and denoted by $E_t^{v,\tau}$, and performance rates are computed for each type t of event and for each vehicle v by:

$$Perf_t^{v,\tau} = 1 - \frac{\sum_{e \in E_t^{v,\tau}} (BetP_e^{v,\tau}(\{\exists\}) - R_e^\tau)^2}{\mid E_t^{\tau,v} \mid} \ ,$$ (3)

where: $R_e^\tau = 1$ if event e is present at time τ, 0 otherwise; $\mid E_t^{v,\tau} \mid$ is the cardinality of $E_t^{v,\tau}$; $BetP_e^{v,\tau}(\{\exists\})$ is the pignistic probability in vehicle v at time τ concerning the presence of the event e (if no message concerns event e in vehicle v database, $Betp_e^{v,\tau}(\{\exists\}) = 0$).

The experiments are realized using a developed Matlab^{TM} simulator [6]. The sampling period $\Delta\tau = 4$ seconds, this means that vehicles exchange their databases and messages are processed every 4 seconds. The range of wireless communication is 200 meters.

Created messages have all the same confidence degree: $m(\{\exists\}) = 0.6$ or $m(\{\nexists\}) = 0.6$.

Accident duration follows a normal distribution $D \sim \mathcal{N}(1800, 300^2)$, the deletion threshold is then obtained $Del_t = 2498$ seconds. Scenario is tested with different values of accident duration obtained from this normal distribution.

In this scenario, an accident occurs at the beginning of each simulation, and 20 different durations are tested.

Only 5 vehicles are present. One vehicle denoted by v receives from distinct sources four messages just after their creation, the first and second messages confirm the accident at 30% and 70% of its duration after its beginning, and the other messages deny the accident at 30% and 50% of its duration after its disappearance. The adequacy to the reality (the average over all the simulation) of vehicle v is illustrated in Figure 2 for each launch (20 durations) and each method. These tests are repeated 9 new times. The mean of the average and the mean of the standard deviation of the adequacy to the reality are presented for each method in Table 2.

These tests show that the used reinforcement mechanism is more in line with the accident disappearance than the discounting operation. In addition, the discounting mechanism does not manage correctly messages denying the event, indeed after the disappearance of an event, discount result tends to the ignorance, which means that the probability of the event presence increases over time while it should remain as low as possible. Before receiving the first message denying the accident, methods n°5 and n°6 give respectively the same result as methods n°1 and n°2. When the vehicle receives messages denying the accident, methods n°5 and n°6 stop considering old messages confirming the presence of the event. This allows to increase the performance when using the discounting mechanism;

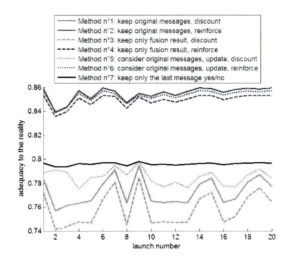

Fig. 2. Accident scenario: the average of the adequacy to the reality for each simulation

Table 2. Accident scenario: means of the average and the standard deviation of the adequacy to the reality

	All the simulation	Before accident disappearance	After accident disappearance
Method n°1	0.771984(0.00997779)	0.666177(0.00224502)	0.82572(0.01586986)
Method n°2	**0.855809**(0.00522433)	0.61829(0.0184514)	**0.975492**(0.01473972)
Method n°3	0.757644(0.01202747)	0.665513(0.00221531)	0.804534(0.01895642)
Method n°4	0.850178(0.00439378)	0.618887(0.0165816)	0.96674(0.01362776)
Method n°5	0.783468(0.00600582)	0.666177(0.00224502)	0.842962(0.00966614)
Method n°6	0.853815(0.00439366)	0.61829(0.0184514)	0.9725(0.01366174)
Method n°7	0.796106(0.000916845)	**0.696715**(0.001044568)	0.846654(0.001000312)

but it is not the case when using the reinforcement mechanism, because at this moment, the result of the old messages reinforced is closer to $m_{\overline{3}}$ than the result of the new message denying the accident. Simple method n°7 gives good results in this scenario for two reasons: created messages have a confidence equal to 100% and tell the reality; and messages denying the accident are received. Note that this method has bad results after the disappearance of the accident until receiving a first message denying the accident. Methods where only the fusion result is kept in vehicle database do not allow managing finely the obsolescence of messages before their combination. For this reason, they give a worse result than the other methods using belief functions.

3   A Credal Method for Handling Traffic Jam Events

3.1   Method Description

Traffic jam is a very dynamic event, for this reason it is important to update information in vehicle database when receiving more recent information contradicting the acquired knowledge in vehicle database. The first step of the proposed method for handling traffic jam events is the same as the methods n°5 and n°6 proposed for accident events, but in this method no ageing mechanism is employed. The threshold Del_t is used only to delete obsolete messages, it can be fixed according to a maximal value known from a historic knowledge (4 hours for example).

In order to predict the overall road situation when the vehicle database contains information about only some parts of the road, a secondary mechanism called *influence mechanism* is proposed to smooth and improve the overview of the situation given to driver. The result of this mechanism is not communicated to other vehicles. Traffic jam (TJ) is an extensive event evolving in the reverse direction of roads, and disappearing in the same direction of the traffic. The influence mechanism can be explained in the following manner:

– Let β_t be the influence rate.
– For each event (TJ, c) result obtained from the first step of the method:
  • If it informs that the cell c is occupied by a traffic jam, generate influences on following cells (Figure 3(a)) by discounting with a rate equal to $1 - \beta_t$, and stop this operation when arriving to a slowing down event like an accident (known in vehicle database) or a roundabout.
  • If it informs that the cell c is not occupied by a traffic jam, generate influences on previous cells (Figure 3(b)).

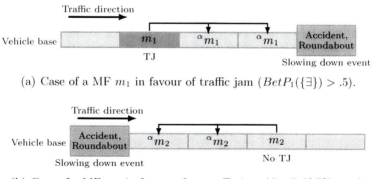

(a) Case of a MF m_1 in favour of traffic jam $(BetP_1(\{\exists\}) > .5)$.

(b) Case of a MF m_2 in favour of no traffic jam $(BetP_2(\{\not\exists\}) > .5)$.

Fig. 3. Illustrations of influences computations in the method dealing with traffic jams

For each cell, results of the first step and obtained influences are combined using the conjunctive rule of combination, and the pignistic probability is then computed.

In previous work [10,3], the spatiality of events are managed by considering the distance between the observed point and the points where information telling about the event presence is available. These methods do not take into consideration how traffic jam evolve and disappear according to the roads and their traffic direction.

3.2   Experiments

The scenario described in Figure 4 has been developed. A traffic jam appears progressively on a road, and disappears a few minutes later. A message is created to confirm the traffic jam, and another one is created to deny it after its disappearance.

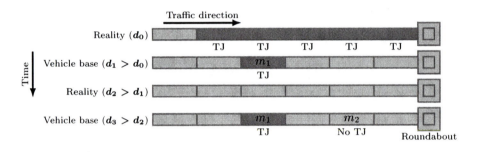

Fig. 4. Scenario: a traffic jam appears on the road and disappears a few minutes later

The proposed method is tested with and without applying the influence mechanism: $\beta = 0.8$ (which means that "the method know that a traffic jam is present, but it is not absolutely sure) and $\beta = 0$ respectively. The obtained mean of the adequacy to the reality for all vehicles present in the map (the map is 1.2km x 1.2km, so the traffic jam interests all vehicles) is equal to 0.6389 when applying the influence mechanism, and 0.2442 without the influence mechanism. This experiment shows the interest of the influence mechanism.

This scenario is also tested where vehicles create and receive messages concerning the traffic jam on all cells (confirm or deny). The proposed method for handling traffic jam event is compared to the second method for handling accident event. The obtained mean of the adequacy to the reality is respectively 0.9285 and 0.7452. This experiment shows the interest of considering world update, cells are considered not occupied once a first method denying the event is received (or created).

4   Conclusion and Future Work

In this paper, methods are proposed to exchange and manage information about accident and traffic jam events on the road in V2V communications using belief functions. Different strategies are compared concerning messages ageing; influences mechanisms and information considered and kept in internal databases.

Future work must consider irregular areas, other types of spatial events such as flog blanket, and links between different types of event. The used simulator is a research tool; a more realistic one has to be used in future work.

References

1. Car 2 car communication consortium C2C-CC, http://www.car-to-car.org/
2. Olariu, S., Weigle, M.C.: Vehicular networks: from theory to practice. 1st edn. Chapman & Hall/CRC (2009)
3. Cherfaoui, V., Denoeux, T., Cherfi, Z.L.: Distributed data fusion: application to confidence management in vehicular networks. In: International Conference on Information Fusion (FUSION 2008), Germany, pp. 846–853 (2008)
4. Ducourthial, B., Cherfaoui, V., Denoeux, T.: Self-stabilizing Distributed Data Fusion. In: Richa, A.W., Scheideler, C. (eds.) SSS 2012. LNCS, vol. 7596, pp. 148–162. Springer, Heidelberg (2012)
5. Bou Farah, M., Mercier, D., Lefèvre, É., Delmotte, F.: Towards a robust exchange of imperfect information in inter-vehicle ad-hoc networks using belief functions. In: IEEE Intelligent Vehicles Symposium, IV 2011, Baden-Baden, Germany, June 5-9, pp. 436–441 (2011)
6. Bou Farah, M., Mercier, D., Lefèvre, É., Delmotte, F.: A high-level application using belief functions for exchanging and managing uncertain events on the road in vehicular ad-hoc networks. Annals of Telecommunications: Special Issue on Belief Functions and Uncertainty Management in Networks and Telecommunication 69, 185–199 (2014)
7. Shafer, G.: A Mathematical Theory of Evidence. Princeton University Press, N.J. (1976)
8. Smets, P., Kennes, R.: The Transferable Belief Model. Artificial Intelligence 66, 191–243 (1994)
9. Katsuno, H., Mendelzon, A.: On the difference between updating a knowledge base and revising it. In: 2nd International Conference on Principles of Knowledge Representation and Reasoning (KR 1991), pp. 387–394 (1991)
10. Lang, J., Muller, P.: Plausible reasoning from spatial observations. In: 17th Conference in Uncertainty in Artificial Intelligence, Seattle, Washington, USA, pp. 285–292 (2001)
11. Bou Farah, M., Mercier, D., Lefèvre, É., Delmotte, F.: Exchanging dynamic and imprecise information in V2V networks with belief functions. In: 16th International IEEE Conference on Intelligent Transport Systems (ITSC 2013), The Hague, The Netherland, pp. 967–972 (2013)
12. Mercier, D., Denœux, T., Masson, M.-H.: Belief function correction mechanisms. In: Bouchon-Meunier, B., Magdalena, L., Ojeda-Aciego, M., Verdegay, J.-L., Yager, R.R. (eds.) Foundations of Reasoning under Uncertainty. STUDFUZZ, vol. 249, pp. 203–222. Springer, Heidelberg (2010)
13. Denœux, T.: The cautious rule of combination for belief fonctions and some extensions. In: 9th International Conference on Information Fusion (FUSION 2006), Florence, Italy, pp. 1–8 (2006)

Designing a Belief Function-Based Accessibility Indicator to Improve Web Browsing for Disabled People

Jean-Christophe Dubois, Yolande Le Gall, and Arnaud Martin

DRUID-IRISA, University of Rennes 1, rue Edouard Branly,
22300 Lannion, France
{Jean-Christophe.Dubois,Yolande.Le-Gall,Arnaud.Martin}@univ-rennes1.fr

Abstract. The purpose of this study is to provide an accessibility measure of webpages, in order to draw disabled users to the pages that have been designed to be accessible to them. Our approach is based on the theory of belief functions, using data which are supplied by reports produced by automatic web content assessors that test the validity of criteria defined by the WCAG 2.0 guidelines proposed by the World Wide Web Consortium (W3C) organization. These tools detect errors with gradual degrees of certainty and their results do not always converge. For these reasons, to fuse information coming from the reports, we choose to use an information fusion framework which can take into account the uncertainty and imprecision of information as well as divergences between sources. Our accessibility indicator covers four categories of deficiencies. To validate the theoretical approach in this context, we propose an evaluation completed on a corpus of 100 most visited French news websites, and 2 evaluation tools. The results obtained illustrate the interest of our accessibility indicator.

Keywords: Belief functions, Web accessibility, Human factors, Measurement, Document analysis.

1 Introduction

The Web constitutes today an essential source of information and communication. While users have a growing interest in terms of social, cultural and economic value, and in spite of legislations and recommendations of the W3C community for making websites more accessible, its accessibility remains hardly efficient for some disabled or ageing users. Actually, making websites accessible and usable by disabled people is a challenge [8] that society needs to overcome [1].

To measure the accessibility of a webpage, several accessibility metrics have been developed [16]. Evaluations are based on the failure to comply with the recommendations of standards, using automatic evaluation tools. They often give a final value, continuous or discrete, to represent content accessibility. However, the fact remains that tests on accessibility criteria are far from being trivial [2].

F. Cuzzolin (Ed.): BELIEF 2014, LNAI 8764, pp. 134–142, 2014.

Evaluation reports of automatic assessors contain errors considered as certain, but also warnings or potential problems which are uncertain. Moreover there are differences between assessor evaluations, even for errors considered as certain.

This work provides a new measure of accessibility and an information fusion framework to fuse information coming from the reports of automatic assessors allowing search engines to re-rank their results according to an accessibility level, as some users would like [10]. This accessibility indicator considers several categories of deficiencies. Our approach is based on the theory of the belief functions adapted to take into account the defects of accessibility given by several automatic assessors seen as information sources, the uncertainty of their results, as well as the possible conflicts between the sources.

In the sections 2 and 3 we will give a description of accessibility tools based on a recent standard and of data provided in their reports. In the 4th section, we will describe the principles of our indicator and develop how we implement the belief functions. In the 5th part, we will present an experiment before concluding.

2   Defect Detection of Webpage Accessibility

Various accessibility standards propose recommendations for improving accessibility of webpages. The Web Content Accessibility Guidelines (WCAG 2.0) [3] proposed by the W3C normalization organization, constitutes an international reference in the field. These guidelines cover a wide range of disabilities (visual, auditory, physical, speech, cognitive, etc.) and several layers of guidance are provided:

– 4 overall principles: perception, operability, understandability & robustness;
– testable success criteria: for each guideline, testable success criteria are provided. Every criterion is associated to one of the 3 defined conformance levels (A, AA and AAA), each representing a requirement of accessibility for users.

Several automatic accessibility assessors, based on various accessibility standards, have been developed [5] for IT professionals. Their limits depend on the automatic tests. Because it is at present not possible to test some criteria about the quality of some pages, some assessor results are given with ambiguity. Consequently, the existing automatic assessors look for the criteria which are not met and give the defects according to 3 levels of validity: the number of errors, which are estimated certain, the number of likely problems (warnings) whose reality is not guaranteed and the number of potential problems (also called generic or non testable) which leads to a complete uncertainty on the tested criterion accessibility.

Finally, even though the results obtained by different assessors match for some tested common criteria, results can differ, even for errors considered as certain.

3   Proposed Accessibility Indicator

After a request, the indicator has to supply information describing to users the accessibility level of each webpage proposed by a search engine. Presented simultaneously with these pages, the indicators' information cover two aspects:

- the accessibility for categories of deficiencies: as previously proposed for accessibility estimation [6] we use 4 major categories: visual, hearing, motor and cognitive deficiencies, as defined by [15]. They are called "deficiency frames";
- the level of accessibility for each deficiency frame.

Collecting results from several assessors has allowed us to benefit from each of their performance. In addition, it strengthens accessibility evaluation for similar results and manages conflicts in case of disagreements. Automatic assessors check a set of criteria which correspond to many deficiencies. As our accessibility evaluation varies for every deficiency frame, our method consists in selecting the relevant criteria for each deficiency frame and then balancing each criterion to consider the difficulties met by users in case of failure. This weighting is based on the criterion conformance level (A, AA, AAA), which corresponds to decreasing priorities (A: most important, etc.). The errors and problems detected for every criterion of the accessibility standard affect the accessibility indicator of the Web content tested according to the deficiency frame the criterion belongs to, its weighting within the frame, the number of occurrences when it is analyzed as a defect in the webpage and the defect's degree of certainty (error, likely or potential problem).

4   Defect Detection and Accessibility Evaluation

After collecting webpage Uniform Resource Locators (URL_p) selected by a search engine from a request, these addresses are supplied to the accessibility assessors and successively for each page, we detect accessibility defects, then estimate accessibility level by deficiency frame for each assessor, before fusing the data by deficiency frame and taking the decision for every deficiency frame [7].

4.1   Assessor Evaluations of Selected Pages

Each URL_p is submitted to the accessibility evaluation tests by each assessor i that tests all the criteria k of the WCAG 2.0 standard, and the following data are collected by a filter that extracts the required data for each deficiency frame:

- $N_{k,i}^e$: errors observed for a criterion k by an assessor i;
- $N_{k,i}^c$: correct checkpoints for a criterion k by an assessor i;
- $T_{k,i}^e$: tests that can induce errors for a criterion k by an assessor i;
- $N_{k,i}^l$: likely problems detected for a criterion k by an assessor i;
- $T_{k,i}^l$: tests that can induce likely problems for a criterion k by an assessor i;
- $N_{k,i}^p$: potential problems suspected for a criterion k by an assessor i;
- $T_{k,i}^p$: tests that can induce potential problems for a criterion k by an assessor i;
- T_i : total tests by an assessor i, with:

$$T_i = \sum_k (N_{k,i}^e + N_{k,i}^l + N_{k,i}^p + N_{k,i}^c) \tag{1}$$

4.2   Accessibility Indicator Level of the Pages

To model initial information including uncertainties, the reliability of the assessors seen as information sources and their possible conflicts, we use the theory
of belief functions [4] [13]. Our objective is to define if a webpage is accessible
(Ac) or not accessible ($\overline{Ac}$) and to supply an indication by deficiency frame.
Consequently, these questions can be handled independently for every deficiency
frame $\Omega_h = \{Ac, \overline{Ac}\}$. We can consider every power set $2^{\Omega_h} = \{\emptyset, Ac, \overline{Ac}, \Omega\}$.

The estimation of the accessibility Ac for a deficiency frame h and a source i
(assessor) is estimated from the number of correct tests for each of the criteria
k occurring in this frame, and from their conformance level represented by α_k:

$$E(Ac)_{h,i} = \frac{\sum\limits_{k}(N_{k,i}^c * \alpha_k)}{T_i} \tag{2}$$

The estimation of the non accessibility $\overline{Ac}$ for a deficiency frame h and a source
i is estimated from the number of errors for each of the criteria k occurring in this
frame, and from the α_k coefficient. A weakening β_i^e coefficient is also introduced
to model the degree of certainty of the error:

$$E(\overline{Ac})_{h,i} = \frac{\sum\limits_{k}(N_{k,i}^e * \alpha_k * \beta_i^e)}{T_{k,i}^e} \tag{3}$$

The estimation of the ignorance Ω_h for a deficiency frame h and a source i is
estimated from the number of likely and potential problem for each of the criteria
k occurring in this frame, and from the α_k coefficient. The weakening coefficients
β_i^l or β_i^p are also used to model the degree of certainty of the problem:

$$E(\Omega_{h,i}) = \frac{\sum\limits_{k}(N_{k,i}^l * \alpha_k * \beta_i^l + N_{k,i}^p * \alpha_k * \beta_i^p)}{\sum\limits_{k}(T_{k,i}^l + T_{k,i}^p)} \tag{4}$$

The mass functions of the subsets of 2^{Ω_h} are computed from the estimations:

$$m(Ac)_{h,i} = \frac{E(Ac)_{h,i}}{E(Ac)_{h,i} + E(\overline{Ac})_{h,i} + E(\Omega)_{h,i}} \tag{5}$$

$$m(\overline{Ac})_{h,i} = \frac{E(\overline{Ac})_{h,i}}{E(Ac)_{h,i} + E(\overline{Ac})_{h,i} + E(\Omega)_{h,i}} \tag{6}$$

$$m(\Omega)_{h,i} = \frac{E(\Omega)_{h,i}}{E(Ac)_{h,i} + E(\overline{Ac})_{h,i} + E(\Omega)_{h,i}} \tag{7}$$

In addition, the source reliability can be modeled [11] with a δ_i coefficient, which constitutes a benefit when some assessors are more efficient than others:

$$
\begin{cases}
m^{\delta_i}(Ac)_{h,i} = \delta_i * m(Ac)_{h,i} \\
m^{\delta_i}(\overline{Ac})_{h,i} = \delta_i * m(\overline{Ac})_{h,i} \\
m^{\delta_i}(\Omega)_{h,i} = 1 - \delta_i * (1 - m(\Omega)_{h,i})
\end{cases}
\tag{8}
$$

4.3   Merging Assessor Results and Decision-Making

Once the masses for each assessor have been obtained, a fusion of the results is conducted by deficiency frame, using the conjunctive rule [14], to combine them and give information in the form of a mass function. These rule properties, which strengthen common results and manage conflicts between sources, are particularly relevant in this context, to deal with divergences between assessor evaluations. To calculate the final decision $D_h(URL_p)$ for a page by deficiency frame, we use the pignistic probability [14].

There are several ways of presenting the accessibility indicator to users. To visualize the deficiency frames, existing specific pictograms are effective. To present the accessibility level we discretize the decision into 5 levels (very good, good, moderate, bad or very bad accessibility) using thresholds and visualized it by an "arrow":

- if $D_h < S_1$, the Web content accessibility is very bad ($\downarrow$),
- if $S_1 < D_h < S_2$, the Web content accessibility is bad ($\searrow$),
- if $S_2 < D_h < S_3$, the Web content accessibility is moderate ($\rightarrow$),
- if $S_3 < D_h < S_4$, the Web content accessibility is good ($\nearrow$),
- if $S_4 < D_h$, the Web content accessibility is very good ($\uparrow$).

5   Experiments

To validate our approach, we present here the results obtained on a set of 100 news Websites, among the most visited ones, all referenced by the OJD[1] organization which provides certification and publication of attendance figures for websites. We test their homepages, following a study [12] concluding that their usability is predictive of the whole site. We chose two open source assessors AChecker, (source 1) [9], and TAW (source 2) from which we extract automatically the accessibility test results. Weight and threshold values given in Table 1 were previously empirically defined from Webpages[2] assumed to be accessible.

The results of these sources are summarized in Fig. 1 for the 3 levels of certainty defects. The box plots present how their defects are distributed: minimum

---

[1] OJD: `http://www.ojd.com/Chiffres/Le-Numerique/Sites-Web/Sites-Web-GP`
[2] Sites labeled by Accessiweb: `http://www.accessiweb.org/index.php/galerie.html`

Table 1. Constant values for our accessibility metric

		A, AA, AAA conformance levels	1 ; 0.8 ; 0.6
Weightings	α_1 ; α_2 ; α_3		
	β_i^e ; β_i^l ; β_i^p	Certainty levels of errors or problems	1 ; 0.5 ; 1
	δ_1 ; δ_2 ; α_3	AChecker and TAW reliabilities (sources)	1 ; 1
Thresholds	S1; S2; S3; S4	Accessibility indicator levels	0.6; 0.7; 0.8; 0.9

and maximum (whiskers), 1st (bottom box plot) and 3rd quartiles (top box plot) and average (horizontal line). We observe similarities between the assessors' results for the errors detected as certain, but also huge differences for the likely (warnings) and potential (non testable) problems. The number of likely problems is almost null for AChecker and the potential one remains always the same for TAW.

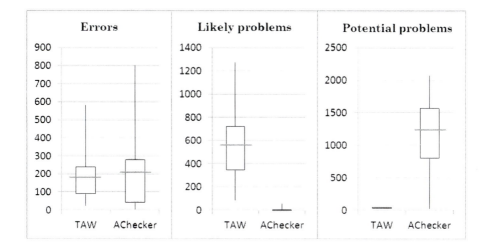

Fig. 1. Results of automatic assessors

The detected defects are taken into account in our accessibility indicator results presented in Fig. 2. The mass function values of accessibility $m(Ac)$ for the 2 sources, TAW and AChecker, and the fusion result are visualized for 3 deficiency frames among the 4, and globally for all deficiencies.

Firstly, we can see that $m(Ac)$ is not evenly distributed between the 2 sources: their distributions of errors are comparable even if there is a larger range for AChecker; however the mass function of accessibility is smaller for AChecker compared to TAW. This is due to the more numerous potential problems (non testable criteria) detected by the AChecker assessor, increasing substantially the denominator in the computation of $m(Ac)$ (Eq. 5). By the way, the values of $E(\Omega)$ and consequently of $m(\Omega)$, are more important, as the β_i^p weight for potential problems is 2 times higher than β_i^l for the likely problems (warnings).

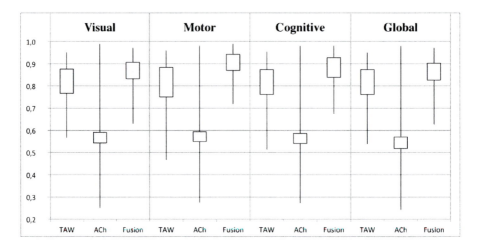

Fig. 2. Accessibility indicator results

We can also notice that the fusion result obtained by the conjunctive rule strengthens the mass functions of the 2 assessors.

In this corpus, visual and cognitive deficiencies have a higher impact on content accessibility than the motor ones. This is logical for news websites, as their homepages include a large number of images. By the way, the motor indicator is less impacted, in particular by the lack of alternatives for images, useful for visual and cognitive deficiencies. Finally, we observe a similarity between the visual and global indicators, as around 80% of all the checkpoints concern visual deficiencies and also because these controls are properly taken into account by assessors.

Table 2. Examples of detailed accessibility results by deficiency frame

Web content (URL_p)	Decision			
	Visual	Motor	Cognitive	Global
LeParisien.fr	0.972 ↑	0.989 ↑	0.974 ↑	0.971 ↑
Famili.fr	0.769 →	0.924 ↑	0.838 ↗	0.766 ↗
Arte.tv	0.701 →	0.718 →	0.717 →	0.686 ↘
LePoint.fr	0.630 ↘	0.725 →	0.673 ↘	0.627 ↘

In Table 2 are presented detailed results for several sites with significant indicator result differences. For examples, *LePoint.fr* and *Arte.tv*, respectively 19th and 33th most consulted websites in France, obtain only 0.627 and 0.686 for the global result, whereas *LeParisien.fr*, ranked 12th, reaches 0.971.

For *Family.fr* we observe differences between the deficiencies, nevertheless focus on accessibility generally benefits all deficiencies on the whole corpus.

6   Conclusion

We present an indicator estimating webpage accessibility levels for distinct categories of deficiencies, in order to supply easily understandable accessibility information to users on pages proposed by a search engine. Our method based on belief function theory fuses results from several automatic assessors and considers their uncertainties. An accurate modelization of the assessor characteristics and of the impact of defect guideline criteria on accessibility is proposed. An experiment performed on a set of 100 news websites validates the method, which benefits from each of the assessor performances on specific criterion tests. Our future research will focus on the implementation of a user's personal weighting to balance the importance of criteria.

References

1. Abascal, J., Arrue, M., Fajardo, I., Garay, N., Tomhas, J.: The use of guidelines to automatically verify web accessibility. Universal Access in the Information Society 3(1), 71–79 (2004)
2. Brajnik, G.: Comparing accessibility evaluation tools: a method for tool effectiveness. Universal Access in the Information Society 3(3-4), 252–263 (2004)
3. Brajnik, G.: Web Accessibility Testing: When the Method is the Culprit. In: International Conference on Computers Helping People with Special Needs, ICCHP 2006, pp. 156–163 (2006)
4. Brajnik, G.: Validity and Reliability of Web Accessibility Guidelines. In: Proceedings of the 11th International ACM SIGACCESS Conference on Computers and Accessibility, ASSETS, pp. 131–138 (2009)
5. Caldwell, B., Cooper, M., Guarino Reid, L., Vanderheiden, G.: Web Content Accessibility Guidelines (WCAG) 2 (December 11, 2008),
   http://www.w3.org/TR/WCAG20/
6. Dempster, A.P.: Upper and Lower probabilities induced by a multivalued mapping. Annals of Mathematical Statistics 38, 325–339 (1967)
7. Dubois, J.-C., Le Gall, Y., Martin, M.: Software Engineering System for the Analysis of Accessibility Data. Patent No. 1451562, Filed February 26th 2014
8. European Disability Strategy 2010-20: A Renewed Commitment to a Barrier-Free Europe. COM 636 final (2010)
9. Gay, G., Qi Li, C.: AChecker: open, interactive, customizable, web accessibility checking. In: W4A International Cross Disciplinary Conference on Web Accessibility, vol. 33, ACM Press (2010)
10. Ivory, M.Y., Yu, S., Gronemyer, K.: Search result exploration: a preliminary study of blind and sighted users' decision making and performance. CHI Extended Abstracts, pp. 1453–1456. ACM Press (2004)
11. Martin, A., Osswald, C., Dezert, J., Smarandache, F.: General combination rules for qualitative and quantitative beliefs. Journal of Advances in Information Fusion 3(2), 67–82 (2008)

12. Nielsen, J., Tahir, M.: Homepage Usability: 50 Websites Deconstructed. New Riders Publishing (2001)
13. Shafer, G.: A mathematical theory of evidence. Princeton University Press (1976)
14. Smets, P.: Belief Functions: the Disjunctive Rule of Combination and the Generalized Bayesian Theorem. International Journal of Approximate Reasoning 9, 1–35 (1993)
15. Vanderheiden, G.C., Vanderheiden, K.R.: Accessible design of consumer products: guidelines for the design of consumer products to increase their accessibility to people with disabilities or who are aging. Madison - WI, Trace R&D Center (1991)
16. Vigo, M., Brajnik, G.: Automatic web accessibility metrics: where we are and where we can go. Interacting with Computers 3(2), 137–155 (2011)

Belief Reasoning Model for Mapping Public Participation in Transport Planning

Nopadon Kronprasert[1,*] and Antti P. Talvitie[2]

[1] Excellence Center in Infrastructure Technology and Transportation Engineering,
Department of Civil Engineering, Chiang Mai University, Chiang Mai, Thailand
`nopkron@gmail.com`
[2] Aalto University, Espoo, Finland
`antti.talvitie@aalto.fi`

Abstract. Public inquiry plays an essential role in the planning process of transport investment and improvement projects. It helps to ensure that decisions are made to achieve project's goals and meet public needs. In public inquiries of transport planning process, policy-makers engage in dialogue in which the reasonableness and beliefs in their judgments are often questioned. Different stakeholders reason and provide evidence in support of their preferences, but these opinions are normally conflicting and ambiguous. This ambiguity is usually expressed as a "I don't know" opinion, but ignored in the analyses. This paper proposes a belief reasoning model as a goal-oriented decision-making method for finding a transport alternative that best achieves the project's goals. The proposed method is applied to evaluate a real-world public transport alternatives analysis. The proposed method provides a means for the planners and citizens to present their own logic and justifications during the public inquiry process.

Keywords: transport planning, decision-making, public participation, belief reasoning, evidence theory, uncertainty.

1 Introduction

Planning of highway, rail, and public transport projects is a multidisciplinary process governed by laws and policies in many countries, which asks for the consideration of a comprehensive set of factors and inclusion of stakeholder inputs and feedbacks. This makes transport planning and decision-making processes complex and requires negotiations among stakeholders. Often transport planning cannot advance because there is a lack of agreement about goal achievement, predicted outcomes, and expected performances of the project.

This study considers the planning of transport investment and improvement projects as a reasoning-building process to advance a desirable course of actions. A series of actions which achieve goals give details of chained relations in a reasoning structure. The study approaches public transport decisions as decisions under

---

* Corresponding author.

F. Cuzzolin (Ed.): BELIEF 2014, LNAI 8764, pp. 143–152, 2014.

uncertainty of which transport analysts and planners have incomplete knowledge or lack of information [6]. A new approach for goal-oriented transport planning deliberations is proposed that models decision systems in a logical manner and employs available even if uncertain knowledge and inconsistent opinions in supporting decision-making.

2   Issues of Current Transport Planning Process

In a comprehensive transport planning and decision-making practices, multi-criteria decision-making approaches have been commonly used for evaluating transport alternatives. The decision tree structure and deterministic values are often favored by planners and analysts because of its visualization of the decision structure and the simplicity of mathematical operation used in the analyses.

These traditional transport project evaluation approaches lack transparency, and clearly reasoned justifications for preferring a specific transport alternative, in the presence of complicated chains of reasoning and uncertainty of information. In reality, transport analysts and planners develop implicit reasoning chains when evaluating transport alternatives; but, that reasoning is unstructured and undocumented [10]. This causes difficulties in knowing and understanding the real reasons for complex decisions because there are no measures for inconsistency, conflicts, omissions and achievement of goals. Therefore, in practice, current evaluation and planning approaches are not sufficient for communicating decisions because the decision variables and criteria are not supported in a fact-based manner.

This paper views evaluation of transport alternatives as a complex reasoning process, which consists of various elements of both transportation and non-transportation nature and involves diverse groups of stakeholders and conflicting opinions and incomplete information.

3   Belief Reasoning Method

3.1   Structure of Belief Reasoning

This study uses 'belief reasoning' method, and applies a reasoning mapping structure [5, 8, 11] and a propagation of belief values in evidence theory [1, 2, 3, 7] for reasoning process.

A reasoning map shown in Fig. 1 is constructed for evaluating the alternatives. It consists of boxes connected with links, which present the chain of reasoning of a collection of propositions and describe the presumed cause-and-effect relationships among them. For evaluating transport alternatives, the reasoning map connects the set of transport system characteristics (Di) to the project's goals (Gi). The relationships between the two are described by a series of performances and impacts (Ci). The reasoning map is useful in decision analysis because it is easy to explain and is applicable in brainstorming and discussions, and for clarifying relationships, issues and uncertainties.

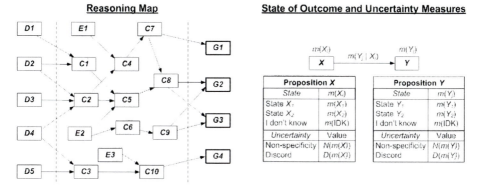

Fig. 1. Structure of reasoning map

Two steps are needed for constructing the reasoning maps how the proposed transport alternatives would support and influence the achievement of goals of the project. First, the transport project's goals (G_i), the collection of variables that describe the characteristics of the systems (D_i) and the exogenous factors, such as forecast travel conditions (E_i) are identified in the planning process. The goals (G_i) reflect the purposes of the proposed projects. The designation of the alternatives and the project description define the variables $(D_i$ and $E_i)$ in the reasoning map.

Second, the reasoning chains that determine the causalities are developed by bridging the relationships between the alternatives and the project's goals. The chains of reasoning are developed using performance measures and arguments about alternatives (documented or developed in the planning process). They can be input-output relations, cause-and-effect relations, or inferences for particular actions. The reasoning maps are scrutinized by the planners and informed by public input before further analysis.

Once the reasoning chains are developed, knowledge (or evidence) about every premise and every relation in the reasoning chains are elicited from experts and planners and citizen groups. These "informants" assign belief values to every state in premise $(D_i$ and $E_i)$ and every state in relation shown in Fig. 1.

Belief in an outcome for which two reasoning chains contribute or two belief distributions (points of view) can also be combined using the aggregate operator [7]. It builds up the belief values (or reduces the degree of ignorance, "I don't know") of stakeholders when supporting pieces of evidence are combined.

3.2 Mathematical Formulation of Belief Reasoning

The following calculation processes are performed to evaluate the transportation alternatives.

- The transportation alternatives are evaluated based on the belief values for achieving the specified goals.

- The trustworthiness of the reasoning process is evaluated based on the measures of uncertainty, non-specificity, and discord associated with available information.
- The critical reasoning chains that significantly influence the outcome are determined based on the sensitivity analysis.

Belief Propagation. Using the belief inference process, the belief values (m) as shown in Fig. 1 are propagated from the input (X_i) to the consequences/outcomes (Y_j) as expressed in Eq.(1) and the process is repeated all the way to the individual goals (G_i). Once the belief value for achieving the individual goals, $m(G_i)$, are calculated, Belief measure (*Bel*) and Plausibility (*Pl*) measure can be calculated by Eqs.(2) and (3), which indicate the conservative and optimistic measures of achieving the goals. These two measures are derived from the distributions of belief values (m). $Bel(G_i)$ is measured by summing all the consistent evidence pointing to goal G_i. $Pl(G_i)$ is the weight of non-conflicting evidence toward goal G_i, obtained by summing the non-conflicting belief values for outcome G_i.

$$m(Y_j) = \sum_{Xi \subseteq X} m(X_i) \times m(Y_j/X_i) \tag{1}$$

$$Bel(G_i) = \sum_{Gk|Gk \subseteq Gi} m(G_k) \tag{2}$$

$$Pl(Gi) = \sum_{Gk|Gk \cap Gi \neq \varnothing} m(G_k) \tag{3}$$

Uncertainty Propagation. This step is to measure the trustworthiness of reasoning process. Uncertainty is the lack of knowledge (or ambiguity of information used). Measuring uncertainty of information and knowledge helps identify information needs in the reasoning chains and promotes discourse in the decision-making process. In this step, the amount of information-based uncertainty in a reasoning chain is quantified using the non-specificity and discord measures in evidence theory as shown in Eqs.(4) and (5). Non-specificity, $N(m(X))$, refers to uncertainty due to imprecise knowledge about X. $N(m(X))$ increases when the belief value of "I don't know" increases and the belief values on the specific states decreases. The discord measure, $D(m(X))$, refers to uncertainty due to conflicting opinions about X. $D(m(X))$ increases when the belief values of two or more states are the same [7]. They measure the quality of information given to the transport analysts.

$$N(m(X)) = \sum_{Xi \subseteq X} \{m(X_i) \times \log_2 |X_i|\} \tag{4}$$

$$D(m(X)) = \sum_{Xi \subseteq X} \{m(X_i) \times \log_2(\sum_{Xj \subseteq X} [m(X_j) \times |X_i \cap X_j|/|X_j|])\} \tag{5}$$

where Xi is the set of outcome associated with each box in a reasoning map, $|Xi|$ is the size of subset X, and $\log_2|Xi|$ is the bit of information needed to find the solution for the binary problem.

Identification of Critical Reasoning Chains. This step is to identify the strong and weak reasoning chains, which is necessary to gauge validity of reasoning. This helps determine which characteristics of alternatives affect the decision most, and provide information on how to improve the alternatives in order to improve goal achievement. Given the belief distributions attached to each attribute in a reasoning map, one can determine whether a reasoning chain is more influential than the other chains. To identify the critical chain in the reasoning map involves finding the variable that most influence the degree of goal achievement. This sensitivity analysis is done by comparing the degree of goal achievement when a particular variable is removed from the reasoning map. The larger the difference of the degrees of goal achievement between 'with and without' a particular variable, the more that variable affects goal achievement. The determination of critical reasoning chains is conducted backward (from the goal node to the decision nodes) by comparing the importance measures among its preceding nodes and selecting that preceding node, which has the highest difference.

4   Application to Transport Planning

The proposed method was applied in Alternatives Analysis in a case study of an evolving public transport investment project in Virginia, USA. The Streetcar alternative is evaluated and compared to the Bus Rapid Transit alternative with respect to five goals of the project—mobility, economic development, livability and sustainability, multimodal transport system, and safety [9].

The reasoning map represents opinions of planners from transit and regional planning entities and allows "I don't know" opinion; ideally citizen views would also be collected. The reasoning map was first drawn up by ten transport experts. The belief values, which represent the confidence of opinions associated with each causal link, were assigned next. The mechanism for propagating the belief values along the chains was applied, and the degree of belief for achieving the goals was obtained. Finally, a measure of uncertainty associated with each variable and goal was calculated to assess the quality of information and the reasons for the preferred alternative.

The study presents the model results as follows. First, the reasoning map configuration is shown. Second, the degrees of goal achievement and their uncertainty measures are discussed. Finally, the critical reasons supporting the goals are determined.

4.1   Reasoning Maps for Goal Achievement

The reasoning map that was developed is composed of 91 variables (22 decision variables, 2 exogenous variables, 62 consequences/outcomes, and 5 goals). For each variable, two possible states of outcomes exist: "Agree" and "Disagree." The "I don't know" state is added for non-specific opinion.

Fig. 2 is an example of the reasoning map for the goal of "Economic Development". The reasoning maps for the other goals are not shown. The boxes on the left column present the decision variables of the transit technology, and the box on the right column shows the goal chosen for illustration purpose. The intermediate boxes which connect the decision variables and goals are a series of interrelated consequences and performances. In the analyses, some variables in one map may be connected to the reasoning maps for the other four goals.

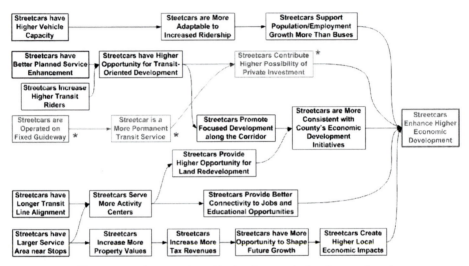

Fig. 2. Reasoning map for achieving "economic development" goal

4.2   Degrees of Goal Achievement and Uncertainty Measures

Two transit mode alternatives are compared: Streetcar and Bus Rapid Transit (BRT). The belief values that the Streetcar achieves the goals of the project relative to the BRT alternative are evaluated.

Table 1 presents the degrees of goal achievement and their associated uncertainty measures of the Streetcar alternative relative to the BRT alternative. There is agreement among the planners that the Streetcar alternative supports most of the goals of the corridor project at high degrees of achievement: 0.803-0.953 for "Mobility," 0.911-0.982 for "Economic development," 0.949-0.999 for "Livability and Sustainability." The exception is for "Multi-modal Transport System," for which the agreement is low (0.149-0.352). Achieving "Safe Environment" is about the same (no difference between two alternatives). The lower values of the degrees of achievement of individual goals represents the conservative values (Bel) and the upper values represent the optimistic values (Pl), the sum of belief values attached to "Agree" and "IDK."

Table 1. Belief and uncertainty measures of goal achievement (Streetcar vs. BRT)

Goals	Degrees of goal achievement			Uncertainty measures		
	Agree	Disagree	IDK	N(m)	D(m)	Total[c]
Mobility	0.803	0.047	0.150	0.150	0.293	0.443
Economic development	0.911	0.018	0.071	0.071	0.148	0.219
Livability and sustainability	0.949	0.001	0.050	0.050	0.041	0.091
Multi-modal transport	0.149	0.648[a]	0.203	0.203	0.567	0.770
Safe environment	0.012	0.961[b]	0.027	0.027	0.099	0.126

[a] It is not believed that Streetcar would support multi-modal transport compared to the BRT.

[b] It is not believed that Streetcar would provide safer environment than BRT.

[c] The maximum uncertainty of opinions associated with individual goal is $\log_2(2) = 1.000$ as there are two possible outcomes: "Agree" and "Disagree."

The high degree of consensus among the planners was not shared by the affected interest along the project corridor. In the public meetings there was a distinct division: the older people favored the BRT while the younger favored the Streetcar. There were some young renters in the meeting for whom Streetcar and TOD meant "transit oriented displacement"—and not transit-oriented development—and economic development in the corridor would require low income residents to move further out from the city to a more affordable rent location.

5   Discussion

The proposed approach has practical value in two respects. First, it quantitatively measures the degree that the selected alternative achieves individual goals. This enables the affected interest to understand and assess the strength not only of the reasoning process, but also of the planning process and the alternatives considered. Because it incorporates the notion of "I don't know" in the calculation of the 'truth', both the conservative and optimistic views of the degree of goal achievement are obtained.

The reasoning map, the associated belief values of each variable and interrelationship help identify the critical links that would make the most important contributions to the degree of goal achievement. Once the critical nodes and links are identified, the planners can pinpoint the relationships which should be studied more to improve the strength of the reasoning process.

5.1   Effects of "I Don't Know" Opinions

Fig. 3 shows the effects of the "I don't know" opinion on the achievement of individual goals measured by Belief (Bel) and Plausibility (Pl) measures. The sensitivity of "I don't know" opinion is tested by increasing the belief value of "I don't know," m(IDK), for all input variables from 0 to 1 with an increment of 0.1, and proportionally decreasing the belief values of other outcomes. When the "Experts" are very certain about their opinions, m(IDK)=0, then the Belief (Bel) and Plausibility (Pl) measures are equal. When "I don't know" increases the difference between Bel and Pl measures increases rapidly. The Bel value decreases since evidence is less certain. The Pl value increases because it represents "optimism" about the outcome ("if you don't know, then everything is possible"). The Bel measure is a conservative one ("if you don't know, then it is unlikely that the possible happens"). The difference between the two measures indicates the degree of non-specificity about goal achievement.

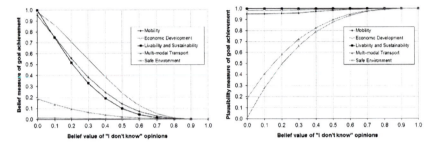

Fig. 3. Effects of ignorance (I don't know) on belief and plausibility of goal achievement

5.2   Critical Reasons

A sensitivity analysis was performed to identify the critical link(s) that most influence the support of the Streetcar alternative. The critical chains contain the variables that highly support the belief of achieving a goal. The critical reasoning chain that influenced the most the achievement of goals is highlighted in red in Fig. 2. Should there be much uncertainty in achieving a goal by a particular alternative; the critical chain would indicate where more resources should be employed to increase knowledge and to reduce the uncertainty or ambiguity.

In Fig. 2, showing the "Economic Development" goal, Streetcar would enhance higher economic development than BRT as shown in Table 1. It is believed that a fixed rail infrastructure is a permanent and long-term transit investment. It would become a corridor landmark and community resource. It would bring more private investment and would encourage more economic activities along the corridor.

6   Conclusions

The principal advantages of the belief reasoning method in transport planning process are: (i) potential to model the planners' and stakeholders' reasoning process in the evaluation of transport alternatives; (ii) flexibility to handle different opinions which may be incomplete, uninformed or informed, or conflicting elicited from multiple actors; (iii) capability to measure uncertainty associated with information or knowledge to focus debates and improve analyses; and (iv) documented paper trail and record about the reasoning process leading to the recommendation for the selection of an alternative. All of these are useful for before-and-after studies and analyses of anticipated or predicted outcomes and will improve the scientific knowledge-base on how decisions are reasoned. The proposed approach clarifies transport decision-making processes where multiple experts or actors are involved, and knowledge of individual experts is fragmented and possibly conflicting.

There are two possible drawbacks of the proposed approach in transport planning. First, the reasoning map can be manipulated by the analysts/planners. This manipulation is mitigated by the greater transparency of the process than in the traditional approaches in which the analysts/planners' reasoning is not revealed in a reasoning map. It may be an advantage to the planners to know the stakeholders' evaluations and have opportunity to understand their concerns and reasoning patterns. It is also possible to customize the map to reflect different stakeholders' reasoning paths. This is an important issue. The advantage of the reasoning map and process is the possibility to conduct plan development and plan evaluation in parallel. The planner can legitimately use the reasoning map in planning for several purposes: study the proposed plans weak links; tailor the plan fit the stakeholders' priorities; to develop complementary policies and so on.

Second, the mechanism to calculate the degree of goal achievement is susceptible to 'group think'. This indeed may have been the case in the case study project. The underlying concept of the proposed mechanism leads to believing the stronger opinions and suspecting the weaker opinions. The stronger opinions dominate the calculations. This seems to be true in any decision-making process. Therefore, for the method to be constructive, it is important that "strong beliefs" are close to the "truth" or at least frank. The other side of this issue is that opinions of the stakeholders need not be combined and the strong voice need not necessarily dominate, but even the weak voice can be heard.

It is desirable in applying the belief reasoning model during public inquiry process that several groups of stakeholders, possibly representing different views and values, are involved. The success of the proposed approach depends on the agreement on the reasoning maps and the integrity of knowledge used on assigning belief values on those maps. During the public inquiry process, the reasoning map should be reviewed by several stakeholder groups for reasonableness, comprehensiveness, clarity, and economy (parsimony) for clarity of the evaluation. The experts and participating citizens should speak out honestly and genuinely about their judgments and openly admit their understanding and degree of uncertainty in their opinions.

The belief reasoning method developed in the paper assists transport planners to evaluate alternatives, to reason about them, and to measure the validity of reasoning in the evaluation. The decision model was created using the reasoning map structure and the evaluation was developed using the evidence theory.

The following two observations are important in the context of this application. Detailed information about characteristics of the alternatives was available and professionally worked through by experts before their interviews and in drawing up the reasoning map. Significant consequences, which contribute to the goals of the project, were discussed and anticipated. They are reflected in the reasoning map and show the underlying thinking of the consulted experts. It is likely that in a real-world application a smaller reasoning map would evolve over time and would not only be justified for planning purposes, but would also clarify the decision situation.

The credibility of the proposed approach does not, however, depend only on the assignment of beliefs on the various elements of the plans. Although the experts and the participating citizens should be honest about their degrees of "I don't know," there is value just drawing up the reasoning maps of the plans and discuss and clarify the relationships among the plan elements. The method bears similarity to Forrester's systems dynamics [3], but it is not restricted to models and regressions from past data and behavior.

References

1. Beynon, M., Curry, B., Morgan, P.: The Dempster-Shafer theory of evidence An alternative approach to multicriteria decision modeling. Omega 28, 37–50 (2009)
2. Dempster, A.P.: A generalization of Bayesian inference (with discussion). J. R. Stat. Soc. 30, 205–247 (1968)
3. Dubois, D., Prade, H.: Representation and combination of uncertainty with belief functions and possibility measures. Comp. Inte. 4, 244–264 (1988)
4. Forrester, J.W.: Urban Dynamics. Pegasus Communications, Portland (1969)
5. Halpern, J.Y.: Reasoning about uncertainty. MIT Press, London (2003)
6. Kanafani, A., Khattak, A., Dahlgren, J.: A planning methodology for intelligent urban transportation systems. Transport Res. C 2, 197–215 (1994)
7. Klir, G.J., Wierman, M.J.: Uncertainty-Based Information-—Elements of Generalized Information Theory. Physica-Verlag, Helidelberg (1999)
8. Kronprasert, N., Talvitie, A.P.: Reasoning-building process for transportation project evaluation and decision-making: Use of reasoning map and evidence theory, Transport Res. Rec. (in press, 2014)
9. Pike Transit Initiative: Columbia Pike Transit Alternatives Analysis, Available via DIALOG (2005), http://www.piketransit.org (Cited January 1, 2010)
10. Rittel, H., Weber, M.: Dilemma in general theory of planning. Policy Sci. 4, 155–169 (1973)
11. Talvitie, A.P., Kronprasert, N., Kikuchi, S.: Transportation decision-making—Comparison of hierarchical tree and reasoning map structures. WCTR, Rio de Janeiro, Brazil (2013)

Some Notes on Canonical Decomposition and Separability of a Belief Function

Xiaolu Ke, Liyao Ma, and Yong Wang

Department of Automation, University of Science and Technology of China
Hefei, China
{kxlu,liyma,yongwang}@mail.ustc.edu.cn

Abstract. The separable support function is a subclass of belief function, and it plays an important role in evidence theory. Although many properties of separable support function have been analyzed, the problem that how to judge whether a belief function is separable has not been solved. Through the canonical decomposition, any belief function could be decomposed into a set of generalized simple support functions. A judgment could be made from the decomposition result by checking all the weights, being a little cumbersome. Thus an alternative is provided. Some notes are made on the canonical decomposition, based on which two sufficient conditions to judge a separable support function are established. It is shown that whether a belief function is separable or not is not only decided by the relations between focal elements, but also influenced by the mass distributions among focal elements. Using the proposed conditions, one could directly make a judgment in certain cases from the basic probability assignment.

Keywords: Evidence thoery, Canonical decomposition, Separability, Simple support function.

1 Introduction

Evidence theory, being able to distinguish disbelief from loss of belief, is an efficient tool to model and process uncertain and imprecise data and is more frequently used in the field of information fusion for decision making. It was first proposed by Dempster[1], and later extended by Shafer [7] to a systematic theorem. In his monograph, Shafer defined the separable support function as a simple support function or the orthogonal sum of two or more simple support functions. It was studied further that some properties and concepts were established based on this function, such as the weight of internal conflict and impingement function. Though the definition for separability was given, no criterion has been put forward to judge which belief function is separable.

By generalizing the concept of simple support function, Smets [8] defined the general simple support function and put forward the canonical decomposition, which can decompose any belief function into a set of general simple support functions. From the definition of separable support function, a belief function is

F. Cuzzolin (Ed.): BELIEF 2014, LNAI 8764, pp. 153–160, 2014.

separable if all generalized simple support functions generated by the canonical decomposition have weights less than 1. But this means that a belief function should be decomposed so as to make a judgment. This may be a little cumbersome, especially when the frame of discernment is large.

In this paper, we try to find some criteria to help judge a separable support function directly from its basic probability assignment (BPA). To do this, the canonical decomposition is further analyzed. Some simple properties are summarized for it, and then some sufficient conditions are provided based on these properties to judge whether a belief function is separable in certain cases. These conditions facilitate the judgment of a separable support function, especially in the case where the frame is large while the focal elements are not that many. It is also shown that both the relations between focal elements and the mass distributions among them can influence the separability of a belief function. An illustrative example intuitively shows the proposed properties.

The organization of the rest paper is as follows. In section 2, some necessary preliminaries about the canonical decomposition are introduced. In section 3, several properties are concluded and proved for the canonical decomposition. Based on these properties, sufficient conditions to judge whether a belief function is separable are put forth in section 4. Then in section 5, a simple example is used to illustrate the results more intuitively, and a conclusion is drawn in section 6.

2   Preliminaries

Let Θ, a finite set of N mutually exclusive and exhaustive hypotheses, be the frame of discernment. Over this frame, a basic probability assignment (BPA) m is defined as a mapping from 2^{Θ} to $[0, 1]$ verifying $\sum_{A \subseteq \Theta} m(A) = 1$. Subsets A of Θ such that $m(A) > 0$ are called focal elements of m. A BPA is said to be non-dogmatic if $m(\Theta) > 0$, and normal if $m(\emptyset) = 0$. In this paper, only the normal belief function is considered. The commonality function Q could be calculated from m through the Mobius transform: $Q(A) = \sum_{A \subseteq B \subseteq \Theta} m(B)$, $A \subset \Theta$.

Suppose m is the basic probability assignment corresponding to belief function Bel. If there exists a subset A of Θ such that m has the following expression:

$$m(B) = \begin{cases} w & B = \Theta \\ 1 - w & B = A \\ 0 & otherwise \end{cases}$$

where $w \in [0, 1]$, then Bel is called a simple support function (SSF) focused on A, and can be denoted as A^w for simplicity. A belief function is said to be separable if it is a SSF or it is the conjunctive combination of some SSFs. By extending the weight w to $[0, \infty)$, Smets [8] defined the generalized simple support function (GSSF), and those GSSF with $w \in (1, \infty)$ are called inverse simple support functions (ISSF).

The canonical decomposition proposed by Smets is defined as follows: for any non-dogmatic belief function Bel over Θ, there exists a unique set of GSSF defined over Θ such that

$$Bel = \bigoplus_{A \subset \Theta} A^{w_A}, \ w_A \in [0, \infty) \text{ for } \forall A \in \Theta, \text{ and}$$

$$w_A = \prod_{X:A\subset X\subseteq\Theta} Q(X)^{(-1)^{|X|-|A|+1}}. \tag{1}$$

Here $\oplus$ stands for the normalized conjunctive rule, i.e., the Dempster's rule of combination. From the definition of separability, a belief function is separable if $w_A < 1$ for all subsets $A \subset \Theta$. This decomposition could also be extended to dogmatic belief functions by assigning a positive small value ϵ to $m(\Theta)$.

3   Some Properties of the Canonical Decomposition

The canonical decomposition can decompose a belief function into a set of GSSF, thus providing an alternative to some problems, such as evidence conflict [4,6], evidence combination [2,3] and evidence clustering [5]. In this section, this technique itself is studied further. Some properties are summarized and proved for special cases.

Property 1. Suppose Bel is a non-dogmatic belief function over Θ, and m, Q are its corresponding BPA and commonality function, respectively. Suppose Bel has n+1 focal elements denoted by $A_1, \cdots, A_n$, and Θ. For all $1 \leq i \leq n$, if $A_i \not\subset A_j$ for all $j \neq i$, then $w_A < 1$.

Proof. Since A_i is not contained in any other focal elements, we have
$Q(A_i) = \sum_{B \supset A_i} m(B) = m(A_i) + m(\Theta)$, and
$Q(B) = m(\Theta)$ for all $B \supset A_i$.
Suppose $|A_i| = N_i, |\Theta| = N$, by the canonical decomposition,

$$w_{A_i} = \prod_{X:A_i\subset X\subseteq\Theta} Q(X)^{(-1)^{|X|-|A_i|+1}}$$

$$= \frac{m(\Theta)^{\binom{N-N_i}{1}} m(\Theta)^{\binom{N-N_i}{3}}\dots}{Q(A_i)m(\Theta)^{\binom{N-N_i}{2}} m(\Theta)^{\binom{N-N_i}{4}}\dots}$$

$$= \frac{1}{Q(A_i)}m(\Theta)^{\binom{N-N_i}{1}-\binom{N-N_i}{2}+\binom{N-N_i}{3}-\binom{N-N_i}{4}+-\cdots}$$

By the binomial theorem,

$$(1-1)^{N-N_i} = \binom{N-N_i}{0} - \binom{N-N_i}{1} + \binom{N-N_i}{2} - + \cdots + (-1)^{N-N_i}\binom{N-N_i}{N-N_i} = 0,$$

when $N - N_i$ is a positive integer. Thus

$$\binom{N-N_i}{1} + \binom{N-N_i}{2} - \binom{N-N_i}{3} + \binom{N-N_i}{4} - + \cdots = \binom{N-N_i}{0} = 1,$$

$$w_{A_i} = \frac{m(\Theta)}{Q(A_i)} = \frac{m(\Theta)}{m(\Theta)+m(A_i)} < 1. \tag{2} \qquad \square$$

This property reflects that each focal element that not contained in other focal elements will correspond to a SSF if decomposed by the canonical decomposition. Then if the focal elements of a belief function do not contain each other, whether is it separable? This cannot be answered by property 1 since weights of those subsets that are not focal elements are unknown. The following property will solve this problem.

Property 2. Suppose Bel is a non-dogmatic belief function over Θ, and m, Q are its corresponding BPA and commonality function, respectively. And suppose Bel has $n + 1$ focal elements denoted by $A_1, \cdots, A_n$, and Θ. If $m(B) = 0$, and $B \neq A_i \cap A_j$ for all $1 \leq i, j \leq n$, then $w_A < 1$.

Proof. (i) If $B \not\subset A_i$ for all $1 \leq i \leq n$, then by setting $m(B) = 0$ in Eq. (2) one has $w_B = 1$.

(ii) If $B \subset A_i$, then If $B \not\subset A_j$ for all $1 \leq j \leq n, j \neq i$, otherwise $B = A_i \cap A_j$. Thus $Q(B) = m(A_i) + m(\Theta)$, and for all $C \supset B$, one has

$$Q(C) = \begin{cases} Q(B) & C \subset A_i, \\ m(\Theta) & C \not\subset A_i, C \subset \Theta. \end{cases}$$

By the canonical decomposition,

$$w_B = \Pi_{X : B \subset X \subset \Theta} Q(X)^{(-1)^{|X| - |B| + 1}}$$

$$= \frac{\left(\prod_{\substack{C : |C| = |B| + 1, \\ B \subset C \subset A_i}} Q(C) \prod_{\substack{C : |C| = |B| + 1, \\ B \subset C \subset \Theta, C \not\subset A_i}} Q(C) \right) \left(\prod_{\substack{C : |C| = |B| + 3, \\ B \subset C \subset A_i}} Q(C) \prod_{\substack{C : |C| = |B| + 3, \\ B \subset C \subset \Theta, C \not\subset A_i}} Q(C) \right) \cdots}{\left(Q(B) \prod_{\substack{C : |C| = |B| + 2, \\ B \subset C \subset A_i}} Q(C) \prod_{\substack{C : |C| = |B| + 2, \\ B \subset C \subset \Theta, C \not\subset A_i}} Q(C) \right) \left(\prod_{\substack{C : |C| = |B| + 4, \\ B \subset C \subset A_i}} Q(C) \prod_{\substack{C : |C| = |B| + 4, \\ B \subset C \subset \Theta, C \not\subset A_i}} Q(C) \right) \cdots}$$

$$= \frac{\left(Q(B)^{\binom{|A_i| - |B|}{1}} m(\Theta)^{\binom{|\Theta| - |A_i|}{1}} \right) \left(Q(B)^{\binom{|A_i| - |B|}{3}} m(\Theta)^{\binom{|\Theta| - |B|}{3} - \binom{|A_i| - |B|}{3}} \right) \cdots}{Q(B) \left(Q(B)^{\binom{|A_i| - |B|}{2}} m(\Theta)^{\binom{|\Theta| - |B|}{2} - \binom{|A_i| - |B|}{2}} \right) \left(Q(B)^{\binom{|A_i| - |B|}{4}} m(\Theta)^{\binom{|\Theta| - |B|}{4} - \binom{|A_i| - |B|}{4}} \right) \cdots}$$

$$= \frac{1}{Q(B)} Q(B)^{\binom{|A_i| - |B|}{1} - \binom{|A_i| - |B|}{2} + \cdots} m(\Theta)^{\binom{|\Theta| - |A_i|}{1} - \left[\binom{|\Theta| - |B|}{2} - \binom{|A_i| - |B|}{2} \right] + \cdots}$$

Again by the binomial theorem, one has

$$\binom{|A_i| - |B|}{1} - \binom{|A_i| - |B|}{2} + \cdots = \binom{|A_i| - |B|}{0} = 1, \text{ and}$$

$$\binom{|\Theta| - |A_i|}{1} - \left[\binom{|\Theta| - |B|}{2} - \binom{|A_i| - |B|}{2} \right] + \left[\binom{|\Theta| - |B|}{3} - \binom{|A_i| - |B|}{3} \right] - + \cdots$$

$$= \binom{|\Theta| - |A_i|}{1} - \left[\binom{|\Theta| - |B|}{2} - \binom{|\Theta| - |B|}{3} + \cdots \right] + \left[\binom{|A_i| - |B|}{2} - \binom{|A_i| - |B|}{3} + \cdots \right]$$

$$= \binom{|\Theta| - |A_i|}{1} - \left[-\binom{|\Theta| - |B|}{0} + \binom{|\Theta| - |B|}{1} \right] + \left[-\binom{|A_i| - |B|}{0} + \binom{|A_i| - |B|}{1} \right]$$

$$= (|\Theta| - |A_i|) - (-1 + |\Theta| - |B|) + (-1 + |A_i| - |B|)$$

$$= 0.$$

Hence,

$$w_B = \frac{1}{Q(B)} Q(B)^1 m(\Theta)^0 = 1. \qquad \square$$

This property means that only focal elements and their intersections could be foci of non-vacuous GSSF using the canonical decomposition.

Property 1 says that the weight of any focal element not contained in others is less than 1. In fact, this constraint could be further relaxed.

Property 3. Suppose Bel is a non-dogmatic belief function over Θ, and m, Q are its corresponding BPA and commonality function, respectively. And suppose Bel has $n + 1$ focal elements denoted by $A_1, \cdots, A_n$, and Θ. If $A_k \neq A_i \cap A_j$ for $1 \leq i, j \neq k \leq n$, then $w_{A_k} < 1$.

Proof. (i) If $A_k \not\subset A_i$ small for all $1 \leq i \neq k \leq n$, then it follows from property 1 that $w_{A_k} < 1$.

(ii) If $A_k \subset A_i$, then $A_k \not\subset A_i$ for all $1 \leq j \leq n, j \neq i, k$, otherwise $A_k = A_i \cap A_j$.

Thus $Q(A_k) = m(A_k) + m(A_i) + m(\Theta), Q(\Theta) = m(\Theta)$, and

$$Q(C) = m(A_i) + m(\Theta) \text{ for every } C \subset A_i, C \neq A_k, \Theta.$$

Then similar to the proof of property 2, we have

$$w_B = \frac{1}{Q(A_k)} Q(C)^1 m(\Theta)^0 = \frac{m(A_i) + m(\Theta)}{m(A_k) + m(A_i) + m(\Theta)} < 1. \qquad \square$$

This indicates that a focal element will correspond to a SSF if it is not contained by two or more other focal elements. However, the inverse usually does not hold. We cannot say a belief function separable or not by its focal elements separately, while neglecting the mass distribution among them.

4   When is a Belief Function Separable?

It is not an easy task to judge whether a belief function is separable or not in a general case. For several special cases, some sufficient conditions are put forth to make such a judgment in this section.

Theorem 1. *Suppose Bel is a non-dogmatic belief function over Θ, and it has $n + 1$ focal elements denoted by $A_1, \cdots, A_n$, and Θ. If these focal elements can be divided into two classes: $A_1, \cdots, A_k, A_{k+1}, \cdots, A_n$, such that*
  (1) $A_i \cap A_j = \emptyset$, for all $1 \leq i \leq k, 1 \leq j(\neq i) \leq n$;
  (2) $A_{k+1} \subset A_{k+2} \subset \cdots \subset A_n$.
Then Bel is a separable support function.

Proof. It follows from property 3 that $w_{A_i} < 1, i = 1, \cdots n$. Since $A_i \cap A_j = A_i$ for all $k + 1 \leq i, j \leq n$, it follows from property 2 that $w_B = 1$ for all other subsets B of Θ that are not focal elements. Thus Bel is separable.   □

As special cases, the following corollaries follow immediately from this theorem.

Corollary 1. *Suppose Bel is a non-dogmatic belief function over Θ. If the intersection of any two focal elements (except the frame) is empty, then Bel is separable.*

Corollary 1.1. *All non-dogmatic belief functions with $|\Theta| = 2$ are separable.*

Corollary 1.2. *All Bayesian alike belief functions, i.e., those only assign positive mass to elements of Θ and Θ itself, are separable.*

Corollary 2. *All non-dogmatic consonant belief functions are separable support functions.*

It should be noted that the same statement as Corollary 2 has been made and proved in another way in [2].

Since this is a sufficient condition to judge a separable support function, a belief function may still be separable if the condition is not satisfied. The following theorem could be seen as a supplement that it can detect a non-separable support function in some cases. If we cannot directly judge a belief function as separable, then we could check whether it is non-separable.

Theorem 2. *Suppose Bel is a non-dogmatic belief function over θ, and m, Q are its corresponding BPA and commonality function, respectively. And suppose Bel has $n + 1$ focal elements denoted by $A_1, \cdots, A_n$, and Θ. If there exists A_i and A_j such that $A_i \cap A_j = B$, and $m(B) = 0, B \not\subset A_k$, for $k \neq i, j$, then Bel is not separable.*

Proof. From the given conditions, the commonality function Q satisfies:
$$Q(B) = m(A_i) + m(A_j) + m(\Theta) \text{ , and}$$

$$\left.\begin{array}{ll} Q(C) = m(A_i) + m(\Theta), & C \subset A_i, C \not\subset A_j \\ Q(D) = m(A_j) + m(\Theta), & D \subset A_j, D \not\subset A_i \\ Q(E) = m(\Theta), & E \not\subset A_i, A_j, E \subset \Theta \end{array}\right\} \quad (3)$$

Then similar to the proof of property 2, the subsets that contain B could be divided into three classes according to Eq. (3). And one has

$$\begin{aligned} w_B &= \frac{Q(C)Q(D)}{Q(B)Q(E)} = \frac{(m(A_i)+m(\Theta))(m(A_j)+m(\Theta))}{(m(A_i)+m(A_j)+m(\Theta))m(\Theta)} \\ &= \frac{(m(A_i)+m(A_j)+m(\Theta))m(\Theta)+m(A_i)m(A_j)}{(m(A_i)+m(A_j)+m(\Theta))m(\Theta)} > 1. \end{aligned}$$

Thus Bel is not a separable support function.

Note that this theorem can be further extended to the case where subset B is the intersection of more than two focal elements, while none of them is contained in more than one other focal element. Besides, from the expression of w_B in the proof, the case where $m(B) > 0$, i.e., B is also a focal element, could also be discussed according to its relative value. However, this discussion would be very complex in some cases and the result is hard to generalize. This theorem could also be explained from another point of view. From the given conditions and property 1, one has $w_{A_i} < 1$ and $w_{A_j} < 1$. Then the combination of these two SSF would assign a positive mass to subset B according to the Dempsters rule. However, B is not a focal element of Bel, which means that the mass assigned to B is zero. This positive mass could not be removed through combing any SSF other by an ISSF focused on B. Thus the weight of B should be bigger than 1.

5   Example

Using the theorems proposed in the above section, some belief functions can be classified into the separable class and some can be rule out of this class. However, both of them are sufficient conditions that there still exists a case where a judgment cannot be made through these two theorems. A conclusion for a general case is rather complex since both the relations of focal elements and mass distributions among them contribute to the separability of a belief function. A simple example is illustrated in the following to show the results intuitively.

Example 1. Let Bel be a belief function over $\Theta = \{\theta_1, \theta_2, \theta_3\}$ with BPA defined as
$$m(\theta_1) = a, m(\{\theta_1, \theta_2\}) = b, m(\{\theta_1, \theta_3\}) = c, m(\Theta) = 1 - a - b - c,$$
where $a, b, c \geq 0$, $a + b + c < 1$.

From the proposed properties, only $\{\theta_1\}, \{\theta_1, \theta_2\} and \{\theta_1, \theta_3\}$ may have weights not equal to one, and they are expressed using a, b, c as follows:
$$w_{\{\theta_1\}} = \frac{(1-a-c)(1-a-b)}{1-a-b-c}, w_{\{\theta_1,\theta_2\}} = \frac{1-a-b-c}{1-a-c}, w_{\{\theta_1,\theta_3\}} = \frac{1-a-b-c}{1-a-b}.$$

The commonality function and decomposition results corresponding to different values of a, b, c are listed in Table 1.

Table 1. Decompositions of belief function in example 1

Focal	m	Q	w(0.4, 0, 0.4)	w(0,0.4,0.4)	w(0.2,0.4,0.4)	w(0.4,0.2,0.2)
$\emptyset$	0	1	1	1	1	1
θ_1	a	1	3/5	9/5	6/5	4/5
θ_2	0	$1 - a - c$	1	1	1	1
θ_3	0	$1 - a - b$	1	1	1	1
θ_1, θ_2	b	$1 - a - c$	1	1/3	1/2	1/2
θ_1, θ_3	c	$1 - a - b$	1/3	1/3	1/3	1/2
θ_2, θ_3	0	$1 - a - b - c$	1	1	1	1
Θ	$1 - a - b - c$	$1 - a - b - c$				

By property 2, the weights of $\{\theta_2\}, \{\theta_3\}, \{\theta_2, \theta_3\}$ will be 1, not matter a, b and c take what values. This could be seen in Tab. 1 that they are equal to 1 in all four cases.

By property 1, $\{\theta_1, \theta_2\}$ will be the focus of a SSF if $b > 0$, which could be seen in the last three cases in Tab. 1. Similarly, $\{\theta_1, \theta_3\}$ will be the focus of a SSF if $c > 0$ as shown in all four cases.

By property 3, if $a > 0$ and one of b and c is equal to zero, then the weight of $\{\theta_1\}$ will be less than 1. This is shown in the 4th column in Tab. 1.

By theorem 1, if $a > 0$ and one of b and c is equal to zero, then Bel is a constant belief function, thus is separable. This could be seen from column 4 that no weight is bigger than 1.

By theorem 2, if $a = 0$ and $b > 0, c > 0$, then Bel is not a separable support function. The 5th column in Tab. 1 shows this case.

Comparing the results of above two cases, one can find that the relations between focal elements contribute to the separability of a belief function.

As to the case where none of a, b and c is equal to zero, neither of the two theorem works. One still does not know whether Bel is separable or not directly from the BPA. The last two columns in Tab. 1 list two such cases where the first one is not separable while the second is separable. This shows that the mass distributions among focal elements also influence the separability of a belief function.

6 Conclusion

Separable support function is an important subclass of belief function. Although much work has been done on its properties, no method has been given to judge whether a belief function is separable or not. The canonical decomposition provides such an alternative by checking the weights of the generated GSSF. But this method is rather cumbersome, especially when the frame is large. Thus two sufficient conditions are proposed in this paper to judge a separable support function directly from its basic probability assignment. They are still based on the canonical decomposition, while some of its properties are used rather than checking weights of GSSF. These properties are summarized and proved for some special cases, leading the proposed conditions to be sufficient only. It is also shown that a sufficient and necessary condition for a general case may be too complex since both focal elements and mass distributions among them contribute to the separability of a belief function. A simple example with variants explains all these properties and conditions intuitively.

References

1. Dempster, A.P.: Upper and lower probabilities induced by a multivalued mapping. Annals of Mathematical Statistics 38, 325–340 (1967)
2. Denoeux, T.: Conjunctive and disjunctive combination of belief functions induced by nondistinct bodies of evidence. Artificial Intelligence 172, 234–264 (2008)
3. Fu, C., Yang, S.: Conjunctive combination of belief functions from dependent sources using positive and negative weight functions. Expert Systems with Applications 41, 1964–1972 (2014)
4. Roquel, A., Le Hégarat-Mascle, S., Bloch, I., Vincke, B.: A new local measure of disagreement between belief functions – application to localization. In: Denœux, T., Masson, M.-H. (eds.) Belief Functions: Theory & Appl. AISC, vol. 164, pp. 335–342. Springer, Heidelberg (2012)
5. Schubert, J.: Clustering decomposed belief functions using generalized weights of conflict. International Journal of Approximate Reasoning 48, 466–480 (2008)
6. Schubert, J.: The internal conflict of a belief function. In: 2nd International Conference on Belief Functions, Compiegne, France, pp. 169–177 (2012)
7. Shafer, G.A.: A Mathematical Theory of Evidence. Princeton University Press (1976)
8. Smets, P.: The canonical decomposition of a weighted belief. In: 14th International Joint Conference on Artificial Intelligence, San Mateo, USA, pp. 1896–1901 (1995)

A Relational Representation of Belief Functions

Liping Liu

The University of Akron
liu@acm.org

Abstract. Set operations are one of the most difficult tasks in implementing belief functions for knowledge based systems. The problem becomes intractable because the number of subsets increases exponentially as the frame size increases. In this paper, I propose representing a subset as an integer, and reduce set operations to bitwise operations. I show the superiority of such a representation and demonstrate how, despite its simplicity, the technique has a profound implication in reducing the complexity of belief function computations and makes it possible to organize and store belief functions using relational databases for large projects.

1 A Relational Representation

Let $\Theta = \{\theta_1, \theta_2, ..., \theta_n\}$ denote the frame of discernment. Relational representation starts with representing a subset $A \subset \Theta$ as a binary number $A = a_1 a_2 ... a_n$ such that

$$a_i = \begin{cases} 0 & \theta_i \notin A \\ 1 & \theta_i \in A \end{cases}$$

for $i = 1, 2, ..., n$. It is easy to see that all subsets of Θ are in one-to-one correspondence to all the n-bits binary numbers if we fix the order of the elements in Θ. For example, let $\Theta = \{H, T\}$. Then we have the following correspondence: empty set $\phi \Longleftrightarrow 00$, $A = \{H\} \Longleftrightarrow 10$, $B = \{T\} \Longleftrightarrow 01$, and the whole set $\Theta \Longleftrightarrow 11$. To avoid using extra notations, we will use the same symbol for a subset and its corresponding binary number. For example, let $\Theta = \{rainy, sunny, cloudy\}$. Then $A = \{rainy, cloudy\}$ is equivalently represented as a binary number $A = 101$.

Note that the trick of binary representation is not new. For example, Smets [7] used it to re-express the formulas in the transferable belief model using matrices. Haenni and Lehmann [2] discussed its implications on combination and marginalization of multivariate belief functions. The correspondence between subsets and binary numbers, however, lies not only at the format but also the operations and relations. Bitwise operations include AND (&), OR (|), and complement (~), which respectively correspond to set intersection, union, and complement. Suppose $A = a_n a_{n-1} ... a_1$ and $B = b_n b_{n-1} ... b_1$. The bitwise operations are defined as follows:

- Bitwise AND (&): $A \& B = c_n c_{n-1} ... c_1$ such that $c_i = 1$ iff $a_i b_i = 1$, for $i = 1, 2, ..., n$. This corresponds to $A \cap B$; $\theta_i \in A \cap B$ if and only if $a_i b_i = 1$.

F. Cuzzolin (Ed.): BELIEF 2014, LNAI 8764, pp. 161–170, 2014.

- Bitwise OR (|): $A|B = c_n c_{n-1}...c_1$ such that $c_i = 1$ iff $a_i + b_i \geq 1$, for $i = 1, 2, ..., n$. This corresponds to $A \cup B$; $\theta_i \in A \cup B$ if and only if $a_i = 1$ ($\theta_i \in A$) or $b_i = 1$ ($\theta_i \in B$), i.e., $a_i + b_i \geq 1$.
- Bitwise Complement ($\sim$): $\sim A = c_n c_{n-1}...c_1$ such that $c_i = 1$ iff $a_i = 0$, for $i = 1, 2, ..., n$. This corresponds to $\neg A$; $\theta_i \in \neg A$ if and only if $a_i = 0$ ($\theta_i \notin A$).

In terms of these bitwise operations, set difference can be also expressed as composite bitwise operations as follows: $A - B = A\&(\sim B)$. Set relations such as containment correspond to bitwise comparisons as follows:

- Bitwise Comparison ($\succeq$ and $\succ$): $A \succeq B$ if and only if $a_i \geq b_i$ for all i. $A \succ B$ if and only if $a_i \geq b_i$ for all i and $a_i > b_i$ for some i.

Then, usual set containment relations can be equivalently expressed as bitwise comparisons. $A \supset B$ ($A \supseteq B$) is equivalent to $A \succ B$ ($A \succeq B$).

It is known that a binary number is a native representation of any data in the computer. Binary numbers and decimal integers have deeper relationships. First, they are one-to-one correspondent. Second, the conversion between binary numbers and decimal integers is implicit in modern operating systems; an integer is internally stored in memory and operated in processors as a binary number. Third, native bitwise operations apply equivalently to integers in modern programming languages such as C, C++, C#, and Java. For example, given any two integers A and B, applying &,|, or ˜operation will implicitly treat the operands as binary, but applying $+$, $-$, $\times$, and $\div$ will treat them as decimals.

Taking advantage of these relationships, I further represent subsets as integers. This is the second step toward the relational representation of belief functions. It is easy to see that, if the frame of discernment is fixed and ordered, subsets, binary numbers, and integers are all equivalent; from one we can come up with a unique other. For example, let the frame $\Theta = \{rainy, sunny, cloudy\}$. Then $A = \{rainy, cloudy\}$ corresponds to binary number 101 or integer 5. Similarly, integer 7 corresponds to binary number 111, which represents subset $\Theta = \{rainy, sunny, cloudy\}$. Therefore, in the future, we can use integers, binary numbers, and subset interchangeably.

One caveat with the relational representation is the bitwise comparisons. Clearly, $A \succeq B$ ($A \succ B$) is not equivalent to $A \geq B$ ($A > B$). For example, as integers 6 is greater than 5 but as binary numbers it is not true that $110 \succ 101$ by bitwise comparisons. In fact, it is easy to prove the following lemmas:

Lemma 1. *For any integers A and B, if $A \succeq B$ ($A \succ B$), then $A \geq B$ ($A > B$). However, the converse is not true.*

Lemma 2. *For any integers A and B, $A = B$ for binary comparison iff $A = B$ for decimal comparison.*

Bitwise comparison is not a native relation defined in programming languages. However, it can be defined or programmed easily using bitwise Bitwise AND ($\&$): It may be also programmed using bitwise shifts as follows.

- Bitwise Shifts ($\ll$ and $\gg$): For any binary number A and integer k, $A \ll k$ (left shift) is a binary number by adding k zeros to the end of A. Conversely, $A \gg k$ (right-shift) is a binary number by removing k ending digits of A. Treated as integers, $A \ll k = A \times 2^k$ and $A \gg k = A \div 2^k$, here division is an integer one.

Using bitwise right shifts, we can then define bitwise comparison $\succeq$ using one line code in C or other modern programming languages as follows. Operation $\succ$ can be similarly defined.

```
bool operator ⪰(int A, int B){return (((A & 01)
>= (B & 01)) ? (A≫ 1) ⪰ (B≫1) : false); }
```

With bitwise operations and comparisons, the basic constructs of the Dempster-Shafer theory may be re-expressed into functions of integers. For example, we may state that a function of integers $Bel(A)$ is a belief function if and only if there is another function $m(A)$ of integers such that $m(0) = 0$, $m(A) \geq 0$ for any integer A, $\sum_{A \succ 0} m(A) = 1$, and $Bel(A) = \sum_{0 < B \preceq A} m(B)$. We could still call an integer a focal element if $m(A) > 0$. Similarly, plausibility and commonality functions can be equivalently expressed as follows:

$$Pl(A) = \sum_{A \& B \neq 0} m(B), \quad Q(A) = \sum_{0 \neq B \succeq A} m(B). \tag{1}$$

Given two independent belief functions symbolized as m_1 and m_2. Then their combination in terms of Dempster's rule is expressed as follows:

$$(m_1 \otimes m_2)(C) = \frac{\sum_{A \& B = C} m_1(A) m_2(B)}{\sum_{A \& B \neq 0} m_1(A) m_2(B)}. \tag{2}$$

The counterpart, according to the transferable belief model [6], is the disjunctive combination that replace $A \& B$ with $A|B$ as follows:

$$(m_1 \oplus m_2)(C) = \sum_{A|B = C} m_1(A) m_2(B). \tag{3}$$

Due to Lemmas 1 and 2, bitwise comparison $=$ is identical to decimal comparison $=$ but bitwise comparisons $\succeq$ and $\succ$ is not simply decimal comparisons $\geq$ and $>$.

2   Combination as Vector Multiplications

Using the relational representation, each belief function is expressed as a map between two vectors: one vector of integers for focal elements and the other vector of real numbers for mass values. For any mass function m, let I be its vector of integer focal elements and M be the vector of corresponding mass values. Then we may represent $m = (I, M)$. Combining two mass functions is essentially the multiplication of these vectors: the first between the integer vectors using bitwise & and the second between mass value vectors using regular algorithmic product. Let us define the two products formally:

Definition 1. *Given two mass functions $m_1 = (I_1, M_1)$ and $m_2 = (I_2, M_2)$. Assume $I_k = (i_{k1}, i_{k2}, ..., i_{kl_k})$ and $M_k = (m_{k1}, m_{k2}, ..., m_{kl_k})$ for $k = 1, 2$. Then $m_1 \times m_2 = (I_1 \& I_2, M_1 \times M_2)$,*

$$I_1 \& I_2 = (i_{11}\&i_{21}, ...i_{11}\&i_{2l_2}, ..., i_{1l_1}\&i_{21}, ...i_{1l_1}\&i_{2l_2}), \tag{4}$$

$$M_1 \times M_2 = (m_{11}m_{21}, ...m_{11}m_{2l_2}, ..., m_{1l_1}m_{21}, ...m_{1l_1}m_{2l_2}). \tag{5}$$

Note that, by transposing I_1 and M_1, the above vector multiplications may be expressed as standard matrix multiplications except that the results are $l_1 \times l_2$ matrices instead of vectors.

Example 1. Assume m_1 and m_2 are two mass functions with focal elements expressed as integers: $m_1(2) = 0.3$, $m_1(7) = 0.7$, $m_2(4) = 0.1$, $m_2(5) = 0.6$, and $m_2(6) = 0.3$. Alternatively, $m_1 = ((2,7),(0.3,0.7))$ and $m_2 = ((4,5,6),(0.1,0.6,0.3))$. Then $m_1 \times m_2 = ((2,7)\&(4,5,6),(0.3,0.7) \times (0.1,0.6,0.3))$ with $(2,7)\&(4,5,6) = (2\&4, 2\&5, 2\&6, 7\&4, 7\&5, 7\&6) = (0,0,2,4,5,6)$ and $(0.3,0.7) \times (0.1,0.6,0.3) = (0.03, 0.18, 0.09, 0.07, 0.42, 0.21)$.

$m_1 \times m_2$, as defined and illustrated above, is a *denormalized mass function* of $m_1 \oplus m_2$, i.e., the sum of masses do not add up to one. To be normalized, first, the cell values in the second vector are summed up for each integer in the first matrix. For example, values 0.03 and 0.18 in Example 1 corresponding to integer 0 will add up to 0.21. Second, the sum for each integer is divided by a number that is one minus the sum corresponding to 0, e.g., 1 - 0.21. After the normalization, the result is the combined mass function. In general, let N denote the normalization operation. Then we have:

$$m_1 \oplus m_2 = N(m_1 \times m_2). \tag{6}$$

For any mass function m, let $N^-(m)$ denote a denormalized m in a general manner: 1) it includes a list of arbitrary non-negative real numbers $m^{(1)}(0)$, $m^{(2)}(0)$, ..., $m^{(l_0)}(0)$ such that $0 \leq \sum_{j=1}^{j=l_0} m^{(j)}(0) < 1$; and 2) each focal integer i corresponds to non-negative real number $m^{(1)}(i)$, $m^{(2)}(i)$, ..., $m^{(l_i)}(i)$ such that

$$m(i) = \frac{\sum_{k=1}^{k=l_i} m^{(k)}(i)}{1 - \sum_{k=1}^{k=l_0} m^{(k)}(0)}. \tag{7}$$

This equation leads to the following statement:

Lemma 3. *The sum of all denormalized mass values for each belief function is one:*

$$\sum \{ \sum_{k=1}^{k=l_i} m^{(k)}(i) \mid i = 0 \text{ or } i \text{ is focal integer} \} = 1. \tag{8}$$

There are many ways to denormalize a mass function. I.e., N^- is not unique. However, they are all equivalent; they all recover the same normalized mass function. Thus, we have

Lemma 4. *For any mass function m and its denormalized version $N^-(m)$,*

$$m = N(N^-(m)). \tag{9}$$

The equivalence lies not only in the form but also in behavior. It is easy to see that one can use $N^-(m)$ instead of m to derive belief, plausibility, and commonality functions. For example, belief function $Bel(A)$ may be derived as

$$Bel(A) = \frac{\sum_{0 < B \preceq A} N^-(m)(B)}{1 - \sum_{B=0} N^-(m)(B)}. \tag{10}$$

Similarly, for any two mass functions m_1 and m_2, their combination can be also equivalently performed by multiplying their denormalized forms as shown in the following lemma:

Lemma 5. *For any two mass functions m_1 and m_2,*

$$m_1 \oplus m_2 = N[N^-(m_1) \times N^-(m_2)]. \tag{11}$$

Theorem 1. *Let m_1, m_2, ..., m_k be a series of mass functions. Then*

$$m_1 \oplus m_2 \oplus ... \oplus m_k = N(m_1 \times m_2 \times ... \times m_k). \tag{12}$$

This theorem has two important implications. First, for combination, a denormalized mass function is an equivalent representation of a mass function for the purpose of combination. Second, combination may be carried out as vector multiplications and the normalization operation is not needed for intermediate products. Normalization is probably never needed unless one needs to interpret a product.

Bayesian probabilities has traditionally enjoyed the blind multiplications of probability tables. The combination of belief functions can do the same; the beauty arises naturally from the relational representation. Note that, by using set operations, one may also employ the tabular form to carry out Dempster's rule as done in Kong [4]. However, the tabular form is for illustration or manual computation only. It is difficult, if not impossible, to implement it in automatic reasoning systems without introducing more complicated data structures and expansive text or symbolic manipulations.

3   Implementation Costs

The standard approach to implementing combination is to use list structures for both focal elements and mass values. Cycling through the lists, we intersect each pair of focal elements and multiply the corresponding mass values. Then we handle the mass product in three cases. If the intersection is empty, add the product into a value for conflicts. Otherwise, add the intersection and the product to the new lists for the combination or update the existing lists if the intersection already exists. The following shows the pseudo code of such an implementation using relational representations assuming $m_1 = (I_1, M_1)$, $m_2 = (I_2, M_2)$, and $m_1 \oplus m_2 = (I, M)$:

```
initialize lists I₁, M₁, I₂, M₂;
declare two empty lists I and M;
float v, m₀ := 0;
int k;
boolean isIn := false;
for (int i = 0; i < |I₁|; i + +) {
    for (int j = 0; j < |I₂|; j + +) {
        k := I₁[i]&I₂[j];
        v := M₁[i]M₂[j];
        if (k == 0) m₀ += v;
        else {
            for (int l = 0; l < |I|; l + +){
                if (k == I[l]) {
                    isIn := true;
                    M[l]+ = v;
                    break;
                }
            }
            if (isIn == false) {
                insert k to I;
                insert v to M;
            }
        }
    }
}
for (int l = 0; l < |I|; l + +) M[l] := M[l]/(1 − m₀);
```

Without using the relational representation, the implementation is similar but becomes more complex in two aspects. First, I_1, I_2, and I will be the list of subsets rather than integers. Second, it takes more operations to perform set intersections and comparisons. The following theorem compares the costs of implementation via the list structure with and without the relational representation.

Theorem 2. *Assume the cardinality of the frame of discernment is n. Then, the ratio of the cost of combination using the relational representation to that with subset representation is between the lower bound $1/n^2$ and the upper bound $7/(3n^2+4)$. Also, as the number of focal elements increases, the ratio approaches to the lower bound.*

Note that the upper bound of the cost ratio is obtained by assuming there is only one focal element in both m_1 and m_2, i.e., they are vacuous. The more reasonable upper bound should be the following, obtained by setting $|I_1||I_2| = 4$, i.e., m_1 and m_2 both have at least two focal elements,

$$\frac{C_{r-list}}{C_{s-list}} \leq \frac{10}{6n^2+4}. \tag{13}$$

The following table shows the bounds of the cost ratio for a few sample frame sizes. As it shows, relational representation saves the cost of combination in the range between 56.25% and 99.90% assuming the frame sizes range from 2 to 32.

	C_{r-list}/C_{s-list}		
n	lower bound	practical upper bound	upper bound
2	25.0%	35.71%	43.75%
3	11.11%	17.24%	22.58%
4	6.25%	10.00%	13.46%
32	0.10%	0.16%	0.22%

The list structure is flexible and expressive, and it is necessary when using subsets representing focal elements. However, a list is not efficient for lookups; the lookup performance depends on the size of the list and it may take $|I_1||I_2|$ time to decide if a new intersection is already in the list I. With the relational representation, lists may be replaced by dictionaries (or equivalently hash tables). A dictionary stores each item as a key-value pair and the key's hash value is used to look up the item in constant time $O(1)$. Thus, each mass function $m = (I, M)$ (or similarly a belief, plausibility, commonality function) may be stored in one dictionary with each focal integer and mass value to form a key-value pair.

The combination of two mass functions can be then reduced to the combination of two dictionary structures, which produces a new dictionary for the result of combination. Thus, Dempster's rule may be implemented as a program module that takes in two dictionaries, and output a new dictionary as the combined mass function as follows:

```
Dictionary<int, float> Combination(Dictionary<int, float> m₁, Dictionary<int,
float> m₂){
        Dictionary<int, float> m = new Dictionary<int, float>();
        float v, m₀ := 0;
        int k;
        foreach (KeyValuePair p₁ in m₁) {
                foreach (KeyValuePair p₂ in m₂) {
                        k = p₁.key & p₂.key;
                        v = p₁.value * p₂.value;
                        if (k ==0) m₀ += v;
                        else {
                                float v₀;
                                if (m.TryGetValue(k, out v₀)) m[k] = v₀ + v;
                                else m.Add(k, v);
                        }
                }
        }
        foreach (KeyValuePair p in m) p.value = p.value/(1 − m₀);
        return m;
}
```

Note that in the above algorithm, TryGetValue checks if dictionary m contains k and gets the corresponding value if it does, thus reducing two lookups into one. Assume m_1 and m_2 have $|I_1|$ and $|I_2|$ focal elements. The combination involves $|I_1||I_2|$ iterations. At each step, it does one bitwise AND and one addition. Then it does one integer comparison to check if $k = 0$, in which case, adds v to m_0. In the case of $k \neq 0$, it takes constant c or $O(1)$ operations to compute the hash value of k to see if m contains k and does one addition if it does. Otherwise, it inserts (k, v) into m. The latter also involves computing the hash value of k but may be avoided by modifying TryGetValue so that it can output the hash value of k. Finally, it involves $|I_1||I_2|$ divisions; it loops through each key-value pair one at a time and there is no lookup or hash value computation. Therefore, the cost of combination using dictionaries is $C_{r-hash} = |I_1||I_2|(5 + c)$, here c is a constant, independent of $|I_1|$ and $|I_2|$. Thus, we have

Theorem 3. *Assume m_1 and m_2 have $|I_1|$ and $|I_2|$ focal elements. Then the ratio of the cost of implementing combination via dictionaries (or has tables) to that via list structures is*

$$\frac{C_{r-hash}}{C_{r-list}} = \frac{c + 5}{|I_1||I_2| + 6}. \tag{14}$$

Theorem 4. *Assume m_l has $|I_l|$ focal elements ($l = 1, 2, ..., L$). Using hash tables or dictionaries, the cost of computing $m_1 \oplus m_2 \oplus ... \oplus m_L$ is $O(1)|I_1||I_2|...|I_{L-1}||I_L|$.*

The cost of a dictionary lookup is determined by hash computation and memory access. While memory access cost due to collisions may be reduced by using more sophisticated hash functions, the hash computation cost will increase [5]. For example, some hashing may take up to 64 clock cycles and the fastest one for integer hashing takes 11 bitwise operations, additions, and multiplications. In fact, the dictionary structure has a clear advantage over the list for combination when $|I_1||I_2|$ is large. Informal benchmark tests show that the lookup time in a dictionary is about 690 ms constant, whereas in a list it is linearly increasing with $|I_1||I_2|$ as empirically described as $67|I_1||I_2|+450$ ms. The lookup times are about the same when $|I_1||I_2| = 3$ but the difference increases as $|I_1||I_2|$ increases; for example, when, $|I_1||I_2| = 12$, the lookup time in a list almost doubles that in a dictionary. Thus, using hash tables or dictionaries, the cost of computing $m_1 \oplus m_2$ is $C_{r-hash} = |I_1||I_2|O(1)$.

There is a still another data structure that is less flexible but more efficient than both list and dictionary structures. In terms of lookup costs, a lookup in an array is about eight times faster than a dictionary lookup. An informal benchmark test involving 1000 values shows that a lookup in an array takes 367 ms whereas it takes 2419 ms in a dictionary with integer keys. The difference partially attributes to their different costs of computing memory addresses; an array involves just two machine cycles of memory location computation (base_pointer + offset * size) followed by a pointer dereference whereas a hash table computes the hash value of a key, taking 11-64 machine cycles. The flipside of the array structure, however, is resizing; it is expansive to adjust the size of an array if it is not initialized correctly in the first place. This is why the array structure may not be used for combining belief functions; the machine cannot determine the number of focal elements or the size of the array before it actually performs the combination.

Besides mass functions, other similar constructs such as belief, plausibility, and commonality functions can be also coded in dictionary structures. Therefore, all the operations involving belief functions may be implemented as program modules that take in one dictionary structure and produce a new dictionary. For example, the following is the pseudo code for computing a belief function from a mass function for all focal elements:

```
Dictionary<int,decimal> MassToBel(Dictionary<int,decimal>m) {
    Dictionary<int, decimal> belief = new Dictionary<int, decimal>();
    decimal beliefValue;
    foreach (DictionaryEntry x in m) {
        beliefValue = 0;
        foreach (DictionaryEntry y in m) {
            if (x.key⪰y.key) beliefValue += y.value;
        }
        belief.add(x.key, beliefValue);
    }
    return belief;
}
```

This code is to compute the belief function values for all focal elements. It can be simplified if we were to compute the belief for a specific proposition or integer since we do not need to cycle through all the focal elements in m.

Computing plausibility and commonality functions can be similarly implemented by changing the test of $x.key \succeq y.key$ in the above code into $x.key \& y.key \neq 0$ and $x.key \preceq y.key$ respectively.

4 Conclusion

This paper shows that, by using integers to represent subsets or focal elements, we can represent a belief function as a simple relation between integers and decimal mass values. The relational representation leverages modern operating systems's native binary representations and bitwise operations, improving the computational efficiency. It also allows more efficient algorithms to implement combinations. As I showed, using list structures, the relational representation allows up to 99.9% computation cost reduction compared to the usual subset representation. By using hash table structures, the relational representation can be further improved to the cost of $|I_1||I_2|O(1)$, where $|I_1|$ and $|I_2|$ are respectively the number of focal elements of the two belief functions to be combined. This is a huge reduction compared to the costs of using lists, which is $|I_1||I_2|(|I_1||I_2|+6)$ for the relational representation and $|I_1||I_2|(|I_1||I_2|n^2 + 2n^2 + 4)$, where n is the frame size, if focal elements are represented as subsets. The efficiency becomes even more obvious when computing belief functions in the power set in problems such as Möbius Transformation [3,8] or combining non-independent pieces of evidence using the cautious rule [1]. In addition, the relational representation allows us to use the classic relational database as knowledge bases to organize and store belief functions.

References

1. Denoeux, T.: Conjunctive and disjunctive combination of belief functions induced by non distinct bodies of evidence. Artificial Intelligence 172, 234–264 (2006)
2. Haenni, R., Lehmann, N.: Implementing belief function computations. International Journal of Intelligent Systems 18 (2003)
3. Kennes, R.: Computational aspects of the möbius transform of a graph. IEEE Transactions on SMC 22, 201–223 (1992)
4. Kong, A.: Multivariate belief functions and graphical models. Ph.D. thesis, Department of Statistics, Harvard University, Cambridge, MA (1986)
5. Maurer, W.D., Lewis, T.G.: Hash table methods. ACM Computing Surveys 7(1), 5–19 (1993)
6. Smets, P.: Belief funcions: the disjunctive rule of combination and the generalized bayesian theorem. International Journal of Approximate Reasoning 9, 1–35 (1993)
7. Smets, P.: The application of the matrix calculus to belief functions. Int. J. Approximate Reasoning 31, 1–30 (2002)
8. Thoma, H.M.: Factorization of belief functions. Ph.D. thesis, Dept. Statistics, Harvard Univ., Cambridge, MA (1989)

Modeling Qualitative Assessments under the Belief Function Framework

Amel Ennaceur[1,2], Zied Elouedi[1], and Éric Lefevre[2]

[1] LARODEC, University of Tunis, Institut Supérieur de Gestion, Tunisia
amel_naceur@yahoo.fr, zied.elouedi@gmx.fr
[2] Univ. Lille Nord of France, UArtois EA 3926 LGI2A, France
eric.lefevre@univ-artois.fr

Abstract. This paper investigates the problem of preference modeling under the belief function framework. In this work, we introduce a new model that is able to generate quantitative information from qualitative assessments. Therefore, we suggest to represent the decision maker preferences in different levels where the indifference, strict preference, weak preference and incompleteness relations are considered. Introducing the weak preference relation separates the preference area from the indifference one by inserting an intermediate zone.

1 Introduction

Modeling the decision maker preferences is not an easy task because he usually prefers to express his opinions qualitatively, based on knowledge and experience that he provides in response to a given question rather than direct quantitative information. Therefore, preferences need to be implemented in an assessment, which reflects as accurate as possible the human mind.

In other words, solving a problem dealing with expert preferences is usually characterized by a high degree of uncertainty. Besides, in some cases, the decision maker may be unable to express his opinions due to his lack of knowledge. He is then forced to provide incomplete or even erroneous information. Obviously, rejecting this difficulty in eliciting the expert preference is not a good practice.

To tackle the problem, a numerical representation under the belief function framework is introduced. Our main aim is to propose numerical values that represent the portion of belief expressed by the decision maker. Some researchers have already dealt with this problem and generate associated quantitative belief functions like [1] [13]. However, these approaches introduced only two fundamental preference relations called indifference and strict preferences.

One can overcome these difficulties as follows: we propose a new model including the weak preference relation, that separates the preference area from the indifference area by inserting an intermediate zone called weak-preference area [9]. A possible interpretation is an hesitation between strict preference and indifference.

Formally, consider two discrimination threshold functions: the indifference threshold ε, and the preference threshold γ. So, including the weak preference

F. Cuzzolin (Ed.): BELIEF 2014, LNAI 8764, pp. 171–179, 2014.

relation allows for more flexibility and nuance to the decision maker while expressing his preferences.

This leads to define crisp binary relations called strict preference $(P, \succ)$, indifference $(I, \sim)$, and weak preference $(Q, \succeq)$.

The originality of our model is to allow the expert to easily express his preferences and to provide a convenience framework for constructing quantitative belief functions from qualitative assessments by using different preference relations.

In this paper, section 2 and 3 describe an overview of the basic concepts of respectively the belief function theory and the qualitative belief function methods. Then, in the main body of the paper, we present our new contribution namely the preference modeling in the belief function framework. Finally, our method will be illustrated by an example.

2   Belief Function Theory

In this section, we briefly review the main concepts underlying the belief function theory as interpreted by the Transferable Belief Model (TBM). The latter is a useful model to represent quantified belief functions. Details can be found in [10] [12] [11].

2.1   Basic Concepts

The TBM is a model to represent quantified belief functions [12]. Let Θ be the frame of discernment representing a finite set of elementary hypotheses related to a problem domain. We denote by 2^{Θ} the set of all the subsets of Θ [10].

The impact of a piece of evidence on the different subsets of the frame of discernment Θ is represented by the so-called basic belief assignment (bba), denoted by m [10]:

$$\sum_{A \subseteq \Theta} m(A) = 1. \tag{1}$$

The value $m(A)$, named a basic belief mass (bbm), represents the portion of belief committed exactly to the event A. The events having positive bbm's are called focal elements. Let $\mathcal{F}(m) \subseteq 2^{\Theta}$ be the set of focal elements of the bba m.

Associated with m is the belief function is defined for $A \subseteq \Theta$ and $A \neq \emptyset$ as:

$$bel(A) = \sum_{\emptyset \neq B \subseteq A} m(B) \text{ and } bel(\emptyset) = 0. \tag{2}$$

The degree of belief $bel(A)$ given to a subset A of the frame Θ is defined as the sum of all the basic belief masses given to subsets that support A without supporting its negation.

2.2   Decision Making

The TBM considers that holding beliefs and making decision are distinct processes. Hence, it proposes a two level model:

- The credal level where beliefs are entertained and represented by belief functions.
- The pignistic level where beliefs are used to make decisions and represented by probability functions called the pignistic probabilities, denoted $BetP$ [11]:

$$BetP(A) = \sum_{B \subseteq \Theta} \frac{|A \cap B|}{|B|} \frac{m(B)}{(1 - m(\emptyset))}, \forall A \in \Theta. \tag{3}$$

2.3   Uncertainty Measures

In the case of the belief function framework, different uncertainty measures (UM) have been defined, such as [5] [6]:

$$H(m) = \sum_{A \in \mathcal{F}(m)} m(A) \log_2(\frac{|A|}{m(A)}). \tag{4}$$

The measure H is aimed at assessing the total uncertainty arising in a body of evidence due to both randomness (ignorance and inconsistency) and nonspecificity associated with a bba.

The measure H attains its global maximum when the bba distributes both randomness and nonspecificity uniformly over the largest possible set of focal elements.

3   Constructing Belief Functions from Qualitative Preferences

The problem of eliciting qualitatively expert opinions and generating basic belief assignments have been addressed by many researchers [1] [2] [3] [13].

In this section, we present Ben Yaghlane et al.'s method [1]. This approach is chosen since it handles the issue of inconsistency in the pair-wise comparisons.

So giving two alternatives, an expert can usually express which of the propositions is more likely to be true, thus they used two binary preference relations: the preference and the indifference relations.

The objective of this method is then to convert these preferences into constraints of an optimization problem whose resolution, according to some uncertainty measures (UM) (nonspecificity measures, conflict measures, composite measures), allows the generation of the least informative or the most uncertain belief functions defined as follows [1]:

$$a \succ b \Leftrightarrow bel(a) - bel(b) \geq \varepsilon \tag{5}$$

$$a \sim b \Leftrightarrow |bel(a) - bel(b)| \leq \varepsilon. \tag{6}$$

ε is considered to be the smallest gap that the expert may discern between the degrees of belief in two propositions a and b. Note that ε is a constant specified by the expert before beginning the optimization process.

Ben Yaghlane et al. proposed a method that requires that propositions are represented in terms of focal elements, and they assume that Θ (where Θ is the frame of discernment) should always be considered as a potential focal element. Then, a mono-objective technique was used to solve a constrained optimization problem.

The preference assessment is transformed into constraint according to the following relation:

$$bel(a) - bel(b) \geq \varepsilon \quad \forall(a, b) \text{ for which } a \succ b$$

Then, the indifference assessment is transformed into constraint according to this relation:

$$bel(a) - bel(b) \geq -\varepsilon \text{ and } bel(a) - bel(b) \leq \varepsilon \quad \forall(a, b) \text{ for which } a \sim b$$

Consequently, we obtain the following constrained optimization model:

$$Max_m UM(m)$$
$$s.t.$$
$$bel(a) - bel(b) \geq \varepsilon \quad \forall(a, b) \text{ for which } a \succ b$$
$$bel(a) - bel(b) \geq -\varepsilon \quad \forall(a, b) \text{ for which } a \sim b \qquad (7)$$
$$bel(a) - bel(b) \leq \varepsilon \quad \forall(a, b) \text{ for which } a \sim b$$
$$\sum_{a \in \mathcal{F}(m)} m(a) = 1, m(a) \geq 0, xzssss\forall a \subseteq \Theta; m(\emptyset) = 0$$

Furthermore, the proposed method addresses the problem of inconsistency. In fact, if the preference relations are consistent, then the optimization problem is feasible. Otherwise no solutions will be found. Thus, the expert may be guided to reformulate his preferences.

In the following section, we propose a method that deals with Ben Yaghlane et al. approach. Our model introduces new preference relations.

4   The Preference Modeling in the Belief Function Framework

We present now one way of introducing the qualitative belief approach to model and process preference information. It leads to a model which can be seen as an extension of the crisp model obtained by replacing pseudo-orders (I: indifference; Q: weak preference; P: preference) by belief informations.

Let us detail the typical features of these belief preference structures and their interpretations as significant quantitative information.

4.1   Preference Articulation

Let A be a set of alternatives, where a and b are two alternatives. Besides, crisp binary relations are based on two basic relations called strict preference P and indifference I [8]. They are defined as follows:

1. a is preferred to b $((a, b) \in P)$ iff $(a \succ b) \wedge \neg (b \succ a)$
2. a is indifferent to b $((a, b) \in I)$ iff $(a \succ b) \wedge (b \succ a)$

However, by using our model, we want to response to the question "The alternative a is at least as good as the alternative b?". We can have then the following answers:

− Either yes or no. The decision maker responses to the previous question by "yes" or "no".
− I don't know: The decision maker can also express his ignorance.
− Answers including the intensity of preference: for example, "a has strongly - weakly, moderately - preferred to b".

For these reasons, a richer model other than standard binary relation is a crucial step. We will assume that the comparison of a and b gives a choice between two other possible cases:

− a is weakly preferred to b $((a, b) \in Q)$ iff $(a \succeq b)$, means that the decision maker thinks that a is at least as good as b;
− the relation between a and b is unknown;

From this relation $\succeq$, we can derive two other important relations on A:

1. Strict preference relation, $\succ$, defined by:

$$a \succ b \Leftrightarrow a \succeq b \text{ and not } (b \succeq a)$$

2. Strict Indifference relation, $\sim$, defined by:

$$a \sim b \Leftrightarrow a \succeq b \text{ and } b \succeq a$$

Under the previous approach [1], in general, when comparing two alternatives a and b, the expert uses two binary relations the preference and indifference relations. Not matter of how large the difference is.

In real-life problems, however, a small positive difference of scores is not always a justification for a preference. A classical attitude is to assess discrimination thresholds to distinguish between significant and not significant differences of scores. Therefore, the indifference threshold ε was introduced [1]. If the performances of two alternatives differ by less than ε, then there is an indifference relation (see Equation (6)) and not a preference relation.

However, this model presents some drawbacks [4]. Suppose two alternatives a and b are such that:

$$bel(a) - bel(b) = \varepsilon - \frac{\mu}{2} \tag{8}$$

where μ is a positive quantity very small compared to ε.

If a slightly superior score (μ) was attached to a, we would obtain:

$$bel(a) - bel(b) = \varepsilon + \frac{\mu}{2} \qquad (9)$$

transforming the previous indifference ($a\ I\ b$) into strict preference ($a\ P\ b$).

We may overcome these difficulties by separating the preference and the indifference relations by inserting an intermediate zone called weak preference relation [7]. A possible interpretation is an hesitation between strict preference and indifference.

Formally, one may consider a strict preference threshold γ to distinguish between strict preference and weak preference. This strict preference threshold is a value such as if the performances of a and b differ by at least γ, then we are in a situation when one alternative is strongly preferred to the other. This is illustrated as follows:

$$a \succ b \Leftrightarrow bel(a) - bel(b) \geq \gamma \qquad (10)$$

$$a \succeq b \Leftrightarrow 0 \leq bel(a) - bel(b) \leq \gamma. \qquad (11)$$

However, when comparing two alternatives, we might want to use both the indifference and the strict preference thresholds, where $\gamma \geq \varepsilon$:

$$a \succ b \Leftrightarrow bel(a) - bel(b) \geq \gamma \qquad (12)$$

$$a \succeq b \Leftrightarrow \varepsilon \leq bel(a) - bel(b) \leq \gamma \qquad (13)$$

$$a \sim b \Leftrightarrow |bel(a) - bel(b)| \leq \varepsilon. \qquad (14)$$

Nevertheless, there exist different ways for choosing the preference and indifference threshold. For instance, Roy et al. [7] believe that the fixing of thresholds involves not only the estimation of error in a physical sense, but also a significant subjective input by the decision-maker himself. They assume that these two thresholds can be constant values or can take the linear form. Besides, in other works [7], γ and ε are derived from mathematical equations.

In this work, we assume that the thresholds γ and ε can be constant values. We interpret the indifference threshold as the minimum margin of uncertainty associated with a given alternative, and the preference threshold as the maximum margin of error associated with the alternative in question.

4.2   Computational Procedure

Now and after modeling the different preference relation, we propose to use the same model as Ben Yaghlane et al. method [1]. We transform these preferences relations into constraints as presented in section 3.2. We get:

$$Max_m UM(m)$$
$$s.t.$$
$$bel(a) - bel(b) \geq \gamma \quad \forall(a,b) \text{ for which } a \succ b$$
$$bel(a) - bel(b) \leq \gamma \quad \forall(a,b) \text{ for which } a \succeq b$$
$$bel(a) - bel(b) \geq \varepsilon \quad \forall(a,b) \text{ for which } a \succeq b \qquad (15)$$
$$bel(a) - bel(b) \leq \varepsilon \quad \forall(a,b) \text{ for which } a \sim b$$
$$bel(a) - bel(b) \geq -\varepsilon \quad \forall(a,b) \text{ for which } a \sim b$$
$$\sum_{a \in \mathcal{F}(m)} m(a) = 1; m(a) \geq 0; \forall a \subseteq \Theta; m(\emptyset) = 0.$$

Where the first constraint of the model is derived from the preference relation. The second and third constraints model the weak preference relation. The fourth and fifth constraints correspond to the indifference relation.

ε and γ are constants specified by the expert before beginning the optimization process.

The choice of thresholds intimately affects whether a particular binary relationship holds. While the choice of appropriate thresholds is not easy, in most realistic decision making situations there are good reasons for choosing non-zero values for ε and γ.

Figure 1 summarizes the obtained transformation. These thresholds define five different intervals in the domain of preference of two alternatives.

Fig. 1. Belief relations built from thresholds and crisp scores

5   Illustrative Example

Let us consider a problem of eliciting the weight of the candidate alternatives. The problem involves five alternatives:

$$\Theta = \{a, b, c, d, e\}.$$

The focal elements are:

$$F1 = \{a\}, F2 = \{a, b, c\}, F3 = \{b, d\}, F4 = \{e\}, F5 = \{a, e\}.$$

Next, the expert opinions should be elicitated. For this purpose, an interview with the expert is realized in order to model his preferences. Consequently, he has validated the following relations:

$$F2 \succ F1 \,,\, F1 \succeq F3 \,,\, F4 \sim F1, F5 \succ F1 \,,\, F5 \succ F4,$$

Now and after eliciting his preferences, the next step is to transform the obtained relations into optimization problem according to our proposed method.

We assume that $\varepsilon = 0.01$, $\gamma = 0.02$ and the uncertainty measures is H since it has a unique maximum as defined in Equation (4).

The following step is then to transform the obtained relations into constraints. We obtain:

1. $F2 \succ F1 \Leftrightarrow bel(F2) - bel(F1) \geq 0.02$
2. $F1 \succeq F3 \Leftrightarrow bel(F1) - bel(F3) \leq 0.02$
3. $F1 \succeq F3 \Leftrightarrow bel(F1) - bel(F3) \geq 0.01$
4. $F4 \sim F1 \Leftrightarrow bel(F4) - bel(F1) \leq 0.01$
5. $F4 \sim F1 \Leftrightarrow bel(F4) - bel(F1) \geq -0.01$
6. $F5 \succ F1 \Leftrightarrow bel(F5) - bel(F1) \geq 0.02$
7. $F5 \succ F4 \Leftrightarrow bel(F5) - bel(F4) \geq 0.02$

Then, we obtain the following optimization problem example:

$$Max_m H(m) = m(F1) * log_2(1/m(F1)) + m(F2) * log_2(3/m(F2))$$
$$+ m(F3) * log_2(2/m(F3)) + m(F4) * log_2(1/m(F4))$$
$$+ m(F5) * log_2(2/m(F5)) + m(\Theta) * log_2(5/m(\Theta));$$
$$s.t.$$
$$bel(F2) - bel(F1) \geq 0.02$$
$$bel(F1) - bel(F3) \leq 0.02$$
$$bel(F1) - bel(F3) \geq 0.01 \qquad (16)$$
$$bel(F4) - bel(F1) \leq 0.01$$
$$bel(F4) - bel(F1) \geq -0.01$$
$$bel(F5) - bel(F1) \geq 0.02$$
$$bel(F5) - bel(F4) \geq 0.02$$
$$\sum_{Fi \in \mathcal{F}(m)} m(Fi) = 1, m(Fi) \geq 0, \forall Fi \subseteq \Theta; m(\emptyset) = 0,$$

Finally, the obtained results are representing in Table 1.

Table 1. The obtained bba using the presented model

Criteria	$\{a\}$	$\{a, b, c\}$	$\{e\}$	$\{b, d\}$	$\{a, e\}$	Θ
m	0.092	0.203	0.082	0.082	0.203	0.338
bel	0.092	0.295	0.082	0.082	0.377	1

Table 1 gives the results of all ordered couples on the basis of their preference relation. Besides, we show that a new subset Θ is introduced that express the part of ignorance.

Indeed, using our model the expert expresses his assessments freely. By applying our presented solution, it is easy to see that our method aggregates all the elicited data.

Here, in the present example, the expert expressed his assessments only in some pairs of alternatives. Thus, a quantitative information is constructed from these incomplete and even uncertain preference relations.

We are then able to represent all the expert knowledge and to transform this information into quantitative data. We have obtained encouraging results since we have the same ranking of alternatives as expressed by the expert.

6   Conclusion

This paper is concerned with preference models including four relations: strict preference (P), weak preference (Q), indifference (I) and incompleteness (J).

The purpose was to establish conditions allowing to represent these four relations by numerical functions and thresholds under the belief function framework. Under this perspective, the paper proposes a new method based on Ben Yaghlane et al. approach and takes into account distinct levels of preferences.

As a future work, we will apply our method in multi-criteria decision making field, which can be interesting in eliciting expert judgments. Our proposed model will be applied through real application: Catering selection problem.

References

1. Ben Yaghlane, A., Denoeux, T., Mellouli, K.: Constructing belief functions from expert opinions. In: Proceedings of the 2nd International Conference on Information and Communication Technologies: from Theory to Applications (ICTTA 2006), Damascus, Syria, pp. 75–89 (2006)
2. Bryson, N., Mobolurin, A.: A process for generating quantitative belief functions. European Journal of Operational Research 115, 624–633 (1999)
3. Ennaceur, A., Elouedi, Z., Lefevre, E.: Introducing incomparability in modeling qualitative belief functions. In: Torra, V., Narukawa, Y., López, B., Villaret, M. (eds.) MDAI 2012. LNCS, vol. 7647, pp. 382–393. Springer, Heidelberg (2012)
4. Fodor, J., Roubens, M.: Fuzzy strict preference relations in decision making. In: Proceedings of the Second IEEE International Conference on Fuzzy Systems, pp. 1145–1149 (1993)
5. Pal, N., Bezdek, J., Hemasinha, R.: Uncertainty measures for evidential reasoning I: A review. International Journal of Approximate Reasoning 7, 165–183 (1992)
6. Pal, N., Bezdek, J., Hemasinha, R.: Uncertainty measures for evidential reasoning II: A review. International Journal of Approximate Reasoning 8, 1–16 (1993)
7. Perny, P., Roy, B.: The use of fuzzy outranking relations in preference modelling. Fuzzy Sets and Systems 49(1), 33–53 (1992)
8. Roubens, M., Vincke, P.: Preference modelling. Springer, Berlin (1985)
9. Roy, B.: Pseudo-orders: Definition, properties and numerical representation. Mathematical Social Sciences 14, 263–274 (1987)
10. Shafer, G.: A Mathematical Theory of Evidence. Princeton University Press (1976)
11. Smets, P.: The application of the Transferable Belief Model to diagnostic problems. International Journal of Intelligent Systems 13, 127–158 (1998)
12. Smets, P., Kennes, R.: The Transferable Belief Model. Artificial Intelligence 66, 191–234 (1994)
13. Wong, S., Lingras, P.: Representation of qualitative user preference by quantitative belief functions. IEEE Transactions on Knowledge and Data Engineering 6, 72–78 (1994)

A Study on Generalising Bayesian Inference
to Evidential Reasoning

Jian-Bo Yang and Dong-Ling Xu

Decision and Cognitive Sciences Research Centre
The University of Manchester, Manchester M15 6PB, UK
{jian-bo.yang,ling.xu}@mbs.ac.uk
Key Laboratory of Process Optimization and Intelligent Decision-making,
Ministry of Education, Hefei 230009, Anhui, P.R. China

Abstract. In this paper the relationship between Bayes' rule and the *Evidential Reasoning* (*ER*) rule is explored. The *ER* rule has been uncovered recently for inference with multiple pieces of uncertain evidence profiled as a belief distribution and takes Dempster's rule in the evidence theory as a special case. After a brief introduction to the *ER* rule the conditions under which Bayes' rule becomes a special case of the *ER* rule are established. The main findings include that the normalisation of likelihoods in Bayesian paradigm results in the degrees of belief in the *ER* paradigm. This leads to *ER*-based probabilistic (likelihood) inference with evidence profiled in the same format of belief distribution. Numerical examples are examined to demonstrate the findings and their potential applications in probabilistic inference. It is also demonstrated that the findings enable the generalisation of Bayesian inference to evidential reasoning with inaccurate probability information with weight and reliability.

Keywords: Evidential reasoning, Belief distribution, Bayesian inference, Probabilistic reasoning, Likelihood inference, Decision making.

1   Introduction

The evidential reasoning (*ER*) rule has been established recently for conjunctive combination of independent evidence with weights and reliabilities [16]. It constitutes a general conjunctive probabilistic reasoning process and reveals that the combined degree of joint support for a proposition from two pieces of independent evidence constitutes two parts in general: the bounded sum of their individual support and the orthogonal sum of their collective support. The *ER* rule is based on the orthogonal sum operation and as such inherits the basic properties of being associative and commutative, which means that it can be used to combine multiple pieces of evidence in any order without changing the final results. It also satisfies common sense synthesis axioms that any rational probabilistic reasoning process should follow.

The *ER* rule takes the original *ER* algorithm [12, 13, 14, 15] as a special case when the reliability of evidence is equal to its weight and the weights of all pieces of evidence are normalised. It is proven that Dempster's rule in the theory of evidence

F. Cuzzolin (Ed.): BELIEF 2014, LNAI 8764, pp. 180–189, 2014.

[2, 3, 7, 9] is also a special case of the *ER* rule when each piece of evidence is fully reliable. The *ER* rule enhances Dempster's rule for combining pieces of fully reliable evidence that are highly or completely conflicting through a new reliability perturbation analysis, thus resolving the non-definition and counter intuitive problems associated with Dempster's rule [5, 6, 17].

In the *ER* rule, a frame of discernment is composed of a set of hypotheses that are mutually exclusive and collectively exhaustive as in the theory of evidence [7]. It is assumed that basic probabilities can be assigned to not only singleton hypotheses but also to any of their subsets, thereby allowing a piece of evidence to be profiled by a belief distribution (*BD*) defined on the power set of the frame of discernment. *BD* is regarded as the most natural and flexible generalisation of conventional probability distribution in the sense that the former allows inexact reasoning at whatever level of abstraction [4] and on the other hand reduces to the latter precisely if basic probabilities are assigned to singleton hypotheses only.

Bayesian inference is regarded as a classical and rigorous probabilistic reasoning process. Much attention has been paid to generalise Bayesian inference. Dempster's pioneer work [2, 3] is among the most prominent, in which Dempster asserted that the ordinary likelihood function based on a sample from a general multinomial population is proportional to the upper probability of the hypothesis. Shafer [7, 8] and Smets [11] proposed belief functions to show that the application of Dempster's rule on these belief functions can approximate Bayesian inference in general when sample size is very large [8] but only lead to the same result as Bayes' rule for a rather special case with a single frequency distribution, which however is rare in practice if any. Aickin [1] proposed to construct credibility functions and modify Dempster's rule to make likelihood inference very nearly a special case of the Dempster–Shafer theory, which leads to computations that are quite different from those of Smets. In Aickin's approach, a credibility function is generated by dividing all likelihoods with the maximum likelihood for each sample, which is consistent with Demspter's aforementioned assertion but is not meant to show that Dempster's rule can be reduced to Bayes' rule for equivalent likelihood inference from sample data.

Our research is rooted in Dempster's original work on multivalued mapping from sample space to hypothesis space. In this paper, we intend to show the novel results generated from our new research that the *ER* rule, which takes Dempster's rule as a special case when all observations are fully reliable, is the same as Bayes' rule in likelihood inference if likelihoods are normalised for mapping observations from sample space to hypothesis space. In this way, any evidence generated from observations can be equivalently profiled in the same format as belief distribution for consistent knowledge representation and inference, whilst in Bayesian inference evidence is represented in different formats of *prior* probability and likelihood. The generalisation of Bayesian inference to evidential reasoning is also investigated in the context of information acquisition from ambiguous observations and inaccurate diagnoses. Numerical examples are examined to show how evidential reasoning can be conducted to implement and generalise Bayesian inference in situations where data are not accurate. It is also shown how important evidence reliability can be in inference.

The rest of the paper is organised as follows. In Section 2, the concepts and properties of the *ER* rule are briefly introduced. In Section 3, the conditions under which the *ER* rule reduces to Bayes' rule are established. Section 4 presents a study on generalising Bayesian inference to evidential reasoning. Two numerical examples are examined. The paper is concluded in Section 5.

2   Brief Introduction to the *ER* Rule

In this section, the *ER* rule established recently [16] is briefly introduced. Suppose $\Theta = \{h_1, \cdots, h_N\}$ is a set of mutually exclusive and collectively exhaustive hypotheses. Θ is referred to as a frame of discernment. The power set of Θ consists of 2^N subsets of Θ, denoted by 2^Θ or $P(\Theta)$, as follows

$$P(\Theta) = 2^\Theta = \{\varnothing, \{h_1\}, \cdots, \{h_N\}, \{h_1, h_2\}, \cdots, \{h_1, h_N\}, \cdots, \{h_1, \cdots, h_{N-1}\}, \Theta\} \tag{1}$$

In the framework of the *ER* rule, a piece of evidence e_j is represented as a random set and profiled by a belief distribution (*BD*) as follows

$$e_j = \left\{ (\theta, p_{\theta.j}), \forall \theta \subseteq \Theta, \sum_{\theta \subseteq \Theta} p_{\theta.j} = 1 \right\} \tag{2}$$

where $(\theta, p_{\theta.j})$ is an element of evidence e_j, representing that the evidence points to proposition θ, which can be any subset of Θ or any element of $P(\Theta)$ except for the empty set, to the degree of $p_{\theta.j}$, referred to as probability or degree of belief in general. $(\theta, p_{\theta.j})$ is referred to as a focal element of e_j if $p_{\theta.j} > 0$.

Associated with evidence e_j is a reliability, denoted by r_j, which represents the ability of the information source, where e_j is generated, to provide correct assessment or solution for a given problem (Smarandache et al., 2010). The reliability of a piece of evidence is the inherent property of the evidence, and in the *ER* framework measures the degree of support for or opposition against a proposition given that the evidence points to the proposition. In other words, the unreliability of a piece of evidence sets a bound within which another piece of evidence can play a role in support for and opposition against different propositions.

On the other hand, evidence e_j can also be associated with a weight, denoted by w_j. The weight of a piece of evidence shares the same definition as that of its reliability. The former is not different from the latter if all pieces of evidence are measured in the same joint space. When different pieces of evidence are acquired from different sources and measured in different ways, however, the weight of evidence can be used to reflect its relative importance in comparison with other evidence and determined according to who uses the evidence. This means that weight w_j can be subjective and different from reliability r_j in situations where different pieces of evidence are generated from different sources and measured in different ways.

To combine a piece of evidence with other evidence, it is necessary to take into account the above three elements of the evidence: its belief distribution, reliability and weight. In the *ER* rule, this is achieved by defining a so-called weighted belief distribution with reliability as follows

$$m_j = \left\{ (\theta, \tilde{m}_{\theta,j}), \forall \theta \subseteq \Theta; (P(\Theta), \tilde{m}_{P(\Theta),j}) \right\} \tag{3}$$

where $\tilde{m}_{\theta,j}$ measures the degree of support for θ from e_j with both the weight and reliability of e_j taken into account, defined as follows

$$\tilde{m}_{\theta,j} = \begin{cases} 0 & \theta = \varnothing \\ c_{rw,j} m_{\theta,j} & \theta \subseteq \Theta, \theta \neq \varnothing \\ c_{rw,j}(1 - r_j) & \theta = P(\Theta) \end{cases} \tag{4}$$

where $m_{\theta,j} = w_j p_{\theta,j}$. $c_{rw,j} = 1/(1 + w_j - r_j)$ is a normalisation factor, which is uniquely determined to satisfy $\sum_{\theta \subseteq \Theta} \tilde{m}_{\theta,j} + \tilde{m}_{P(\Theta),j} = 1$ given that $\sum_{\theta \subseteq \Theta} p_{\theta,j} = 1$. Note that there would be $w_j = r_j$ or $m_{\theta,j} = r_j p_{\theta,j}$ if all pieces of evidence are measured in a joint space, or $p_{\theta,j}$ for each piece of evidence is given by the same probability function. Compared with Shafer's discounting method, the critical difference is that in the *ER* rule, the degree of residual support (after discounting) is earmarked to the power set for redistribution instead of assigning it specifically to the frame of discernment.

If two pieces of evidence e_0 and e_1 are independent in that the information that e_0 carries does not depend on whether e_1 is known or not and vice versa, the combined degree of belief to which e_0 and e_1 jointly support proposition θ, denoted by $p_{\theta,e(2)}$, is then generated by the orthogonal sum of their weighted belief distributions with reliability (i.e. m_0 and m_1), given as follows

$$p_{\theta,e(2)} = \begin{cases} 0 & \theta = \varnothing \\ \dfrac{\hat{m}_{\theta,e(2)}}{\sum_{D \subseteq \Theta} \hat{m}_{D,e(2)}} & \theta \subseteq \Theta, \theta \neq \varnothing \end{cases}$$

$$\hat{m}_{\theta,e(2)} = \left[(1 - r_1)m_{\theta,0} + (1 - r_0)m_{\theta,1} \right] + \sum_{B \cap C = \theta} m_{B,0} m_{C,1} \quad \forall \theta \subseteq \Theta \tag{5}$$

The recursive formulae of the *ER* rule are also given to combine multiple pieces of evidence in any order.

It is proven that Dempster's rule is a special case of the above *ER* rule when each piece of evidence e_j in question is assumed to be fully reliable, or $r_j = 1$ for all j.

3 Equivalence between the *ER* Rule and Bayes' Rule

This section is aimed to provide the exact conditions under which a special case of the *ER* rule, the same as Dempster's rule, reduces to Bayes' rule.

Let e_0 stand for old evidence that is profiled with the *prior* probabilities of the hypotheses in the frame of discernment $\Theta = \{h_1, \cdots, h_N\}$, or

$$e_0 = \left\{ (h_i, p_{i0}), i = 1, \cdots, N, \sum_{i=1}^{N} p_{i0} = 1 \right\} \tag{6}$$

where p_{i0} is the probability to which evidence e_0 points to hypothesis h_i, or $p_{i0} = p(h_i | e_0)$.

Let c_{ij} stand for the likelihood to which the jth test result (e_j) is expected to occur given that the ith hypothesis (h_i) is true and evidence e_0 is known, or $c_{ij} = p(e_j | h_i, e_0)$, with $\sum_{j=1}^{L} c_{ij} = 1$ for $i = 1, \cdots, N$, as shown in Table 1. Given that a test result e_1 is observed as new evidence, Bayes' rule can be used to generate *posterior* probability that both e_0 and e_1 support hypothesis h_i as follows

$$p(h_i | e_1, e_0) = \frac{p(e_1 | h_i, e_0) p(h_i | e_0)}{\sum_{n=1}^{N} p(e_1 | h_n, e_0) p(h_n | e_0)} \qquad (7)$$

Table 1. Likelihoods

Hypothesis	Test result				
	e_1	...	e_j	...	e_L
h_1	c_{11}	...	c_{1j}	...	c_{1L}
$\vdots$	$\vdots$	$\ddots$	$\vdots$	$\ddots$	$\vdots$
h_i	c_{i1}	...	c_{ij}	...	c_{iL}
$\vdots$	$\vdots$	$\ddots$	$\vdots$	$\ddots$	$\vdots$
h_N	c_{N1}	...	c_{Nj}	...	c_{NL}

While Bayes' rule is rigorous, the combination of old evidence e_0 with new evidence e_1 in Equation (7) is not symmetrical [7], in the sense that the old evidence is profiled as a probability distribution over the set of hypotheses h_i for $i = 1, \cdots, N$, whilst the new evidence is characterised by likelihoods over the set of test results e_j ($j = 1, \cdots, L$) for a given hypothesis. This asymmetry underpins Bayesian inference as a process of updating knowledge once new evidence becomes available. However, this can cause confusion if multiple pieces of evidence are not particularly classified as old and new and need to be combined in any order. Nevertheless, it is desirable that both old and new evidence is represented in the same format for combination.

Let p_{ij} stand for the degree of belief that test result e_j points to hypothesis h_i, with $\sum_{i=1}^{N} p_{ij} = 1$ for $j = 1, \cdots, L$. Test result e_j can then be profiled over the set of hypotheses symmetrically in the same way as for evidence e_0 as follows

$$e_j = \left\{ (h_i, p_{ij}), i = 1, \cdots, N, \sum_{i=1}^{N} p_{ij} = 1 \right\} \qquad j = 1, \cdots, L \qquad (8)$$

p_{ij} can be generated from likelihood c_{ij}. The following results establish the equivalence conditions under which Bayes' rule is a special case of the *ER* rule with $r_j = 1$ for all j, which constitutes a symmetrical evidence combination process.

Theorem 1. If all tests to generate likelihoods in Table 1 are conducted independently, the relationship between likelihood c_{ij} and degree of belief p_{ij} is given by

$$p_{ij} = c_{ij} \Big/ \sum_{n=1}^{N} c_{nj} \qquad \text{for } i = 1, \cdots, N \text{ and } j = 1, \cdots, L \qquad (9)$$

Let $p_{h_i.e(2)}$ stand for the combined degree of belief to which both e_0 and e_j support hypothesis h_i. We then have the following result.

Corollary 1. Under the same conditions as for Theorem 1, if probability is assigned only to singleton hypothesis, each piece of evidence is fully reliable and the degrees of belief are given by Equations (9), the *ER* rule reduces to Bayes' rule, or

$$p_{h_i.e(2)} = p(h_i | e_j, e_0) \qquad (10)$$

The numerical example below is used to demonstrate how the above results could be applied to symmetrical Bayesian inference via equivalent evidential reasoning.

Example 1. Suppose independent tests and diagnoses for a sample of 10000 persons in a population are shown in Table 2. We are interested to find the probability to which a person from the population already has *AIDS* if the person has his first *HIV* test that is positive.

Table 2. Experimental Data

Sample Data		Test Result		Total Diagnosis
		HIV Positive (e_1)	HIV Negative (e_2)	
Hypotheses	AIDS (h_1)	95	5	100
	No AIDS (h_2)	990	8910	9900
Total Test		1085	8915	10000

What needs to be identified is the degree of belief, denoted by $p_{h_1.e(2)}$, to which h_1 is supported by both pieces of evidence: the *prior AIDS* distribution of the population as revealed by the experiment (e_0) and a positive *HIV* test result (e_1). From Equation (9), the *prior* probabilities $p_{10} = p(h_1 | e_0)$ and $p_{20} = p(h_2 | e_0)$, and likelihoods c_{11} and c_{21} for the two pieces of evidence e_0 and e_1 can be generated from the experimental data given in Table 2 as follows

$$p_{10} = p(h_1 | e_0) = \frac{100}{10000} = 0.01, \qquad p_{20} = p(h_2 | e_0) = \frac{9900}{10000} = 0.99;$$

$$c_{11} = p(e_1 | h_1, e_0) = \frac{95}{100} = 0.95, \qquad c_{21} = p(e_1 | h_2, e_0) = \frac{990}{9900} = 0.1$$

$$p_{11} = \frac{c_{11}}{c_{11} + c_{21}} = \frac{0.95}{0.95 + 0.1} = \frac{0.95}{1.05} = 0.9048, \qquad p_{21} = \frac{c_{21}}{c_{11} + c_{21}} = \frac{0.1}{1.05} = 0.0952$$

Equation (5) with $r_0 = r_1 = 1$ can then be used to calculate $p_{h_1, e(2)}$ as follows

$$p_{h_1, e(2)} = \frac{p_{11} p_{10}}{p_{11} p_{10} + p_{21} p_{20}} = \frac{0.9048 \times 0.01}{0.9048 \times 0.01 + 0.0952 \times 0.99} = 0.0876$$

From the conventional Bayesian analysis, the same result can be generated as follows

$$p(h_1 | e_1, e_0) = \frac{p(e_1 | h_1, e_0) p(h_1 | e_0)}{p(e_1 | h_1, e_0) p(h_1 | e_0) + p(e_1 | h_2, e_0) p(h_2 | e_0)} = \frac{0.95 \times 0.01}{0.95 \times 0.01 + 0.1 \times 0.99} = 0.0876$$

4   Generalisation of Bayesian Inference to Evidential Reasoning

Bayesian inference as shown in the previous section is rigorous but requires accurate *prior* probabilities and likelihoods in the sense that each test must lead to exactly one of the L test results and each test result must be diagnosed to belong to exactly one of the N hypotheses. Such accuracy is desirable and should always be pursued. However, ambiguous test results and inaccurate diagnoses are common in real experiments. This section is aimed to investigate how the above "accurate" and "rigorous" Bayesian inference can be generalised for rigorous reasoning with evidence generated from ambiguous tests and inaccurate diagnoses.

Let θ stand for a proposition representing a set of diagnoses, $c_{\theta, j}$ for the generalised likelihood to which the jth test result (e_j) is expected to occur given proposition θ, with $\sum_{j=1}^{L} c_{\theta, j} = 1$ for any $\theta \subseteq \Theta = \{h_1, \cdots, h_N\}$, and $p_{\theta, j}$ for the belief degree to which the jth test result points to proposition θ, with $\sum_{\theta \subseteq \Theta} p_{\theta, j} = 1$ for any $j = 1, \cdots, L$. Belief degree $p_{\theta, j}$ can be generated from generalised likelihood $c_{\theta, j}$ as follows.

Corollary 2. Suppose the same conditions as for Theorem 1 are held. If all tests for generating generalised likelihood $c_{\theta, j}$ are conducted independently, the relationship between $c_{\theta, j}$ and $p_{\theta, j}$ is given by:

$$p_{\theta, j} = c_{\theta, j} \Big/ \sum_{A \subseteq \Theta} c_{A, j} \qquad \text{for } \theta \subseteq \Theta \text{ and } j = 1, \cdots, L \qquad (11)$$

Example 2. Suppose there are imprecise experimental data for a population, as shown in Table 3. It is also assumed that the experimental data can represent the *prior AIDS* distribution of the population with a 95% level of reliability and an *AIDS* diagnosis from a *HIV* test can be regarded to be 98% reliable. What is the probability to which a person from the population already has *AIDS* if the person's first *HIV* test turns out to be positive, given that the person's *HIV* test result and the experimental data are regarded to be of equal importance in the inference?

Table 3. Experimental Data under Uncertainty

Diagnosis		HIV test result			Total diagnosis
		Positive e_1	Negative e_2	Unknown e	
AIDS	h_1	95	5	0	100
No AIDS	h_2	980	8860	10	9850
Unknown	$\Theta = \{h_1, h_2\}$	5	7	38	50
Total test		1080	8872	48	10000

The belief degrees for the evidence of the *prior AIDS* distribution (e_0) for the population are given by $p_{10} = 100/10000 = 0.01$, $p_{20} = 9850/10000 = 0.985$, $p_{\Theta 0} = 50/10000 = 0.005$, as shown in Table 3.

The generalised likelihood $c_{\theta 1}$ and belief degree $p_{\theta 1}$ for the evidence of positive *HIV* test result (e_1) are calculated in Table 3 by $c_{11} = 95/100 = 0.95$, $c_{21} = 980/9850 = 0.0995$, $c_{\theta 1} = 5/50 = 0.1$, and then

$$p_{11} = \frac{c_{11}}{c_{11} + c_{21} + c_{\theta 1}} = \frac{0.95}{1.1495} = 0.8264, \ p_{21} = \frac{0.0995}{1.1495} = 0.0866, \ p_{\theta 1} = \frac{0.1}{1.1495} = 0.087.$$

The reliabilities and weights of e_0 and e_1 are given by $r_0 = 0.95$, $r_1 = 0.98$ and $w_0 = w_1 = 0.5$. Note that the weights are normalized here with $w_0 + w_1 = 1$ for illustration purpose. In general, such normalisation is not always required. The degrees of individual support for θ from e_0 and e_1 are calculated by

$$m_{h_1.0} = w_0 p_{10} = 0.5 \times 0.01 = 0.005, \ m_{h_2.0} = w_0 p_{20} = 0.4925, \ m_{\theta 0} = w_0 p_{\theta 0} = 0.0025;$$

$$m_{h_1.1} = w_1 p_{11} = 0.5 \times 0.826 = 0.4132, \ m_{h_2.1} = w_1 p_{21} = 0.0433, \ m_{\theta 1} = w_1 p_{\theta 1} = 0.0435$$

Equation (5) can then be used to combine e_0 and e_1 to count their joint support by

$$\hat{m}_{h_1.e(2)} = (1 - r_1)m_{h_1.0} + (1 - r_0)m_{h_1.1} + m_{h_1.0}m_{h_1.1} + m_{h_1.0}m_{\theta 1} + m_{\theta 0}m_{h_1.1} = 0.0241$$

$$\hat{m}_{h_2.e(2)} = (1 - r_1)m_{h_2.0} + (1 - r_0)m_{h_2.1} + m_{h_2.0}m_{h_2.1} + m_{h_2.0}m_{\theta 1} + m_{\theta 0}m_{h_2.1} = 0.0549$$

$$\hat{m}_{\theta.e(2)} = (1 - r_1)m_{\theta 0} + (1 - r_0)m_{\theta 1} + m_{\theta 0}m_{\theta 1} = 0.0023$$

The belief degrees to which e_0 and e_1 both support θ are finally generated by

$$p_{h_1.e(2)} = \frac{\hat{m}_{h_1.e(2)}}{\hat{m}_{h_1.e(2)} + \hat{m}_{h_2.e(2)} + \hat{m}_{\theta.e(2)}} = \frac{0.0241}{0.0241 + 0.0549 + 0.0023} = \frac{0.0241}{0.0813} = 0.2964$$

$$p_{h_2.e(2)} = \frac{0.0549}{0.0813} = 0.6753, \text{ and } p_{\theta.e(2)} = \frac{0.0023}{0.0813} = 0.0283$$

The ambiguity and inaccuracy in the experiment are retained by $p_{\theta.e(2)}$ in the above final results. As such, the probability to which the person has *AIDS* is not precise but between 0.2964 and 0.3247 ($p_{h_1.e(2)} + p_{\theta.e(2)}$). The probability to which the person does not have *AIDS* is between 0.6753 and 0.7036 ($p_{h_2.e(2)} + p_{\theta.e(2)}$).

It should be noted that the reliability of evidence plays an important role in inference and should be estimated with care and rigor. For instance, if both pieces of evidence are assumed to be fully reliable in Example 2, or $r_0 = r_1 = 1$, it can be shown that there will be $p_{h_1,e(2)} = 0.0716$, $p_{h_2,e(2)} = 0.926$ and $p_{\theta,e(2)} = 0.0024$, meaning a much smaller probability (0.0716 to 0.0740) of having *AIDS* with much smaller ambiguity (0.0024). Such results are quite different from the results generated above for $r_0 = 0.95$ and $r_1 = 0.98$, but justifiable as evidence e_0 is against the first hypothesis "*AIDS*" much more than evidence e_1 against the second hypothesis "*No AIDS*".

5   Concluding Remarks

In this paper, the recently established evidential reasoning (*ER*) rule was briefly introduced. The relationship between Bayes' rule and the *ER* rule was then investigated and their equivalence conditions were provided. This study shows that Bayesian inference can be conducted in a symmetrical process in the *ER* paradigm where each piece of evidence is profiled in the same format of belief distribution. This on one hand facilitates the combination of evidence in any order for Bayesian inference. On the other hand, experimental data can be used to acquire evidence. In this study, Bayesian inference was generalised to take into account ambiguous test results and inaccurate diagnoses in experiment. This can help conduct inference in a realistic yet rigorous manner without having to make unnecessary assumptions about inaccurate or missing data. The two examples demonstrated the implementation processes of Bayesian inference in the *ER* paradigm. Finally, it is important to note that the reliability of evidence plays an important role in inference and needs to be estimated using domain specific knowledge with care and rigor.

Acknowledgement. This work was partly supported by the European Commission under the grant No.: EC- GPF-314836.

References

1. Aickin, M.: Connecting Dempster-Shafer belief functions with likelihood-based inference. Synthese 123(3), 347–364 (2000)
2. Dempster, A.P.: Upper and lower probabilities induced by a multi-valued mapping. Annals of Mathematical Statistics 38, 325–339 (1967)
3. Dempster, A.P.: A generalization of Bayesian inference. Journal of the Royal Statistical Society, Series B 30, 205–247 (1968)
4. Gordon, J., Shortliffe, E.H.: A method for managing evidential reasoning in a hierarchical hypothesis space. Artificial Intelligence 26(3), 323–357 (1985)
5. Haenni, R.: Shedding new light on Zadeh's criticism of Dempster's rule of combination. In: The 7th International Conference on Information Fusion (FUSION) (2005)
6. Murphy, C.K.: Combining belief functions when evidence conflicts. Decision Support Systems 29, 1–9 (2000)
7. Shafer, G.: A Mathematical Theory of Evidence. Princeton University Press, Princeton (1976)

8. Shafer, G.: Belief functions and parametric models. Journal of the Royal Statistical Society, Series B 44, 322–352 (1982)
9. Shafer, G., Pearl, J.: Readings in Uncertain Reasoning. Morgan Kaufmann Publishers, Inc., San Mateo (1990)
10. Smarandache, F., Dezert, J., Tacnet, J.M.: Fusion of sources of evidence with different importances and reliabilities. In: The 2010 13th IEEE Conference on Information Fusion (FUSION), pp. 1–8 (2010)
11. Smets, P.: Belief functions: The disjunctive rule of combination and the generalized Bayesian theorem. International Journal Approximate Reasoning 9(1), 1–35 (1993)
12. Xu, D.L., Yang, J.B., Wang, Y.M.: The ER approach for multi-attribute decision analysis under interval uncertainties. European Journal of Operational Research 174(3), 1914–1943 (2006)
13. Yang, J.B.: Rule and utility based evidential reasoning approach for multiattribute decision analysis under uncertainties. European Journal of Operational Research 131, 31–61 (2001)
14. Yang, J.B., Xu, D.L.: On the evidential reasoning algorithm for multiattribute decision analysis under uncertainty. IEEE Transactions on Systems, Man, and Cybernetics Part A: Systems and Humans 32(3), 289–304 (2002)
15. Yang, J.B., Wang, Y.M., Xu, D.L.: The Evidential reasoning approach for MADA under both probabilistic and fuzzy uncertainties. European Journal of Operational Research 171(1), 309–343 (2006)
16. Yang, J.B., Xu, D.L.: Evidential reasoning rule for evidence combination. Artificial Intelligence 205, 1–29 (2013)
17. Zadeh, L.A.: A mathematical theory of evidence. AI Magazine 55, 81–83 (1984)

Partial Ranking by Incomplete Pairwise Comparisons Using Preference Subsets

Johan Schubert

Department of Decision Support Systems, Division of Information and Aeronautical Systems,
Swedish Defence Research Agency,SE-164 90 Stockholm, Sweden
schubert@foi.se
http://www.foi.se/fusion

Abstract. In multi-criteria decision making the decision maker need to assign weights to criteria for evaluation of alternatives, but decision makers usually find it difficult to assign precise weights to several criteria. On the other hand, decision makers may readily provide a number of preferences regarding the relative importance between two disjoint subsets of criteria. We extend a procedure by L. V. Utkin for ranking alternatives based on decision makers' preferences. With this new method we may evaluate and rank partial sequences of preferences between two subsets of criteria. To achieve this ranking it is necessary to model the information value of an incomplete sequence of preferences and compare this with the belief-plausibility of that sequence in order to find the partial ranking of preferences with maximum utility.

Keywords: belief function, Dempster-Shafer theory, preferences, multi-criteria decision making, pairwise comparison, ranking.

1   Introduction

In multi-criteria decision making (MCDM) decision makers needs to evaluate and rank different alternatives using several criteria (e.g., measures of effectiveness; MOEs). To be able to rank the alternatives they usually seek a weighting of these criteria, but weights may be unavailable and decision makers may find it impossible to assign precise weights to all criteria. An initial step can be to filter all alternatives under consideration by Pareto filtering [6, 16]. This will eliminate all alternatives that can never be selected regardless of which weight assignment is adopted for the criteria. This will reduce the problem size, but the same problem with assigning weights remains. However, it is often possible for decision makers to express an order of importance between all different criteria, or at least to express a preference between two different

---

* This work was supported by the FOI research project "Simulation-based Defense Planning", which is funded by the R&D programme of the Swedish Armed Forces.

F. Cuzzolin (Ed.): BELIEF 2014, LNAI 8764, pp. 190–198, 2014.

subsets of all criteria.

In this paper we develop an extension to a procedure by Utkin [20] for ranking alternatives based on multiple decision makers' preferences in MCDM. We let a group of decision makers express any number of preferences regarding the relative importance between any two disjoint subsets of criteria. We derive a method for finding a partial preference order of all measures of effectiveness. This method will accept any preference expression about the MOEs from multiple decision makers. For example, expressions such as "*measure of effectiveness* MOE_i *is more important than measure of effectiveness* MOE_j"; $MOE_i \succcurlyeq MOE_j$, or expressions regarding two different subsets of all measures such as "*measures* MOE_i *and* MOE_j *are more important than measures* MOE_k *and* MOE_l"; $\{MOE_i, MOE_j\} \succcurlyeq \{MOE_k, MOE_l\}$. As we extend the preference assignment approach developed by Utkin we combine it with a preference ranking approach by Schubert [12] to derive a partial ranking of all MOEs. When the best sequence of preferences (of measures of effectiveness) is found we can weight all alternatives and select the best alternative with the highest value. This alternative can be further analysed to explain the cause of success [14].

Another approach is provided by Masson and Denœux [11] that extends a methodology by Tritchler and Lockwood [19]. In [19] simple support functions regarding each singleton pair of preferences $m^{\Theta_{ij}}$ are assigned on individual frames Θ_{ij} by experts. After all assignments are extended to a common frame of discernment and combined the most plausible linear ordering of all preference is found. In [11] a linear programming approach is proposed to solve the problem in an efficient way. The methodology is further extended to some partial rankings of preferences where a hierarchical clustering approach selects which partial orders of preferences are evaluated based on plausibility. The final choice of preferred partial order is left to the user.

In Sec. 2 we assign basic belief masses based on all decision makers' pairwise preferences of any two subsets of all measures of effectiveness. In Sec. 3 we calculate a decision maker's belief and plausibility in partial sequences of preferences. In Sec. 4 we derive the information value of a partial sequence of preferences. Based on the results of the previous two sections we calculate the utility of each partial sequence of preferences as a product of two functions corresponding, on the one hand, to belief and plausibility in the proposition and, on the other hand, the information value of the proposition (Sec. 4). Finally, conclusions are drawn (Sec. 5).

2   Assignment of Decision Makers' Preferences

We will keep track of all preferences expressed by all decision makers. This includes both preferences about the order of importance among single measures and among subsets of measures. For each expression we count the number of decision makers giving the same preferences and sum-up the total number of assigned preferences by all decision makers

$$c_{AB}(\{MOE_i\}_{i \in A} \succcurlyeq \{MOE_j\}_{j \in B}), \tag{1}$$

where $\varnothing \neq A, B \subseteq \{i\}_{i=1}^{|\{MOE_i\}|} = I$, i.e., A and B are subsets of and index set I of indices corresponding to the set of all MOEs. Any number of these c_{AB} may be equal to zero due to a lack of assigned preferences regarding some subsets of MOEs.

The preferences assigned between two subsets of measures can be simplified to a set of preferences among single pairs of measures [20]. We have,

$$\{MOE_i\}_{i \in A} \succcurlyeq \{MOE_j\}_{j \in B} = \{MOE_i \succcurlyeq MOE_j\}_{i \in A, j \in B}. \tag{2}$$

From the counts of assigned preferences (1) we derive a basic belief assignment within belief function theory [3, 4, 17]. In this setting of our problem representation, the frame of discernment (i.e., the set of all possible preference rankings) is

$$\Theta = 2^{\{MOE_i \succcurlyeq MOE_j\}_{i,j \in I}}. \tag{3}$$

However, only a subset of Θ corresponding to chains of preferences will be under investigation in this approach (see (8) in Sec. 3).

We have the following basic belief assignment, using (1),

$$m_{AB}(\{MOE_i \succcurlyeq MOE_j\}_{i \in A, j \in B}) = \frac{1}{N} c_{AB}(\{MOE_i \succcurlyeq MOE_j\}_{i \in A, j \in B}) \tag{4}$$

where N is the total sum of all counts

$$N = \sum_{AB} c_{AB}(\{MOE_i \succcurlyeq MOE_j\}_{i \in A, j \in B}). \tag{5}$$

While it is possible to change the representation in (4) and (5) using (2), it is not possible to divide the basic belief mass among the different preferences in $\{MOE_i \succcurlyeq MOE_j\}_{i \in A, j \in B}$ as we have no information on how to divide it among the different preferences. Instead the entire mass must remain on the whole set.

3   A Decision Maker's Belief in Preferences

From the basic belief assignments (4) we may calculate belief and plausibility for any element of the frame of discernment.

While it is possible to calculate belief and plausibility in each single measures of performance such as,

$$\{MOE_j\} \succcurlyeq \{MOE_i\}_{i \in I}, \forall j \tag{6}$$

where $|\{MOE_j\}| = 1$ (as was done in [15]) we will instead calculate belief and plausibility in incomplete rankings of all measures. Utkin [20] considered complete rankings B of all measure as an alternative approach to calculating belief and plausibility in (6) where plausibility was calculated for a sequence of preferences

$$B_{i_1 i_n} = \{(MOE_{i_1} \succcurlyeq MOE_{i_2}) \cap (MOE_{i_2} \succcurlyeq MOE_{i_3}) \cap \ldots \cap (MOE_{i_{n-1}} \succcurlyeq MOE_{i_n})\}, \tag{7}$$

containing all preferences once. Here belief in any complete sequence is zero as we only have basic belief assignments in sets of preference relations (4) that are all proper supersets to (7) even in the case when the supported set in (4) is a singleton set, as (7) is a sequence of intersections (*not* unions).

We will derive an extension of (7) where we allow any sequence that is an intersection of subsets of all preference relations, including but not limited to singleton sets,

$$B^*_{i_1 i_n} = \{(B_{i_1} \geqslant B_{i_2}) \cap (B_{i_2} \geqslant B_{i_3}) \cap \ldots \cap (B_{i_{n-1}} \geqslant B_{i_n})\}, \tag{8}$$

where B_{i_j} is a subset of all measures $\{MOE_i\}_{i \in A}$ such that the intersection $B_{i_j} \cap B_{i_k} = \varnothing$ and $\cup B_{i_j} = \{MOE_i\}_{i \in I}, \ \forall j$.

Using the representation of (8) we have focal elements $m(B_{i_j} \geqslant B_{i_k})$ for many (but *not* necessarily all) indices i_j, i_k, and may calculate belief and plausibility in $B^*_{i_1 i_n}$. We get beliefs,

$$\mathrm{Bel}(B^*_{i_1 i_2}) = m(B_{i_1} \geqslant B_{i_2}). \quad n = 2, \tag{9}$$

$$\mathrm{Bel}(B^*_{i_1 i_n}) = 0, \qquad\qquad n \geq 3 \tag{10}$$

where belief in any nonsingleton preferences is always zero (as mentioned above), and may in addition calculate plausibility in any partial sequence of preference as

$$\mathrm{Pls}(B^*_{i_1 i_n}) = \sum_{(B_{i_j} \geqslant B_{i_k}) \in \{B_{i_l} \geqslant B_{i_m}\}_{lm} \mid \cap \{B_{i_l} \geqslant B_{i_m}\}_{lm} = B^*_{i_1 i_n}} m(B_{i_j} \geqslant B_{i_k}) \tag{11}$$

where the sum is taken over all focal elements $(B_{i_j} \geqslant B_{i_k})$, $1 \leq j$, $k = j + 1 \leq n$, that are included in $B^*_{i_1 i_n}$.

Given the calculated belief and plausibility we may compare all partial sequences of preferences $B^*_{i_1 i_n}$. If the belief intervals of two different sequences of partial preferences are not overlapping then clearly the higher believed sequence is more preferred.

When an interval $[\mathrm{Bel}(B^*_{i_j i_k}), \mathrm{Pls}(B^*_{i_j i_k})]$ is fully included in an interval $[\mathrm{Bel}(B^*_{i_j i_m}), \mathrm{Pls}(B^*_{i_j i_m})]$ it is not immediately clear which is the preferred partial sequence of preferences; $B^*_{i_j i_k}$ or $B^*_{i_j i_m}$. We can interpolate with a parameter $\rho \in [0, 1]$ in each belief-plausibility interval in order to find the preferred partial sequence of preferences [12]. However, we have no information regarding the value of ρ, and any assumption about ρ will be unwarranted.

Instead we may calculate the point ρ_{jklm} where the two partial sequences of preferences $B^*_{i_j i_k}$ and $B^*_{i_j i_m}$ are equally preferred. When

$$[\mathrm{Bel}(B^*_{i_j i_m}), \mathrm{Pls}(B^*_{i_j i_m})] \supset [\mathrm{Bel}(B^*_{i_j i_k}), \mathrm{Pls}(B^*_{i_j i_k})] \tag{12}$$

we have

$$\rho_{jklm} = \frac{\mathrm{Bel}(B^*_{i_j i_k}) - \mathrm{Bel}(B^*_{i_j i_m})}{[\mathrm{Pls}(B^*_{i_j i_m}) - \mathrm{Bel}(B^*_{i_j i_m})] - [\mathrm{Pls}(B^*_{i_j i_k}) - \mathrm{Bel}(B^*_{i_j i_k})]}. \tag{13}$$

If $\rho_{jklm} < 0.5$ then $B^*_{i_j i_m}$ is more preferred than $B^*_{i_j i_k}$. The requirement that we must have $\rho_{jklm} < 0.5$ is equivalent to having the mid-point in the belief-plausibility interval of $B^*_{i_j i_m}$ is higher than that of $B^*_{i_j i_k}$.

This implies that we can obtain an exact order of all partial sequence of preferences (of measures of performance) using a standard sorting algorithm based on the belief-plausibility interval mid-points for each sequence.

It is obvious from the representation of $B^*_{i_1 i_n}$ (8) that there is of partial sequence of preferences with sequence length 1 ($n = 2$)

$$B^*_{i_1 i_2} = \{(B_{i_1} \succcurlyeq B_{i_2})\} \tag{14}$$

where $|\{(B_{i_1} \succcurlyeq B_{i_2})\}| = 1$, $B_{i_1} \cap B_{i_2} = \varnothing$ and $B_{i_1} \cup B_{i_2} = \{MOE_i\}_{i \in I}$, i.e., B_{i_j} and B_{i_k} are exclusive and exhaustive.

When

$$B_{i_1} = \{MOE_i\}_{i \in I} \tag{15}$$

we have

$$\mathrm{Bel}(B^*_{i_1 i_2}) = \mathrm{Pls}(B^*_{i_1 i_2}) = 1. \tag{16}$$

This makes it necessary to put a value on the information content of $B^*_{i_1 i_n}$ that is valued against the belief and plausibility of the partial sequence of preferences (of measures of effectiveness; MOEs), otherwise we will always prefer a fully nonspecific proposition with belief of 1 but with no information value (i.e., a vacuous belief function).

4   A Decision Maker's Value of Preferences

The value to a decision maker of a partial sequence of preferences $B^*_{i_1 i_n}$ (8) is obviously less than that of a complete sequence of preferences $B_{i_1 i_n}$ (7). As the sequence of preference is intended to be used for weight assignment for the different MOEs, where the weights assigned abide by the preference order, it is not possible to say which weight should be higher of MOE_{i_j} and MOE_{i_k} if they belong to the same subset, e.g., if

$$B^*_{i_1 i_n} = \{(B_{i_1} \succcurlyeq B_{i_2}) \cap (B_{i_2} \succcurlyeq B_{i_3})\}, \tag{17}$$

where

$$(B_{i_1} \succcurlyeq B_{i_2}) = (\{MOE_1, MOE_2\} \succcurlyeq \{MOE_3\})$$

$$(B_{i_2} \succcurlyeq B_{i_3}) = (\{MOE_3\} \succcurlyeq \{MOE_4\}) \tag{18}$$

we can only state that we must have $\{w_1, w_2\} \geq w_3 \geq w_4$ when weighing the preferences in MCDM, but we cannot say anything regarding the relative values of w_1 and w_2.

Finding the best partial sequence of preferences (of measures of effectiveness) becomes a balance between finding sequences with high belief-plausibility and high information value [13]. A measure that calculates a type of information value is the *aggregated uncertainty* (*AU*). The functional *AU* was independently discovered by several authors about the same time [2, 7, 10]. In general, *AU* is defined as

$$AU(\mathrm{Bel}) = \max_{\{p_x\}_{x \in \Theta}} \left\{ -\sum_{x \in \Theta} p(x)\log_2 p(x) \right\} \tag{19}$$

where $\{p_x\}_{x \in \Theta}$ is the set of all probability distributions such that $p_x \in [0, 1]$ for all $x \in \Theta$.

Abellán et al. [1] suggested that AU could be disaggregated in separate measures of nonspecificity and scattering that generalize Hartley information [8] and Shannon entropy [18], respectively, for any mass function, i.e., $AU(m) = I(m) + GS(m)$. Dubois and Prade [5] defined such a measure of nonspecificity as

$$I(m) = \sum_{A \in F} m(A)\log_2|A| \qquad (20)$$

where $F \subseteq 2^\Theta$ is the set of focal elements.

The problem studied in this paper is a special case. We have a partial sequence of preferences where each set of preferences $(B_{i_j} \succeq B_{i_k})$ in the sequence corresponds to a mass function with one, usually nonspecific, focal element A with mass 1 and cardinality greater or equal than 1. Thus, with $m(A) = 1$ we have no scattering of information (i.e., $GS(m) = 0$) and AU specializes to $I(m)$ where the nonspecificity (20) simplifies further to the traditional Hartley function [8]

$$H(m) = \log_2|A| , \qquad (21)$$

as $m(A) = 1$, for each set of preferences in the sequence of $B^*_{i_1 i_n}$.

Using the problem representation of $B^*_{i_1 i_n}$ (8) the joint Hartley information of an entire sequence of multiple preference relations is formulated as

$$
\begin{aligned}
H(B^*_{i_1 i_n}) &= \log_2 \prod_{(B_{i_j} \succeq B_{i_k}) \in \{B_{i_j} \succeq B_{i_m}\}_{lm} \mid \cap \{B_{i_j} \succeq B_{i_m}\}_{lm} = B^*_{i_1 i_n}} \left| (B_{i_j} \succeq B_{i_k}) \right| \\
&= \log_2 \prod_{(B_{i_j} \succeq B_{i_k}) \in \{B_{i_j} \succeq B_{i_m}\}_{lm} \mid \cap \{B_{i_j} \succeq B_{i_m}\}_{lm} = B^*_{i_1 i_n}} |B_{i_j}||B_{i_k}| \\
&= \log_2 \prod_{j=1}^{n} |B_{i_j}| = \sum_{j=1}^{n} \log_2 |B_{i_j}| , \qquad (22)
\end{aligned}
$$

where the first equality use the definition of the Hartley function for multiple variables, the second equality use the fact that subsets of measures can be simplified to a set of preferences among single measures (2) [20].

Furthermore, we have

$$0 \leq H(B^*_{i_1 i_n}) < \left|\{MOE_i\}_{i \in I}\right| \frac{\log_2 e}{e} \qquad (23)$$

where the upper limit is reached when the number of preference subsets in the sequence is $n = \frac{1}{e}\left|\{MOE_i\}_{i \in I}\right|$, and the number of preference relations in each subset $|B_{i_j}| = \log_2 e, \forall j$ (ignoring that $n, |B_{i_j}| \in \mathbb{Z}^+$).

Note, that the best information value for the decision maker is when $H(B^*_{i_1 i_n})$ is minimized, i.e., when the sequence of preference is as specific as possible with one preference relation per subset (7). The only reason to prefer a partial sequence of preferences before a complete sequence is if its belief-plausibility is higher.

5   The Decision Maker's Choice of Preference Order

The utility U for a decision maker of knowing a sequence of preferences $B^*_{i_1 i_n}$ is a trade-off between finding a sequence of preferences that on the on hand maximize the belief and plausibility, and on the other hand maximize the value of the information itself for the decision maker.

A function that tries to achieve both task simultaneously by calculating the utility of $B^*_{i_1 i_n}$ is the product of the belief-plausibility midpoint, i.e., $\rho = \frac{1}{2}$ (13), with a function of the Hartley function of $B^*_{i_1 i_n}$.

We define

$$U(B^*_{i_1 i_n}) = \frac{1}{2}\left[\mathrm{Bel}(B^*_{i_1 i_n}) + \mathrm{Pls}(B^*_{i_1 i_n})\right]\left[1 - \frac{H(B^*_{i_1 i_n})}{|\{MOE_i\}_{i \in I}|\dfrac{\log_2 e}{e}}\right], \qquad (24)$$

where both terms on the right hand side of the equality belong to [0, 1]. Thus, the utility $U(B^*_{i_1 i_n}) \in [0, 1]$ and will serve as the basis for comparing different alternative partial sequences of preferences (of measures of performance; MOEs).

All partial sequences of preferences $B^*_{i_1 i_n}$ are evaluated based on their utility $U(B^*_{i_1 i_n})$. The partial sequence with highest utility is considered the best sequence and is the partial preference order that will be used in MCDM. Although (24) is exponential in the number of MOEs, the number of measures in the MCDM is usually not very large which makes this a calculation with low computational cost. In a previous paper [15] we developed a method for assigning weights by a Monte Carlo approach to the set of all MOEs for multiple criteria evaluation. When we have a partial sequence of preferences, e.g.,

$$B^*_{i_1 i_4} = \{(B_{i_1} \succcurlyeq B_{i_2}) \cap (B_{i_2} \succcurlyeq B_{i_3})\}, \qquad (25)$$

where

$$(B_{i_1} \succcurlyeq B_{i_2}) = (MOE_1 \succcurlyeq \{MOE_2, MOE_3\})$$

$$(B_{i_2} \succcurlyeq B_{i_3}) = (\{MOE_2, MOE_3\} \succcurlyeq MOE_4) \qquad (26)$$

we may assign any weight to the MOEs that abide by the constraints $1 \geq w_1 \geq \{w_2, w_3\} \geq w_4 \geq 0$ where w_i is the weight of MOE_i and there is no constraint between w_2 and w_3.

Other authors have considered different approaches to weight assignment. Huang et al. [9] consider the assignment of weights to criteria based on the consistency and similarity of the opinions from decision makers regarding these criteria. In addition it is also possible to let the decision makers themselves be weighted. Yue [21] suggest using the decision makers' experience regarding the topic under consideration as a basis for assigning weights. A third approach, is to let each decision maker use a weighting of his own as an expression of the importance placed on a pairwise comparison of two disjoint subsets of MOEs.

6   Conclusions

We show that it is possible to extend Utkin's methodology for complete ranking of all single preferences between different alternatives [20] in MCDM, to a new methodology that evaluates all partial rankings of all subsets of these measures. Both methods use the same pairwise comparisons of preference subsets assigned by experts. While Utkin's method use only plausibility for a complete ranking (of singletons), we show that this is not possible when extending the solution to incomplete ranking (of all possible subsets). Instead, it is necessary to calculate the utility by modelling the information value of an incomplete ranking and compare this, in a trade-off, against the belief-plausibility of the same incomplete ranking of all possible subsets of preferences (of measures of effectiveness; MOEs). Only then can we find the best partial ranking of preferences that combine high belief-plausibility with high information value to maximize utility for the decision maker.

References

1. Abellán, J., Klir, G.J., Moral, S.: Disaggregated total uncertainty measure for credal sets. International Journal of General Systems 35, 29–44 (2006)
2. Chau, C.W.R., Lingras, P., Wong, S.K.M.: Upper and lower entropies of belief functions using compatible probability functions. In: Komorowski, J., Raś, Z.W. (eds.) ISMIS 1993. LNCS, vol. 689, pp. 306–315. Springer, Heidelberg (1993)
3. Dempster, A.P.: A generalization of Bayesian inference. Journal of the Royal Statistical Society Series B 30, 205–247 (1968)
4. Dempster, A.P.: The Dempster-Shafer calculus for statisticians. International Journal of Approximate Reasoning 48, 365–377 (2008)
5. Dubois, D., Prade, H.: A note on measures of specificity for fuzzy sets. International Journal of General Systems 10, 279–283 (1985)
6. Ehrgott, M., Wiecek, M.M.: Multiobjective programming. In: Figueira, J., Greco, S., Ehrgott, M. (eds.) Multiple Criteria Decision Analysis: State of the Art Surveys, pp. 667–722. Springer, New York (2005)
7. Harmanec, D., Klir, G.J.: Measuring total uncertainty in Dempster-Shafer theory: A novel approach. International Journal of General Systems 22, 405–419 (1994)
8. Hartley, R.V.L.: Transmission of information. The Bell System Technical Journal 7, 535–563 (1928)
9. Huang, S., Su, X., Hu, Y., Mahadevan, S., Deng, Y.: A new decision-making method by incomplete preferences based on evidence distance. Knowledge-Based Systems 56, 264–272 (2014)
10. Maeda, Y., Ichihashi, H.: An uncertainty measure with monotonicity under the random set inclusion. International Journal of General Systems 21, 379–392 (1993)
11. Masson, M.-H., Denœux, T.: Ranking from pairwise comparisons in the belief function framework. In: Proceedings of the Second International Conference on Belief Functions, pp. 311–318 (2012)
12. Schubert, J.: On ρ in a decision-theoretic apparatus of Dempster-Shafer theory. International Journal of Approximate Reasoning 13, 185–200 (1995)

13. Schubert, J.: Constructing and evaluating alternative frames of discernment. International Journal of Approximate Reasoning 53, 176–189 (2012)
14. Schubert, J., Hörling, P.: Explaining the impact of actions. In: Proceedings of the 15th International Conference on Information Fusion, pp. 354–360 (2012)
15. Schubert, J., Hörling, P.: Preference-based Monte Carlo weight assignment for multiple-criteria decision making in defense planning. In: Proceedings of the 17th International Conference on Information Fusion (to appear, 2014)
16. Sen, A.K.: Markets and freedom: Achievements and limitations of the market mechanism in promoting individual freedoms. Oxford Economic Papers 45, 519–541 (1993)
17. Shafer, G.: A Mathematical Theory of Evidence. Princeton University Press, Princeton (1976)
18. Shannon, C.E.: A mathematical theory of communication. The Bell System Technical Journal 27, 379–423, 623–656 (1948)
19. Tritchler, D., Lockwood, G.: Modelling the reliability of paired comparisons. Journal of Mathematical Psychology 35, 277–293 (1991)
20. Utkin, L.V.: A new ranking procedure by incomplete pairwise comparisons using preference subsets. Intelligent Data Analysis 13, 229–241 (2009)
21. Yue, Z.: An extended TOPSIS for determining weights of decision makers with interval numbers. Knowledge-Based Systems 24, 146–153 (2011)

Mathematical Theory of Evidence in Navigation

Włodzimierz Filipowicz*

Gdynia Maritime University,
ul. Morska 81/83, 81-225 Gdynia, Poland
w.filipowicz@wn.am.gdynia.pl
http://www.gdynia.am.pl/

Abstract. Mathematical Theory of Evidence (MTE), also known as Belief Theory, exploits belief and plausibility measures and operates on belief assignments and belief structures. The theory also offers combination mechanisms in order to increase the informative context of the initial evidence. The evidence is meant as a collection of facts and knowledge. In navigation, facts are position indications delivered by various aids, and also results of observations such as taking bearings, distances or horizontal angles. Those facts are random variables governed by various distributions. Nautical knowledge embraces features of such distributions as well as discrepancies in their estimations. Awareness of systematic errors is also a part of a seafarer's knowledge. Whichever the conditions MTE combination scheme is expected to enable position fixing of the ship.

Keywords: nautical evidence, belief assignments, position fixing, normalization.

1 Introduction

This paper is focused on the practicality and functionality Dempster-Shafer concepts [3], [13] of evidence representation and reasoning and the possibility of application of belief theory in geodetic positioning and navigational position fixing. Many authors point to numerous applications involving the Bayesian approach while examples employing other concepts are rather scarce. It is said that there are only a few practical problems solved with theory of Evidence [2]. Meaningful applications are related to risk analyses [15], expert system inference engine implementation [14] or satellite services demand forecast [11]. It should noted that maritime application of the theory was successful while solving multi-target detection problem [1].

It is the navigator who has to handle a set of random points delivered by various navigational aids from which he is supposed to indicate a point as being the position of his ship. Dispersions of points are governed by two dimensional approximate distributions. The fixed position is located somewhere in vicinity of

* The author thanks Dr Fabio Cuzzolin from Oxford Brookes University for his patience and gentle insisting on preparing final version of this paper.

F. Cuzzolin (Ed.): BELIEF 2014, LNAI 8764, pp. 199–208, 2014.

indications at hand. It is very similar, in case of measured distances, bearings or horizontal angles. The ship's position is located within the area of crossings of appropriate isolines[1] that intersect inside the confined area. The area of the true position is spanned over isolines' crossing points provided the available evidence features random errors and might be outside the area once systematic deflection prevail. It is supposed that the navigator is able to resolve all dilemmas thanks to his knowledge, experience and also intuition.

Practical navigation is based upon probability theory. The basis is enough to define distributions of random variables that are assumed to be of measured value. It also enables a priori evaluation of fixes taken according to certain schemata since accuracy is calculated with formulas designated for selected schedules of observations taking into account the constellation of landmarks and approximate measurements error [10].

Expectations regarding flexibility of the upgraded models are greater. Items that should affect fixed position should also include the kind of distributions of measurements taken with a particular navigational aid and discrepancies in the parameters of such distributions. It is popular to state that the mean error of a bearing taken with radar is interval valued within the range of $[\pm 1, \pm 2.5°]$. The presented evaluation of the mean error appears as a fuzzy figure and as such, fuzziness should be accepted and taken into account during computations. Subjective assessment, also in form of linguistic terms, of each observation should be accepted and processed. Empirical distributions are also supposed to be included into calculations. The most important thing is the embedded ability for objective evaluation of the obtained fix along with measures indicating the probability of its locations within the surrounding area [7]. Meeting the above stated expectations is impossible with traditional formal apparatus. Its ability is almost exhausted in the considered applications. Research and published works devoted to a new platforms and modern environments put attention on Evidence Theory that delivers a wide range of new opportunities.

The theory extended for possibilistic platform creates new opportunities for modelling uncertainty [17]. In the presented applications doubtfulness is due to erroneous observations. It is widely known that random and systematic errors are included in measurements.

2   Nautical Evidence Encoding

In nautical applications evidence refers to collection of indications and measurements also known as observations and knowledge regarding these observations. Available data are assumed to be random variables governed by known distributions. It is widely accepted that the distributions are empirical that are usually

---

[1] In navigation an isoline is a function related to measurement also referred to as an observation. Graph of an isoline projected to the plane (chart) is a set of points of equal bearings, distances or another measurement. Isoline of a distance to a landmark is a circle with the centre in the landmark position. Isoline of a bearing to an object is a straight line that passes through the object position.

approximated by the Gaussian ones. Therefore confidence intervals in the vicinity of the given data may be established and probability of a true measurement being located there easily calculated.

Belief assignments embrace relations between evidence and hypothesis items. It tells how a piece of evidence with reference set $\{o_{ij}\}$ supports each of the hypothesis points $\{x_k\}$. Relations between evidence and hypothesis frames take the form of Eq. 1.

$$
\begin{aligned}
\mathrm{m}(e_i) &= \{(\mu_{i1}(x_k),\, m(\mu_{i1})),\, ...,\, (\mu_{in}(x_k),\, m(\mu_{in})) \\
m(\mu_{i1}) &= f(e_i \rightarrow \mu_{i1}(x_k))
\end{aligned}
\tag{1}
$$

Hereafter function $f(e_i \rightarrow \mu_{i1}(x_k))$ that defines mass assigned to each vector $\mu_{ij}(x_k)$, is assumed known for each referential item (element of the set $\{o_{ij}\}$) linked to i-th measurement or indication [8], [9]. Values returned by this function are obtained based on statistical investigations of observations sets of test values regarding particular source of nautical data. Function that returns membership grades $\mu_{ij}(x_k)$ for each of k-th hypothesis elements, takes the form of Eq. 2. It can be read that location grades are degrees of inclusion of hypothesis points within evidence frame. In the formula $C = 1$ for binary approach, $C \in [0, 1]$ when using fuzzy membership. Sets embrace grades expressing possibilities of consecutive hypothesis items being located within the sets related to each piece of evidence.

$$
\mu_{ij}(x_k) = \begin{cases} C & if \quad x_k \in o_{ij} \\ 0 & \text{otherwise} \end{cases}
\tag{2}
$$

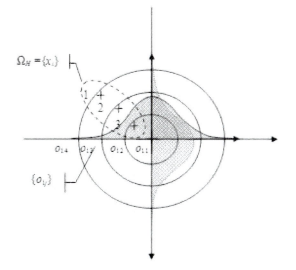

Fig. 1. Graphic interpretation of binary nautical evidence representations

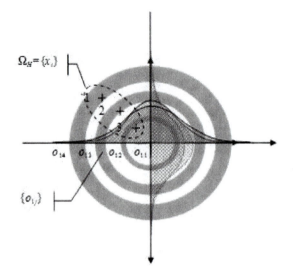

Fig. 2. Graphic interpretation of fuzzy nautical evidence representations

Figure 1 shows scheme of areas around indication delivered by a navigational aid. Crisp valued limits of confidence intervals are presented. In nautical science crisp valued standard deviations of measurements are considered inadequate. In recent navigation book [10] indication mean error is described as imprecise interval value usually as: $[\pm\sigma^-, \pm\sigma^+]$. Thus appropriate limits are interval valued as presented at Fig. 2. It should be also noticed that presented areas are circular what can be observed under assumption of the same distributions for both axis.

Each set has an assigned credibility mass also considered as a degree of belief. It expresses support for given hypothesis space items embedded within particular piece of evidence. Therefore, evidence mapping consists of (location set – mass of its confidence from particular piece of evidence point of view) pairs.

$$
m_i = \{m_{ij}\} \cup \{m_{in}\} = \left\{ \int_{j \cdot \sigma}^{(j+1) \cdot \sigma} P_i(x)\, dx \cdot (1 - m_{in}) \right\} \cup \{m_{in}\}
$$

where:

$$j = (-3,\ -2,\ -1,\ 0,\ 1,\ 2)$$

$\qquad(3)$

Belief mass is considered as a probability that the true indicated value falls within given credibility interval and can be calculated with Formula 3. The expression splits the whole set of masses related to i-th evidence into two components. One embraces cumulated probabilities attributed to selected confidence intervals. Another one is a level of doubtfulness assigned to given piece of evidence.

Seafarers know that mean error of particular aid is, for example, inside the range of $[\pm 1, \pm 1.5]$ cables. It means fuzzy value with core of [-1, 1] cables and support of [-1.5, 1.5] cables [5], [6].

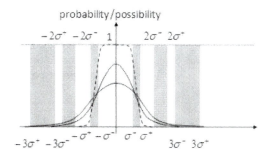

Fig. 3. Modelling imprecise measurements data invokes probabilistic and possibilistic approaches

Figure 3 shows dashed line that is membership function that returns possibility of certain point inclusion into $[-\sigma^-, +\sigma^+]$ range. Mean error estimates standard deviation (square root of a variance) of the distribution. Figure 3 also shows interval valued limits of confidence intervals related to two distribution functions. In confidence range a measurement falls with certain probability. It is assumed that confidence intervals are symmetrically placed around the mean.

Table 1. Binary (left) and fuzzy (right) representations of evidence related to navigational aid indication

	binary			fuzzy			
	$\{x_1$	x_2	$x_3\}$	$\{x_1$	x_2	$x_3\}$	m
$\mu_{11}(x_k)$	$\{$ 0	0	1 $\}$	$\{$ 0	0	0.91 $\}$	$m_{11}=0.615$
$\mu_{12}(x_k)$	$\{$ 0	1	0 $\}$	$\{$ 0	0.85	0.09 $\}$	$m_{12}=0.245$
$\mu_{13}(x_k)$	$\{$ 1	0	0 $\}$	$\{$ 0.90	0.15	0 $\}$	$m_{13}=0.036$
$\mu_{14}(x_k)$	$\{$ 0	0	0 $\}$	$\{$ 0.10	0	0 $\}$	$m_{14}=0.004$
$\mu_{1n}(x_k)$	$\{$ 1	1	1 $\}$	$\{$ 1	1	1 $\}$	$m_{1u}=0.100$

Table 1 presents two belief assignments that are representations of evidence related to the example navigational aid indication. At the left side there are binary locations for hypothesis space embracing three points and shown in Fig. 1. Selected circular confidence areas have crisp limits. At the right side the table embraces fuzzy location vectors. Fuzziness is due to uncertainty in evaluation of random errors distribution parameters. Selected circular areas have interval valued limits. In fuzzy approach evidence representation consists of pairs: fuzzy vectors representing uncertain locations of a set of points within sets related to each piece of evidence – degrees of confidence assigned to these vectors.

Empirical type of random variables distribution is encountered very often in navigation. They are usually converted to Gaussian ones although it so happens that conversions are not theoretically justified. Thus empirical distribution direct inclusion into evidence representation seems natural and necessary. In this case, confidence intervals are substituted by histogram bins and cumulative probabilities are replaced by relative frequencies of observations falling within the bin. Since available histograms differ, calculated frequencies are rather ranges of values than single figures. Thus belief assignments upgraded with empirical distributions are interval valued.

2.1   Evidence Related to Nautical Observations

Result of a nautical observation (taking distance for example) delivers imprecise value. The measurement contains random error as well as systematic deflection very often. In practical navigation results of observations are converted to their isolines, functions that are measurement projections on a chart. Terrestrial or celestial navigation involves dealing with isolines and their gradients. Hereto confidence intervals are to be established along gradient directions. The most frequently used are isolines of bearings, distances and horizontal angles. Crisp valued standard deviation of a measurement is substituted by imprecise interval valued written usually as: $[\pm\sigma_i^-, \pm\sigma_i^+]$. Being interested in an isoline deflection one considers $[\pm m_i^-, \pm m_i^+]$. Random mean error of a distance measured with radar variable range marker is a function of the obtained value and are said to be within the interval of $[\pm1, \pm1.5]$ percent of the measurement. Taken distance of 10 Nm is random variable with mean error inside the range of $[\pm1, \pm1.5]$ cables. The concept of exploiting evidence, that is meant as encoded facts and knowledge, in supporting decisions in navigation is based on measurement distribution. Introduced confidence intervals define the probabilities of true isolines being located within appropriate strips established along gradient directions.

3   Position Fixing

Practical navigation exploits graphical and analytical methods, its scientific background is based upon probability theory. The basis is enough to enable a priori evaluation of fixes taken according to certain schemata since accuracy is calculated with formulas designated for selected schedules of observations taking into account the constellation of landmarks and random valued measurements.

In MTE structures combination is carried out [4]. During association all pairs of location vectors are associated and product of involved masses is assigned to the result set. Obtained assignment is supposed to increase informative context of the initial structures. Combination of structures embracing measurements data is assumed to result in position fixing. The goal can be achieved provided association of sets enables selection of common points located within intersection of introduced ranges. Adequate selection can be done with T-norm operations[2] [12] used during association. The simplest T-norm results in smaller values

---

[2] T-norms are used as fuzzy logics conjunction operators, they are a generalization of the two-valued logical conjunction. Hereto T-norms are used to calculate the intersection of fuzzy sets.

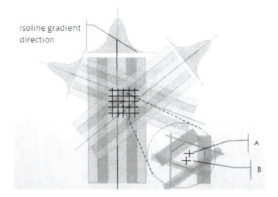

isoline gradient
direction

Fig. 4. Position fixing based on three observations

being taken from consecutive pairs of elements in associating vectors. This operation is used in implemented software dealing with fuzzy reasoning in nautical science. In the presented applications, the association of two location vectors with T-norm select hypothesis frame points situated within a common area. A null result vector means that there are no points within intersection and might indicate poor quality evidence.

Figure 4 illustrates three fragments of isolines intended for position fixing. Contours of imprecise confidence internals limits are marked for each observation. The figure shows intersection of three fragments of isolines related to three randomly distorted measurements. Presented situation is typical for position fixing. The illustration also include exploded insertion showing single cell confined by imprecise limits of considered strips. There are two points: A and B that are potential true locations of the ship. Let us assume that both points location degree within shown area are equal to one. For each of them plausibility and belief measures are to be calculated. Formulae that enable calculation of plausibility and belief measures were derived in publication [4], [8]. To calculate belief value one has to find minimum among complemented location grades for each element within considered set. Therefore belief for the two points, that they represent fixed position, is zeroed. One can conclude that multiple point presence within intersections of ranges causes that belief for each of points is close to zero. It should be noted that hypothesis frame points are to be arranged with respect to isolines mean errors or width of considered strips. Plausibility support measure does not feature the same disadvantage. Therefore it was proposed as primary factor deciding on fixed position selection.

Grid (mesh) is usually used to define hypothesis frame during iterative calculations. The repetitive search for the fixed position explores decreasing the area in order to achieve required accuracy. In each loop, for a given search area, new belief assignments are created, normalized and combined. In the final stage, the search area should be small enough to guarantee a satisfying quality of the solution. The quality of the solution depends on the size of the mesh. It should be noted that the quality is also determined by other, widely known factors. Let us mention number and quality of observations as well as constellation of observed landmarks.

Scheme of position fixing with intersected isolines is very much the same as this for indications association. Fixed position is somewhere inside isolines intersection area provided absence of fixed error. In case of systematic distortion location of the fix should be found in different way. The way to handle systematic errors will be published shortly. Both cases involving position indications and isolines are exploited in navigation. With MTE they can be mixed up and readily considered jointly.

The traditional way of position fixing takes advantage of available measurements, their approximate random distributions and diversification of observations once the analytical approach is used. The main disadvantage of the concept is the lack of a built-in universal method of the fix a posteriori evaluation. Traditional meaning of the fix accuracy is related to a regular area around the fixed position. Within the area the true position of the ship is located with certain degree of credibility. It is assumed that the area is of circular or elliptical shape within which the fix is located with the same probability.

In the suggested approach, distribution of probabilities of the fix being located within explored area is embedded into processing scheme. Therefore, accuracy evaluation can be made a posteriori and is to be perceived as a cohesive area within which probability (plausibility) of the fix location is higher than the required threshold value.

4   Notes on Normalization

Position fixing can be achieved provided the association of sets enables the selection of common points located within intersection of introduced ranges. Adequate selection can be done with T-norm operations [12] used during association. Thus result of association may be empty or sub-normal. Therefore, a certain amount of mass is assigned to null set which means the conflicting situation that can also be referred to as an inconsistency. In position fixing inconsistency means the absence of a hypothesis space point within intersection area. This might indicate poor quality of considered set of measurements as well as scarce, consequently wrongly distributed, hypothesis points. Thus it is important to record all conflicting cases and evaluate its final uncorrupted value.

A pseudo belief structure is said to be a belief assignment that does not fulfil a certain set of conditions. Normality of the assignment is achieved via normalization. The main reason for this transformation is to avoid belief being greater than plausibility measure. These measures are meant as limits of interval valued probability expressing support for the given hypothesis item. Belief is the lower boundary of the interval, plausibility is meant as the higher limit. Unfortunately contradictory results can be obtained based on pseudo belief structures [16].

It is supposed that evidence representations should be normalized at the initial and intermediate stages of processing in order to avoid contradictory results.

The most popular normalization procedures feature serious disadvantages. The Yager method disables detection of inconsistency cases. In the Dempster concept, all masses assigned to non-empty sets are increased by a factor that is a function of the total inconsistency mass. It leads to the unacceptable proposition that "the higher inconsistency mass the greater probability assigned to non-empty sets" or referring to position fixing, "the poorer quality data, the higher credibility attributed to the fix". Therefore the author's proposal of conversion has been submitted.

The main advantage of the approach is the ability to maintain unchanged value of the plausibility measure, the primary factor deciding on selection of the final solution. It also assures that belief and plausibility measures remain in proper relation, the first is not greater than the second one. The transformation was discussed in details in recent paper delivered by the author [7].

5   Summary

Fuzzy approach is used to include knowledge into a mathematical model. It is a tool that enable human observers to transform their observations into an adequate model. In nautical science observers usually use linguistic terms and imprecise data in order to describe and explain their activity. Information on measurement accuracy appears as a fuzzy figures, discrepancies in distributions parameters evaluation are interval valued.

Dealing with uncertain and imprecise evidence is a challenge in nautical science and practice. Formal descriptions of problems encountered in navigation involve models that accept imprecise, erroneous and therefore uncertain values. The concept should be followed regarding position fixing and its accuracy evaluation. It is the navigator who has to handle a set of random points delivered by various navigational aids or distorted data that are output of observations. Based on available evidence he is supposed to indicate a point as being the position of his ship.

Models that include uncertainty can be created with MTE. The theory can be perceived as an extension of the Bayesian concept. It also offers combination mechanism, enabling the enrichment of informative context of the initial evidence. Despite its broad ability, the theory still remains unpopular in the presented scope of interest.

Measurement and indication data, along with nautical knowledge, can be encoded into belief functions. Both knowledge and data are considered as evidence that is exploited in navigation. Belief functions in nautical applications represent evidence and are subject to combination in order to increase their informative context. Evidence representations and results of their combinations could include inconsistencies wherever T-norm operations are involved. Inconsistency must be removed to avoid conflicting final results.

Presented approach creates an opportunity to revise the fix quality evaluation. Traditional meaning of the fix accuracy is related to an area around the fixed position. Within the area the true position of the ship is located with a certain degree of credibility. It is often assumed that the area is of circular or elliptical shape. Formulas enabling calculation of its radius were derived for typical schemes followed while making a fix.

References

1. Ayoun, A., Smets, P.: Data Association in Multi-Target Detection Using the Transferable Belief Model. International Journal of Intelligent Systems 16, 1167–1182 (2001)
2. Burrus, N., Lesage, D.: Theory of Evidence. Technical Report no. 0307 - 07/07/03. Activity: CSI Seminar, Place: EPITA Research and Development Laboratory, Cedex France (2004) (published)
3. Dempster, A.P.: A generalization of Bayesian inference. Journal of the Royal Statistical Society B 30, 205–247 (1968)
4. Denoeux, T.: Modelling Vague Beliefs using Fuzzy Valued Belief Structures. Fuzzy Sets and Systems 116, 167–199 (2000)
5. Filipowicz, W.: Belief Structures in Position Fixing. In: Mikulski, J. (ed.) TST 2010. CCIS, vol. 104, pp. 434–446. Springer, Heidelberg (2010)
6. Filipowicz, W.: Evidence Representation and Reasoning in Selected Applications. In: Jędrzejowicz, P., Nguyen, N.T., Hoang, K. (eds.) ICCCI 2011, Part II. LNCS, vol. 6923, pp. 251–260. Springer, Heidelberg (2011)
7. Filipowicz, W.: Fuzzy evidence reasoning and navigational position fixing. In: Tweedale, J.W., Jane, L.C. (eds.) Recent advances in Knowledge-Based Paradigms and Applications. AISC, vol. 234, pp. 87–102. Springer, Heidelberg (2014)
8. Filipowicz, W.: New Approach towards Position Fixing. Annual of Navigation 16, 41–54 (2010)
9. Filipowicz, W.: Belief Structures and their Application in Navigation. Methods of Applied Informatics 3, 53–82 (2009)
10. Jurdziński, M.: Principles of Marine Navigation. WAM, Gdynia (2008) (in Polish)
11. McBurney, P., Parsons, S.: Using Belief Functions to Forecast Demand for Mobile Satellite Services. In: Srivastava, R.P., Mock, T. (eds.) Belief Functions in Business Decisions, pp. 281–315. Physica-Verlag, Heidelberg. Springer-Verlag Company (2002)
12. Rutkowski, L.: Methods and Techniques of the Artificial Intelligence. PWN, Warsaw (2009) (in Polish)
13. Shafer, G.: A Mathematical Theory of Evidence. Princeton University Press, Princeton (1976)
14. Srivastava, R.P., Dutta, S.K., Johns, R.: An Expert System Approach to Audit Planning and Evaluation in the Belief-Function Framework. International Journal of Intelligent Systems in Accounting, Finance and Management 5(3), 165–183 (1996)
15. Sun, L., Srivastava, R.P., Mock, T.: An Information Systems Security Risk Assessment Model under Dempster-Shafer Theory of Belief Functions. Journal of Management Information Systems 22(4), 109–142 (2006)
16. Yager, R.: On the Normalization of Fuzzy Belief Structures. International Journal of Approximate Reasoning 14, 127–153 (1996)
17. Yen, J.: Generalizing the Dempster–Shafer Theory to Fuzzy Sets. IEEE Transactions on Systems, Man and Cybernetics 20(3), 559–570 (1990)

Application of Belief Functions Theory to Non Destructive Testing of Industrial Pieces

Ahmad Osman[1], Valerie Kaftandjian[2], and Ulf Hassler[1]

[1] Fraunhofer Development Center X-ray Technologies EZRT, Flugplatzstrasse 75,
90768 Fuerth, Germany
{ahmad.osman,ulf.hassler}@iis.fraunhofer.de
[2] National Institute of Applied Sciences INSA- Lyon,
Laboratory of Vibrations and Acoustics (LVA), University of Lyon, Bat. St. Exupery,
25 Avenue Capelle, 69621 Villeurbanne, France
valerie.kaftandjian@insa-lyon.fr

Abstract. In this contribution we present a classification method based on the evidence theory where a comparison between modeling with and without conflict is presented as well as a comparison between the orthogonal and cautious fusion rules. The classification rules are compared to the state of the art support vector machine classifier on an industrial ultrasonic dataset.

Keywords: Evidence theory, non-destructive testing, defects classification.

1 Introduction: Context of the Study

In the field on Non Destructive Testing (NDT) of industrial pieces such as castings, welds, or composites, the general aim is to detect defects as small as possible, while preventing the detection of false alarms due to noise or artefacts. Over the last several years, we have started to develop a classifier based on Dempster-Shafer (DS) theory in which features measured on the segmented objects (such as contrast, area, etc$\cdots$) are considered as information sources and fused. The feature values are translated into mass values thanks to a mass assignment procedure based on a learning approach. The frame of discernment consists of two single hypotheses (true defect H_1 and false defect H_2) and the compound one thus corresponds to ignorance ($H_3{=}H_1{\cup}H_2$). In our initial work, the data fusion approach was used in the aim to improve the detection of weld defects in [1], and in castings inspection [2]. The obtained results proved to be precise and reliable decisions were obtained. However, the supervision of the expert was necessary to assign the confidence levels (or mass values). Then, a new mass value attribution procedure was developed, without expert supervision. The method, introduced in [3], allows converting from the space of feature values to the mass values space. This method is divided into two processes: learning and validation process. A choice was made to avoid conflict between sources by assigning masses only to H_1 and H_3. By that way, the Dempster rule of combination can be applied without

F. Cuzzolin (Ed.): BELIEF 2014, LNAI 8764, pp. 209–218, 2014.
© Springer International Publishing Switzerland 2014

the risk to increase the fused mass when conflict appears. Several applications cases in NDT have been tested with success [4], [5]. In the present paper, we compare this "no conflict "approach with another possible choice, where only H_1 and H_2 are considered (Bayesian masses). In this case, the Dempster rule without normalization is preferred, and conflict is computed. A specific decision rule is developed involving a conflict threshold. As the features are considered as sources of information, their independence needs to be discussed. For this purpose we use the cautious rule to fuse the sources and compare its output with the output of the orthogonal rule. Moreover, the orthogonal rule is used not only to fuse all sources together, but also pairwise, and we have introduced a specific procedure to select best sources in terms of performances. Thus, when a pair of feature is selected, their independence is checked a posteriori. Finally, support vector machine classifier was selected as a gold standard to compare our results with a state of the art method.

2   Principle of the DS Classifier

2.1   Mass Assignment Learning Phase

After segmentation and feature extraction on the segmented objects, the spatial repartition of features values is divided into regions of confidence. To build these regions, the global histogram of class A (true defects TD) and class B (false defects FD) is used, on a learning database, i.e. a set of objects of known class (classification by an expert). Firstly, this histogram is divided into a set I of intervals. For each interval denoted $i \in I$, the percentage of TD (instances of the class A) present in this region is calculated using the following equation:

$$P_{A,B} = \frac{h_A(i)}{h_A(i) + h_B(i)} \tag{1}$$

Where $h_A(i)$ and $h_B(i)$ represent respectively the number of instances of A and B inside i.

Secondly, subsequent intervals are merged to form a region of confidence.

In this step, a constraint is imposed on the degree of variation of $P_{A,B}(i)$ between two adjacent regions with a fixed threshold denoted DV. If $\bigtriangledown P_{A,B} = |P_{A,B}(i+1) - P_{A,B}(i)| < DV$, then the interval i is merged with the interval $i+1$, and they form a region of confidence. Figure 1 shows the regions found after merging in the example histogram.

The influence of this threshold DV (called Derivation Variation) on the system performance and stability was studied [6] and a value of $DV = 0.2$ was selected. At the end of this step, some obtained regions contain a number of points too small to be considered as significant. Therefore a second constraint on the number of points existing in each region is imposed: a region should contain at least a certain percentage of points denoted $Perc$, which we specify. Let M be the region which contains the biggest number of points N_M inside it, and the minimal number of points to be respected inside each region is: $N_c = Perc \cdot N_M$.

The influence of $Perc$ on the systems performance was also studied in [6] and a value of $Perc = 0.1$ was selected. Once the regions are built, mass attribution is done with two possible choices, either using only the H_1 and the ignorance hypothesis (in this case no conflict is possible), or using Bayesian masses (table 1). In both cases, the mass assigned to the "true defect" hypothesis H_1 is directly the proportion of TD in the region of confidence R_i. Masses obtained on the H_1 hypothesis are illustrated in figure 1 for the three regions of the example histogram.

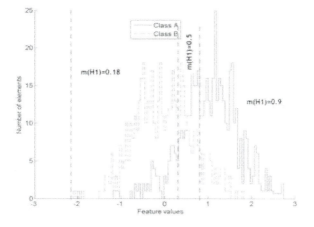

Fig. 1. Illustration of the regions of confidence after merging of intervals in the histogram. In this example, three regions are found for which the mass on H1 is indicated.

Table 1. Mass functions assignment

Without conflict	With possible conflict
$m(H_1) = P_{A,B}(R_i)$	
$m(H_2) = 0$	$m(H_2) = 1 - m(H_1)$
$m(H_3) = 1 - m(H_1)$	$m(H_3) = 0$

Finally, the last stage of the mass value assignment is to ensure a continuous transition between the regions of confidence. One fuzzy set is defined for each region with a classical trapezoidal shape membership function. The slope of the membership function is chosen to be proportional to the difference between the mass values of the two adjacent regions. Let f_k be a source of information used to classify an object in class A or B according to its feature x and R_1, $R_2, \cdots R_s$, be the set of regions of confidence. $k = 1 \cdots Q$ is the number of features considered as information sources. Each object has a set of degrees of membership μ_{R_i}, $i = 1 \cdots s$ to each region R_i with $\sum_{i=1}^{s} \mu_{R_i}(x) = 1$. The final mass $m(H_1)$ attributed by a source f_k to the object from its feature x is calculated by weighting the mass values of each region R_i by its degree of membership μ_{R_i}:

$$m(\text{object} \in H_1) = m(x/f_k) = \sum_{i=1}^{s} \mu_{R_i}(x) \cdot m(R_i) \tag{2}$$

The three fuzzy sets obtained for the example histogram and the corresponding final mass function is illustrated in figure 2.

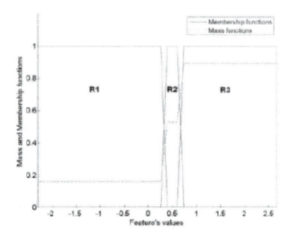

Fig. 2. For each region of confidence, a fuzzy set is defined with a corresponding trapezoidal membership function (blue line). The final mass function is computed from equation (2) (red dotted line). The histogram of figure 1 is used in this example.

2.2   Fusion of Features Learning Phase

After the estimation of regions of confidence and their corresponding mass values assignment, the fusion process takes place. Each feature being considered as a source of information, mass values are combined using different rules. The normalised Dempster orthogonal rule is used to fuse features pairwise, three or all features together (equation 3). Dempster's rule [7] is defined as follows: considering Q mass distributions $m_1 \cdots m_Q$ from different information sources $B_1, B_2 \cdots B_Q$, the Dempster's rule of combination results in a new distribution, $m = m_1 \oplus m_2 \oplus \cdots m_Q$, which carries the joint information provided by the sources:

$$m(A_i) = \frac{\sum_{B_1 \cap B_2 \cdots B_Q = A_i} m_1(B_1) m_2(B_2) \cdots m_Q(B_Q)}{1 - K} \tag{3}$$

where

$$K = \sum_{B_1 \cap B_2 \cdots B_Q = \Phi} m_1(B_1) m_2(B_2) \cdots m_Q(B_Q) \tag{4}$$

K is a measure of conflict between the sources and is introduced in equation 4 as a normalization factor. As it can be deduced, the larger K, the more conflicting are the sources and the less sense makes their combination. As a consequence some authors, Smets in particular [8], require the use of the Dempsters combination rule without normalization. Thus, in our case, we must distinguish the two cases, with and without conflict. When the masses are distributed on H_1 and H_3, no conflict can occur, and the Dempsters rule is perfectly adapted. On the contrary, when Bayesian masses are defined, the conflict is computed and kept for the decision step, and the non-normalized orthogonal sum is preferred. In addition to the Dempster rule, the cautious rule [9] is used to fuse all sources together.

2.3   Decision Rule at the Learning Stage

Here, the two cases with and without conflict must be distinguished.

Without Conflict: to classify an object using the information source f_k threshold S_m is applied on its mass value (H_1) . The object is classified as a defect if $m(H_1) \geq S_m$, or unknown (defect or not) if $m(H_1) < S_m$. Several thresholds S_m are tested at the learning phase from 0.6 to 0.9, and best values are selected using defined performance criterion in paragraph 2.3.

With Conflict: in this case, to classify an object using the information source f_k two thresholds are considered. If the conflict K is above a threshold T_K (chosen at 0.6), then it is considered that the decision is not reliable, and the object is classified as "unknown ". If the conflict K is under the conflict threshold T_K, then the object is classified as a defect if $m(H_1) > m(H_2)$, or false defect elsewise.

Selection of "successful" Sources Learning Stage. First of all, some metrics should be defined to characterize the classification performance of a source. Let P be the total of positives (true defects), N be the to-tal of negatives (false defects), TP be the total number of positives correctly classified, TN be the to-tal number of negatives correctly classified, FN be the total number of positives incorrectly classified and FP be the total number of negatives incorrectly classified. Two performance metrics are defined to select best combination of features as:

– True Defects classification rate:

$$\text{PTD} = \frac{\text{TP}}{\text{P}}$$

– False Defects classification rate[1]:

$$\text{PFD} = \frac{\text{TN}}{\text{N}}$$

---

[1] In the case without conflict, the PFD is computed as the total number of objects classified as unknown divided by the total number of negatives, whereas when the conflict is considered, PFD is equal to the total number of objects correctly classified as false defects divided by the total number of negatives.

The user indicates which are the PTD and PFD required rates to consider a source as "successful" (90% are the default values). Only those sources will then be considered for the validation phase. All single features, all combination of two features and the combination of the whole set of features are considered at this stage. The "successful" set is then composed of all combinations which are above the required performance. It is worth noting that the number of combination of pairwise features can be high, but the whole process being automatic, this selection is very powerful. This selection procedure is our warranty that only useful and informative sources are used afterwards in the classifier (independence of the selected sources is checked a posteriori). Thus, this selection of successful sources is a very important part of the learning stage.

2.4   Validation Phase

Validation is done on a test database of manually classified objects and the following steps take place:

- Selected features extraction.
- Translation from feature values to mass values using the regions of confidence obtained during the learning phase.
- Mass values fusion using only the "successful" selected features.
- Decision rule using the threshold value S_m selected as the best one for these features during learning (case without conflict) or using the decision rule with conflict.
- Performances on the validation database are then compared to the learning database.

3   Experimental Results with and without Conflict

For this contribution, we dispose of a 3D ultrasound datasets composed of 419 binary objects (blobs or potential defects) manually classified by an expert as true or false defects. For automatic classification purpose, a total number of 35 geo-metrical and intensity based features are measured on each blob (or object). These features represent the input sources of information for the classifiers to automatically classify the entry blob as a TD or FD.
For the learning and testing processes, the complete dataset is divided into:

- Learning dataset: 212 potential defects consisting of 164 FDs and 48 TDs.
- Testing dataset: 207 potential defects consisting of 164 FDs and 43 TDs.

3.1   Comparison of the with and without Conflict Approaches

The learning phase took at first place for the DS based classifier with and without conflict. At a preliminary comparison stage, the two different approaches were evaluated based on the number of successful sources. We remind that a successful source is a source whose performance metrics are higher that a given threshold.. As demonstrated in table 2, while the threshold rates vary between 0.9 and 0.6, the number of successful sources increased correspondently for both ap-proaches. This is normal because it is more easy to respect the required perfor-mance rates when the rate is lower. The important fact to mention is that the DS classifier without conflict allowed obtaining a clearly higher number of successful sources for each required PTD and PFD. This can be interpreted as follows: in the case without conflict, the hesitation between sources is modelled as an ignorance via the H3 mass. This ignorance can add some information when it is fused with another source whose part of belief completes the information. In the case with conflict, the hesitation is shared between the two hypothesis H_1 and H_2, so that only completely redundant sources can become successful (i.e. can see their masses increasing after fusion). Complementary sources will appear as conflicting.

Table 2. Comparison of the number of successful sources (learning phase) given by the approaches with and without conflict for different PTD and PFD rates

$DV = 0$, $Perc = 0.1$	Without conflict ($S_m = 0.9$)	With conflict ($T_K = 0.6$)
Number of sucessful sources (PTD, PFD ≥ 0.9)	14	0
Number of sucessful sources (PTD, PFD ≥ 0.8)	90	14
Number of sucessful sources (PTD, PFD ≥ 0.7)	198	88
Number of sucessful sources (PTD, PFD ≥ 0.6)	282	161

For a more precise comparison, ten combinations of two independent features were selected to investigate their performances with and without conflict. These combinations were considered to classify the blobs of the testing dataset. The graph in figure 3 presents the combinations performances on the testing dataset. As it can be noticed, the consideration of conflict resulted in a clear reduction of the PTD rates for all combinations on the testing dataset. As for the PFD rates, the two approaches with and without conflict give approximately the same results. The fact that the two populations do not have the same behavior is nor-mal. In the first modelling approach, the emphasis is put of the true defects (hypothesis H_1). When a lot of false defects are present in a region of the his-togram, the ignorance is preferred to the hypothesis H_2, because it means that it is still possible that a true defect is there. By that way, after fusion, the H1 mass is expected to increase and true defects are classified if their mass on H_1 is high, otherwise they are considered as unknown (i.e. ignorance), and the PFD rate is computed using this number of unknown objects. In the second case, the two populations are considered equally, and their masses after fusion can increase only if the fused features are in agreement. Defects are then classified in TD and FD (giving respectively the PTD and PFD rates), or unknown if the sources are in conflict (this number is considered apart). The fact that the two PFD rates are the same with the two approaches means that we have as many objects whose ignorance is high or whose mass on H_2 is high after fusion. The fact that PTD is higher without conflict means that a certain number of objects had a part of ignorance with one source and a part of belief with another source, which gives a higher mass on H_1 after fusion, while the same case gives a conflict with Bayesian masses. Another important aspect is the reliability of the sources which can be assessed by regarding the frequency of occurrence of conflicts for each combination. As previously mentioned, in the case of a conflict, the object is classified as unknown. Among the considered 10 combinations, the smallest number of unknown objects occurred for the combination number 5, with 10 occurrences (total of objects is 212) in the learning phase and 13 occurrences (total is 207) in the testing phase. This source can be considered as more reliable with respect to the number of conflicts than the other 9 combinations (having between 16 and 38 unknown objects).

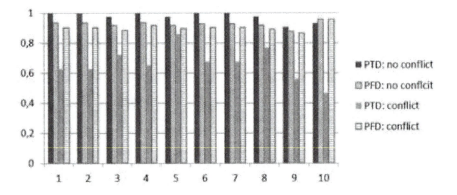

Fig. 3. Testing phase: Performances in terms of PTD and PFD rates of the randomly selected 10 combinations of independent features in conflict and without conflict cases

As output of this study, it is clear the classification approach without conflict gives better classification rates than the approach with conflict and Bayesian masses.

3.2   Comparison of the Fusion Rules

Next we compare all the considered classifiers: the DS orthogonal without conflict fusion rule (DSF), the Cautious rule and the SVM classifier. The results are presented in table 3. As it can be seen, SVM performs better when the two classification rates PTD and PFD are considered equally, but the best PTD rate is obtained with the DSF classifier using only a combination of two independent features (elongation of the blob in the transverse plane E_{xy} and its contrast CS_{Max}) instead of 35 features for SVM. The cautious rule performs also perfectly with a PTD rate of 1, but gives the lowest PFD rate.

Table 3. Performances of the considered classifiers on the learning and testing datasets

	Learning phase		Testing phase	
Combination rule	**PTD**	**PFD**	**PTD**	**PFD**
SVM Classifier	-	-	0.98	0.97
DSF(E_{xy}, CS_{Max})	0.96	0.98	1	0.93
Cautious rule ($S_m = 0.9$)	0.98	0.98	1	0.79

4   Conclusion

The choice to give a mass value to the hypothesis true defects H_1 and igno-rance H_3 without permitting a source to give mass to false defects hypothesis H_2 allowed not only to avoid conflicts but also to maximize the true defects classification rates as it was proven in this study. The reason is that, without conflict, the mass value attributed to the hypothesis H_1 is higher than in the case with conflict resulting in a better separation of the distribution of the mass values of the class of true defects from the other(s) class(es), thus the output is a higher classification rate of true defects. An important part of the whole pro-cedure is the selection of successful sources on the basis of their performances on the learning database: it appeared that several combinations of two features were successful, and their independence was checked a posteriori. For this reason, the orthogonal rule has high performances. The fact that the cautious rule applied on the whole set of features performed less well than the orthogonal rule comes from the fact that in our case, the cautious rule is equivalent to the maximal value of the masses, which means that finally only one feature is used. The SVM performed globally better than the other classifiers however the highest PTD rate was given by the DSF non normalized orthogonal fusion rule. In the field of non-destructive testing, this is an important result because in most industrial cases, PTD rate is considered with more importance than PFD rate. Although the results shown here come from one application case (ultrasonic 3D testing of composites), the same method was tested with success on 2D and 3D X-ray testing [3], [4].

References

1. Kaftandjian, V., Dupuis, O., Babot, D., Zhu, Y.: Uncertainty modeling using Dempster–Shafer theory for improving detection of weld defects. Pattern Recog-nition Letters 24, 547–564 (2003)
2. Lecomte, G., Kaftandjian, V., Cendre, E.: Combination of information from several x-ray images for improving defect detection performances-application to castings in-spection. In: Proc. 9th European Conference on Non-Destructive Testing (ECNDT), Berlin, Germany, September 25-29 (2006)

3. Osman, A., Kaftandjian, V., Hassler, U.: Improvement of X-ray castings inspection reliability by using Dempster-Shafer data fusion theory. Pattern Recognition Letters 32(2), 168–180 (2011)
4. Osman, A., Kaftandjian, V., Hassler, U.: Automatic classification of 3D segmented CT data using data fusion and support vector machine. Journal of Electronic Imaging of Spie 21 (2012)
5. Osman, A.: Automated evaluation of three dimensional ultrasonic datasets. Phd thesis, university of Erlangen-Nuremberg and INSA-Lyon (2013)
6. Osman, A., Kaftandjian, V., Hassler, U.: Application of data fusion theory and support vector machine to X-ray castings inspection. In: Proceedings of 10th European Conference on Non-Destructive Testing (ECNDT), Moscow, Russia (2010)
7. Dempster, A.: Upper and lower probabilities induced by multivalued mapping. Ann. Math. Statist. 38, 32–339 (1967)
8. Smets, P.: The combination of evidence in the transferable belief model. IEEE Trans. Pattern Anal. Machine Intell. 12(5), 447–458 (1990)
9. Denoeux, T.: Conjunctive and disjunctive combination of belief functions in-duced by nondistinct bodies of evidence. Artificial Intelligence 172(2-3), 234–264 (2008)

Predicting Stock Returns in the Capital Asset Pricing Model Using Quantile Regression and Belief Functions

Kittawit Autchariyapanitkul[1], Somsak Chanaim[2], Songsak Sriboonchitta[1], and Thierry Denoeux[3]

[1] Kittawit Autchariyapanitkul, Songsak Sriboonchitta
Faculty of Economics, Chiang Mai University, Chiang Mai 52000, Thailand
kittawit_autchariya@cmu.ac.th,
[2] Somsak Chanaim
Faculty of Science, Chiang Mai University, Chiang Mai 52000, Thailand
[3] Thierry Denoeux
UMR 7253 Heudiasyc, Université de Technologie de Compiègne, CNRS, France

Abstract. We consider an inference method for prediction based on belief functions in quantile regression with an asymmetric Laplace distribution. Specifically, we apply this method to the capital asset pricing model to estimate the beta coefficient and measure volatility under various market conditions at given levels of quantile. Likelihood-based belief functions are calculated from historical data of the securities in the S&P500 market. The results give us evidence on the systematic risk, in the form of a consonant belief function specified from the asymmetric Laplace distribution likelihood function given recorded data. Finally, we use the method to forecast the return of an individual stock.

Keywords: Asymmetric Laplace distribution, Capital Asset Pricing, Dempster-Shafer Theory, Financial data, Likelihood-based belief functions, Quantile regression.

1 Introduction

The Capital Asset Pricing Model (CAPM) is one of the most useful models in investment. In this model, asset returns are usually assumed to be jointly normally distributed random variables. However, this is not always the case. The CAPM assumes that the variance of returns adequately measures risk. This may be true if returns are normally distributed. In this paper, we propose to use quantile regression with an asymmetric Laplace distribution (ALD), coupled with an inference method based on belief functions, to estimate the parameters of the model and predict stock returns.

Quantile regression can characterize the entire conditional distribution of the outcome variable and is more robust to outliers and misspecification of the error distribution. It can also handle heteroscedasticity, as shown by Koenger. For the application of quantile regression to the CAPM, the reader is referred

F. Cuzzolin (Ed.): BELIEF 2014, LNAI 8764, pp. 219–226, 2014.

to, e.g., [1]. It was found that the market price of beta risk is significant in both tails of the conditional distribution of returns.

We present a likelihood-based approach to the estimation of regression quantiles based on the asymmetric Laplace distribution. In [8], this distribution is used to model the distribution of currency exchange rates and is shown to capture the peakedness, leptokurticity (Fat tails) and skewness inherent in such data. Similarly, it is shown in [6] that the Laplace distribution has a geometric stability to represent the weekly and monthly distributions of stock returns and also models the high peak, fat tails and skewness of the returns.

Here, we use the Dempster-Shafer theory of belief functions introduced by Dempster [3] and Shafer [7]. In this approach, a piece of evidence is modeled by a belief function, which can be viewed as the distribution of a random set. This method is applied to estimation using the likelihood-based approach introduced in [7] and recently justified in [4], and to prediction using the method introduced in [5]. The main contribution of this paper is thus to propose an alternative method for drawing inferences about conditional quantiles via a likelihood-based belief function approach.

The remainder of the paper is organized as follows. Section 2 provides the background on quantile regression with asymmetric Laplace distribution and Section 3 introduces the prediction machinery using belief functions. Section 4 discusses the empirical solutions to the forecasting problem. The last section summarizes the paper.

2 Quantile Regression with an Asymmetric Laplace Distribution

Let Y be a response variable and X a vector of explanatory variables. In linear quantile regression, the conditional α-quantile $q_\alpha(Y|X)$ of Y given X is assumed to be linearly related to X through the equation $q_\alpha(Y|X) = X'\beta_\alpha$, where β_α is a vector of unknown parameters and X' is the transpose of X. Denoting the error by ε_α, we can write the quantile regression model as

$$Y = X'\beta_\alpha + \varepsilon_\alpha. \tag{1}$$

We have

$$q_\alpha(Y|X) = q_\alpha[(X'\beta_\alpha + \varepsilon_\alpha)|X] = q_\alpha(X'\beta_\alpha + \varepsilon_\alpha|X) = X'\beta_\alpha + q_\alpha(\varepsilon_\alpha|X), \tag{2}$$

since given X, $X'\beta_\alpha$ is a constant. Thus, $q_\alpha(\varepsilon_\alpha|X) = 0$, which is the counterpart of the standard condition $E(\varepsilon|X) = 0$ in the mean linear regression model. If ε_α is independent of X, the α-quantile of the noise ε_α is zero, that is, $\int_{-\infty}^{0} dF_{\varepsilon_\alpha}(u) = \alpha$. For $q_\alpha(Y|X) = X'\beta_\alpha$, we see that β_α minimize $E[\rho_\alpha(Y - X'\beta)]$ over β, where $\rho_\alpha(\cdot)$ is the so-called check (or loss) function defined by

$$\rho_\alpha(u) = u(\alpha - 1_{(u<0)}), \tag{3}$$

with $1_{(u<0)}$ denoting the usual indicator function. Thus, given i.i.d (X_i, Y_i), a plausible estimator of β_α is

$$\widehat{\beta_\alpha} = \arg\min \frac{1}{n}\{\sum_{i=1}^{n} \rho_\alpha(Y_i - X_i'\beta)\}. \tag{4}$$

This estimator is called the Least Absolute Deviation (LAD) estimator.

Suppose that the error term ε_α has an ALD with mean 0 and standard deviation σ_α:

$$f_{\sigma_n}(\varepsilon_\alpha) = \frac{\alpha(1-\alpha)}{\sigma_\alpha} \exp\left\{-\rho_\alpha\left(\frac{\varepsilon_\alpha}{\sigma_\alpha}\right)\right\}. \tag{5}$$

Then, minimizing the absolute deviation is equivalent to maximizing the likelihood and the LAD estimator of β_α is a maximum likelihood estimator (MLE). The likelihood function for $\beta_\alpha, \sigma_\alpha$ after observing the data $D = (X_1, Y_1), \ldots, (X_n, Y_n)$ is

$$L_D(\beta_\alpha, \sigma_\alpha) = \frac{\alpha^n(1-\alpha)^n}{\sigma_\alpha^n} \exp\left\{-\sum_{i=1}^{n} \rho_\alpha\left(\frac{Y_i - X_i'\beta_\alpha}{\sigma}\right)\right\}. \tag{6}$$

3 Statistical Inference and Prediction Using Belief Functions

3.1 Likelihood-Based Belief Functions

Suppose we observe a realization x of the random vector X with probability density function (pdf) $p_\theta(x)$, where $\theta \in \Theta$ is an unknown parameter. In this paper, we use the method proposed by Shafer [7], which can be derived from the Likelihood Principle (LP) and the Least Commitment Principle (LCP) [4]. According to the LP, all the information about Θ is represented by the likelihood function defined by $L_x(\theta) = p_\theta(x)$ for all $\theta \in \Theta$. In statistics, the likelihood ratio has the meaning of a "relative plausibility", which can be written as:

$$\frac{pl_x(\theta_1)}{pl_x(\theta_2)} = \frac{L_x(\theta_1)}{L_x(\theta_2)}, \tag{7}$$

for all $(\theta_1, \theta_2) \in \Theta^2$ or, equivalently, $pl_x(\theta) = cL_x(\theta)$, for all $\theta \in \Theta$ and some positive constant c. The LCP then implies that the highest possible value should be given to constant c [4], which leads us to equating the contour function pl_x with the relative likelihood:

$$pl_x(\theta) = \frac{L_x(\theta)}{\sup_{\theta \in \Theta} L_x(\theta)}. \tag{8}$$

The information about θ is represented by the consonant belief function Bel_x^Θ with contour function pl_x, i.e., with corresponding plausibility function

$Pl_x^\Theta(A) = \sup_{\theta \in A} pl_x(\theta)$, for all $A \subseteq \Theta$. The focal sets of Bel_x^Θ are the levels sets of pl_x defined as follows:

$$\Gamma_x(\omega) = \{\theta \in \Theta | pl_x(\theta) \geq \omega\}, \tag{9}$$

for $\theta \in [0, 1]$. These sets are also called *plausibility regions*. The consonant belief function Bel_x^Θ is equivalent to the random set induced by the Lebesgue measure λ on $[0,1]$ and the multi-valued mapping Γ_x from $[0, 1] \rightarrow 2^\Theta$ (see, [5]). We remark that the MLE of θ is the value of θ with highest plausibility.

3.2   Prediction Using Belief Functions

Let X be a random variable with parametric density function $f_\theta(x)$ for $\theta \in \Theta$ and assume that we have observed $X = x$. Given the belief function Bel_x^Θ about θ, we can predict the future value of a random variable Y whose pdf $g_\theta(y)$ also depends on θ. In the approach introduced in [5], Y is written as a function of the parameter θ and an unobserved auxiliary variable $u \in \mathbb{U}$ with known probability measure μ not depending on θ:

$$Y = \varphi(\theta, u). \tag{10}$$

Using Equations (9) and (10), we can compose the multi-valued mapping Γ_x from $[0, 1] \rightarrow 2^\Theta$ with φ to get a new multi-valued mapping Γ_x' from $[0, 1] \times \mathbb{U}$ to $2^\mathbb{Y}$ defined as

$$\Gamma_x' : [0, 1] \times \mathbb{U} \rightarrow 2^\mathbb{Y}$$
$$(\omega, u) \rightarrow \varphi(\Gamma_x(\omega), u).$$

We can then define the predictive belief $(Bel_x^\mathbb{Y})$ and plausibility $(Pl_x^\mathbb{Y})$ functions on $\mathbb{Y}$ as

$$Bel_x^\mathbb{Y}(A) = (\lambda \otimes \mu)(\{(\omega, u) \in [0, 1] | \varphi(\Gamma_x(\omega, u) \subseteq A\}). \tag{11a}$$
$$Pl_x^\mathbb{Y}(A) = (\lambda \otimes \mu)(\{(\omega, u) \in [0, 1] | \varphi(\Gamma_x(\omega, u) \cap A \neq \emptyset\}), \tag{11b}$$

for all $A \subseteq \mathbb{Y}$.

4   Application to Stock Market Prediction

4.1   Model

The CAPM measures the sensitivity of the expected excess return on security to expected market risk premium. The equation of CAPM is a linear function of the security market line:

$$E(R_A) - R_F = \beta_0 + \beta_1 E(R_M - R_F), \tag{12}$$

where $E(R_A)$ is the expected return of the asset, R_M is the expected market portfolio return, R_F is the risk free rate, β_0 is the intercept and β_1 is the equity beta, representing market risk. Suppose we have observed the historical returns of stock $R_A = (r_{a1}, \cdots, r_{an})$ and returns from market $R_M = (r_{m1}, \cdots, r_{mn})$. The errors will be assumed to be iid with density function (5). The likelihood function is given by (6).

4.2   Experimental Results

The data contain the weekly log returns of the integrated oil and gas company, Chesapeake Energy (CHK), during 2010-2013. The ML estimates of the parameters are shown in Table 1 for different values of α.

Table 1. Parameter estimation results. Standard errors are given in parentheses.

Stock Name	Parameters	$\alpha = 0.40$	$\alpha = 0.50$	$\alpha = 0.60$
CHK	β_0	-0.011 (0.002)	-0.004 (0.003)	0.005 (0.000)
	β_1	1.379 (0.163)	1.442 (0.005)	1.304 (0.017)
	σ	0.002 (0.001)	0.016 (0.001)	0.016 (0.010)

We used a nonlinear optimization algorithm to maximize the likelihood (6) with respect to $\theta = (\beta_{(0,\alpha)}, \beta_{(1,\alpha)}, \sigma_\alpha)$. The plausibility function on θ is then defined by the relative likelihood (8) and the marginal contour function on a specific parameter is obtained by take the supremum with respect to the others parameters, e.g.,

$$pl_{R_\Lambda}(\beta_{(0,\alpha)}) = \sup_{\beta_{(1,\alpha)},\sigma} pl_{R_\Lambda}(\beta_{(0,\alpha)}). \tag{13}$$

Figure 1 displays two-dimensional marginal contour functions and Figure 2 shows the marginal contour functions for parameters β_0, β_1 and σ. The 0.15 threshold corresponds to an approximate 95% confidence interval and gives us an interval of plausible values of each of the three parameters.

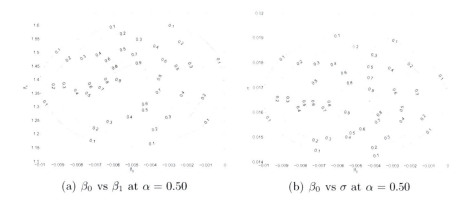

(a) β_0 vs β_1 at $\alpha = 0.50$ (b) β_0 vs σ at $\alpha = 0.50$

Fig. 1. Marginal contour functions $pl_x(\theta_1, \theta_2)$ in two-dimensional parameter subspaces

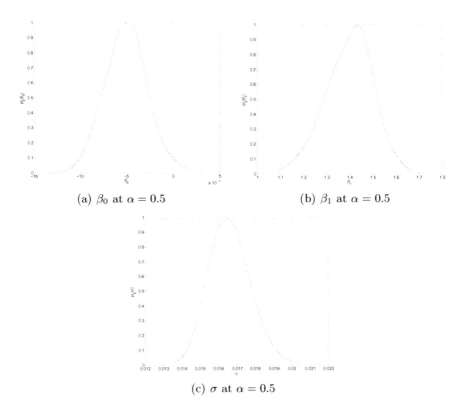

(a) β_0 at $\alpha = 0.5$

(b) β_1 at $\alpha = 0.5$

(c) σ at $\alpha = 0.5$

Fig. 2. Marginal plausibility of $\beta_0^{0.5}$ (a), $\beta_1^{0.5}$ (b) and $\sigma^{0.5}$ (c)

To predict the expected return of the asset $r_{a,n+1}$ for a new market portfolio return $r_{m,n+1}$, we compute the minimum and maximum of $r_{a,n+1}$ given $r_{m,n+1}$ at fixed α by

$$r_{a,n+1} = \beta_{0,\alpha} + \beta_{1,\alpha} r_{m,n+1} + \sigma_\alpha F_{\varepsilon_\alpha}^{-1}(u), \tag{14}$$

under the constraint $pl_{R_A}(\beta_{i,\alpha}, \sigma_\alpha) > \omega$, where $F_{\varepsilon_\alpha}^{-1}$ is the inverse cumulative distribution function (cdf) of the asymmetric Laplace distribution $ALD(\alpha, 0, 1)$ and u, ω are independent random variables with the same uniform distribution $U([0,1])$. Given (14), we randomize independently N pairs of the random number $(\omega_i, u_i), i = 1, 2, \cdots, N$ resulting in N intervals $[r_a^L(\omega_i, u_i), r_a^U(\omega_i, u_i)]$. For any $A \subseteq \mathbb{R}$, the stock returns $Bel_{r_{ai}}(A)$ and $Pl_{r_{ai}}(A)$ can be estimated by equation (11). The estimated lower and upper expectations of $r_{a,n+1}$ are then:

$$\overline{R}_A^L = \sum_{i=1}^{N} \frac{r_a^L(\omega_i, u_i)}{N} \tag{15a}$$

$$\overline{R}_A^U = \sum_{i=1}^{N} \frac{r_a^U(\omega_i, u_i)}{N}. \tag{15b}$$

Figures 3 displays the lower and upper cdfs $Bel_{R_A}((-\infty, R_A])$ and $Pl_{R_A}((-\infty, R_A])$ at given $r_m = 0.05$. This function give us the summary of the predictive belief function Bel_{R_A}. Figure 4 shows the upper and lower predictive quantiles of the stock returns (see [5]), defined by the inequalities $pl(R_A \geqslant q_{\alpha'}^L) = \alpha'$ and $pl(R_A \leqslant q_{\alpha'}^U) = \alpha'$. As shown in [5], the following inequalities hold:

$$Bel(q_{\alpha'}^L \leqslant R_A \leqslant q_{1-\alpha'}^U) \geqslant 1 - 2\alpha'. \tag{16}$$

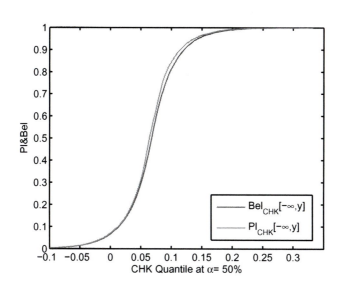

Fig. 3. Upper and lower cumulative distribution function given $r_m = 0.05$

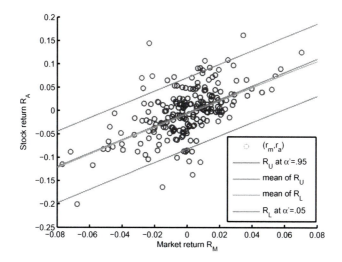

Fig. 4. Lower and upper quantiles of stock returns at $\alpha = 0.5$

Lower-upper expectations and quantiles are other representations of prediction uncertainty, taking into account both parameter estimation uncertainty and randomness. For these data, the very narrow gap between the lower and upper cdfs shows that estimation uncertainty is small as compared to random uncertainty. In practice, these results can be used to increase the performance of the investment portfolio.

5 Conclusions

In this paper, we studied the method of quantile CAPM with ALD for stocks in S&P500 in the belief function framework. We used the Dempster-Shafer theory of belief functions to model the uncertainty referring to the statistical prediction based on historical data and a financial model. This method consists of two steps. First, a consonant belief function representing the uncertainty on the parameter vector θ is defined from the normalized likelihood function given the past data. The return of individual stock R_A is then expressed as $\varphi(\theta, u)$, where u is a stochastic variable with known distribution and the beliefs on θ and u are transferred through φ, resulting in a belief function on R_A. This approach has been adapted to the prediction of stock returns. A possible extension of this work is to consider uncertainty on the independent variable r_m, which can also be expressed as a belief function and combined with other uncertainties to compute a belief function on R_A. This issue will be addressed in future work.

Acknowledgments. The authors thank Prof. Dr. Hung T. Nguyen for his helpful comments and suggestions on the connection between belief functions and random sets.

References

1. Barnes, L.M., Hughes, W.A.: A Quantile Regression Analysis of the Cross Section of Stock Market Returns. Federal Reserve Bank of Boston, working paper (2002)
2. Ben Abdallah, N., Mouhous Voyneau, N., Denoeux, T.: Combining statistical and expert evidence using belief functions: Application to centennial sea level estimation taking into account climate change. International Journal of Approximate Reasoning 55, 341–345 (2014)
3. Dempster, A.P.: Upper and lower probabilities induced by a multivalued mapping. Annals of Mathematical Statistics 38, 325–339 (1967)
4. Denoeux, T.: Likelihood-based belief function: justification and some extensions to low-quality data. International Journal of Approximate Reasoning (2013) (accepted for publication), http://dx.doi.org/10.1016.j.ijar.2013.06.007
5. Kanjanatarakul, O., Sriboonchitta, S., Denoeux, T.: Forecasting using belief functions: an application to marketing econometrics. International Journal of Approximate Reasoning 55(5), 1113–1128 (2014)
6. Linden, M.: A Model for Stock Return Distribution. International Journal of Finance and Economics 6, 159–169 (2001)
7. Shafer, G.: A mathematical theory of evidence. Princeton University Press, Princeton (1976)
8. Sánchez, B.L., Lachos, H.V., Labra, V.F.: Likelihood Based Inference for Quantile Regression Using the Asymmetric Laplace Distribution. Journal of Statistical Computation and Simulation 81, 1565–1578 (2013)

Evidential Object Recognition
Based on Information Gain Maximization

Thomas Reineking and Kerstin Schill

Cognitive Neuroinformatics, University of Bremen,
Enrique-Schmidt-Str. 5, 28359 Bremen, Germany
reineking@uni-bremen.de

Abstract. This paper presents an object recognition approach based on belief function inference and information gain maximization. A common problem for probabilistic object recognition models is that the parameters of the probability distributions cannot be accurately estimated using the available training data due to high dimensionality. We therefore use belief functions in order to make the reliability of the evidence provided by the training data an explicit part of the recognition model. In contrast to typical classification approaches, we consider recognition as a sequential information-gathering process where a system with dynamic beliefs actively seeks to acquire new evidence. This acquisition process is based on the principle of maximum expected information gain and enables the system to perform optimal actions for reducing uncertainty as quickly as possible. We evaluate our system on a standard object recognition dataset where we investigate the effect of the amount of training data on classification performance by comparing different methods for constructing belief functions from data.

Keywords: belief functions, object recognition, information gain.

1 Introduction

Object recognition is an inherently uncertain problem because of ambiguous relations between features and classes, which is why probabilistic classification approaches are very popular [4]. However, oftentimes the training set is too small in comparison to the number of model parameters, which is why the underlying probability distributions cannot be accurately estimated and overfitting occurs. In this case, belief functions can be used in order to make the lack of evidence caused by limited amounts of training data explicit, which helps to reduce the problem of overfitting.

In this paper, a recognition system is presented which combines bottom-up processing of sensory information with top-down reasoning based on information gain maximization. Note that some of the results shown in this paper were originally presented in [9]. The system is inspired by the one proposed in [10], which has been applied to problems ranging from self-localization [19] to scene categorization [11]. Here, the focus is on object recognition where the system

F. Cuzzolin (Ed.): BELIEF 2014, LNAI 8764, pp. 227–236, 2014.

successively collects features over time by actively extracting information from different parts of an image. Belief functions are used for fusing the collected evidence while taking into account the amount of available training data for each class. The action selection process follows an information-theoretic approach where the system, at each point in time, executes the action with the highest expected information gain with respect to the current belief distribution over possible object classes.

An important characteristic of the proposed system is that actions are not simply means for acquiring sensory evidence because, in conjunction with sensory information, they also provide evidence and are therefore an explicit part of the representation. This is motivated by results from perceptual psychology and neurobiology which indicate that the separation of sensory and motor signals in biological systems is not strict and that motor information plays not only an important but a constituting role for perception [6]. For this reason, the system learns the joint distribution over sensory and motor information for representing object classes.

The remainder of this paper is structured as follows: The recognition system with the evidential inference and the information gain strategy are presented in the next section along with different methods for constructing belief functions from limited amounts of training data. In Sect. 3, the system is applied to an object recognition problem where the different belief construction methods are compared empirically. The paper concludes with a discussion of the presented system in Sect. 4.

2   Recognition System

The proposed system is based on a continuous cycle of retrieving the "most informative" feature from an image and using this feature to update the current belief distribution. This distribution is successively updated by the combined evidence of extracted sensory information and the corresponding motor information based on a previously-learned sensorimotor model. At each point in time, the system determines an optimal next action by maximizing the expected information gain with respect to the current belief distribution using the sensorimotor model in order to predict the effect of actions. The action with the highest expected information gain is then executed which leads to the collection of a new piece of sensory evidence, after which the cycle starts over. A schematic overview of this process is shown in Fig. 1.

Let $X \subseteq \Theta_x$ be the evidential variable representing the class and let $\Theta_x = \{x_1, x_2, \ldots\}$ be the corresponding finite frame of discernment where each x_i represents an object class. Furthermore, let $z_{1:t} = z_1, \ldots, z_t$ denote the sequence of sensory features collected up to time t and let $u_{1:t}$ denote the sequence of performed actions. Each tuple (z_k, u_k) forms a sensorimotor feature. The corresponding frames of discernment $z_k \in \Theta_z$ and $u_k \in \Theta_u$ are finite and time-invariant. Sensorimotor features are assumed to be conditionally independent given the class, which resembles a Naive Bayes model. The basis for recognition

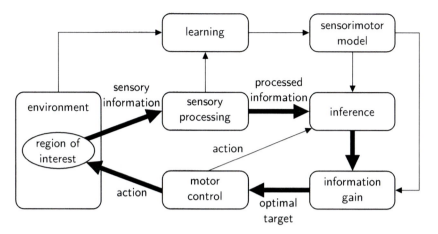

Fig. 1. Schematic overview of the recognition process. The continuous evidence selection and update cycle is indicated by the thick arrows. Here, sensory information from the image is actively selected based on the current belief (computed by the inference module) and the information gain strategy. The newly collected evidence is then used to update the current belief which, in turn, leads to another information-gathering action.

is thus the computation of the class belief distribution $m_{\Theta_x}[z_{1:t}, u_{1:t}]$ given all collected evidence.

2.1   Inference

Inference is based on a generative classification scheme where the generalized Bayesian theorem [12] is used to compute the posterior class distribution from the class-conditional distributions over the sensorimotor features [13]. Because of the assumption of conditional independence of sensorimotor features, the final belief distribution can be decomposed into a series of distributions (each induced by a single sensorimotor feature) using Dempster's rule of combination. The update can then be performed recursively over time where the belief at time $t-1$ is used to compute the belief at time t.

$$m_{\Theta_x}[z_{1:t}, u_{1:t}] = m_{\Theta_x}[z_{1:t-1}, u_{1:t-1}] \oplus m_{\Theta_x}[z_t, u_t] \qquad (1)$$

The class prior m_{Θ_x} at $t = 0$ is assumed to be vacuous here, although this is not a necessary assumption. The belief $m_{\Theta_x}[z_t, u_t]$ induced by sensorimotor feature (z_t, u_t) can be computed from the likelihoods $pl_{\Theta_z \times \Theta_u}[x](z_t, u_t)$ using the generalized Bayesian theorem.

$$m_{\Theta_x}[z_t, u_t](X) = \eta \prod_{x \in X} pl_{\Theta_z \times \Theta_u}[x](z_t, u_t) \prod_{x \in \overline{X}} (1 - pl_{\Theta_z \times \Theta_u}[x](z_t, u_t)) \qquad (2)$$

Here, η represents a normalization constant. By assuming that the a priori belief for u_t is vacuous, each likelihood can be expressed as a marginal distribution

$pl_{\Theta_z}[x, u_t](z_t)$ over z_t. These likelihoods form the basis for inference and different methods for constructing them from data are described in Sect. 2.3.

In practice, solving the above equations exactly is infeasible because the frames of discernment are too large. This is why the importance-sampling-based Monte-Carlo algorithm presented in [8] is applied for updating the belief distribution. Using this algorithm, the belief update can be performed with linear time complexity $O(K |\Theta_x|)$ where K denotes the number of samples drawn from the prior distribution (we use $K = 10,000$ in Sect. 3). In order to obtain the final class label, the pignistic transformation [14] is applied to the final belief distribution and the singleton with the highest pignistic probability is returned. Note that the pignistic transformation is only one way of determining the final class label and other decision rules, like ones based on imprecise probabilities, would be interesting to consider as well [16].

2.2   Information Gain

As described above, the system selects the action with the highest expected information gain. For measuring information gain, a measure of uncertainty applicable to belief functions is required. Here, we use the Shannon entropy of the pignistic transformation (denoted by H_{BetP}) of the underlying belief function. The reason for using the pignistic entropy is that the final classification is also based on the pignistic transformation, though other measures could be used as well [5]. The expected information gain $I(u_t)$ of action u_t is defined as the expected reduction in uncertainty after having performed action u_t [15].

$$I(u_t) = H_{BetP}(m_{\Theta_x}[z_{1:t-1}, u_{1:t-1}]) - E_{z_t}(H_{BetP}(m_{\Theta_x}[z_{1:t}, u_{1:t}])) \qquad (3)$$

Because the sensory feature z_t is not known prior to executing the corresponding action u_t, the expected value of the resulting uncertainty $H_{BetP}(m_{\Theta_x}[z_{1:t}, u_{1:t}])$ with respect to z_t has to be considered.

Finding the action u_t^* associated with the highest expected information gain simply requires computing the gain for every possible action u_t and choosing the one that maximizes $I(u_t)$. Let $\Theta_{u;t} \subseteq \Theta_u$ denote the set of actions that have not been performed up to time t (executing the same action twice would cause the same piece of evidence to be counted twice, which is why only the subset $\Theta_{u;t}$ is considered). Maximizing the expected information gain $I(u_t)$ with $u_t \in \Theta_{u;t}$ is equivalent to minimizing the expected uncertainty after having executed action u_t because the current uncertainty is constant.

$$u_t^* = \arg\max_{u_t \in \Theta_{u;t}} I(u_t) = \arg\min_{u_t \in \Theta_{u;t}} E_{z_t}(H_{BetP}(m_{\Theta_x}[z_{1:t}, u_{1:t}])) \qquad (4)$$

Computing this expected value consists of two parts: Computing the uncertainty after having observed a particular value z_t, which can be done using (1), and computing the pignistic probability of z_t given all previous pieces of evidence.

$$E_{z_t}(H_{BetP}(m_{\Theta_r}[z_{1:t}, u_{1:t}]))$$
$$= \sum_{z_t \in \Theta_z} H_{BetP}(m_{\Theta_r}[z_{1:t}, u_{1:t}]) \, BetP_{\Theta_z}[z_{1:t-1}, u_{1:t}](z_t) \tag{5}$$

The mass function $m_{\Theta_z}[z_{1:t-1}, u_{1:t}]$ underlying the pignistic probability of z_t can be obtained by conditioning on class X and by exploiting independence for feature z_t (it only depends on class X and action u_t) and for class X (action u_t does not influence the class belief without the corresponding feature z_t).

$$m_{\Theta_z}[z_{1:t-1}, u_{1:t}] = \sum_{X \subseteq \Theta_r} m_{\Theta_z}[X, u_t] \, m_{\Theta_r}[z_{1:t-1}, u_{1:t-1}](X) \tag{6}$$

Mass function $m_{\Theta_r}[z_{1:t-1}, u_{1:t-1}]$ simply represents the belief at time $t-1$ and is thus directly available. Because the feature distribution $m_{\Theta_z}[X, u_t]$ is conditioned on a set of classes $X \subseteq \Theta_x$, the disjunctive rule of combination is applied in order to construct it from the singleton-conditioned distributions $m_{\Theta_z}[x_i, u_t]$ with $x_i \in X$ [12]. For this, the sum over all possible unions of sets $Z_{t;i} \subseteq \Theta_z$ resulting in Z_t has to be computed.

$$m_{\Theta_z}[X, u_t](Z_t) = \sum_{(\bigcup_{i:x_i \in X} Z_{t;i}) = Z_t} \prod_{x_i \in X} m_{\Theta_z}[x_i, u_t](Z_{t;i}) \tag{7}$$

The above equations can be used to find the optimal action at any given time, however, solving them exactly is usually intractable. Like for inference, the solution can be approximated though, and in [9], an efficient Monte-Carlo algorithm with time complexity $O(K'|\Theta_u||\Theta_z||\Theta_x|)$ for finding the optimal action is presented (K' denotes the number of samples). Usually, K' is chosen to be smaller than the number of samples K used for inference because the effects of approximation errors are not as severe for determining the next action.

2.3 Model Construction

The basis for inference are the likelihoods $pl_{\Theta_z}[x, u_t](z_t)$ where the sensory feature z_t and the corresponding action u_t are assumed to be discrete. The likelihoods have to be estimated from training data, which is problematic if the number of model parameters is large compared to the available data (for the object recognition problem described in the next section, there are 50,000 parameters resulting from $|\Theta_x| = 10$, $|\Theta_z| = 100$, and $|\Theta_u| = 50$). This problem is the motivation for using belief functions to model the distribution over z_t because belief functions can make the reliability of the different likelihood estimates explicit. Intuitively, this means that for the extreme case of a complete absence of training samples, the corresponding belief function should be vacuous whereas more training samples should result in a more committed belief function.

We consider different methods from the literature for constructing the likelihoods and we compare them empirically in next section.[1] In particular, we use the methods proposed in [2] (denoted by BelMax*) and [1] (denoted by MCD*), which are both based on the idea of constructing confidence intervals and then solving an optimization problem in order to derive a belief function from these intervals. In both methods, solving the full optimization problem is intractable for larger spaces which is why approximations are used in both cases (see (30) in [2] and (28) in [1]). In addition, we use the Imprecise Dirichlet Model (IDM) presented in [17], which was originally proposed in the context of the imprecise probability framework. For comparison, we also consider the two most common probabilistic methods, namely the maximum likelihood estimate (MLE; the relative frequencies are directly accepted as probabilities) and Laplace smoothing (an additive term is used to smooth each feature count).

3   Application to Object Recognition

In this section, we apply the system to an object recognition problem where it classifies an image by sequentially processing regions of interest in the image. This resembles the way humans analyze scenes via saccadic eye movements and the information gain strategy can be interpreted as a model for attention in this context [10]. For each region of interest, a descriptor is extracted which is used in conjunction with the performed action to update the belief distribution over possible object classes. Note that the aim here is to demonstrate how the recognition system functions and to compare the different model construction methods rather than to compete with state-of-the-art object recognition approaches (e.g., [18]).

We use the Caltech-256 dataset [3] where we randomly select a subset of 10 classes in order to limit the computational effort (the only selection criterion is that the class contains at least 100 images). The results presented below are obtained using 10-fold cross validation where, for each class, 80 images are used for training and 20 for testing. Before processing, all images are scaled and cropped to a common size of 256×256 pixels. A region of interest corresponds to a 64×64 pixel patch, from which a gist feature vector [7] is extracted. Gist features are based on histograms of orientation-selective band-pass filter responses and are usually used as global image descriptors. However, they also work well for describing local image patches, which is how they are used here. Each feature vector is then discretized using k-means clustering trained on 20,000 randomly sampled image patches (with $k = 100$). Clustering is also performed for actions where an action simply represents the image coordinates of a region of interest (with $k = 50$). An example of how the system performs recognition is shown in Fig. 2.

The basis for constructing the likelihoods $pl_{\Theta_z}[x, u_t]$ are sensorimotor histograms where, for each combination of a class x and a quantized action u_t, the

---

[1] All of the methods are implemented in the open source library *PyDS* available at https://github.com/reineking/pyds.

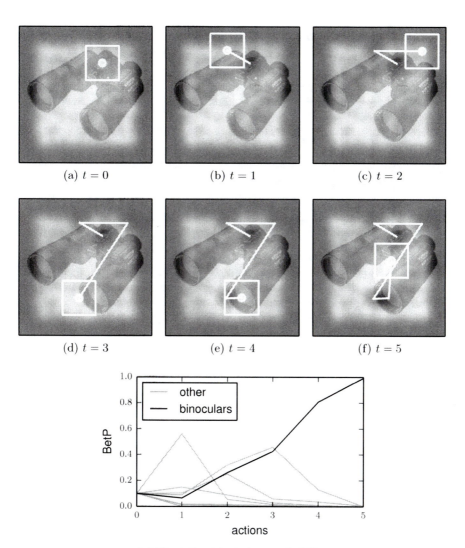

(a) $t = 0$ (b) $t = 1$ (c) $t = 2$

(d) $t = 3$ (e) $t = 4$ (f) $t = 5$

(g) Pignistic object class probability

Fig. 2. Object recognition example. Plots (a) to (f) show performed actions over time where the white square represents the current fixation while the white lines indicate previous fixations. The information gain distribution over possible target positions is superimposed over the image where higher brightness values indicate higher expected information gain values (a Gaussian located at each clustered prototype position is used to interpolate between prototype positions). Plot (g) shows the corresponding pignistic object class probability over time. The true class "binoculars" is correctly recognized with high confidence after the system has performed 6 actions.

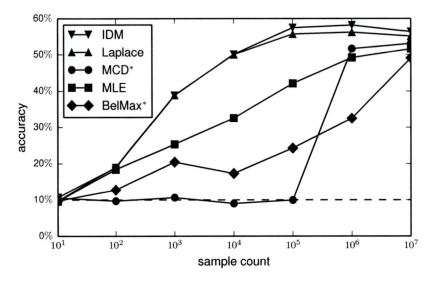

Fig. 3. Mean recognition rate on Caltech-256 (using 10 classes) for different model construction methods and different training sample counts. The sample count is plotted on a logarithmic scale. Chance level is indicated by the dashed line.

number of occurrences of each quantized gist vector z_t is counted. With 100 discretized gist vectors and 50 discretized actions, there are 5,000 histogram entries for each class. By applying one of the belief construction methods described in Sect. 2.3, the required plausibility can then be computed. In order to investigate the influence of the amount of available training data for the different model construction methods, we measure the recognition rate for different numbers of training samples used for computing the sensorimotor histograms. The number of samples states how many sensorimotor features are extracted in total from all 80 training images for each class.

The results of this investigation are shown in Fig. 3. As expected, all construction methods result in higher recognition rates for larger sample counts. Overall, the IDM method performs best with Laplace smoothing being a close second. Both methods significantly outperform the MLE solution. The MCD* method only performs at chance level until reaching 10^6 samples, at which point it also outperforms the MLE solution.[2] The reason for this performance jump is that, for smaller samples counts, the constructed belief functions are usually vacuous. Despite this fact, the MCD* method is the only one that performs robustly on all classes for higher sample counts (see [9] for details). In contrast, the BelMax* method consistently performs worse than the MLE solution in this experiment. In general, there appears to be a limit when approaching 60% accuracy where additional samples do not improve accuracy. This limit is likely due to the fact

---

[2] We use $\alpha = 0.5$ for the confidence intervals in the BelMax* and the MCD* method. Although the original papers suggest using smaller values, larger ones tend to significantly improve the recognition rate here.

that there are only 80 training images for each class, which is why drawing additional samples only results in redundant information at some point. Perhaps surprisingly, even for a very large sample count of 10^7, the MLE solution is still being outperformed by the other methods (except for BelMax*). A possible explanation for this effect is that that the other methods never estimate a likelihood to be strictly zero. Assigning a likelihood of zero is always problematic because it causes the corresponding class to be categorically rejected.

4   Discussion

In the comparison of the different model construction methods, the IDM approach resulted in the highest recognition rate. However, a simple probabilistic approach like Laplace smoothing yields almost equally good results in this particular experiment. An interesting direction for future research on belief function construction would be to consider specialized methods for generative classification models. This is because all of the considered methods construct full belief functions over the feature space whereas only plausibilities of singletons are actually used during classification. As a result, it is not necessary to consider the full power set over the feature space and strong restrictions like the assumption of consonance in the case of the MCD* method could be avoided.

Regarding the use of the pignistic transformation, both for determining the final class label as well as for measuring the expected information gain, it would be very interesting to consider alternative decision rules that do not attempt to reduce the available information to a probabilistic representation. With respect to the information gain, one could, for example, investigate how measures based on non-specificity would affect the system's information gathering behavior.

Overall, it was shown that belief functions provide a sound theoretical basis for performing inference when there is insufficient training data for reliably estimating the underlying probability distributions. For the problem of object recognition, it was shown that a belief function model can outperform probabilistic models in terms of recognition rate because belief functions can take the number of training samples into consideration. We expect that this effect becomes even stronger if there are different numbers of samples for different classes but this is a subject of future work. The system presented in this paper combines evidential inference with an information gain maximization strategy for actively collecting evidence over time in order to reduce uncertainty as quickly as possible. This information-driven cycle of acquisition and processing is essentially domain independent though and it would therefore be interesting to apply the same principles in other domains.

Acknowledgments. This work was supported by DFG (SFB/TR 8 Spatial Cognition, project "A5-[ActionSpace]").

References

1. Aregui, A., Denœux, T.: Constructing consonant belief functions from sample data using confidence sets of pignistic probabilities. International Journal of Approximate Reasoning 49(3), 575–594 (2008)
2. Denœux, T.: Constructing belief functions from sample data using multinomial confidence regions. International Journal of Approximate Reasoning 42(3), 228–252 (2006)
3. Griffin, G., Holub, A., Perona, P.: Caltech-256 object category dataset. Tech. rep., California Institute of Technology (2007)
4. Hoiem, D., Efros, A.A., Hebert, M.: Putting objects in perspective. International Journal of Computer Vision 80(1), 3–15 (2008)
5. Klir, G.J.: Uncertainty and information: foundations of generalized information theory. Wiley (2005)
6. Noë, A.: Action in Perception. MIT Press (2004)
7. Oliva, A., Torralba, A.: Modeling the shape of the scene: A holistic representation of the spatial envelope. International Journal of Computer Vision 42(3), 145–175 (2001)
8. Reineking, T.: Particle filtering in the Dempster-Shafer theory. International Journal of Approximate Reasoning 52(8), 1124–1135 (2011)
9. Reineking, T.: Belief Functions: Theory and Algorithms. Ph.D. thesis, University of Bremen (February 2014)
10. Schill, K., Umkehrer, E., Beinlich, S., Krieger, G., Zetzsche, C.: Scene analysis with saccadic eye movements: Top-down and bottom-up modeling. Journal of Electronic Imaging 10(1), 152–160 (2001)
11. Schill, K., Zetzsche, C., Hois, J.: A belief-based architecture for scene analysis: From sensorimotor features to knowledge and ontology. Fuzzy Sets and Systems 160(10), 1507–1516 (2009)
12. Smets, P.: Belief functions: The disjunctive rule of combination and the generalized Bayesian theorem. International Journal of Approximate Reasoning 9, 1–35 (1993)
13. Smets, P.: The application of the transferable belief model to diagnostic problems. International Journal of Intelligent Systems 13, 127–157 (1998)
14. Smets, P.: Decision making in the TBM: the necessity of the pignistic transformation. International Journal of Approximate Reasoning 38, 133–147 (2005)
15. Thrun, S., Burgard, W., Fox, D.: Probabilistic robotics. MIT Press, Cambridge (2005)
16. Troffaes, M.C.: Decision making under uncertainty using imprecise probabilities. International Journal of Approximate Reasoning 45(1), 17–29 (2007)
17. Walley, P.: Inferences from multinomial data: learning about a bag of marbles. Journal of the Royal Statistical Society 58(1), 3–57 (1996)
18. Zeiler, M.D., Fergus, R.: Visualizing and understanding convolutional neural networks. arXiv preprint arXiv:1311.2901 (2013)
19. Zetzsche, C., Wolter, J., Schill, K.: Sensorimotor representation and knowledge-based reasoning for spatial exploration and localisation. Cognitive Processing 9, 283–297 (2008)

Evidence-Based Modelling of Organizational Social Capital with Incomplete Data: An NCaRBS Analysis

Malcolm J. Beynon and Rhys Andrews

Cardiff Business School, Cardiff University,
Colum Drive, Cardiff, CF10 3EU, Wales, UK
{BeynonMJ,AndrewsR4}@cardiff.ac.uk

Abstract. Organizational social capital is critical to effective organizational functioning. Yet, different aspects of social capital are likely to be present to varying degrees within any given organization. In this study, alternative blends of structural, relational and cognitive social capital are modelled using a range of key organizational variables drawn from an incomplete dataset. A novel evidence-based approach to the ambiguous classification of objects (N-state Classification and Ranking Belief Simplex or NCaRBS) is used for the analysis. NCaRBS is uniquely able to capture the full range of ambiguity in the antecedents and effects of social capital, and to do so by incorporating incomplete data without recourse to the external management of the missing values. The study therefore illustrates the multi-faceted potential of analytical techniques based on uncertain reasoning, using the Dempster-Shafer theory of evidence methodology.

Keywords: Dempster-Shafer theory, Incomplete data, NCaRBS, Social Capital, Validation.

1 Introduction

Positive relationships amongst organization members are essential for efficient knowledge transfer and creation [8]. Nevertheless, the social capital within organizations may be contingent upon internal structural characteristics, such as size, decentralization and staffing cutbacks. In this study, NCaRBS [4], a development on the original CaRBS technique introduced in [1, 2], is used to model alternative combinations of three key dimensions of social capital: structural (connections among actors); relational (trust among actors); and cognitive (shared goals and values) [9].

As a technique whose rudiments are based on the Dempster-Shafer theory of evidence [5, 11], NCaRBS undertakes *n*-state classification analysis based on uncertain reasoning. One of the strengths of NCaRBS (and CaRBS in general) is that it can be applied directly to incomplete data without having to manipulate or exclude cases with missing values. Using a large-scale survey dataset with a sizeable number of missing values, the results of two NCaRBS models of alternative social capital data sets are compared, namely when all missing values are included and when using a case deletion approach to the management of missing values.

F. Cuzzolin (Ed.): BELIEF 2014, LNAI 8764, pp. 237–246, 2014.

Graphical analysis of the contribution of size, decentralization and staffing cutbacks towards social capital blends affirms the value of including missing values and the ability of NCaRBS to undertake such types of analysis. Added confidence in these results comes from a re-sampling procedure that identifies near-identical relationships.

2   NCARBS

NCaRBS [4] models the ambiguous classification of n_O objects (o_1, o_2, ..), to n_D decision outcomes (d_1, d_2, ..), based on their description by n_C characteristics (c_1, c_2, ..). The characteristics' evidence is expressed through the construction of *constituent* BOEs (bodies of evidence) from a characteristic value $v_{i,j}$ (i^{th} object, j^{th} characteristic), to discern between an object's association to a decision outcome (say d_h), its complement ($\neg d_h$) and a level of concomitant ignorance ($\{d_h, \neg d_h\}$).

The construction of a constituent BOE, defined $m_{i,j,h}(\cdot)$ (i^{th} object, j^{th} characteristic, h^{th} outcome), discerning between $\{d_h\}$ and $\{\neg d_h\}$, is described Fig. 1.

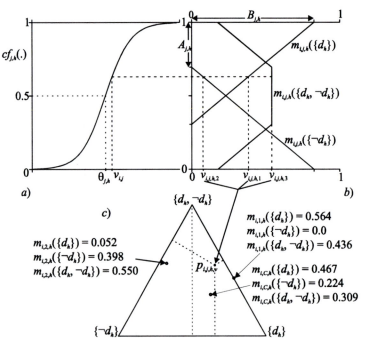

Fig. 1. Stages within the NCaRBS technique

In Fig. 1, stage a) shows the transformation of a characteristic value $v_{i,j}$ into a confidence value $cf_{j,h}(v_{i,j})$, using $cf_{j,h}(v_{i,j}) = 1/(1 + \exp(-k_{j,h}(v_{i,j} - \theta_{j,h}))$, with control parameters $k_{j,h}$ and $\theta_{j,h}$. Stage b) transforms a $cf_{j,h}(v_{i,j})$ into a constituent BOE $m_{i,j,h}(\cdot)$, made up of the three mass values (see [10]);

$$m_{i,j,h}(\{d_h\}) = \max\left(0, \frac{B_{j,h}}{1-A_{j,h}}cf_{j,h}(v_{i,j}) - \frac{A_{j,h}B_{j,h}}{1-A_{j,h}}\right),$$

$$m_{i,j,h}(\{\neg d_h\}) = \max\left(0, \frac{-B_{j,h}}{1-A_{j,h}}cf_{j,h}(v_{i,j}) + B_{j,h}\right),$$

and $m_{i,j,h}(\{d_h, \neg d_h\}) = 1 - m_{i,j,h}(\{d_h\}) - m_{i,j,h}(\{\neg d_h\})$,

where $A_{j,h}$ and $B_{j,h}$ are two further control parameters. Stage c) shows a BOE $m_{i,j,h}(\cdot)$; $m_{i,j,h}(\{d_h\}) = v_{i,j,h,1}$, $m_{i,j,h}(\{\neg d_h\}) = v_{i,j,h,2}$ and $m_{i,j,h}(\{d_h, \neg d_h\}) = v_{i,j,h,3}$, can be represented as a simplex coordinate $(p_{i,j,h,v})$ in a simplex plot (equilateral triangle).

Dempster's rule of combination is used to combine these BOEs. To illustrate, the combination of two constituent BOEs, $m_{i,j_1,h}(\cdot)$ and $m_{i,j_2,h}(\cdot)$, for the same object (o_i) and single outcome (d_h), defined $(m_{i,j_1,h} \oplus m_{i,j_2,h})(\cdot)$, results in a combined BOE with mass values (and focal elements) given by:

$$(m_{i,j_1,h} \oplus m_{i,j_2,h})(\{d_h\}) = \frac{\begin{array}{c}m_{i,j_1,h}(\{d_h\})m_{i,j_2,h}(\{d_h\}) + m_{i,j_2,h}(\{d_h\})m_{i,j_1,h}(\{d_h, \neg d_h\}) \\ + m_{i,j_1,h}(\{d_h\})m_{i,j_2,h}(\{d_h, \neg d_h\})\end{array}}{1 - (m_{i,j_1,h}(\{\neg d_h\})m_{i,j_2,h}(\{d_h\}) + m_{i,j_1,h}(\{d_h\})m_{i,j_2,h}(\{\neg d_h\}))}$$

$$(m_{i,j_1,h} \oplus m_{i,j_2,h})(\{\neg d_h\}) = \frac{\begin{array}{c}m_{i,j_1,h}(\{\neg d_h\})m_{i,j_2,h}(\{\neg d_h\}) \\ + m_{i,j_2,h}(\{d_h, \neg d_h\})m_{i,j_1,h}(\{\neg d_h\}) \\ + m_{i,j_2,h}(\{\neg d_h\})m_{i,j_1,h}(\{d_h, \neg d_h\})\end{array}}{1 - (m_{i,j_1,h}(\{\neg d_h\})m_{i,j_2,h}(\{d_h\}) + m_{i,j_1,h}(\{d_h\})m_{i,j_2,h}(\{\neg d_h\}))}$$

$$(m_{i,j_1,h} \oplus m_{i,j_2,h})(\{d_h, \neg d_h\}) = 1 - (m_{i,j_1,h} \oplus m_{i,j_2,h})(\{d_h\}) - (m_{i,j_1,h} \oplus m_{i,j_2,h})(\{\neg d_h\}).$$

This combination process is graphically demonstrated for two example BOEs, $m_{i,1,h}(\cdot)$ and $m_{i,2,h}(\cdot)$, see Fig. 1c.

The combination process can be performed iteratively to combine the characteristic based evidence, constituent BOEs $m_{i,j,h}(\cdot)$ $j = 1, .., n_C$, for an object o_i to a single outcome d_h, producing a *outcome* BOE, defined $m_{i,-,h}(\cdot)$ (other ways of combining the evidence can be considered). The respective outcome BOEs can also be combined to bring together the evidence contained in them, the result termed an *object* BOE, for object o_i it is defined $m_{i,-,-}(\cdot)$ (reduced to $m_i(\cdot)$), contains the evidence on the associations of the object to the n_D decision outcomes.

The object BOEs are made up of mass values associated with focal elements, which are the power set of $\{d_1, d_2, ..\}$ (minus the empty set). To enable the assignment of values to individual outcomes, the pignistic probability function

$$BetP_i(d_h) = \sum_{\substack{s_j \subseteq \{d_1, d_2 ...\} \\ s_j \cap \{d_h\} \neq \varnothing}} m_i(s_j)/|s_j|$$ for object o_i, it represents the level of pignistic

probability associated with the outcome d_h from the object BOE $m_i(\cdot)$. The series of pignistic probability values $BetP_i(d_h)$ $h = 1, .., n_D$ (see [6]), dictates the association of the object o_i to each of the outcomes d_h $h = 1, .., n_D$.

The effectiveness of the NCaRBS technique, is governed by the values assigned to the incumbent control parameters $k_{j,h}$, $\theta_{j,h}$, $A_{j,h}$ and $B_{j,h}$, $j = 1, .., n_C$ and $h = 1, .., n_D$.

This necessary configuration is considered as a constrained optimization problem, solved here using trigonometric differential evolution (TDE) [7]. The configured NCaRBS system can be measured by a defined objective function (OB^{NCaRBS}), the OB^{NCaRBS} defined is given as:

$$OB^{NCaRBS} = \frac{1}{3n_O} \sum_{i=1}^{n_O} \sqrt{\sum_{h=1}^{n_D} \left(BetP_i(d_h) - v_{d_h,i} \right)^2} \, ,$$

in the limit, $0 \leq OB^{NCaRBS} \leq 1$ (see [3, 4]).

3   Social Capital

The social capital analysis considered here utilises data from a comparative large-N survey of senior public sector executives conducted in ten European countries (Austria, Estonia, France, Germany, Hungary, Italy, Netherlands, Norway, Spain, United Kingdom) in 2012. The survey was sent to over 21,000 executives via post and email. There were 4,814 valid answers, with a response rate of 22.6%. Missing values are present for a range of questions that some respondents chose not to answer.

Table 1. Organizational social capital dimensions (and items)

People in my organization....	
Structural (S_socap)	Engage in open and honest communication with one another
	Share and accept constructive criticisms
	Willingly share information with one another
Relational (R_socap)	Have confidence in one another
	Have a good team spirit
	Are trustworthy
Cognitive (C_socap)	Share the same ambitions and vision for the organization
	Enthusiastically pursue collective goals and mission
	View themselves as partners in charting the organization's direction

Within the survey (see Table 1 and in text), the *structural* dimension of social capital (S_socap) was gauged by asking informants to score on seven-point scales, ranging from 1 (strongly disagree) to 7 (strongly agree), three questions about the exchange of information between organization members. Three further questions dealing with the strength of working relationships were used to assess *relational* social capital (R_socap). The *cognitive* dimension (C_socap) was then evaluated by posing three questions about the extent to which values and objectives are shared by all staff within the organization.

Alternative combinations, or blends, of the different dimensions of social capital may be the product of key internal organizational characteristics, such as organization size, decentralization of decisions and staffing cutbacks. The *size* of the organizations for which executives worked is measured using a survey question asking respondents to indicate the approximate overall number of employees within the organization in which they worked. Executives were also asked about the presence of 'decentralization of financial decisions' and 'decentralization of staffing decisions' within their organizations on a 7-point scale, and an index of *decentralization* was then constructed from the responses. *Staffing cutbacks* is measured using a question asking respondents to indicate from 1 (not at all) to 7 (to a great extent) to what extent their organization had applied staff layoffs in response to the fiscal crisis.

As mentioned earlier, the original data set is incomplete, see Table 2, which shows the number of cases which have a certain number of missing characteristic values for the analysis that is undertaken.

Table 2. Levels of incompleteness across considered 4,814 cases

Number Missing	0	1	2	3
Number Cases	3144	1017	112	541

From Table 2, 4,273 respondents have at least 1 value present amongst the characteristics, then using case deletion to deal with the missing values (for example), would mean that only 3,144 respondents would be considered in the analysis of organizational social capital. By contrast, NCaRBS is able to analyse fully the incomplete dataset, thereby permitting the inclusion of over 1,000 further cases in the modelling process.

Prior to undertaking comparative analysis of the incomplete and managed datsets, the separate S_socap, R_socap and C_socap values are transformed into a hybrid vector, which accounts for the distribution of the three values (to reduce the effects of social desirability bias for relational social capital for instance), see Table 3 (following the approach in [4]).

Table 3. Example of social capital blend vector construction

Details	S_socap	R_socap	C_socap
Mean	4.855	5.013	4.532
Standard deviation	1.209	1.20	1.302
Original Capital values (o_{16})	5.667	5.333	5.000
Transformed Capital values (o_{16})	0.354	0.319	0.327

In Table 3 the mean and standard deviation values associated with the three social capital dimensions are presented, showing the general differences in their scores. An example transformation case is shown, for o_{16}, where consideration of the R_socap and C_socap value demonstrates the mitigation of social desirability bias. As the individual social capital blend vectors are made up of three values, which add up to one, they can be represented as points in a simplex plot, see Fig. 2.

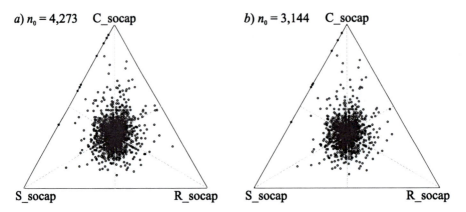

Fig. 2. Social capital blend vectors of cases (a – incomplete, b – managed)

Fig. 2 shows the social capital blend vectors in their simplex coordinate format, for the incomplete (a - n_O = 4,273) and managed (b - n_O = 3,144) data sets. There is slight variation in the simplex coordinate positions shown across the two different sets of hybrid social capital values (coming from the different numbers of cases considered in each version of the data set).

4   NCaRBS Analyses of Social Capital Data Set

This section presents the comparative NCaRBS analyses of the original incomplete social capital data set and an alternative version that is managed through case deletion. To analyse the incomplete data set there has to be a process to model a missing characteristic value, say $v_{i,j}$. Within NCaRBS, and CaRBS in general, from [2], the associated constituent BOE describing a missing value is defined as:

$$m_{i,j,h}(\{d_h\}) = 0, \ m_{i,j,h}(\{\neg d_h\}) = 0 \text{ and } m_{i,j,h}(\{d_h, \neg d_h\}) = 1.$$

This constituent BOE is fixed, and does not change depending on the control parameters found when configuring NCARBS (see for example Fig 1).

The results from the two NCaRBS analyses are restricted here to the level of model fit (based on respective OB^{NCaRBS} values) and contributions of organizational characteristics to the objects' social capital blend vectors. Each model was run 10 times, with best fit for the incomplete data being OB^{NCaRBS} = 0.070779 and for the managed data set OB^{NCaRBS} = 0.070336, indicating that the model fit for the incomplete data set exhibits the slightly worse predictive fit. To understand the variation in fit values, we should consider the actual numbers of available organizational characteristics to configure on. For the incomplete and managed data sets there are 11,578 and 9,432 characteristic values respectively to model social capital. Hence with 81.465% of the data to work with, it is not entirely surprising that the OB^{NCaRBS} value is lower for the managed data set.

The results in terms of characteristics' contributions are explored here through their graphical representation; see Fig. 3 and Fig. 4.

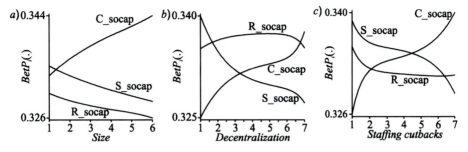

Fig. 3. Characteristic contribution based on incomplete data set

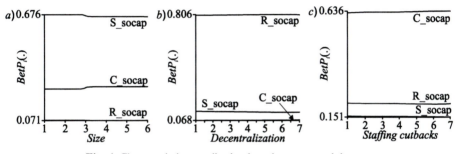

Fig. 4. Characteristic contribution based on managed data set

It can be clearly seen that alternative forms of information are gained from the NCaRBS analysis of the incomplete data (Fig. 3) and the managed data (Fig. 4). Generally, NCaRBS is able to fully demonstrate the nonlinearity in the associations between objects (respondents) and outcomes (social capital blend). Concentrating on the results from Fig. 3 (incomplete data set), Fig. 3a indicates that as organization size increases structural and relational capital decline, but cognitive social capital becomes stronger. Fig. 3b illustrates that as decentralization increases structural social capital declines, but relational and (especially) cognitive social capital grow. Finally, Fig. 3c highlights that staff cutbacks are associated with declining intra-organizational communication and interpersonal trust, but higher levels of shared mission.

5   Validation Analysis of NCaRBS results (Using Re-sampling)

The results presented in section 4 are from a one-off analysis using all the available data (3,144 cases for incomplete data set and 4,273 for managed data set). To add further confidence in the validity of the results from this analysis, a re-sampling procedure is undertaken and the models recalculated (see for example [12]). Due to page limitation this validation exercise is undertaken on the incomplete data set only.

The re-sampling undertaken here was based on performing multiple runs of the NCaRBS technique using identified in-samples and out-of-samples of cases. Here, 10 runs were performed, in each run 90% of cases (3,846) were used as the in-sample on which the NCaRBS was run to configure a model, and 10% of cases (427) were used an out-of-sample.

For each pair of in-sample and out-of-sample sets of data, levels of fit can be found based on the objective function (OB^{NCaRBS}), see Fig. 5.

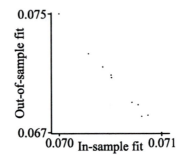

Fig. 5. Scatter-plot of in-sample and out-of-sample fit values (based on incomplete data set)

In Fig. 5, the two axes depict the OB^{NCaRBS} fit value for in-sample (horizontal) and out-of-sample (vertical). Clearly, there is a relatively consistent inverse relationship between the pairs of fit values, namely as the level of in-sample fit increases so the level of out-of-sample fit decreases. Beyond this relationship, whether there is significant difference between the in-sample and out-of-sample fit values are considered using a paired-sample t-test. From the test there was not a significant difference between the fit values for in-sample (M = 0.0708, SD = 0.000270) and out-of-sample (M = 0.0705, SD = 0.00236) sets of data; t(9) = 0.372, p = 0.718. Briefly, for the managed data set, similar analysis also suggested not a significant different between the fit values for in-sample (M = 0.0703, SD = 0.000270) and out-of-sample (M = 0.0711, SD = 0.000270) sets of data; t(9) = −0.682, p = 0.512. The results suggest the configured NCaRBS models in each of the 10 runs fit the out-of-sample cases.

The contribution of the individual variables to the social capital blends following the re-sampling procedure can be illustrated graphically as for the one-off analysis using all of the data (see Fig. 6).

In Fig. 6, the ten contribution lines associated with each separate social capital dimension derived from the re-sampling runs are plotted together to illustrate the general trends found through the re-sampling process. Comparison of these graphs with those for the one-off analysis presented in Fig. 3, reveals very similar patterns in the relationship between the structural characteristics and each dimension of social capital.

For example, comparing Fig. 3a with Fig. 6a, 6b and 6c, as organization size increases, structural and relational capital decline, but cognitive social capital becomes stronger; as decentralization increases, structural social capital declines, but relational and (especially) cognitive social capital grow; staff cutbacks are associated with declining intra-organizational communication and interpersonal trust, but higher levels of shared mission.

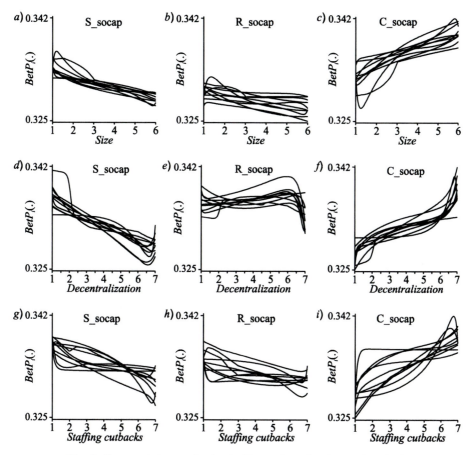

Fig. 6. Characteristic contribution in 10 runs (based on incomplete data)

6   Conclusions

The NCaRBS technique, along with all the family of CaRBS based techniques, offer an almost unique opportunity to analyze incomplete data without the need to manipulate or exclude cases with missing values. The results for the evidence-based modelling of organizational social capital blends presented here dramatically illustrate the impact of this facility for incorporating incompleteness. Nevertheless, the full potential of the technique has yet to be explored. Further research could investigate the sensitivity of the technique to alternative ways of capturing the impact of ignorance in the data. In particular, it would be interesting to evaluate the effect of weighting the impact of cases in the objective functions depending on how incomplete the information associated with them is.

For now though, this paper concludes by observing that NCaRBS offers organizational analysts and scientists in other fields a powerful means for incorporating data with missing values in their research. In this respect, we concur with others who call for more and better work developing and demonstrating novel applications of Dempster-Shafer theory of evidence based analysis techniques.

References

1. Beynon, M.J.: A novel technique of object ranking and classification under ignorance: An application to the corporate failure risk problem. European Journal of Operational Research 167, 493–517 (2005a)
2. Beynon, M.J.: Optimizing object classification under ambiguity/ignorance: Application to the credit rating problem. International Journal of Intelligent Systems in Accounting, Finance and Management 13, 113–130 (2005b)
3. Beynon, M.J., Andrews, R.A., Boyne, G.: Evidence-based Modelling of Strategic Fit: An Introduction to RCaRBS. European Journal of Operational Research 207(2), 886–896 (2010)
4. Beynon, M.J., Andrews, R.A., Boyne, G.: Evidence-based Modelling of Hybrid organizational strategies. Computational and Mathematical Organization Theory Journal (2014), doi:10.1007/s1058801491745
5. Dempster, A.P.: Upper and lower probabilities induced by a multiple valued mapping. Ann. Math. Statistics 38, 325–339 (1967)
6. Denœux, T., Zouhal, L.M.: Handling possibilistic labels in pattern classification using evidential reasoning. Fuzzy Sets and Systems 122, 409–424 (2001)
7. Fan, H.-Y., Lampinen, J.: A trigonometric mutation operation to differential evolution. Journal of Global Optimization 27, 105–129 (2003)
8. Kogut, B., Zander, U.: What do firms do? Coordination, identity and learning. Organization Science 7, 502–518 (1996)
9. Nahapiet, J., Ghoshal, S.: Social capital, intellectual capital and the organizational advantage. Academy of Management Review 23, 242–266 (1998)
10. Safranek, R.J., Gottschlich, S., Kak, A.C.: Evidence accumulation using binary frames of discernment for verification vision. IEEE Transactions on Robotics and Automation 6, 405–417 (1990)
11. Shafer, G.A.: Mathematical theory of evidence. Princeton University Press, Princeton (1976)
12. Twomey, J.M., Smith, A.E.: Bias and Variance of Validation Methods for Function Approximation Neural Networks Under Conditions of Sparse Data. IEEE Transaction on Systems, Man and Cybernetics – Part C: Applications and Reviews 28(3), 417–430 (1998)

Outliers in Evidential C-Means:
An Empirical Exploration Using Survey Data on Organizational Social Capital

Malcolm J. Beynon and Rhys Andrews

Cardiff Business School, Cardiff University,
Colum Drive, Cardiff, CF10 3EU, Wales, UK
{BeynonMJ,AndrewsR4}@cardiff.ac.uk

Abstract. Evidential C-Means (ECM) is a technique for cluster analysis, which has a methodology based on the Dempster-Shafer theory of evidence (DST). To date this technique has been theoretically discussed but has had limited application. Based on DST, ECM facilitates the association of objects to sets of clusters, rather than simply a single cluster. One feature of ECM is the facility for classifying cases to no cluster, the level of which is effected by the parameters in ECM (in particular δ, which controls for the datapoints considered outliers). In this study, the substantive effects of varying δ are explored by investigating the relationship between organziational social capital and employee engagement. Drawing on a large-N survey of senior public sector executives, the clustering of different dimensions of organizational social capital is undertaken, and the relationship between those clusters and employee engagement analysed at varying levels of δ. The implications of the findings are discussed.

Keywords: Clustering, Dempster-Shafer theory, Evidential C-Means, Engagement, Evidential C-Means, Social Capital

1 Introduction

The Evidential C-Means (ECM) clustering technique [11], is based on the Dempster-Shafer theory of evidence (DST - [5, 14]), and is a development on the well-known crisp k-means and fuzzy c-means non-hierarchical clustering techniques ([4, 10]). Its development, in particular, is to enable consideration of levels of association of objects not only to single clusters but to sets of clusters and even no clusters (potential outliers).

In this paper, the substantive effects of varying the parameter determining the inclusion of outliers in ECM (δ - see later) is illustrated by investigating the relationship between three different dimensions of organizational social capital and the work engagement of senior managers.

The management of outliers is a key concern within applied research ([6, 8]). A pertinent consideration (statement) in regard to outliers, within the context of clustering, as in this study, was given in [3], noting that outliers may be considered as noise points lying outside a set of defined clusters or alternatively outliers may be defined

F. Cuzzolin (Ed.): BELIEF 2014, LNAI 8764, pp. 247–255, 2014.
© Springer International Publishing Switzerland 2014

as the points that lie outside of the set of clusters but are also separated from the noise. In [6], in their introduction to a cluster approach to outlier detection, they do point out that not only a single point but also a small cluster can probably be an outlier. This study contributes to debates around the inclusion or exclusion of outliers in cluster analysis by examining how this issue plays out when using ECM.

First, senior public sector executives' perceptions of the degree to which structural, relational and cognitive social capital are present within the organizations in which they work are clustered at different levels of δ. Next, the validation of the different clusters that are derived is established by comparing levels of employee engagement for different social capital clusters. Finally, whether different results are observed when δ, takes a low or high value is evaluated, before conclusions are drawn on the basis of the findings.

2   Evidential C-Means

ECM ([11]) is based on a finite set of c elements $\Theta = \{C_1, C_2, ..., C_c\}$, called a frame of discernment (here c clusters). Based on the notion of partial knowledge, a *basic belief assignment* (bba), defined as a function m from 2^Θ (subset of Θ) to [0, 1], has

$$\sum_{A_j \subseteq \Theta} m(A_j) = 1.$$ A subset A_j of the frame of discernment Θ ($A_j \subseteq \Theta$), for which $m(A_j)$

is non-zero, is called a focal set and represents the exact belief in the proposition depicted by A_j (allocated to A_j from the given evidence).

In ECM, for each object x_i and the bbas $m_{ij} = m_i(A_j)$ ($A_j \neq \varnothing$, $A_j \subseteq \Theta$), the m_{ij} is low (resp. high) when the distance d_{ij} between x_i and the focal set A_j is high (resp. low). ECM assumes that each cluster C_k is represented by a center $c_k \in \Re^p$ (p dimensions of object x_i). For each subset A_j of Θ (set of clusters) the barycenter $\overline{c}_j$ of the center

associated to the clusters composing A_j is given by $\overline{c}_j = \dfrac{1}{|A_j|}\sum_{k=1}^{c} s_{kj}c_k$, where $|A_j|$

denotes the cardinal of A_j and $s_{kj} = \begin{cases} 1 & \text{if } C_k \in A_j, \\ 0 & \text{else,} \end{cases}$. The distance d_{ij} is then defined

by $d_{ij}^2 \triangleq \left\| x_i - \overline{c}_j \right\|^2$. Considering the credal partition $M = (m_1, ..., m_n) \in \Re^{n \times 2^c}$ and the matrix C of size $(c \times p)$ of cluster centers, which minimize the following objective function:

$$J_{ECM}(M,C) \triangleq \sum_{i=1}^{n} \sum_{\{j|A_j \neq \varnothing, A_j \subseteq \Theta\}} |A_j|^\alpha m_{ij}^\beta d_{ij}^2 + \sum_{i=1}^{n} \delta^2 m_{i\varnothing}^\beta,$$

subject to $\sum_{\{j|A_j \neq \varnothing, A_j \subseteq \Theta\}} m_{ij} + m_{i\varnothing} = 1 \ \forall i = 1,...,n$, where $m_{i\varnothing}$ denotes $m_i(\varnothing)$ the belief in

membership to no clusters. Within the $J_{ECM}(M, C)$ expression, the impacts of the three parameters α, β and δ can be interpreted as follows (see [11]): α - controls the level of penalization of cluster subsets (A_j) with high cardinality (here $\alpha = 2$),

β (> 1) - controls the fuzziness of the partition across focal elements (here $\beta = 2$) and δ - controls the amount of data considered as outliers (choice of δ described later). For an object x_i, its credal partition m_i is made up of the levels of exact belief (bba) allocated to each subset of the considered c clusters ($A_j \subseteq \Theta$ has bba $m_i(A_j)$), including no clusters (the empty set $\varnothing$ with bba $m_i(\varnothing)$).

A number of concomitant functions exist within Dempster-Shafer theory that enable variations in the final cluster membership results to be created for objects when using ECM, subject to a credal partition having been constructed. Without loss of generality (for a focal set A_j and an object x_i), we consider the Belief function,

$$\text{Bel}(\{A_j\}) = \sum_{A_h \subseteq A_j \,(A_h \subseteq \Theta)} m_i(\{A_h\}) \quad \text{for } A_j \subseteq \Theta,$$ representing the confidence in an object's

membership to the focal set cluster A_j (subset of clusters).

This, and other functions, can be used to identify the majority association of objects to a single cluster or to possible subsets of clusters. In this study, a level of sensitivity analysis is undertaken, by considering different values of the δ parameter, when constructing the credal partition (previously also considered in [1]). In doing so, the substantive effects of varying the δ parameter are explored by investigating the relationship between organizational social capital and employee engagement.

3   The Survey Data

The exploration of dealing with outliers in ECM presented here utilises data from a comparative large-N survey of senior public sector executives conducted in ten European countries (Austria, Estonia, France, Germany, Hungary, Italy, Netherlands, Norway, Spain, United Kingdom) in 2012. The survey was sent to over 21,000 executives via post and email. There were 4,814 valid answers, with a response rate of 22.6%, this was reduced to 3,177 cases which had the complete data for the needs of the intended analysis.

Respondents answered nine questions relating to three dimensions of social capital within the civil service organizations in which they work, namely i) *Structural* (S_socap) - exchange of information between organization members, ii) *Relational* (R_socap) - strength of working relationships and iii) *Cognitive* (C_socap) – the extent to which values and objectives are shared by all staff within the organization [12]. The respondents were also asked three questions relating to their engagement with their work (*Engagement*).

Before carrying out the ECM of the different dimensions of social capital, three separate values for each dimension are constructed and then transformed into a social capital vector (see details in [2]), which takes account of the levels of each of the three values, see Table 1. That is, the derivation of the social capital vector includes the aim to remove the potential for social desirability bias to influence relative levels of each dimension. Moreover, the vector is relative to the individual case, after removal of general external influences (social bias).

Table 1. Example construction of social capital vector

Details	S_socap	R_socap	C_socap
Mean	4.855	5.013	4.532
Standard deviation	1.209	1.200	1.302
Original Capital values (o_{16})	5.667	5.333	5.000
Transformed Capital values (o_{16})	0.354	0.319	0.327

In Table 1, the mean and standard deviation values associated with the three social capital variables are presented, showing the differences in their scores. An example transformation case is also shown, for o_{16}, where consideration of the R_socap and C_socap value demonstrates the mitigation of social bias.

As the social capital vectors are made up of three values which add up to one, they can each be represented as a point in a simplex plot, which graphically depicts the ratios of the three values as positions in an equilateral triangle - see Fig. 1.

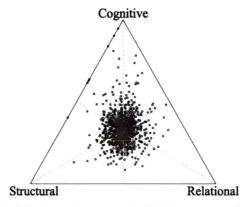

Fig. 1. Social capital vectors for 3,144 senior executives

Each point in the simplex plot describes a respondent's perception of the different dimensions of social capital within the organization in which they work. The nearer a point is to one of the three vertices, the more a respondent associates their organization with that dimension of social capital. A point at the centre of the simplex plot would show a consistent level of association to the three dimensions of social capital (whatever that level is).

4   The ECM Cluster Analysis

This section presents a cluster analysis of the social capital data depicted in Fig. 1. The number of clusters to be derived is a key consideration when carrying out cluster analysis [9]. Here, two, three, four and five cluster solutions were examined (over only one δ parameter value), with the three cluster based solution offering the clearest conceptual connection with the analytical requirements of the study (a non-statistical approach advocated by Ketchen and Shook [9]).

Using ECM requires the assignment of values to control parameters (see section 2). Here, α (the level of penalization of cluster subsets) and β (the fuzziness of the partition across focal elements) are assigned default values given in [11], namely $\alpha = 2$ and $\beta = 2$.   For the control parameter δ (the amount of datapoints considered as outliers), a number of different values are evaluated.   With respect to the three cluster solution, the impact of the value of δ over a continuous sub-domain can be seen in Fig. 2.

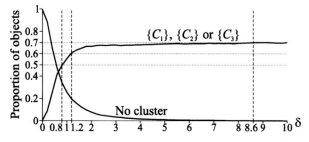

Fig. 2. Levels of association to singleton clusters and no cluster (δ changes)

The impact of changes in the value of δ is here interpreted in two ways: *i*) the percentage of the data associated with no cluster (potential outliers); and *ii*) the percentage of the data associated with a single cluster (here $\{C_1\}$, $\{C_2\}$ and $\{C_3\}$), in terms of their exact belief (see section 2 and [11]).

In Fig. 2, holding α and β constant, as δ goes from 1 to 10, there is a decrease in the proportion of objects associated with no cluster (from 1 down to 0), and an increase in the association of the objects with singleton clusters (from 0 up to near 0.7 proportion of objects).   This latter impact ($0.7 < 1$) is a by-product of trying to move objects from association with no cluster (outlier) to association with a subset of clusters of some sort (note it reaches a limit of just above 0.7, suggesting that about 0.3 of objects for the high values of δ are associated with sets of two or three clusters – also acknowledging the role of the α and β parameters here).

Based on the results in Fig. 2, ECM was undertaken with three separate δ values, namely $\delta = 0.8$, 1.2 and 8.6, which are associated with previously identified proportion values near 0.5, 0.6 and 0.7 of objects associated with single clusters (not without loss of generality to other rubrics for choosing specific δ values), see Fig. 3.   The resultant series of $Bel(\{A_j\})$ values are used to identify the focal elements (from power set of $\{C_1, C_2, C_3\}$), that represents a majority association (see [1]).

Fig. 3 provides an overview of the constituent cluster means (the means of the three social capital vector values for the single clusters $\{C_1\}$, $\{C_2\}$ and $\{C_3\}$) under each cluster solution (using *a*) $\delta = 0.8$, *b*) 1.2 and *c*) 8.6).   Comparison of these constituent means permits the identification of patterns in the combination of the different dimensions of social capital.   In Fig. 3, the constituent cluster means are the points joined by the lines labelled '1', '2' and '3' (for clusters $\{C_1\}$, $\{C_2\}$ and $\{C_3\}$, respectively).

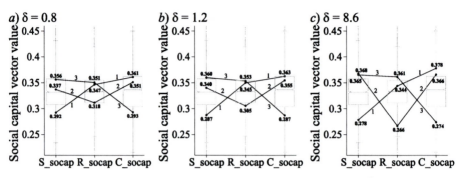

Fig. 3. Constituent cluster means for clusters $\{C_1\}$, $\{C_2\}$ and $\{C_3\}$ (δ changes)

To establish whether the $\{C_1\}$, $\{C_2\}$ and $\{C_3\}$ constituent cluster means shown in Fig. 3 represent distinctive combinations of social capital values, it is necessary to establish whether the clusters are genuinely different from one another. Accordingly, Table 2 reports ANOVA and post-hoc results showing the statistical differences between the $\{C_1\}$, $\{C_2\}$ and $\{C_3\}$ clusters for the three different values of δ (see [9]).

Table 2. Differences between social capital dimensions across clusters

ECM	Statistic		S_socap	R_socap	C_socap
$\delta = 0.8$	ANOVA		64.15 (0.00)	42.16 (0.00)	57.75 (0.00)
$C_1 - 418$	Post-hoc Bonferroni	C_1 and C_2	**.0031 (0.00)**	**.0030 (0.00)**	.0038 (0.33)
$C_2 - 610$		C_1 and C_3	**.0032 (0.00)**	.0031 (1.00)	**.0040 (0.00)**
$C_3 - 527$		C_2 and C_3	**.0029 (0.00)**	**.0028 (0.00)**	**.0036 (0.00)**
$\delta = 1.2$	ANOVA		113.4 (0.00)	83.6 (0.00)	101.8 (0.00)
$C_1 - 530$	Post-hoc Bonferroni	C_1 and C_2	**.0027 (0.00)**	**.0026 (0.00)**	.0033 (0.46)
$C_2 - 727$		C_1 and C_3	**.0027 (0.00)**	.0027 (1.00)	**.0034 (0.00)**
$C_3 - 650$		C_2 and C_3	**.0025 (0.00)**	**.0024 (0.00)**	**.0031 (0.00)**
$\delta = 8.6$	ANOVA		493.7 (0.00)	487.8 (0.00)	638.2 (0.00)
$C_1 - 845$	Post-hoc Bonferroni	C_1 and C_2	**.0020 (0.00)**	**.0020 (0.00)**	**.0023 (0.00)**
$C_2 - 502$		C_1 and C_3	**.0018 (0.00)**	**.0017 (0.00)**	**.0020 (0.00)**
$C_3 - 859$		C_2 and C_3	.0020 (1.00)	**.0019 (0.00)**	**.0023 (0.00)**

In Bold $p \le 0.05$ (two-tailed tests)

Table 2 shows that there are large number of statistically significant differences between the singleton clusters, indicating that the ECM has identified distinctive combinations of the different dimensions of organizational social capital. Returning to Fig 3a), and taking into account the results in Table 2, for $\delta = 0.8$, the three clusters are defined by their cluster means, namely; $\{C_1\}$ is described by low S_socap, high R_socap and high C_socap, $\{C_2\}$ described by medium S_socap, low R_socap and medium C_socap, and $\{C_3\}$ described by high S_socap, high R_socap and low C_socap. In Fig 3b) and Fig 3c) slight variations are shown, most noticeably in the position of S_socap (for $\{C_2\}$) and R_socap (for $\{C_1\}$) in Fig 3c).

Due to the transformation-based construction of the social capital vector (see Fig 1), attention has to be given to values of these constituent means below or above the average values of 0.333, indicating the below or above average association of that cluster of respondents on that dimension of social capital.

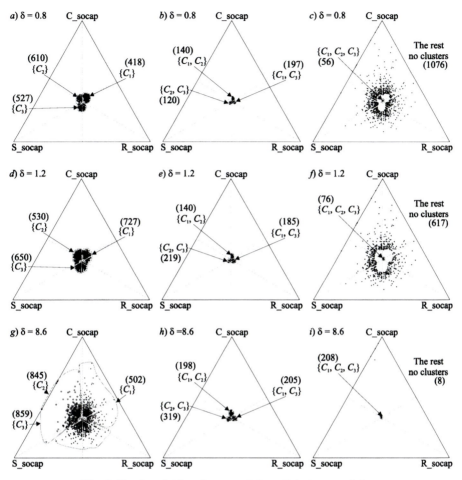

Fig. 4. Simplex plot based representation of cluster associations

The inclusion of more datapoints within the ECM by increasing the value of δ does not seem to have dramatically altered the differences between the social capital values for the different clusters, though as one might expect there are more statistical significant differences between the clusters when more datapoints are included in the cluster solution. The impact of this clustering process can be further illustrated by visualising the positions of the objects associated with each of the singleton clusters and their potential subsets, namely, $\{C_1\}$, $\{C_2\}$, $\{C_3\}$, $\{C_1, C_2\}$, $\{C_1, C_3\}$, $\{C_2, C_3\}$, $\{C_1, C_2, C_3\}$, $\{\}$, see Fig 4.

In Fig 4, over the three different values δ considered, there are variations in the objects associated with each of the subsets of clusters. The results for associations with $\{C_1\}$, $\{C_2\}$ and $\{C_3\}$, are shown in a), d) and g). Critically, as the value of δ increases so the notion of an outlier becomes more and more parsimonious, until in Fig 4i), once the singleton clusters and cluster sub-sets are all plotted, there are only eight datapoints associated with no cluster at all (overlapping points in simplex plot).

To validate the three cluster solution and to explore the substantive effects of changes in the value of δ further, the values of an external variable are compared across each cluster [11], namely employee engagement, which research has shown is associated with high levels of social capital [13], see Table 3.

Table 3. Social capital clusters and employee engagement

ECM	Statistic		Engagement	
$\delta = 0.8$	Order (Means)		C_3 (5.30) $< C_2$ (5.54) $< C_1$ (5.56)	
	ANOVA		F. 31.752 (Sig. 0.00)	
	Post-hoc Bonferroni	C_1 and C_2	Mn. Diff. 0.075 (Sig. 1.000)	
		C_1 and C_3	**Mn. Diff. 0.078 (Sig. 0.027)**	
		C_2 and C_3	**Mn. Diff. 0.071 (Sig. 0.023)**	
$\delta = 1.2$	Order (Means)		C_3 (5.21) $< C_2$ (5.47) $< C_1$ (5.48)	
	ANOVA		F. 35.646 (Sig. 0.000)	
	Post-hoc Bonferroni	C_1 and C_2	Mn. Diff. 0.068 (Sig. 1.000)	
		C_1 and C_3	**Mn. Diff. 0.069 (Sig. 0.006)**	
		C_2 and C_3	**Mn. Diff. 0.064 (Sig. 0.002)**	
$\delta = 8.6$	Order (Means)		C_2 (5.05) $< C_3$ (5.14) $< C_1$ (5.29)	
	ANOVA		F. 19.625 (Sig. 0.000)	
	Post-hoc Bonferroni	C_1 and C_2	**Mn. Diff. 0.068 (Sig. 0.015)**	
		C_1 and C_3	Mn. Diff. 0.058 (Sig. 0.250)	
		C_2 and C_3	Mn. Diff. 0.068 (Sig. 1.000)	

[F.- F statistic, Sig.- Significance, Mn Diff.- Mean Difference]. **In Bold** $p \leq 0.05$ (two-tailed tests)

The results shown in Table 3 highlight that when $\delta = 0.8$ and $\delta = 1.2$, there is a consistent pattern of no statistically significant differences between the engagement values associated with clusters C_1 and C_2 against those of C_3. However, when $\delta = 8.6$ the pattern of statistically significant results completely reverses, with differences observed only between C_1 and C_2 and none between C_3 and the other clusters.

These findings then underline that the criteria for the inclusion of outliers can have dramatic effects on the substantive interpretation of the findings of applied research studies. More importantly, within the context of ECM, they highlight the importance of the careful calibration of the parameters for cluster analysis, and the need to explain and justify the reasons behind the choice of the δ value that is adopted.

5   Conclusions

This paper has demonstrated that how outliers are dealt with when undertaking ECM cluster analysis can have important implications for the substantive interpretation of the findings from applied research studies. With ECM able to associate objects with single as well as groups of clusters, and also no clusters, these early results show how changes in one of the key parameters of ECM can lead to different findings, especially when clusters are used to explain other phenomena. Given the limited number of applications of ECM to date, the analysis presented here therefore provides researchers interested in using the technique with some initial pointers for ensuring that their work is robust and defensible.

Although this study has begun to investigate some of the key methodological considerations underpinning ECM, there are a number of other important areas for further exploration. At the technical and empirical levels, changes in the δ value clearly matter. As a result, it will be interesting to see in subsequent studies how changing the other two parameters in ECM (α and β) impacts on the interpretation of the findings. Given that *prima facie* changes in all three parameters seem likely to have the potential to generate highly divergent results, it will be crucial that researchers pay more attention to this issue in the future.

References

1. Beynon, M.J., McDermott, A., Heffernan, M.: Psychological Contract and Job Satisfaction: Clustering Analysis using Evidential C-Means and Comparison with other Techniques. Intelligent Systems in Accounting, Finance and Management 19(4), 247–273 (2013)
2. Beynon, M.J., Andrews, R.A., Boyne, G.: Evidence-based Modelling of Hybrid organizational strategies. Computational and Mathematical Organization Theory Journal (2014), doi:10.1007/s1058801491745
3. Aggarwal, C.C., Yu, P.S.: Outlier Detection for High Dimensional Data. In: Proceedings of the ACM SIGMOD Conference (2001)
4. Bezdek, J.C.: A convergence theorem for the fuzzy ISODATA clustering algorithms. IEEE Transactions on Pattern Analysis and Machine Intelligence 2, 1–8 (1980)
5. Dempster, A.P.: Upper and lower probabilities induced by a multiple valued mapping. Ann. Math. Statistics. 38, 325–339 (1967)
6. Duan, L., Xu, L., Liu, Y., Lee, J.: Cluster-based outlier detection. Annals of Operations Research 168(1), 151–168 (2009)
7. Hair, J.F., Anderson, R.E., Tatham, R.L., Black, W.C.: Multivariate Data Analysis with Readings. MacMillan, New York (1998)
8. Hodge, V.J., Austin, J.: A Survey of Outlier Detection Methodologies. Artificial Intelligence Review 22, 85–126 (2004)
9. Ketchen Jr., D.J., Shook, C.L.: The application of cluster analysis in strategic management research: an analysis and critique. Strategic Management Journal 17, 441–445 (1996)
10. MacQueen, J.B.: Some methods for classification and analysis of multivariate observations. In: Le Cam, L.M., Neyman, J. (eds.) Proceedings of the 5th Berkeley Symposium on Mathematical Statistics and Probability, vol. 1, pp. 281–297. University of California Press, Berkeley (1967)
11. Masson, M.-H., Denœux, T.: ECM: An evidential version of the fuzzy *c*-means algorithm. Pattern Recognition 41, 1384–1397 (2008)
12. Nahapiet, J., Ghoshal, S.: Social capital, intellectual capital and the organizational advantage. Academy of Management Review 23, 242–266 (1998)
13. Parzefall, M.-R., Kuppelweiser, V.G.: Understanding the antecedents, the outcomes and the mediating role of social capital. Human Relations 65, 447–472 (2012)
14. Shafer, G.A.: Mathematical theory of evidence. Princeton University Press, Princeton (1976)

Causal Compositional Models
in Valuation-Based Systems

Radim Jiroušek[1] and Prakash P. Shenoy[2]

[1] Faculty of Management, University of Economics, Jarošovská 1117/II,
377 01 Jindřichův Hradec, Czech Republic
`radim@utia.cas.cz`
[2] University of Kansas School of Business, 1300 Sunnyside Ave., Summerfield Hall,
Lawrence, KS 66045-7601, USA
`pshenoy@ku.edu`

Abstract. This paper shows that Pearl's causal networks can be described using compositional models in the valuation-based systems (VBS) framework. There are several advantages of using the VBS framework. First, VBS is a generalization of several uncertainty theories (e.g., probability theory, a version of possibility theory where combination is the product t-norm, Spohn's epistemic belief theory, and Dempster-Shafer belief function theory). This implies that causal compositional models, initially described in probability theory, are now described in all uncertainty calculi that fit in the VBS framework. Second, using the operators of VBS, we describe how causal inference can be made in causal compositional models in an elegant and unifying algebraic way. This includes the computation of conditioning, and the computation of the effect of interventions.

Keywords: Valuation-based system, causality, conditionals, intervention, compositional model.

1 Introduction

In many situations we are faced with the question of what will happen if we make some changes, such as if we intervene by an action that changes the status quo. In [5], Pearl shows that such questions can be answered using *causal probabilistic models* because of their ability *to represent and respond to external or spontaneous changes.* In [3], causal probabilistic models were described by causal compositional models in the probabilistic framework. In this paper we show that such causal compositional models can be described in the valuation-based systems (VBS) framework [7], so that they apply to all uncertainty calculi that fit in the VBS framework.

An outline of the paper is as follows. Section 2 reviews the VBS framework. Section 3 reviews the composition operator and its basic properties in the VBS framework. Section 4 describes causal compositional models in the VBS framework, and making inferences in such models. We distinguish between conditioning and the effect of interventions. We also describe a small illustrative example.

F. Cuzzolin (Ed.): BELIEF 2014, LNAI 8764, pp. 256–264, 2014.

2   Valuation-Based Systems

We use notation from [7] and [4] that have a detailed introduction to VBS and to compositional models in VBS. Φ denotes a set whose elements are called *variables* that are denoted by upper-case Roman alphabets (e.g., X, Y, and Z). Subsets of Φ are denoted by lower-case Roman alphabets (e.g., r, s, and t). Ψ denotes a set whose elements are called *valuations*. Elements of Ψ are denoted by lower-case Greek alphabets (e.g., ρ, σ, and τ). Each valuation is associated with a subset of variables, and represents some knowledge about the variables in the subset. Thus, we say that ρ is a valuation for r, where $r \subseteq \Phi$ is the subset associated with ρ.

It is useful to identify a subset of valuations $\Psi_n \subset \Psi$, whose elements are called *normal*. Normal valuations are those that are *coherent* in some sense. For example, in D-S belief function theory, normal valuations are basic probability assignment potentials whose values for non-empty subsets add to one.

We describe a specific VBS model by a pair (Φ_S, Ψ_S). This pair must be consistent in the sense that for each $X \in \Phi_S$ there exists a valuation $\rho \in \Psi_S$ for r such that $X \in r$, and that each valuation $\rho \in \Psi_S$ must be for variables $r \subseteq \Phi_S$. The VBS framework includes three operators — *combination*, *marginalization*, and *removal* — that are used to make inferences from the knowledge encoded in a VBS.

Combination. The combination operator $\oplus \colon \Psi \times \Psi \to \Psi_n$ represents aggregation of knowledge. It satisfies the following three axioms:

1. (*Domain*) If ρ is a valuation for r, and σ is a valuation for s, then $\rho \oplus \sigma$ is a normal valuation for $r \cup s$.
2. (*Commutativity*) $\rho \oplus \sigma = \sigma \oplus \rho$.
3. (*Associativity*) $\rho \oplus (\sigma \oplus \tau) = (\rho \oplus \sigma) \oplus \tau$.

Marginalization. The marginalization operator $-X \colon \Psi \to \Psi$ allows us to coarsen knowledge by marginalizing X out of the domain of a valuation. It satisfies the following four axioms:

1. (*Domain*) If ρ is a valuation for r, and $X \in r$, then ρ^{-X} is a valuation for $r \setminus \{X\}$.
2. (*Normal*) ρ^{-X} is normal if and only if ρ is normal.
3. (*Order does not matter*) If ρ is a valuation for r, $X \in r$, and $Y \in r$, then $(\rho^{-X})^{-Y} = (\rho^{-Y})^{-X}$, which is denoted by $\rho^{-\{X,Y\}}$.
4. (*Local computation*) If ρ and σ are valuations for r and s, respectively, $X \in r$, and $X \notin s$, then $(\rho \oplus \sigma)^{-X} = (\rho^{-X}) \oplus \sigma$.

Sometimes it is useful to use the notation $\rho^{\downarrow r \setminus \{X,Y\}}$ to denote $\rho^{-\{X,Y\}}$, when we wish to emphasize the variables that remain (instead of the variables that are marginalized out).

The set of all normal valuations with the combination operator $\oplus$ forms a commutative semigroup. We let $\iota_\emptyset$ denote the (unique) identity valuation of this semigroup. Thus, for any normal valuation ρ, $\rho \oplus \iota_\emptyset = \rho$.

The set of all normal valuations for $s \subseteq \Phi$ with the combination operator $\oplus$ also forms a commutative semigroup (which is different from the semigroup discussed in the previous paragraph). Let ι_s denote the (unique) identity for this semigroup. Thus, for any normal valuation σ for s, $\sigma \oplus \iota_s = \sigma$.

Notice that, in general, $\rho \oplus \rho \neq \rho$. Thus, it is important to ensure that we do not double count knowledge when it matters. This can be ensured, e.g., when defining the composition operator in Section 3, by the removal operator that is defined next.

Removal. This operator $\ominus \colon \Psi \times \Psi_n \to \Psi_n$ represents removing knowledge in the second valuation from the knowledge in the first valuation. It must satisfy the following three axioms:

1. (*Domain*): Suppose σ is a valuation for s and ρ is a normal valuation for r. Then $\sigma \ominus \rho$ is a normal valuation for $r \cup s$.
2. (*Identity*): For each normal valuation ρ for r, $\rho \oplus \rho \ominus \rho = \rho$. Thus, $\rho \ominus \rho$ acts as an identity for ρ, and we denote $\rho \ominus \rho$ by ι_ρ. Thus, $\rho \oplus \iota_\rho = \rho$.
3. (*Combination and Removal*): Suppose π and θ are valuations, and suppose ρ is a normal valuation. Then, $(\pi \oplus \theta) \ominus \rho = \pi \oplus (\theta \ominus \rho)$.

We call $\sigma \ominus \rho$ the valuation resulting after removing ρ from σ. The identity axiom defines the removal operator as an inverse of the combination operator.

In [7], a number of properties of combination, marginalization, and removal operators are stated and proved. For example, for valuations σ and θ for s and t, respectively, a normal valuation ρ for r, and $X \in s \setminus r$ it holds that

1. $(\sigma \oplus \theta) \ominus \rho = (\sigma \ominus \rho) \oplus \theta$.
2. $(\sigma \ominus \rho)^{-X} = \sigma^{-X} \ominus \rho$.

Domination. As defined in the identity property of removal, $\rho \oplus \iota_\rho = \rho$. In general, if ρ' is a normal valuation for r that is distinct from ρ, then $\rho' \oplus \iota_\rho$ may not equal ρ'. However, there may exist a class of normal valuations for r such that if ρ' is in this class, then $\rho' \oplus \iota_\rho = \rho'$. We will call this class of normal valuations as valuations that are *dominated* by ρ. Thus, if ρ dominates ρ', written as $\rho \gg \rho'$, then $\rho' \oplus \iota_\rho = \rho'$.

3   Composition Operator

The composition operator aggregates knowledge encoded in two normal valuations while adjusting for the double counting of knowledge when it does matter. Suppose ρ and σ are normal valuations for r and s, respectively, and suppose that $\sigma^{\downarrow r \cap s} \gg \rho^{\downarrow r \cap s}$. The composition of ρ and σ, written as $\rho \triangleright \sigma$, is defined as follows:

$$\rho \triangleright \sigma = \rho \oplus \sigma \ominus \sigma^{\downarrow r \cap s}. \tag{1}$$

The following theorem summarizes the most important properties of the composition operator.

Theorem 1. *Suppose ρ, σ and τ are normal valuations for r, s, and t, respectively, and suppose that $\sigma^{\downarrow r \cap s} \gg \rho^{\downarrow r \cap s}$, $\tau^{\downarrow(r \cup s) \cap t} \gg (\rho \triangleright \sigma)^{\downarrow(r \cup s) \cap t}$ and $\tau^{\downarrow r \cap t} \gg \rho^{\downarrow r \cap t}$. Then the following statements hold:*

1. (Domain): $\rho \triangleright \sigma$ *is a normal valuation for* $r \cup s$.
2. (Composition preserves first marginal): $(\rho \triangleright \sigma)^{\downarrow r} = \rho$.
3. (Reduction:) *If* $s \subseteq r$ *then,* $\rho \triangleright \sigma = \rho$.
4. (Non-commutativity): *In general,* $\rho \triangleright \sigma \neq \sigma \triangleright \rho$.
5. (Commutativity under consistency): *If ρ and σ have a common marginal for* $r \cap s$, *i.e.,* $\rho^{\downarrow r \cap s} = \sigma^{\downarrow r \cap s}$, *then* $\rho \triangleright \sigma = \sigma \triangleright \rho$.
6. (Non-associativity): *Suppose τ is a normal valuation for t, and suppose* $\tau^{\downarrow(r \cup s) \cap t} \gg (\rho \triangleright \sigma)^{\downarrow(r \cup s) \cap t}$. *Then, in general,* $(\rho \triangleright \sigma) \triangleright \tau \neq \rho \triangleright (\sigma \triangleright \tau)$.
7. (Associativity under special condition I): *If* $r \supset (s \cap t)$ *then,* $(\rho \triangleright \sigma) \triangleright \tau = \rho \triangleright (\sigma \triangleright \tau)$.
8. (Associativity under special condition II): *If* $s \supset (r \cap t)$ *then,* $(\rho \triangleright \sigma) \triangleright \tau = \rho \triangleright (\sigma \triangleright \tau)$.
9. (Stepwise composition): *If* $(r \cap s) \subseteq t \subseteq s$ *then,* $(\rho \triangleright \sigma^{\downarrow t}) \triangleright \sigma = \rho \triangleright \sigma$.
10. (Exchangeability): *If* $r \supset (s \cap t)$ *then,* $(\rho \triangleright \sigma) \triangleright \tau = (\rho \triangleright \tau) \triangleright \sigma$.
11. (Simple marginalization): *If* $(r \cap s) \subseteq t \subseteq r \cup s$ *then,* $(\rho \triangleright \sigma)^{\downarrow t} = \rho^{\downarrow r \cap t} \triangleright \sigma^{\downarrow s \cap t}$.
12. (Irrelevant combination): *If* $t \subseteq r \setminus s$ *then,* $\rho \triangleright (\sigma \oplus \tau) = \rho \triangleright \sigma$.

Proof. All properties are proved in [4] with the exception of Properties 3, 7 and 12.

Property 3 is a direct consequence of Property 2. To prove Property 7, it is sufficient to use the definition of the composition operator (Equation 1), simple marginalization (Property 11), the commutativity and associativity of combination, and the fact that under the specified condition $(r \cup s) \cap t = r \cap t$:

$$\rho \triangleright (\sigma \triangleright \tau) = \rho \oplus (\sigma \triangleright \tau) \ominus (\sigma \triangleright \tau)^{\downarrow r \cap (s \cup t)}$$
$$= \rho \oplus \sigma \oplus \tau \ominus \tau^{\downarrow s \cap t} \ominus (\sigma \triangleright \tau)^{\downarrow r \cap (s \cup t)}$$
$$= \rho \oplus \sigma \oplus \tau \ominus \tau^{\downarrow s \cap t} \ominus (\sigma^{\downarrow r \cap s} \triangleright \tau^{\downarrow r \cap t}) \oplus \sigma^{\downarrow r \cap s} \ominus \sigma^{\downarrow r \cap s} \oplus \tau^{\downarrow r \cap t} \ominus \tau^{\downarrow r \cap t}$$
$$= \rho \oplus \sigma \oplus \tau \ominus (\sigma^{\downarrow r \cap s} \triangleright \tau^{\downarrow r \cap t}) \oplus (\sigma^{\downarrow r \cap s} \triangleright \tau^{\downarrow r \cap t}) \ominus \sigma^{\downarrow r \cap s} \ominus \tau^{\downarrow r \cap t}$$
$$= (\rho \triangleright \sigma) \oplus \tau \ominus \tau^{\downarrow(r \cup s) \cap t} = (\rho \triangleright \sigma) \triangleright \tau.$$

To prove Property 12 we use the definition of the composition operator (Equation 1), simple marginalization (Property 11), and the commutativity and associativity of combination:

$$\rho \triangleright (\sigma \oplus \tau) = \rho \oplus (\sigma \oplus \tau) \ominus (\sigma \oplus \tau)^{\downarrow r \cap (s \cup t)} = \rho \oplus (\sigma \oplus \tau) \ominus (\sigma^{\downarrow r \cap s} \oplus \tau)$$
$$= \rho \oplus \sigma^{\downarrow r \cap s} \ominus \sigma^{\downarrow r \cap s} \oplus \sigma \oplus \tau \ominus (\sigma^{\downarrow r \cap s} \oplus \tau)$$
$$= \rho \oplus \sigma \ominus \sigma^{\downarrow r \cap s} \oplus (\sigma^{\downarrow r \cap s} \oplus \tau) \ominus (\sigma^{\downarrow r \cap s} \oplus \tau) = \rho \triangleright \sigma. \quad \blacksquare$$

In designing computational procedures for probabilistic compositional models in [1], we compensated the lack of associativity of the composition operator by the so-called *anticipating composition operator*. Its name is suggestive from the fact that it introduces an additional conditional independence relation into the result of composition—it *anticipates* the independence relation that is necessary for associativity, and therefore it must take into account the set of variables, for which the preceding distribution is defined. In this paper we introduce the anticipating operator of composition for VBS in the following way. Suppose ρ and σ are normal valuations for r and s, respectively, and suppose t is a subset of variables. Then,

$$\rho \bigotimes_t \sigma = (\rho \oplus \sigma^{\downarrow(t\backslash r)\cap s}) \triangleright \sigma. \tag{2}$$

Notice that, as explained above, this composition operator is parameterized by subset t. If $(t \backslash r) \cap s = \emptyset$ then $\rho \bigotimes_t \sigma = \rho \triangleright \sigma$. The importance of this operator stems from the following assertion.

Theorem 2. *Suppose τ, ρ, and σ are normal valuations for t, r, and s, respectively, and suppose that $\sigma^{\downarrow r\cap s} \gg \rho^{\downarrow r\cap s}$ and $\rho^{\downarrow r\cap t} \gg \tau^{\downarrow r\cap t}$. Then*

$$(\tau \triangleright \rho) \triangleright \sigma = \tau \triangleright (\rho \bigotimes_t \sigma). \tag{3}$$

Proof. The proof uses irrelevant combination (Property 12 of Theorem 1), and associativity under special condition I (Property 7 of Theorem 1):

$$(\tau \triangleright \rho) \triangleright \sigma = (\tau \triangleright (\rho \oplus \iota_{(t\backslash r)\cap s})) \triangleright \sigma$$
$$= \tau \triangleright ((\rho \oplus \iota_{(t\backslash r)\cap s}) \triangleright \sigma) = \tau \triangleright (\rho \bigotimes_t \sigma). \qquad \blacksquare$$

4   Causal Compositional Models

Suppose $\Phi = \{X_1, X_2, \ldots, X_n\}$. For each variable X_i, let $\mathcal{C}(X_i)$ denote the subset of the variables that are causes of X_i. We assume that $X_i \notin \mathcal{C}(X_i)$. $\{\mathcal{C}(X_i)\}_{i=1}^n$ constitutes a *causal model*. Using Pearl's terminology [5], we say that a causal model is *Markovian* if there exists an ordering of variables (without loss of generality we assume that it is the ordering $X_1, X_2, \ldots, X_n$) such that $\mathcal{C}(X_1) = \emptyset$, and for $i = 2, 3, \ldots, n$, $\mathcal{C}(X_i) \subseteq \{X_1, \ldots, X_{i-1}\}$. Markovian causal models are causal models without feedback relations.

Let r_i denote $\mathcal{C}(X_i) \cup \{X_i\}$. From here onwards, the symbol τ exclusively denotes causal models, i.e. if we have valuations ρ_i for r_i for $i = 1, \ldots, n$ a causal compositional model (CCM) τ is defined as follows:

$$\tau = (\ldots((\rho_1 \triangleright \rho_2) \triangleright \rho_3) \triangleright \ldots \triangleright \rho_{n-1}) \triangleright \rho_n = \rho_1 \triangleright \rho_2 \triangleright \ldots \triangleright \rho_n. \tag{4}$$

(To increase legibility of the formulae, we will not include parentheses if the composition operator is successively performed from left to right.)

Notice that all the properties of the composition operator, including Property 10, describe Markovian preserving modifications. For example, if $\rho_1 \triangleright \rho_2 \triangleright \rho_3$ is a Markovian CCM, then $r_1 \supseteq r_2 \cap r_3$ guarantees that $\rho_1 \triangleright \rho_3 \triangleright \rho_2$ is also Markovian (it follows from the fact that under this assumption $r_3 \cap (r_1 \cup r_2) = r_3 \cap r_1$).

Readers familiar with Pearl's causal networks [5] have certainly noticed that for the probabilistic case, CCM τ defined by formula (4) is exactly the causal network represented by an acyclic directed graph $G = (V, E)$ with $V = \Phi$, and there is an edge $(X_j \rightarrow X_i) \in E$ *iff* $X_j \in \mathcal{C}(X_i)$. The conditional probability distributions necessary to define the probabilistic causal network are $\rho(X_i | \mathcal{C}(X_i))$ for $i = 1, \ldots, n$.

4.1   Conditioning and Intervention

In causal models, there is a difference between conditioning and intervention. Suppose $S = 1$ denotes a person who smokes, $Y = 1$ denotes (nicotine-stained) yellow teeth, and $C = 1$ denotes presence of lung cancer. We assume $\mathcal{C}(S) = \emptyset$, $\mathcal{C}(Y) = \{S\}$, and $\mathcal{C}(C) = \{S\}$. Conditioning on $Y = 0$ means including evidence that teeth are not stained (which lowers the chances that the person has cancer). On the other hand, the intervention denoted by $do(Y = 0)$ means a changed universe where the person gets his teeth whitened (e.g., from his dentist), but the chances of cancer remains unchanged.

To simplify the exposition, in the rest of this subsection, let s denote $r_1 \cup \ldots \cup r_n$ and t denote $s \setminus \{X\}$ for some $X \in s$. Thus, in CCM $\tau = \rho_1 \triangleright \rho_2 \triangleright \ldots \triangleright \rho_n$, conditioning by $X = \mathbf{x}$ leads to a valuation $\tau(t | X = \mathbf{x})$ for t.

As shown in [3], we can realize both the conditioning and intervention as a composition of the causal compositional model $\rho_1 \triangleright \ldots \triangleright \rho_n$ with a valuation $\nu_{|X;\mathbf{x}}$, which is a valuation for variable X expressing knowledge that $X = \mathbf{x}$. Using this notation we can apply the following simple formulae that were proved for the probabilistic framework in [3]:

$$\tau(t | X = \mathbf{x}) = \left(\nu_{|X;\mathbf{x}} \triangleright (\rho_1 \triangleright \rho_2 \triangleright \ldots \triangleright \rho_n) \right)^{-X}, \tag{5}$$

and

$$\tau(t | do(X = \mathbf{x})) = \left(\nu_{|X;\mathbf{x}} \triangleright \rho_1 \triangleright \rho_2 \triangleright \ldots \triangleright \rho_n \right)^{-X}. \tag{6}$$

Notice the importance of the pair of brackets by which the formulae above differ from each other. This difference arises from the fact that the operator of composition is not associative.

To clarify these formulae, consider for a moment, again, probabilistic interpretation. Then, the expression in formula (5) equals

$$\nu_{|X;\mathbf{x}} \triangleright (\rho_1 \triangleright \rho_2 \triangleright \ldots \triangleright \rho_n) = \nu_{|X;\mathbf{x}} \triangleright \tau(s) = \frac{\nu_{|X;\mathbf{x}} \cdot \tau(s)}{\tau(X)},$$

which is a probability distribution for variables s, and equals $\tau(t | X = \mathbf{x})$ for those combinations of values of variables s for which $X = \mathbf{x}$, and 0 for all the remaining combinations of values. Therefore $\tau(t | X = \mathbf{x}) = \left(\nu_{|X;\mathbf{x}} \triangleright \tau(s) \right)^{-X}$.

To explain formula (6) we have to make a reference to Pearl's causal networks [5], and to consider CCM

$$\sigma = \rho_0 \triangleright \rho_1 \triangleright \rho_2 \triangleright \ldots \triangleright \rho_n, \tag{7}$$

for a one-dimensional distribution $\rho_0(X)$ (ρ_0 may be considered uniform). At the end of the preceding section we said that CCM τ defined by formula (4) corresponds to the causal network with an acyclic directed graph $G = (\Phi, E)$, where $(X_j \rightarrow X_i) \in E$ iff $X_j \in \mathcal{C}(X_i)$. Obviously, CCM σ defined by formula (7) corresponds to the causal network with an acyclic directed graph $\bar{G} = (\Phi, \bar{E})$, in which there is no edge heading to X and all the remaining edges from E are preserved; i.e., $\bar{E} = \{(X_j \rightarrow X_i) \in E : X_i \neq X\}$.

Following Definition 3.2.1 in [5] (or formula (3.11) from the same source), we can see that the result of intervention performed in the causal model τ can be computed as a conditioning in the model σ:

$$\tau(t|do(X = \mathbf{x})) = \sigma(t|X = \mathbf{x}) = \left(\nu_{|X;\mathbf{x}} \triangleright \sigma(s)\right)^{-X}$$
$$= \left(\nu_{|X;\mathbf{x}} \triangleright (\rho_0 \triangleright \rho_1 \triangleright \ldots \triangleright \rho_n)\right)^{-X} .$$

Applying Property 8 of Theorem 1 n-times (it is possible because $\nu_{|X;\mathbf{x}}$ and ρ_0 are defined for the same variable X) we get:

$$\nu_{|X;\mathbf{x}} \triangleright (\rho_0 \triangleright \rho_1 \triangleright \ldots \triangleright \rho_{n-1} \triangleright \rho_n) = \nu_{|X;\mathbf{x}} \triangleright (\rho_0 \triangleright \rho_1 \triangleright \ldots \triangleright \rho_{n-1}) \triangleright \rho_n = \ldots$$
$$= \nu_{|X;\mathbf{x}} \triangleright \rho_0 \triangleright \rho_1 \triangleright \ldots \triangleright \rho_{n-1} \triangleright \rho_n,$$

from which the formula (6) is obtained using Property 3 of Theorem 1.

Readers familiar with the Pearl's causal networks [5] have certainly noticed an advantage of CCM. In CCM, we can compute both conditioning and intervention from one causal compositional model as shown above. In Pearl's causal networks, we have to consider two different networks. Conditioning is computed from the complete causal network. For the computation of intervention, we have to consider a reduced causal network where all the arrows heading to the intervention variable are deleted.

4.2 An Example: Elimination of Hidden Variables

In this subsection, as an illustration, we derive formulae for computation of conditioning and intervention in a simple causal compositional model with four variables U, Y, X, Z, the first of which is assumed to be hidden (unobservable). Suppose that $\mathcal{C}(U) = \emptyset$, $\mathcal{C}(Y) = \{U\}$, $\mathcal{C}(X) = \{Y\}$, $\mathcal{C}(Z) = \{U, X\}$, so that the causal model is Markovian. Also, suppose that the situation is described by a causal compositional model as follows:

$$\tau(U, Y, X, Z) = \rho_1(U) \triangleright \rho_2(U, Y) \triangleright \rho_3(Y, X) \triangleright \rho_4(U, X, Z).$$

In the CCM above, $\rho_1(U)$ denotes a normal valuation for U, etc., and $\tau(U, Y, X, Z)$ denotes the joint normal valuation for $\{U, Y, X, Z\}$. As U is a hidden variable, only $\rho_3(Y, X)$ can be estimated from data, all others include U in their domains. To simplify notation, we will let, e.g., $\tau(Y, X, Z)$ denote $\tau(U, Y, X, Z)^{-U}$, etc.

Computation of the conditional $\tau(Z|Y = \mathbf{y})$ is simple.

$$\tau(Z|Y = \mathbf{y}) = \left(\nu_{|Y;\mathbf{y}} \triangleright \tau(U, Y, X, Z)\right)^{\downarrow\{Z\}} \overset{(11)}{=} \left(\nu_{|Y;\mathbf{y}} \triangleright \tau(U, Y, X, Z)^{-\{U\}}\right)^{\downarrow\{Z\}}$$
$$\overset{(11)}{=} \left(\nu_{|Y;\mathbf{y}} \triangleright \tau(Y, X, Z)^{-\{X\}}\right)^{\downarrow\{Z\}} = \left(\nu_{|Y;\mathbf{y}} \triangleright \tau(Y, Z)\right)^{\downarrow\{Z\}} .$$

Thus we can estimate $\tau(Z|Y = \mathbf{y})$ by $\left(\nu_{|Y:\mathbf{y}} \triangleright \hat{\tau}(Y, Z)\right)^{\downarrow\{Z\}}$, which includes only observable variables. Notice that during these computations we used Property 11 of Theorem 1 twice. This is why the symbol (11) appears above the respective equality signs. This type of explanation will also be used in the subsequent computations.

To compute $\tau(Z|do(Y = \mathbf{y}))$ we use the properties of the composition and the anticipating operators defined in the preceding section. To simplify the exposition, we do just one elementary modification at each step, and thus the following computations may appear more cumbersome than they really are.

$$
\begin{aligned}
\tau(Z|do(Y = \mathbf{y})) &= \left(\nu_{|Y:\mathbf{y}} \triangleright \rho_1(U) \triangleright \rho_2(U, Y) \triangleright \rho_3(Y, X) \triangleright \rho_4(U, X, Z)\right)^{\downarrow\{Z\}} \\
&\overset{(3)}{=} \left(\nu_{|Y:\mathbf{y}} \triangleright \rho_1(U) \triangleright \rho_3(Y, X) \triangleright \rho_4(U, X, Z)\right)^{\downarrow\{Z\}} \\
&\overset{(10)}{=} \left(\nu_{|Y:\mathbf{y}} \triangleright \rho_3(Y, X) \triangleright \rho_1(U) \triangleright \rho_4(U, X, Z)\right)^{\downarrow\{Z\}} \\
&\overset{\text{Th } 2}{=} \left(\nu_{|Y:\mathbf{y}} \triangleright \rho_3(Y, X) \triangleright \left(\rho_1(U) \oslash_{\{Y,X\}} \rho_4(U, X, Z)\right)\right)^{\downarrow\{Z\}} \\
&\overset{(11)}{=} \left(\nu_{|Y:\mathbf{y}} \triangleright \rho_3(Y, X) \triangleright \left(\rho_1(U) \oslash_{\{Y,X\}} \rho_4(U, X, Z)\right)^{-U}\right)^{\downarrow\{Z\}}.
\end{aligned}
$$

To express $\left(\rho_1(U) \oslash_{\{Y,X\}} \rho_4(U, X, Z)\right)^{-U}$ we take advantage of the idea of extension used by Pearl in [5]. It is one way of taking into account the mutual dependence of variables X, Y, and Z. It plays the same role as the inheritance of parents property of Shachter's arc reversal rule [6].

$$
\begin{aligned}
\left(\rho_1(U) \oslash_{\{Y,X\}} \rho_4(U, X, Z)\right)^{-U} &= \left(\rho_1(U) \oslash_{\{X\}} \rho_4(U, X, Z)\right)^{-U} \\
&\overset{(11)}{=} \left(\left(\rho_2(U, Y) \oslash_{\{X\}} \rho_4(U, X, Z)\right)^{-Y}\right)^{-U} \\
&= \left((\rho_4(X) \oplus \rho_2(U, Y)) \triangleright \rho_4(U, X, Z)\right)^{\downarrow\{X,Z\}} \\
&= \left((\rho_4(X) \oplus \rho_2(Y)) \triangleright \rho_2(U, Y) \triangleright \rho_4(U, X, Z)\right)^{\downarrow\{X,Z\}} \\
&\overset{(3)}{=} \left((\rho_4(X) \oplus \rho_2(Y)) \triangleright \rho_2(U, Y) \triangleright \rho_3(Y, X) \triangleright \rho_4(U, X, Z)\right)^{\downarrow\{X,Z\}} \\
&\overset{(7)}{=} \left((\rho_4(X) \oplus \rho_2(Y)) \triangleright (\rho_2(U, Y) \triangleright \rho_3(Y, X)) \triangleright \rho_4(U, X, Z)\right)^{\downarrow\{X,Z\}} \\
&\overset{(8)}{=} \left((\rho_4(X) \oplus \rho_2(Y)) \triangleright (\rho_2(U, Y) \triangleright \rho_3(Y, X) \triangleright \rho_4(U, X, Z))\right)^{\downarrow\{X,Z\}} \\
&= \left((\rho_4(X) \oplus \rho_2(Y)) \triangleright \tau(U, Y, X, Z)\right)^{\downarrow\{X,Z\}} \\
&\overset{(11)}{=} \left((\rho_4(X) \oplus \rho_2(Y)) \triangleright \tau(Y, X, Z)\right)^{\downarrow\{X,Z\}} \\
&= \left((\tau(X) \oplus \tau(Y)) \triangleright \tau(Y, X, Z)\right)^{\downarrow\{X,Z\}} = \left(\tau(Y) \oslash_{\{X\}} \tau(Y, X, Z)\right)^{-Y},
\end{aligned}
$$

which eventually leads to

$$\hat{\tau}(Z|do(Y = \mathbf{y}))$$

$$= \left(\nu_{|Y;\mathbf{y}} \triangleright \rho_3(Y, X) \triangleright \left((\rho_4(X) \oplus \rho_2(Y)) \triangleright \tau(Y, X, Z) \right)^{\downarrow\{X,Z\}} \right)^{\downarrow\{Z\}}$$

$$= \left(\nu_{|Y;\mathbf{y}} \triangleright \hat{\tau}(Y, X) \triangleright \left((\hat{\tau}(X) \oplus \rho_2(Y)) \triangleright \hat{\tau}(Y, X, Z) \right)^{\downarrow\{X,Z\}} \right)^{\downarrow\{Z\}}$$

$$= \left(\nu_{|Y;\mathbf{y}} \triangleright \hat{\tau}(Y, X) \triangleright \left(\hat{\tau}(Y) \oslash_{\{X\}} \hat{\tau}(Y, X, Z) \right)^{-Y} \right)^{\downarrow\{Z\}}$$

$$= \left(\nu_{|Y;\mathbf{y}} \triangleright \hat{\tau}(Y, X) \triangleright \left(\hat{\tau}(Y) \oslash_{\{X\}} \hat{\tau}(Y, X, Z) \right)^{-Y} \right)^{\downarrow\{Z\}} .$$

5   Conclusions

We have described causal compositional models, originally introduced in [3] in the probabilistic framework, in the VBS framework. Both conditioning and interventions can be described easily using the composition operator. A simple example illustrates the use of the composition operator for conditioning and intervention.

Acknowledgments. This work has been supported in part by funds from grant GAČR 403/12/2175 to the first author, and from the Ronald G. Harper Distinguished Professorship at the University of Kansas to the second author.

References

1. Bína, V., Jiroušek, R.: Marginalization in multidimensional compositional models. Kybernetika 42(4), 405–422 (2006)
2. Jiroušek, R.: Foundations of compositional model theory. Int. J. of General Systems. 40(6), 623–678 (2011)
3. Jiroušek, R.: On causal compositional models: Simple examples. In: Laurent, A., Strauss, O., Bouchon-Meunier, B., Yager, R.R., et al. (eds.) IPMU 2014, Part I. CCIS, vol. 442, pp. 517–526. Springer, Heidelberg (2014)
4. Jiroušek, R., Shenoy, P.P.: Compositional models in valuation-based systems. Int. J. of Approximate Reasoning 55(1), 277–293 (2014)
5. Pearl, J.: Causality: Models, Reasoning, and Inference. Cambridge Univ. Press, NY (2009)
6. Shachter, R.: Evaluating influence diagrams. Operations Research 34(6), 871–882 (1986)
7. Shenoy, P.P.: Conditional independence in valuation-based systems. Int. J. of Approximate Reasoning 10(3), 203–234 (1994)
8. Shenoy, P.P.: No double counting semantics for conditional independence. In: Cozman, F.G., Nau, R., Seidenfeld, T. (eds.) Proc. of the 4th Int. Symposium on Imprecise Probabilities and Their Applications (ISIPTA 2005), pp. 306–314. SIPTA (2005)

Merging Possibilistic Networks
through a Disjunctive Mode

Faiza Titouna and Salem Benferhat

University of Batna, Computer Sciences Department, Algeria
CRIL-CNRS, University of Artois Rue Jean Souvraz 62307 Lens, France

Abstract. This paper addresses the problem of merging a number of expert opinions which have expressed by means of possibilistic networks in order to make additional decision more reliable and precise. We have considered the fusion of graphical possibilistic models through a disjunctive mode. For this purpose, we have chosen the maximum operator which generally used when information issued from different sources are totally in conflict. So, we have proposed a new combination approach when initial models shared the same variables.

Keywords: Possibility theory, possibilistic networks, maximum operator.

1   Introduction

Possibility theory provides a good framework for dealing with merging problems when information is pervaded with uncertainty and inconsistency. One of the important aims in merging uncertain information is to exploit complementarities between the sources in order to get a more complete and precise global point of view. Many different merging operators have been proposed [10], [13], [18]. In [2], [3] a conjunctive operator is introduced to exploit the symbolic complementarities between pieces of information provided by different sources and to deal with conflict the authors use a disjunctive operator to merge inconsistent knowledge bases.

Information fusion issued from multiple sources has an increasing interest in diverse areas applications. For instance, the information provided by individual sensors is incomplete, inaccurate and/or unreliable. Therefore, a fusion based estimate provides a more effective approach towards traffic speed estimation [1]. In [20], a combination of multi-agent systems and information fusion technology in target recognition system has been used. Agents are informed by information sources of varying levels of reliability. The information provided by an agent can be viewed as his belief. However, the beliefs of different agents may be conflicting and partially inconsistent. Therefore, to establish a global point of view about the real world, it is important to merge beliefs of different agents according to their levels of reliability. Uncertain pieces of information are assumed to be represented by possibilistic networks. So, the integration or the merging of distributed heterogeneous networks is a challenging problem. This problem is

F. Cuzzolin (Ed.): BELIEF 2014, LNAI 8764, pp. 265–274, 2014.

difficult because different networks to be merged may have different structures and data from different networks may be conflicting.

There are few works that deal with the problem of fusing probabilistic [6], [16] or possibilistic networks, [12], [14], [15]. The context of this paper concerns merging uncertain information represented by graphical models. We explore a fusion method through a disjunctive mode expressed by the maximum operator. It extends and completes results presented in [4],[5].

After some preliminaries introduced in Section 2, Section 3 discusses the combination modes in particular the disjunctive mode. In Section 4, we present how to merge conflicting information defined by different possibilsitic networks. Finally, we conclude.

2   Formal Preliminaries

The possibility theory introduced by Zadeh [19] and by Dubois and Prade [9] is a theoretical framework for modeling uncertainty in a qualitative way.

Let $V = \{A_1, A_2, ..., A_n\}$ be a set of variables. We denote by $D_A = \{a_1, ..., a_n\}$ the domain associated with the variable A. By a we denote any instance of A. $\Omega = \times_{A_i \in V} D_{A_i}$ denotes the universe of discourse, which is the cartesian product of all variables domains. Each element $\omega \in \Omega$ is called a state or an interpretation or a solution. Subsets of Ω are simply called events. In the following, we only give a brief background on possibility theory; for more details see [9].

2.1   Possibility Theory

Possibility theory introduces the notion of possibility distribution denoted by π and corresponding to a mapping from Ω to the scale [0,1] encoding our knowledge on the real world, denoted by u, which is generally ill known. The possibilistic scale can be interpreted in an ordinal and numerical manners.

Two dual measures, called possibility and necessity, are used in order to model available information. The possibility measure $\Pi(\phi) = max_{\omega \in \phi, \phi \subset \Omega} \pi(\omega)$ is called the possibility degree of ϕ and it corresponds to the possibility degree to have one of the models of ϕ as the real world. This measure evaluates at which level ϕ is consistent with our knowledge represented by π. The necessity measure $N(\phi) = 1 - \Pi(\neg\phi) = min_{\omega \nvDash \phi}(1 - \pi(\omega))$ called the necessity degree of ϕ, this measure evaluates at which level ϕ is certainly implied by our knowledge represented by π. A possibility distribution π is said to be normalized (or coherent), if $max_\omega \pi(\omega) = 1$.

2.2   Possibilistic Networks

In possibility theory [9], [19], there are two kinds of possibilistic networks depending if possibilistic conditioning[1] is based on the minimum (it is then called

---

[1] The notion of conditioning consists in modifying initial knowledge, encoded by a possibility distribution π, by the arrival of a new certain piece of information.

ordinal or min-based possibilistic networks) or on the product operator (it is called numerical or quantitative networks).

A possibilistic network $\mathbb{N}$ is composed of two principles parts. The first one, it is a graphical structure called a DAG (Directed Acyclic Graph) and denoted by $\mathbb{G}$, it represents a set of nodes (variables) linked by arcs. The latter encode the influence relation between variables. In the second part, uncertainties are quantified by a priori and conditional possibility distributions $\pi(a)$ and $\pi(a|U_A)$ for each instance $a \in D_A$ respectively, where U_A represents the parents of A.

When, we use the product form of possibilistic conditioning, we get a possibilistic network close to the probabilistic one sharing the same features and having the same theoretical and practical results [17]. A possibilistic network encodes independence assertions, which do not depend on how the network is quantified. An independence assertion is a statement of the form X and Y are independent given Z, namely : $\forall X, \forall Y, \forall Z, \pi(X|Y \wedge Z) = \pi(X|Z)$ (see [11] and [7]). The independence assertions in a belief network are important because it allows to reduce the complexity of inference. In this paper, the joint possibility distribution π_J is defined via the chain rule based on the minimum as follows :

Definition 1. *Let* $\mathbb{N} = (\pi, \mathbb{G})$ *be a possibilistic network. The joint possibility distribution associated with* $\mathbb{N}$*, denoted by* π_J*, is expressed by the following chain rule:*

$$\pi_J(A_1, .., A_N) = min_{i=1..N}\pi(A_i \mid U_{A_i}). \tag{1}$$

3   Disjunctive Combination

When sources are in conflict, we usually use a T-conorm to combine them. A T-conorm is an operation Tc from $[0, 1] \times [0, 1]$ to $[0,1]$ such as :

$Tc(a, b) = Tc(b, a)$ (commutativity),
$Tc(a, Tc(b, c)) = Tc(Tc(a, b), c)$ (associativity),
$b \leq c, Tc(a, b) \leq Tc(a, c)$ (monotonicity),
$Tc(a, 0) = a$ (neutral element 0).

For any T-conorm, the following inequality holds: $\forall(a, b) \in [0, 1]^2$, Tc(a,b)$\geq$ max(a,b). This shows that the maximum operator is the smallest T-conorm and that any T-conorm has a disjunctive behavior which satisfies the following property : $\forall a \in [0, 1]$, Tc(a,1) = 1.

Unlike the conjunctive mode, the disjunctive fusion corresponds to a lower reliability, in the sense where among elements of a group, there is at least a fully reliable element. However, we do not know which elements is reliable and which is not. So, to keep the whole information, it is preferable to use the disjunctive mode expressed generally by the maximum operator. Moreover, when pieces of information provided by different sources have the same degree of reliability and in conflict, it is absurd to prefer one source rather than another. Such behavior cannot be obtained by applying the conjunctive operator, only the disjunctive operator gives a reasonable result. The disjunctive operator can be viewed as a

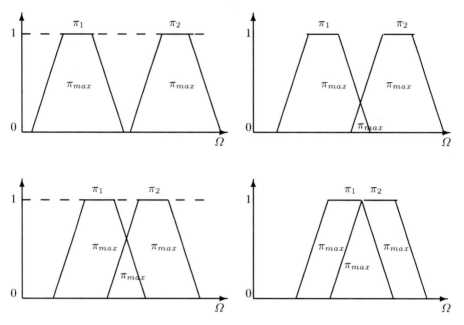

Fig. 1. Cases of disjunctive fusion

logical union. Different cases are represented in Fig. 1, to explain the behavior of this operator. The disjunction will favor the reliable source as the one which gives the higher degree of confidence. Indeed, the maximum operator is appropriate when the sources are highly conflicting with each other and the minimum operator is meaningful when the sources are consistent. The reason that the maximum operator is chosen because the inconsistency is viewed as a bad thing and needs to be avoided.

4   Graphical-Model Based Merging

Before presenting our approach of disjunctive combination by applying the *maximum* operator, we need to give some important and necessary definitions which are useful to extend any possibilistic network.

In the rest of paper, we restrict our work to binary variables. The following proposition provides an interesting way to explain how initial information is preserved.

Proposition 1. *Let* $\mathbb{N} = (\mathbb{G}, \pi)$ *be the possibilistic network defined over the set of variables denoted by* $\mathbb{V}$. *Let* A *be a variable such that* $A \notin \mathbb{V}$ *and* U_A *the parents of* A. *Let* $\mathbb{N}' = (\mathbb{G}', \pi')$ *be the network obtained by adding a new variable* A *to the initial network* $\mathbb{N}$ *such as :*

- $\mathbb{G}' = \mathbb{G} \cup \{A\}$,

- $\forall a_i \in D_A, \pi'(a_i) = 1,$
- $\forall X \in \mathbb{V}, \forall x_i \in D_X, \pi'(x_i|U_X) = \pi(x_i|U_X).$

Then, we have :

$$\forall \omega \in \Omega, \pi_J(\omega) = max_{a \in D_A} \pi'_J(a\omega). \tag{2}$$

In the next definition, we present how to augment a network.

Definition 2. *(**Augmented Network**) Let $\mathbb{N} = (\mathbb{G}, \pi)$ be a possibilistic network defined over a set of variables $\mathbb{V}$. Let $\mathbb{N}' = (\mathbb{G}', \pi')$ be an augmented possibilistic network obtained as follows :*

- *Adding a new variable A according to Proposition 1,*
- *Adding a new link from the new variable A to each variable of the initial network $\mathbb{N}$.*
  The possibility distributions associated with the augmented network are defined as follows :
- $\forall a_i \in D_A, \pi'(a_i) = 1,$
-

$$\forall X \in \mathbb{V}, X \neq A, \forall x_i \in D_X, \pi'(x_i|U_X, a_j) = \begin{cases} \pi(x_i|U_X) \; if \quad j{=}1 \\ 1 \qquad\qquad otherwise. \end{cases}$$

We recall that the joint possibility distribution is computed via the chain rule based on the minimum.

Example 1. Let $\mathbb{N}$ be a possibilistic network. Let $\mathbb{G}$ be the DAG associated with $\mathbb{N}$, and represented by Fig. 2(a). The possibility distributions associated with $\mathbb{N}$ are given respectively in Table 1. Let C be a new binary variable. Namely, $D_C = \{c_1, c_2\}$. Let $\mathbb{N}'$ be the augmented possibilistic network obtained from $\mathbb{N}$ such that:

- $\mathbb{G}' = \mathbb{G} \cup \{C\},$
- $\forall c_i \in D_C, \pi'(c_i) = 1,$
- $\forall X \in \mathbb{V}, \forall x_i \in D_X, \forall c_j \in D_C, \pi'(x_i \mid U_X, c_j) = \pi(x_i \mid U_X)$ for j=1,
- $\forall X \in \mathbb{V}, \forall x_i \in D_X, \forall c_j \in D_C, \pi'(x_i \mid U_X, c_j) = 0$ for $j = 2$.

The first step of the construction of the augmented DAG depicted in Fig. 2(b) represents the extension of the initial DAG Fig. 2(a) by adding a new variable C according to Proposition 1. Then, the equation 2 is well checked. For instance, let $\omega = a_2b_1$ be an interpretation and let c_1 and c_2 be two states of the variable C. So, $\pi'_J(c_1a_2b_1) = min(\pi'(c_1), \pi'(a_2|c_1), \pi'(b_1|a_2, c_1)) = min(1, \pi(a_2), \pi(b_1|a_2)) = min(1, 0.3, 0.5) = 0.3$. Likewise for $\pi'(c_2a_2b_1) = min(1, 0.3, 0.5) = 0.3$. Indeed, $max_c\pi'_J(c\omega) = \pi_J(\omega) = 0.3$.

In the second step (Fig. 2(c)), we have added a new link from the variable C to A and another link from C to B according to Definition 2. Table 2 gives the conditional possibility distributions π' associated with the augmented network.

The next definition shows how to merge two possibilistic networks based on the *maximum* operator. This fusion process reveals the relationship between the semantic combination and its graphical counterpart.

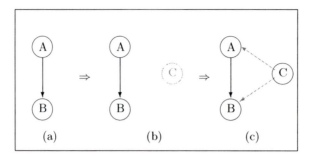

Fig. 2. Construction steps of an augmented DAG

Table 1. Initial possibility distributions π associated with $\mathbb{N}$

A	$\pi(A)$	A	B	$\pi(B \mid A)$
a_1	1	a_1	b_1	1
a_2	0.3	a_1	b_2	0.2
		a_2	b_1	0.5
		a_2	b_2	1

Table 2. Conditional possibility distributions π' associated with $\mathbb{N}'$

C	$\pi'(C)$	A	C	$\pi'(A \mid C)$	A	B	C	$\pi'(B \mid A \wedge C)$	A	B	C	$\pi'(B \mid A \wedge C)$
c_1	1	a_1	c_1	1	a_1	b_1	c_1	1	a_2	b_1	c_1	0.5
c_2	1	a_1	c_2	1	a_1	b_1	c_2	1	a_2	b_1	c_2	1
		a_2	c_1	0.3	a_1	b_2	c_1	0.2	a_2	b_2	c_1	1
		a_2	c_2	1	a_1	b_2	c_2	1	a_2	b_2	c_2	1

Definition 3. *Let* $\mathbb{N}1 = (\mathbb{G}_1, \pi_1)$ *and* $\mathbb{N}2 = (\mathbb{G}_2, \pi_2)$ *be two possibilistic networks having the same graphical model. Let* $\mathbb{N}_{max} = (\mathbb{G}_{max}, \pi_{max})$ *be the merged network obtained by applying the maximum operator.*

At the graphical level, the merged graph $\mathbb{G}_{max}$ *is obtained by applying the following steps :*

a. *Choose anyone of the initial graphs. For example* $\mathbb{G}_2$,
b. *Rename each variable* X *in* $\mathbb{G}_2$. *Let* X' *be the new variable,*
c. *Augment separately* $\mathbb{G}_1$ *and* $\mathbb{G}_2$ *by adding new nodes* C *and* C' *respectively according to Proposition 1 and Definition 2,*
d. *Create a link from each variable* X *in* $\mathbb{G}_1$ *to its associated* X' *in* $\mathbb{G}_2$. *Namely:* $X \to X'$.
e. *Create a Link from the variable* C *to the variable* C'. *Namely :* $C \to C'$.

At the semantic level, *the conditional possibility distributions of the merged network are computed as:*

1.

$$\forall c_i \in D_C, \pi_{max}(c_i) = 1.$$

2.

$$\forall c_j \in D_C, \forall c_i' \in D_{C'}, \pi_{max}(c_i'|c_j) = \begin{cases} 1 \ if \ \ i \neq j, \\ 0 \ otherwise. \end{cases}$$

3.

$$\forall x_i \in D_X, \forall c_j \in D_C, \pi_{max}(x_i|U_X, c_j) = \begin{cases} \pi_1(x_i|U_X) \ if \ \ j=1, \\ 1 \quad\quad\quad\quad otherwise. \end{cases}$$

4. $\forall x_i' \in D_{X'}, \forall x_j \in D_X, \forall c_k' \in D_{C'},$

$$\pi_{max}(x_i'|U_X, x_j, c_k') = \begin{cases} \pi_2(x_i|U_X) \ if \ i=j \ and \ k=1, \\ 1 \quad\quad\quad\quad if \ i=j \ and \ k=2, \\ 0 \quad\quad\quad\quad if \ i \neq j. \end{cases}$$

The interesting specification of the augmented network consists in preserving all information through the marginal possibility distributions of the initial network.

Proposition 2. *Given two possibilistic networks* $\mathbb{N}1$ *and* $\mathbb{N}2$ *associated with* π_1 *and* π_2 *respectively. let* Π_{max} *be the marginal possibility distribution associated with the fused possibilistic network* $\mathbb{N}_{max}$ *the result of merging* $\mathbb{N}1$ *and* $\mathbb{N}2$ *using the* maximum *operator. Then, we have:*

$$\forall \omega \in \Omega, \Pi_{max}(\omega) = max(\pi_1(\omega), \pi_2(\omega)). \tag{3}$$

Proof. Suppose that $\omega = a_1, ..., a_n$ and a_i is an instance of $A_i \in V$. Let $a_1', ..., a_n'$ be instances of renamed variables. Let c and c' instances of added variable in the augmented networks. The marginal possibility distribution associated with the fused network is computed as follows: $\Pi_{max}(a_1, ..., a_n) =$
$max_{a_1', ..., a_n', c, c'} \pi_{max}(a_1, ..., a_n, a_1', ..., a_n', c, c') =$
$max_{a_1', ..., a_n', c, c'} min(\pi_{max}(a_1|U_{A_1}, c), ..., \pi_{max}(a_n|U_{A_n}, c), \pi_{max}(a_1'|U_{A_1}, a_1, c'), ...,$
$\pi_{max}(a_n'|U_{A_n}, a_n, c'), \pi_{max}(c'|c))$ (1).
Using Definition 3. the term $\pi_{max}(c'|c) = 1$ if the instances of c and c' are opposite, otherwise $\pi_{max}(c'|c) = 0$. In this case, either $\pi_{max}(a_i|U_{A_i}, c) = \pi_1(a_1|U_{A_1})$ or $\pi_{max}(a_j'|U_{A_j}, a_j, c') = \pi_2(a_1|U_{A_1})$. Moreover, some terms are eliminated due to the third condition of equation 4. Hence, at the final step, we obtain :
$\Pi_{max}(a_1, ..., a_n) = max(\pi_1(a_1, ..., a_n), \pi_2(a_1, ..., a_n)).$
We remark that to compute the obtained expression (1), we apply the variable elimination algorithm (see [8]).

The next example illustrates Definition 3 and shows how to construct the merged network $\mathbb{N}_{max}$. It also illustrates the Proposition 2 showing that the global joint distribution is preserved.

Table 3. Initial possibility distributions

A	$\pi_1(A)$	$\pi_2(A)$	A B	$\pi_1(B \mid A)$	$\pi_2(B \mid A)$
a_1	1	1	$a_1\, b_1$	1	1
a_2	0.3	0.4	$a_1\, b_2$	0.2	0.6
			$a_2\, b_1$	0.5	0.1
			$a_2\, b_2$	1	1

Example 2. Let be two possibilistic networks N1 and N2. The DAGs associated to these networks have the same graphical structure and they are represented by the initial graph in Fig. 2(a). The conditional possibility distributions associated with N1 and N2 are defined by the Table 3. Now, we will apply the construction process of fusion network based on the maximum operator. For this purpose, we should follow the steps given in Definition 2. Then, at the graphical level, we obtain the DAG presented in Fig. 3. First, we rename each variable of G2. Indeed, A is replaced by A' and B is replaced by B'. Next, we add a link from A to A' and another one from B to B'. The third step consists to add new variables C and C'. Finally, we link the variable C and the variable C' belonging to each of graphs G1 and G2 respectively. At the semantic level, we apply the equations, formalized in the Definition 2, to compute the conditional possibility distributions associated with the fused network. These distributions are showed in Table 4.

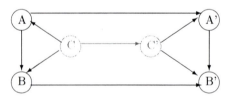

Fig. 3. The fused network

The conditional possibility distributions associated with the node B' are computed by applying the last equation given in Definition 3. For instance, we have: $\pi_{max}(b'_1|a'_2, b_2, c'_1) = 0$ and $\pi_{max}(b'_2|a'_2, b_2, c'_1) = \pi_2(b_2|a_2) = 0.1$.

Also, $\pi_{max}(b'_2|a'_2, b_2, c'_2) = 1$. Based on conditional possibility distributions π_{max} given in different tables, the equation 3 is well verified. For example, we have:
$\pi_1(a_2b_1) = \min(\pi_1(a_2), \pi_1(b_1|a_2)) = 0.3$ and $\pi_2(a_2b_1) = \min(\pi_2(a_2), \pi_2(b_1|a_2)) = 0.1$. On the other hand, we compute the marginal distribution associated with the merged network as follows : $\forall i, j,\ \Pi_{max}(a_2b_1) = max_{a', b', c, c'}\pi_{max}(a_2, b_1, a', b'c, c')$
$= max_{a', b'}(max(max(\pi_{max}(a_2, b_1, a', b', c_1, c'_1), \pi_{max}(a_2, b_1, a', b', c_1, c'_2)),$

Table 4. Conditional possibility distributions π_{max}

A C C'	$\pi_{max}(A\|C)$	$\pi_{max}(C'\|C)$	B A C	$\pi_{max}(B\|A,C)$	B A C	$\pi_{max}(B\|A,C)$
$a_1\ c_1\ c_1'$	1	0	$b_1\ a_1\ c_1$	1	$b_2\ a_1\ c_1$	0.2
$a_1\ c_2\ c_1'$	0	1	$b_1\ a_1\ c_2$	1	$b_2\ a_1\ c_2$	1
$a_2\ c_1\ c_2'$	0.3	1	$b_1\ a_2\ c_1$	0.5	$b_2\ a_2\ c_1$	1
$a_2\ c_2\ c_2'$	1	0	$b_1\ a_2\ c_2$	1	$b_2\ a_2\ c_2$	1

C	$\pi_{max}(C)$	A' A C'	$\pi_{max}(A'\|A,C')$	A' A C'	$\pi_{max}(A'\|A,C')$
c_1	1	$a_1'\ a_1\ c_1'$	1	$a_2'\ a_1\ c_1'$	0
c_1	1	$a_1'\ a_1\ c_2'$	1	$a_2'\ a_1\ c_2'$	0
		$a_1'\ a_2\ c_1'$	0	$a_2'\ a_2\ c_1'$	0.4
		$a_1'\ a_2\ c_2'$	0	$a_2'\ a_2\ c_2'$	1

$max(\pi_{max}(a_2, b_1, a', b', c_2, c_1'), \pi_{max}(a_2, b_1, a', b', c_2, c_2')))$ =
Applying the second equation in Definition 3, we obtain:
$max_{a',b'}(max(max(0, \pi_{max}(a_2, b_1, a', b', c_1, c_2'),$
$max(\pi_{max}(a_2, b_1, a', b', c_2, c_1'), 0))))$
$= max(max(max(max(0, \pi_{max}(a_2, b_1, a', b', c_1, c_2'),$
$max(\pi_{max}(a_2, b_1, a', b', c_2, c_1'), 0)))) = max(0, 0.3, 0.1, 0) = 0.3$.
Using Definition 3, we apply the third and the fourth equations and by developing this expression according to the variables a' and b', we can show that the result is checked. So, we have: $\Pi_{max}(a_2, b_1) = max(\pi_1(a_2 b_1), \pi_2(a_2 b_1))$.

The computations of the process of merging via the maximum operator is achieved in linear time. Moreover, inference algorithms applied on the merged network, requires adding new links in the step of moralization in the junction tree.

5 Conclusion

Information issued from different sources must be combined to reduce uncertainty and inconsistency. This paper has provided a new approach of data fusion in the framework of possibility theory. So, conflicting information is modeled by possibilistic networks and it is merged using the maximum operator in order to produce a consistent possibilistic network. The main feature of this mode of combination is that it takes into consideration all available information.

References

1. Bachmann, C., Abdulhai, B., Roorda, M., Moshiri, B.: A comparative assessment of multi-sensor data fusion techniques for freeway traffic speed estimation using microsimulation modeling. Transportation Research Part C: Emerging Technologies (2013)
2. Benferhat, S., Dubois, D., Kaci, S., Prade, H.: A principled analysis of merging operations in possibilistic logic. Uncertainty in Artificial Intelligence Proceedings (200)

3. Benferhat, S., Kaci, S.: Fusion of possibilistic knowledge bases from a postulate point of view. In: FLAIRS Conference (2002)
4. Benferhat, S., Titouna, F.: Aggregating quantitative possibilistic networks. In: Proceedings of the 9th International Florida Artificial Intelligence Research (Flairs 2006) (2006)
5. Benferhat, S., Titouna, F.: Fusion and normalization of quantitative networks. Applied Intelligence (2009)
6. Benferhat, S., Titouna, F.: On the fusion of probabilistic networks. In: Mehrotra, K.G., Mohan, C.K., Oh, J.C., Varshney, P.K., Ali, M. (eds.) IEA/AIE 2011, Part I. LNCS, vol. 6703, pp. 49–58. Springer, Heidelberg (2011)
7. De Cooman, G.: Possibility theory - parti: Measure and integral theoretics groundwork; partii: Conditional possibility; partiii: Possibilistic independence. International Journal of General Systems (1997)
8. Dechter, R.: Bucket elimination: A unifying framework for probabilistic inference algorithms. In: Uncertainty in Artificial Intelligence (UAI 1996) (1996)
9. Dubois, D., Prade, H.: Possibility theory: An approach to computerized processing of uncertainty. Plenium Press, New York (1988)
10. Dubois, D., Prade, H.: On the use of aggregation operations in information fusion processes. Fuzzy Sets and Systems (2004)
11. Fonck, P.: Conditional independence in possibility theory. Conditional independence in possibility theory (1994)
12. JoseDel, S., Moral, S.: Qualitative combination of bayesian networks. International Journal of Intelligent Systems (2003)
13. Konieczny, S., Perez, R.: On the logic of merging. In: Proceedings of the 6th International Conference on Principles of Knowledge Representation and Reasoning (KR 1998) (1998)
14. Matzkevich, I., Abramson, B.: The topological fusion of bayes nets. In: Proceedings of the 8th Conference on Uncertainty in Artificial Intelligence (UAI 1992), Stanford, CA, USA (1992)
15. Matzkevich, I., Abramson, B.: Some complexity considerations in the combination of belief networks. In: Proceedings of the 9th Conference on Uncertainty in Artificial Intelligence (UAI 1993), San Fransisco, CA (1993)
16. de Oude, P., Ottens, B., Pavlin, G.: Information fusion with distributed probablistic networks. Artificial Intelligence and Applications (2005)
17. Pearl, J.: Probabilistic reasoning in intelligent systems: Networks of plausible inference. Morgan Kaufmann, San Fransisco (1988)
18. Qi, G., Liu, W., Glass, D.: A split-combination method for merging inconsistent possibilistic knowledge bases. In: Proceedings of 9th International Conference on Principles of Knowledge Representation and Reasoning (KR 2004) (2004)
19. Zadeh, L.: Fuzzy sets as a basis for a theory of possibility. Fuzzy Sets ans Systems (1978)
20. Zhou, Y.: Intelligent processing research for target fusion recognition system based on multi-agents. In: International Conference on Computational Intelligence and Software Engineering (CiSE) (2010)

On the Estimation of Mass Functions Using Self Organizing Maps

Imen Hammami[1], Jean Dezert[2], Grégoire Mercier[1], and Atef Hamouda[3]

[1] Telecom Bretagne, Brest 29238, France
imen.hammammi@gmail.com, gregoire.mercier@telecom-bretagne.eu
[2] The French Aerospace Lab, F-91761 Palaiseau, France
jean.dezert@onera.fr
[3] Faculty of Sciences of Tunis, El Manar Tunis 2092, Tunisie
atef.hamouda@fst.rnu.tn

Abstract. In this paper, an innovative method for estimating mass functions using Kohonen's Self Organizing Map is proposed. Our approach allows a smart mass belief assignment, not only for simple hypotheses, but also for disjunctions and conjunctions of hypotheses. This new method is of interest for solving estimation mass functions problems where a large quantity of multi-variate data is available. Indeed, the use of Kohonen map that allows to approximate the feature space dimension into a projected 2D space (so called map) simplifies the process of assigning mass functions. Experimentation on a benchmark database shows that our approach gives similar or better results than other methods presented in the literature so far, with an ability to handle large amount of data.

Keywords: Evidence Theory, Belief assignment, Kohonen map, Estimation.

1 Introduction

When it comes to exploit the redundancy and the complementarity of information stemming from very varied sources to give a unique representative information, the belief function theory, introduced by Dempster [1] and formalized by Shafer [2], is considered as an appealing formalism in information fusion domain. Indeed, it offers a mathematical framework that allows the processing of both imprecise and uncertain information.

The initial theory was improved in different directions, for example through the work of Dezert-Smarandache [3], a paradoxical reasoning has been proposed. Despite, the fact that belief function theory performs well in extracting the most truthful proposition from a multisource context, it nevertheless presents a major difficulty that is the estimation of basic belief assignments.

If we take a look at the various works that deal with this problem of belief function estimation, we distinguish two main family approaches. Likelihood based approaches [2,4], require the knowledge, or the estimation, of the conditional probability density for each class. The second family is the distance-based

F. Cuzzolin (Ed.): BELIEF 2014, LNAI 8764, pp. 275–283, 2014.

approaches [5,6]. However, these two types of estimation present some limits: among them we can mention the need of the *a priori* knowledge on the hypotheses which is not always easy to know, especially, for compound hypotheses.

An original method is presented in this paper to estimate mass functions when a large quantity of multi-variate data is available. In the feature space (in $\mathbb{R}^p$), operations on Basic Belief Assignment (BBA) can be much more complex and may not be feasible due to computing time or accuracy consideration. The proposed method to overcome this limitation is based on Kohonen's Map that allows to approximate the feature space dimension into a projected 2D space (so called map). Then, the use of Kohonen's map simplifies the process of assigning mass functions on conjunctions and disjunctions of hypotheses when considering relative distance of an observation to the map. Thus, it can model at the same time ignorance, imprecision, paradox as result exploits all the conceptual contribution of the theory.

2   Evidence Theory

Dempster-Shafer Theory (DST) is used for representing belief on imperfect observation through the Basic Belief Assignment (BBA), defined on all the subsets of the frame of discernment Θ, noted 2^Θ. In our context, $m(\cdot)$ will have to be built from the observation provided by a sensor, that is from a sample $\boldsymbol{x} \in \mathbb{R}^p$. A BBA $m(\cdot)$ is the mapping from elements of the power set 2^Θ onto $[0,1]$ under constraints:

$$\begin{cases} m(\boldsymbol{x} \in \emptyset) = 0 \\ \sum_{A \subseteq 2^\Theta} m(\boldsymbol{x} \in A) = 1. \end{cases} \tag{1}$$

The frame of discernment Θ is the set of possible answers of the problem under concern. It is composed of exhaustive and exclusive hypotheses: $\Theta = \{\theta_1, \theta_2, \ldots, \theta_N\}$. From this frame of discernment, the power set noted 2^Θ can be built, including all the disjunctions of hypotheses θ_i such as $\theta_i \cup \theta_j$ or $\theta_i \cup \theta_j \cup \theta_k$... As discussed above, Dezert-Smarandache theory (DSmT) [3] is considered as amelioration of beliefs theory. The main idea of DSmT is to work on the hyper-powerset of the frame of discernment. The hyper-power set D^Θ is defined as the Dedekind's lattice built from Θ whith $\cap$ and $\cup$ operators. For decision making from mass function, the Generalized Pignistic Transformation [3] noted $BetP_g$ is frequently used:

$$BetP_g(\boldsymbol{x} \in A) = \sum_{B \in D^\Theta} \frac{C_M(B \cap A)}{C_M(B)} m(\boldsymbol{x} \in B), \quad \forall A \in D^\Theta \tag{2}$$

where C_M is the cardinality within DSmT. The decision is taken by the maximum of pignistic probability function $BetP(\cdot)$. Similarly, the Pignistic Transformation $BetP$ can be used within DST framework for decision making.

3   Overview on Kohonen's Map

There exist many versions of the Self Organizing Maps (SOM). However, the basic philosophy is very simple and already effective [7]. A SOM defines a mapping from the input space (say $\mathbb{R}^p$) onto a regular array of $M \times N$ nodes (see Fig. 1) [8].

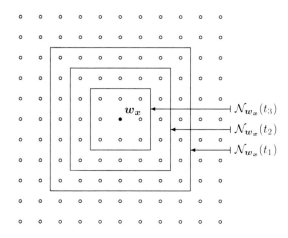

Fig. 1. A schematic view of a 11×11 Kohonen's Self Organizing Map. Several topological neighborhoods $\mathcal{N}_{\boldsymbol{w_x}}(t_i)$ of the winning neuron $\boldsymbol{w_x}$ are drawn. The size is decreasing with the number of iterations ($t_1 < t_2 < t_3$) during the training phase.

A reference vector, also called weighting vector, $\boldsymbol{w}(i,j) \in \mathbb{R}^p$ is associated to the node at each position (i,j) with $1 \leqslant i \leqslant N$ and $1 \leqslant j \leqslant M$. An input vector $\boldsymbol{x} \in \mathbb{R}^p$ is to be compared to each $\boldsymbol{w}(i,j)$. The best match is defined as output of the SOM: thus, the input data $\boldsymbol{x}$ is mapped onto the SOM at location $(i_{\boldsymbol{x}}, j_{\boldsymbol{x}})$ where $\boldsymbol{w}(i_{\boldsymbol{x}}, j_{\boldsymbol{x}})$ is the neuron the most similar to $\boldsymbol{x}$ according to a given metric. SOM performs a non linear projection of the probability density function $p(\boldsymbol{x})$ from the high-dimensional input data onto the two-dimensional array.

In practical applications, the Euclidean distance is usually used to compare $\boldsymbol{x}$ and $\boldsymbol{w}(i,j)$. The node that minimizes the distance between $\boldsymbol{x}$ and $\boldsymbol{w}(i,j)$ defines the best-matching node (or the so-called winning neuron), and is denoted by the subscript $\boldsymbol{w_x}$:

$$\|\boldsymbol{x} - \boldsymbol{w_x}\| = \min_{\substack{1 \leqslant i \leqslant M \\ 1 \leqslant j \leqslant N}} \|\boldsymbol{x} - \boldsymbol{w}(i,j)\|. \tag{3}$$

An optimal mapping would be the one that maps the probability density function $p(\boldsymbol{x})$ in the most faithful fashion, preserving at least the local structures of $p(\boldsymbol{x})$.

It can be considered also that the SOM achieves a non-uniform quantization that transforms $\boldsymbol{x}$ to $\boldsymbol{w_x}$ by minimizing the given metric. Nevertheless, thanks to the training phase (detailed below) the neurons $\boldsymbol{w}$ are located on the map according to their similarity. Then, when considering neurons $\boldsymbol{w}(i,j)$ located not *too far* from the winning neuron $\boldsymbol{w_x}$, the distance in $\mathbb{R}^p$ between $\boldsymbol{x}$ and $\boldsymbol{w}(i,j)$ is not dramatically different from the one between $\boldsymbol{x}$ and $\boldsymbol{w_x}$. That means that in the neighborhood of $\boldsymbol{w_x}$ on the map, are located the wining neurons of the neighbors (in $\mathbb{R}^p$) of $\boldsymbol{x}$. Hence, a class in $\mathbb{R}^p$ is projected into the map at the same area, remaining homogeneous. Moreover, whatever the initial shape of the class in the $\mathbb{R}^p$ feature space is, the projected class is highly likely to be of isotropic shape in the map.

4   Feature Space for Smart BBA

The proposed smart BBA intends to evaluate the mass of each class in 2^Θ or 2^D according to the topology of the observed manifold. Then, two sets of data may be handled (see Fig. 2): on the first hand the initial observations $\boldsymbol{x}$ and class centers $\{C_1, C_2, \ldots, C_K\}$ in $\mathbb{R}^p$ and, on the other hand the so-called *winning neurons* $\boldsymbol{w_x}$ and the projected class centers $\boldsymbol{w}_{C_k}$.

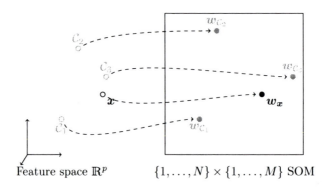

Fig. 2. Observations in the feature space and their projections into Kohonen's map. Note that the neurons $\boldsymbol{w_x}$ and $\boldsymbol{w}_{C_k}$ can be located on the map through their location index (n, m) or in $\mathbb{R}^p$ with their p component value.

Then, Kohonen's map can be used to build easily BBA and to balance between conjunction and disjunction when considering relative distance of an observation to the map. Moreover, the use of Kohonen's map simplifies the evaluation of the masses since operations on the maps require calculation on index only, while operations on the feature space (in $\mathbb{R}^p$) may be much more complex (when dealing with stochastic divergence for instance). So two kinds of distances will be considered and their related difference will induce uncertainty:

1. $d_{\mathbb{R}^p}(\cdot, \cdot)$ which is the distance in $\mathbb{R}^p$. It can be defined through the Euclidean norm $\mathcal{L}^2(\mathbb{R}^p)$ but also through a spectral point of view such as the spectral angle mapper or the spectral information divergence [9]. It may also be based on the Kullback-Leibler divergence or the mutual information when dealing with Synthetic Aperture Radar (SAR) [10].

2. $d_{\mathrm{map}}(\cdot,\cdot)$ which is the distance along Kohonen's map. It is mainly based on the Euclidean norm and uses the index that locates the 2 vectors on the map:
$d_{\mathrm{map}}(\boldsymbol{w_1},\boldsymbol{w_2}) = \sqrt{(n_1-n_2)^2 + (m_1-m_2)^2}$ if $\boldsymbol{w_1}$ (resp. $\boldsymbol{w_2}$) is located at position (n_1,m_1) (resp. (n_2,m_2)) on the map.

5   A New Method to Build BBA

This section details a strategy for building a BBA by using Kohonen's map and an initial classifier on $\mathbb{R}^p$.

Mass of simple hypotheses: The definition of masses of focal elements could be based on the distance on the feature space. Nevertheless, an appropriated definition should take into account the variance of the classes to weight each of them, as it is the case in a likelihood point of view. This weighting is already performed by the projection onto Kohonen's map so that, the mass of focal class is defined as:

$$\begin{cases} m(\boldsymbol{x} \in \theta_k) & \sim 1 \quad\ \text{if } \boldsymbol{w_x}{=}\boldsymbol{w}_{\mathcal{C}_k} \\ m(\boldsymbol{x} \in \theta_k) & \sim \dfrac{d_{\mathrm{map}}(\boldsymbol{w_x},\boldsymbol{w}_{\mathcal{C}_k})^{-1}}{\sum_{\ell=1}^{K} d_{\mathrm{map}}(\boldsymbol{w_x},\boldsymbol{w}_{\mathcal{C}_\ell})^{-1}} \quad \text{otherwise} \end{cases} \tag{4}$$

where $k = 1,2,\ldots,K$, $\boldsymbol{w}_{\mathcal{C}_k}$ is the projected class, $\boldsymbol{w_x}$ is the winning neurons.

According to eq. (4), we consider that the more the distance $d_{\mathrm{map}}(\boldsymbol{w_x},\boldsymbol{w}_{\mathcal{C}_k})$ (relatively to the other distances between $\boldsymbol{x}$ and $\mathcal{C}_\ell$ on the map) the less the mass $m(\boldsymbol{x} \in \theta_k)$.

Total ignorance case: From the feature space, we may consider that the mass evaluation of an observation falls into ignorance if its distance to the map is much more important that the distance of its related class center to the map. Then, it can be expressed as follows:

$$m(\boldsymbol{x} \in \Theta) \sim 1 - \min\left(\frac{d_{\mathbb{R}^p}(\boldsymbol{x},\boldsymbol{w_x})}{d_{\mathbb{R}^p}(\mathcal{C}_{\boldsymbol{x}},\boldsymbol{w}_{\mathcal{C}_{\boldsymbol{x}}})}, \frac{d_{\mathbb{R}^p}(\mathcal{C}_{\boldsymbol{x}},\boldsymbol{w}_{\mathcal{C}_{\boldsymbol{x}}})}{d_{\mathbb{R}^p}(\boldsymbol{x},\boldsymbol{w_x})} \right) \tag{5}$$

where $\mathcal{C}_{\boldsymbol{x}}$ is the class center of $\boldsymbol{x}$, $\boldsymbol{w}_{\mathcal{C}_{\boldsymbol{x}}}$ is its projection on the map.

Mass of the conjunction between two classes: The conjunction between two classes may be defined into the feature space as the space in-between the two classes. But, one has to account for the variance of each classes that increases the complexity of this measure. Once again, it is much more convenient to define the $\phi_k \cap \phi_\ell$ mass into Kohonen's map, as:

$$m(\boldsymbol{x} \in \theta_k \cap \theta_\ell) \sim e^{-\gamma(z-1)^2} \tag{6}$$

where $z = d_{\mathrm{map}}(\boldsymbol{w_x}, \frac{\boldsymbol{w}_{\mathcal{C}_k}+\boldsymbol{w}_{\mathcal{C}_\ell}}{2}), 0 < k,\ell \leqslant K, \ell \neq k$. By adopting eq. (6) we consider that the value of $m(\boldsymbol{x} \in \theta_k \cap \theta_\ell)$ becomes maximal when $\boldsymbol{x}$ reaches the middle of $[\boldsymbol{w}_{\mathcal{C}_k}, \boldsymbol{w}_{\mathcal{C}_\ell}]$ segment. Eq. (6) yields a value of $m(\boldsymbol{x} \in \phi_k \cap \phi_\ell)$ closed to 1 in the middle. Moreover, $m(\boldsymbol{x} \in \phi_k \cap \phi_\ell)$ vanishes when $\boldsymbol{x}$ is far away from the $[\boldsymbol{w}_{\mathcal{C}_\ell}, \boldsymbol{w}_{\mathcal{C}_k}]$ segment. The γ parameter tunes this vanishing behavior. For example, if we want eq. (6) be over $\frac{1}{2}$ between the 1st and the 3rd quartile of $[\boldsymbol{w}_{\mathcal{C}_k}, \boldsymbol{w}_{\mathcal{C}_\ell}]$ segment, then γ should be equal to $2\sqrt{2}$. For a smaller domain around the median of $[\boldsymbol{w}_{\mathcal{C}_k}, \boldsymbol{w}_{\mathcal{C}_\ell}]$ segment, γ should be greater.

Mass of disjunction between two classes: The ignorance in the decision making between two classes $\mathcal{C}_k$ and $\mathcal{C}_\ell$ may be considered to a dual of eq. (6), but here by considering distances in the feature space. When a sample $\boldsymbol{x}$ is not *too far* from class $\mathcal{C}_k$ or $\mathcal{C}_\ell$, it is not *too difficult* to decide if it has too be associated to the class k or ℓ. But if $\boldsymbol{x}$ is *far* from $\mathcal{C}_k$ and $\mathcal{C}_\ell$, it comes the disjunction. Then, disjunction mass may be related to:

$$m(\boldsymbol{x} \in \theta_k \cup \theta_\ell) \sim 1 - \tanh(\beta h) \qquad (7)$$

where $h = \frac{d_{\mathbb{R}^p}(\mathcal{C}_k, \mathcal{C}_\ell)}{d_{\mathbb{R}^p}(\boldsymbol{x}, \mathcal{C}_k) + d_{\mathbb{R}^p}(\boldsymbol{x}, \mathcal{C}_\ell)}, 0 < k, \ell \leqslant K, k \neq \ell$. Here, the β parameter stands for the level of ambiguity. When $\boldsymbol{x}$ is close, in $\mathbb{R}^p$, to the segment $[\mathcal{C}_k, \mathcal{C}_\ell]$, $d(\mathcal{C}_k, \mathcal{C}_\ell) \simeq d_{\mathbb{R}^p}(\boldsymbol{x}, \mathcal{C}_k) + d_{\mathbb{R}^p}(\boldsymbol{x}, \mathcal{C}_\ell)$ so that z is close to 1, and $m(\boldsymbol{x} \in \theta_k \cup \theta_\ell)$ has to vanish. The more the β, the less the ambiguous mass.

Conjunction and disjunction for more than 2 classes: This construction that takes into consideration the ratio of distance between 2 classes or the distance to the middle of 2 classes can be extended to more than 2 classes. For instance, eq. (6) can be based on the centroid of more than 2 class. Eq. (7) can be generalized by the composition of one against one class from a set of K classes, divided by the sum of distance of $\boldsymbol{x}$ to each of the K class centers. Nevertheless, this part has not been deeper investigated since those compositions should not have significative impact on the fusion or the classification results.

Final mass belief function: The complete BBA has to respect eq. (1) constraint so that is it necessary to apply a normalization step to the unnormalized BBA obtained by separately calculates the belief masses on simple and compound hypotheses.

6   Experiments on Benchmark Dataset

In order to highlight some advantages and possible drawbacks of the proposed SOM-based BBA, the performance of the SOM-based BBA is compared to EV-CLUS [11] and ECM [6] ones by using dataset provided by the University of California - Irvine (UCI) Machine Learning Repository[1]. Seven numerical data sets out of 270 have been taken into consideration with various amounts of features (that correspond to the feature space dimension $\mathbb{R}^p$) and number of classes (from 2 to 7) as detailed in Table 1.

---

[1] The dataset is available at http://archive.ics.uci.edu/ml

Kohonen's map has been trained with the following parameters: a size of 20×20 neurons, trained with 200 iterations. An initial neighborhood size $\mathcal{N}_{\boldsymbol{w}}(t_0)$ of 10 neurons and a learning rate $\alpha(t_0)$ of 0.9. It appears that the SOM-based BBA yields most of the time the highest classifications results (put in boldface in the results of Table 2). In each row of Table 2, the first line corresponds to the number of correctly classified samples, the second line corresponds to the proportion of samples correctly classified, and the last line shows the computation time. It is worth noting that when ECM performs better, the SOM-based approach is close to the best accuracy (73.52 % versus 74.11 % for the benefit of ECM with the Wine database, and 69.24 % versus 69.62 % with the Statlog Landsat satellite images database). Equivalent results prove that SOM-based BBA is just a simplified (*i.e.* quantized) version of the feature space ECM work with. Better results are due to the fact that distances on the map (in 2D) are more appropriated for complex (or non isotropic) class (in pD). EVCLUS is always below. It seems that the performance ranking between ECM and SOM-based BBA is not depending on the feature space dimension nor the number of classes since the Wine and Statlog Landsat satellite image data bases are very different to each other. Since the SOM-based approach considers a projected feature space of dimension 2, it may induce on those cases a too coarse approximation of the manifold in comparison to ECM. Nevertheless, it is worth noting that the benefit in using a SOM-based approach for BBA is related to the number of samples to be handled. Fig. 3 shows that the more the number of sample the fastest the SOM-based approach in comparison to the ECM while yielding the same level of accuracy. Then the SOM-based approach appears to be a valuable alternative to handle large data set such as real images for classification purpose. In fact, distance in $\mathbb{R}^p$ is more computational demanding than in $\mathbb{R}^2$. Indeed, the form of the class in the SOM is more isotropic, so that no consideration on the shape of the manifold is to be considered. On the contrary, ECM has to care of the standard deviation of the classes to build the mass distribution.

Table 1. Characteristics of the UCI datasets used for comparison

Dataset	Features	classes	samples
Banknote authentication	4	2	1372
Pima Indians Diabetes	8	2	768
Seeds	7	3	210
Wine	13	3	170
Statlog (Landsat Satellite)	36	6	6435
Statlog (Image Segmentation)	19	7	2130
Synthetic control chart time series	60	6	600

Table 2. Classification results of EVCLUS, ECM with decision by *BetP* and SOM-based BBA with decision by *BetP$_g$*

Dataset	Banknote authentication	Pima Indians Diabetes	Seeds	Wine	Statlog (Landsat Satellite)	Statlog (Image Segmentation)	Synthetic control chart time series
EVCLUS	843	475	157	103	3027	895	384
	61.44 %	61.84 %	74.76 %	60.58 %	47.03 %	42.01 %	64.0 %
	1172.2sec	181.7sec	34.3sec	6.7 sec	5857 sec	3657 sec	370 sec
ECM	848	506	189	126	4480	1282	453
	61.80 %	65.88 %	90.0 %	**74.11 %**	**69.62 %**	55.49 %	72.5 %
	3.4sec	3.2sec	0.3sec	0.9sec	480sec	161sec	6.9sec
SOM-based	1090	549	191	125	4456	1431	501
	79.44 %	**71.48 %**	**90.95 %**	73.52 %	69.24 %	**67.18 %**	**83.5 %**
	8.6sec	6.7sec	5.8sec	5.9sec	163sec	84sec	8.0sec

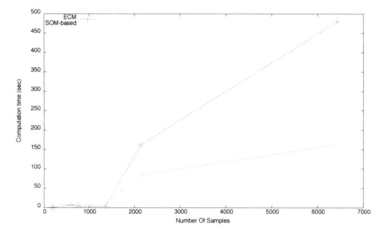

Fig. 3. Computation time depending on the feature space dimension

7   Conclusion

In this article, a new method for mass function construction through Kohonen's map has been proposed. Our method performs the assignment of belief masses on simple, conjunctive and disjunctive hypotheses. So, unlike the other approaches, it exploits all the conceptual contribution of the theory thanks to its ability to deal with uncertain and paradoxical data through the proposed BBA. Experiments on a set of benchmark database showed that our approach yields better accuracy as stated by the confusion matrices. Moreover, the overall SOM-based BBA algorithm is much less demanding in term of computation so that it is possible to handle large data set.

References

1. Dempster, A.P.: Upper and Lower Probabilities Induced by a Multivalued Mapping. Annals of Mathematical Statistics 38, 325–339 (1967)
2. Shafer, G.: A Mathematical Theory of Evidence. Princeton University Press, NJ (1976)
3. Smarandache, F., Dezert, J.: Advances and Applications of DSmT for Information Fusion (Collected works), vol. 1, 2 & 3. American Research Press, Rehoboth (2004-2009), http://www.gallup.unm.edu/~smarandache/DSmT.htm
4. Smets, P.: Belief functions: The Disjunctive Rule of Combination and the Generalized Bayesian Theorem. In: Yager, R.R., Liu, L. (eds.) Classic Works of the Dempster-Shafer Theory of Belief Functions. STUDFUZZ, vol. 219, pp. 633–664. Springer, Heidelberg (2008)
5. Zouhal, L.M., Denœux, T.: An Evidence-Theoretic K-NN Rule with Parameter Optimization. IEEE Transactions on Systems, Man, and Cybernetics, Part C 28(2), 263–271 (1998)
6. Masson, M.H., Denœux, T.: ECM: An Evidential Version of the Fuzzy C-means Algorithm. Pattern Recogn. 41(4), 1384–1397 (2008)
7. Kohonen, T.: The Self-Organizing Map. Proceedings of the IEEE 78(9), 1464–1480 (1990)
8. Kraaijveld, M.A., Mao, J., Jain, A.K.: A Nonlinear Projection Method Based on Kohonen's Topology Preserving Maps. IEEE Trans. Neural Networks 6(3), 548–559 (1995)
9. Chang, C.: An Information Theoretic-based Measure for Spectral Similarity and Discriminability. IEEE Trans. on Information Theory 46(5), 1927–1932 (2000)
10. Inglada, J., Mercier, G.: A New Statistical Similarity Measure for Change Detection in Multitemporal SAR Images and its Extension to Multiscale Change Analysis. IEEE Trans. on Geosci. Remote Sensing 45(5), 1432–1446 (2007)
11. Denœux, T., Masson, M.H.: EVCLUS: EVidential CLUSstering of Proximity Data. IEEE Trans. on Systems, Man, and Cybernetics, Part B 34(1), 95–109 (2004)

Second-Order Belief Hidden Markov Models

Jungyeul Park[1], Mouna Chebbah[1,2], Siwar Jendoubi[1,2], and Arnaud Martin[1]

[1] UMR 6074 IRISA, Université de Rennes1, Lannion, France
[2] LARODEC Laboratory, University of Tunis, ISG Tunis, Tunisia
{jungyeul.park,mouna.chebbah,arnaud.martin}@univ-rennes1.fr,
jendoubi.siwar@etudiant.univ-rennes1.fr

Abstract. Hidden Markov Models (HMMs) are learning methods for pattern recognition. The probabilistic HMMs have been one of the most used techniques based on the Bayesian model. First-order probabilistic HMMs were adapted to the theory of belief functions such that Bayesian probabilities were replaced with mass functions. In this paper, we present a second-order Hidden Markov Model using belief functions. Previous works in belief HMMs have been focused on the first-order HMMs. We extend them to the second-order model.

Keywords: Belief functions, Dempster-Shafer theory, first-order belief HMM, second-order belief HMM, probabilistic HMM.

1   Introduction

A Hidden Markov Model (HMM) is one of the most important statistical models in machine learning [15]. A HMM is a classifier or labeler that can assign label or class to each unit in a sequence [10]. It has been successfully utilized over several decades in many applications for processing text and speech such as Part-of-Speech (POS) tagging [11], named entity recognition [29] and speech recognition [7]. However, such works in the early part of the period are mainly based on first-order HMMs. As a matter of fact, the assumption in the first-order HMM, where the state transition and output observation depend only on one previous state, does not exactly match with the real applications [13]. Therefore, they require a number of sophistications. For example, even though the first-order HMM for POS tagging in early 1990s performs reasonably well, it captures a more limited amount of the contextual information than is available [27]. As consequence, most modern statistical POS taggers use a second-order model [3].

Uncertainty theories can be integrated in statistical models such as HMMs: The probability theory has been used to classify units in a sequence with the Bayesian model. Then, the theory of belief functions is employed to this statistical model because the fusion proposed in this theory simplifies computations of *a posteriori* distributions of hidden data in Markov models. This theory can provide rules to combine evidences from different sources to reach a certain level of belief [21,28,24,4,23]. Belief HMMs introduced in [6,12,14,16,25,19,2,8,18], use

F. Cuzzolin (Ed.): BELIEF 2014, LNAI 8764, pp. 284–293, 2014.

combination rules proposed in the framework of the theory of belief functions. This paper is an extension of previous ideas for second-order belief HMMs. For the current work, we focus on explaining a second-order model. However, the proposed method can be easily extended to higher-order models.

This paper is organized as follows: In Sections 2 and 3, we detail probabilistic HMMs for the problem of POS tagging where HMMs have been widely used. Then, we describe the first-order belief HMM in Section 4. Finally, before concluding, we propose the second-order belief HMM.

2   First-Order Probabilistic HMMs

POS tagging is a task of finding the most probable estimated sequence of n tags given the observation sequence of v words. According to [15], a first-order probabilistic HMM can be characterized as follows:

N The number of states in a model $S_t = \{s_1^t, s_2^t, \cdots s_N^t\}$.

M The number of distinct observation symbols.
      $V = \{v_1, v_2, \cdots, v_M\}$.

$A = \{a_{ij}\}$ The set of N transition probability distributions.

$B = \{b_j(o_t)\}$ The observation probability distributions in state j.

$\pi = \{\pi_i\}$ The initial probability distribution.

Figure 1 illustrates the first-order probabilistic HMM allowing to estimate the probability of the sequence s_i^{t-1} and s_j^t where a_{ij} is the transition probability from s_i^{t-1} to s_j^t and $b_j(o_t)$ is the observation probability on the state s_j^t. Regarding POS tagging, the number of possible POS tags that are hidden states S_t of the HMM is N. The number of words in the lexicons V is M. The transition probability a_{ij} is the probability that the model moves from one tag s_i^{t-1} to another tag s_j^t. This probability can be estimated using a training data set in supervised learning for the HMM. The probability of a current POS tag appearing in the first-order HMM depends only on the previous tag. In general, first-order probabilistic HMMs should be characterized by three fundamental problems as follows [15]:

- Likelihood: Given a set of transition probability distributions A, an observation sequence $O = o_1, o_2, \cdots, o_T$ and its observation probability distribution B, how do we determine the likelihood $P(O|A, B)$? The first-order model relies on only one observation where $b_j(o_t) = P(o_j|s_j^t)$ and the transition probability based on one previous tag where $a_{ij} = P(s_j^t|s_i^{t-1})$. Using the forward path probability, the likelihood $\alpha_t(j)$ of a given state s_j^t can be computed by using the likelihood $\alpha_{t-1}(i)$ of the previous state s_i^{t-1} as described below:

$$\alpha_t(j) = \sum_i \alpha_{t-1}(i) a_{ij} b_j(o_t) \tag{1}$$

Fig. 1. First-order probabilistic and belief HMMs

- Decoding: Given a set of transition probability distributions A, an observation sequence $O = o_1, o_2, \cdots, o_T$ and its observation probability distribution B, how do we discover the best hidden state sequence? The Viterbi algorithm is widely used for calculating the most likely tag sequence for the decoding problem. The Viterbi algorithm can calculate the most probable path $\delta_t(j)$ which contains the sequence of $\psi_t(j)$. It can select the path that maximizes the likelihood of the sequence as described below:

$$\begin{aligned} \delta_t(j) &= \max \delta_{t-1}(i)a_{ij}b_j(o_t) \\ \psi_t(j) &= \operatorname{argmax} \psi_{t-1}(i)a_{ij} \end{aligned} \tag{2}$$

- Learning: Given an observation sequence $O = o_1, o_2, \cdots, o_T$ and a set of states $S = \{s_1^t, s_2^t, \cdots, s_N^t\}$, how do we learn the HMM parameters for A and B? The parameter learning task usually uses the Baum-Welch algorithm which is a special case of the Expectation-Maximization (EM) algorithm.

In this paper, we focus on the likelihood and decoding problems by assuming a supervised learning paradigm where labeled training data are already available.

3   Second-Order Probabilistic HMMs

Now, we explain the extension of the first-order model to a *trigram*[1] in the second-order model. Figure 2 illustrates the second-order probabilistic HMM allowing to estimate the probability of the sequence of three states s_i^{t-2}, s_j^{t-1} and s_k^t where a_{ijk} is the transition probability from s_i^{t-2} and s_j^{t-1} to s_k^t, and $b_k(o_t)$ is the observation probability on the state s_k^t. Therefore, the second-order probabilistic HMM is characterized by three fundamental problems as follows:

- Likelihood: The second-order model relies on one observation $b_k(o_t)$. Unlike the first-order model, the transition probability is based on two previous tags where $a_{ijk} = P(s_k^t | s_i^{t-2}, s_j^{t-1})$ as described below:

$$\alpha_t(k) = \sum_j \alpha_{t-1}(j)a_{ijk}b_k(o_t) \tag{3}$$

However, it will be more difficult to find a sequence of three tags than a sequence of two tags. Any particular sequence of tags s_i^{t-2}, s_j^{t-1}, s_k^t that occurs

---

[1] The trigram is the sequence of three elements, *i.e.* three states in our case.

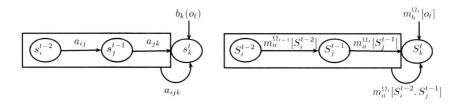

Fig. 2. Second-order probabilistic and belief HMMs

in the test set may simply never have occurred in the training set because of data sparsity [10]. Therefore, a method for estimating $P(s_k^t | s_i^{t-2}, s_j^{t-1})$, even if the sequence s_i^{t-2}, s_j^{t-1}, s_k^t never occurs, is required. The simplest method to solve this problem is to combine the trigram $\hat{P}(s_k^t | s_i^{t-2}, s_j^{t-1})$, the bigram $\hat{P}(s_k^t | s_j^{t-1})$, and even the unigram $\hat{P}(s_k^t)$ probabilities [3]:

$$P(s_k^t | s_i^{t-2}, s_j^{t-1}) = \lambda_1 \hat{P}(s_k^t | s_i^{t-2}, s_j^{t-1}) + \lambda_2 \hat{P}(s_k^t | s_j^{t-1}) + \lambda_3 \hat{P}(s_k^t) \quad (4)$$

Note that $\hat{P}$ is the maximum likelihood probabilities which are derived from the relative frequencies of the sequence of tags. Values of λ are such that $\lambda_1 + \lambda_2 + \lambda_3 = 1$ and they can be estimated by the *deleted interpolation* algorithm [3]. Otherwise, [27] describes a different method for values of λ as below:

$$\begin{aligned}
\lambda_1 &= k_3 \\
\lambda_2 &= (1 - k_3) \cdot k_2 \\
\lambda_3 &= (1 - k_3) \cdot (1 - k_2)
\end{aligned} \quad (5)$$

where $\quad k_2 = \frac{log(C(s_j^{t-1}, s_k^t) + 1) + 1}{log(C(s_j^{t-1}, s_k^t) + 1) + 2}, \quad k_3 = \frac{log(C(s_i^{t-2}, s_j^{t-1}, s_k^t) + 1) + 1}{log(C(s_i^{t-2}, s_j^{t-1}, s_k^t) + 1) + 2}, \quad$ and $C(s_i^{t-2}, s_j^{t-1}, s_k^t)$ is the frequency of a sequence $s_i^{t-2}, s_j^{t-1}, s_k^t$ in the training data. Note that $\lambda_1 + \lambda_2 + \lambda_3$ is not always equal to one in [27]. The likelihood of the observation probability for the second-order model uses B where $b_k(o_t) = P(o_k | s_k^t, s_j^{t-1})$.

– Decoding: For second-order model we require a different Viterbi algorithm. For a given state s at the time t, it would be redefined as follows [27]:

$$\begin{aligned}
\delta_t(k) &= \max \delta_{t-1}(j) a_{ijk} b_k(o_t) \\
&\text{where } \delta_t(j) = \max P(s^1, s^2, \cdots, s^{t-1} = s_i, s^t = s_j, o_1, o_2, \cdots, o_t) \\
\psi_t(k) &= \operatorname{argmax} \psi_{t-1}(j) a_{ijk} \\
&\text{where } \psi_t(k) = \operatorname{argmax} P(s^1, s^2, \cdots, s^{t-1} = s_i, s^t = s_j, o_1, o_2, \cdots, o_t)
\end{aligned} \quad (6)$$

– Learning: The problem of learning would be similar to the first-order model except that parameters A and B are different.

With respect to performance measures, different transition probability distributions in [3] and [27] obtain 97.0% and 97.09% tagging accuracy for known words, respectively for the same data (the Penn Treebank corpus). Even though probabilistic HMMs perform reasonably well, belief HMMs can learn better under certain conditions on observations [8].

4   First-Order Belief HMMs

In probabilistic HMMs, A and B are probabilities estimated from the training data. However, A and B in belief HMMs are mass functions (bbas) [16,8]. According to previous works on belief HMMs, a first-order HMM using belief functions can be characterized as follows[2]:

N	The number of states in a model $\Omega_t = \{S_1^t, S_2^t, \cdots, S_N^t\}$.
M	The number of distinct observation symbols V.
$A = \{m_a^{\Omega_t}[S_i^{t-1}](S_j^t)\}$	The set of conditional bbas to all possible subsets of states.
$B = \{m_b^{\Omega_t}[o_t](S_j^t)\}$	The set of bbas according to all possible observations O_t.
$\pi = \{m_\pi^{\Omega_1}(S_i^{\Omega_1})\}$	The bba defined for the the initial state.

Difference between the first-order probabilistic and belief HMMs is presented in Figure 1, the transition and observation probabilities in belief HMMs are described as mass functions. Therefore, we can replace a_{ij} by $m_a^{\Omega_t}[S_i^{t-1}](S_j^t)$ and $b_j(o_t)$ by $m_b^{\Omega_t}[o_t](S_j^t)$. The set Ω_t has been used to denote states for HMMs using belief functions [16,8]. Note that s_i^t is the single state for probabilistic HMMs and S_i^t is the multi-valued state for belief HMMs. First-order belief HMMs should also be characterized by three fundamental problems as follows:

– Likelihood: The likelihood problem in belief HMMs is not solved by *likelihood*, but by using the combination. The first-order belief model relies on (i) only one observation $m_b^{\Omega_t}[o_t](S_j^t)$ and (ii) a transition conditional mass function based on one previous tag $m_a^{\Omega_t}[S_i^{t-1}](S_j^t)$. Mass functions of sets A and B are combined using the Disjunctive Rule of Combination (DRC) for the forward propagation and the Generalized Bayesian Theorem (GBT) for the backward propagation [22]. Using the forward path propagation, the mass function of a given state S_j^t can be computed as the combination of mass functions on the observation and the transition as described below:

$$q_\alpha^{\Omega_t}(S_j^t) = \sum m_\alpha^{\Omega_{t-1}}(S_i^{t-1}) \cdot q_a^{\Omega_t}[S_i^{t-1}](S_j^t) \cdot q_b^{\Omega_t}(S_j^t) \tag{7}$$

Note that the mass function of the given state S_j^t is derived from the commonality function $q_\alpha^{\Omega_t}$.

– Decoding: Several solutions have been proposed to extend the Viterbi algorithm to the theory of belief functions [16,20,17]. Such solutions maximize the plausibility of the state sequence. In fact, the *credal* Viterbi algorithm

---

[2] In the model Ω_t, S^t are focal elements.

starts from the first observation and estimates the commonality distribution of each observation until reaching the last state. For each state S_j^t, the estimated commonality distribution $(q_\delta^{\Omega_t}(S_j^t))$ is converted back to a mass function that is conditioned on the previous state. Then, we apply the *pignistic* transform to make a decision about the current state $(\psi_t(s_j^t))$:

$$
\begin{aligned}
q_\delta^{\Omega_t}(S_j^t) &= \sum_{S_i^{t-1} \subseteq A^{t-1}} m_\delta^{\Omega_{t-1}}(S_i^{t-1}) \cdot q_a^{\Omega_t}[S_i^{t-1}](S_j^t) \cdot q_b^{\Omega_t}(S_j^t) \\
\psi_t(s_j^t) &= \text{argmax}_{S_i^{t-1} \in \Omega_{t-1}} (1 - m_\delta^{\Omega_t}[S_i^{t-1}](\emptyset)) \cdot P_t[S_i^{t-1}](S_j^t)
\end{aligned}
\tag{8}
$$

where $A^t = \cup_{S_j^{t-1} \in \Omega_t} \psi_t(S_j^t)$ [16].

- Learning: Instead of the traditional EM algorithm, we can use the E^2M algorithm for the belief HMM [18].

To build belief functions from what we learned using probabilities in the previous section, we can employ the least commitment principle by using the inverse pignistic transform [26,1].

5   Second-Order Belief HMMs

Like the first-order belief HMM, N, M, B and π are similarly defined in the second-order HMM. The set A is quite different and is defined as follows:

$$
A = \{m_a^{\Omega_t}[S_i^{t-2}, S_j^{t-1}](S_k^t)\}
\tag{9}
$$

where A is the set of conditional bbas to all possible subsets of states based on the two previous states. Second-order belief HMMs should also be characterized by three fundamental problems as follows:

- Likelihood: The second-order belief model relies on one observation $m_b^{\Omega_t}[o_t](S_k^t)$ in a state S_k at time t and the transition conditional mass function based on two previous states S_i^{t-2} and S_j^{t-1}, defined by $m_a^{\Omega_t}[S_i^{t-2}, S_j^{t-1}](S_k^t)$. Using the forward path propagation, the mass function of a given state S_k^t can be computed as the disjunctive combination (DRC) of mass functions on the transition $m_a^{\Omega_t}[S_i^{t-2}, S_j^{t-1}](S_k^t)$ and the observation $m_b^{\Omega_t}(S_k^t)$ as described below:

$$
q_\alpha^{\Omega_t}(S_k^t) = \sum m_\alpha^{\Omega_{t-1}}(S_j^{t-1}) \cdot q_a^{\Omega_t}[S_i^{t-2}, S_j^{t-1}](S_k^t) \cdot q_b^{\Omega_t}(S_k^t)
\tag{10}
$$

where $q_a^{\Omega_t}[S_i^{t-2}, S_j^{t-1}](S_k^t)$ is the commonality function derived from the conjunctive combination of mass functions of two previous transitions. The conjunctive combination is used to have the conjunction of observations on previous two states S_i^{t-2} and S_j^{t-1}. The combined mass function $m_a^{\Omega_t}[S_i^{t-2}, S_j^{t-1}](S_k^t)$ of two transitions $m_a^{\Omega_{t-1}}[S_i^{t-2}](S_j^{t-1})$ and $m_a^{\Omega_t}[S_j^{t-1}](S_k^t)$ is defined as follows:

$$
m_a^{\Omega_t}[S_i^{t-2}, S_j^{t-1}](S_k^t) = m_a^{\Omega_{t-1}}[S_i^{t-2}](S_j^{t-1}) \; \textcircled{\tiny{$\bigcirc$}} \; m_a^{\Omega_t}[S_j^{t-1}](S_k^t)
\tag{11}
$$

The conjunctive combination is required to obtain the conjunction of both transitions. Note that the mass function of the given state S_k^t is derived from the commonality function $q_\alpha^{\Omega_t}$. We use DRC with commonality functions like in [16]. Note that the observation only on one previous state is taken into account in the first-order belief HMM, but the conjunction of observations on two previous states is considered in the second-order belief HMM.

- Decoding: We accept our assumption of the first-order belief HMM for the second-order model. Similarly to the first-order belief HMM, we propose a solution that maximizes the plausibility of the state sequence. The credal Viterbi algorithm estimates the commonality distribution of each observation from the first observation till the final state. For each state S_k^t, the estimated commonality distribution $(q_\delta^{\Omega_t}(S_k^t))$ is converted back to a mass function that is conditioned on a mass function of the two previous states. This mass function is the conjunctive combination of mass functions of the two previous states. Then, we apply the pignistic transform to make a decision about the current state $(\psi_t(s_j^t))$ as before:

$$
\begin{aligned}
q_\delta^{\Omega_t}(S_k^t) &= \textstyle\sum_{S_j^{t-1} \subseteq A^{t-1}} m_\delta^{\Omega_{t-1}}(S_j^{t-1}) \cdot q_a^{\Omega_t}[S_i^{t-2}, S_j^{t-1}](S_k^t) \cdot q_b^{\Omega_t}(S_k^t) \\
\psi_t(s_k^t) &= \mathrm{argmax}_{S_j^{t-1} \in \Omega_{t-1}} \, (1 - m_\delta^{\Omega_t}[S_j^{t-1}](\emptyset)) \cdot P_t[S_i^{t-2}, S_j^{t-1}](S_k^t)
\end{aligned}
\tag{12}
$$

- Learning: Like the first-order belief model, we can still use the E^2M algorithm for the belief HMM [18].

Since the combination of mass functions in the belief HMM is required where the previous observation is already considered in the set of conditional bbas $m_a^{\Omega_t}[S_i^{t-2}, S_j^{t-1}]$, we do not need to refine the observation probability for the second-order model as in the second-order probabilistic model.

6   Conclusion and Future Perspectives

The problem of POS tagging has been considered as one of the most important tasks for natural language processing systems. We described such a problem based on HMMs and tried to apply our idea to the theory of belief functions. We extended previous works on belief HMMs to the second-order model. Using the proposed method, we will be able to easily extend the higher-order model for belief HMMs. Some technical aspects still remain to be considered. Robust implementation for belief HMMs are required where in general we can find over one million observations in the training data to deal with the problem of POS tagging. As described before, the choice of inverse pignistic transforms would be empirically verified.[3] We are planning to implement these technical aspects in near future.

---

[3] For example, [5] used the inverse pignistic transform in [26] to calculate belief functions from Bayesian probability functions. As matter of fact, the problem of POS tagging can be normalized and inverse pignistic transforms in [26] did not propose the case for $m(\emptyset)$.

The current work is described to rely on a supervised learning paradigm from labeled training data. Actually, the forward-backward algorithm in HMMs can do completely unsupervised learning. However, it is well known that EM performs poorly in unsupervised induction of linguistic structure because it tends to assign relatively equal numbers of tokens to each hidden state [9].[4] Therefore, the initial conditions can be very important. Since the theory of belief functions can take into consideration of uncertainty and imprecision, especially for the lack of data, we might obtain a better model using belief functions on an unsupervised learning paradigm.

References

1. Aregui, A., Denœux, T.: Constructing consonant belief functions from sample data using confidence sets of pignistic probabilities. International Journal of Approximate Reasoning 49(3), 575–594 (2008)
2. Boudaren, M.E.Y., Monfrini, E., Pieczynski, W., Aïssani, A.: Dempster–Shafer fusion of multisensor signals in nonstationary Markovian context. EURASIP Journal on Advances in Signal Processing 134, 1–13 (2012)
3. Brants, T.: TnT – A Statistical Part-of-Speech Tagger. In: Proceedings of the Sixth Conference on Applied Natural Language Processing, pp. 224–231. Association for Computational Linguistics, Seattle (2000),
   http://www.aclweb.org/anthology/A00-1031
4. Dubois, D., Prade, H.: Representation and combination of uncertainty with belief functions and possibility measures. Computational Intelligence 4(3), 244–264 (1988), http://onlinelibrary.wiley.com/doi/10.1111/
   j.1467-8640.1988.tb00279.x/abstract
5. Fayad, F., Cherfaoui, V.: Object-Level Fusion and Confidence Management in a Multi-Sensor Pedestrian Tracking System. Lecture Notes in Electrical Engineering 35, 15–31 (2009)
6. Fouque, L., Appriou, A., Pieczynski, W.: An evidential Markovian model for data fusion and unsupervised image classification. In: Proceedings of the Third International Conference on Information Fusion, FUSION 2000, Paris, France, July 10-13, vol. 1, pp. 25–32 (2000)
7. Huang, X.D., Ariki, Y., Jack, M.A.: Hidden Markov Models for Speech Recognition. Edinburgh University Press (1990)
8. Jendoubi, S., Yaghlane, B.B., Martin, A.: Belief Hidden Markov Model for Speech Recognition. In: Proceedings of the International Conference on Modeling, Simulation and Applied Optimization (ICMSAO 2013), Hammamet, Tunisia, April 28-30 (2013)
9. Johnson, M.: Why Doesn't EM Find Good HMM POS-Taggers? In: Proceedings of the 2007 Joint Conference on Empirical Methods in Natural Language Processing and Computational Natural Language Learning (EMNLP-CoNLL), pp. 296–305 (2007), http://www.aclweb.org/anthology/D/D07/D07-1031
10. Jurafsky, D., Martin, J.H.: Speech and Language Processing, 2nd edn. Prentice Hall (2008)

---

[4] The actual distribution of POS tags would be highly skewed as in heavy-tail distributions.

11. Kupiec, J.: Robust part-of-speech tagging using a hidden Markov model. Computer Speech and Language 6(3), 225–242 (1992)
12. Lanchantin, P., Pieczynski, W.: Unsupervised restoration of hidden nonstationary Markov chain using evidential priors. IEEE Transactions on Signal Processing - Part II 53(8), 3091–3098 (2005)
13. Lee, L.M., Lee, J.C.: A Study on High-Order Hidden Markov Models and Applications to Speech Recognition. In: Ali, M., Dapoigny, R. (eds.) IEA/AIE 2006. LNCS (LNAI), vol. 4031, pp. 682–690. Springer, Heidelberg (2006)
14. Pieczynski, W.: Multisensor triplet Markov chains and theory of evidence. International Journal of Approximate Reasoning 45(1), 1–16 (2007)
15. Rabiner, L.R.: A Tutorial on Hidden Markov Models and Selected Applications in Speech Recognition. Proceedings of the IEEE 77(2), 257–286 (1989)
16. Ramasso, E.: Reconnaissance de séquences d'états par le Modèle des Croyances Transférables. Application à l'analyse de vidéos d'athlétisme. Ph.D. thesis, Universit Joseph-Fourier - Grenoble I (2007)
17. Ramasso, E.: Contribution of belief functions to hidden Markov models with an application to fault diagnosis. In: Proceedings of 2011 IEEE Conference on Prognostics and Health Management (PHM), Grenoble, France, September 1-4, pp. 1–6 (2011)
18. Ramasso, E., Denœux, T.: Making Use of Partial Knowledge About Hidden States in HMMs: An Approach Based on Belief Functions. IEEE Transactions on Fuzzy Systems 22(2), 395–405 (2014)
19. Ramasso, E., Denœux, T., Zerhouni, N.: Partially-Hidden Markov Models. In: Proceedings of the 2nd International Conference on Belief Functions, Compiègne, France, May 9-11 (2012)
20. Serir, L., Ramasso, E., Zerhouni, N.: Time-Sliced Temporal Evidential Networks: The case of Evidential HMM with application to dynamical system analysis. In: Proceedings of 2011 IEEE Conference on Prognostics and Health Management (PHM), Montreal, Canada, June 20-23, pp. 1–10 (2011)
21. Shafer, G.: A Mathematical Theory of Evidence. Princeton University Press (1976)
22. Smets, P.: Belief functions: The disjunctive rule of combination and the generalized Bayesian theorem. International Journal of Approximate Reasoning 9(1), 1–35 (1993), http://www.sciencedirect.com/science/article/pii/0888613X9390005X
23. Smets, P.: Analyzing the combination of conflicting belief functions. Information Fusion 8(4), 387–412 (2007), http://www.sciencedirect.com/science/article/pii/S1566253506000467
24. Smets, P., Kennes, R.: The Transferable Belief Model. Artificial Intelligence 66, 191–234 (1994)
25. Soubaras, H.: On Evidential Markov Chains. In: Bouchon-Meunier, B., Magdalena, L., Ojeda-Aciego, M., Verdegay, J.-L., Yager, R.R. (eds.) Foundations of Reasoning under Uncertainty. STUDFUZZ, vol. 249, pp. 247–264. Springer, Heidelberg (2010), http://dx.doi.org/10.1007/978-3-642-10728-3_13
26. Sudano, J.J.: Inverse Pignistic Probability Transforms. In: Proceedings of the Fifth International Conference on Information Fusion, Annapolis, MD, USA, July 8-11, vol. 2, pp. 763–768 (2002)

27. Thede, S.M., Harper, M.P.: A Second-Order Hidden Markov Model for Part-of-Speech Tagging. In: Proceedings of the 37th Annual Meeting of the Association for Computational Linguistics, pp. 175–182. Association for Computational Linguistics, College Park (1999), http://www.aclweb.org/anthology/P99-1023
28. Yager, R.R.: On the Dempster-Shafer Framework and New Combination rules. Information Sciences 41(2), 93–137 (1987)
29. Zhou, G., Su, J.: Named Entity Recognition using an HMM-based Chunk Tagger. In: Proceedings of 40th Annual Meeting of the Association for Computational Linguistics, pp. 473–480. Association for Computational Linguistics, Philadelphia (2002), http://www.aclweb.org/anthology/P02-1060

Learning Parameters in Directed Evidential Networks with Conditional Belief Functions

Narjes Ben Hariz and Boutheina Ben Yaghlane

LARODEC Laboratory - Institut Supérieur de Gestion de Tunis, Tunisia
narjes.benhariz@gmail.com,
boutheina.yaghlane@ihec.rnu.tn

Abstract. Directed evidential networks with conditional belief functions are one of the most commonly used graphical models for analyzing complex systems and handling different types of uncertainty. A crucial step to benefit from the reasoning process in these models is to quantify them. So, we address, in this paper, the issue of estimating parameters in evidential networks from evidential databases, by applying the maximum likelihood estimation generalized to the evidence theory framework.

Keywords: Belief Functions, Parameters Estimation, Evidential models, Evidential DataBases.

1   Introduction

Evidential graphical models have gained, in recent years, an expanding interest as a powerful tool for modeling and analyzing complex systems and reasoning under different types of uncertainty based on the belief functions theory.

One of the most commonly applied models in the evidential framework are the Directed EVidential Networks with conditional belief functions (DEVNs) [3]. On one hand, these models generalize the evidential networks with conditional belief functions [18] by handling n-ary relations between variables, on the other hand, unlike probabilistic models such as Bayesian networks [10], they are able to handle different levels of uncertainty in data.

A DEVN is based on two parts: the graphical part that consists on a directed acyclic graph with a set of nodes and a set of edges and the numeric parameters represented by conditional belief functions. Another point of interest of these networks is their flexibility in representing beliefs. In fact, conditional beliefs in these models can be expressed according to two different manners: for each node in the context of its parents (per child node) or for each dependency relation between a parent node an a child node (per edge).

The majority of works concerning DEVNs address inference algorithms and reasoning in these networks [3,2,8]. Nevertheless, an essential step before being able to reason with evidential networks is to quantify them. The data needed in the quantification process are generally derived from expert opinions or from data stored in databases.

F. Cuzzolin (Ed.): BELIEF 2014, LNAI 8764, pp. 294–303, 2014.

Thus, we address in this paper the problem of learning parameters in DEVNs from uncertain data stored in Evidential DataBases (EDB) [1], and this, by applying the maximum likelihood principle, one of the most statistical methods generally used in learning BNs [6,7,12].

The paper is organized as follow: In Section 2, we remaind briefly the most important background notions regarding the belief functions theory. The evidential data bases are recalled in Section 3. We recall the basic concepts related to the directed evidential networks with conditional belief functions in section 4. Section 5 concerns the maximum likelihood and its use in learning BNs. In Section 6, we present the main purpose of the paper which is the algorithm of learning parameters in DEVNs with its two variants, per child node and per edge. In the last Section, we explain the proposed approach through an illustrative example.

2   Belief Functions Theory: Basic Concepts

The belief functions theory, also known as evidence theory or Dempster-Shafer theory is a general and flexible framework for handling and modeling different types of uncertainty [13]. In the following, we remind some basic concepts of this theory, more details can be found in [13,15].

Let Ω be a finite set of exclusive and exhaustive elements called the frame of discernment and 2^{Ω} its power set.

The portion of belief supporting exactly a proposition A is called the basic belief assignment (bba), which is a function from 2^{Ω} to $[0,1]$ such that:

$$\sum_{A \subseteq \Omega} m^{\Omega}(A) = 1 \tag{1}$$

Any subset $A \in \Omega$ with $m^{\Omega}(A) > 0$ is called a focal element, and the set of all these elements is denoted by $F(m^{\Omega})$.

With each mass function m^{Ω} is associated a belief (bel^{Ω}) and plausibility (pl^{Ω}) functions from 2^{Ω} to $[0,1]$, which give the minimum and maximum amount of support attributed to A, respectively. These functions are defined as follows:

$$bel^{\Omega}(A) = \sum_{\emptyset \neq B \subseteq A} m^{\Omega}(B) \tag{2}$$

$$pl^{\Omega}(A) = \sum_{\emptyset \neq B \cap A} m^{\Omega}(B) \tag{3}$$

Let $m^{\Omega}[B](A)$ denote the conditional basic belief assignment of A given B, it is defined by Dempster's rule of conditioning as:

$$m^{\Omega}[B](A) = \sum_{C \subseteq \overline{B}} m^{\Omega}(A \cap C), \tag{4}$$

where $\bar{B}$ is the complement of the proposition B. More details about the rules of conditioning in the belief functions theory can be found in [14,16].

3   Evidential DataBases

An Evidential DataBase (EDB) or a Dempster-Shafer (DS) database is a database storing certain or/and uncertain data modeled using the belief functions framework [1].

In an EDB with L lines and C columns (attributes), each attribute $c \in [1, C]$ has a frame of discernment Ω_c including its possible values.

Let V_{lc} be the value of cell in the lth line and c^{th} column, V_{lc} is an evidential value defined by a mass function m_{lc} from 2^{Ω_c} to $[0, 1]$ such as:

$$m_{lc}(\emptyset) = 0 \; and \; \sum_{A \subseteq \Omega_c} m_{lc}(A) = 1 \qquad (5)$$

Data in an EDB, can take different levels of imperfection:

- Certain data: when the focal element is a singleton with a mass equal to one.
- Probabilistic data: when all focal elements are singletons.
- Possibilistic data: when focal elements are nested.
- Missing data: when the total amount of evidence is affected to one focal element which is the frame of discernment.
- Evidential data: including any other type of information.

4   Directed Evidential Networks with Conditional Belief Functions

Directed EVidential Networks with conditional belief functions (DEVNs) are proposed in [3] to generalize the evidential networks with conditional belief functions (ENCs) [18] that generalize Bayesian Networks (BNs) [10] for handling different types of uncertainty using evidence theory framework.

As it is derived from ENCs and BNs, a DEVN is based on two principal parts:

The qualitative level which is modeled by a Directed Acyclic Graph (DAG) $G = (N, E)$, where $N = \{N_1, ..., N_x\}$ is the set of nodes (variables), and $E = \{E_1, ..., E_y\}$ is the set of edges coding the different conditional dependencies between variables.

The quantitative level which is represented by a set of parameters θ modeled by conditional belief functions. Each node in the DEVN is associated with an a priori mass function. If it is a root node, adding to this function, the node is associated with a conditional mass function defined per edge or per child node.

Each node N_i in a DEVN is a representation of a random variable taking its values on a frame of discernment Ω_{N_i}. Let $PA(N_i)$ and $CH(N_i)$ denote the set of its parent nodes and the set of its child nodes, respectively. Like in BNs, each root node in a DEVN is associated with an a priori bbm, but unlike in BNs, child nodes in DEVNs are associated with both an a priori mass function and a conditional one.

Conditional belief functions in DEVNs can be defined in two manners:

- **Per child node**, as in BNs: for each child node N_c is associated a conditional belief function given all its parent nodes $PA(N_c)$. This conditional mass is denoted by $m^{\Omega_{N_c}}[PA(N_c)](N_c)$.
- **Per edge**, as in ENCs: the conditional relation between a child node N_c and a parent node $N_p \in PA(N_c)$, represented by an edge, is weighted with a conditional mass function $m^{\Omega_{N_c}}[N_p](N_c)$.

These to ways of modeling conditional beliefs makes DEVNs more flexible than BNs and ENCs and make the quantification of the network easier to an expert.

5   Maximum Likelihood and Learning in BNs

The issue of parameter estimation from data sets remains an important subject in statistics and knowledge management problems. One of the well known statistic methods for estimating parameters of a statistical model is the Maximum Likelihood (ML) principle [11]. This method is the center of the majority of approaches of learning parameters in probabilistic models from databases containing both complete and missing data.

When all variables are observed perfectly, the simplest and most used method for estimating probabilities in BNs is the ML which measure the probability of an event by its frequency of occurrence in the database. The estimated probability to a random variable[1] X_i conditionally to its parent nodes $PA(X_i)$ is calculated as follows:

$$P(X_i = x_k | PA(X_i) = x_j) = \frac{N_{i,j,k}}{\sum_k N_{i,j,k}}, \tag{6}$$

where $N_{i,j,k}$ is the number of events for which X_i takes the value x_k and its parents takes the configuration of values x_j. More details concerning the statistical learning in BNs can be found in [6,7,12].

Many other learning approaches are developed to estimate parameters from databases containing missing data, one of the most popular is the Expectation Maximization (EM) algorithm [4] which is based mainly on the ML estimation.

The likelihood principle and the EM algorithm were generalized, under the belief functions framework, to the Credal EM [17] and the Evidential EM [5] in order to handle the imprecision and the uncertainty in data.

The main idea of the extension of the likelihood notion to the evidence framework is to take the classical likelihood, defined originally in the probability framework, weighted by the mass function associated to each variable [5].

Thus, we apply, in the rest of the paper, the maximum likelihood principle and its generalization in the evidence theory, to develop a new algorithm for estimating the a priori mass function and the conditional beliefs in a directed evidential network from data bases storing different types of data: complete, missing, certain and/or uncertain.

---

[1] Each random variable corresponds to a node in the Bayesian network.

6   Learning Parameters in DEVNs

We present in this part, the main purpose of the paper which is learning parameters in directed evidential networks with conditional belief functions from an evidential database by applying the maximum likelihood estimation principle.

As mentioned previously, in a DEVN, each node is associated with an a priori *bba* and each child node is quantified by a conditional belief function modeled according to two different approaches: per child node, when the mass function of each child node is calculated given all its parent nodes, or per edge, when the relation between a child node and a parent node is evaluated by a conditional belief.

Let us consider a DEVN with a set of nodes N and a set of edges E and an EDB with L lines and C columns such that each column corresponds to a random variable (node) in the DEVN.

Building on the generalization idea of the likelihood principle in the evidence theory and analogically to the ML in the probability framework expressed by equation (6), the a priori mass function of a node $N_i \in N$ can be calculated as follows:

$$m^{\Omega_{N_i}}(N_i = A_k) = \frac{\sum_{l=1}^{|L|} m_{lc}^{\Omega_{N_i}}(N_i = A_k)}{\sum_{l=1}^{|L|} m_{lc}^{\Omega_{N_i}}(N_i)}, \tag{7}$$

where A_k is a proposition from $2^{\Omega_{N_i}}$, c denotes the column corresponding to the node N_i and $m_{lc}^{\Omega_{N_i}}$ is the mass function defining the cell in the lth line and c^{th} column.

Similarly, we define in equation (8) the conditional mass function of a node N_i given its parent nodes $PA(N_i) = \{pa_1(N_i), ..., pa_z(N_i)\}$:

$$m^{\Omega_{N_i}}[PA(N_i) = x](N_i = A_k) = \frac{\sum_{l=1}^{|L|} m_{lc}^{\Omega_{N_i}}(N_i = A_k) * \prod_j m_{lcj}^{\Omega_{pa_j}}(pa_j(N_i) = x_j)}{\sum_{l=1}^{|L|} \prod_j m_{lcj}^{\Omega_{pa_j}}(pa_j(N_i) = x_j)}, \tag{8}$$

where x is a configuration of values in which each parent node takes a possible proposition from its frame of discernment.

These equations are the core of the learning parameters algorithms in directed evidential networks.

6.1   Learning Algorithm Per Child Node

The process of estimating parameters per child node in a DEVN is based on two main steps: the estimation of an a priori mass function for each node and the estimation of the conditional mass function of each child node given all its parent nodes. This process is detailed formally by Algorithm 1.

Note that this algorithm can be used for learning parameters in Bayesian networks from probabilistic data.

Algorithm 1. Learning parameters per child node

Require: $DAG = (N, E), Data$
Ensure: $DEVN = (N, E, \theta_p, \theta_c)$

for each node $N_i \in N$ **do**
   1. Calculate the a priori mass function $m^{\Omega_{N_i}}(N_i)$
   $c \leftarrow SelectColumn(Ni, C)$

   for each proposition A_k in $2^{\Omega_{N_i}}$ **do**
     $m^{\Omega_{N_i}}(A_k) \leftarrow Result\_of\_equation(7)$
   end for
   $N_i.\theta_p \leftarrow m^{\Omega_{N_i}}(A)$
   2. Calculate the conditional mass function $m^{\Omega_{N_i}}[PA](N_i)$

   if N_i is a child node **then**
     $cPA = SelectColumns(PA, C)$

     for each proposition A_k in $2^{\Omega_{N_i}}$ **do**

       for each possible configuration $conf_j$ **do**
         $m^{\Omega_{N_i}}[PA = conf_j](A_k) \leftarrow Result\_of\_equation(8)$
       end for
     end for
     $N_i.\theta_c \leftarrow m^{\Omega_{N_i}}[PA](A)$
   else
     $N_i.\theta_c \leftarrow \emptyset$
   end if
end for

6.2 Learning Algorithm Per Edge

The approach of learning parameters per edge, described in Algorithm 2, aims to quantify each dependency relation between a parent node and a child node by a conditional mass function. The step of estimation the a priori mass function for each node is similar to the first step in Algorithm 1.

Note that this algorithm can be also used for learning parameters in evidential networks with conditional belief functions from any type of data.

7 Illustrative Example

In order to explain the learning algorithm detailed previously, we present in the following an illustrative example focusing on a part from "ASIA" network[2] and a part from a corresponding evidential database modeled in figure 1.

---

[2] The Bayesian network of the classical problem Asia Chest Clinic first described in [9]

Algorithm 2. Learning parameters per edge

Require: $DAG = (N, E), Data$
Ensure: $DEVN = (N, E, \theta_p, \theta_c)$

  for each node $N_i \in N$ **do**
    1. Calculate the a priori mass function $m^{\Omega_{N_i}}(N_i)$
    2. Calculate the conditional mass function $m^{\Omega_{N_i}}[pa(Ni)](N_i)$

    if N_i is not a root node **then**
      $PA \leftarrow Parents(N_i)$

      for each proposition A_j in $2^{\Omega_{N_i}}$ **do**

        for each parent node $pa \in PA$ **do**
          $c \leftarrow SelectColumn(pa, C)$
          $m^{\Omega_{N_i}}[pa = x_q](A_j) \leftarrow Result\_of\_equation(8)$
          $N_i.pa.\theta_c \leftarrow m^{\Omega_{N_i}}[pa](A)$
        end for
      end for
    else
      $N_i.\theta_c \leftarrow \emptyset$
    end if
  end for

All variables in "ASIA" network are binary, we consider in this example, as shown in figure 1, four variables $\{A, T, O, L\}$ having the power sets, respectively: $\{a, \bar{a}, a \cup \bar{a}\}$; $\{t, \bar{t}, t \cup \bar{t}\}$; $\{o, \bar{o}, o \cup \bar{o}\}$ and $\{l, \bar{l}, l \cup \bar{l}\}$.

Data used in this example are composed from 20 instances and contain different levels of imperfection: uncertain attributes, certain attributes and imprecise attributes.

The different results of applying the learning process to the selected part of "ASIA" network are shown in figure 2. For each root node (A and L) is associated an a priori mass function. The node T is quantified by an a priori mass function $m^{\Omega_T}(T)$ and a conditional belief knowing its parent node $m^{\Omega_T}[A](T)$. Note that in the case of a node having one parent (such as T), the result of learning parameters per child node or per edge is the same. For the node O is associated an a priori mass function $m^{\Omega_O}(O)$, a conditional mass function given all its parent nodes $m^{\Omega_O}[T, L](O)$ and a conditional mass function given one parent node $m^{\Omega_O}[T](O)$ and $m^{\Omega_O}[L](O)$.

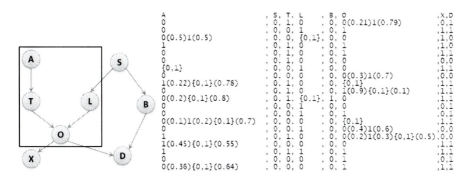

Fig. 1. The graphical structure and the EDB of the network for the Asia Chest Clinic problem

In the following we present some examples of calculation details in order to further clarify equations (7) and (8):

- $m^{\Omega_A}(A = a) = \dfrac{\sum_1^{20} m_{lc}^{\Omega_A}(A=a)}{\sum_1^{20}(m_{lc}^{\Omega_A}(A=a)+m_{lc}^{\Omega_A}(A=\bar{a})+m_{lc}^{\Omega_A}(A=a\cup\bar{a}))} = \dfrac{0+0+0.5+...+1}{1+1+0.5+0.5+...+1} = 0.2185$

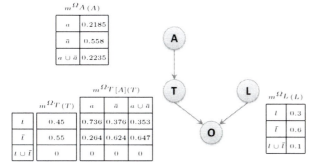

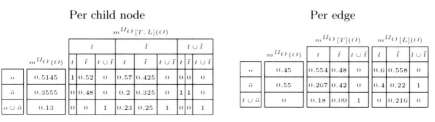

Fig. 2. The result of applying the learning parameters algorithms on a part of ASIA network

- $m^{\Omega_T}[A = a](T = \bar{t}) = \dfrac{\sum_1^{20} m_{lc}^{\Omega_T}(T=\bar{t})*m_{lc}^{\Omega_A}(A=a)}{\sum_1^{20} m_{lc}^{\Omega_A}(A=a)} = \dfrac{1*0.5+1*0.2+1*0.45}{0.5+1+0.22+0.2+0.45+1+1} =$

  0.264

- $m^{\Omega_O}[T = \bar{t}, L = l](O = o) = \dfrac{\sum_1^{20} m_{lc}^{\Omega_O}(O=o)*m_{lc}^{\Omega_T}(T=\bar{t})*m_{lc}^{\Omega_L}(L=l)}{\sum_1^{20} m_{lc}^{\Omega_T}(T=\bar{t})*m_{lc}^{\Omega_L}(L=l)} =$

  $\dfrac{1*1+1*1+1*1+1*0.6}{1*1+1*1+1*1+1*1} = 0.52$

Note that if we use probabilistic data (as in node T), then these equations give the same result as equation (6) which explains the fact that applying our first algorithm (for the case per child node) to learn the parameters of the DEVNs from a complete database gives the same results as the algorithm based in the maximum likelihood for learning parameters in Bayesian networks.

It is important to mention that if a configuration value of a parent node does not exist in the database, then the total amount of belief will be assigned to the total ignorance. For instance the proposition $\{t \cup \bar{t}\}$ does not appear in the database (the value $\{0, 1\}$ in T column), this makes $m^{\Omega_O}[T = t \cup \bar{t}, L = l](O = o \cup \bar{o})$ equal to $m^{\Omega_O}[T = t \cup \bar{t}, L = \bar{l}](O = o \cup \bar{o})$ equal to $m^{\Omega_O}[T = t \cup \bar{t}, L = l \cup \bar{l}](O = o \cup \bar{o})$ equal to 1. This can be a simple solution for the problem of zero counts in the data.

8   Conclusion

We have proposed, in this paper, new algorithms for learning parameters in directed evidential networks with conditional belief functions by applying the generalization of the maximum likelihood estimation in the evidence theory for handling uncertainty in data, stored in evidential databases.

As a future work, we intend to study the complexity of the proposed algorithm by applying it to complex systems and big databases. Another center of interest will be to improve the equation used in the proposed algorithms to deal with some problems such as zero counts and overfitting.

References

1. Bach Tobji, M.A., Ben Yaghlane, B., Mellouli, K.: A new algorithm for mining frequent itemsets from evidential databases. In: Proceeding of Information Processing and Management of Uncertainty (IPMU 2008), Malaga, Spain, pp. 1535–1542 (2008)
2. Ben Yaghlane, B., Mellouli, K.: Updating directed belief networks. In: Hunter, A., Parsons, S. (eds.) ECSQARU 1999. LNCS (LNAI), vol. 1638, pp. 43–54. Springer, Heidelberg (1999)
3. Ben Yaghlane, B., Mellouli, K.: Inference in Directed Evidential Networks Based on the Transferable Belief Model. IJAR 48(2), 399–418 (2008)
4. Dempster, A.P., Laird, N.M., Rubin, D.B.: Maximum Likelihood from incomplete data via the EM algorithm. Journal of the Royal Statistical Society, SERIES B 39, 1–38 (1977)
5. Denœux, T.: Maximum Likelihood Estimation from Uncertain Data in the Belief Function Framework. Knowledge and Data Engineering 25, 119–113 (2013)

6. Jordan, M.: Learning in Graphical Models. Kluwer Academic Publisher (1998)
7. Krause, P.J.: Learning probabilistic networks. The Knowledge Engineering Review 13(4), 321–351 (1998)
8. Laâmari, W., Ben Yaghlane, B.: Reasoning in Singly-Connected Directed Evidential Networks with Conditional Beliefs. In: Likas, A., Blekas, K., Kalles, D. (eds.) SETN 2014. LNCS, vol. 8445, pp. 221–236. Springer, Heidelberg (2014)
9. Lauritzen, S.L., Spiegelhalter, D.J.: Local computation with probabilities and graphical structures and their application to expert systems. J. Royal Statistical Society B 50, 157–224 (1988)
10. Murphy, K.: Probabilistic Graphical Models. Michael Jordan (2002)
11. Myung, I.J.: Tutorial on maximum likelihood estimation. Journal of Mathematical Psycology 47, 90–100 (2003)
12. Naim, P., Wuillemin, P.H., Leray, P., Pourret, O., Becker, A.: Réseaux Bayésiens. Eyrolles (2004)
13. Shafer, G.: A Mathematical Theory of Evidence. Princeton Univ. Press, Princeton (1976)
14. Smets, P.: Jeffrey's rule of conditioning generalized to belief functions. In: Proceedings of the Ninth international conference on Uncertainty in artificial intelligence (UAI 1993), Washington, DC, USA, pp. 500–505 (1993)
15. Smets, P., Kennes, R.: The transferable belief model. Artificial. Intelligence 66, 191–234 (1994)
16. Tang, Y., Zheng, J.: Dempster Conditioning and Conditional Independence in Evidence Theory. In: Zhang, S., Jarvis, R.A. (eds.) AI 2005. LNCS (LNAI), vol. 3809, pp. 822–825. Springer, Heidelberg (2005)
17. Vannoorenberghe, P., Smets, P.: Partially supervised learning by a credal **EM** approach. In: Godo, L. (ed.) ECSQARU 2005. LNCS (LNAI), vol. 3571, pp. 956–967. Springer, Heidelberg (2005)
18. Xu, H., Smets, P.: Evidential Reasoning with Conditional Belief Functions. In: Heckerman, D., et al. (eds.) Proceedings of Uncertainty in Artificial Intelligence (UAI 1994), Seattle, Washington, USA, pp. 598–606 (1994)

Econometric Forecasting Using Linear Regression and Belief Functions

Orakanya Kanjanatarakul[1], Philai Lertpongpiroon[1], Sombat Singkharat[1], and Songsak Sriboonchitta[2]

[1] Department of Economics, Faculty of Management Sciences, Chiang Mai Rajabhat University, Thailand
orakanyaa@gmail.com
[2] Faculty of Economics, Chiang Mai University, Thailand

Abstract. We describe a method for quantifying the uncertainty in statistical forecasts using belief functions. This method consists in two steps. In the estimation step, uncertainty on the model parameters is described by a consonant belief function defined from the relative likelihood function. In the prediction step, parameter uncertainty is propagated through an equation linking the quantity of interest to the parameter and an auxiliary variable with known distribution. This method allows us to compute a predictive belief function that is an alternative to both prediction intervals and Bayesian posterior predictive distributions. In this paper, the feasibility of this approach is demonstrated using a model used extensively in econometrics: linear regression with first order autoregressive errors. Results with macroeconomic data are presented.

Keywords: Dempster-Shafer theory, evidence theory, prediction, statistical inference.

1 Introduction

Forecasting can be defined as the task that consists in making statements about events that have not yet been observed. Such a task is of the utmost importance in many areas, in particular in economics. This is the reason why a vast literature has been devoted to this subject (see, e.g., [11]). Typically, there is a distinction between judgmental forecasting that relies on expert opinions, and statistical forecasting, which is based on past data and statistical models. In practice, both sources of knowledge (expert opinions and data) are often used jointly to achieve more reliable forecasts.

Usually, statements about future events cannot be made with full confidence. It is thus very important to quantify the uncertainty of such statements. In statistical forecasting, this is usually achieved using either prediction intervals or Bayesian posterior predictive distributions. Prediction intervals at level α are intervals that would contain the quantity of interest $100\alpha\%$ of the time if they were repeatedly computed for an infinite number of data sets drawn from the same distribution as the one that is postulated to have generated the observed

F. Cuzzolin (Ed.): BELIEF 2014, LNAI 8764, pp. 304–312, 2014.
© Springer International Publishing Switzerland 2014

data. However, their use to quantify the uncertainty pertaining to predictions based on a single dataset can be questioned (see, e.g., a thorough discussion in [7] on this issue). Also, it is not clear how prediction intervals can be combined with uncertain information from other sources such as expert opinions, and their use in a decision making context with utilities is also problematic. Bayesian posterior distributions do not have these limitations, but they require the specification of a prior probability distribution on the parameters, which poses some theoretical and practical difficulties when prior knowledge of parameter values is actually weak or even inexistent.

The Dempster-Shafer theory of belief functions is now a well established formal framework for modeling uncertainty. Recently, applications to statistical inference have gained revived interest [4,5,10]. The belief function approach does not have the same limitation as Bayesian inference as it does not require to specify a prior probability distribution. Both approaches coincide, though, when a probabilistic prior is available. Recently, a statistical forecasting method based on a parametric model and belief functions has been introduced [10]. This method is based on two steps: estimation and prediction. In the estimation step, a consonant belief function is built from the likelihood function, as initially proposed by Shafer [12] and recently justified in Ref. [5]. In the prediction step, the uncertainty on the parameter value is propagated through an equation linking the quantity of interest to the parameter and auxiliary variables with known distribution. The result is a predictive belief function quantifying the uncertainty on the prediction.

In [10], the above approach was applied to a very specific model in the field of marketing econometrics. In this paper, we further develop the approach and apply it to econometric forecasting using a widely used model: multiple regression with serial correlation. The rest of this paper is organized as follows. The inference and general forecasting method will first be recalled in Section 2. The approach will then be particularized to the linear regression model in Section 3. Finally, Section 4 will conclude the paper.

2   Inference and Prediction Using Belief Functions

Basic knowledge of the theory of belief functions will be assumed throughout this paper. A complete exposition in the finite case can be found in Shafer's book [12]. The reader is referred to [2] for a quick introduction on those aspects of this theory needed for statistical inference. In this section, the definition of a belief function from the likelihood function and the general forecasting method introduced in [10] will be recalled in Sections 2.1 and 2.2, respectively.

2.1   Inference

Let $Z \in \mathbb{Z}$ denote the observable data, $\theta \in \Theta$ the parameter of interest and $f_\theta(z)$ the probability mass or density function describing the data-generating mechanism. Statistical inference has been addressed in the belief function framework by many authors, starting from Dempster's seminal work [3]. In [12], Shafer proposed, on intuitive grounds, a more direct approach in which a belief function Bel_z^Θ on Θ is built from the likelihood function. This approach was applied to statistical tests for auditing in [14,8]. It was further elaborated by Wasserman [15] and discussed by Aickin [1], among others. It was recently justified by Denœux in [5], from three basic principles: the likelihood principle, compatibility with Bayesian inference and the least commitment principle [13]. The least committed belief function verifying the first two principles, according to the commonality ordering [6] is the consonant belief function Bel_z^Θ, the contour function of which is the relative likelihood function

$$pl_z(\theta) = \frac{L_z(\theta)}{\sup_{\theta' \in \Theta} L_z(\theta')}. \tag{1}$$

This belief function is called the likelihood-based belief function on Θ induced by z. The corresponding plausibility function can be computed from pl_z as

$$Pl_z^\Theta(A) = \sup_{\theta \in A} pl_z(\theta), \tag{2}$$

for all $A \subseteq \Theta$. The focal sets of Bel_z^Θ are the levels sets of $pl_z(\theta)$ defined as

$$\Gamma_z(\omega) = \{\theta \in \Theta | pl_z(\theta) \geq \omega\}, \tag{3}$$

for $\omega \in [0, 1]$. These sets may be called plausibility regions and can be interpreted as sets of parameter values whose plausibility is greater than some threshold ω. The belief function Bel_z^Θ is equivalent to the random set induced by the Lebesgue measure λ on $[0, 1]$ and the multi-valued mapping Γ_z from $[0, 1]$ to 2^Θ. In particular, the following equalities hold:

$$Bel_z^\Theta(A) = \lambda(\{\omega \in [0, 1] | \Gamma_z(\omega) \subseteq A\}) \tag{4a}$$

$$Pl_z^\Theta(A) = \lambda(\{\omega \in [0, 1] | \Gamma_z(\omega) \cap A \neq \emptyset\}), \tag{4b}$$

for all $A \subseteq \Theta$ such that the above expressions are well-defined.

2.2 Forecasting

The forecasting problem can be defined as follows: given some knowledge about θ obtained by observing past data z (represented here by a belief function), we wish to make statements about some random new data $W \in \mathbb{W}$ whose conditional distribution $g_{z,\theta}(w)$ given $Z = z$ depends on θ. For instance, in a time series forecasting problem, $z = (y_1, \ldots, y_T)$ may denote the observed data until time T and $w = (y_{T+1}, \ldots, y_{T+h})$ the future data to be forecasted.

A solution to the forecasting problem can be found using the sampling model used by Dempster [3] for inference. In this model, the new data W is expressed as a function of the parameter θ and an unobserved auxiliary variable ξ taking values in Ξ with known probability distribution μ independent of θ:

$$W = \varphi(\theta, \xi), \tag{5}$$

where φ is defined in such a way that the distribution of W for fixed θ is $g_{z,\theta}(w)$. When W is a real random variable, a canonical model of the form (5) can be obtained as $W = G_{z,\theta}^{-1}(\xi)$, where $G_{z,\theta}$ is the conditional cumulative distribution function (cdf) of W given $Z = z$, $G_{z,\theta}^{-1}$ is its generalized inverse and ξ has a continuous uniform distribution in $[0, 1]$.

The belief function Bel_z^{Θ} on Θ, the probability measure μ and relation (5) between W, θ and ξ joinly define a belief function on W. This belief function is induced by a random set defined as follows. Let Γ_z' be the multi-valued mapping from $[0, 1] \times \Xi$ to 2^W that maps each pair (ω, ξ) to the set of values $\varphi(\theta, \xi)$ such that $\theta \in \Gamma_z(\omega)$; formally,

$$\begin{aligned} \Gamma_z' : [0, 1] \times \Xi &\to \quad 2^W \\ (\omega, \xi) &\to \varphi(\Gamma_z(\omega), \xi). \end{aligned} \tag{6}$$

As the distribution of ξ does not depend on θ, ξ and the underlying random variable ω associated with Bel_z^{Θ} are independent. We thus have a random set defined by the product measure $\lambda \otimes \mu$ on $[0, 1] \times \Xi$ and the multi-valued mapping Γ_z'. This random set induces predictive belief and plausibility functions on W defined as

$$Bel_z^W(A) = (\lambda \otimes \mu)\left(\{(\omega, \xi) | \Gamma_z'(\omega, \xi) \subseteq A\}\right), \tag{7a}$$

$$Pl_z^W(A) = (\lambda \otimes \mu)\left(\{(\omega, \xi) | \Gamma_z'(\omega, \xi) \cap A \neq \emptyset\}\right), \tag{7b}$$

for all $A \subseteq W$. When closed-form expressions for these quantities are not available, they can be approximated by Monte Carlo simulation [10].

3   Application to Linear Regression

In this section, the approach summarized above will be applied to the multiple linear regression model. When using this model for time series forecasting, the errors cannot usually be assumed to be independent. We will thus consider the case where the error terms are serially correlated and follow a first order autoregressive [AR(1)] process (see, e.g., [11]). The corresponding linear model is

$$Y_t = \mathbf{x}_t'\boldsymbol{\beta} + \epsilon_t, \quad t = 1, \ldots, T, \tag{8}$$

where Y_t is the dependent variable at time t, $\mathbf{x}_t = (1, x_{1t}, \ldots, x_{pt})'$ is the vector of independent variables at time t (considered to be fixed), $\boldsymbol{\beta} = (\beta_0, \ldots, \beta_p)'$ is the vector of regression coefficients and ϵ_t is the error at time t, assumed to be related to the error at the previous time step by the equation

$$\epsilon_t = \rho\epsilon_{t-1} + U_t, \tag{9}$$

where ρ is a correlation parameter such that $|\rho| < 1$ and U_t is an error term. It is assumed that $U_t \sim \mathcal{N}(0, \sigma^2)$ and $\text{Cov}(U_t, U_s) = 0$ whenever $t \neq s$. The vector of parameters is thus $\boldsymbol{\theta} = (\boldsymbol{\beta}, \sigma, \rho)' \in \mathbb{R}^{p+3}$. Inference and prediction for this model will be addressed in Sections 3.1 and 3.2, respectively.

3.1   Inference

Let $\mathbf{z} = (y_1, \ldots, y_T)$ be the observed data. The likelihood function for the above model can be written as:

$$L_{\mathbf{z}}(\boldsymbol{\theta}) = f_{\boldsymbol{\theta}}(y_1) \prod_{t=2}^{T} f_{\boldsymbol{\theta}}(y_t | y_{t-1}). \tag{10}$$

Now, we can notice that $\rho y_{t-1} = \rho \mathbf{x}'_{t-1}\boldsymbol{\beta} + \rho \epsilon_{t-1}$. Subtracting this expression from (8), we get $Y_t - \rho y_{t-1} = (\mathbf{x}_t - \rho \mathbf{x}_{t-1})'\boldsymbol{\beta} + U_t$. Hence,

$$Y_t | y_{t-1} \sim \mathcal{N}(\rho y_{t-1} + (\mathbf{x}_t - \rho \mathbf{x}_{t-1})'\boldsymbol{\beta}, \sigma^2). \tag{11}$$

Now, it is easy to see that $\mathbb{E}(\epsilon_t) = 0$ and $\mathrm{Var}(\epsilon_t) = \sigma^2/(1 - \rho^2)$. Consequently, we can take $Y_1 \sim \mathcal{N}\left(\mathbf{x}'_1\boldsymbol{\beta}, \frac{\sigma^2}{1-\rho^2}\right)$, from which the expression of the likelihood function (10) can easily be obtained. The contour function (1) is then $pl_{\mathbf{z}}(\boldsymbol{\theta}) = L_{\mathbf{z}}(\boldsymbol{\theta})/L_{\mathbf{z}}(\widehat{\boldsymbol{\theta}})$, where $\widehat{\boldsymbol{\theta}}$ is the maximum likelihood estimate (MLE) of $\boldsymbol{\theta}$. Several specific iterative procedures have been proposed to maximize the likelihood for this model [11]. However, any non linear optimization algorithm can be used.

Given $J \subset \{1, \ldots, p+3\}$, the marginal contour function for $\boldsymbol{\theta}_J$ is

$$pl_{\mathbf{z}}(\boldsymbol{\theta}_J) = \max_{\{\theta_j, j \notin J\}} pl_{\mathbf{z}}(\boldsymbol{\theta}), \tag{12}$$

which can be computed numerically using a non linear constrained optimization algorithm. More generally, the plausibility of any hypothesis $H \subset \Theta$ can be computed as

$$Pl_{\mathbf{z}}(H) = \max_{\boldsymbol{\theta} \in H} pl_{\mathbf{z}}(\boldsymbol{\theta}). \tag{13}$$

It thus makes sense to reject H if its plausibility is smaller than some threshold. An interesting connection with the classical theory of significance tests can be made if we notice that $Pl_{\mathbf{z}}(H)$ is exactly the likelihood ratio statistic for H. It is known that, under regularity conditions and under H, the large sample distribution of $-2 \ln Pl_{\mathbf{z}}(H)$ is chi-squared, with degrees of freedom equal to the number r of restrictions imposed. Consequently, rejecting hypothesis H if its plausibility is smaller than $\exp(-\chi^2_{r;1-\alpha}/2)$, where $\chi^2_{r;1-\alpha}$ is the $1 - \alpha$-quantile of the chi-square distribution with r degrees of freedom, is a testing procedure with significance level approximately equal to α. Of particular interest in linear regression are hypotheses of the form $H : \rho = 0$ and $H : \beta_j = 0$.

Example 1. *As an example, let us consider the wage-productivity data from [9, page 460]. These data consist in indexes of real compensation per hour (Y) and output per hour (x) in the business sector of the U.S. economy for the period 1959 to 1998. The base of the indexes is 1992=100. We consider the following model:*

$$Y_t = \beta_0 + \beta_1 x_t + \beta_2 x_t^2 + \epsilon_t. \tag{14}$$

The MLEs are $\widehat{\beta}_0 = -12.9$, $\widehat{\beta}_1 = 1.85$, $\widehat{\beta}_2 = -7.13 \times 10^{-3}$, $\widehat{\sigma} = 0.680$ and $\widehat{\rho} = 0.559$. The marginal contour functions for parameters β_0, β_1, β_2 and ρ are shown in Figure 1. The 0.15 horizontal line corresponds to the 5% critical value $\exp(-\chi^2_{1;0.95}/2)$. We can see that both β_2 and ρ are significantly different from 0, which means that the relation between wages and productivity is certainly non linear and autocorrelation is very likely to be present. The intercept β_0, however, is not significantly different from 0.

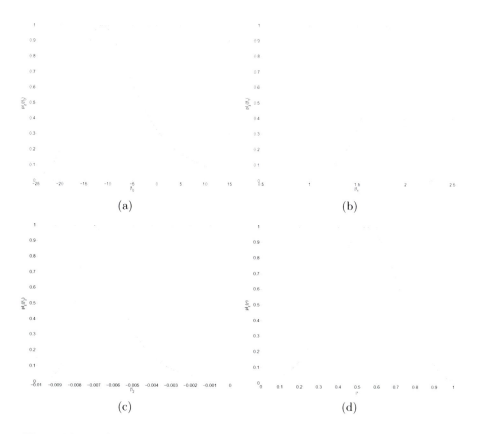

(a)

(b)

(c)

(d)

Fig. 1. Marginal contour functions for parameters β_0 (a), β_1 (b), β_2 (c) and ρ (d)

3.2   Forecasting

Let us assume that we have observed the data $\mathbf{z} = (y_1, \ldots, y_T)$ up to time T and we wish to predict future values of the dependent variable $W = (Y_{T+1}, \ldots, Y_{T+h})$ from time $T+1$ to $T+h$. We can easily show by induction that

$$Y_{T+j} = \rho^j y_T + (\mathbf{x}_{T+j} - \rho^j \mathbf{x}_T)' \boldsymbol{\beta} + \sigma \sum_{k=1}^{j} \rho^{j-k} \xi_k, \tag{15}$$

for $j = 1, \ldots, h$, where $\xi_1, \ldots, \xi_h$ are independent random variable with standard normal distribution. We thus have a φ-equation of the form (5) with $\xi = (\xi_1, \ldots, \xi_h) \in \Xi = \mathbb{R}^h$ following an h-dimensional standard normal distribution.

As explained in Section 2.2, this equation allows us to define a belief function on $\mathbb{W} = \mathbb{R}^h$. Here, the focal sets $\Gamma'_{\mathbf{z}}(\omega, \xi)$ are subsets of $\mathbb{R}^h$, which cannot be easily described exactly. They can be approximated by boxes, i.e., Cartesian products of intervals of the form

$$B(\omega, \xi) = [Y^L_{T+1}(\omega, \xi), Y^U_{T+1}(\omega, \xi)] \times \ldots \times [Y^L_{T+h}(\omega, \xi), Y^U_{T+h}(\omega, \xi)], t \quad (16)$$

where $Y^L_{T+j}(\omega, \xi)$ and $Y^U_{T+j}(\omega, \xi)$ are, respectively, the minimum and maximum of (15) under the constraint $pl_{\mathbf{z}}(\boldsymbol{\theta}) \geq \omega$, for $j = 1, \ldots, h$. As explained in [10], the plausibility of any proposition $W \in A$ for $A \subset \mathbb{R}^h$ can be approximated by Monte Carlo simulation as

$$Pl^{\mathbb{W}}_{\mathbf{z}}(A) \approx \frac{1}{N} \# \{i \in \{1, \ldots, N\} | B(\omega_i, \xi_i) \cap A \neq \emptyset\}, \quad (17)$$

where $\#$ denotes cardinality and (ω_i, ξ_i), $i = 1, \ldots, N$ are N independent draws of (ω, ξ).

Example 2. *Let us consider again the wage-productivity data of Example 1. Figure 2 displays the forecasts made at time $T = 1988$ for the period 1989-1998. To make these predictions, the parameters have been estimated using the data from 1959 to 1988. The graph shows the point predictions*

$$\widehat{y}(T + h) = \widetilde{\rho}^j y_T + (\mathbf{x}_{T+j} - \widetilde{\rho}^j \mathbf{x}_T)' \widehat{\boldsymbol{\beta}}, \quad (18)$$

as well as predictive quantile intervals [10] at levels 50%, 25% and 5%. We recall that the predictive quantile interval at level α for Y_{T+j} is $(q^L_\alpha, q^U_{1-\alpha}]$, where q^L_α is the α-quantile of Y^L_{T+j} and $q^U_{1-\alpha}$ is the $(1 - \alpha)$-quantile of Y^U_{T+j}. By definition, the plausibility that Y_{T+j} is below q^L_α and the plausibility that Y_{T+j} is above $q^U_{1-\alpha}$ are both equal to α. We can see that the true values y_{T+j} remain most of the time within the 25% quantile intervals, and always within the 5% quantile intervals. Figure 3 shows the plausibility that Y_{1993} lies in the interval $[y - \delta, y + \delta]$ as a function of y, for different values of δ.

4   Conclusions

In business and economics, forecasts are typically used for decision-making and strategic planning. When aggregating predictions from numerical models with other information, decision-makers need to assess the uncertainty of the forecasts. Describing this uncertainty in a faithful and accurate way is thus a very important issue. In this paper, this issue has been addressed in the Dempster-Shafer framework. Our method for computing predictive belief functions has been applied to a relatively simple but widely used model for time series forecasting: linear regression with serial correlation. We note that, for this model,

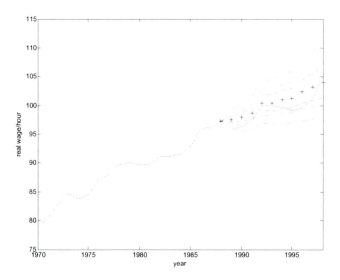

Fig. 2. Predictions for the wage-productivity data. The solid line represents the true values of real wage/hour as a function of time, the crosses show the point predictions and the interrupted lines correspond to the predictive quantile intervals at levels 50%, 25% and 5%.

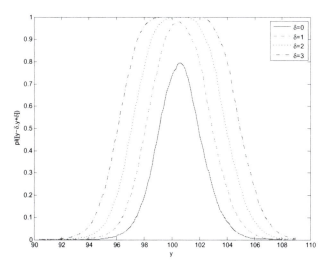

Fig. 3. Plausibility $Pl([y - \delta, y + \delta])$ as a function of y for Y_{1993} for $\delta \in \{0, 1, 2, 3\}$

the variance of prediction errors cannot be determined exactly, making it difficult to compute prediction intervals [11, page 215]. The proposed method can be
easily implemented using Monte Carlo simulation. Bayesian posterior predictive
distributions are recovered when a prior distribution on the model parameter is
specified. Model combination using this approach as well as theoretical analysis
of the asymptotic properties of the method are left for further study.

References

1. Aickin, M.: Connecting Dempster-Shafer belief functions with likelihood-based inference. Synthese 123, 347–364 (2000)
2. Ben Abdallah, N., Mouhous Voyneau, N., Denœux, T.: Combining statistical and
   expert evidence using belief functions: Application to centennial sea level estimation taking into account climate change. International Journal of Approximate
   Reasoning 55(1), Part 3, 341–354 (2014)
3. Dempster, A.P.: Upper and lower probabilities induced by a multivalued mapping.
   Annals of Mathematical Statistics 38, 325–339 (1967)
4. Dempster, A.P.: The Dempster-Shafer calculus for statisticians. International Journal of Approximate Reasoning 48(2), 365–377 (2008)
5. Denœux, T.: Likelihood-based belief function: justification and some extensions
   to low-quality data. International Journal of Approximate Reasoning 55(7),
   1535–1547 (2014), http://dx.doi.org/10.1016/j.ijar.2013.06.007
6. Dubois, D., Prade, H.: A set-theoretic view of belief functions: logical operations
   and approximations by fuzzy sets. International Journal of General Systems 12(3),
   193–226 (1986)
7. Edwards, A.W.F.: Likelihood (expanded edition). The John Hopkins University
   Press, Baltimore (1992)
8. Gillet, P., Srivastava, R.P.: Attribute sampling: A belief-function approach to statistical audit evidence. Auditing: A Journal of Practice and Theory 19(1), 145–155
   (1994)
9. Gujarati, D.N.: Basic Econometrics, 4th edn. McGraw-Hill, Boston (2003)
10. Kanjanatarakul, O., Sriboonchitta, S., Denœux, T.: Forecasting using belief func-
    tions: an application to marketing econometrics. International Journal of Approx-
    imate Reasoning 55(5), 1113–1128 (2014)
11. Pindyck, R.S., Rubinfeld, D.L.: Econometric models and economic forecasts, 4th
    edn. McGraw-Hill, Boston (1998)
12. Shafer, G.: A mathematical theory of evidence. Princeton University Press, Prince-
    ton (1976)
13. Smets, P.: Belief functions: the disjunctive rule of combination and the generalized
    Bayesian theorem. International Journal of Approximate Reasoning 9, 1–35 (1993)
14. Srivastava, R.P., Shafer, G.: Integrating statistical and non-statistical audit evi-
    dence using belief functions: A case of variable sampling. International Journal of
    Intelligent Systems 9, 519–539 (1994)
15. Wasserman, L.A.: Belief functions and statistical evidence. The Canadian Journal
    of Statistics 18(3), 183–196 (1990)

Modelling and Fusion of Imperfect Implication Rules

Janith N. Heendeni[1], Kamal Premaratne[1], Manohar N. Murthi[1],
and Matthias Scheutz[2]

[1] Elect. & Comp. Eng., Univ. of Miami, Coral Gables, FL, USA
j.anuja@umiami.edu, {kamal,mmurthi}@miami.edu
[2] Comp. Sci., Tufts Univ., Medford, MA, USA
mscheutz@cs.tufts.edu

Abstract. In this paper, we develop a method to find the uncertain consequent by fusing the uncertain antecedent and the uncertain implication rule. In particular with Dempster-Shafer theoretic models utilized to capture the uncertainty intervals associated with the antecedent and the rule itself, we derive bounds on the confidence interval associated with the rule consequent. We derive inequalities for the belief and plausibility values of the consequent and with least commitment choice they become equations. We also demonstrate the consistency of our model with probability and classical logic.

Keywords: Belief, Plausibility, Fusion, Implication rule, Antecedent, Consequent, Uncertainty.

1 Introduction

Implication rules, which take the form "if A, then B" or, as is often expressed, $A \implies B$, constitute the backbone of reasoning and inference engines. A large volume of existing work addresses the extraction of such rules from databases and their use in various application scenarios. However, most of these works assume that the evidence/information at hand is "perfect", which, in practice, is far from the truth. Databases are rife with imperfect (e.g., ambiguous, vague, or incomplete) entries rendering the rule antecedent A, the rule $\implies$ itself, and hence the rule consequent B to be imperfect. Even otherwise, one cannot expect to get "perfect" rules when only *finite* databases are available for rule extraction.

Probabilistic and fuzzy models are perhaps the two most commonly used approaches to capture imperfect rules [4],[10]. This current work of ours is based on *Dempster-Shafer (DS) theory* [12] which can capture a wider variety of imperfections, provide interval-based models of the underlying uncertainties, and can be considered a generalization of probability mass functions (p.m.f.s). Several previous works deal with DS theory (DST) based modeling of imperfect rules: in [6],[7], DST fusion/combination strategies are employed to get results that are most similar to ours, but general *bounds* and inequalities that we derive are absent and the approach is different; in [2], emphasis is placed on satisfying the

F. Cuzzolin (Ed.): BELIEF 2014, LNAI 8764, pp. 313–320, 2014.

material implications of propositional logic statements; [11] designs a complete uncertain logic framework (imperfect rules being a special case) which is compatible with classical (perfect) logic [10]. We take a different view: we do not impose compatibility with classical logic in imperfect domains; rather, we expect compatibility only when the domain is perfect, so that our model is very general and all probability and classical logic are special cases.

We model our imperfect rules via DST Fagin-Halpern (FH) conditionals [5]. While the use of the Bayesian conditional has been criticized as a model of probabilistic imperfect rules [9],[2], we demonstrate that the DST FH conditionals can be used as an effective interval-based model of imperfect rules to fuse with imperfect antecedent. Given the uncertainty intervals associated with the rule antecedent and the rule itself, we derive explicit lower and upper bounds for the uncertainty interval of the rule consequent. Then we explicitly show its consistency with Bayesian inference and classical logic.

2   Preliminaries

Basic DST Notions. Let $\Theta = \{\theta_1, \cdots, \theta_M\}$ denote the *Frame of Discernment (FoD)* which contains the discrete set of mutually exclusive and exhaustive propositions. The power set 2^Θ, i.e., the set containing all the possible subsets of Θ, is 2^Θ. For arbitrary $A \subseteq \Theta$, $\overline{A}$ denotes those singletons that are not in A.

As usual, $m_\Theta(\cdot) : 2^\Theta \mapsto [0,1]$ is a *basic belief assignment (BBA)* or *mass assignment* where $\sum_{A \subseteq \Theta} m_\Theta(A) = 1$ and $m_\Theta(\emptyset) = 0$. Propositions that receive non-zero mass are the *focal elements;* the set of focal elements is the *core* $\mathcal{F}_\Theta$. The triplet $\mathcal{E} = \{\Theta, \mathcal{F}_\Theta, m_\Theta\}$ is the *body of evidence (BoE)*.

Given a BoE, $\mathcal{E} \equiv \{\Theta, \mathcal{F}_\Theta, m_\Theta\}$, the *belief* function $Bl_\Theta : 2^\Theta \mapsto [0,1]$ is $Bl_\Theta(A) = \sum_{B \subseteq A} m_\Theta(B)$. The *plausibility* function $Pl_\Theta : 2^\Theta \mapsto [0,1]$ is $Pl_\Theta(A) = 1 - Bl_\Theta(\overline{A})$. The *uncertainty interval* associated with A is $[Bl_\Theta(A), Pl_\Theta(A)]$.

Of the various notions of DST conditionals abound in the literature, the Fagin-Halpern (FH) conditional [5] possesses several attractive properties and offers a unique probabilistic interpretation and hence a natural transition to the Bayesian conditional notion [5], [3], [14].

Definition 1 (FH Conditionals). *For the BoE $\mathcal{E} = \{\Theta, \mathcal{F}_\Theta, m_\Theta\}$ and $A \subseteq \Theta$ s.t. $Bl_\Theta(A) \neq 0$, the conditional belief $Bl_\Theta(B/A) : 2^\Theta \mapsto [0,1]$ and conditional plausibility $Pl_\Theta(B/A) : 2^\Theta \mapsto [0,1]$ of B given A are*

$$Bl_\Theta(B/A) = \frac{Bl_\Theta(A \cap B)}{Bl_\Theta(A \cap B) + Pl_\Theta(A \cap \overline{B})}; \quad Pl_\Theta(B/A) = \frac{Pl_\Theta(A \cap B)}{Pl_\Theta(A \cap B) + Bl_\Theta(A \cap \overline{B})}.$$

3   Modelling and Fusion

3.1   Model Assumption

We model the implication rule by FH conditionals. Consider the implication rule $A \Longrightarrow B$, where A denotes the antecedent, B denotes the consequent, and $\Longrightarrow$

denotes the rule R. There might be situations where A and B belong to two different BoEs. In that case a common BoE which contains both A and B has to be considered. Therefore without loss of generality we assume antecedent and consequent are in same BoE. We consider the uncertainty of the rule R and it is modeled as follows;

$$Bl(R) = Bl(B/A); \quad Pl(R) = Pl(B/A) \tag{1}$$

Additionally if we have evidence on $\overline{A} \Longrightarrow B$, which we model by $Bl(B/\overline{A})$ and $Pl(B/\overline{A})$, more finer results can be obtained for the consequent. Later with results, we conclude that these conditionals are a good way to model the implication rules.

3.2 Fusion

The purpose of this paper is to find the uncertainty intervals of the consequent given the uncertainty intervals of antecedent and the rule. For simplicity, we will use the following notation:

$$Bl(A) = \alpha_1; \quad Pl(A) = \beta_1; \quad Bl(B) = \alpha_2; \quad Pl(B) = \beta_2;$$
$$Bl(B/A) = \alpha_r; \, Pl(B/A) = \beta_r; \, Bl(B/\overline{A}) = \overline{\alpha}_r; \, Pl(B/\overline{A}) = \overline{\beta}_r, \tag{2}$$

Results: We obtain following relations for belief and plausibility of the consequent.
If knowledge of antecedent and knowledge of both $A \Longrightarrow B$ and $\overline{A} \Longrightarrow B$ are available, following lower and upper bounds can be obtained for the belief and plausibility respectively.

$$\alpha_2 \geq \alpha_1\alpha_r + (1 - \beta_1)\overline{\alpha}_r. \tag{3}$$

$$\beta_2 \leq \alpha_1\beta_r + (1 - \beta_1)\overline{\beta}_r + (\beta_1 - \alpha_1). \tag{4}$$

We call them **General Bounds**.

Least Commitment (LC) Choice. The principle of minimum or least commitment (LC) [13], [1] dictates that we are least committed and rely on available evidence only, i.e., select the lower bound for α_2 and the upper bound for β_2. The corresponding LC choice;

$$\alpha_2 = \alpha_1\alpha_r + (1 - \beta_1)\overline{\alpha}_r. \tag{5}$$

$$\beta_2 = \alpha_1\beta_r + (1 - \beta_1)\overline{\beta}_r + (\beta_1 - \alpha_1). \tag{6}$$

If knowledge of antecedent and knowledge of only $A \Longrightarrow B$ are available the relations become;

$$\alpha_2 \geq \alpha_1\alpha_r. \tag{7}$$

$$\beta_2 \leq 1 - \alpha_1(1 - \beta_r). \tag{8}$$

We call them **Relaxed Bounds.** Since we are using only the implication $A \Longrightarrow B$, these are the bounds for the **imperfect implication**. With the LC choice these bounds become following equations.

$$\alpha_2 = \alpha_1 \alpha_r. \tag{9}$$

$$\beta_2 = 1 - \alpha_1(1 - \beta_r). \tag{10}$$

Uncertainty. The upper bound for the uncertainty of the General Bounds;

$$\beta_2 - \alpha_2 \leq (\beta_1 - \alpha_1) + \alpha_1(\beta_r - \alpha_r) + (1 - \beta_1)(\overline{\beta}_r - \overline{\alpha}_r). \tag{11}$$

The above term for the upper bound of the uncertainty has an interesting intuitive interpretation: the uncertainty interval of the consequent is bounded above by the uncertainty of the antecedent plus the uncertainties of the rules $A \Longrightarrow B$ and $\overline{A} \Longrightarrow B$ weighted by their corresponding belief terms; $Bl(A) = \alpha_1$ and $Bl(\overline{A}) = 1 - \beta_1$. And it can be easily shown that this term, the upper bound for the uncertainty, is always less than or equal to 1, which is correct and intuitive. The lower bound for the uncertainty is 0 since by definition $\beta_2 \geq \alpha_2$. (Note that we define α_2 and β_2 as belief functions and then find relations for them). And also it is clear that the relations which were obtained for β_2 are always greater than or equal to the relations which were obtained for α_2.

The inequalities can be written in one line;
$0 \leq \alpha_1 \alpha_r \leq \alpha_1 \alpha_r + (1 - \beta_1)\overline{\alpha}_r \leq \alpha_2 \leq \beta_2 \leq \alpha_1 \beta_r + (1 - \beta_1)\overline{\beta}_r + (\beta_1 - \alpha_1) \leq 1 - \alpha_1(1 - \beta_r) \leq 1$ and it is apparent that when more knowledge (The term knowledge refers to the knowledge of belief and plausibility values.) is available the bounded uncertainty interval of the consequent gets narrower. When there is no knowledge of implication rules, the uncertainty interval of the consequent is $[0, 1]$, when knowledge of antecedent and $A \Longrightarrow B$ is available the interval becomes $[\alpha_1 \alpha_r, 1 - \alpha_1(1 - \beta_r)]$, when antecedent and both $A \Longrightarrow B$, $\overline{A} \Longrightarrow B$ are available the interval becomes $[\alpha_1 \alpha_r + (1 - \beta_1)\overline{\alpha}_r, \alpha_1 \beta_r + (1 - \beta_1)\overline{\beta}_r + (\beta_1 - \alpha_1)]$ and the knowledge of consequent is available it is $[\alpha_2, \beta_2]$.

Proofs: Without loss of generality we assumed that A and B are in same BoE. Therefore;

$$Bl(B) = Bl(B \cap A) + Bl(B \cap \overline{A}) + \sum_{\substack{\emptyset \neq P \subseteq (B \cap A) \\ \emptyset \neq Q \subseteq (B \cap \overline{A})}} m(P \cup Q). \tag{12}$$

$$Bl(B) \geq Bl(B \cap A) + Bl(B \cap \overline{A}), \tag{13}$$

We know that [8] $Bl(A) \leq Bl(B \cap A) + Pl(\overline{B} \cap A)$. This, together with the FH conditionals (where $Bl(A) \neq 0$) can then be used to write

$$Bl(A) \, Bl(B/A) \leq Bl(B \cap A). \tag{14}$$

This inequality holds true for $Bl(A) = 0$ as well. Substitute $\overline{A}$ for A in (14):

$$Bl(\overline{A})\,Bl(B/\overline{A}) \leq Bl(B \cap \overline{A}). \tag{15}$$

Use (13), (14) and (15), and use the fact that $Bl(\overline{A}) = 1 - Pl(A)$ with notation (2) to get (3);

$$\alpha_2 \geq \alpha_1\alpha_r + (1 - \beta_1)\,\overline{\alpha}_r.$$

Substitute $\overline{B}$ for B in (13),(14), and (15) to get,

$$Bl(\overline{B}) \geq Bl(A)\,Bl(\overline{B}/A) + Bl(\overline{A})\,Bl(\overline{B}/\overline{A}). \tag{16}$$

Use the facts; $Bl(\overline{B}) = 1 - Pl(B)$, $Bl(\overline{B}/A) = 1 - Pl(B/A)$ and $Bl(\overline{B}/\overline{A}) = 1 - Pl(B/\overline{A})$ with notation (2) to get (4);

$$\beta_2 \leq \alpha_1\beta_r + (1 - \beta_1)\,\overline{\beta}_r + (\beta_1 - \alpha_1).$$

If the knowledge of $\overline{A} \Longrightarrow B$ is unavailable, we relax the rule by assuming total uncertainty which is $[\overline{\alpha}_r, \overline{\beta}_r] = [0, 1]$ in (3) and (4) to get (7) and (8);

$$\alpha_2 \geq \alpha_1\alpha_r.$$

$$\beta_2 \leq 1 - \alpha_1(1 - \beta_r).$$

4   Consistency with Probability and Classical Logic

4.1   Consistency with Probability

For p.m.f.s, we have (a) $Pr(B) = Pr(B \cap A) + Pr(B \cap \overline{A})$, which corresponds to (12), except that the additional summation term vanishes and the inequality (13) reduces to an equality; and (b) $Pr(B \cap A) = Pr(A)\,Pr(B|A)$, which corresponds to (14), except that the inequality reduces to an equality. Therefore, instead of the bounds for α_2 and β_2, we get equalities identical to the LC choice.

$$\alpha_2 = \alpha_1\alpha_r + (1 - \beta_1)\,\overline{\alpha}_r; \quad \beta_2 = \alpha_1\beta_r + (1 - \beta_1)\,\overline{\beta}_r + (\beta_1 - \alpha_1). \tag{17}$$

When the belief and plausibility are equal for each proposition, DST models reduce to p.m.f.s. The belief and plausibility (which are now identical) of each proposition then yield the probability of that same proposition. Suppose the antecedent and the rules $A \Longrightarrow B$ and $\overline{A} \Longrightarrow B$ are probabilistic, i.e.,

$$\alpha_1 = \beta_1 = Pr(A); \quad \alpha_r = \beta_r = Pr(B/A); \quad \overline{\alpha}_r = \overline{\beta}_r = Pr(B/\overline{A}). \tag{18}$$

Substitute in (17) to get $\alpha_2 = \beta_2 = \alpha_1\alpha_r + (1 - \alpha_1)\,\overline{\alpha}_r$. This corresponds to $Pr(B) = Pr(A)\,Pr(B|A) + Pr(\overline{A})\,Pr(B|\overline{A})$.

4.2   Consistency with Classical Logic

Note that $\alpha_1 = \beta_1 = 1$ and $\alpha_1 = \beta_1 = 0$ imply the occurrence or non-occurrence of proposition A with 100% confidence. Though FH conditionals are not defined when $\alpha_1 = \beta_1 = 0$ [5] we have shown that our relations are valid even $\alpha_1 = \beta_1 = 0$, further if we take a limiting argument and let $\alpha_1 = \beta_1$ tend to 0 in the limit and the result will be same as if we substitute 0 for both α_1 and β_1 in the equations. We associate the two cases $\alpha_1 = \beta_1 = 1$ and $\alpha_1 = \beta_1 = 0$ with the logical 'Truth' and logical 'False' in classical logic. For example, with $\alpha_1 = \beta_1 = \{0,1\}$ and $\alpha_2 = \beta_2 = \{0,1\}$, Table 1 shows the truth table of $A \Longrightarrow B$. To see the consistency with classical logic, we now use $\alpha_1 = \beta_1 = \{0,1\}$, $\alpha_r = \beta_r = \{0,1\}$, and $\overline{\alpha}_r = \overline{\beta}_r = \{0,1\}$ with (5) and (6) (Note that (3) and (4) become (5) and (6) in classical logic case as in probabilistic case). See Table 2. The results for $\alpha_2 = \beta_2$ in Table 2 can be expressed as $(A \wedge (A \Longrightarrow B)) \vee (\neg A \wedge (\neg A \Longrightarrow B)) = (A \wedge (\neg A \vee B)) \vee (\neg A \wedge (A \vee B)) = B$.

Table 1. Truth Table for $A \Longrightarrow B$ in Classical Logic

$\alpha_1 = \beta_1$	$\alpha_2 = \beta_2$	$A \Longrightarrow B$
0	0	1
0	1	1
1	0	0
1	1	1

Table 2. When we have both $A \Longrightarrow B$ and $\overline{A} \Longrightarrow B$ for the Classical Logic Case obtained from (5) and (6)

$\alpha_1=\beta_1$	$\alpha_r=\beta_r$	$\overline{\alpha}_r=\overline{\beta}_r$	α_2	β_2		$\alpha_2=\beta_2$
0	0	0	0	0	$\Longrightarrow$	0
0	0	1	1	1	$\Longrightarrow$	1
0	1	0	0	0	$\Longrightarrow$	0
0	1	1	1	1	$\Longrightarrow$	1
1	0	0	0	0	$\Longrightarrow$	0
1	0	1	0	0	$\Longrightarrow$	0
1	1	0	1	1	$\Longrightarrow$	1
1	1	1	1	1	$\Longrightarrow$	1

Now consider the implication case; (9) and (10). (Note that (7) and (8) become (9) and (10) in classical logic case).

Let us compare the entries of Table 3 (obtained from (9) and (10)) and Table 1 (truth table for $A \Longrightarrow B$ in classical logic). *(a) Antecedent is true:* See lines 3-4 where both tables show identical behavior. *(b) Antecedent is false:* See lines 1-2 where the tables behave differently. *(b.1) When rule is true:* the consequent can take 0 or 1 in both tables. Note that the information in lines 1-2 of Table 1 are

Table 3. When we have only $A \Longrightarrow B$ for the Classical Logic Case obtained from (9) and (10)

| | | | | | $\alpha_2 \neq \beta_2$ in general | |
$\alpha_1 = \beta_1$	$\alpha_r = \beta_r$	α_2	β_2		α_2	β_2
0	0	0	1	$\Longrightarrow$	0	1
0	1	0	1	$\Longrightarrow$	0	1
1	0	0	0	$\Longrightarrow$	0	0
1	1	1	1	$\Longrightarrow$	1	1

captured in line 2 of Table 3 which explains when antecedent is false though implication rule is true the consequent can be true or false. *(b.2) When rule is false:* this is not in Table 1 whereas line 1 of Table 3 not only allows this, but it also allows the consequent to take either 0 or 1 value which explains when antecedent is false and the implication rule is false the consequent can be true or false.

From these tables it is clear that the relations we developed are consistent with classical logic as well as they better explain the classical logic behaviour of implication rules than conventional implication truth table.

5   Illustrative Example

As an illustrative simple example, consider red and black balls, and 3 urns A, B, and C: urn A has 3 red, 5 black, plus 2 additional balls; urn B has 5 red, 2 black, plus 3 additional balls; and urn C has 3 red, 5 black, plus 2 additional balls. The additional balls could be any combination of red and black balls.

First we select urn A and randomly take out a ball (first trial). If we get a red ball (RB), we select urn B; otherwise, if we get a black ball (BB), we select urn C. Then we take out a ball from the selected urn (second trial). What are the belief and plausibility values of getting a RB in the second trial?

In the DST framework, let $[\alpha_1, \beta_1]$, $[\alpha_r, \beta_r]$, and $[\alpha_2, \beta_2]$ denote the belief and plausibility values corresponding to getting a RB in the first trial, getting a RB in the second trial given that the first trial yields a RB, and getting a RB in the second trial, respectively. Therefore, $[\alpha_1, \beta_1] = [0.3, 0.5]$, $[\overline{\alpha}_1, \overline{\beta}_1] = [0.5, 0.7]$, $[\alpha_r, \beta_r] = [0.5, 0.8]$, $[\overline{\alpha}_r, \overline{\beta}_r] = [0.3, 0.5]$, and $[\alpha_2, \beta_2] = [0.36, 0.65]$ (computed by accounting for all the possibilities).

Let us now see what our results yield: the general bounds yield $0.30 \leq \alpha_2 \leq \beta_2 \leq 0.69$; the relaxed bounds yield $0.15 \leq \alpha_2 \leq \beta_2 \leq 0.94$. Both these contain $[\alpha_2, \beta_2] = [0.36, 0.65]$. Also note that the general bounds are much tighter than the relaxed bounds (which ignore the information in $[\overline{\alpha}_r, \overline{\beta}_r]$).

6   Conclusion

We have derived mathematical relations to belief and plausibility values of a consequent when the belief and plausibility values of corresponding antecedent and implication rule are given, by modelling the implication rule with DST FH conditionals. The results and their consistency with probability and classical logic demonstrate the reasonability of modelling the uncertain implication rules by DST FH conditionals.

Further the results are more general and flexible than the previous works since the derivations are not imposed by any probabilistic or classical logic relations which are special cases of this model.

Acknowledgment. This work is based on research supported by the US Office of Naval Research (ONR) via grants #N00014-10-1-0140. and #N00014-11-1-0493, and the US National Science Foundation (NSF) via grant #1038257.

References

1. Aregui, A., Denoeux, T.: Constructing consonant belief functions from sample data using confidence sets of pignistic probabilities. Int. J. of Approx. Reasoning 49(3), 574–594 (2008)
2. Benavoli, A., et al.: Modelling uncertain implication rules in evidence theory. In: Proc. FUSION, Cologne, Germany, pp. 1–7 (2008)
3. Denneberg, D.: Conditioning (updating) non-additive measures. Ann. of Oper. Res. 52(1), 21–42 (1994)
4. Dubois, D., Hullermeier, E., Prade, H.: Toward the representation of implication-based fuzzy rules in terms of crisp rules. In: Proc. Joint IFSA World Congress and NAFIPS Int. Conf. vol. 3, pp. 1592–1597 (2001)
5. Fagin, R., Halpern, J.Y.: A new approach to updating beliefs. In: Bonissone, P.P., Henrion, M., Kanal, L.N., Lemmer, J.F. (eds.) Proc. UAI, pp. 347–374. Elsevier Science, New York (1991)
6. Ginsberg, M.L.: Nonmonotonic reasoning using Dempster's rule. In: Proc. National Conf. Artificial Intell., pp. 126–129 (1984)
7. Hau, H.Y., Kashyap, R.L.: Belief combination and propagation in a lattice-structured inference network. IEEE Trans. on Syst., Man and Cyber. 20(1), 45–57 (1990)
8. Kulasekere, E.C., et al.: Conditioning and updating evidence. Int. J. of Approx. Reasoning 36(1), 75–108 (2004)
9. Lewis, D.: Probabilities of conditionals and conditional probabilities. The Phil. Rev. LXXXV (3), 297–315 (1976)
10. Nguyen, H., Mukaidono, M., Kreinovich, V.: Probability of implication, logical version of Bayes theorem, and fuzzy logic operations. In: Proc. IEEE Int. Conf. on Fuzzy Syst (FUZZ-IEEE), Honolulu, HI, vol. 1, pp. 530–535 (2002)
11. Nunez, R.C., et al.: Modeling uncertainty in first-order logic: a Dempster-Shafer theoretic approach. In: Proc. Int. Symp. on Imprecise Prob.: Theories and Appl (ISIPTA), Compiegne, France (2013)
12. Shafer, G.: A Mathematical Theory of Evidence. Princeton Univ. Press, Princeton (1976)
13. Smets, P.: What is Dempster-Shafer's model? In: Yager, R.R., Fedrizzi, M., Kacprzyk, J. (eds.) Advances in the Dempster-Shafer Theory of Evidence, pp. 5–34. John Wiley and Sons, New York (1994)
14. Wickramarathne, T.L., Premaratne, K., Murthi, M.N.: Toward efficient computation of the Dempster-Shafer belief theoretic conditionals. IEEE Trans. on Cyber. 43(2), 712–724 (2013)

Conflict between Belief Functions: A New Measure Based on Their Non-conflicting Parts

Milan Daniel

Institute of Computer Science, Academy of Sciences of the Czech Republic
Pod Vodárenskou věží 2, 182 07 Prague 8, Czech Republic
milan.daniel@cs.cas.cz

Abstract. When combining belief functions by conjunctive rules of combination, conflicts often appear, which are assigned to empty set by the non-normalised conjunctive rule or normalised by Dempster's rule of combination in Dempster-Shafer theory. Combination of conflicting belief functions and interpretation of their conflicts is often questionable in real applications; hence a series of alternative combination rules were suggested and a series of papers on conflicting belief functions have been published and conflicts of belief functions started to be investigated.

This theoretical contribution introduces a new definition of conflict between two belief functions on a general finite frame of discernment. Its idea is based on Hájek-Valdés algebraic analysis of belief functions, on our previous study of conflicts of belief functions, where internal conflicts of belief functions are distinguished from a conflict between belief functions, and on the decomposition of a belief function into its conflicting and non-conflicting parts. Basic properties of this newly defined conflict are presented, analyzed and briefly compared with our previous approaches to conflict as well as with Liu's degree of conflict.

Keywords: belief functions, Dempster-Shafer theory, uncertainty, Dempster's semigroup, internal conflict, conflict between belief functions, non-conflicting part of belief function, conflicting part of belief function.

1   Introduction

Complications of highly conflicting belief function combination, see e.g., [2, 6, 27], have motivated a theoretical investigation of conflicts between belief functions (BFs) [8, 16, 21–25]. The problematic issue of an essence of conflict between belief functions (BFs), originally defined as $m_{\bigcirc}(\emptyset)$ by the non-normalised version of Dempster's rule $\bigcirc$, was first mentioned by Almond [1] in 1995, and discussed further by Liu [22] in 2006. Almond's counter-example has been overcome by Liu's progressive approach. Unfortunately, the substance of the problem has not thus been solved as positive conflict value still may be detected in a pair of mutually non-conflicting BFs.

Further steps ahead were presented in our previous study [8]. New ideas concerning interpretation, definition, and measurement of conflicts of BFs were introduced there. Three new approaches to interpretation and computation of

F. Cuzzolin (Ed.): BELIEF 2014, LNAI 8764, pp. 321–330, 2014.

conflicts were presented: combinational conflict, plausibility conflict, and comparative conflict. Unfortunately, none of those captures the nature of conflict sufficiently enough yet; thus these approaches need further elaboration. Nevertheless, the very important distinction between conflict between BFs and internal conflicts in individual BFs is pointed out there; and the necessity to distinguish between a conflict and difference among BFs is emphasized.

When the mathematical properties of the three approaches to BF conflicts were analyzed, there appeared a possibility of expressing a BF Bel as Dempster's sum of non-conflicting BF Bel_0 with the same plausibility decisional support as the original BF Bel has and of indecisive BF Bel_S which does not prefer any of the elements in the corresponding frame of discernment — see [9]. A new measure of conflict between BFs is based on that approach.

2 Preliminaries

We assume classic definitions of basic notions from theory of *belief functions* (BFs) [26] on a finite frame of discernment $\Omega_n = \{\omega_1, \omega_2, ..., \omega_n\}$, see also [5–7]. We say that BF Bel is *non-conflicting* when conjunctive combination of Bel with itself does not produce any conflicting belief masses (when $(Bel \ominus Bel)(\emptyset) = 0$, i.e., $Bel \ominus Bel = Bel \oplus Bel$), i.e. whenever $Pl(\omega_i) = 1$ for some $\omega_i \in \Omega_n$. Otherwise, BF is *conflicting*, i.e., it contains some internal conflict [8].

Let us recall *normalised plausibility of singletons*[1] of Bel: Pl_P is the Bayesian BF (i.e., probability distribution on Ω_n in fact) $Pl\_P(Bel)$ (or simply Pl_P if corresponding Bel is obvious) such, that $Pl\_P(\omega_i) = \frac{Pl(\{\omega_i\})}{\sum_{\omega \in \Omega} Pl(\{\omega\})}$, where Pl is plausibility corresponding to Bel [3, 7] and alternative Smets' *pignistic probability* $BetP(\omega_i) = \sum_{\omega_i \in X} \frac{m(X)}{|X|}$. An *indecisive BF* (or non-discriminative BF) is a BF which does not prefer any $\omega_i \in \Omega_n$, i.e., a BF which gives no decisional support for any $\omega_i \in \Omega_n$ (it either gives no support as the vacuous BF (VBF), gives the same support to all elements as symmetric BFs give, or $Pl\_P(Bel) = U_n$ ($Pl\_P(\omega) = \frac{1}{n}$ for any $\omega \in \Omega_n$). $S_{Pl} = \{Bel \,|\, Pl\_P(Bel) = U_n\}$.

We can represent BFs by enumeration of their m-values, i.e., by (2^n-1)-tuples or by (2^n-2)-tuples as $m(\Omega_n) = 1 - \sum_{X \subsetneq \Omega_n} m(X)$; thus we have pairs $(a,b) = (m(\{\omega_1\}), m(\{\omega_2\}))$ for BFs on Ω_2.

Hájek-Valdés algebraic structure $\mathbf{D}_0$ of these pairs (called *d-pairs*) with Dempster's rule $\oplus$ (called *Dempster's semigroup*) and its analysis [19, 20, 28] were further studied and generalised by the author, e.g., in [5, 10]. There are distinguished d-pairs $0 = (0,0)$ (i.e., *vacuous BF*) and $0' = (\frac{1}{2}, \frac{1}{2})$, $-(a,b) = (b,a)$, homomorphisms[2][3] $h : h(a,b) = (a,b) \oplus 0' = (\frac{1-b}{2-a-b}, \frac{1-a}{2-a-b})$ and $f : f(a,b) = (a,b) \oplus -(a,b) = (\frac{a+b-a^2-b^2-ab}{1-a^2-b^2}, \frac{a+b-a^2-b^2-ab}{1-a^2-b^2})$. We will use the following subsets of d-pairs: $S = \{(a,a)\}$, $S_1 = \{(a,0)\}$, $S_2 = \{(0,b)\}$, and $G = \{(a, 1-a)\}$.

---

[1] Plausibility of singletons is called *contour function* by Shafer [26], thus $Pl\_P(Bel)$ is a normalisation of contour function in fact (thus $\sum_{\omega \in \Omega} Pl\_P(\omega) = 1$).

[2] Note that $h(a,b)$ is an abbreviation for $h((a,b))$, similarly for $f(a,b)$.

[3] $0'$ and h are generalised by $U_n = (\frac{1}{n}, \frac{1}{n}, ..., \frac{1}{n}, 0, 0, ..., 0)$ and $h(Bel) = Bel \oplus U_n$ on Ω_n.

We can express BFs on Ω_2 (d-pairs) by a 2-dimensional triangle, see Fig. 1. Complexity of the structure grows exponentially with cardinality of the frame of discernment, e.g., we have a 6-dimensional structure on Ω_3, see [9, 10].

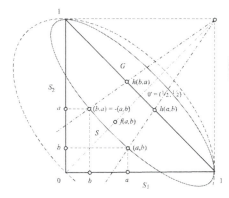

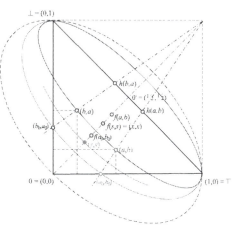

Fig. 1. $\mathbf{D}_0$. Homomorphism h is in this representation a projection of $\mathbf{D}_0$ to group $\mathbf{G}$ on $G = \{(a, 1 - a)\}$ along the straight lines running through the point $(1, 1)$. All of the d-pairs lying on the same ellipse (running through points $(0, 1)$ and $(1, 0)$) are mapped by homomorphism f to the same d-pair in semigroup on $S = \{(s, s)\}$.

Fig. 2. Non-conflicting part (a_0, b_0) and conflicting part (s, s) of a BF (a, b) on a 2-element frame of discernment Ω_2

3   Conflicts of Belief Functions

Internal conflicts $IntC(m)$ which are included in particular individual BFs are distinguished from *conflict between BFs* $C(m_1, m_2)$ in [8]; the entire sum of conflicting masses is called *total conflict* $TotC(m_1, m_2)$; and three approaches to conflicts were introduced: combinational, plausibility and comparative.

Unfortunately, there are not yet any precise formulas, but only bounding inequalities for *combinational conflicts*: $\frac{1}{2}TotC(m, m)) \leq IntC(m) \leq TotC(m, m)$, $TotC(m_1, m_2) - (IntC(m_1) + IntC(m_2)) \leq C(m_1, m_2) \leq TotC(m_1, m_2)$.

Internal plausibility conflict of BF Bel is defined as $Pl\text{-}IntC(Bel) = 1 - max_{\omega \in \Omega} Pl(\{\omega\})$, where Pl is the plausibility equivalent to Bel.

Plausibility conflict between BFs Bel_1 and Bel_2 is defined by the formula $Pl\text{-}C(Bel_1, Bel_2) = min(\sum_{\omega \in \Omega_{PlC}(Bel_1, Bel_2)} \frac{1}{2}|PLP(Bel_1)(\omega) - PLP(Bel_2)(\omega)|, (m_1 \odot m_2)(\emptyset))$, where *conflicting set* $\Omega_{PlC}(Bel_1, Bel_2)$ is the set of elements $\omega \in \Omega$ with conflicting Pl_P values [8]. For an analysis and improvement of $Pl\text{-}C$ and analogously defined *pignistic conflict* $Bet\text{-}C$ see [11, 12, 15].

The idea of comparative conflictness / non-conflictness is a specification of basic belief masses (m-values) to smaller focal elements, which fit focal elements of the other BF as much as possible. *The comparative conflict between BFs Bel_1 and Bel_2 is defined as the smallest difference of such more specified basic belief assignments derived from the input m_1 and m_2.*

The above three approaches were compared with Liu's degree of conflict cf in [8]; cf is defined as $cf(m_i, m_j) = (m_{\ominus}(\emptyset), difBetP_{m_i}^{m_j})$ in [22], $difBetP_{m_i}^{m_j}$ is defined as $difBetP_{m_i}^{m_j} = max_{A \subseteq \Omega}(|BetP_{m_i}(A) - BetP_{m_j}(A)|)$.

Analysing these three approaches to conflicts [8], especially plausibility conflict *Pl-C*, the most elaborated of the approaches, a possibility of decomposition of a belief function into its conflicting and non-conflicting parts was observed.

We can use the important property of Dempster's combination, which is respecting the homomorphisms h and f, i.e., respecting the h-lines and f-ellipses, when two BFs are combined on a two-element frame of discernment [5, 19, 20, 28], see Fig 2. Using this property and two technical lemmata from [9] we obtain:

Theorem 1. *Any BF (a, b) on a 2-element frame of discernment Ω_2 is Dempster's sum of its unique non-conflicting part $(a_0, b_0) \in S_1 \cup S_2$ and of its unique conflicting part $(s, s) \in S$, which does not prefer any element of Ω_2, i.e., $(a, b) = (a_0, b_0) \oplus (s, s)$. It holds true that $s = \frac{b(1-a)}{1-2a+b-ab+a^2} = \frac{b(1-b)}{1-a+ab-b^2}$ and $(a, b) = (\frac{a-b}{1-b}, 0) \oplus (s, s)$ for $a \geq b$; and similarly that $s = \frac{a(1-b)}{1+a-2b-ab+b^2} = \frac{a(1-a)}{1-b+ab-a^2}$ and $(a, b) = (0, \frac{b-a}{1-a}) \oplus (s, s)$ for $a \leq b$.*

An algebraic analysis of Dempster's semigroup on Ω_3 is currently in development. We have only a simple description of the set of indecisive BFs, the most basic algebraic substructures on Dempster's semigroup on Ω_3 now [10]. Thus we do not have an analogy of Theorem 1 for BFs defined on general finite frames, and existence of their unique conflicting part is still an open problem.

On the other hand, we have already proven homomorphic properties of h : $h(Bel) = Bel \oplus U_n$ and also existence of a unique non-conflicting part Bel_0 for any BF Bel on any finite frame of discernment Ω_n [9].

Theorem 2. *For any BF Bel defined on a general finite Ω_n there exists a unique consonant BF Bel_0 such that,*

$$h(Bel_0 \oplus Bel_S) = h(Bel)$$

for any BF Bel_S for which $Bel_S \oplus U_n = U_n$ (Especially also $h(Bel_0) = h(Bel)$).

Algorithm 1. *(Computing the non-conflicting part of a BF).* Take all element(s) with maximal contour value (plausibility of singletons); they create the least focal element of Bel_0; assign to it the m-value equal to the difference between the max and max but one (different) contour values. A cycle: among the remaining elements (if any remains) take again all the element(s) with maximal contour value and add them to the previous focal element, thus you obtain a new focal element of Bel_0 (m-value: the corresponding difference between different contour values again). Repeat the cycle until Ω_n is obtained with m-value equal to min contour value. For a positive minimal contour value include Ω_n among focal elements of Bel_0. For a non-consistent BF Bel $(Pl(\{\omega_i\}) < 1$ for any $\omega_i \in \Omega_n)$ we need final normalisation of Bel_0.

More formally (a construction of the set of focal elements SFE and basic belief assignment m defined on SFE):

FE := $\emptyset$; SFE := $\emptyset$; Ω := Ω_n
Max_Pl := $Pl(\{\omega\})$, where $\omega \in \Omega_n$ s. t. $Pl(\{\omega\}) \geq Pl(\{\omega'\})$ for any $\omega' \in \Omega_n$
Min_Pl := $Pl(\{\omega\})$ where $\omega \in \Omega_n$ s. t. $Pl(\{\omega\}) \leq Pl(\{\omega'\})$ for any $\omega' \in \Omega_n$
Max1 := $\{\omega \in \Omega \mid Pl(\{\omega\}) = \text{Max\_Pl}\}$
Ω := $\Omega \setminus$ Max1
Max2 := $\{\omega \in \Omega \mid Pl(\{\omega\}) \geq Pl(\{\omega'\})$ for any $\omega' \in \Omega\}$
while Max2 $\neq \emptyset$ **do**
    FE := FE $\cup$ Max1; SPE := SPE $\cup$ {FE}
    $m(\text{FE})$:= $Pl(\{\omega_1\}) - Pl(\{\omega_2\})$, where $\omega_1 \in$ Max1, $\omega_2 \in$ Max2
    Max1 := Max2; Ω := $\Omega \setminus$ Max1
    Max2 := $\{\omega \in \Omega \mid Pl(\{\omega\}) \geq Pl(\{\omega'\})$ for any $\omega' \in \Omega\}$
end while
if Min_Pl > 0 **then**
    SFE := SPE $\cup$ Ω_n (as FE $\cup$ Max1 $= \Omega_n$ now)
    $m(\Omega_n)$:= Min_Pl
end if
if Max_Pl < 1 **then** normalisation of m (because $\sum_{X \subseteq \Omega_n} m(X) = \text{Max\_Pl}$)
end if

4   Conflict between Belief Functions Based on Their Non-conflicting Parts

4.1   Motivation and Definition of a New Measure of Conflict

One of the main problems of the previous definitions of conflict between BFs is the fact that the defined conflict usually includes some part (or even entire in the original Shafer's definition) of internal conflicts which are included inside the BFs in question. The other frequent problem is that the definitions of conflict between BFs are incorrectly related to distance or difference between the BFs.

In the following Theorem 1 we have unique decomposition of any belief function Bel on Ω_2 into its non-conflicting and conflicting parts $Bel = Bel_0 \oplus Bel_S$. There is no conflict in Bel_0 and entire internal conflict of Bel is included in Bel_S (as we suppose Bel_S to be non-conflicting with any BF for all Bel_S such that $h(Bel_S) = 0'$). Unfortunately, we do not have such a decomposition for BFs on a general finite frame of discernment Ω_n (this topic is still under investigation). Nevertheless, according to Theorem 2, we have a unique non-conflicting part Bel_0 for any BF Bel on Ω_n, such that Bel_0 does not include any part of internal conflict of the original BF Bel.

Thus $(m'_0 \odot m''_0)(\emptyset) = TotC(Bel'_0, Bel''_0) = C(Bel'_0, Bel''_0)$ holds true for any couple of BFs Bel', Bel'' on Ω_n, their con-conflicting parts Bel'_0, Bel''_0 and the related bbas m'_0, m''_0. Using these facts, we can define the conflict between BFs

Bel' and Bel'' as the conflict between their non-conflicting parts Bel'_0 and Bel''_0 (as conflicting parts Bel'_S, Bel''_S are mutually non-conflicting and both of them are non-conflicting with both non-conflicting parts Bel'_0 and Bel''_0):

Definition 1. *Let Bel', Bel'' be two belief functions on n-element frame of discernment $\Omega_n = \{\omega_1, \omega_2, ..., \omega_n\}$. Let Bel'_0 and Bel''_0 be their non-conflicting parts and m'_0, m''_0 the related basic belief assignments (bbas). We define* conflict *between BFs Bel' and Bel'' as*

$$Conf(Bel', Bel'') = m_{Bel'_0 \circledcirc Bel''_0}(\emptyset) = (m'_0 \circledcirc m''_0)(\emptyset).$$

Example 1. Let us suppose Ω_3, now; and four BFs m', m'', m''', and m'''' given as follows:

X :	$\{\omega_1\}$	$\{\omega_2\}$	$\{\omega_3\}$	$\{\omega_1,\omega_2\}$	$\{\omega_1,\omega_3\}$	$\{\omega_2,\omega_3\}$	Ω_3
$m'(X)$:	0.375	0.100	0.225	0.10			0.20
$m''(X)$:	0.250	0.175	0.175	0.20	0.05	0.05	0.10
$m'''(X)$:	0.350	0.250		0.25	0.05		0.10
$m''''(X)$:	0.100	0.200		0.40	0.00	0.00	0.30

$Pl\_P' = (0.45, 0.20, 0.35)$, $Pl\_P'' = (0.40, 0.35, 0.25)$, $Pl\_P''' = (0.50, 0.40, 0.10)$, $Pl\_P'''' = (0.40, 0.45, 0.15)$, $m'_0 = (\frac{10}{45}, 0, 0, 0, \frac{15}{45}, 0; \frac{20}{45})$, $m''_0 = (0.125, 0, 0, 0.25, 0, 0; 0.625)$, $m'''_0 = (0.20, 0, 0, 0.60, 0, 0; 0.20)$, $m''''_0 = (0, \frac{5}{45}, 0, \frac{25}{45}, 0, 0; \frac{15}{45})$. Thus, $Conf(Bel', Bel'') = 0 = Conf(Bel', Bel''') = Conf(Bel'', Bel''')$; and $Conf(Bel', Bel'''') = \frac{10}{45} \cdot \frac{5}{45} + \frac{5}{45} \cdot \frac{15}{45} = \frac{5}{81}$; $Conf(Bel'', Bel'''') = \frac{5}{45} \cdot \frac{5}{40} = \frac{1}{72}$; $Conf(Bel''', Bel'''') = \frac{10}{50} \cdot \frac{5}{45} = \frac{1}{45}$.

Let us also present some highly conflicting examples. For simplicity we consider Ω_3 again; for examples on larger frames of discernment see [14].

Example 2. Let us suppose Ω_3, again; and two pairs of highly conflicting BFs m', m'', and m''', m'''' now:

X :	$\{\omega_1\}$	$\{\omega_2\}$	$\{\omega_3\}$	$\{\omega_1,\omega_2\}$	$\{\omega_1,\omega_3\}$	$\{\omega_2,\omega_3\}$	Ω_3
$m'(X)$:	0.9			0.1			
$m''(X)$:		0.9		0.1			
$m'''(X)$:			1.0				
$m''''(X)$:	0.3	0.1		0.6			

$Pl\_P' = (0.9, 0.0, 0.1)$, $Pl\_P'' = (0.0, 0.9, 0.1)$, $Pl\_P''' = (0.0, 0.0, 1.0)$, $Pl\_P'''' = (\frac{9}{16}, \frac{7}{16}, 0.0)$, $m'_0 = (\frac{8}{9}, 0, 0, 0, \frac{1}{9}, 0; 0)$, $m''_0 = (0, \frac{8}{9}, 0, 0, 0, \frac{1}{9},; 0)$, $m'''_0 = (0, 0, 1.0, 0, 0, 0; 0)$, $m''''_0 = (\frac{2}{9}, 0, 0, \frac{7}{9}, 0, 0; 0)$.

Thus, $Conf(Bel', Bel'') = \frac{8}{9} \cdot \frac{8}{9} + \frac{8}{9} \cdot \frac{1}{9} + \frac{8}{9} \cdot \frac{1}{9} = \frac{80}{81} = 0.98765432$.
$Conf(Bel', Bel''') = \frac{8}{9} = Conf(Bel'', Bel''')$; and $Conf(Bel''', Bel'''') = \frac{2}{9} + \frac{7}{9} = 1.0$.
(Of course there is $Conf(Bel', Bel'''') = 0$ and small conflict $Conf(Bel'', Bel'''')$.)

4.2   An Analysis of Properties of the Measure of Conflict *Conf*

Let us present properties of *Conf* now, for proofs of the statements see [14].

Lemma 1. *Conflict Conf between belief functions is symmetric:* $Conf(Bel', Bel'') = Conf(Bel'', Bel')$.

Lemma 2. *Any BF $Bel_{SPl} \in S_{Pl}$ is non-conflicting with any other BF on Ω_n:* $Conf(Bel_{SPl}, Bel) = 0$ *for any Bel defined on Ω_n and any BF $Bel_{SPl} \in S_{Pl} = \{Bel \mid P\_LP(Bel) = U_n\}$.*

Corollary 1. *(i) Any BF $Bel_{S0} \in S_0 = \{(a, a, ..., a, 0, 0, ...0; 1-na) \mid 0 \le a \le \frac{1}{n}\}$ is non-conflicting with any other BF Bel defined on Ω_n, i.e., $Conf((a, a, ..., a, 0, 0, ...0; 1 - na), Bel) = 0$. This specially holds true also for 0 and U_n.*
(ii)   Any symmetric BF $Bel_S \in S = \{Bel \mid m(X) = m(Y)$ for $|X| = |Y|\}$ is non-conflicting with any other BF Bel defined on Ω_n, i.e., $Conf(Bel_S, Bel) = 0$.

Theorem 3. *Let Bel' and Bel'' be general BFs defined on an n-element frame of discernment Ω_n, let Bel'_0 and Bel''_0 be their unique non-conflicting parts, and $X' = \{\omega \in \Omega_n \mid Pl'(\{\omega\}) \ge Pl'(\{\omega'\})$ for any $\omega' \in \Omega_n\}$, $X'' = \{\omega \in \Omega_n \mid Pl''(\{\omega\}) \ge Pl''(\{\omega'\})$ for any $\omega' \in \Omega_n\}$. The following statements are equivalent:*
(i) BFs Bel' and Bel'' are mutually non-conflicting, i.e. $Conf(Bel', Bel'') = 0$,
(ii)   The least focal elements of Bel'_0 and Bel''_0 have non-empty intersection,
(iii) $X' \cap X'' \ne \emptyset$.

Corollary 2. *(i) For any BF Bel on Ω_n the following holds: $Conf(Bel, Bel) = 0$.*
(ii)   For any couple of BF Bel' and Bel'' defined on Ω_n such that $Pl\_P' = Pl\_P''$ the following holds true: $Conf(Bel', Bel'') = 0$.
(iii) For any couple of BFs (a, b) and (c, d) defined on Ω_2 such that $BetP(a, b) = BetP(c, d)$ the following holds true: $Conf((a, b), (c, d)) = 0$.

Note that assertion (iii) holds true just for BFs defined on Ω_2. Thus, on general Ω_n, there exist mutually conflicting BFs with same pignistic probabilities, see Example 3.

Example 3. Let us suppose Ω_3, now; and two BFs m' and m'' given as follows:

X :	$\{\omega_1\}$	$\{\omega_2\}$	$\{\omega_3\}$	$\{\omega_1, \omega_2\}$	Ω_3
$m'(X)$:	0.21	0.22	0.44	0.10	0.03
$m''(X)$:	0.01	0.02	0.44	0.50	0.03

$BetP' = (0.27, 0.28, 0.45) = BetP''$, $Pl\_P' = (\frac{34}{116}, \frac{35}{116}, \frac{47}{116})$, $Pl\_P'' = (\frac{54}{156}, \frac{55}{156}, \frac{47}{156})$, $m'_0 = (0, 0, \frac{12}{47}, 0, 0, \frac{1}{47}; \frac{34}{47})$, $m''_0 = (0, \frac{1}{55}, 0, \frac{47}{55}, 0, 0; \frac{47}{55})$, $Conf(Bel', Bel'') = \frac{8 \cdot 12}{47 \cdot 55} = \frac{96}{2585} = 0.037137$. Thus the conflict between BFs is small, but it is positive.

Theorem 4. *Let Bel' and Bel'' be arbitrary BFs on a general finite frame of discernment Ω_n given by bbas m' and m''. For conflict Conf between Bel' and Bel'' it holds that*

$$Conf(Bel', Bel'') \le (m' \textcircled{\odot} m'')(\emptyset).$$

Despite a simple idea and the simple definition of conflict *Conf* between BFs, there are many variants of explicit formulas for computation of the conflict, due to different ordering of m-values of focal elements of the BFs. For illustration, we present only the simplest case of BFs on a 2-element frame of discernment:

$$Conf((a,b),(c,d)) = \frac{a-b}{1-b} \cdot \frac{d-c}{1-c} \quad \text{if} \quad a>b \,\&\, c<d,$$

analogously for $a<b \,\&\, c>d$, $Conf((a,b),(c,d)) = 0$ otherwise.

In general, we have just to follow Definition 1: to compute non-conflicting parts Bel'_0 and Bel''_0 of both BFs in question (Algorithm 1) and simply apply $\odot$.

Martin's Axioms of Conflict between Belief Functions. There are the following axioms of conflict between belief functions presented in [23]:

(A1) : $Conf(Bel', Bel'') \geq 0$,
(A2) : $Conf(Bel, Bel) = 0$,
(A3) : $Conf(Bel', Bel'') = Conf(Bel'', Bel')$,
(A4) : $Conf(Bel', Bel'') \leq 1$.

All of these axioms[4] are satisfied by the conflict *Conf* according our Definition 1. Martin underlines, that he does not assume triangle inequality $Conf(Bel', Bel''') \leq Conf(Bel', Bel'') + Conf(Bel'', Bel''')$. Note, that our definition of the conflict is the case, where triangle inequality does not hold true, see Example 4.

In addition to these axioms, we should mention also important properties from Theorem 4 and Lemma 1 resp. its corollary on symmetric belief functions.

Example 4. Let $Bel' = (0.4, 0.1, 0.1, 0.2, 0, 0.1; 0.1)$, $Pl\_P' = (\frac{7}{15}, \frac{5}{15}, \frac{3}{15})$, $Bel'' = (0.3, 0.2, 0.1, 0.1, 0, 0.1; 0.2)$, $Pl\_P'' = (\frac{6}{16}, \frac{6}{16}, \frac{4}{16})$, $Bel''' = (0.1, 0.2, 0.3, 0.1, 0, 0.2; 0.1)$, $Pl\_P''' = (\frac{3}{15}, \frac{6}{15}, \frac{6}{15})$, $Bel'_0 = (\frac{2}{7}, 0, 0, \frac{2}{7}, 0, 0; \frac{3}{7})$, $Bel''_0 = (0, 0, 0, \frac{2}{6}, 0, 0; \frac{4}{6})$, $Bel'''_0 = (0, 0, 0, 0, 0, \frac{3}{6}; \frac{3}{6})$, $Conf(Bel'_0, Bel'''_0) = \frac{1}{7} \nleq 0 = Conf(Bel'_0, Bel''_0) + Conf(Bel''_0, Bel'''_0)$.

5   Open Problems for Future Research

We have a simply defined conflict between two belief functions on a general finite frame of discernment. Nevertheless, to complete this study of conflicts of BFs we will have to define and analyze also internal conflicts of individual BFs.

Two main open issues remain: The first one is a question of precise interpretation of the conflicting part of a belief function and its relationship to the internal conflict of the BF on a 2-element frame of discernment. First results are presented in [13].

The second, more complex issue is a study of internal conflict of BFs on a general finite frame of discernment. This also includes a question whether a decomposition of a general BF exists to its non-conflicting and conflicting parts; consequently, a generalisation of Hájek-Valdés algebraic analysis of BFs to a general frame of discernment is concerned, namely a generalisation of the operation $-(a, b) = (b, a)$ and of homomorphism f.

As another open question remains a further elaboration of the theoretic principles of the presented results with those from [16] and [23].

---

[4] There is also (A5), unfortunately mistyped or incorrectly formulated in [23], see [14].

6   Conclusion

In this study, we introduced a new definition of conflict *Conf* between belief functions on a general finite frame of discernment. Its properties were compared with our previous approaches [8], and also with Liu's approach [22]. *Conf* is a simplification of plausibility conflict *Pl-C*, while keeping its nature. *Conf* also specifies the size of the conflict between belief functions in a way which is compatible with the combinational conflict. Thus, we can consider *Conf* as an improvement of both the combinational- and the plausibility-conflict approaches.

The presented theoretical results improve general understanding of conflict between belief functions and the entire nature of belief functions. Correct understanding of conflicts may, consequently, improve combination of conflicting belief functions in their practical applications.

Acknowledgments. This research is supported by the grant P202/10/1826 of the Czech Science Foundation (GAČR). The partial institutional support of RVO 67985807 from the Institute of Computer Science is also acknowledged.

References

1. Almond, R.G.: Graphical Belief Modeling. Chapman & Hall, London (1995)
2. Ayoun, A., Smets, P.: Data association in multi-target detection using the transferable belief model. International Journal of Intelligent Systems 16(10), 1167–1182 (2001)
3. Cobb, B.R., Shenoy, P.P.: A Comparison of Methods for Transforming Belief Function Models to Probability Models. In: Nielsen, T.D., Zhang, N.L. (eds.) ECSQARU 2003. LNCS (LNAI), vol. 2711, pp. 255–266. Springer, Heidelberg (2003)
4. Cuzzolin, F.: Lp consonant approximation of belief functions. IEEE Transactions on Fuzzy Systems 22(2), 420–436 (2014)
5. Daniel, M.: Algebraic structures related to Dempster-Shafer theory. In: Bouchon-Meunier, B., Yager, R.R., Zadeh, L.A. (eds.) IPMU 1994. LNCS, vol. 945, pp. 51–61. Springer, Heidelberg (1995)
6. Daniel, M.: Distribution of Contradictive Belief Masses in Combination of Belief Functions. In: Bouchon-Meunier, B., Yager, R.R., Zadeh, L.A. (eds.) Information, Uncertainty and Fusion, pp. 431–446. Kluwer Academic Publishers, Boston (2000)
7. Daniel, M.: Probabilistic Transformations of Belief Functions. In: Godo, L. (ed.) ECSQARU 2005. LNCS (LNAI), vol. 3571, pp. 539–551. Springer, Heidelberg (2005)
8. Daniel, M.: Conflicts within and between Belief Functions. In: Hüllermeier, E., Kruse, R., Hoffmann, F. (eds.) IPMU 2010. LNCS (LNAI), vol. 6178, pp. 696–705. Springer, Heidelberg (2010)
9. Daniel, M.: Non-conflicting and Conflicting Parts of Belief Functions. In: Coolen, F., de Cooman, G., Fetz, T., Oberguggenberger, M. (eds.) ISIPTA 2011: Proceedings of the 7th ISIPTA, pp. 149–158. Studia Universitätsverlag, Innsbruck (2011)
10. Daniel, M.: Introduction to an Algebra of Belief Functions on Three-Element Frame of Discernment — A Quasi Bayesian Case. In: Greco, S., Bouchon-Meunier, B., Coletti, G., Fedrizzi, M., Matarazzo, B., Yager, R.R. (eds.) IPMU 2012, Part III. CCIS, vol. 299, pp. 532–542. Springer, Heidelberg (2012)

11. Daniel, M.: Properties of Plausibility Conflict of Belief Functions. In: Rutkowski, L., Korytkowski, M., Scherer, R., Tadeusiewicz, R., Zadeh, L.A., Zurada, J.M. (eds.) ICAISC 2013, Part I. LNCS (LNAI), vol. 7894, pp. 235–246. Springer, Heidelberg (2013)

12. Daniel, M.: Belief Functions: A Revision of Plausibility Conflict and Pignistic Conflict. In: Liu, W., Subrahmanian, V.S., Wijsen, J. (eds.) SUM 2013. LNCS (LNAI), vol. 8078, pp. 190–203. Springer, Heidelberg (2013)

13. Daniel, M.: An Interpretation of Conflicting Parts of Belief Functions on Two-Element Frame of Discrement. In: Kratochvíl, V., Vejnarová, J. (eds.) Proceedings of the 16th Czech-Japan Seminar on Data Analysis and Decision Making under Uncertainty (CJS 2013), pp. 187–196. University of Economics (2013)

14. Daniel, M.: Conflicts of Belief Functions: about a New Measure Based on their Non-Conflicting Parts. Technical report V-1205, ICS AS CR, Prague (2014)

15. Daniel, M., Ma, J.: Conflicts of Belief Functions: Continuity and Frame Resizement. In: Straccia, U., Cali, A. (eds.) SUM 2014. LNCS (LNAI), vol. 8720, pp. 106–119. Springer, Heidelberg (2014)

16. Destercke, S., Burger, T.: Toward an axiomatic definition of conflict between belief functions. IEEE Transactions on Cybernetics 43(2), 585–596 (2013)

17. Dubois, D., Prade, H.: Representation an combination of uncertainty with belief functions and possibility measures. Computational Intelligence 4, 244–264 (1988)

18. Dubois, D., Prade, H.: Consonant Approximations of Belief Functions. International Journal of Approximate Reasoning 4, 419–649 (1990)

19. Hájek, P., Havránek, T., Jiroušek, R.: Uncertain Information Processing in Expert Systems. CRC Press, Boca Raton (1992)

20. Hájek, P., Valdés, J.J.: Generalized algebraic foundations of uncertainty processing in rule-based expert syst (dempsteroids). Computers and Artificial Intelligence 10(1), 29–42 (1991)

21. Lefèvre, E., Elouedi, Z.: How to preserve the conflict as an alarm in the combination of belief functions? Decision Support Systems 56(1), 326–333 (2013)

22. Liu, W.: Analysing the degree of conflict among belief functions. Artificial Intelligence 170, 909–924 (2006)

23. Martin, A.: About Conflict in the Theory of Belief Functions. In: Denœux, T., Masson, M.-H. (eds.) Belief Functions: Theory & Appl. AISC, vol. 164, pp. 161–168. Springer, Heidelberg (2012)

24. Roquel, A., Le Hégarat-Mascle, S., Bloch, I., Vincke, B.: Decomposition of conflict as a distribution on hypotheses in the framework on belief functions. International Journal of Approximate Reasoning 55(5), 1129–1146 (2014)

25. Schubert, J.: The Internal Conflict of a Belief Function. In: Denœux, T., Masson, M.-H. (eds.) Belief Functions: Theory & Appl. AISC, vol. 164, pp. 169–177. Springer, Heidelberg (2012)

26. Shafer, G.: A Mathematical Theory of Evidence. Princeton University Press, Princeton (1976)

27. Smets, P.: Analyzing the combination of conflicting belief functions. Information Fusion 8, 387–412 (2007)

28. Valdés, J.J.: Algebraic and logical foundations of uncertainty processing in rule-based expert systems of Artificial Intelligence. PhD Thesis, ČSAV, Prague (1987)

29. Yager, R.R.: On the Demspter-Shafer framework and new combination rules. Information Sciences 41, 93–138 (1987)

On Marginal Problem in Evidence Theory

Jiřina Vejnarová*

Institute Information Theory and Automation of the AS CR,
Pod Vodárenskou věží 4, Prague, Czech Republic
vejnar@utia.cas.cz

Abstract. Marginal problem in the framework of evidence theory is
introduced in a way analogous to probabilistic one, to address the question of whether or not a common extension exists for a given set of
marginal basic assignments. Similarities between these two problem types
are demonstrated, concerning necessary condition for the existence of an
extension and sets of all solutions. Finally, product extension of the set
of marginal basic assignments is introduced as a tool for the expression
of a representative in a closed form.

Keywords: Marginal problem, extension, product extension.

1 Introduction

The marginal problem – which addresses the question of whether or not a common extension exists for a given set of marginal distributions – is one of the most
challenging problem types in probability theory. The challenges lie not only in
a wide range of the relevant theoretical problems (probably the most important
among them is to find conditions for the existence of a solution to this problem), but also in its applicability to various problems of statistics [4], computer
tomography [7], and artificial intelligence [12]. Recently it has also been studied in other frameworks, for example, in possibility theory [10] and quantum
mathematics [8].

In this paper we will introduce an evidential marginal problem analogous
to that encountered in the probabilistic framework. We will demonstrate the
similarities between these frameworks concerning necessary conditions, and sets
of solutions; finally we will also introduce product extension of the set of marginal
basic assignments.

The paper is organised as follows: after a brief overview of necessary concepts
and notation (Section 2), we will introduce the evidential marginal problem,
necessary condition, and the set of solutions in Section 3; and in Section 4 we
will deal with product extension.

2 Basic Concepts and Notation

In this section we will, as briefly as possible, recall basic concepts from evidence
theory [9] concerning sets and set functions.

* The support of Grant GAČR 13-20012S is gratefully acknowledged.

F. Cuzzolin (Ed.): BELIEF 2014, LNAI 8764, pp. 331–338, 2014.
© Springer International Publishing Switzerland 2014

For an index set $N = \{1, 2, \ldots, n\}$, let $\{X_i\}_{i \in N}$ be a system of variables, each X_i having its values in a finite set $\mathbf{X}_i$. In this paper we will deal with a *multidimensional frame of discernment* $\mathbf{X}_N = \mathbf{X}_1 \times \mathbf{X}_2 \times \ldots \times \mathbf{X}_n$, and its *subframes* (for $K \subseteq N$)

$$\mathbf{X}_K = \times_{i \in K} \mathbf{X}_i.$$

Throughout this paper, X_K will denote a group of variables $\{X_i\}_{i \in K}$ when dealing with groups of variables on these subframes.

For $M \subset K \subseteq N$ and $A \subset \mathbf{X}_K$, we denote by $A^{\downarrow M}$ a *projection* of A into $\mathbf{X}_M$:

$$A^{\downarrow M} = \{y \in \mathbf{X}_M \mid \exists x \in A : y = x^{\downarrow M}\},$$

where, for $M = \{i_1, i_2, \ldots, i_m\}$,

$$x^{\downarrow M} = (x_{i_1}, x_{i_2}, \ldots, x_{i_m}) \in \mathbf{X}_M.$$

In addition to the projection, in this text we will also need its inverse operation that is usually called a cylindrical extension. The *cylindrical extension* of $A \subset \mathbf{X}_K$ to $\mathbf{X}_L$ ($K \subset L$) is the set

$$A^{\uparrow L} = \{x \in \mathbf{X}_L : x^{\downarrow K} \in A\} = A \times \mathbf{X}_{L \setminus K}.$$

A more complex instance is to make a common extension of two sets, which will be called a join [1]. By a *join* of two sets $A \subseteq \mathbf{X}_K$ and $B \subseteq \mathbf{X}_L$ ($K, L \subseteq N$), we will understand a set

$$A \bowtie B = \{x \in \mathbf{X}_{K \cup L} : x^{\downarrow K} \in A \ \& \ x^{\downarrow L} \in B\}.$$

Let us note that, for any $C \subseteq \mathbf{X}_{K \cup L}$, it naturally holds $C \subseteq C^{\downarrow K} \bowtie C^{\downarrow L}$, but generally $C \neq C^{\downarrow K} \bowtie C^{\downarrow L}$.

Let us also note that if K and L are disjoint, then the join of A and B is just their Cartesian product, $A \bowtie B = A \times B$, and if $K = L$ then $A \bowtie B = A \cap B$. If $K \cap L \neq \emptyset$ and $A^{\downarrow K \cap L} \cap B^{\downarrow K \cap L} = \emptyset$ then $A \bowtie B = \emptyset$ as well. Generally, $A \bowtie B = A^{\uparrow K \cup L} \cap B^{\uparrow K \cup L}$), i.e., a join of two sets is the intersection of their cylindrical extensions.

In evidence theory [9], two dual measures are used to model the uncertainty: belief and plausibility measures. Each of them can be defined with the help of another set function called a *basic (probability or belief) assignment* m on $\mathbf{X}_N$, i.e., $m : \mathcal{P}(\mathbf{X}_N) \longrightarrow [0, 1]$, where $\mathcal{P}(\mathbf{X}_N)$ is the power set of $\mathbf{X}_N$, and $\sum_{A \subseteq \mathbf{X}_N} m(A) = 1$. Furthermore, we assume that $m(\emptyset) = 0$.[1] A set $A \in \mathcal{P}(\mathbf{X}_N)$ is a *focal element* if $m(A) > 0$.

For a basic assignment m on $\mathbf{X}_K$ and $M \subset K$, a *marginal basic assignment* of m on $\mathbf{X}_M$ is defined (for each $A \subseteq \mathbf{X}_M$) by the equality

$$m^{\downarrow M}(A) = \sum_{\substack{B \subseteq \mathbf{X}_K \\ B^{\downarrow M} = A}} m(B). \tag{1}$$

---

[1] This assumption is not generally accepted, e.g., in [2] it is omitted.

3   Marginal Problem

Let $\{X_i\}_{i\in N}$ be a finite system of finite-valued variables with values in $\{\mathbf{X}_i\}_{i\in N}$. Using the procedure of marginalisation (1) one can always uniquely restrict a basic assignment m on $\mathbf{X}_N$ to the basic assignment m_K on $\mathbf{X}_K$ for $K \subset N$. However, the opposite process, the procedure of an *extension* of a system of basic assignments m_{K_i}, $i = 1, \ldots, m$ on $\mathbf{X}_{K_i}$ to a basic assignment m_K on $\mathbf{X}_K$ $(K = K_1 \cup \cdots \cup K_m)$, is not unique (if it exists) and can be done in many ways.

Let us demonstrate this fact with two simple examples.

Example 1. Consider, for $i = 1, 2$, two basic assignments m_i on $\mathbf{X}_i = \{a_i, b_i\}$, specified in the left-hand side of Table 1. Our task is to find a basic assignment m

Table 1. Example 1: basic assignments m_1 and m_2 and m and m'

$A \subseteq \mathbf{X}_1$	$m_1(A)$	$A \subseteq \mathbf{X}_2$	$m_2(A)$	$A \subseteq \mathbf{X}_1 \times \mathbf{X}_2$	$m(A)$	$A \subseteq \mathbf{X}_1 \times \mathbf{X}_2$	$m'(A)$
$\{a_1\}$	0.2	$\{a_2\}$	0.6	$\{a_1 a_2\}$	0.2	$\{a_1\} \times \mathbf{X}_2$	0.2
$\{b_1\}$	0.3	$\{b_2\}$	0	$\{b_1 a_2\}$	0.3	$\{b_1\} \times \mathbf{X}_2$	0.2
$\mathbf{X}_1$	0.5	$\mathbf{X}_2$	0.4	$\mathbf{X}_1 \times \{a_2\}$	0.1	$\{b_1 a_2\}$	0.1
				$\{a_1 a_2, b_1 b_2\}$	0.4	$\mathbf{X}_1 \times \mathbf{X}_2$	0.5

on $\mathbf{X}_1 \times \mathbf{X}_2$ satisfying these marginal constraints. It is easy to realise that, e.g., m or m' contained in the left-hand side of Table 1 is a solution to this problem. It is obvious that one can find numerous different solutions to this problem.   ◇

The following example is devoted to a (more interesting) case of overlapping marginals.

Example 2. Consider two basic assignments m_i (for $i = 1, 2$) on $\mathbf{X}_i \times \mathbf{X}_3$ $(\mathbf{X}_i = \{a_i, b_i\}, i = 1, 2, 3)$ specified in Table 2. It is again easy to realise that both

Table 2. Example 2: basic assignments m_1 and m_2.

$A \subseteq \mathbf{X}_1 \times \mathbf{X}_3$	$m_1(A)$	$A \subseteq \mathbf{X}_2 \times \mathbf{X}_3$	$m_2(A)$
$\{a_1 a_3\}$	0.5	$\{a_2 a_3\}$	0.5
$\{a_1 a_3, b_1 b_3\}$	0.3	$\{a_2 a_3, b_2 b_3\}$	0.3
$\mathbf{X}_1 \times \{a_3\}$	0.2	$\mathbf{X}_2 \times \{a_3\}$	0.2

joint basic assignments m and m' contained in Table 3 satisfy these constraints. And it is again obvious that one can find numerous different solutions to this problem.   ◇

Table 3. Example 2: basic assignments m and m'

$A \subseteq \mathbf{X}_1 \times \mathbf{X}_2 \times \mathbf{X}_3$	$m(A)$	$A \subseteq \mathbf{X}_1 \times \mathbf{X}_2 \times \mathbf{X}_3$	$m'(A)$
$\{a_1 a_2 a_3\}$	0.5	$\{a_1 a_2 a_3\}$	0.3
$\{a_1 a_2 a_3, b_1 b_2 b_3\}$	0.3	$\{a_1 a_2 a_3, b_1 b_2 b_3\}$	0.3
$\mathbf{X}_1 \times \mathbf{X}_2 \times \{a_3\}$	0.2	$\{a_1\} \times \mathbf{X}_2 \times \{a_3\}$	0.2
		$\mathbf{X}_1 \times \{a_2 a_3\}$	0.2

The evidential marginal problem can be, analogous to probability theory, understood as follows: Let us assume that X_i, $i \in N$, $1 \leq |N| < \infty$ are finitely-valued variables, $\mathcal{K}$ is a system of nonempty subsets of N and

$$S = \{m_K, K \in \mathcal{K}\} \tag{2}$$

is a family of basic assignments, where each m_K is a basic assignment on $\mathbf{X}_K$.

The problem we are interested in is the existence of an *extension*, i.e., a basic assignment m on $\mathbf{X}$ whose marginals are basic assignments from S; or, more generally, the set

$$\mathcal{E} = \{m : m^{\downarrow K} = m_K, K \in \mathcal{K}\} \tag{3}$$

is of interest.

Let us note that we will not be able to find any basic assignment on $\mathbf{X}_1 \times \mathbf{X}_2 \times \mathbf{X}_3$ with prescribed two-dimensional marginals in Example 2 if these marginals do not satisfy quite a natural condition called a projectivity (or compatibility) condition.

Having two basic assignments m_1 and m_2 on $\mathbf{X}_K$ and $\mathbf{X}_L$, respectively ($K, L \subseteq N$), we say that these assignments are *projective* if

$$m_1^{\downarrow K \cap L} = m_2^{\downarrow K \cap L},$$

which occurs if and only if there exists a basic assignment m on $\mathbf{X}_{K \cup L}$ such that both m_1 and m_2 are marginal assignments of some m on $\mathbf{X}_{K \cup L}$ (cf. also Theorem 2).

This condition is clearly necessary, but not sufficient, as demonstrated in Example 3.

Example 3. Let $\mathbf{X}_i$ be the same as in Example 2, and m_1, m_2 and m_3 be defined as shown in Table 4.

Although these three basic assignments are projective, more exactly, $m_i(\{a_j\}) = 0.5$ and $m_i(\mathbf{X}_j) = 0.5$ for $i = 1, 2, 3$ and $j = i, i+1 (mod 3)$, no basic assignment m on $\mathbf{X}_1 \times \mathbf{X}_2 \times \mathbf{X}_3$ exists that would have them as its marginals . From the first two marginals one can derive that the only focal elements of m are $\{a_1 a_2 a_3\}$ and $\mathbf{X}_1 \times \mathbf{X}_2 \times \mathbf{X}_3$, but none of them is projected to any of the focal elements of m_3.   ◇

Table 4. Example 3: basic assignments m_1, m_2 and m_3

$A \subseteq \mathbf{X}_1 \times \mathbf{X}_2$	$m_1(A)$	$A \subseteq \mathbf{X}_2 \times \mathbf{X}_3$	$m_2(A)$	$A \subseteq \mathbf{X}_1 \times \mathbf{X}_3$	$m_1(A)$
$\{a_1 a_2\}$	0.5	$\{a_2 a_3\}$	0.5	$\{a_1\} \times \mathbf{X}_3$	0.5
$\mathbf{X}_1 \times \mathbf{X}_2$	0.5	$\mathbf{X}_2 \times \mathbf{X}_2$	0.5	$\mathbf{X}_1 \times \{a_3\}$	0.5

In the probabilistic framework, projectivity is a necessary condition for the existence of an extension, too, and becomes a sufficient condition if the index sets of the marginals can be ordered in such a way that it satisfies a special property called the running intersection property (see, e.g., [6]), or equivalently, if the model is decomposable. We conjure that a similar result also holds in evidential framework; nevertheless, it will remain a topic for our future research.

If a solution of an evidential marginal problem exists, it is (usually) not unique, as we have already seen in Examples 1 and 2. This fact is completely analogous to the probabilistic framework. And the following theorem reveals another analogy in this respect.

Theorem 1. *The set $\mathcal{E}(\mathcal{S})$ is a convex set of basic assignments.*

Proof. Let $m_1, m_2 \in \mathcal{E}(\mathcal{S})$ and m be such that

$$m(C) = \alpha m_1(C) + (1 - \alpha) m_2(C)$$

for any $C \subset \mathbf{X}_N$. Since $m_1^{\downarrow K}(C^{\downarrow K}) = m_2^{\downarrow K}(C^{\downarrow K}) = m_K^{\downarrow K}(C^{\downarrow K})$ for any $K \in \mathcal{K}$, we get

$$m^{\downarrow K}(C^{\downarrow K}) = \alpha m_1^{\downarrow K}(C^{\downarrow K}) + (1 - \alpha) m_2^{\downarrow K}(C^{\downarrow K}) = m_K^{\downarrow K}(C^{\downarrow K})$$

for any $K \in \mathcal{K}$. Therefore, $m \in \mathcal{E}(\mathcal{S})$.   □

A convex combination of basic assignments m and m' usually leads to a more complex basic assignment with a higher number of focal elements, as can be seen from the following simple example.

Example 1. *(Continued)* Combining m and m' with $\alpha = 0.5$, we obtain the basic assignment contained in Table 4.   ◇

This fact is again analogous to a probabilistic framework, but contrary to the probabilistic case, where the number of focal elements is limited to the cardinality of $\mathbf{X}_N$, in evidence theory the increase of the number of focal elements may lead to intractable tasks.

4   Product Extensions

It is evident that it is rather hard to deal with the whole sets of extensions; hence it seems to be reasonable to look for a representative of each such set.

Table 5. Example 1: basic assignment m^*

$A \subseteq \mathbf{X}_1 \times \mathbf{X}_2$	$m^*(A)$	$A \subseteq \mathbf{X}_1 \times \mathbf{X}_2$	$m^*(A)$	$A \subseteq \mathbf{X}_1 \times \mathbf{X}_2$	$m^*(A)$
$\{a_1 a_2\}$	0.1	$\{a_1\} \times \mathbf{X}_2$	0.1	$\mathbf{X}_1 \times \{a_2\}$	0.05
$\{b_1 a_2\}$	0.2	$\{b_1\} \times \mathbf{X}_2$	0.1	$\mathbf{X}_1 \times \mathbf{X}_2$	0.25
$\{a_1 a_2, b_1 b_2\}$	0.2				

Dempster's rule of combination [9] is a standard way to combine (in the framework of evidence theory) information from different sources. It has been frequently criticised since the time it first appeared. That is why many alternatives to it have been suggested by various authors.

From the viewpoint of this paper, the most important among them is the *conjunctive combination rule* [2], which is, in fact, a non-normalised Dempster's rule defined for m_1 and m_2 on the same space $\mathbf{X}_K$ by the formula

$$(m_1 \textcircled{\odot} m_2)(C) = \sum_{A, B \subseteq \mathbf{X}_K\, A \cap B = C} m_1(A) m_2(B).$$

The result of this rule is one of the examples of a non-normalised basic assignment.

It can easily be generalised [3] to the case when m_1 is defined on X_K and m_2 is defined on X_L ($K \neq L$) in the following way (for any $C \in \mathbf{X}_{K \cup L}$):

$$(m_1 \textcircled{\odot} m_2)(C) = \sum_{\substack{A \subseteq \mathbf{X}_K, B \subseteq \mathbf{X}_L \\ A^{\uparrow L \cup K} \cap B^{\uparrow L \cup K} = C}} m_1(A) m_2(B). \tag{4}$$

Another possible way to solve this problem is to use the product extension of marginal basic assignments defined as follows:

Definition 1. *Let m_1 and m_2 be projective basic assignments on $\mathbf{X}_K$ and $\mathbf{X}_L$ ($K, L \subseteq N$), respectively. We will call basic assignment m on $\mathbf{X}_{K \cup L}$ product extension of m_1 and m_2 if for any $A = A^{\downarrow K} \bowtie A^{\downarrow L}$*

$$m(A) = \frac{m_1^{\downarrow K}(A^{\downarrow K}) \cdot m_2^{\downarrow L}(A^{\downarrow L})}{m_1^{\downarrow K \cap L}(A^{\downarrow K \cap L})}, \tag{5}$$

whenever the right-hand side is defined, and $m(A) = 0$ otherwise.

Let us note that the definition is only seemingly non-commutative, as m_1 and m_2 are supposed to be projective. Therefore, it is irrelevant which marginal is used in the denominator.

In the following example we will show that a product extension is more appropriate than Dempster's rule of combination.

Table 6. Example 4: basic assignments m_1, m_2Z

$A \subseteq \mathbf{X}_1 \times \mathbf{X}_3$	$m_1(A)$	$A \subseteq \mathbf{X}_2 \times \mathbf{X}_3$	$m_2(A)$
$\mathbf{X}_1 \times \{b_3\}$	0.5	$\mathbf{X}_2 \times \{b_3\}$	0.5
$\{(a_1 b_3, b_1 a_3)\}$	0.5	$\{(a_2 b_3, b_2 b_3)\}$	0.5

Example 4. Let $\mathbf{X}_i, i = 1, 2, 3$, be the same as in previous examples and m_1 and m_2 be two basic assignments defined as shown in Table 6.

Since their marginals are projective, as can easily been checked, there exists (at least one) common extension of both of them.

Applying the conjunctive combination rule to the marginals, one obtains values contained in the left-hand part of Table 7 with the marginal basic assignments different from the originals.

Table 7. Example 4: basic assignments obtained by Dempster's combination rule and product extension

$A \subseteq \mathbf{X}_1 \times \mathbf{X}_3$	$m_1(A)$	$A \subseteq \mathbf{X}_2 \times \mathbf{X}_3$	$m_2(A)$
$\mathbf{X}_1 \times \mathbf{X}_2 \times \{b_3\}$	0.25	$\mathbf{X}_1 \times \mathbf{X}_2 \times \{b_3\}$	0.5
$\{(a_1 a_2 b_3, b_1 b_2 a_3)\}$	0.25	$\{(a_1 a_2 b_3, b_1 b_2 a_3)\}$	0.5
$\mathbf{X}_1 \times \{a_2\} \times \{b_3\}$	0.25		
$\{a_1\} \times \mathbf{X}_2 \times \{b_3\}$	0.25		

On the other hand, product extensions of basic assignments m_1 and m_2 contained in the right-hand side of Table 7 keep both marginals.   ◇

The difference consists in assigning values to joins of focal elements of the marginal basic assignments. While in (4) the original basic assignments are used even in instances in which focal elements have different projections; at least one of the marginals is equal to zero in (5) in this case, which means that these sets cannot be focal elements of the joint basic assignment.

This result was not obtained by chance, as the following assertion implies.

Theorem 2. Let m_1 and m_2 be two projective basic assignments on $\mathbf{X}_K$ and $\mathbf{X}_L$ ($K, L \subseteq N$), respectively, and m be their product extension. Then

$$m^{\downarrow K}(B) = m_1(B),$$
$$m^{\downarrow L}(C) = m_2(C)$$

for any $B \in \mathbf{X}_K$ and $C \in \mathbf{X}_L$, respectively.

Proof. It follows directly from Theorem 1 in [11].   □

The next step would be to prove an analogous result for a more general system of basic assignments (as suggested in the previous section). Results form [5] indicate that it could be done.

5 Conclusions

We have introduced an evidential marginal problem in a way analogous to a probability setting, where marginal probabilities are substituted by marginal basic assignments.

We presented the necessary conditions for the existence of a solution to this problem and also dealt with the sets of all solutions. Finally, we introduced a so-called product extension, which enables us to express an extension of the problem in a closed form.

There are still many problems to be solved in the future, such as the structure of the set of extensions of the problem as well as a generalisation of the product extension to a more general index set of marginal basic assignments.

References

1. Beeri, C., Fagin, R., Maier, D., Yannakakis, M.: On the desirability of acyclic database schemes. J. of the Association for Computing Machinery 30, 479–513 (1983)
2. Ben Yaghlane, B., Smets, P., Mellouli, K.: Belief functions independence: I. the marginal case. Int. J. Approx. Reasoning 29, 47–70 (2002)
3. Ben Yaghlane, B., Smets, P., Mellouli, K.: Belief functions independence: II. the conditional case. Int. J. Approx. Reasoning 31, 31–75 (2002)
4. Janžura, M.: Marginal problem, statistical estimation, and Möbius formula. Kybernetika 43, 619–631 (2007)
5. Jiroušek, R., Vejnarová, J.: Compositional models and conditional independence in Evidence Theory. Int. J. Approx. Reasoning 52, 316–334 (2011)
6. Malvestuto, F.M.: Existence of extensions and product extensions for discrete probability distributions. Discrete Mathematics 69, 61–77 (1988)
7. Pougazaa, D.-B., Mohammad-Djafaria, A., Berchera, J.-F.: Link between copula and tomography. Pattern Recognition Letters 31, 2258–2264 (2010)
8. Schilling, C.: The quantum marginal problem. In: Proceedings of the Conference QMath 12, Berlin (2013)
9. Shafer, G.: A Mathematical Theory of Evidence. Princeton University Press, Princeton (1976)
10. Vejnarová, J.: On possibilistic marginal problem. Kybernetika 43(5), 657–674 (2007)
11. Vejnarová, J.: On conditional independence in evidence theory. In: Augustin, T., Coolen, F.P.A., Moral, S., Troffaes, M.C.M. (eds.) Proceedings of ISIPTA 2009, Durham, UK, pp. 431–440 (2009)
12. Vomlel, J.: Integrating inconsistent data in a probabilistic model. Journal of Applied Non-Classical Logics 14, 367–386 (2004)

Multi-Sensor Fusion Using Evidential SLAM for Navigating a Probe through Deep Ice

Joachim Clemens and Thomas Reineking

Cognitive Neuroinformatics, University of Bremen,
Enrique-Schmidt-Str. 5, 28359 Bremen, Germany
{clemens,reineking}@uni-bremen.de

Abstract. We present an evidential multi-sensor fusion approach for navigating a maneuverable ice probe designed for extraterrestrial sample analysis missions. The probe is equipped with a variety of sensors and has to estimate its own position within the ice as well as a map of its surroundings. The sensor fusion is based on an evidential SLAM approach which produces evidential occupancy grid maps that contain more information about the environment compared to probabilistic grid maps. We describe the different sensor models underlying the algorithm and we present empirical results obtained under controlled conditions in order to analyze the effectiveness of the proposed multi-sensor fusion approach. In particular, we show that the localization error is significantly reduced by combining multiple sensors.

Keywords: SLAM, Mulit-Sensor Fusion, Evidence Theory, Navigation, Mapping.

1 Introduction

The Cassini spacecraft has provided strong evidence that there is a subglacial sea of liquid water under the ice crust of Saturn's moon Enceladus. Because water is an essential prerequisite for the existence of life, Enceladus is considered to be one of the most promising candidates for finding extraterrestrial life. The goal of the "Enceladus Explorer" project is therefore to develop a maneuverable ice probe that is capable of autonomously navigating through deep ice in order to obtain a sample from a subsurface water reservoir. As a first step towards an extraterrestrial mission, the probe was tested on several glaciers in Europe and Antarctica.

The probe is equipped with multiple sensors that need to be fused in order to estimate a map of the surrounding ice and the probe's position. When a mobile robot navigates through an unknown environment, it has to solve a similar problem of jointly estimating a map of the environment while localizing itself with respect to this map. This problem is commonly known as simultaneous localization and mapping (SLAM) [5] and it forms the basis for the sensor fusion approach presented in this paper. We use a fusion approach based on belief functions because it allows us to cope with the uncertainty resulting from the fact

F. Cuzzolin (Ed.): BELIEF 2014, LNAI 8764, pp. 339–347, 2014.

that many of the underlying parameters are difficult to model probabilistically, especially in the context of an extraterrestrial mission with an unknown environment. A particular advantage of the evidential approach is that the generated maps provide additional information about uncertainty compared to probabilistic maps.

2   Hardware Platform

The ice probe shown in Fig. 1 uses a melting head to penetrate the ice while a screw assures close contact to the ice. The probe is maneuverable by differential heating and can navigate through ice at a speed of up to 1.1 m/h using a number of different sensors. A combination of a tactical grade fiber optical gyro (FOG) inertial measurement unit (IMU) and a differential magnetometer system measure the current attitude. To estimate the absolute position of the probe, an acoustic positioning system (APS) was developed. It consists of 6 transducer stations arranged above the operation area which send synchronized ultrasonic pulses that can be received by the probe. In addition, the melting head carries an acoustic close-proximity reconnaissance system (ARS) for mapping the surroundings in order to detect obstacles like stones as well as water-filled crevasses as a target for sampling. The ARS uses 4 ultrasonic phased arrays whose signals can penetrate the ice up to a distance of 6 meters. A full description of the melting probe itself is presented in [2] while the navigation subsystems including details regarding the hardware and preprocessing steps as well as a rough outline of the sensor fusion algorithm are described in [6]. In contrast, the focus in this paper is on the problem of multi-sensor fusion based on an evidential SLAM approach.

Fig. 1. The maneuverable melting probe "IceMole" in the launchpad on the Commonwealth Glacier in Antarctica. (Figure reprinted from [6].)

3   Multi-Sensor Fusion

The goal of the sensor fusion is to simultaneously estimate a map of the environment and the probe's trajectory (including position and attitude). We use grid maps where the space is discretized into cells and each cell can be either occupied or empty (denoted by o and e). For SLAM, the state of a cell is usually modeled as a single probability $P(o)$. In our approach, each cell is instead described by a belief function where mass can not only be assigned to the singletons but also to the union $\Theta = \{o, e\}$ and the empty set [7]. Effectively, this allows representing additional dimensions of uncertainty with the mass assigned to Θ representing a lack of evidence and the mass assigned to $\emptyset$ representing conflicting measurements.

In order to solve the joint estimation problem of localization and mapping, the evidential FastSLAM algorithm from [9] is used. It uses a Rao-Blackwellized particle filter [3] to approximate the joint belief distribution $m[z_{0:t}, u_{1:t}](x_{0:t}, Y)$ over the map Y and the probe's trajectory $x_{0:t}$ (a sequence of poses $x_0, \ldots, x_t$) given the probe's controls $u_{1:t}$ and all measurements $z_{0:t}$. Due to the fact that motion dynamics can usually be modeled probabilistically, the assumption is made that the marginal distribution over the trajectory is Bayesian. This makes it possible to factorize the joint belief distribution into a probabilistic trajectory estimation part and a conditional evidential mapping part.[1]

$$m[z_{0:t}, u_{1:t}](x_{0:t}, Y) = p(x_{0:t}|z_{0:t}, u_{1:t})\, m[x_{0:t}, z_{0:t}](Y) \qquad (1)$$

Using the generalized Bayesian theorem (GBT) [11], the posterior of the trajectory can be further factorized into a plausibility $pl[x_{0:t}, z_{0:t-1}](z_t)$ of the current measurement and a proposal distribution $p(x_{0:t}|z_{0:t-1}, u_{1:t})$. The proposal distribution can be updated probabilistically using a motion model $p(x_t|x_{t-1}, u_t)$ that incorporates the current control u_t.

$$p(x_{0:t}|z_{0:t}, u_{1:t}) \propto pl[x_{0:t}, z_{0:t-1}](z_t)\, p(x_{0:t}|z_{0:t-1}, u_{1:t}) \qquad (2)$$

$$p(x_{0:t}|z_{0:t-1}, u_{1:t}) = p(x_t|x_{t-1}, u_t)\, p(x_{0:t-1}|z_{0:t-1}, u_{1:t-1}) \qquad (3)$$

Because the map Y is conditioned on the entire trajectory $x_{0:t}$ in Eq. (1), the grid cells Y_i are approximately independent of each other (there is no pose uncertainty). This allows factorizing the joint map distribution into M marginal cell distributions where M denotes the total number of grid cells.

$$m[x_{0:t}, z_{0:t}](Y) = \prod_{i=1}^{M} m[x_{0:t}, z_{0:t}](Y_i) \qquad (4)$$

As a result, each marginal cell distribution can be updated independently based on the belief $m[x_t, z_t](Y_i)$ induced by the current measurement using an appropriate combination rule (here, only the conjunctive rule of combination is considered).

$$m[x_{0:t}, z_{0:t}](Y_i = \cdot) = m[x_{0:t-1}, z_{0:t-1}](Y_i = \cdot) \ominus m[x_t, z_t](Y_i = \cdot) \qquad (5)$$

---

[1] See [8] for a proof of this factorization.

The algorithm used to approximate the joint distribution in Eq. (1) is based on a particle filter where each particle represents a complete trajectory and a corresponding map belief function. Measurements are incorporated using importance sampling where the particles are updated recursively over time as follows:

1. For each particle, sample a new pose x_t in order to incorporate control u_t.
2. Compute importance weights $pl[x_{0:t}, z_{0:t-1}](z_t)$ using measurement z_t.
3. For each particle, update the map with measurement z_t.
4. Resample particles with probability proportional to the importance weights.

The state of the probe at time t is a vector comprised of position and attitude. The control u_t represents the screw feed and z_t is a vector consisting of measurements $z_{t;q}$ from the IMU/differential magnetometer system, of measurements $z_{t;p}$ from the APS, and of measurements $z_{t;r}$ from the ARS. Because measurements from different sensors are assumed to be independent given the current pose x_t and the map Y, the product of the individual measurement plausibilities can be used in Eq. (2) to compute the importance weights in step 2. Furthermore, only the ARS is used to update the map in step 3 because the other sensors do not provide any information about the environment.

4   Motion and Sensor Models

In this section, the motion and sensor models needed to perform steps 1 to 3 of the fusion algorithm are described in more detail.

Motion Model

The motion model $p(x_t|x_{t-1}, u_t)$ in Eq. (2) describes the probe's state transition from $t-1$ to t given control u_t and the previous state x_{t-1}. The covered distance between $t-1$ and t is computed from the control commands given to the screw step motor. The gear transmission ratio and the pitch of the ice screw are known and the screw is assumed to be nearly slip-free with additive Gaussian noise. Hence, the prediction can be performed using standard motion equations [1].

IMU and Differential Magnetometer System

After preprocessing the raw data from the IMU and the magnetometers with appropriate algorithms [6], they provide an absolute, drift-free attitude estimate $z_{t;q}$ with high accuracy for roll and pitch, and moderate accuracy for the heading. The error is assumed to be normally distributed where the covariance matrix Σ_{z_q} is estimated in the preprocessing step. The measurement plausibility $pl[x_{0:t}, z_{0:t-1}](z_{t;q})$ used in Eq. (2) is thus given by a multivariate Gaussian where $x_{t;q}$ represents the expected attitude of the current state estimate and normalization constant α_q guaranties that the density values do not exceed 1 [10].

$$pl[x_{0:t}, z_{0:t-1}](z_{t;q}) = \alpha_q \mathcal{N}(z_{t;q}; x_{t;q}, \Sigma_{z_q}) \tag{6}$$

Acoustic Positioning System

The acoustic positioning system (APS) measures the time that a signal requires for traveling from one of the transducers to the probe. Knowing the speed of sound in ice, this can be used to localize the probe. In general, it would be possible to estimate a position from the APS measurements $z_{t;p}$ using standard trilateration techniques. However, the geometric constellation, with all transducers almost aligned in a single plane, would lead to high inaccuracies. In addition, tritlateration needs measurements from at least 3 transducers, which are not always available. Instead, a tightly coupled update is used to incorporate the measurements for each transducer separately. Similar to the attitude model in Eq. (6), the measurement plausibility for the k-th transducer is given by a scaled Gaussian (with variance $\sigma_{z_p}^2$). The expected travel time results from the speed of sound c_{ice} and the Euclidean distance between the transducer position x_{p_k} and the probe's position $x_{t;p}$.

$$pl[x_{0:t}, z_{0:t-1}](z_{t;p_k}) = \alpha_p \mathcal{N}(z_{t;p_k}; \|x_{t;p} - x_{p_k}\| \cdot c_{ice}^{-1}, \sigma_{z_p}^2) \tag{7}$$

Acoustic Reconnaissance System

Each acoustic reconnaissance system (ARS) measurement $z_{t;r}$ is an array of values representing how strongly the ultrasonic waves were reflected for a given distance and angle inside the 2D measurement cone. At a specific frequency, the waves are able to penetrate ice while they are reflected by obstacles likes stones, which is why the ARS data is suitable for mapping the environment. In addition, the data is also used for localization because the degree of mismatch between the map estimated from previous measurements and the map resulting from the current measurement can be used as a measure for the plausibility of $z_{t;r}$.

In order to perform mapping, an inverse sensor model $m[x_t, z_{t;r}](Y_i)$ is needed in Eq. (5) which provides a belief distribution for each cell Y_i given pose x_t and measurement $z_{t;r}$. Here, we learn a logistic regression model in order to obtain an occupancy probability for the i-th cell (denoted by $P_{LR}(Y_i = o|x_t, z_{t;r})$) from an ARS scan based on labeled training data. The occupancy probability resulting from logistic regression is transformed into a belief function $m_{LR}[x_t, z_{t;r}](Y_i)$ by discounting with factor $1 - \epsilon_r$, which reflects the fact that measurements are very noisy and that the learned logistic regression model does not capture all the underlying effects. In addition, it has to be taken into account that the ultrasonic signals are not able to penetrate massive obstacles. Therefore, the final belief for each cell Y_i is furthermore discounted by the masses assigned to $\{o\}$ for all cells Y_j ($j < i$) located between the sensor and cell Y_i (cells are assumed to be arranged in ascending ordered by their distance to the sensor). For singletons $Y_i = \{o\}$ and $Y_i = \{e\}$, the mass is computed as follows (the mass on Θ is implicitly given due to normalization):

$$m[x_t, z_{t;r}](Y_i) = m_{LR}[x_t, z_{t;r}](Y_i) \prod_{j=1}^{i-1} \left(1 - m_{LR}[x_t, z_{t;r}](Y_j = \{o\})\right), \quad (8)$$

$$m_{LR}[x_t, z_{t;r}](Y_i) = \begin{cases} (1 - \epsilon_r)P_{LR}(Y_i = o|x_t, z_{t;r}) & \text{if } Y_i = \{o\}, \\ (1 - \epsilon_r)(1 - P_{LR}(Y_i = o|x_t, z_{t;r})) & \text{if } Y_i = \{e\}, \\ \epsilon_r & \text{else.} \end{cases} \quad (9)$$

For the non-ARS sensors, the plausibility $pl[x_{0:t}, z_{0:t-1}](z_t)$ in Eq. (2) used for localization can be directly computed from the corresponding measurements. In contrast, for the ARS, the measurement plausibility $pl[x_{0:t}, z_{0:t-1}](z_{t;r})$ has to be computed from the information provided by $z_{t;r}$ about the map. Intuitively, the plausibility (i.e., the importance weight) should reflect how well the scan represented by $z_{t;r}$ matches the previously estimated map. Here, we use the degree of conflict between the normalized map belief $\eta \, m[x_{0:t-1}, z_{0:t-1}](Y)$ at time $t - 1$ and the map belief induced by measurement $z_{t;r}$ according to the inverse sensor model $m[x_t, z_{t;r}](Y)$ as a measure of mismatch. The conflict con_i for each cell Y_i is given by the mass assigned to $\emptyset$ when applying the conjunctive rule of combination to the map belief and the inverse model. The overall amount of conflict results from multiplying the cell conflicts, meaning that the importance weight is given by:

$$pl[x_{0:t}, z_{0:t-1}](z_{t;r}) = 1 - \prod_{i=1}^{M} con_i, \quad (10)$$

$$con_i = \left(m[x_t, z_{t;r}](Y_i) \, \circledcirc \, \eta \, m[x_{0:t-1}, z_{0:t-1}](Y_i)\right)(Y_i = \emptyset). \quad (11)$$

5   Results

While the probe has been tested on several glaciers already, the results presented here are based on a test conducted in an indoor swimming pool in order to have controlled conditions and ground truth data. Fixated balls filled with air and concrete (with a diameter of ca. 20 cm) were used to act as obstacles. Furthermore, 4 APS transducers were placed in the corners of the pool. The obstacles, the transducers, and the probe were attached to floats hanging at a depth of 2 m and laser trilateration was used to determine their position. In case of the probe, front and back were measured in order to obtain the heading as well. All objects where aligned in a horizontal plane, hence a 2D grid map was used. Because the ice screw and magnetometer system could not be used during the test, their measurements were simulated based on ground true with additional noise. All results were computed with 1000 particles.

The localization error resulting from different sensor combinations is shown in Fig. 2. As expected, performing only dead reckoning (DR) results in the highest error. When updating the DR estimate with absolute distance measurements from the APS, the error is significantly smaller. Because of the higher accuracy of the IMU and differential magnetometer (IMU/Mag), the performance is even better when correcting with these sensors, although they only provide attitude information. The lowest error is obtained when using the APS in combination with IMU/Mag because absolute position and attitude estimates are provided. Additionally updating the position with respect to the estimated map based on the ARS currently does not significantly improve the localization performance because further optimizations of the ARS sensors and models are needed.

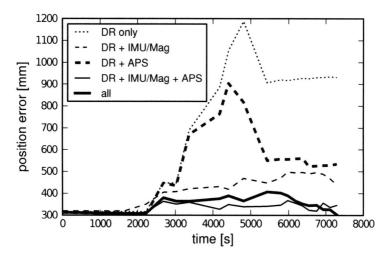

Fig. 2. Mean position error of all particles over time for different sensor combinations. The highest error results from only performing dead reckoning (DR) while each additional sensor (IMU and magnetometers, acoustic positioning system (APS) and acoustic reconnaissance system (ARS)) leads to an error reduction.

Fig. 3 shows the estimated map with the highest cumulative importance weight over time. The high mass values for occupied in (a) indicate detected obstacles while the area between the probe and the obstacles are believed to be empty as shown in (b). For the areas behind obstacles as well as for the area that was not covered by ARS measurements, most mass is assigned to Θ (see (c)), which corresponds to ignorance about the true state of these cells. Finally, (d) shows the mass on $\emptyset$, which results from conflicting measurements in the vicinity of obstacles. These different dimensions of uncertainty can provide additional information to the probe's guidance system or to an operator. In particular, areas with high mass on $\emptyset$ may require more measurements to determine the exact size and position of obstacles while mass on Θ indicates that there is no information about obstacles at all.

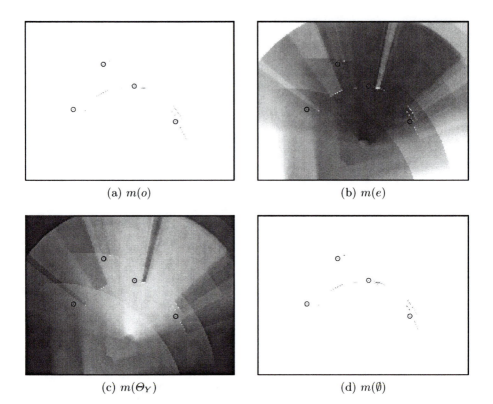

(a) $m(o)$ (b) $m(e)$

(c) $m(\Theta_Y)$ (d) $m(\emptyset)$

Fig. 3. Grid map computed by the evidential FastSLAM algorithm. (a) and (b) show the mass values for occupied and empty while (c) and (d) show the mass values for Θ and $\emptyset$ (black indicates a value of one and white a value of zero). The circles indicate the ground truth positions of the obstacles.

6   Summary

In this paper, we have presented a multi-sensor fusion approach for navigating a maneuverable melting probe through deep ice in order to obtain samples from subsurface water reservoirs in terrestrial as well as in extraterrestrial settings. It is based on a SLAM algorithm that produces evidential occupancy grid maps and utilizes a Rao-Blackwellized particle filter to estimate the joint distribution over the probe's trajectory and the map. Different sensor models were presented as well as results from an empirical evaluation under controlled conditions. We showed that the localization performance improved when using multiple sensors and that the resulting map contains the obstacles in the environment along with additional information about uncertainty compared to a probabilistic approach. A quantitative comparison with other recent fusion techniques is one of the next steps and further researches have to be done regarding some difficulties that may occur when using the GBT and Dempster's rule for fusion (see [4] for a recent discussion). While the results presented in this paper were obtained in a rather artificial setting, more realistic tests will be conducted in Antarctica at the end of the year, and the long term goals are Enceladus' ice crust and Mars' polar regions.

Acknowledgements. This work was supported by DLR (project "Enceladus Explorer") and DFG (SFB/TR 8 Spatial Cognition, project "A5-[ActionSpace]").

References

1. Bar-Shalom, Y., Li, X.R., Kirubarajan, T.: Estimation with applications to tracking and navigation: theory algorithms and software. John Wiley & Sons (2004)
2. Dachwald, B., Feldmann, M., Espe, C., Plescher, E., Xu, C.: The Enceladus Explorer Collaboration: Development and testing of a maneuverable subsurface probe that can navigate autonomously through deep ice. In: Proceedings of the 9th International Planetary Probe Workshop (2012)
3. Doucet, A., De Freitas, N., Murphy, K., Russell, S.: Rao-Blackwellised particle filtering for dynamic Bayesian networks. In: Proceedings of the Sixteenth Conference on Uncertainty in Artificial Intelligence, pp. 176–183 (2000)
4. Dubois, D., Denœux, T.: Conditioning in dempster-shafer theory: Prediction vs. Revision. In: Denœux, T., Masson, M.-H. (eds.) Belief Functions: Theory & Appl. AISC, vol. 164, pp. 385–392. Springer, Heidelberg (2012)
5. Durrant-Whyte, H., Bailey, T.: Simultaneous localization and mapping: part i. IEEE Robotics & Automation Magazine 13(2), 99–110 (2006)
6. Niedermeier, H., Clemens, J., Kowalski, J., Macht, S., Heinen, D., Hoffmann, R., Linder, P.: Navigation system for a research ice probe for antarctic glaciers. In: IEEE/ION PLANS 2014. IEEE (2014)
7. Pagac, D., Nebot, E., Durrant-Whyte, H.: An evidential approach to map-building for autonomous vehicles. IEEE Transactions on Robotics and Automation 14(4), 623–629 (1998)
8. Reineking, T.: Belief Functions: Theory and Algorithms. Ph.D. thesis, University of Bremen (February 2014),
   http://nbn-resolving.de/urn:nbn:de:gbv:46-00103727-16
9. Reineking, T., Clemens, J.: Evidential FastSLAM for grid mapping. In: 16th International Conference on Information Fusion (FUSION), pp. 789–796 (July 2013)
10. Smets, P.: Belief functions on real numbers. International Journal of Approximate Reasoning 40(3), 181–223 (2005)
11. Smets, P.: Belief functions: The disjunctive rule of combination and the generalized Bayesian theorem. International Journal of Approximate Reasoning 9, 1–35 (1993)

Belief Fusion of Predictions of Industries in China's Stock Market

Yongjun Xu[1], Lin Wu[1,2], Xianbin Wu[1,2], and Zhiwei Xu[1]

[1] Institute of Computing Technology, Chinese Academy of Sciences, Beijing, 100190
[2] University of Chinese Academy of Sciences, Beijing, 100049
{xyj,wulin,wuxianbin,zxu}@ict.ac.cn

Abstract. This contribution presents the application of Dempster-Shafer theory to the prediction of China's stock market. To be specific, we predicted the most promising industry in the next month every trading day. This prediction can help investors to select stocks, but is rarely seen in previous literatures. Instead of predicting the fluctuation of the stock market from scratch all by ourselves, we fused ratings of 44 industries from China's securities companies using Shafer's evidence theory. Our preliminary experiment is a daily prediction since 2012-05-02 with ratings published 10 days before that day. Our predicted industries have an average rank of 19.85 in earnings, 11.8% better than random guessing (average rank is 22.5). The average rise rate of predicted industries in a month is 0.59%, 0.86% higher than overall (which is -0.274%), and nearly 0.7% higher than simple voting (which is -0.097%). Our predictions are posted on Weibo every day since 2014-04-28.

Keywords: Belief Fusion, Stock Market, Dempster-Shafer Theory, Prediction.

1 Introduction

A prediction of the most promising industry in the medium term can help investors select stocks or industry index funds[1] if the accuracy is better than random guessing. But this kind of prediction is rarely seen in literatures.

Previous prediction methods include statistics, technical analysis [5], fundamental analysis [5], and linear regression [12]. State-of-the-art in stock prediction techniques is surveyed in [1]. Instead of predicting the fluctuation of stock market from scratch all by ourselves, we fuse beliefs from experts — China's securities companies. These securities companies can be seen as soft data sensors [4] that observe related phenomena, and give ratings for some industries as the output of analysis. With their ratings as input, we try to predict the most promising

---

[1] "An index fund (also index tracker) is a collective investment scheme (usually a mutual fund or exchange-traded fund) that aims to replicate the movements of an index of a specific financial market, or a set of rules of ownership that are held constant, regardless of market conditions. As of 2007, index funds made up 11.5% of equity mutual fund assets in the US." — http://en.wikipedia.org/wiki/Index_fund.

F. Cuzzolin (Ed.): BELIEF 2014, LNAI 8764, pp. 348–355, 2014.
© Springer International Publishing Switzerland 2014

industry in the next month, which is expected to have the highest average rise in stock price.

As [1] states, "information regarding a stock is normally incomplete, complex, uncertain and vague". A securities company usually publishes ratings on less than 2 industries every trading day. These ratings consist of "buy", "overweight" and "neutral", representing different degrees of belief about the investment value. For industries with no ratings, its investment value is ignorant other than neutral. To combine ratings from different securities companies, we use the Dempster-Shafer theory [8,9], which is a powerful tool for uncertainty reasoning. In this theory, different sources express their uncertainty about the question of interest with belief functions. Then those functions are fused by Dempste's rule to arrive at the final degree of belief.

This paper is structured as follows. In Sect. 2, we present our model and formalization. We also describe our methods to predict. In Sect. 3, we introduce our experiment. Section 4 demonstrates our results. In Sect. 5, we draw the conclusion and discuss future work.

2   Problem Formalization and Methods

In this section, we describe the formalization and methods of our prediction of the most promising industry.

2.1   Question of Interest and Frame of Discernment

Under the framework of Dempster-Shafer theory, the answer to the question of interest is one element of a finite set called Frame of Discernment. It's composed of an exhaustive list of mutually exclusive answers.

In our problem, the question of interest is: "Which is the most promising industry in the medium term". There are 44 possible answers according to East-Money[2], which is one of China's largest financial website. Let's denote the frame of discernment by Ω. Then

$$\Omega = \{\text{electricity, electronic, culture and media, pharmaceuticals}\ldots\} \qquad (1)$$

$$|\Omega| = 44 \qquad (2)$$

2.2   Evidence and Basic Belief Assignment (BBA)

As far as we know, there is no direct answer to the question of interest. But ratings of industries published by securities companies can be seen as evidence for this question, which is available on the website [3].

---

[2] http://www.eastmoney.com/
[3] http://data.eastmoney.com/report/hyyb.html

A securities company may rate an industry as "buy", "overweight" or "neutral". There is no rating "sell" on the website. This special situation maybe results from government policies and China's special culture. As a securities company publishes ratings of limited industries on a single day (usually less than two industries on average), we combine its ratings from 10 consecutive trading days as a single report. From such a report, we can get 4 sets, which usually have intersections:

$$S_{buy} = \{\text{industry } I | I \text{ is rated as "buy"}\} \tag{3}$$

$$S_{overweight} = \{\text{industry } I | I \text{ is rated as "overweight"}\} \tag{4}$$

$$S_{neutral} = \{\text{industry } I | I \text{ is rated as "neutral"}\} \tag{5}$$

$$S_{others} = \Omega - S_{buy} - S_{overweight} - S_{neutral} \tag{6}$$

When securities companies give different ratings for a particular industry during these 10 days, only the latest one is adopted.

We haven't taken the freshness of data into consideration, for the purpose of reduction in computation burden. In our method, all the industries with the same rating from a securities company are in a single set. So the number of focal elements is only 4 in a securities company's report. After combination, the number will grow exponentially. To reduce it, we discard those focal elements whose masses are under a threshold, which is set experientially as 0.0001.

Our subjective judgment is that, S_{buy} is very likely to contain the most promising industry, $S_{overweight}$ is also likely to contain it, and $S_{neutral}$ is not likely to contain the most promising industry. According to this judgment, basic belief assignment is calculated as follows when $S_{neutral}$ is not empty:

$$m(S_{buy}) = \frac{44 - |S_{others}|}{44} * \frac{4 * |S_{buy}|}{4 * |S_{buy}| + |S_{overweight}| + |\overline{S_{neutral}}|} \tag{7}$$

$$m(S_{overweight}) = \frac{44 - |S_{others}|}{44} * \frac{|S_{overweight}|}{4 * |S_{buy}| + |S_{overweight}| + |\overline{S_{neutral}}|} \tag{8}$$

$$m(\overline{S_{neutral}}) = \frac{44 - |S_{others}|}{44} * \frac{|\overline{S_{neutral}}|}{4 * |S_{buy}| + |S_{overweight}| + |\overline{S_{neutral}}|} \tag{9}$$

$$m(\Omega) = \frac{|S_{others}|}{44} \tag{10}$$

When $S_{neutral}$ is empty, $\overline{S_{neutral}}$ equals Ω, basic belief assignment is calculated as follows:

$$m(S_{buy}) = \frac{44 - |S_{others}|}{44} * \frac{4 * |S_{buy}|}{4 * |S_{buy}| + |S_{overweight}|} \tag{11}$$

$$m(S_{overweight}) = \frac{44 - |S_{others}|}{44} * \frac{|S_{overweight}|}{4 * |S_{buy}| + |S_{overweight}|} \tag{12}$$

$$m(\Omega) = \frac{|S_{others}|}{44} \tag{13}$$

These formulas are representations of evidence. We'll modify them according to statistics in the future.

After obtaining the basic belief assignment of each securities company, we combine them one by one with Dempster's combination rule [8]:

$$m(A) = \frac{\sum_{A_1 \subseteq \Omega, A_2 \subseteq \Omega} \{m_1(A_1)m_2(A_2)|A_1 \cap A_2 = A\}}{\sum_{A_1 \subseteq \Omega, A_2 \subseteq \Omega} \{m_1(A_1)m_2(A_2)|A_1 \cap A_2 \neq \varnothing\}} \tag{14}$$

In the above equation, m_1 and m_2 correspond to the evidence from the two securities companies that are being combined, see Fig. 1. The prominent advantage of Dempster's combination rule over others [13,14] is its simplicity, which is important in our scenario with 44 singleton sets and 25 data sources. Besides, the result shouldn't be influenced when we change the order of combination. So we need a rule with features of associativity and commutativity.

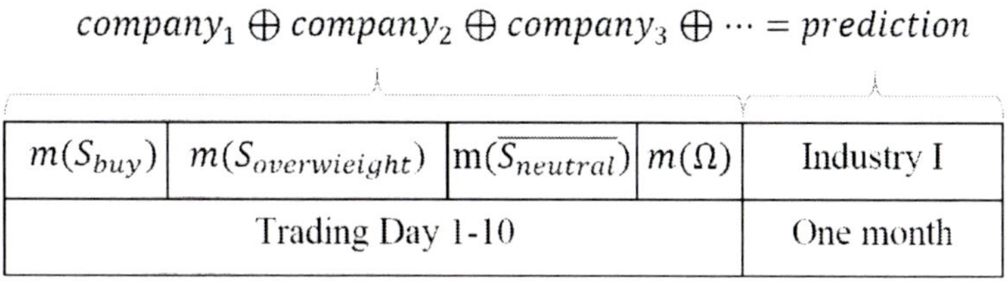

$$company_1 \oplus company_2 \oplus company_3 \oplus \cdots = prediction$$

$m(S_{buy})$	$m(S_{overwieight})$	$m(S_{neutral})$	$m(\Omega)$	Industry I
	Trading Day 1-10			One month

Fig. 1. Prediction of the most valuable industry in the following 30 days by combining ratings from each securities company

2.3   Decision

There is no agreement about how to make decision with final belief functions. Candidate methods include choosing the hypothesis with the maximum BBA, belief, plausibility or pignistic probability.

Smets proposed making decisions based on maximizing pignistic probabilities [11]. Pignistic probability is derived from BBA by pignistic transformation [11]:

$$BetP(\omega) = \sum_{W \subseteq \Omega, \omega \subseteq W} \frac{1}{|W|} \frac{m(w)}{1 - m(\phi)}, \forall \omega \subseteq \Omega \tag{15}$$

This method is widely used in literatures [2,6,7,10].

In our experiment, we found that decisions based on maximum beliefs have the best performance and we adopted it in our paper.

3   Experiment

There are about 50 to 150 ratings published on the website[4] every trading day since 2012-04-25. On other days, there are usually less than 10 ratings every day. We have collected all of these historical ratings, and made historical predictions every day, supposing that we were in the past. Besides, we are making new predictions every trading day, which are posted on Weibo[5](China's Twitter).

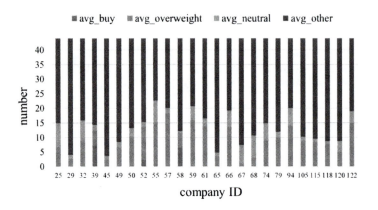

Fig. 2. Average number of industries with ratings "buy", "overweight", "neutral" and without ratings for each of the selected 25 companies in 10 consecutive trading days during the last two years

There are 78 securities companies who have published their ratings in the last two years. But some of them are not active, we manually selected the top 25 active companies as our data sources, see Fig. 2.

To evaluate our predictions, we supposed that an investor would spend 1 dollar to buy the stocks of each industry every trading day, and sell them after 30 days. And we supposed that money spent for each stock is proportional to the trading volume of it on that day (This is similar to index funds). Then we calculated the earnings for each industry in the next month and got the rank of our predicted industries. At the same time, we summed up the monthly rise rates of predicted industries on every trading day during the last two years and compare it with the average of all industries. The historical data of all the stocks (more than 2,000) in the last two years was provided by Shanghai Wind Information Co., Ltd.

We also compared our methods with simple voting: if an industry is ranked as "buy", "overweight" or "neutral", it gets 4, 1 or -1 vote respectively. If more than one industries has the largest votes, we chose one of them randomly.

---

[4] http://data.eastmoney.com/report/hyyb.html
[5] http://weibo.com/u/3915945698

4   Results

4.1   Computation Burden

The number of focal elements after the combination of 25 companies is usually below 1000, see Fig. 3. We ran our python program on a computer with a 4-core 2.4GHz CPU and 2GB RAM. The combination of 25 data sources took 1.98 seconds on average.

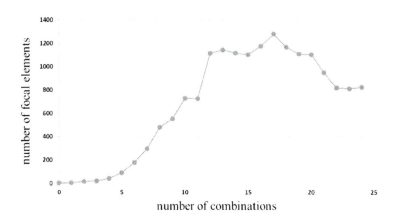

Fig. 3. The trend of the number of focal elements after each combination. The declination results from the threshold of minimum mass, which we set as set experientially as 0.0001.

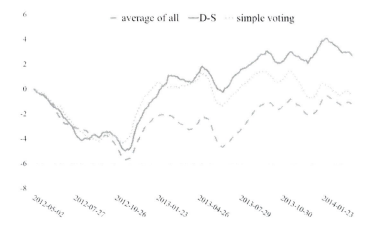

Fig. 4. Accumulated monthly rise rate of predicted industries by D-S and simple voting, and the average of all the industries

4.2 Accuracy

Every day, we ranked industries according to their rise rate in stock price in the previous month. The average rank of our predicted industries is 19.85 in the last two years, 11.8% better than random guessing (average rank is 22.5). The average rise rate of predicted industries in a month is 0.59%, 0.86% higher than overall (which is -0.274%), and nearly 0.7% higher than simple voting (which is -0.097%). The accumulated monthly rise rate day by day is shown in Fig. 4. To put it simple, this figure shows how many dollars you would have earned if you bought 1 dollar of the predicted industry's index fund every trading day and sold it after 30 days since 2012-05-02. From this figure, we can see that on 2014-04-28, you would have earned 2.715 and -0.45 dollars if the industry is chosen according to D-S and simple voting respectively.

5 Conclusion and Future Work

We have introduced the application of Dempster-Shafer theory to the prediction of industries in China's stock market in this paper. Instead of forecasting stock market by technical analysis or fundamental analysis, we fused output of soft data sensors C reports from securities companies. Our predicted industries have an average rank of 19.85 in earnings, 11.8% better than random guessing (average rank is 22.5). The average rise rate of predicted industries in a month is 0.59%, 0.86% higher than overall (which is -0.274%), and nearly 0.7% higher than simple voting (which is -0.097%). Our predictions are posted on Weibo every day since 2014-04-28.

In the future, we will continue collecting data for further evaluation and improvement of our methods. The basic belief assignment is determined according to our subjective judgment at present. When more data is available, we plan to adjust it on the basis of statistical information, such as using the probabilistic representation of evidence presented by [3].

Acknowledgments. This paper is supported in part by National Natural Science Foundation of China (NSFC) under grant No.(61173132).

References

1. Agrawal, J., Chourasia, V., Mittra, A.: State-of-the-art in stock prediction techniques. International Journal of Advanced Research in Electrical, Electronics and Instrumentation Engineering 2, 1360–1366 (2013)
2. Fiche, A., Martin, A., Cexus, J.-C., Khenchaf, A.: A comparison between a bayesian approach and a method based on continuous belief functions for pattern recognition. In: Denœux, T., Masson, M.-H. (eds.) Belief Functions: Theory & Appl. AISC, vol. 164, pp. 53–60. Springer, Heidelberg (2012)
3. Halpern, J.Y., Fagin, R.: Two views of belief: belief as generalized probability and belief as evidence. Artificial Intelligence 54(3), 275–317 (1992)

4. Jenkins, M.P., Gross, G.A., Bisantz, A.M., Nagi, R.: Towards context aware data fusion: Modeling and integration of situationally qualified human observations to manage uncertainty in a hard+ soft fusion process. Information Fusion (2013)
5. Kara, Y., Acar Boyacioglu, M., Baykan, M.K.: Predicting direction of stock price index movement using artificial neural networks and support vector machines: The sample of the istanbul stock exchange. Expert Systems with Applications 38(5), 5311–5319 (2011)
6. Karem, F., Dhibi, M., Martin, A.: Combination of supervised and unsupervised classification using the theory of belief functions. In: Denœux, T., Masson, M.-H. (eds.) Belief Functions: Theory & Appl. AISC, vol. 164, pp. 85–92. Springer, Heidelberg (2012)
7. Senouci, M.R., Mellouk, A., Oukhellou, L., Aissani, A.: Using the Belief Functions Theory to Deploy Static Wireless Sensor Networks. In: Denœux, T., Masson, M.-H. (eds.) Belief Functions: Theory & Appl. AISC, vol. 164, pp. 425–432. Springer, Heidelberg (2012)
8. Shafer, G.: A mathematical theory of evidence, vol. 1. Princeton University Press, Princeton (1976)
9. Shafer, G.: Perspectives on the theory and practice of belief functions. International Journal of Approximate Reasoning 4(5), 323–362 (1990)
10. Shoyaib, M., Abdullah-Al-Wadud, M., Zahid Ishraque, S.M., Chae, O.: Facial Expression Classification Based on Dempster-Shafer Theory of Evidence. In: Denœux, T., Masson, M.-H. (eds.) Belief Functions: Theory & Appl. AISC, vol. 164, pp. 213–220. Springer, Heidelberg (2012)
11. Smets, P.: Decision making in the tbm: the necessity of the pignistic transformation. International Journal of Approximate Reasoning 38(2), 133–147 (2005)
12. Upadhyay, A., Bandyopadhyay, G., Dutta, A.: Forecasting stock performance in indian market using multinomial logistic regression. Journal of Business Studies Quarterly 3(3) (2012)
13. Yang, J.B., Xu, D.L.: Evidential reasoning rule for evidence combination. Artificial Intelligence 205, 1–29 (2013)
14. Yong, D., WenKang, S., ZhenFu, Z., Qi, L.: Combining belief functions based on distance of evidence. Decision Support Systems 38(3), 489–493 (2004)

An Evidential Fusion Rule for Ambient Intelligence for Activity Recognition

Faouzi Sebbak[1], Farid Benhammadi[1], Sofiane Bouznad[2], Abdelghani Chibani[2], and Yacine Amirat[2]

[1] Ecole Militaire Polytechnique, Algiers, Algeria
[2] UPEC, LISSI Laboratory, Paris, France

Abstract. These last years, a lot of combination rules emerged in order to model the situations of belief fusion. These rules can be classified in two different classes. However, these rules do not differentiate between focal elements in the combination step which produce counterintuitive results in some situations. Motivated by this observation, we propose a new combination rule which hybrids the strategies of these two classes. Our rule is two-step operator where the averaging step comes first, and then the conflict redistribution step. Experimental studies are conducted on a real smart home dataset to show the accuracy of our rule in ubiquitous-assisted living situation.

Keywords: Dempster–Shafer theory, belief functions, conflict redistribution, combination rules, activity recognition.

1 Introduction

The Dempster-Shafer Theory (DST) has been popular because it seems well suited for dealing with uncertainty [1]. However, the rule combination used in this theory appears inadequate for some situation of belief fusion [2, 3]. Motivated by solving this inadequateness numerous authors have proposed several combination rules which can be broadly classified in two classes [4–10]. The first class attempts to reduce or suppress the conflict before the combination step by modifying the original evidences. In this context, Murphy proposed a combination rule [5] based on the arithmetic average of belief functions associated with the evidences to be combined. This method is a commutative but not associative trade-off rule [10]. The second class aims to eliminate evidential conflict in the combination rule by managing this conflict in order to give no negative impact in the combination rule. The idea behind these rules is to transfer total or partial conflicting masses proportionally to non-empty set and the partial ignorance involved in the model according to some constraints [9]. Many rules were developed around the propositionally conflict redistribution. In some approaches, the proportionalization uses only the masses assigned to each set by the sources of information [8] or according to the results of the conjunctive rule [7]. In the Proportional Conflict Redistribution Rules (PCR1-5) [10], this proportionalization uses both the sources of information and the masses obtained from the

F. Cuzzolin (Ed.): BELIEF 2014, LNAI 8764, pp. 356–364, 2014.

conjunctive rule. However, the conflict is not proportionally redistributed on the whole focal set elements with respect to the masses assigned to each focal set obtained after conjunctive rule application. A similar work that combines bodies of evidence has been proposed in [9]. This approach is the generalization of the PCR rules. However, these two classes do not treat the cardinality of focal sets in a combination process since the results can not reflect the difference between combined bodies of evidence in the situation belief functions.

This paper aims to address the above limitations and to propose a new combination rule called Conflict Redistribution based on the Cardinality of focal elements (CRC). The idea behind is based on a mixture between presented previously two classes. Our combination rule is two-step operator where the evidence correction step comes first, and then the conflict redistribution step. The evidence correction of each body of evidence is based on the arithmetic average of belief computed in respect of the corresponding others sources. However, the global conflict proportionalization uses the masses computed from the conjunctive rule to determine weighting factors. These factors represent the weighted sum computed from the basic belief assignments (bpas) weighted by the cardinalities of focal elements used in the conjunctive rule. The proposed combination alternative is evaluated with a real-world smart home dataset proposed in [11] and our mapping technique [12] to translate uncertain contextual information from the pervasive environment to the high-level activity layer.

The rest of this paper is organized as follows: In Section 2, we briefly recall basic notions of evidence theory. Section 3 describes the proposed rule for multiple sources. Simulation and comparison studies based on both numerical examples and real-world smart home dataset are reported and discussed in Section 4.

2   DS Theory

The first combination rule proposed by Dempster and Shafer [1] is the normalized conjunctive combination rule given for two bodies of evidences. In the following, we recall the grounds of the main concepts and principles of this rule. The frame of discernment is a set of mutually exclusive and exhaustive hypotheses H_n. The subsets $H \in 2^\Theta$ is called the focal set elements of $m(\cdot)$. From a frame of discernment Θ correspondingly 2^Θ the power set of Θ, a basic belief assignment (bba) is defined as a mapping $m(\cdot)$ satisfying the following proprieties:

$$m(\emptyset) = 0 \text{ and } \sum_{H \in 2^\Theta} m(H) = 1$$

Based on Shafer's model of the frame; Dempster's rule for two sources, $m = m_1 \oplus m_2$ is defined by Eq.1:

$$m_{DS}(H) = \frac{m_{12}(H)}{1 - m_{12}(\emptyset)} \tag{1}$$

$$m_{12}(H) = \sum_{\substack{H_1, H_2 \in 2^\Theta \\ H_1 \cap H_2 = H}} m_1(H_1) m_2(H_2) \tag{2}$$

where $m_{12}(H)$ represents the conjunctive consensus operator and $m_{12}(\emptyset)$ reflects the conflicting mass of the combination between the two sources.

3   The Proposed Combination Rule

In the Dempster's and Murphy's combination rules, the conflict is proportionally redistributed on all focal set elements. Murphy [5] suggests that, if belief functions associated with the evidences are available, the arithmetic average of these beliefs can be combined in multiple times by Dempster's rule. However, in conflict redistribution approaches [7–10], the conflict is redistributed only on the original focal elements. The proportionalization of PCR6 rule [9] uses both the sources information and the masses obtained from the conjunctive rule. But the conflict is not proportionally distributed to all focal set elements (all meaningful propositions). The major disadvantage of these rules is that they do not make the difference between bodies of evidence in combination step which yields counterintuitive results in decision-making process. Let's illustrate this disadvantage by the following example. Consider an example of activity recognition with three interfered sensors. Suppose that these sensors have made observations of the occurring activity, and ensure that it's an activity A_1, A_2, A_3 or A_4: $\Theta = \{A_1, A_2, A_3, A_4\}$, with the following bba's:

$$m_1(A_1) = 0.5 \qquad\qquad m_1(A_2 \cup A_3 \cup A_4) = 0.5$$
$$m_2(A_1 \cup A_2) = 0.5 \qquad\qquad m_2(A_3) = 0.5$$
$$m_3(A_1 \cup A_2 \cup A_4) = 0.5 \qquad\qquad m_3(A_2 \cup A_3 \cup A_4) = 0.5$$

Now we combine these masses using a given rule from each class: Dempster's, Murphy's and PCR6 rules. As it can be seen from Table 1, the existing rules do not redistribute a fraction of the conflicting mass effectively on the focal set elements A_i. For example, in all rules the conflict redistribution process assigns the same mass to focal elements $\{A_1\}$ and $\{A_3\}$ although there is a difference between the cardinality of original evidences used in combination step. The combined mass of the activity A_1 ($m_{123}(A_1)$) is obtained from the masses $m_1(A_1)$, $m_2(A_1 \cup A_2)$ and $m_3(A_1 \cup A_2 \cup A_4)$ while, the combined mass of A_3 ($m_{123}(A_3)$) is obtained from $m_2(A_3)$, $m_1(A_2 \cup A_3 \cup A_4)$ and $m_3(A_2 \cup A_3 \cup A_4)$. So the belief part of $\{A_1\}$ in $\{A_1 \cup A_2\}$ is greater than the belief part of $\{A_3\}$

Table 1. Combination results of masses

Fused masses	Rules		
	Dempster's	Murphy's	PCR6
$m_{123}(\{A_1\})$	0.25	0.1863	0.25
$m_{123}(\{A_2\})$	0.5	0.2941	0.25
$m_{123}(\{A_3\})$	0.25	0.1863	0.25
$m_{123}(\{A_4\})$	0	0	0

in $\{A_2 \cup A_3 \cup A_4\}$. Thus the certainty in $\{A_1 \cup A_2\}$ of 0.5 for A_1 might give some additional support in $\{A_1\}$ compared to the certainty in $\{A_2 \cup A_3 \cup A_4\}$ of 0.5 for A_3. We suppose that this result is not accordant to the objective of reasoning over evidences accumulation since the results can not reflect the difference between bodies of evidence.

To overcome the drawbacks of the preceding rules, we propose an alternative rule which is two-step operator where the evidence correction step comes first, and then the conflict redistribution step. The evidence correction uses the weighted average mass between sources observations through other respective masses. This correction assumes the independence and the dependence between the bodies of evidence at the same time because we believe that the certainty about the most correct judgment increases by having more accumulated independent evidence with the highest belief. Based on the conjunctive operator, the conflict redistribution step uses the cardinality of the bodies of evidence.

First, we introduce the Weighted Average Mass (WAM) definition used in the proposed combination rule.

Let Θ be a frame of discernment with n elements, and let $m_s(\cdot)$ be $bbas$ defined on 2^Θ. We define the WAM associated to the focal element X as:

$$\widetilde{m}_i(X) = \frac{m_i(X) + \overline{m}_i(X)}{2} \tag{3}$$

where $\overline{m}_i(X)$ denotes the average mass of the focal element. X computed using the other bodies of evidence of X:

$$\overline{m}_i(X) = \frac{1}{s-1} \sum_{j \neq i} m_j(X) \tag{4}$$

where s is the number of independent sources.

We propose a method to modify each original body of evidence according to its arithmetic average mass using other sources. This WAM allows to preserve the mass distribution in the same way as the original mass distribution. It means that, if a bba for focal set element is bigger and other $bbas$ are all small, a WAM of this focal set get the same tendency. So this mechanism offers a good weighted average mass correspondence as well as convergence.

Now, we describe our combination rule for multiple sources $s \geq 2$ as follows:

$$m_{12\cdots s|CRC}(X) = \sum_{\substack{X_1, X_2 \cdots, X_s \in 2^\Theta \\ X_1 \cap X_2 \cap \cdots X_s = X}} \prod_{i=1}^{s} \widetilde{m}_i(X_i) \tag{5}$$
$$+ w_{1,2,\cdots,s}(X) \, k_{1,2,\cdots,s}$$

where $k_{1,2,\cdots,s}$ represents the total conflicting mass while $w_{1,2,\cdots,s}(X)$ is the weighting factor defined by as follows:

$$w_{1,2,\cdots,s}(X) = \frac{|X|}{\lambda} \sum_{\substack{X_1, X_2 \cdots, X_s \in 2^\Theta \\ X_1 \cap X_2 \cap \cdots X_s = X}} \prod_{i=1}^{s} \frac{\widetilde{m}_i(X_i)}{|X_i|} \tag{6}$$

where λ is the normalization coefficient of the weighting factors.

Table 2. The weighted average masses computation

WAMs	$\{A_1\}$	$\{A_3\}$	$\{A_1 \cup A_2\}$	$\{A_1 \cup A_2 \cup A_4\}$	$\{A_2 \cup A_3 \cup A_4\}$
			Focal element		
$\widetilde{m}_1(\cdot)$	0.250	0.125	0.125	0.125	0.375
$\widetilde{m}_2(\cdot)$	0.125	0.250	0.250	0.125	0.25
$\widetilde{m}_3(\cdot)$	0.125	0.125	0.125	0.25	0.375

Let's reconsider the preceding example: Using the above definition, we obtained the WAMs reported in Table 2. Clearly, the WAMs are different from the arithmetic average used in Murphy's rule. So these WAMs have a similar tendency as the original bodies of evidence and show a more realistic averaging of the original bodies of evidence.

$m_{123}(A_1) = 0.0898, m_{123}(A_2) = 0.1445, m_{123}(A_3) = 0.0898$
$m_{123}(A_1 \cup A_2) = 0.0313, m_{123}(A_2 \cup A_4) = 0.0781$
$m_{123}(A_1 \cup A_2 \cup A_4) = 0.0039, m_{123}(A_2 \cup A_3 \cup A_4) = 0.0352$
with the total conflicting mass $k_{123} = 0.5273$.

Now, we compute the weighted factors in respect to the results of the conjunctive rule and the cardinality of focal elements.

$w_{123}(A_1) = 0.1884 \qquad w_{123}(A_2) = 0.0651 \qquad w_{123}(A_3) = 0.1446$
$w_{123}(A_1 \cup A_2) = 0.1414 \qquad w_{123}(A_2 \cup A_4) = 0.1714$
$w_{123}(A_1 \cup A_2 \cup A_4) = 0.0289 \, w_{123}(A_2 \cup A_3 \cup A_4) = 0.2603$

As it can be seen from these results, the weighted factor of the focal set $\{A_1\}$ is bigger than the weighted factors of the focal sets $\{A_2\}$ and $\{A_3\}$. This is due to the fact that the combined mass $m_{123}(A_1)$ according to the conjunctive rule is computed in respect to the WAM masses of the focal sets $\{A_1, A_1 \cup A_2, A_1 \cup A_2, \cup A_4\}$. Whereas the combined masses $m_{123}(A_2)$ and $m_{123}(A_3)$ of focal sets $\{A_2\}$ and $\{A_3\}$ are computed from the WAM masses of $\{A_1 \cup A_2 \cup A_4, A_1 \cup A_2, A_2 \cup A_3 \cup A_4\}$ and $\{A_2 \cup A_3 \cup A_4, A_3, A_2 \cup A_3 \cup A_4\}$ respectively.

We proportionalize the total conflicting mass using these weighting factors. Consequently, the combination results are as follows:

$m_{123|CRC}(\{A_1\}) = 0.1892 \quad m_{123|CRC}(\{A_2\}) = 0.1788 \quad m_{123|CRC}(\{A_3\}) = 0.1661$
$m_{123|CRC}(\{A_1 \cup A_2\}) = 0.1058 \quad m_{123|CRC}(\{A_2 \cup A_4\}) = 0.1685$
$m_{123|CRC}(\{A_1 \cup A_2 \cup A_4\}) = 0.0192 \{A_2 \cup A_3 \cup A_4\} = 0.1724$

These results are different from those reported in Table 1. Therefore, our rule makes the difference between masses of focal sets $\{A_1\}$, $\{A_2\}$ and $\{A_3\}$ in the combination step.

Unfortunately, our rule is commutative, not associative and a part of the family of weighted operators such the weighted average operator [8]. It converges toward Murphys rule when the conflict is approaching 0. In addition, our rule does not preserve the vacuous belief assignment (Disappearing Ignorance. The disappearing ignorance propriety in Dempster's rule is an advantage in combination process because only the evidences without ignorance are combined. We presume that the disappearing ignorance is not justified in all situation of belief fusion [5]. As illustration, let's consider again the activity recognition situation and the following two bba's: $m_1(A_1) = 0.5$, $m_1(A_3 \cup A_4) = 0.5$, and $m_2(\Theta) = 1$. In this example, Dempster's rule yields the first belief assignments ($m_1(\cdot)$). However in our rule we obtained the following results: $m_{12|CRC}(A_1) = 0.3403$, $m_{12|CRC}(A_3 \cup A_4) = 0.3542$ and $m_{12|CRC}(\Theta) = 0.3056$. Thus, we cannot suppress or neglect the weaker belief committed to the activity A_2 which can be supported by the second totally ignorant source.

4   Performance Evaluation

In ambient intelligence applications, context reasoning aims to build new knowledge from existing context data. Recently, a variety of evidential reasoning approaches have been proposed to treat contextual information [13–17]. The use of dempster's rule in [13,14] will get negative impact on the accuracy of activity recognition since the conflicting masses are eliminated due to the normalization factor. McKeever et al. [15] propose to include temporal information in the reasoning process. They propose also to extend the lifetime of the triggered sensor evidence for the activity duration, and as a consequence inference continues over the activity duration. For the combination they used Murphy's rule. In [14], Hong et al. generated an ontology for activities of daily living and used the D-S theory to reason about the activity recognition. In [16], Sebbak et al. have proved that an adequate mapping techniques to translate uncertain contextual information from the pervasive environment to the high-level activity layer can provide an efficient way to increase the efficiency and the accuracy of activity recognition. In [17], Liao et al. propose a framework with a lattice structure based on the evidence theory to manage the uncertainty in smart homes according to an object, a context and an activity layers. Their approach aims to incorporate the historical information and the patterns related to the activities being considered to improve the reasoning performance.

In this section, we evaluate and compare the proposed combination rule using a real-life smart home dataset proposed in [11] and the mapping technique [12] for aggregating the raw data, which is captured using a wireless senor network, into high-level activity knowledge. This evaluation aims to show how activity recognition is improved using the proposed combination rule. It aims also to compare the obtained results among other combination rules in evidential-based approaches. The Van Kasteren's dataset captures the activities of a 26 years old man over a period of 28 day in his apartment. Over the 28 days, seven different activities were recorded: 'sleeping', 'leave home', 'use toilet','take shower','get

Table 3. Activity recognition accuracy using different combination rules

Combination rule	Accuracy
CRC	0.6918
Murphy	0.6813
Mean	0.6593
PCR6	0.6534
Dempster-Shafer	0.5441
Smets / Yager / Dubois et Prade	0.5369
Disjunctive	0.3341

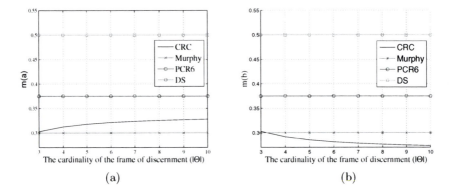

(a)   (b)

Fig. 1. The cardinality effect on conflict redistribution for two activities

drink', 'prepare breakfast' and *'prepare dinner'*. Data are gathered from 14 binary sensors installed in doors, cupboards, the refrigerator and toilet flush.

In this evaluation, we use the same masses construction process introduced in [15]. These masses are build by examining for each activity occurrence the number of times the sensors are used. For example, if in ten occurrences of *'get drink'* activity the sensor *cup* is used nine times, then the corresponding masses are 0.9 for the focal element get drink and 0.1 is allocated to the total ignorance: $\Theta = \{get\ drink,\ \neg get\ drink\}$. These masses can be discounted if we have more information about sensor reliability.

Based on the Extended Dempster-Shafer Theory proposed in [15], Table 3 presents the results of activity recognition using the proposed rule and other well-known combination rules. At the head of the this table, the CRC rule gives the best activity accuracy and improves the performance of activity recognition by improving F-measure metrics. The proposed rule manage and redistribute the conflicting mass on the corresponding activities according to the original sensor's masses.

Dempster's rule of combination did not show a good result because it completely ignores all the conflicts through the normalization factor. If a single sensor is *off* at a given time, the majority opinion of other sensors will be lost. Therefore, unless all sensors are fired at the same time, the evidence from any firing sensors will be lost. Murphy's rule shows competent results by combining the average of the multiple sensor masses. Fig. 1 shows the impact of the frame of discernment scalability on conflict redistribution for two activities. As shown, with the growth of the amount of the size of frame of discernment set, the belief of the mass committed to the activity $\{b\}$ decreases in our approach while it remains constant in Murphy's, PCR6 and Dempster's rules. The reason is that a part of this belief is weaker according to the variation of $|\Theta|$.

5   Conclusion

In this paper, a two-step rule fusion is established where the averaging of evidence step comes first, and then the conflict redistribution step. The latter step considers a new notion of beliefs according to the cardinality of focal set elements. Experimental studies are conducted on a real smart home dataset to show the accuracy of our rule in ubiquitous-assisted living situation where our CRC rule advances some existing evidential rules.

References

1. Shafer, G.: A mathematical theory of evidence. Princeton University Press (1976)
2. Zadeh, L.: On the validity of Dempster's rule of combination of evidence, Electronics Research Laboratory, Univ. of California. Memorandum UCB/ERL-M (1979)
3. Dezert, J., Tchamova, A.: On the behavior of dempster's rule of combination (2011)
4. Yager, R.R.: On the dempster-shafer framework and new combination rules. Inf. Sci. 41, 93–137 (1987)
5. Murphy, C.K.: Combining belief functions when evidence conflicts. Decision Support Systems 29, 1–9 (2000)
6. Lefevre, E., Colot, O., Vannoorenberghe, P.: Belief function combination and conflict management. Information Fusion 3, 149–162 (2002)
7. Daniel, M.: Associativity in combination of belief functions; a derivation of minc combination. Soft Comput., 288–296 (2003)
8. Josang, A., Daniel, M., Vannoorenberghe, P.: Strategies for combining conflicting dogmatic beliefs. In: Proceedings of Fusion 2003, vol. 2, pp. 1133–1140 (2003)
9. Martin, A., Osswald, C.: A new generalization of the proportional conflict redistribution rule stable in terms of decision. CoRR abs/0806.1797 (2008)
10. Smarandache, F., Dezert, J.: Advances and applications of DSmT for information fusion: collected works. Advances and applications of DSmT for information fusion: collected works, vol. 1. American Research Press (2004)
11. Kasteren, T.V., Noulas, A.K., Englebienne, G., Kröse, B.J.A.: Accurate activity recognition in a home setting. In: UbiComp. ACM International Conference Proceeding Series, vol. 344, pp. 1–9. ACM (2008)
12. Sebbak, F., Benhammadi, F., Chibani, A., Amirat, Y., Mokhtari, A.: Dempster-shafer theory-based human activity recognition in smart home environments. Annals of Telecommunications, 1–14 (2013)

13. Zhang, D., Guo, M., Zhou, J., Kang, D., Cao, J.: Context reasoning using extended evidence theory in pervasive computing environments. Future Generation Comp. Syst. 26, 207–216 (2010)
14. Hong, X., Nugent, C.D., Mulvenna, M.D., McClean, S.I., Scotney, B.W., Devlin, S.: Evidential fusion of sensor data for activity recognition in smart homes. Pervasive and Mobile Computing 5, 236–252 (2009)
15. McKeever, S., Ye, J., Coyle, L., Bleakley, C.J., Dobson, S.: Activity recognition using temporal evidence theory. JAISE 2, 253–269 (2010)
16. Sebbak, F., Amirat, Y., Chibani, A., Mokhtari, A., Benhammadi, F.: An evidential fusion approach of activity recognition in ambient intelligence environments. Robotic and Autonomous Systems 61, 1235–1245 (2013)
17. Liao, J., Bi, Y., Nugent, C.: Using the dempster-shafer theory of evidence with a revised lattice structure for activity recognition. IEEE Trans. on Information Technology in Biomedicine 15(1), 74–82 (2011)

Evidential Fusion for Sentiment Polarity Classification

Yaxin Bi

School of Computing and Mathematics, University of Ulster
Newtownabbey, Co. Antrim, BT37 0QB, UK
y.bi@ulster.ac.uk

Abstract. This paper presents an evidential fusion approach for sentiment classification tasks and a comparative study with linear sum combination. It involves the formulation of sentiment classifier output in the triplet evidence structure and adaptation of combination formulas for combining simple support functions derived from triplet functions by using Smets's rule, the cautious conjunctive rules and linear sum rule. Empirical comparisons on the performance have been made in individuals and in combinations by using these rules, the results demonstrate that the best ensemble classifiers constructed by the four combination rules outperform the best individual classifiers over two public datasets of MP3 and Movie-Review.

Keywords: Belief functions, combination rules, linear sum and sentiment polarity classification.

1 Introduction

The social media of online reviews, forum discussions and social networks is now pervasive in so many areas of personal, social and economic life, and influences people's opinion toward entities, subjects and events. When used in the analysis of public opinion, such as the automated interpretation of online product reviews, sentiment analysis can be extremely helpful in identifying the polarity of opinions about the success of products. However, identifying opinions gleaned from social media remains a challenging task due to the proliferation of diverse social networks [1] and little is known about evidential fusion approaches in the context of sentiment classification. This paper presents our latest research on an evidential fusion approach for sentiment polarity classification.

Sentiment classification normally involves to assign opinionated texts with a situation in the form of positive, negative or neutral, but supervised machine learning algorithms are not able directly classify inputs to a neutral situation, which could be alternatively obtained through a membership function on numerical scores. In this study, we consider positive and negative situations as binary mutually exclusive propositions for defining a frame of discernment and use the frame to represent the neutral situation in terms of *ignornace*. In this way we can effectively adapt the triplet function to represent sentiment classifier output [6].

F. Cuzzolin (Ed.): BELIEF 2014, LNAI 8764, pp. 365–373, 2014.

Following this we adapt the computational formulas derived to combine multiple triplet functions by the cautious conjunctive combination rule, the normalized version of the cautious rule [3], the Transferable Belief Model(TBM) conjunctive rule [4] and linear sum rule, which could be regarded as a novel piece of work as the application of the cautious rules and Smets's rule to combine the adapted triplet functions has not previously been investigated in the context of sentiment polarity classification. The more comparative studies with other combinations will be included in a future paper. To evaluate the effectiveness of the proposed method two experiments have been conducted on combining eight machine learning algorithms by using these rules in conjunction with the linear sum combination over the online review datasets of MP3 and Movie-Review, the experimental results show that on both of the datasets, the best combined classifiers by using the four rules outperform the best individual classifiers.

2   Basics of Belief Functions

Belief functions were originally developed under the Dempster-Shafer (DS) theory of evidence [5], which have been commonly used for modeling someone's degrees of belief. The TBM model is an alternative to DS with its own interpretations to the conditions imposed in the DS model. TBM also provides mechanisms for representing the quantified beliefs held on a frame of discernment and concerns the same concepts as covered by the Bayesian model, but based on belief functions rather than on probabilistic quantification.

Let Θ denote a finite set called the frame of discernment that is comprised of mutually exclusive propositions. A mass function or called *basic belief assignment* (bba) is defined as a function $m : 2^{\Theta} \to [0, 1]$ with the condition of

$$\sum_{A \subseteq \Theta} m(A) = 1$$

where $m(A)$ measures the amount of belief that someone exactly commits to A, rather than the total support committed to A. The condition of $m(\emptyset) \neq 0$ held in DS is not imposed in TBM. Any subset $A \subseteq \Theta$ is called a focal element or focus if $m(A) > 0$. To obtain the measurements of the total support committed to A and of other situations, the DS provides other related functions, particularly, *commonality function (q)* that can be obtained by a mass function as follows:

$$q(A) = \sum_{B \supseteq A} m(B) \tag{1}$$

As a special case of mass functions, measurements on the frame of discernment are only committed to a specific subset A and Θ. Such a mass function is called a *simple support function*, denoted by A^w, where $m(A) = 1 - w$ and $m(\Theta) = w$ represent the degree of support for proposition $A \subseteq \Theta$ and support for all other possible worlds that are not included in A.

In practice, evidence sources may not be entirely reliable. Support degrees derived from such sources need to be discounted to truly reflect the reliability of the sources. The DS theory also provides a discount mechanism by the following formula.

$$m^r(A) = \begin{cases} (1-r)m(A), & \text{if } A \subset \Theta \\ r + (1-r)m(\Theta), & \text{if } A = \Theta \end{cases} \tag{2}$$

where r represents the discounting rate within the range of $[0, 1]$.

Definition 1. Let m_1 and m_2 be two mass functions on the frame of discernment Θ, and for any subset $A \subseteq \Theta$, the conjunctive combination of m_1 and m_2 on A, denoted by $\bigcirc\!\!\!\!\wedge$, is defined as follows:

$$m_1 \bigcirc\!\!\!\!\wedge m_2(A) = \sum_{X \cap Y = A} m_1(X)m_2(Y) \tag{3}$$

where $X, Y \subseteq \Theta$, the conjunctive rule is also referred to as Smets's rule. If the conjunctive rule is divided by the normalization factor $K = 1 - \sum_{X \cap Y = \emptyset} m_1(X) * m_2(Y)$, thereby resulting in a rule called Dempster's rule of combination, denoted by $\oplus$. Notice that the TBM model lifts the restriction on $m(\emptyset) = 0$ and removes the normalization operation held in the DS model.

Definition 2. Let m_1 and m_2 be two non dogmatic[1] mass functions defined on the frame of discernment Θ. The cautious conjunctive combination of m_1 and m_2, denoted by $m_{1 \bigcirc\!\!\!\wedge 2} = m_1 \bigcirc\!\!\!\wedge m_2$, is defined on the basis of a weight function below [3]:

$$w_{1 \bigcirc\!\!\!\wedge 2}(A) = w_1(A) \wedge w_2(A), \forall A \subset \Theta \tag{4}$$

and then

$$m_1 \bigcirc\!\!\!\wedge m_2 = \bigcirc\!\!\!\!\wedge_{A \subset \Theta} A^{w_1(A) \wedge w_2(A)}. \tag{5}$$

where the weight $w(A)$ can be obtained from the commonalities by the following formula:

$$w(A) = \prod_{B \supseteq A} q(B)^{(-1)^{|B| - |A| + 1}} \tag{6}$$

if the conjunctive operation $\bigcirc\!\!\!\wedge$ in Equation (5) is replaced by the Dempster orthogonal sum $\oplus$, then the revised Equation (5) has to be divided by the normalization factor of $K = 1 - m_1 \bigcirc\!\!\!\wedge m_2(\emptyset)$, resulting in a normalized version of the cautious rule below:

$$m_1 \bigcirc\!\!\!\wedge m_2 = \frac{\bigoplus_{\emptyset \neq A \subset \Theta} A^{w_1(A) \wedge w_2(A)}}{K}. \tag{7}$$

As indicated in [3] that $m_1 \bigcirc\!\!\!\wedge m_2(\emptyset) = 1$ never holds as 'the cautious combination of two non dogmatic BBAs can never be dogmatic'.

---

[1] Dogmatic means that the frame of discernment Θ is not a focal set.

3   Triplet Belief Functions and Combinations

A sentiment polarity classification can simply be as a special case of topic-based text categorization with the polar topics of positive and negative sentiments. Formally let D be a training text collection, $C = \{c, \tilde{c}\}$ be binary class labels and φ be a classifier, then we represent classifier output by $\varphi(d) = C \times [0, 1], d \in D$ and formulate the representation as a piece of evidence in the form of triplet below.

Definition 3. Let $\Theta = \{x_1, x_2, ..., x_n\}$ be a frame of discernment and $\varphi(d) = \{m(\{x_1\}), m(\{x_2\}), ..., m(\{x_n\})\}$ be mass probabilities derived from classifier outputs. An expression in the form of $A = \langle A_1, A_2, A_3 \rangle$ is defined as a *triplet*, where $A_1, A_2 \subset \Theta$ are singletons, A_3 is the whole set Θ. When $n = 2$, the frame of discernment Θ is comprised of only binary focal elements, denoted by $\Theta = \{x, \tilde{x}\}$, such that a triplet mass function on Θ satisfies the following condition:

$$m(\{x\}) + m(\{\tilde{x}\}) + m(\Theta) = 1,$$

where the degrees of support for $\{x\}$, $\{\tilde{x}\}$ and Θ can be obtained by using the discounting function Equation (2). Given multiple triplet mass functions of $m_1, \ldots, m_L$ that are committed to binary focal elements, the general formulas of combining them by using Smets's rule can be obtained below [6] [7]:

$$m(\{x\}) = 1 - \prod_{i=1}^{n}(1 - m_i(\{x\})) \tag{8}$$

$$m(\{\tilde{x}\}) = 1 - \prod_{i=1}^{n}(1 - m_i(\{\tilde{x}\})) \tag{9}$$

$$m(\Theta) = 1 - \prod_{i=1}^{n} m_i(\Theta) \tag{10}$$

To combine $m_1, \ldots, m_L$ by the cautious rule, we arrange these L functions into a group of pairs and combine each pair separately as follows:

$$\underbrace{m_1 \textcircled{\wedge} m_2}_{l_1}, \underbrace{m_3 \textcircled{\wedge} m_4}_{l_2}, \ldots, \underbrace{m_{L-1} \textcircled{\wedge} m_L}_{l_{L/2}} \tag{11}$$

where $l_1+, \ldots l_{L/2} = L$ and L is assumed to be an even number.

Specifically taking the first pair of triplet functions as an example, the combination involves three steps [3]. The first step is to compute the commonality functions q_1 and q_2 from m_1 and m_2 by Equation (1); the second is to compute the weight functions w_1 and w_2 using Equation (6) and then generate (inverse)simple mass functions in the form of $A^{w_1(A) \wedge w_2(A)}$, for all $A \subset \Omega$ such that $w_1 \wedge w_2(A) \neq 1$; and finally compute $m_{1\textcircled{\wedge}2} = m_1\textcircled{\wedge}m_2$ on these simple mass functions by using Smets's rule. From the former two steps, we have,

$$\{x\}^{w_1(\{x\})\wedge w_2(\{x\})} = \{x\}^{min(\{\frac{m_1(\Theta)}{m_1(\{x\})+m_1(\Theta)}\cdot\frac{m_2(\Theta)}{m_2(\{x\})+m_2(\Theta)}\})=w} \quad (12)$$

$$\{\tilde{x}\}^{w_1(\{\tilde{x}\})\wedge w_2(\{\tilde{x}\})} = \{\tilde{x}\}^{min(\{\frac{m_1(\Theta)}{m_1(\{\tilde{x}\})+m_1(\Theta)}\cdot\frac{m_2(\Theta)}{m_2(\{\tilde{x}\})+m_2(\Theta)}\})=\tilde{w}} \quad (13)$$

with w and $\tilde{w}$, two (inverse) simple support functions can be generated as follows,

$$m_{12}^1(\{x\}) = 1 - w; m_{12}^1(\Theta) = w. \quad (14)$$

$$m_{12}^2(\{\tilde{x}\}) = 1 - \tilde{w}; m_{12}^2(\Theta) = \tilde{w}. \quad (15)$$

For the remaining pairs of triplet functions, we can repeat the same process above by using Equations (12)-(15) to subsequently obtain $L/2$ simple support functions that are committed to $\{x\}$ by Equation (14) and $L/2$ simple support functions that are committed to $\{\tilde{x}\}$ by Equation (15). Finally we can calculate the degrees of belief for $\{x\}$, $\{\tilde{x\}}$ and Θ by using Equations (8) - (10). When L is not an even number, it is straightforward to combine the Lth triplet mass function with a simple support function resulting from the $L-1$ triplet functions.

4   Evaluation

To evaluate the performance of ensemble classifiers made by using the four combination rules of the cautious conjunctive rule, the normalized cautious rule, Smets's rule and Linear Sum rule, we conducted the experiments with eight machine learning algorithms to generate base classifier over the two datasets of MP3 and Movie-Review. These learning algorithms include *NaiveBayes, IBk, KStar, DecisionStump, J48, RandomForest, DecisionTable* and *JRip*, which are directly taken from the Waikato Environment for Knowledge Analysis (Weka) version 3.6 [8]. The philosophies behind these algorithms are quite different, but each has been shown to be effective in previous text categorization studies. For our experiments parameters used for each algorithm were set at the default settings.

The MP3 dataset contains MP3 digital camera and player reviews collected in Amazon.com [9]. Each of review consists of short sentences and is labeled with a five star scale. The reviews with 1 and 2 stars are considered very negative and negative, respectively, whereas reviews with 4 and 5 stars are considered positive and very positive, and reviews with 3 stars are regarded as neutral [10]. The Movie-Review are rated with a similar schema. For this work, we concentrated only on discriminating between positive and negative polarity sentiment and discarded the reviews with neutral. As a result the MP3 dataset used in our experiments contains 21519 positive and 6390 negative reviews and the Movie-Review consists of 1000 positive and 1000 negative movie reviews.

The experiments were conducted using a ten-fold cross validation, and the performance of classifiers in individuals and combinations was measured by the

Table 1. The accuracies of best individual classifier, best ensemble classifiers constructed by the cautious conjunctive rule, the normalized cautious rule, Smets's rule and Linear Sum on MP3 and Movie-Review (MR) datasets

Datasets	Best individual	Cautious rule	Normalized rule	Smets's rule	Linear sum
MP3	79.52%	81.74%	81.68%	82.32%	81.79%
MR	75.17%	76.57%	76.57%	76.49%	77.37%
Av	77.34%	79.16%	79.13%	79.41%	79.55%

F-measure. For construction of ensemble classifiers by the four combination rule, all combinations of eight classifiers were generated. Specifically, we first combine any two classifiers, denoted by $C2$, and combine the resulting combination of two classifiers with a third classifier, denoted by $C3$, and the result with a fourth classifier, denoted by $C4$, until combine all eight classifiers, denoted by $C8$, resulting in a 247×3 number of classifier combinations in total for one dataset.

Table 1 presents the summarized accuracies of the best individual and best ensemble classifiers constructed by the four combination rules on the two datasets. On average, the best accuracies increase by 2.36% compared with the best individual on the MP3 dataset, and increase by 1.58% on Movie-Review. These give a totally averaged 1.97% increase on these datasets. The details of each of the experimental results are depicted below.

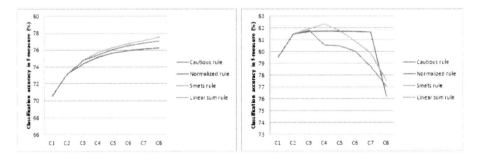

Fig. 1. Averaged (left) and best (right) accuracies of different groups combination of classifiers using the four combination rules over the MP3 dataset

Figure 1 (left) shows the averaged accuracies of different ensemble classifier groups on MP3, where $C1$ on the x-axis represents the averaged accuracy of eight classifiers, $C2$ represents an averaged accuracy of all accuracies of the ensemble classifiers that are comprised of two classifiers by using four combination rules respectively, $C3$ represents an averaged accuracy of all accuracies of the ensemble classifiers made up of three classifiers, and so forth. This figure illustrates that the averaged accuracies of different groups of ensemble classifiers gradually increase with adding more classifiers into classifier ensembles. It can be seen that the averaged performance of the combined classifiers by the cautious conjunctive rule is the same as that of the ensemble classifiers made by the normalized cautious rule, and the ensemble classifiers made by Smets's rule and by Linear Sum outperform that constructed by the cautious rules. Compared with the averaged accuracy of eight base classifiers, the averaged accuracies of all ensemble classifiers made by the cautious rules are 4.69% better, by Smets's rule it is 5.36% better, and by Linear Sum it is 5.16% better.

Figure 1 (right) shows the accuracies of the best ensemble classifiers among the respective groups of ensemble classifiers on MP3, where $C1$, $C2$, ..., $C8$ on the x-axis represent the best individual accuracies among each of the ensemble classifier groups, respectively. Unlike the trends embodying in Figure 1 (left), the best accuracies increase from the combination of two classifiers to four classifiers and then drop down with adding more classifiers into ensemble classifiers. It can be found that the ensemble classifiers made by Smets's rule perform best, the cautious conjunctive rule, the normalized cautious rule and the Linear Sum perform similarly. The best accuracy drawn from all the ensemble classifiers made by Smets's rule is 2.8% better than the accuracy of best individual classifier, by Linear Sum it is 2.27% better, by the cautious conjunctive rule it is 2.22% than better, and by the normalized cautious rule it is 2.21% better.

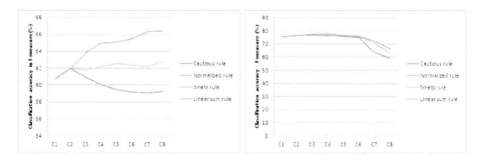

Fig. 2. Averaged (left) and best (right) accuracies of different groups combination of classifiers using the four combination rules over the Movie-Review dataset

Figure 2 (left) presents a similar analysis as depicted in Figure 1 (left) on Movie-Review instead. Compared with the analysis results with those in Figure 1 (left), the trend of the ensemble classifiers made by the Linear Sum is consistent with those presented in Figure 1 (left), but the trends with the cautious rules are opposite to what the cautious rules conducts on MP3. The averaged accuracies of all ensemble classifiers constructed by the cautious rules are 0.79% less than that of the averaged eight base classifiers, but by Smets's rule it is 1.51% better than that of the averaged eight base classifiers, however the averaged accuracy by Linear Sum is 4.08%, marginally better than the averaged performance of eight base classifiers. Figure 2 (right) shows the best accuracies among each of the ensemble classifier groups for the Movie-Review dataset. The performance trends of the ensemble classifiers made by the four combination rules are roughly embodied in a decreasing manner, but the accuracies of the ensemble classifiers made by the cautious rules drop down sharply. The best accuracies achieved are among the combinations of two, three or four classifiers cross four groups of ensemble classifiers made by these combination rules. From the experimental results, it is found that the Linear Sum performs best, the cautious rules performs the second best, the accuracy of best ensemble classifier among seven groups of ensemble classifiers is 1.4% better than that of the best individual classifier, for Smets's rule it is 1.33% better than the best individual classifier, and for Linear Sum it is 2.21% better than the best individual classifier.

5   Conclusions

In this paper we proposed to use the triplet function to represent polarity sentiment classification output and adapted the formulas developed for computing triplet functions to combining multiple triplets in the form of simple support functions with the four combination rules. We empirically compare the proposed approach with the linear sum approach, the results demonstrate that the potential of the proposed method in determining the sentiment polarity of online product reviews.

The experimental results reveal the fact that the best ensemble classifiers, which are made by either the evidential rules or the linear sum, are composed of 2-4 classifiers. This indicates that combining more classifiers represented by triplet mass functions into an ensemble classifier may not result in the best combined accuracy as combining more classifiers may not effectively make the best combination to arrive at a convergent consensus in addition to increasing computational complexity as observed in [2]. From a further examination on the construction of the ensemble classifiers, it is also found that the best base classifier is always a component classifier in the best ensemble classifiers. In opposition to this, the second best base classifier plays in a varied role in constructing the best ensemble classifiers, this means that the role played is depending the combination rules and the datasets. In the best ensemble classifier constructed by Smets's rules on MP3, the second best classifier is one of the component classifiers, by contrast it is not one with the cautious rules and the linear sum. While for Movie-Review, the second best classifier does not play a role in constructing the best ensemble classifiers made by the four combination rules.

In this study, the generation of sentiment classifiers is based on the conventional text categorization approach, where we used the bag of words as a feature representation, and we did not incorporate a set of seed words or part-of-speech tagging as prior knowledge to associate features with aspects/topics. This will be an important next step in an attempt to improve the sentiment classification accuracy. As mentioned previously the sentiment polarity classification involves three possible outcomes: positive, negative and neutral. In this work the neutral category has implicitly been formulated as *ignorance* in the form of a frame of discernment, but the associated mass probabilities were obtained through the discounting function. The justification on such a treatment remains to be addressed in connection with formulating the neutral output as a frame of discernment in future.

References

1. Feldnan, R.: Techniques and Applications for Sentiment Analysis. Communications of the ACM 56(4), 82–89 (2013)
2. Bi, Y., Guan, J.W., Bell, D.: The combination of multiple classifiers using an evidential approach. Artificial Intelligence 17, 1731–1751 (2008)
3. Denoeux, T.: Conjunctive and disjunctive combination of belief functions induced by nondistinct bodies of evidence. Artificial Intelligence 172(2-3), 234–264 (2008)
4. Smets, P., Kennes, R.: The transferable belief model. Artificial Intelligence 66, 191–243 (1994)
5. Shafer, G.: A Mathematical Theory of Evidence, 1st edn. Princeton University Press, Princeton (1976)
6. Bi, Y.: An Efficient Triplet-based Algorithm for Evidential Reasoning. International Journal of Intelligent Systems 23(4), 1–34 (2008)
7. Srivastava, R.: Alternative form of Dempster's rule for binary variables. International Journal of Intelligent Systems 20(8), 789–797 (2005)
8. Witten, I.H., Frank, E.: Data Mining: Practical machine learning tools and techniques, 3rd edn. Morgan Kaufmann, San Francisco (2011)
9. Kim, S., Pantel, P., Chklovski, T., Pennacchiotti, M.: Automatically assessing review helpfulness. In: Proceedings of the Conference on Empirical Methods in Natural Language Processing (EMNLP), Sydney, Australia, pp. 423–430 (July 2006)
10. Internet Movie Database (IMDb) archive, `http://reviews.imdb.com/Reviews/`

On the Quality of Optimal Assignment
for Data Association

Jean Dezert and Kaouthar Benameur

The French Aerospace Lab, Chemin de la Hunière, F-91761 Palaiseau, France
{jean.dezert,Kaouthar.Benameur}@onera.fr

Abstract. In this paper, we present a method based on belief functions to evaluate the quality of the optimal assignment solution of a classical association problem encountered in multiple target tracking applications. The purpose of this work is not to provide a new algorithm for solving the assignment problem, but a solution to estimate the quality of the individual associations (pairings) given in the optimal assignment solution. To the knowledge of authors, this problem has not been addressed so far in the literature and its solution may have practical aspects for improving the performances of multisensor-multitarget tracking systems.

Keywords: Data association, PCR6 rule, Belief function.

1   Introduction

Efficient algorithms for modern multisensor-multitarget tracking (MS-MTT) systems [1,2] require to estimate and predict the states (position, velocity, etc) of the targets evolving in the surveillance area covered by the sensors. The estimations and the predictions are based on sensors measurements and dynamical models assumptions. In the monosensor context, MTT requires to solve the data association (DA) problem to associate the available measurements at a given time with the predicted states of the targets to update their tracks using filtering techniques (Kalman filter, Particle filter, etc). In the multisensor MTT context, we need to solve more difficult multi-dimensional assignment problems under constraints. Fortunately, efficient algorithms have been developed in operational research and tracking communities for formalizing and solving these optimal assignments problems. Several approaches based on different models can be used to establish rewards matrix, either based on the probabilistic framework [1,3], or on the belief function (BF) framework [4,5,6,7]. In this paper, we do not focus on the construction of the rewards matrix[1], and our purpose is to provide a method to evaluate the quality (interpreted as a confidence score) of each association (pairing) provided in the optimal solution based on its consistency (stability) with respect to all the second best solutions.

---

[1] We assume that the rewards matrix is known and has been obtained by a method chosen by the user, either in the probabilistic or in the BF framework.

F. Cuzzolin (Ed.): BELIEF 2014, LNAI 8764, pp. 374–382, 2014.

The simple DA problem under concern can be formulated as follows. We have $m > 1$ targets T_i $(i = 1, \ldots, m)$, and $n > 1$ measurements[2] z_j $(j = 1, \ldots, n)$ at a given time k, and a $m \times n$ rewards (gain/payoff) matrix $\boldsymbol{\Omega} = [\omega(i, j)]$ whose elements $\omega(i, j) \geq 0$ represent the payoff (usually homogeneous to the likelihood) of the association of target T_i with measurement z_j, denoted (T_i, z_j). The data association problem consists in finding the global optimal assignment of the targets to some measurements by maximizing[3] the overall gain in such a way that no more than one target is assigned to a measurement, and reciprocally.

Without loss of generality, we can assume $\omega(i, j) \geq 0$ because if some elements $\omega(i, j)$ of $\boldsymbol{\Omega}$ were negative, we can always add the same maximal negative value to all elements of $\boldsymbol{\Omega}$ to work with a new payoff matrix $\boldsymbol{\Omega}' = [\omega'(i, j)]$ having all elements $\omega'(i, j) \geq 0$, and we get the same optimal assignment solution with $\boldsymbol{\Omega}$ and with $\boldsymbol{\Omega}'$. Moreover, we can also assume, without loss of generality $m \leq n$, because otherwise we can always swap the roles of targets and measurements in the mathematical problem definition by working directly with $\boldsymbol{\Omega}^t$ instead, where the superscript t denotes the transposition of the matrix. The optimal assignment problem consists of finding the $m \times n$ binary association matrix $\mathbf{A} = [a(i, j)]$ which maximize the global rewards $R(\boldsymbol{\Omega}, \mathbf{A})$ given by

$$R(\boldsymbol{\Omega}, \mathbf{A}) \triangleq \sum_{i=1}^{m} \sum_{j=1}^{n} \omega(i, j) a(i, j) \tag{1}$$

$$\text{Subject to} \quad \begin{cases} \sum_{j=1}^{n} a(i, j) = 1 & (i = 1, \ldots, m) \\ \sum_{i=1}^{m} a(i, j) \leq 1 & (j = 1, \ldots, n) \\ a(i, j) \in \{0, 1\} & (i = 1, \ldots, m \text{ and } j = 1, \ldots, n) \end{cases} \tag{2}$$

The association indicator value $a(i, j) = 1$ means that the corresponding target T_i and measurement z_j are associated, and $a(i, j) = 0$ means that they are not associated $(i = 1, \ldots, m$ and $j = 1, \ldots, n)$.

The solution of the optimal assignment problem stated in (1)–(2) is well reported in the literature and several efficient methods have been developed in the operational research and tracking communities to solve it. The most well-known algorithms are Kuhn-Munkres (a.k.as Hungarian) algorithm [8,9] and its extension to rectangular matrices proposed by Bourgeois and Lassalle in [10], Jonker-Volgenant method [11], and Auction [12]. More sophisticated methods using Murty's method [13], and some variants [3,14,15,16,17,18,19], are also able to provide not only the best assignment, but also the m-best assignments. We will not present in details all these classical methods because they have been already well reported in the literature [20,21], and they are quite easily accessible on the web. In this paper, we want to provide a confidence level (i.e. a

---

[2] In a multi-sensor context targets can be replaced by tracks provided by a given tracker associated with a type of sensor, and measurements can be replaced by another tracks set. In different contexts, possible equivalents are assigning personnel to jobs or assigning delivery trucks to locations.

[3] In some problems, $\boldsymbol{\Omega} = [\omega(i, j)]$ represents a cost matrix whose elements are the negative log-likelihood of association hypotheses. In this case, the data association problems consists in finding the best assignment that minimizes the overall cost.

quality indicator) in the optimal data association solution. More precisely, we are searching an answer to the question: how to measure the quality of the pairings $a(i, j) = 1$ provided in the optimal assignment solution $\mathbf{A}$? The necessity to establish a quality indicator is motivated by the following three main reasons:

1. In some practical tracking environment with the presence of clutter, some association decisions $(a(i, j) = 1)$ are doubtful. For these unreliable associations, it is better to wait for new information (measurements) instead of applying the hard data association decision, and making potentially serious association mistakes.
2. In some multisensor systems, it can be also important to save energy consumption for preserving a high autonomy capacities of the system. For this goal, only the most trustful specific associations provided in the optimal assignment have to be selected and used instead of all of them.
3. The best optimal assignment solution is not necessarily unique. In such situation, the establishment of quality indicators may help in selecting one particular optimal assignment solution among multiple possible choices.

Before presenting our solution in Section 2, one must recall that the best, as well as the 2nd-best, optimal assignment solutions are unfortunately not necessarily unique. Therefore, we must also take into account the possible multiplicity of assignments in the analysis of the problem. The multiplicity index of the best optimal assignment solution is denoted $\beta_1 \geq 1$, and the multiplicity index of the 2nd-best optimal assignment solution is denoted $\beta_2 \geq 1$, and we will denote the sets of corresponding assignment matrices by $\mathcal{A}_1 = \{\mathbf{A}_1^{(k_1)}, k_1 = 1 \ldots, \beta_1\}$ and by $\mathcal{A}_2 = \{\mathbf{A}_2^{(k_2)}, k_2 = 1 \ldots, \beta_2\}$. The next simple example illustrates a case with multiplicity of 2nd-best assignment solutions for the reward matrix $\boldsymbol{\Omega}_1$.

Example: $\beta_1 = 1$ and $\beta_2 = 4$ (i.e. no multiplicity of $\mathbf{A}_1$ and multiplicity of $\mathbf{A}_2$)

$$\boldsymbol{\Omega}_1 = \begin{bmatrix} 1 & 11 & 45 & 30 \\ 17 & 8 & 38 & 27 \\ 10 & 14 & 35 & 20 \end{bmatrix}$$

This reward matrix provides a unique best assignment $\mathbf{A}_1$ providing $R_1(\boldsymbol{\Omega}_1, \mathbf{A}_1) = 86$, and $\beta_2 = 4$ second-best assignment solutions providing $R_2(\boldsymbol{\Omega}_1, \mathbf{A}_2^{k_2}) = 82$ $(k_2 = 1, 2, 3, 4)$ given by

$$\mathbf{A}_1 = \begin{bmatrix} 0 & 0 & 1 & 0 \\ 0 & 0 & 0 & 1 \\ 0 & 1 & 0 & 0 \end{bmatrix}$$

$$\mathbf{A}_2^{k_2=1} = \begin{bmatrix} 0 & 0 & 0 & 1 \\ 0 & 0 & 1 & 0 \\ 0 & 1 & 0 & 0 \end{bmatrix}, \quad \mathbf{A}_2^{k_2=2} = \begin{bmatrix} 0 & 0 & 1 & 0 \\ 1 & 0 & 0 & 0 \\ 0 & 0 & 0 & 1 \end{bmatrix}, \quad \mathbf{A}_2^{k_2=3} = \begin{bmatrix} 0 & 0 & 1 & 0 \\ 0 & 0 & 0 & 1 \\ 1 & 0 & 0 & 0 \end{bmatrix}, \quad \mathbf{A}_2^{k_2=4} = \begin{bmatrix} 0 & 0 & 0 & 1 \\ 1 & 0 & 0 & 0 \\ 0 & 0 & 1 & 0 \end{bmatrix}$$

2   Quality of the Associations of the Optimal Assignment

To establish the quality of the specific associations (pairings) (i, j) satisfying $a_1(i, j) = 1$ belonging to the optimal assignment matrix $\mathbf{A}_1$, we propose to use both $\mathbf{A}_1$ and 2nd-best assignment solution $\mathbf{A}_2$. The basic idea is to compare the values $a_1(i,j)$ with $a_2(i,j)$ obtained in the best and in the 2nd-best assignments to identify the change (if any) of the optimal pairing (i,j). Our quality indicator will depend on both the stability of the pairing and its relative impact in the global reward. The proposed method works also when the 2nd-best assignment solution $\mathbf{A}_2$ is not unique (as in our example). The proposed method will also help to select the best (most trustful) optimal assignment in case of multiplicity of $\mathbf{A}_1$ matrices.

2.1 A Simplistic Method (Method I)

Before presenting our sophisticate method based on belief functions, let's first present a simplistic intuitive method (called Method I). For this, let's assume at first that $\mathbf{A}_1$ and $\mathbf{A}_2$ are unique (no multiplicity occurs). The simplistic method uses only the ratio of global rewards $\rho \triangleq R_2(\mathbf{\Omega}, \mathbf{A}_2)/R_1(\mathbf{\Omega}, \mathbf{A}_1)$ to measure the level of uncertainty in the change (if any) of pairing (i,j) provided in $\mathbf{A}_1$ and $\mathbf{A}_2$. More precisely, the quality (trustfulness) of pairings in an optimal assignment solution $\mathbf{A}_1$, denoted[4] $q_I(i,j)$, is simply defined as follows for $i = 1, \ldots, m$ and $j = 2, \ldots, n$:

$$q_I(i,j) \triangleq \begin{cases} 1, & \text{if } a_1(i,j) + a_2(i,j) = 0 \\ 1 - \rho & \text{if } a_1(i,j) + a_2(i,j) = 1 \\ 1, & \text{if } a_1(i,j) + a_2(i,j) = 2 \end{cases} \tag{3}$$

By adopting such definition, one commits the full confidence to the components (i,j) of $\mathbf{A}_1$ and $\mathbf{A}_2$ that perfectly match, and a lower confidence value (a lower quality) of $1 - \rho$ to those that do not match. To take into account the eventual multiplicities (when $\beta_2 > 1$) of the 2nd-best assignment solutions $\mathbf{A}_2^{k_2}$, $k_2 = 1, 2, \ldots, \beta_2$, we need to combine the $\mathbf{Q}_I(\mathbf{A}_1, \mathbf{A}_2^{k_2})$ values. Several methods can be used for this, in particular we can use either:

– **A Weighted Averaging Approach**: The quality indicator component $q_I(i,j)$ is then obtained by averaging the qualities obtained from each comparison of $\mathbf{A}_1$ with $\mathbf{A}_2^{k_2}$. More precisely, one will take:

$$q_I(i,j) \triangleq \sum_{k_2=1}^{\beta_2} w(\mathbf{A}_2^{k_2}) q_I^{k_2}(i,j) \tag{4}$$

where $q_I^{k_2}(i,j)$ is defined as in (3) (with $a_2(i,j)$ replaced by $a_2^{k_2}(i,j)$ in the formula), and where $w(\mathbf{A}_2^{k_2})$ is a weighting factor in $[0,1]$, such that $\sum_{k_2=1}^{\beta_2} w(\mathbf{A}_2^{k_2}) = 1$. Since all assignments $\mathbf{A}_2^{k_2}$ have the same global reward value R_2, then we suggest to take $w(\mathbf{A}_2^{k_2}) = 1/\beta_2$. A more elaborate method would consist to use the quality indicator of $\mathbf{A}_2^{k_2}$ based on the 3rd-best solution, which can be itself computed from the quality of the 3rd assignment solution based on the 4th-best solution, and so on by a similar mechanism. We however don't give more details on this due to space constraints.

---

[4] The subscript I in $q_I(i,j)$ notation refers to Method I.

- **A Belief-Based Approach** (see [22] for basics on belief functions): A second method would express the quality by a belief interval $[q_I^{\min}(i,j), q_I^{\max}(i,j)]$ in $[0,1]$ instead of single real number $q_I(i,j)$ in $[0,1]$. More precisely, one can compute the belief and plausibility bounds of the quality by taking $q_I^{\min}(i,j) \equiv Bel(a_1(i,j)) = \min_{k_2} q_I^{k_2}(i,j)$ and $q_I^{\max}(i,j) \equiv Pl(a_1(i,j)) = \max_{k_2} q_I^{k_2}(i,j)$, with $q_I^{k_2}(i,j)$ given by (3) and $a_2(i,j)$ replaced by $a_2^{k_2}(i,j)$ in the formula. Hence for each association $a_1(i,j)$, one can define a basic belief assignment (BBA) $m_{ij}(.)$ on the frame of discernment $\Theta \triangleq \{T = \text{trustful}, \neg T = \text{not trustful}\}$, which will characterize the quality of the pairing (i,j) in the optimal assignment solution $\mathbf{A}_1$, as follows:

$$\begin{cases} m_{ij}(T) = q_I^{\min}(i,j) \\ m_{ij}(\neg T) = 1 - q_I^{\max}(i,j) \\ m_{ij}(T \cup \neg T) = q_I^{\max}(i,j) - q_I^{\min}(i,j) \end{cases} \tag{5}$$

Remark: In practice, only the pairings[5] (i,j) such that $a_1(i,j) = 1$ are useful in tracking algorithms to update the tracks. Therefore, we don't need to pay attention (compute and store) the qualities of components (i,j) such that $a_1(i,j) = 0$.

2.2   A More Sophisticate and Efficient Method (Method II)

The previous method can be easily applied in practice but it does not work very well because the quality indicator depends only on the ρ factor, which means that all mismatches between the best assignment $\mathbf{A}_1$ and the 2nd-best assignment solution $\mathbf{A}_2$ have their quality impacted in the same manner (they are all taken as $1 - \rho$). As a simple example, if we consider the rewards matrix $\mathbf{\Omega}_1$ given in our example, we will have $\rho = R_2(\mathbf{\Omega}_1, \mathbf{A}_2^{k_2})/R_1(\mathbf{\Omega}_1, \mathbf{A}_1) = 82/86 \approx 0.95$, and we will get using method I with the weighting averaging approach (using same $w(\mathbf{A}_2^{k_2}) = 1/\beta_2 = 0.25$ for $k_2 = 1, 2, 3, 4$) the following quality indicator matrix:

$$\mathbf{Q}_I(\mathbf{A}_1, \mathcal{A}_2) = \frac{1}{\beta_2} \sum_{k_2=1}^{\beta_2} \mathbf{Q}_I(\mathbf{A}_1, \mathbf{A}_2^{k_2}) = \begin{bmatrix} 1.0000 & 1.0000 & \mathbf{0.5233} & 0.5233 \\ 0.5233 & 1.0000 & 0.7616 & \mathbf{0.2849} \\ 0.7616 & \mathbf{0.2849} & 0.7616 & 0.7616 \end{bmatrix} \tag{6}$$

We observe that optimal pairings (2,4) and (3,2) get the same quality value 0.2849 with the method I (based on averaging), even if these pairings have different impacts in the global reward value, which is abnormal. If we use the method I with the belief interval measure based on (5), the situation is worst because the three optimal pairings (1,3), (2,4) and (3,2) will get exactly same belief interval values $[0.0465, 1]$. To take into account, and in a better way, the reward values of each specific association given in the best assignment $\mathbf{A}_1$ and in the 2nd-best assignment $\mathbf{A}_2^{k_2}$, we propose to use the following construction of quality indicators depending on the type of matching (called Method II):

---

[5] Given in the optimal solution found for example with Murty's algorithm.

- When $a_1(i,j) = a_2^{k_2}(i,j) = 0$, one has full agreement on "non-association" (T_i, z_j) in $\mathbf{A}_1$ and in $\mathbf{A}_2^{k_2}$ and this non-association (T_i, z_j) has no impact on the global rewards values $R_1(\boldsymbol{\Omega}, \mathbf{A}_1)$ and $R_2(\boldsymbol{\Omega}, \mathbf{A}_2^{k_2})$, and it will be useless. Therefore, we can set its quality arbitrarily to $q_{II}^{k_2}(i,j) = 1$.

- When $a_1(i,j) = a_2^{k_2}(i,j) = 1$, one has a full agreement on the association (T_i, z_j) in $\mathbf{A}_1$ and in $\mathbf{A}_2^{k_2}$ and this association (T_i, z_j) has different impacts in the global rewards values $R_1(\boldsymbol{\Omega}, \mathbf{A}_1)$ and $R_2(\boldsymbol{\Omega}, \mathbf{A}_2^{k_2})$. To qualify the quality of this matching association (T_i, z_j), we define the two BBA's on $X \triangleq (T_i, z_j)$ and $X \cup \neg X$ (the ignorance), for $s = 1, 2$:

$$\begin{cases} m_s(X) = a_s(i,j) \cdot \omega(i,j)/R_s(\boldsymbol{\Omega}, \mathbf{A}_s) \\ m_s(X \cup \neg X) = 1 - m_s(X) \end{cases} \tag{7}$$

Applying the conjunctive rule of fusion, we get

$$\begin{cases} m(X) = m_1(X)m_2(X) + m_1(X)m_2(X \cup \neg X) + m_1(X \cup \neg X)m_2(X) \\ m(X \cup \neg X) = m_1(X \cup \neg X)m_2(X \cup \neg X) \end{cases} \tag{8}$$

Applying the pignistic transformation[6] [24], we get finally $BetP(X) = m(X) + \frac{1}{2} \cdot m(X \cup \neg X)$ and $BetP(\neg X) = \frac{1}{2} \cdot m(X \cup \neg X)$. Therefore, we choose the quality indicator as $q_{II}^{k_2}(i,j) = BetP(X)$.

- When $a_1(i,j) = 1$ and $a_2^{k_2}(i,j) = 0$, one has a disagreement (conflict) on the association (T_i, z_j) in $\mathbf{A}_1$ and in (T_i, z_{j_2}) in $\mathbf{A}_2^{k_2}$, where j_2 is the measurement index such that $a_2(i, j_2) = 1$. To qualify the quality of this non-matching association (T_i, z_j), we define the two following basic belief assignments (BBA's) of the propositions $X \triangleq (T_i, z_j)$ and $Y \triangleq (T_i, z_{j_2})$

$$\begin{cases} m_1(X) = a_1(i,j) \cdot \frac{\omega(i,j)}{R_1(\boldsymbol{\Omega}, \mathbf{A}_1)} \\ m_1(X \cup Y) = 1 - m_1(X) \end{cases} \text{ and } \begin{cases} m_2(Y) = a_2(i, j_2) \cdot \frac{\omega(i, j_2)}{R_2(\boldsymbol{\Omega}, \mathbf{A}_2^{k_2})} \\ m_2(X \cup Y) = 1 - m_2(Y) \end{cases} \tag{9}$$

Applying the conjunctive rule, we get $m(X \cap Y = \emptyset) = m_1(X)m_2(Y)$ and

$$\begin{cases} m(X) = m_1(X)m_2(X \cup Y) \\ m(Y) = m_1(X \cup Y)m_2(Y) \\ m(X \cup Y) = m_1(X \cup Y)m_2(X \cup Y) \end{cases} \tag{10}$$

Because we need to work with a normalized combined BBA, we can choose different rules of combination (Dempster-Shafer's, Dubois-Prade's, Yager's rule [23], etc). In this work, we recommend the Proportional Conflict Redistribution rule no. 6 (PCR6), proposed originally in DSmT framework [23], because it has been proved very efficient in practice. So, we get with PCR6:

$$\begin{cases} m(X) = m_1(X)m_2(X \cup Y) + m_1(X) \cdot \frac{m_1(X)m_2(Y)}{m_1(X) + m_2(Y)} \\ m(Y) = m_1(X \cup Y)m_2(Y) + m_2(X) \cdot \frac{m_1(X)m_2(Y)}{m_1(X) + m_2(Y)} \\ m(X \cup Y) = m_1(X \cup Y)m_2(X \cup Y) \end{cases} \tag{11}$$

---

[6] We have chosen here BetP for its simplicity and because it is widely known, but DSmP could be used instead for expecting better performances [23].

Applying the pignistic transformation, we get finally $BetP(X) = m(X) + \frac{1}{2} \cdot m(X \cup Y)$ and $BetP(Y) = m(Y) + \frac{1}{2} \cdot m(X \cup Y)$. Therefore, we choose the quality indicators as follows: $q_{II}^{k_2}(i,j) = BetP(X)$, and $q_{II}^{k_2}(i,j_2) = BetP(Y)$.

The absolute quality factor $Q_{abs}(\mathbf{A}_1, \mathbf{A}_2^{k_2})$ of the optimal assignment given in $\mathbf{A}_1$ conditioned by $\mathbf{A}_2^{k_2}$, for any $k_2 \in \{1, 2, \dots, \beta_2\}$ is defined as

$$Q_{abs}(\mathbf{A}_1, \mathbf{A}_2^{k_2}) \triangleq \sum_{i=1}^{m} \sum_{j=1}^{n} a_1(i,j) q_{II}^{k_2}(i,j) \tag{12}$$

Example (continued): If we apply the Method II (using PCR6 fusion rule) to the rewards matrix $\mathbf{\Omega}_1$, then we will get the following quality matrix (using weighted averaging approach)

$$\mathbf{Q}_{II}(\mathbf{A}_1, \mathcal{A}_2) = \frac{1}{\beta_2} \sum_{k_2=1}^{\beta_2} \mathbf{Q}_{II}(\mathbf{A}_1, \mathbf{A}_2^{k_2}) = \begin{bmatrix} 1.0000 & 1.0000 & \mathbf{0.7440} & 0.7022 \\ 0.7200 & 1.0000 & 0.8972 & \mathbf{0.5753} \\ 0.8695 & \mathbf{0.4957} & 0.9119 & 0.8861 \end{bmatrix}$$

with the absolute quality factors $Q_{abs}(\mathbf{A}_1, \mathbf{A}_2^{k_2=1}) \approx 1.66$, $Q_{abs}(\mathbf{A}_1, \mathbf{A}_2^{k_2=2}) \approx 1.91$, $Q_{abs}(\mathbf{A}_1, \mathbf{A}_2^{k_2=3}) \approx 2.19$, $Q_{abs}(\mathbf{A}_1, \mathbf{A}_2^{k_2=4}) \approx 1.51$. Naturally, we get

$$Q_{abs}(\mathbf{A}_1, \mathbf{A}_2^{k_2=3}) > Q_{abs}(\mathbf{A}_1, \mathbf{A}_2^{k_2=2}) > Q_{abs}(\mathbf{A}_1, \mathbf{A}_2^{k_2=1}) > Q_{abs}(\mathbf{A}_1, \mathbf{A}_2^{k_2=4})$$

because $\mathbf{A}_1$ has more matching pairings with $\mathbf{A}_2^{k_2=3}$ than with other 2nd-best assignment $\mathbf{A}_2^{k_2}$ ($k_2 \neq 3$), and those pairings have also the strongest impacts in the global reward value. One sees that the quality matrix $\mathbf{Q}_{II}$ differentiates the qualities of each pairing in the optimal assignment $\mathbf{A}_1$ as expected (contrariwise to Method I). Clearly, with Method I we obtain the same quality indicator value 0.2849 for the specific associations (2,4) and (3,2) which seems intuitively not very reasonable because the specific rewards of these associations impact differently the global rewards result. If the method II based on the belief interval measure computed from (5) is preferred[7], we will get respectively for the three optimal pairings (1,3), (2,4) and (3,2) the three distinct belief interval [0.5956,0.8924], [0.4113,0.7699] and [0.3524,0.6529]. These belief intervals show that the ordering of quality of optimal pairings (based either on the lower bound, or on the upper bound of belief interval) is consistent with the ordering of quality of optimal pairings in $\mathbf{Q}_{II}(\mathbf{A}_1, \mathcal{A}_2)$ computed with the averaging approach. Method II provides a better effective and comprehensive solution to estimate the quality of each specific association provided in the optimal assignment solution $\mathbf{A}_1$.

3   Conclusion

In this paper we have proposed a method based on belief functions for establishing the quality of pairings belonging to the optimal data association (or assignment) solution provided by a chosen algorithm. Our method is independent

---

[7] Just in case of multiplicity of second best assignments.

of the choice of the algorithm used in finding the optimal assignment solution, and, in case of multiple optimal solutions, it provides also a way to select the best optimal assignment solution (the one having the highest absolute quality factor). The method developed in this paper is general in the sense that it can be applied to different types of association problems corresponding to different sets of constraints. This method can be extended to SD-assignment problems. The application of this approach in a realistic multi-target tracking context is under investigations and will be reported in a forthcoming publication if possible.

References

1. Bar-Shalom, Y., Willett, P.K., Tian, X.: Tracking and Data Fusion: A Handbook of Algorithms. YBS Publishing, Storrs (2011)
2. Hall, D.L., Chong, C.Y., Llinas, J., Liggins II, M.: Distributed Data Fusion for Network-Centric Operations. CRC Press (2013)
3. He, X., Tharmarasa, R., Pelletier, M., Kirubarajan, T.: Accurate Murty's Algorithm for Multitarget Top Hypothesis. In: Proc. of Fusion 2011, Chicago, USA (2011)
4. Dezert, J., Smarandache, F., Tchamova, A.: On the Blackman's Association Problem. In: Proc. of Fusion 2003, Cairns, Australia (2003)
5. Tchamova, A., Dezert, J., Semerdjiev, T., Konstantinova, P.: Target Tracking with Generalized Data Association Based on the General DSm Rule of Combination. In: Proc. of Fusion 2004, Stockholm, Sweden (2004)
6. Dezert, J., Tchamova, A., Semerdjiev, T., Konstantinova, P.: Performance Evaluation of Fusion Rules For Multitarget Tracking in Clutter Based on Generalized Data Association. In: Proc. of Fusion 2005, Philadelphia, USA (2005)
7. Denœux, T., El Zoghby, N., Cherfaoui, V., Jouglet, A.: Optimal Object Association in the Dempster- Shafer Framework. To appear in IEEE Trans. on Cybern (2014)
8. Kuhn, H.W.: The Hungarian Method for the Assignment Problem. Naval Research Logistic Quarterly 2, 83–97 (1955)
9. Munkres, J.: Algorithms for the Assignment and Transportation Problems. Journal of the Society of Industrial and Applied Mathematics 5(1), 32–38 (1957)
10. Bourgeois, F., Lassalle, J.C.: An Extension of the Munkres Algorithm for the Assignment Problem to Rectangular Matrices. Comm. of the ACM 14(12), 802–804 (1971)
11. Jonker, R., Volgenant, A.: A shortest augmenting path algorithm for dense and sparse linear assignment problems. J. of Comp. 38(4), 325–340 (1987)
12. Bertsekas, D.: The auction algorithm: A Distributed Relaxation Method for the Assignment Problem. Annals of Operations Research 14(1), 105–123 (1988)
13. Murty, K.G.: An Algorithm for Ranking all the Assignments in Order of Increasing Cost. Operations Research 16(3), 682–687 (1968)
14. Chegireddy, C.R., Hamacher, H.W.: Algorithms for Finding K-best Perfect Matching. Discrete Applied Mathematics 18, 155–165 (1987)
15. Danchick, R., Newnam, G.E.: A Fast Method for Finding the Exact N-best Hypotheses for Multitarget Tracking. IEEE Trans. on AES 29(2), 555–560 (1993)
16. Miller, M.L., Stone, H.S., Cox, I.J.: Optimizing Murty's Ranked Assignment Method. IEEE Trans. on AES 33(3), 851–862 (1997)
17. Pascoal, M., Captivo, M.E., Climaco, J.: A Note on a New Variant of Murty's Ranking Assignments Algorithm. 4OR Journal 1, 243–255 (2003)

18. Ding, Z., Vandervies, D.: A Modified Murty's Algorithm for Multiple Hypothesis Tracking. In: SPIE Sign. and Data Proc. of Small Targets, vol. 6236, (2006)
19. Fortunato, E., et al.: Generalized Murty's Algorithm with Application to Multiple Hypothesis Tracking. In: Proc. of Fusion 2007, Québec, July 9-12, pp. 1–8 (2007)
20. Hamacher, H.W., Queyranne, M.: K-best Solutions to Combinatorial Optimization Problems. Annals of Operations Research (4), 123–143 (1985)
21. Dell'Amico, M., Toth, P.: Algorithms and Codes for Dense Assignment Problems: the State of the Art. Discrete Applied Mathematics 100, 17–48 (2000)
22. Shafer, G.: A Mathematical Theory of Evidence. Princeton University Press, Princeton (1976)
23. Smarandache, F., Dezert, J.: Advances and Applications of DSmT for Information Fusion, vols. 1, 2 & 3. ARP (2004–2009),
    `http://www.gallup.unm.edu/~smarandache/DSmT.htm`
24. Smets, P., Kennes, R.: The Transferable Belief Model. Artificial Intelligence 66(2), 191–234 (1994)

Data Association for Object Enumeration Using Belief Function Theory

Wafa Rekik, Sylvie Le Hégarat-Mascle, Cyrille André,
Abdelaziz Kallel, Roger Reynaud, and Ahmed Ben Hamida

Institute of Fundamental Electronics, 91405 Orsay, cedex, France
University of Sfax, Tunisia, Advanced Technologies for Medicine and Signals
{wafa.rekik,sylvie.le-hegarat,cyrille.andre,roger.reynaud}@u-psud.fr,
abdelaziz.kallel@isecs.rnu.tn,ahmed.benhamida@enis.rnu.tn

Abstract. Several video surveillance applications aim at counting the
objects present in a scene. Using robust background substraction techniques, detections are unlabelled and often correspond to fragments of
objects. Then, a key step for object counting is the association of the fragments representing subparts of a same object. In this work, we model
the uncertainty and the imprecision of the location of the detected fragments using Belief Function Theory. Specifically to the case of a video
sequence, we propose a data association method between the new detections and the objects already under construction. Tests on actual data
were performed. In particular, they allow for the evaluation of the proposed method in term of robustness versus the objects moving.

Keywords: data Association, object enumeration, belief functions.

1 Introduction

Object detection and enumeration is a classical problem in computer vision and
more specifically video surveillance applications. In a typical scene, there may
be several objects of interest, appearing and disappearing from the scene during
the acquisition time period, so that the problem considered in this work is to
enumerate them, for instance in order to be tracked further. Now, neither background substraction techniques nor more sophisticated approaches (e.g., Gaussian mixture models) succeed in avoiding the partial self occlusion of an object
or partial 'camouflage' (when the background looks just like some object parts).
Then, an object having some undetected subparts may appear as divided into
several fragments. In this work, we assume image processing outputs such that,
at each instant, a physical object is generally, given by several detections (blocs
of pixels) and we deal with the problem of object construction and enumeration
from these detections. Now, since detections are unlabelled, the first issue is to
associate them spatially and temporally. Besides probabilistic approaches, many
approaches have been proposed for the data association problem in the framework of belief function theory [3,2,7,9,6,4]. In [3], belief function theory allows
integrating additional information (such as shape constraints, rigid motions.)

F. Cuzzolin (Ed.): BELIEF 2014, LNAI 8764, pp. 383–392, 2014.

into the Joint Probabilistic Data Association Filter to track articulated model objects in the presence of many false detections and occlusions. In [7,6,4], belief functions are defined on an elementary discernment frame $\{yes, no\}$ to model the relevance of each potential association. Then, to obtain a global association, they are vacuously extended to a global discernment frame regarding the set of associations. In those works, beliefs are specified from the object characteristics like speed, class, colour, form, texture etc. In our case, objects are heterogeneous in terms of colour and texture, so that they are characterized by their positions on the image. Besides, considering that at each instant an object may be split-ted into several fragments our problem is basically a multi association problem rather than a $1 - 1$ association problem implying that at most one detection is associated with at most one object. In this paper, we show that, although appar-ently dealing with a different problem namely objects identification (*Combat ID declaration*), the work [9] can be transposed to derive a solution to our problem. We also propose belief operators to take into account specific temporal and spa-tial a priori on our problem. The remainder of the paper is as follows: Section 2 recalls some tools of belief function theory, our approach for data association is described in Section 3 and finally some illustrative results and conclusions are provided in Section 4.

2   Background

In the following, we denote by Ω the discernment frame and by 2^{Ω} the set of its subsets. Three belief functions are defined from 2^{Ω} to [0,1]: the mass (also called basic belief assignment or bba) m, the credibility *bel* and the plausibility *pl* [11]. An element $A \in 2^{\Omega}$ such that $m(A) > 0$ is a focal element of m. A categorical bba is a bba with only one focal element. It is simple if it has two focal elements among them Ω. Assuming a closed world, $m(\emptyset) = 0$. Conversely, for an open world $m(\emptyset) \geq 0$ and $m(\emptyset)$ is often presented as the degree of conflict.

Several operators have been proposed to modify a bba according to new in-formation pieces or bbas. For instance, the discounting operator allows taking into account the reliability of a source quantified by $\alpha \in [0, 1]$:

$$\forall A \in 2^{\Omega}, \hat{m}(A) = \alpha m(A), \hat{m}(\Omega) = \alpha m(\Omega) + (1 - \alpha). \tag{1}$$

Learning that the solution certainly belongs to $C \in 2^{\Omega}$, the bba m is conditioned on C as follows:

$$\forall A \in 2^{\Omega}, m[C](A) = \sum_{B \in 2^{\Omega}/A = B \cap C} m(B). \tag{2}$$

Considering two bbas m_1^{Ω} and m_2^{Ω}, several combination rules have been pro-posed. Let us cite Smets conjunctive rule $\bigcirc$ that allows us to get a specialized bba assuming distinct sources (Eq. 3) [11]. The orthogonal sum $\oplus$, proposed by Dempster [10], assumes a closed world. Then, it normalizes the bba, so that

$m(\emptyset) = 0$ after normalization. The disjunctive rule $\bigcirc[11]$ allows us to get a generalized bba (Eq. 4) [11].

$$\forall C \in 2^{\Omega}, m_{\textcircled{\tiny A}}(C) = \sum_{(A,B) \in 2^{\Omega} \times 2^{\Omega} / A \cap B = C} m_1(A) \, m_2(B). \tag{3}$$

$$\forall C \in 2^{\Omega}, m_{\textcircled{\tiny O}}(C) = \sum_{(A,B) \in 2^{\Omega} \times 2^{\Omega} / A \cup B = C} m_1(A) \, m_2(B). \tag{4}$$

Finally, let us summarize the approach [9] for data association. One of its interest is that the data association criterion is self-contained in the bbas defined for the target identification problem. Since the definition of 'initial' bbas remains an issue for evidential modelling, not defining specific bbas for the data association subproblem appears to us as a major advantage. Let $\Omega = \{\omega_1, ..., \omega_N\}$ be the set of the possible ID for a target. For each target o_{1j}, a bba $m^{\Omega}\{o_{1j}\}$ is defined on Ω representing the belief in the target ID. Then, assuming a target o_{1j} to be associated with a target o_{2i}, the association criterion is as follows: Bbas $m^{\Omega}\{o_{1j}\}$ and $m^{\Omega}\{o_{2i}\}$ are vacuously extended to $\Omega^2 = \Omega \times \Omega$ and conjunctively combined, so that, $\forall C \in 2^{\Omega^2}$,

$$m^{\Omega^2}\{o_{1j}, o_{2i}\}(C) = \begin{cases} m^{\Omega}\{o_{1j}\}(A) m^{\Omega}\{o_{2i}\}(B) & \text{if } C = (A, B) \\ 0 & \text{else.} \end{cases} \tag{5}$$

This bba represents the joint belief in the ID of targets o_{1j} and o_{2i}. Assuming that two targets are the same ($o_{1j} \equiv o_{2i}$) if they have the same ID, the plausibility of their association writes versus the mass on $\emptyset$ issued from the conjunctive combination of bbas $m^{\Omega}\{o_{1j}\}$ and $m^{\Omega}\{o_{2i}\}$ as follows:

$$pl^{\Omega^2}\{o_{1j}, o_{2i}\}(o_{1j} \equiv o_{2i}) = 1 - m_{j\textcircled{\tiny A}i}^{\Omega}(\emptyset), \tag{6}$$

where m_j and m_i are the abbreviations of $m^{\Omega}\{o_{1j}\}$ and $m^{\Omega}\{o_{2i}\}$.

The generalization of this approach to the association of a set of n targets $\{o_{1j}\}_{j=1...n}$ with a second set of n targets $\{o_{2i}\}_{i=1...n}$ is immediate. Targets bbas defined on Ω are vacuously extended to product space Ω^{2n}. The plausibility of each association is then evaluated on Ω^{2n} as follows:

$$pl^{\Omega^{2n}}(o_{1j} \equiv o_{2a_j} : j = 1, ..., n) = \prod_{j=1}^{n} (1 - m_{j\textcircled{\tiny A}a_j}(\emptyset)), \tag{7}$$

where $\mathcal{A} = [a_1, ..., a_n]$ is a permutation vector of size n representing the association of type 1-1 ($o_{1j} \equiv o_{2a_j}$ for $j = 1, ..., n$) [9]. Taking the opposite of the logarithm of expression $pl^{\Omega^{2n}}(o_{1j} \equiv o_{2a_j} : j = 1, ..., n)$, the maximization of the plausibility boils down to a well-known problem of minimization of the sum of positive costs defined in Eq.8, for which efficient solutions exist (e.g., [8]).

$$c_0(a_j = i) = -log(1 - m_{j\textcircled{\tiny A}i}(\emptyset)) = -log \sum_{A \cap B \neq \emptyset} m_j(A) \, m_i(B). \tag{8}$$

3   Proposed Approach

Since, at a given time, the *physical objects* are often only partially detected, they cannot be directly enumerated. The first issue is then to construct them by collecting the unlabelled detections over time. For this, some objects already partially constructed from detections of previous instants have to be associated with the new detections. In the following, the word *object* refers either to the physical object or to its approximation at a given time that is a set of associated detections (i.e. having a same label).

Formally, let us denote by $\mathcal{D} = \{d_1, ..., d_l\}$ the set of the $l = |\mathcal{D}|$ detections at instant t and by $\mathcal{O} = \{o_1, ..., o_n\}$ the set of the $n = |\mathcal{O}|$ objects at the same instant. An association '1-1' is represented by a vector $\mathcal{A} = [a_1...a_n]$ of size n that gives for each object of index $j \in \{1...n\}$, the index $a_j \mid a_j \in \{0...l\}$ of the associated element (detection or object as explained further) if it exists: $a_j = 0$ means the absence of the associated element.

In order to be able to associate several detections with the same object, multiple associations called of type 1-N should be possible. However, this type of association involves rather sensitive parameters, especially threshold (e.g., in [7] threshold is used to discard the associations having 'too' low belief) so that its behaviour may be difficult to control. Here, we propose to rather consider iteratively, two kinds of 1-1 association:

- An association called 'detection-object' between each detection and an object (note that non-association is possible if there is no object compatible with a detection). Objects are then updated based on the new associated detections whereas the non-associated detections initiate new objects.
- An association called 'object-object' between the different objects in order to fuse them if they are subparts of the same physical object. Then, if two detections have to be associated with the same physical object, the first one will be associated during the detection-object association whereas the second one that initiated a new object after 'detection-object' association step, can be associated during the 'object-object' association step.

Both kinds of association are based on the minimization of a cost function computed from belief functions representing the objects (Section. 3.1).

3.1   Credal Object Representation

In this work, an object is represented in term of imprecise location of a detection. Then, the discernment frame is the image lattice (for an image of nl lines and nc columns, Ω is then the product space $\{1...nl\} \times \{1...nc\}$). A bba corresponding to a given object represents the belief in the location of a detection (fragment of this object). Note that, in order to satisfy the exclusivity of the discernment frame hypotheses, the detection locations are exclusive (practically, image processing provides distinct detections, at a given time, that could be for instance indexed by their left upper corner coordinates). Reminding us that a detection d_j may be a seed for a new object (that will be constructed based on further detection associations), its credal representation is simply a categorical bba $m\{d_j\}$ having as unique focal element $A(d_j)$ the set of the pixels belonging to d_j. Then, the bba $m\{o_i\}$ of an object o_i is derived from the bbas of the associated detections. Two mechanisms compete:

- The first one aims at spatially constructing an object from its detections. This mechanism is performed using the disjunctive rule (Eq. 4) to combine the object bba with the bbas of the associated detections.
- The second one aims, in the case of a video sequence and thus time indexed detections, at considering the object possible motion. This mechanism is performed through the temporal conditioning and the spatial conditioning operators.

Disjunctive Combination. According to the first mechanism, the bba $m\{o_j\}$ of an object o_j associated with a detection d_{a_j} is updated by combining it disjunctively (Eq. 4) with $m\{d_{a_j}\}$ as follows:

$$\forall j \in \{1,...,n\} \mid a_j \in \{1,...,l\}, m\{o_j\} \leftarrow m\{o_j\} \oslash m\{d_{a_j}\}. \qquad (9)$$

Considering the object-object association, just replace l by n and d_{a_j} by o_{a_j}. A non associated detection is identified by an index $i \mid \forall j \in \{1...n\}, a_j \neq i$. It initiates a new object whose life time may be very short if it is immediately fused during the object-object association. We also note that the object-object association may be iterated depending on the fragmentation rate, that depends on the image processing algorithm (the more important this rate is, the greater is the number of iterations during the object-object association).

Temporal and Spatial Conditionings. This second mechanism allows us to take into account the temporal dimension of detections. The idea is to give more weights to recent detections when constructing object bbas in order to cope with object displacements and/or disappearances from the scene. In this study, we deal with the construction of an object o_j from its associated detections d_{o_j}. Then, assuming that Δt last instants are sufficient for the estimation of the detection imprecise locations, boils down to a conditioning of the object bba $m\{o_j\}$ on the disjunction of detections of the Δt last instants. In Eq. 10, we denote by $m_{\Delta t}$ the categorical bba allowing this temporal conditioning. We also assume that spatially close detections are also close in time. Then, the locations close to the last observations of the object have their beliefs reinforced using a conjunctive combination (Eq. 3) between the object bba (after conditioning) and a simple bba $m^\alpha_{d_{o_j},t-1}$ defined as follows: Let $m_{d_{o_j},t-1}$ be the categorical bba having as focal element the disjunction of detections associated with o_j at $t-1$. Then, $m^\alpha_{d_{o_j},t-1}$ is the result of its discounting by a factor α. So that the greater α is, the less credible are old detections in term of locations of future detections.

$$\forall j \in \{1,...,n\}, m\{o_j\} \leftarrow m\{o_j\} \oslash m^\alpha_{d_{o_j},t-1} \oslash m_{\Delta t}. \qquad (10)$$

When the temporal conditioning copes with disappeared objects (elimination of the bbas of objects undetected during the period of time Δt), the spatial conditioning handles the objects separation. A typical example is the separation of a group of persons, each one following a different way. Besides, it allows for the separation of objects that are mistakenly fused during their crossing.

Spatial conditioning basic assumption is that an object is a connected mono component so that any other connected component than the main one is 'noise' and can be removed. In practice, the connected components of an object are not estimated on the image lattice but after projection on the column axis. This projection is motivated by the observed symmetry of the objects with respect to the column axis (e.g., case of objects of 'human' type imaged in a vertical plane and we note that such an a priori can be modified depending on the geometry of acquisition and objects) so that the object fragmentation is principally according to the line axis. Let A correspond to the disjunction of detections associated with the object. We denote by $A^{\downarrow X}$ the projection of A on the column axis and by $C^{\downarrow X}$ the greater connected component of $A^{\downarrow X}$. The spatial conditioning is then performed on the disjunction of detections associated with the object such that their projection on the column axis belongs to $C^{\downarrow X}$. In summary, temporal and spatial conditioning operations allow us to cope with the objects moving and changing (e.g., separation in particular versus the column axis) along the video sequence. Practically, both conditionings consist in combining the bba with a bba whose unique focal element is a given hypothesis estimated from detections and basic assumption about temporal and spatial consistency of the objects. These conditionings are intrinsically renormalizations by the belief on the Δt last instants or by the belief on the principal connected component of the object under construction, performed using the orthogonal combination rule.

3.2   Association Criteria

In the presentation of the bba updating, we assume that the association between detections at t and objects (derived from previous detections) is known. A main interest of the proposed representation is the ability to define a simple and efficient data association criterion. Let us remind that for each object, the bba represents the belief about the imprecise location of a future detection. We propose two association criteria one for the detection-object association and the other for the object-object association. The first one is derived transposing the approach [9]. It is used for the definition of the cost of an elementary association between a detection and an object, as the conflict generated by the conjunctive combination of their bbas (Eq.8). Then, the cost matrix M_c is rectangular of size $n \times l$. The Hungarian algorithm [8] allows us to get an efficient solution. In [9], only the minimal number $|n - l|$ of non-associations is allowed. In our case, to not assume a minimal number of associations, we extend the cost matrix to a square matrix of size $2 \times max\{n, l\}$ such that: $\forall (j, i) \in \{1, ..., n\} \times \{1, ..., l\}, M_c(j, i) = c_0(a_j = i)$ and $\forall (j, i) \notin \{1, ..., n\} \times \{1, ..., l\}, M_c(j, i) = c_{na}$, where c_{na} denotes the non association cost. Besides, specifically for the object-object association, we propose to iterate n_{it} times and to monitor the non-association cost. Also, we aim at limiting the fusion of objects corresponding to different physical objects. Thus, a second criterion was defined to take into account the size of the focal elements of the bbas. The implicit assumption is that a bba having focal elements with large cardinalities corresponds to an object already well-reconstructed and that completing it with a new set of detections should be performed carefully, e.g., taking into account the relative size of the intersection between the focal elements. As in the spatial conditioning step, we suppose that the fragmentation mainly occurs along the line axis, so that, in an ad-hoc way we propose an elementary cost involving a weighting coefficient:

$$c_1\left(a_j = i\right) = -log \sum_{A \cap B \neq \emptyset} m_j\left(A\right) m_i\left(B\right) \frac{|A_{\downarrow X} \cap B_{\downarrow X}|}{|A_{\downarrow X}||B_{\downarrow X}|}. \tag{11}$$

where $D_{\downarrow X}$ ($D \in \{A, B\}$) is the projection of $D \subseteq \Omega$ in the column axis.

As for the detection-object association, we define a cost matrix for the object-object association. This latter is square. It is such that the non-diagonal elements are equal to $c_1\left(a_j = i\right)$. The diagonal elements are equal to the non-association cost. In fact, the selection of a diagonal element corresponds to the association of an object with itself and then its non-association with any other object. So, this matrix is symmetrical since the two dimensions of the matrix represent in fact the same set: A matrix element of coordinates (i, j) represents the association of object o_i with object o_j or, equivalently, the association of object o_j with object o_i, that is represented by matrix element (j, i). In order to ensure a symmetrical solution, we have modified the Hungarian algorithm [8] to preserve the symmetry of the cost matrix during its transformations into equivalent matrices. In this case, the convergence time is no longer guaranteed. However, experimentally, we noted that the algorithm rapidly converges in the majority of cases (in the other rare cases, we get a potentially suboptimal solution). Five main steps are then implemented for data association: (i) 1-1 association between detections at t and objects under construction based on costs defined by Eq. 8; (ii) an iterative 1-1 association between objects using costs given by Eq.11; (iii) bbas updating by combination of bbas of the associated elements using Eq.9; (iv) temporal conditioning and refinement using Eq.10; (v) spatial conditioning.

4   Results

To evaluate the proposed method, we tested it on a sequence of real data acquired at 25 images per second. In the presented sequence extract, six persons and one car move in the scene and cross each other, so that until six objects of interest may be simultaneously present. Different image processing algorithms have been used: a variant of [5] for Fig. 1 and [1] for Fig. 2. Fig. 1 illustrates qualitatively main conclusions about the performance of our method, namely: (i) The proposed association process succeeds in handling multiple detections; (ii) Temporal conditioning is able to cope with moving object. For instance, the boy appearing on the right of the image before instant 112 and crossing to leave the scene after instant 167; (iii) Spatial conditioning allows for the object separation like the three girls on the right of the image at instant 134 fused into the same object (group) at instant 167 and separated into three objects at instant 204; (iv) Considering focal element size limits the fusion of objects crossing each other, like the two persons on the left of the image at instant 294. Fig. 2 shows a qualitative comparison of the proposed method (first column) with two variants, either only involving c_0 criterion or only involving c_1 criterion (second and third columns, respectively). When our method globally succeeds in constructing the objects from multiple detections, the c_1 criterion in data association leads to some remaining non-associated detections, e.g., in violet and brown in Fig. 2b and the c_0 criterion in data association sometimes leads to undesirable fusion of some objects, e.g., the two girls in the left side coded

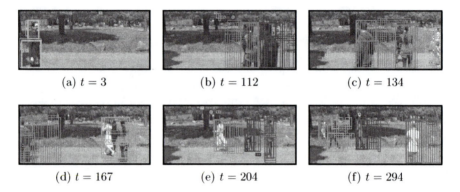

(a) $t = 3$ (b) $t = 112$ (c) $t = 134$

(d) $t = 167$ (e) $t = 204$ (f) $t = 294$

Fig. 1. Object construction: at instant t, detections of the same colour are associated with the same object (in bold lines, detections at t and in fine lines, former detections).

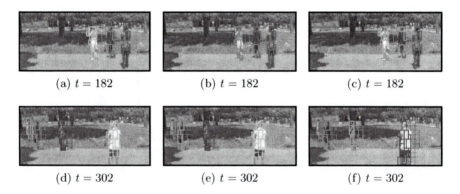

(a) $t = 182$ (b) $t = 182$ (c) $t = 182$

(d) $t = 302$ (e) $t = 302$ (f) $t = 302$

Fig. 2. Example of object construction at 2 instants (respectively 1st and 2nd lines), and considering 3 different association criteria for the detection-object association and the object-object one: 1st column: (c_0, c_1), 2nd column (c_1, c_1), 3rd column (c_0, c_0). At a given instant t, a same colour notifies that the detections are associated with the same object, with the detections at t in bold lines.

in orange in Fig. 2f. Noting the efficiency of the mixed criterion (c_0, c_1) in both cases to both facilitate the first association between detections at t and already existing objects and delaying the fusion between objects even when they overlap (depending on the relative size of the overlap). Quantitatively, given a ground truth (GT), the method has been evaluated in terms of precision $(= \frac{n_{tp}}{n_{tp} + n_{fp}})$ and recall $(= \frac{n_{tp}}{n_{tp} + n_{fn}})$ measures, where n_{tp}, n_{fp} and n_{fn} denote the number of 'true positives' (tp), 'false positives' (fp) and 'false negatives' (fn), respectively. Fig. 3 illustrates their definition in a rather complex case. Fig. 3a shows the GT of the detection labelling (i.e. unique colour for a given object) corresponding to Fig. 2b. Using a bipartite graph representation, Fig. 3b shows the relationships (graph vertices) given by the detection labelling either in the GT or in the result (graph nodes). When two nodes are linked by only one vertex, it is a tp, whereas when several vertices are present, one is counted as a tp and the other(s) either as fp (two or more labels in the result for a unique label in the GT) or fn (one label in the result for several labels in the GT). Fig. 4 shows the 'precision' (y-axis) versus the 'recall' (x-axis) values computed either in terms of labels (Fig. 4a) or in terms of fragments (Fig. 4b). The different curves represent the results of the proposed method for different combinations of the association criteria (c_0 or c_1) for the detection-object association and the object-object one. The points on a given curve correspond to different 'delays in decision', δt varying in $[0, 4]$,

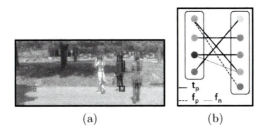

(a)　　　　　　　　　　(b)

Fig. 3. Example illustrating the definition of tp, fp and fn from the GT labelling shown in (a) and the obtained results shown in Fig. 2b: $n_{tp} = 4$, $n_{fp} = 1$ and $n_{fn} = 1$

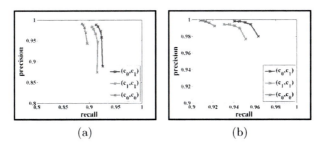

(a)　　　　　　　　　　(b)

Fig. 4. Quantitative performance estimation of the proposed method according to the delay in decision: recall and precision rates computed in terms of labels (a) and fragments (b)

introduced as follows: the fragmentary detections at t are labelled as in the result at $t + \delta t$, so that some fragments not associated at t may be associated at $t + \delta t$. Besides the fact that the results are very promising, we note that, as expected, when δt increases, both n_{fp} decreases and n_{fn} increases so that, both 'precision' increases and 'recall' slightly decreases.

5 Conclusion

In this work, we proposed a method to construct objects present in a video sequence in the perspective of their enumeration and possibly further tracking, from fragmentary detections. The temporal dimension allows for the accumulation of the observations, while technically, multi association of uncertain and imprecise data (in term of location) becomes an issue that we solved using belief functions theory. Future work will deal with more complete tests of the proposed methodology and tracking of the constructed objects.

References

1. Ammar, M., Le Hégarat-Mascle, S., Reynaud, R., Robin, A.: An a-contrario approach for object detection in video sequence. Int. J. of Pure and Applied Math. 89, 173–201 (2013)
2. Ayoun, A., Smets, P.: Data association in multi-target detection using the transferable belief model. Int. J. of Intelligent Systems 16(10), 1167–1182 (2001)
3. Cuzzolin, F.: Visions of a Generalized Probability Theory. Ph.D. thesis, Department of Information Engineering, University of Padova, Italy (2001)
4. Denoeux, T., Zoghby, N.E., Cherfaoui, V., Jouglet, A.: Optimal object association in the dempster-shafer framework. IEEE Trans. on Cyber. (to appear, 2014)
5. Kim, K., Chalidabhongse, T., Harwood, D., Davis, L.: Real-time foreground-background segmentation using codebook model. Real-Time Imaging In Special Issue on Video Object Processing 11(3), 172–185 (2005)
6. Mercier, D., Lefevre, E., Jolly, D.: Object association with belief functions, an application with vehicles. Information Fusion 181(24), 5485–5500 (2011)
7. Mourllion, B., Gruyer, D., Royere, R., Théroude, S.: Multi-hypotheses tracking algorithm based on the belief theory. In: Proc. of Fusion 2005, vol. 2, p. 8 (2005)
8. Munkres, J.: Algorithms for the assignment and transportation problems. J. of the Society for Industrial and Applied Mathematics 5(1), 32–38 (1957)
9. Ristic, B., Smets, P.: Global cost of assignment in the tbm framework for association of uncertain id reports. Aer. Sci. and Tech. 11(4), 303–309 (2007)
10. Shafer, G.: A mathematical theory of evidence. Princeton University Press, Princeton (1976)
11. Smets, P.: Belief functions: the disjunctive rule of combination and the generalized bayesian theorem. Int. J. of Approx. Reason 9(1), 1–35 (1993)

A Novel Methodology for Target Classification Based on Dempster-Shafer Theory

Hasan Ihsan Turhan[1], Mubeccel Demirekler[1], and Melih Gunay[2]

[1] Middle East Technical University, Ankara, Turkey
{hasan.turhan,demirek}@metu.edu.tr
[2] ASELSAN Inc. Ankara, Turkey
mgunay@aselsan.com.tr

Abstract. In this paper, classification of air vehicles according to their types is studied. Demspter-Shafer theory is utilized for this purpose. The target tracker data is used for obtaining the probability masses by comparing it with the prior information. Prior information is modeled as the probability density function of the features used for classification. The prior information models the selected features as Gaussian mixtures while the tracker data models the same features as non-parametric density. This new methodology is tested on real data.

Keywords: Dempster-Shafer Theory, Belief Functions, Basic Probability (Mass) Assignment, Dempster-Shafer Reasoning, Target Tracking, Decision Making, Target Classification.

1   Introduction

Target classification is an important problem, which should be encountered in designing an efficient air defense system. In all classification problems, features are selected according to their discriminating powers and availability. In this study, the available information comes from a radar target tracker that tracks air vehicles. Tracker provides rich information about the state of the target, which is composed of the velocity and the position vectors [1]. Tracker provides the prob-ability density function of the state as a Gaussian density at discrete time instants [1].

Most of the related work that exists in the literature uses Dempster Shafer theory. Classification of a target is made using kinematic features or radar cross section or any other relevant information like electronic support measures [3], [11], [12]. Caramicoli et al. [5] and Ristic and Smets [12] use kinematic features to derive some classification rules. Kinematic information is also used in our study and we develop a new methodology for assigning masses to classes. The main distinction of the mass assignment proposed in this work is that all the information, i.e., the probability density function of the state instead of only mean, provided by the tracker is utilized. The algorithm assumes that the prior probability density functions of all classes and the current measurement are known for some related kinematic features of the target. Furthermore, as a sensible

F. Cuzzolin (Ed.): BELIEF 2014, LNAI 8764, pp. 393–402, 2014.
© Springer International Publishing Switzerland 2014

assumption, we assume that prior probability density functions of the related kinematic features of all classes can be approximated by Gaussian mixtures. Assigning masses using both prior and measurement probability density functions in Dempster-Shafer framework is the main contribution of this study.

Basic mass assignment is one of the main steps in any application of the Dempster-Shafer theory. The methods of mass assignment in the literature are numerous. At the early stages of the theory, masses were assigned according to the expert opinion in various applications. Afterwards, various models were used for this purpose. Yager [17] uses belief functions as a fuzzy measure. Zhu et al. [18] uses membership functions. Florea et al. [6] uses membership values as probability masses. Rmer et al. [13] uses possibility and necessity measures of fuzzy logic theory for defining belief functions. Bloch [4], Jiang et al. [8] and Masson et al. [10] use distances to cluster centers for mass assignment. Utkin [15] uses imprecise Dirichlet model. Bendjebbour et al. [2], Hagarat-Mascle et al. [9], Salzestein et al. [14] and Xu et al. [16] use probabilities for mass assignment.

The organization of the rest of this paper is as follows. Section 2 starts with the problem definition and proposes a solution to the problem. Section 3 investigates the effectiveness of the proposed method. Real data is used in the experiments. Results are compared with another similar method that uses prior probability den-sity functions. Conclusions are made in Section 4.

2   Dempster-Shafer Framework from the Tracking Perspective

In target tracking applications, tracker supplies information about the state vector of the target by giving the probability density function of the state as Gaussian [1]. The state vector usually consists of the position and the velocity of the target. The problem considered here is to classify target as one of the predefined types by using the information provided by the tracker. Tracker output is collected over time, converted to probability masses and probability masses are combined. We use the speed and the altitude of the aircraft as its discriminating features. The proposed method assigns masses to the classes by using a novel method. The combination of the masses is made by using Dempsters rule.

2.1   Basic Mass Assignment

Speed and the altitude of the air vehicle are selected as features that are used for classification. It is assumed that these two variables are independent, hence estimating individual densities is sufficient.

The application classifies the air target as bomber and surveillance plane, helicopter or unmanned air vehicle.

The prior information about the features for different classes has been collected mainly from the Jane's book [7] and the internet. The nominal and the maximum speeds and altitudes of the above defined types of air vehicles are used to generate prior probability density functions as mixtures of Gaussians.

For each class prior speed and altitude is represented by N Gaussians, where N is selected according to the available data and probability density functions are obtained by applying the kernel smoothing method to the collected data. The resultant prior probability density functions are given in Section 3.

Tracker gives the (Gaussian) probability density function of the velocity and the position of the target at each time instant which is considered as the measurement. Altitude, which is one of the features, is already a part of the state vector. Hence its probability density function is available. The probability density function of the speed on the other hand should be calculated from the velocity vector. Speed is defined as:

$$s_k = \sqrt{v_x^2 + v_y^2 + v_z^2} \tag{1}$$

The probability density function of s_k can be approximated as a non-central chi square distribution with 3 degrees of freedom. In this work we obtained the probability density function of the speed using Monte Carlo methods from the given Gaussian distribution of the velocity and equation 1.

2.2   A Novel Basic Mass Assignment Algorithm

We describe the mass assignment algorithm for the three class case. The generalization of the algorithm to any number of classes is trivial. Since the number of classes is three, the universal set contains three elements denoted by A, B and C, that is $\Theta = A, B, C$.

Figure 1 gives typical prior and measurement probability density functions. The points 'a', 'b' and 'c' are the equal likelihood points of the corresponding classes and are used for mass assignments. In order to obtain masses, the measurement probability density function is multiplied by the prior probability density function of each class. The resultant curves are the unnormalized posterior probability density functions, which are shown in Figure 1b. The masses are selected to be proportional to areas under the curves over some selected intervals after multiplication. Formal definitions of the associated masses for a 3 class problem are given below.

Let $p_A(x)$, $p_B(x)$ and $p_C(x)$ be the prior probability density functions of the A, B and C classes respectively. Let $p(x)$ be the probability density function of the measurement. Then the masses assigned to the sets are:

$$m(\{A\}) = \int_{x \in S_A} \frac{p_A(x)p(x)}{p_A(x)p(x) + p_B(x)p(x) + p_C(x)p(x)} dx \tag{2a}$$

$$S_A = \{x | p_A > p_B \text{ and } p_A > p_C\} \tag{2b}$$

$$m(\{B\}) = \int_{x \in S_B} \frac{p_B(x)p(x)}{p_A(x)p(x) + p_B(x)p(x) + p_C(x)p(x)} dx \tag{2c}$$

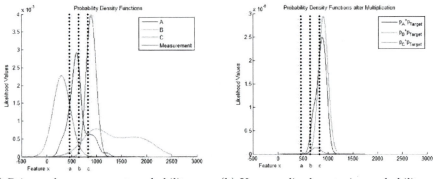

(a) Prior and measurement probability density functions

(b) Unnormalized posterior probability density functions

Fig. 1. Probability Density Functions

$$S_B = \{x | p_B > p_A \text{ and } p_B > p_C\} \tag{2d}$$

$$m(\{C\}) = \int_{x \in S_C} \frac{p_C(x)p(x)}{p_A(x)p(x) + p_B(x)p(x) + p_C(x)p(x)} dx \tag{2e}$$

$$S_C = \{x | p_C > p_A \text{ and } p_C > p_B\} \tag{2f}$$

$$m(\{A, C\}) = \int_{x \in S_{AC}} \frac{p_A(x)p(x)}{p_A(x)p(x) + p_B(x)p(x) + p_C(x)p(x)} dx$$
$$+ \int_{x \in S_{CA}} \frac{p_C(x)p(x)}{p_A(x)p(x) + p_B(x)p(x) + p_C(x)p(x)} dx \tag{2g}$$

$$S_{AC} = \{x | p_A < p_C \text{ and } p_A > p_B\} \text{ and } S_{CA} = \{x | p_C < p_A \text{ and } p_C > p_B\} \tag{2h}$$

$$m(\{A, B\}) = \int_{x \in S_{AB}} \frac{p_A(x)p(x)}{p_A(x)p(x) + p_B(x)p(x) + p_C(x)p(x)} dx$$
$$+ \int_{x \in S_{BA}} \frac{p_B(x)p(x)}{p_A(x)p(x) + p_B(x)p(x) + p_C(x)p(x)} dx \tag{2i}$$

$$S_{AB} = \{x | p_A < p_B \text{ and } p_A > p_C\} \text{ and } S_{BA} = \{x | p_B < p_A \text{ and } p_B > p_C\} \tag{2j}$$

$$m(\{B,C\}) = \int\limits_{x \in S_{BC}} \frac{p_B(x)p(x)}{p_A(x)p(x) + p_B(x)p(x) + p_C(x)p(x)} dx$$

$$+ \int\limits_{x \in S_{CB}} \frac{p_C(x)p(x)}{p_A(x)p(x) + p_B(x)p(x) + p_C(x)p(x)} dx \tag{2k}$$

$$S_{BC} = \{x | p_B < p_C \text{ and } p_B > p_A\} \text{ and } S_{CB} = \{x | p_C < p_B \text{ and } p_C > p_A\} \tag{2l}$$

$$m(\{B,C\}) = \int\limits_{x \in S_{ABC}} \frac{p_A(x)p(x)}{p_A(x)p(x) + p_B(x)p(x) + p_C(x)p(x)} dx$$

$$+ \int\limits_{x \in S_{BAC}} \frac{p_B(x)p(x)}{p_A(x)p(x) + p_B(x)p(x) + p_C(x)p(x)} dx \tag{2m}$$

$$+ \int\limits_{x \in S_{CAB}} \frac{p_C(x)p(x)}{p_A(x)p(x) + p_B(x)p(x) + p_C(x)p(x)} dx$$

$$S_{ABC} = \{x | p_A < p_B \text{ and } p_A < p_C\} \text{ , } S_{BAC} = \{x | p_B < p_A \text{ and } p_B > p_C\} \text{ and}$$
$$S_{CAB} = \{x | p_C < p_A \text{ and } p_C > p_B\} \tag{2n}$$

Note that the procedure formulated above gives the normalized masses and their sum is unity.

2.3 Analysis of the Novel Basic Mass Assignment Method

We analyze the performance of the proposed method by comparing it with Xu et al. [16], as it is the most similar method that exists in the literature. A two class artificial scenario is generated for this purpose. Since Xu et al. [16] uses Gaussian densities, we selected the prior probability density functions of the two classes and a measurement Gaussian as given below:

Prior probability density function of class A : $p_A(x) = N(x; 1000, 300^2)$
Prior probability density function of class B : $p_B(x) = N(x; 2000, 300^2)$
Probability density function of the measurement: $p_M(x) = N(x; 1513, 100^2)$

Under these conditions the proposed method assigns the following masses:
$m(\{A\}) = 0.3062$
$m(\{B\}) = 0.3961$
$m(\{A,B\}) = 0.2977$

To compare the output of the proposed method with Xu et al. [16], we assume that the actual measurement is some x drawn from the measurement

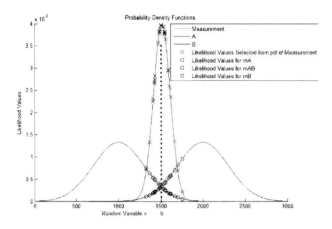

Fig. 2. Prior and measurement probability density functions

probability density function. Xu et al. [16] assigns the masses according to the actual measurement as given below.

$$m(.) = \begin{cases} m(\{A\}) = \alpha p_A(x) \text{ and } m(\{A, B\}) = \alpha p_B(x), & \text{if } p_A(x) > p_B(x) \\ m(\{B\}) = \alpha p_B(x) \text{ and } m(\{A, B\}) = \alpha p_A(x), & \text{if } p_B(x) > p_A(x) \end{cases} \quad (3)$$

Note that in this formulation the uncertainty of the measurement is not used. Table 1 is generated from masses that are assigned by drawing 30 samples from the given measurement probability density function as shown in figure 2 according to Xu et al. [16]. The mass values for these 30 samples are illustrated in Figure 3. Table 1 shows that the mean values coincide with the probability masses that are assigned by the proposed method. However the large standard deviations show that probability masses vary with the incoming data that makes the result susceptible to a realization at a given time. In Section 3, we compare the two methods on a scenario of tracking a real target.

Table 1. Mean and standard deviation values for the method of Xu et al. [16]

	Mean	Standard Deviation
$m(\{A\})$	0.2907	0.3453
$m(\{B\})$	0.3908	0.3618
$m(\{A, B\})$	0.3186	0.1232

3   Experimental Results

We conducted a tracking experiment to analyze the method that we proposed and compared it with the method proposed in Xu et al. [16], which is assumed

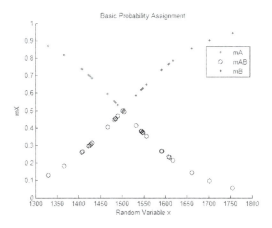

Fig. 3. Basic probability assignments for the randomly selected 30 sample

to use only the mean of the estimated feature. The experiment is conducted by using real data that belongs to a helicopter and is tracked by a radar that has a scan period of 2 seconds. The trajectory of the helicopter in x-y plane and the tracker output are given Figure 5.

Three air vehicle types for classification are defined to be: Bomber and surveillance planes (P), helicopters (H) and unmanned air vehicles (U) so the universal set consists of three elements as $\Theta = \{P, H, U\}$.

The prior probability density functions of speed and altitude are given in Figure 4 as Gaussian mixtures.

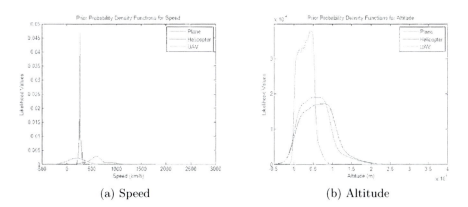

(a) Speed   (b) Altitude

Fig. 4. Prior probability density functions

From the beginning to the end of the trajectory, the system assigns high probability masses to the set H and some probability masses to other sets. To obtain an overall decision, first, the instantaneous masses obtained from the

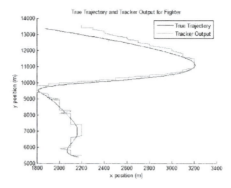

Fig. 5. x-y view of the true trajectory and the tracker output: Helicopter

speed and the altitude are combined. For the ultimate decision all masses, from the initial time to the final time, are also combined and the target is classified as a helicopter at all times greater than 8 seconds with a mass greater than 0.98.

When a measurement comes, algorithm assigns the probability masses instantaneously for every feature and combines them. The computation time spent to reach the overall decision is about 0.2843 seconds in an Intel i7 computer 8 GB RAM with Matlab 2012a. Considering that the air defense radars produce measurement reports with periods in the order of seconds, the algorithm is certainly fast enough for real time operation.

In order to make a comparison, we also applied the method of Xu et al. [16] on the same data by considering the measurements to be the mean value of the features that are provided by the tracker. The instantaneous combined decisions obtained from the speed and the altitude and the final decisions of both methods are shown in Figures 6 and 6. The method that uses only the mean value makes wrong assignments in quite a number of instances since the mean alone may give low likelihood value due to the unsmooth nature of the speed of the helicopter. This results in wrong classification decision.

4   Conclusion

This work utilizes Dempster-Shafer Theory for target classification and the main contribution lies in the task of basic mass assignment. The methodology proposed utilizes all of the information provided by the tracker which is given in the form of a Gaussian probability density function unlike the alternative methods in the literature using only the mean.

The proposed method is tested with real data. Results are compared with another methodology that uses only the mean estimates of the features that can be considered quite similar to the one given in Xu et al. [16]. Test results show that using the whole probability density function of the features provided by the tracker brings significant advantages for classification compared to using only the mean of the features.

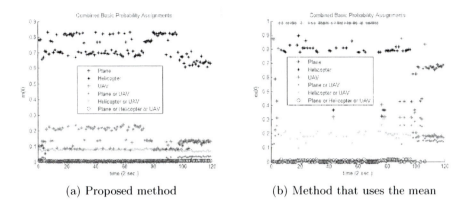

(a) Proposed method   (b) Method that uses the mean

Fig. 6. Instantaneous combined masses of features (speed and altitude)

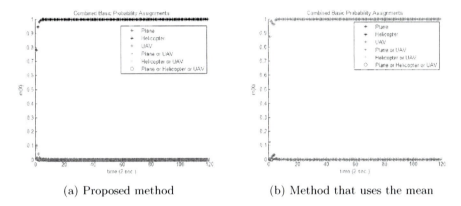

(a) Proposed method   (b) Method that uses the mean

Fig. 7. Combined masses from initial time to final time of features (speed and altitude)

References

1. Bar-Shalom, Y.: Multitarget-multisensor tracking: Applications and advances, vol. III. Artech House, Inc., Norwood (2000)
2. Bendjebbour, A., Delignon, Y., Fouque, L., Samson, V., Pieczynski, W.: Multi-sensor image segmentation using Dempster-Shafer fusion in markov fields context. IEEE Transactions on Geoscience and Remote Sensing 39(8), 1789–1798 (2001)
3. Blackman, S., Popoli, R.: Design and Analysis of Modern Tracking Systems, pp. 967–1068. Artech House, Norwood (1999)
4. Bloch, I.: Some aspects of Dempster — Shafer evidence theory for classification of multi-modality medical images taking partial volume effect into account. Pattern Recogni-tion Letters 17(8), 905–919 (1996)
5. Caromicoli, A., Kurien, T.: Multitarget identification in airborne surveillance. In: International Society for Optics and Photonics Orlando Symposium (1989)

6. Florea, M.C., Jousselme, A.-L., Grenier, D., Bosse, E.: Combining belief functions and fuzzy membership functions. International Society for Optics and Photonics Aero-Sense 2003, 113–122 (2003)
7. Jane, F.: Jane's all the world's aircraft. McGraw-Hill (1999)
8. Jiang, W., Duanmu, D., Fan, X., Deng, Y.: A New Method to Determine Basic Probability Assignment under Fuzzy Environment. In: International Conference on Systems and In-formatics, pp. 758–762 (2012)
9. Le Hegarat-Mascle, S., Bloch, I., Vidal-Madjar, D.: Application of Dempster — Shafer evi-dence theory to unsupervised classification in multisource remote sens-ing. IEEE Transactions on Geoscience and Remote Sensing 35(4), 1018–1031 (1997)
10. Masson, M.H., Denoeux, T.: ECM: An evidential version of the fuzzy c-means algo-rithm. Pattern Recognition 41(4), 1384–1397 (2008)
11. Bogler, P.: Shafer-Dempster reasoning with applications to multisensor target iden-tification systems. IEEE Transactions on Systems, Man and Cybernetics 17(6), 968–977 (1987)
12. Ristic, B., Smets, P.: Target identification using belief functions and implication rules. IEEE Transactions on Aerospace and Electronic Systems 41(3), 1097–1103 (2005)
13. Romer, C., Kandel, A.: Constraints on belief functions imposed by fuzzy ran-dom var-iables. IEEE Transactions on Systems, Man and Cybernetics 25(1), 86–99 (1995)
14. Salzenstein, F., Boudraa, A.: Unsupervised multi sensor data fusion approach. In: Sixth International Symposium on Signal Processing and its Applications, vol. 1, pp. 152–155. IEEE, Kuala Lumpur (2001)
15. Utkin, L.: Extensions of belief functions and possibility distributions by using the im-precise Dirichlet model. Fuzzy Sets and Systems 154(3), 413–431 (2005)
16. Xu, P., Deng, Y., Su, X., Mahadevan, S.: A new method to determine basic proba-bility as-signment from training data. Knowledge-Based Systems 46, 69–80 (2013)
17. Yager, R.R.: A class of fuzzy measures generated from a Dempster — Shafer belief structure. International Journal of Intelligent Systems 14(12), 1239–1247 (1999)
18. Zhu, Y., Bentabet, L., Dupuis, O., Kaftandjian, V., Babot, D., Rombaut, M.: Au-tomatic determination of mass functions in Dempster — Shafer theory using fuzzy c-means and spatial neighborhood information for image segmentation. Optical Engineering 41(4), 760–770 (2002)

A New Parameterless Credal Method
to Track-to-Track Assignment Problem

Samir Hachour, François Delmotte, and David Mercier

Univ. Lille Nord de France, UArtois, EA 3926 LGI2A, Béthune, France

Abstract. This paper deals with the association step in a multi-sensor multi-target tracking process. A new parameterless credal method for track-to-track assignment is proposed and compared with parameter-dependent methods, namely: the well known Global Nearest Neighbor algorithm (GNN) and a credal method recently proposed by Denœux et al.

Keywords: Track-to-track assignment, belief functions, appearance management.

1 Introduction

In a multi-sensor context, the target environment can be observed differently depending on sensors positions and observation capabilities. A centralized fusion process can then help to enhance targets detections and recognitions. To realize the merging of targets data, the central system has amongst other things to order targets estimated data in a common way, which is done through the track-to-track assignment step. Numerous probabilistic methods have been proposed to solve this problem such as the Joint Probabilistic Data Association (JPDA) method [7,3] and the Multi-Hypothesis Tracking (MHT) method [3]. In the latter, probabilities of associations are propagated over time, which makes this method more robust but also more computationally demanding. Other probabilistic methods can also be found in [3,15,2].

The focus of this paper is on mono-hypothesis data assignments where matchings between sensors estimates are computed at each time step and no other hypotheses are conserved. In two dimensional assignment problems, which means data obtained from two sensors, optimal matchings can be provided using the Munkres algorithm [4]. Performances are therefore dependent on the manner that data are represented and given to the optimal Munkres algorithm. In the standard Global Nearest Neighbor algorithm (GNN) [3], data are simply Mahalanobis distances [11] between sensors positions estimates, and a parameter is needed to manage targets which are partially observed (which do not belong to all sensors fields of view). Recently, an equivalent belief-function-based method was proposed by Denœux et al.[6]. Mahalanobis distances in this method are transformed to mass functions. This method has the ability to perform multiple information based assignments but, as in GNN method, it still depends on a fix

F. Cuzzolin (Ed.): BELIEF 2014, LNAI 8764, pp. 403–411, 2014.

parameter in order to build mass functions from distances. Some other equivalent credal solutions can be found in [12,8]. The method proposed in [12] models information in the same way as in [6] and [8] proposes a comparison study of the recent belief functions assignment methods.

In this paper, a new parameterless credal method based on likelihoods calculations is proposed. Using single sensor simulations this method is shown to perform as good as parameter-dependent methods when their parameters are optimally trained.

The multi-sensor multi-target tracking architecture used in this paper is presented in Section 2. The proposed solution for the assignment problem is exposed in Section 3. Comparison results are then provided in Section 4.

2   Multi-sensor multi-target architecture

A centralized multi-sensor multi-target architecture, simplified to two sensors, is illustrated in Figure 1. It represents the solution implemented by the authors, which has been employed in previous works [9,10] and which is used in this paper in Section 4.

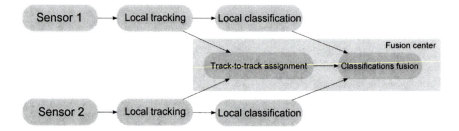

Fig. 1. Track-to-track algorithm based on sensors estimates in a multi-sensor multi-target global scheme.

Each sensor performs a complete tracking and a classification of each target. Details about local tracking and classification algorithms can be found in [10]. Track-to-track assignment can be exclusively performed using distances between sensors estimates, it represents the solution without local classification feedbacks represented in Figure 1.

At each time step k, the set of estimates performed by sensor i is noted $\hat{X}_i(k) = \{\hat{x}_i^1(k), \hat{x}_i^2(k), \ldots, \hat{x}_i^{n_i}(k)\}$, where n_i is the number of targets observed by sensor i at time step k, and $\hat{x}_i^t(k)$, $t \in \{1, \ldots, n_i\}$, is the state estimate of target t.

For each time step k, the distance between the state estimate of target t by sensor i and state estimate of target ℓ by sensor j is defined by:

$$d_{t,\ell}(k) = (\hat{x}_i^t(k) - \hat{x}_j(k)^\ell)^T (Cov_{t,\ell}(k))^{-1} (\hat{x}_i^t(k) - \hat{x}_j^\ell(k)), \tag{1}$$

with $t \in \{1, \ldots, n_i\}$, $\ell \in \{1, \ldots, n_j\}$, n_i and n_j respectively the number of targets observed by sensors i and j at time step k, and the global covariance matrix $Cov_{t,\ell}(k)$ taken equal to the mean value of the covariance matrix of target t estimated by sensor i (noted $P_i^t(k)$) and the covariance matrix of target ℓ estimated by sensor j (noted $P_j^\ell(k)$):

$$Cov_{t,\ell}(k) = \frac{1}{2}(P_i^t(k) + P_j^\ell(k)) . \qquad (2)$$

Local classifications performed by sensors can be used to enhance track-to-track assignment step. This is done using the feedback assignment strategy given in Figure 2.

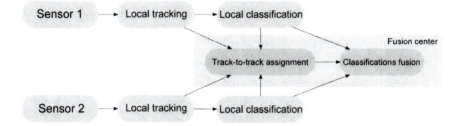

Fig. 2. Track-to-track algorithm based on sensors estimates and local classification results in a multi-sensor multi-target global scheme

Suppose targets local classifications results are given in the form of mass functions m expressed on a the frame 2^C, where $C = \{c_1, c_2, \ldots\}$ represents the set of all the possible classes. Such additional information can then be used in the assignment step as explained in details in [6].

The association methods compared in Section 4 to achieve track-to-track matchings are all based on distances expressed by (1).

3   A Non-parametric Credal Solution for the Assignment Problem

In this section, a parameterless credal method is presented to perform the associations from the distances expressed by (1). In this solution, mass functions modeling does not need any parameter design. It is based on likelihoods seen as plausibility functions as in Smet's works [14] (Similar notions can also be found in [1]).

Time step k has been omitted for the sake of simplicity.

Let $r_{t,\ell} \in \{0, 1\}$ be the relation that $\hat{x}_i^t$ is associated or not with $\hat{x}_j^\ell$ ($r_{t,l} = 1$ means that target t estimated by sensor i corresponds to target ℓ estimated by sensor j, $r_{t,\ell} = 0$ otherwise).

For each estimated target $t \in \{1, \ldots, n_i\}$ given by a sensor i, a plausibility function Pl_t is built on the set $\hat{X}_j^{*t} = \{\hat{x}_j^1, \ldots, \hat{x}_j^{n_j}, *_j\}$ of sensor j known targets, element $*_t$ meaning that a new target is associated with $\hat{x}_i^t$. The set $\hat{X}_j^{*t}$ can be shortly denoted $\{1, \ldots, n_j, *_t\}$. The plausibility Pl_t is defined by:

$$Pl_t(\{\ell\}) = G_{\ell,t}, \quad \forall \ell \in \{1, \ldots, n_j\}, \tag{3}$$

where $G_{\ell,t}$ is a likelihood measure calculated as:

$$G_{\ell,t} = \frac{exp[-d_{\ell,t}^2/2]}{\sqrt{(2\pi)^q |Cov_{\ell,t}|}}, \quad \ell \in \{1, \ldots, n_j\}, \tag{4}$$

with q the dimension of the estimated state vector $\hat{x}$ and $Cov_{\ell,t}$ defined as in (2).

Plausibility $Pl_t(\{\ell\})$ indicates the plausibility that target with state $\hat{x}_i^t$ is associated with target with state $\hat{x}_j^\ell$.

The maximum plausibility that target with state $\hat{x}_i^t$ will be associated to one of the n_j already known targets by sensors j corresponds to $\max\limits_{\ell=1,\ldots,n_j} (Pl_t(\{\ell\})) \leq 1$. This maximum can be lower than one, in particular if the frame of discernment formed by the set of known objects is not exhaustive. Indeed, a target with state $\hat{x}_i^t$ can correspond to a new object ($*_t$). The plausibility of this event is thus defined by:

$$Pl_t(\{*_t\}) = 1 - \max\limits_{\ell=1,\ldots,n_j} (Pl_t(\{\ell\})). \tag{5}$$

Pl_t is then defined on a an exhaustive closed-world $\hat{X}_j \cup \{*_t\}$, the corresponding mass function is denoted by m_t and is obtained by a direct application of the Generalized Bayesian Theorem (GBT)[13,5], recalled here for convenience:

$$m_t(A) = \prod_{\ell \in A} Pl_t(\{\ell\}) \prod_{\ell \in \bar{A}} (1 - Pl_t(\{\ell\})), \quad \forall A \subseteq \hat{X}_j^{*t}. \tag{6}$$

Each mass function m_t, regarding the association of target $\hat{x}_i^t$, can then be combined with any other mass functions based on other additional information (e.g. shape, color, class, etc.) [6].

Once all mass functions m_t have been computed for each estimated target t, they are transformed into pignistic probabilities $BetP_t$ using the pignistic transformation [13].

The best assignment relation is then chosen as the one maximizing the following criterion:

$$\max \sum_{\ell,t} BetP_t(\{\ell\})r_{\ell,t}, \quad \ell = \{1, \ldots, n_i + n_j\}, t = \{1, \ldots, n_j\}. \tag{7}$$

with the following constraints:

$$\sum_{\ell}^{n_i+n_j} r_{\ell,t} \leq 1, \tag{8}$$

$$\sum_{t}^{n_j} r_{\ell,t} = 1 \, , \tag{9}$$

$$r_{\ell,t} \in \{0,1\} \,. \forall \ell \in \{1,\ldots,n_i+n_j\}, \forall t \in \{1,\ldots,n_j\} \tag{10}$$

As Denœux et al.'s and GNN approaches, this problem can be solved using Hungarian or Munkres algorithms [4].

The constraint expressed by (8) means that sensor i's estimation of a given target state can be assigned to sensor j's estimation of a given target state, if not, it is considered as a new target's state. The constraint expressed by (9) means that a target known by sensor j can be matched with a target of sensor i. If the target is not known by sensor i, it is assigned to the extraneous element $(*)$.

The assignment problem is illustrated in Table 1. Note that this description is based on sensor $i's$ point of view (to which elements of sensor i are assigned the elements of sensor j?). The same process may be performed for sensor j point of view (to which elements of sensor j elements of sensor i are associated). As Mercier et al.'s method [12], this process is generally not symmetric.

Table 1. Pignistic probabilities assignment matrix

	$\hat{x}_i^1$	$\hat{x}_i^2$	$\ldots$	$\hat{x}_i^{n_i}$
$\hat{x}_j^1$	$BetP_{1,1}$	$BetP_{1,2}$	$\ldots$	$BetP_{1,n_i}$
$\hat{x}_j^2$	$BetP_{2,1}$	$BetP_{2,2}$	$\ldots$	$BetP_{2,n_i}$
$\vdots$	$\vdots$	$\vdots$	$\ldots$	$\vdots$
$\hat{x}_j^{n_j}$	$BetP_{n_j,1}$	$BetP_{n_j,2}$	$\ldots$	$BetP_{n_j,n_i}$
$*_1$	$BetP_{*_1,1}$	0	$\ldots$	0
$*_2$	0	$BetP_{*_2,2}$	$\ldots$	0
$\vdots$	$\vdots$	$\vdots$	$\ldots$	$\vdots$
$*_{n_i}$	0	0	$\ldots$	$BetP_{*_{n_i},n_i}$

4   Simulations Results

In this section, two scenarios of test are exposed to illustrate comparisons between GNN algorithm, Denoeux et al.'s algorithm and the proposed algorithm.

GNN algorithm depends on a parameter noted λ which allows GNN algorithm to manage objects detection, the real λ being equal to the maximum distance between an observation and a prediction in Munkres algorithm. In Denœux et al.'s algorithm [6], a parameter noted γ is used to transform distances into mass functions: the weight $\exp(-\gamma d_{t,\ell})$, with $d_{t,\ell}$ the distance between objects t and ℓ, supports the belief in favor of the association of t with ℓ, and $1 - \exp(-\gamma d_{t,\ell})$ supports the converse (non-association of t with ℓ).

Formalized in [8], a link between parameters λ and γ can be stated. As λ is the maximum distance from which a non association is established for each observation, the following relation can be considered: $\exp\left(-\gamma\lambda\right) = 1 - \exp\left(-\gamma\lambda\right)$, which means:

$$\gamma = \frac{-\log\left(0.5\right)}{\lambda}. \tag{11}$$

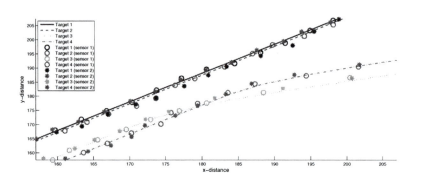

Fig. 3. Scenario 1 description: four conflicting targets. Estimations of sensor 1 are given by circles. Estimations of sensor 2 are given by stars.

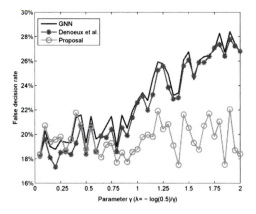

Fig. 4. False decision rates aggregated over 10 noise realizations with different values of parameters γ (and then λ (11)).

A first scenario is illustrated in Figure 3. Four nearby targets have to be tracked. The idea is to match estimations of sensor 1 (circles) to estimations of sensor 2 (stars). This scenario 1 aims to show the impact on the association decision when parameters are not optimally defined. False assignment rates averaged over 10 different measurement noise realizations [10] for each association algorithm for different values of parameters λ and γ are depicted in Figure 4. It can be seen that changes in parameters λ and γ have clearly an effect on the performances of the parameter-dependent algorithms. Indeed, large values of γ correspond to low values of λ which is seen as the detection distance. Low values of the detection distance force the parameter-dependent algorithms to decide that some or all the incoming targets are new ones and some or all known targets are non-detected. This is the reason of the increasing false decision rates of the parameter-dependent algorithms in Figure 3.

Maximizing plausibilities instead of pignistic probabilities in (7) in the proposed approach give similar results in these scenarios.

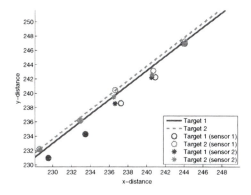

Fig. 5. Scenario 2 description: two nearby targets. Estimations of sensor 1 are given by circles. Estimations of sensor 2 are given by stars.

A second simulation, depicted in Figure 5, aims to illustrate the benefit of the use of additional information in the assignment step (cf Figure 2). In this case, classification mass functions are combined with mass functions provided by distances for the two credal algorithms. Since, the GNN algorithm is based on distances only as entering data, no method allowing the integration of additional information for GNN algorithm was already proposed. In this simulation, optimal parameters λ and γ are used. In Figure 6, it can be observed that additional information enhances the credal algorithms performances. Additional information (classes, velocity, etc.) can help to resolve the conflicting assignment situation. Thanks to the general formel aspect of belief functions theory, multiple information can be modelled and combined, which leads to a more accurate assignment decisions.

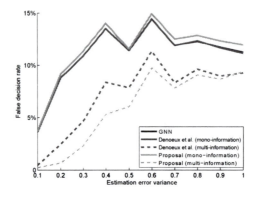

Fig. 6. False decision rates aggregated over 10 noise realizations, mono-information refers to distance and multi-information refers to distance and class

5   Conclusion

This paper provides a new parameterless credal method to the assignment task in multi-target tracking.

Contrarily to equivalent methods which are parameter-dependent, this one does not need any parameter. Parameters in the concerned methods allows new elements appearances to be managed (detection of new targets in the case of observation-to-track assignment or partially observed targets in track-to-track assignment). A more natural appearance management solution is provided in this paper, it is based on a better understanding of targets environment.

Comparisons on conflicting scenarios show that the proposed method performs equally to parameter-dependent methods, when their parameters are optimally trained. Moreover, it is shown that credal algorithms performances can be enhanced, when additional information are available.

The ability of the credal methods to preserve the information on imprecise sets would represent an important advantage for a future multi-scan and multi-hypothesis based approaches.

Acknowledgments. The authors are grateful to Prof. T. Denœux for having shared the Matlab^TM code of Denœux et al.'s assignment algorithm [6].

References

1. Appriou, A.: Multisensor data fusion in situation assessment processes. In: Gabbay, D.M., Kruse, R., Nonnengart, A., Ohlbach, H.J. (eds.) FAPR 1997 and ECSQARU 1997. LNCS, vol. 1244, pp. 1–15. Springer, Heidelberg (1997)
2. Bar-Shalom, Y.: Tracking and data association. Academic Press Professional, San Diego (1987)

3. Blackman, S., Popoli, R.: Design and analysis of modern tracking systems. Artech House, Norwood (1999)
4. Bourgeois, F., Lassalle, J.C.: An extension of the Munkres algorithm for the assignment problem to rectangular matrices. Communications of the ACM 14(12), 802–804 (1971)
5. Delmotte, F., Smets, P.: Target identification based on the Transferable Belief Model interpretation of Dempster-Shafer model. IEEE Transactions on Systems, Man and Cybernetics, Part A: Systems and Humans 34(4), 457–471 (2004)
6. Denœux, T., El Zoghby, N., Cherfaoui, V., Jouglet, A.: Optimal object association in the Dempster-Shafer framework. IEEE Transactions on Cybernetics (to appear)
7. Fortmann, T., Bar-Shalom, Y., Scheffe, M.: Multi-target tracking using joint probabilistic data association. In: Proceedings of the 19th IEEE Conference on Decision and Control including the Symposium on Adaptive Processes, vol. 19, pp. 807–812 (1980)
8. Hachour, S., Delmotte, F., Mercier, D.: Comparison of credal assignment algorithms in kinematic data tracking context. In: Laurent, A., Strauss, O., Bouchon-Meunier, B., Yager, R.R. (eds.) IPMU 2014, Part III. CCIS, vol. 444, pp. 200–211. Springer, Heidelberg (2014)
9. Hachour, S., Delmotte, F., Mercier, D., Lefèvre, E.: Multi-Sensor Multi-Target tracking with robust kinematic data based credal classification. In: 8th Workshop, Sensor Data Fusion: Trends, Solutions, Application, SDF 2013, Bonn, Germany (Octobre, 2013)
10. Hachour, S., Delmotte, F., Mercier, D., Lefèvre, E.: Object tracking and credal classification with kinematic data in a multi-target context. Information Fusion 20, 174–188 (2014),
http://www.sciencedirect.com/science/article/pii/S1566253514000128
11. McLachlan, G.: Mahalanobis distance. Resonance 4(6), 20–26 (1999)
12. Mercier, D., Lefèvre, É., Jolly, D.: Object association with belief functions, an application with vehicles. Information Sciences 181(24), 5485–5500 (2011)
13. Smets, P.: Belief functions: the disjunctive rule of combination and the Generalized Bayesian Theorem. International Journal of Approximate Reasoning 9(1), 1–35 (1993)
14. Smets, P.: Belief functions on real numbers. International Journal of Approximate Reasoning 40(3), 181–223 (2005),
http://www.sciencedirect.com/science/article/pii/S0888613X0500023X
15. Vermaak, J., Godsill, S., Perez, P.: Monte carlo filtering for multi target tracking and data association. IEEE Transactions on Aerospace and Electronic Systems 41(1), 309–332 (2005)

Geometric Interpretations of Conflict: A Viewpoint

Thomas Burger*

iRTSV-BGE (Université Grenoble-Alpes, CNRS, CEA, INSERM), Grenoble, France
thomas.burger@cea.fr

Abstract. Recently, several works have focused on the study of conflict among belief functions with a geometrical approach. In such framework, a corner stone is to endow the set of belief functions with an appropriated metric, and to consider that distant belief functions are more conflicting than neighboring ones. This article discusses such approaches, caveats some of their difficulties and highlights ways to circumvent them.

Keywords: belief functions, conflict, distance.

1 Introduction

Mass functions are rather simple objects from a mathematical point of view: distributions over a finite powerset which add up to one. However, their semantic is rich enough to be used in artificial intelligence to express the subjective opinion of an agent, in versatile frameworks such as imprecisely known statistics or censored data fusion. This difference between the simplicity of the mathematical object, and the subtlety of its interpretation at a high semantic level is probably the curse of belief function theory, as it prevents providing the scientist or engineer with a simple textbook or recipe, that is no longer put into question, on how to use belief functions to model a real world problem. For instance, after few decades of developments, the theory still lacks a unique and well established definition of conflicting belief functions. Since the seminal work of Dempster [8] where the mass in the emptyset has been used as a normalization factor in the orthogonal sum, the traditional *conflict mass* is regularly challenged with alternative definitions [16,17,9].

This never-ending debate on the mathematical definition of conflict has been fed for few years now by a trend, which is discussed in the present paper. This trend is largely based on endowing the set of mass functions with a metric, and on characterizing the degree of conflict between two mass functions according to their pairwise distance. Historically, this direction was first initiated in 1996 by the work of George and Pal [10], which remains seldom cited (40 citations according to Google Scholar), while a few years later (2001), Jousselme

---

* This work was supported by the ANR funding ANR-10-INBS-08, and the Prospectom project (Mastodons 2012 CNRS challenge). The author deeply thanks Sébastien Destercke and Didier Dubois whom discussions with fed this viewpoint.

F. Cuzzolin (Ed.): BELIEF 2014, LNAI 8764, pp. 412–421, 2014.

et al. [12] proposed their famous distance based on Jaccard's index. During the early 2000s, Cuzzolin developed his geometrical framework for belief functions, and Liu proposed to complement the conflict mass by the Chebyshev (or L^∞) distance between pignistic transforms [16]. Jousselme's work being cited 400 times, Liu around 200 times and Cuzzolin three most cited papers [4,5,6] on the subject reaching more than 150 citations, we can fairly acknowledge that the interplay of these works, crystalized in the 2012 survey of Jousselme [14] (a presentation of which was given at BELIEF 2010, in Brest [13]) provided the technical ground, on which these new ways to define conflict has blossomed in the past years.

From that point on, numerous works have focused on providing a distance based definition of conflict. The objective of this article is not to review or to compare them. Rather, it is to go back to the foundation of this trend, and to address the interplays between the very mathematical notion of distance and the concept of conflict as acknowledged in belief function theory. After some definitions (Section 2), these interplays are discussed at a mathematical level (Section 3), and at a semantic one (Section 4).

2   Definition

Let us recall that a *metric space* (E, d) is a set E endowed with a *distance d*. A distance on E is defined as:

1. An application from $E \times E$,
2. onto $\mathbb{R}_+$,
3. so that $\forall x, y \in E^2, d(x, y) = 0 \Leftrightarrow x = y$,
4. $d(x, y) = d(y, x)$,
5. $\forall x, y, z \in E^3, d(x, z) \leq d(x, y) + d(y, z)$.

Usually, (2) is referred to as *non-negativity*, (3) as *separability*, (4) as *symmetry* and (5) as *subadditivity*, or *triangle inequality*. Although the term is not standard, let us refer to (1) as *binarity* for convenience. Beyond algebraic definitions, it is classically assumed in information-related sciences, that the semantic associated to a distance is that of *dissimilarity*: Greater the distance between two elements of E the more dissimilar they are, and the smaller the distance, the more similar. In the particular case of belief function theory, E is generally the set $\mathcal{M}(\Omega)$ of mass functions with frame Ω. To simplify distance definitions, $\mathcal{M}(\Omega)$ is also often assumed to be a $(n - 1)$ standard simplex in a n dimensional *normed vector space* V spanned by the n possible focal elements that are canonically derived from working on Ω (see [6]). Thus, any norm defined on V trivially leads to a distance on $\mathcal{M}(\Omega)$.

Let us now turn to the definition of conflicting belief functions: As explained in the introduction, the belief function community has not accepted a single mathematical definition for it, and scientists may derive *a posteriori* the mathematical definition which fit with the particular situation they face. It means that the definition is somehow clear at a "modeling" level, as everyone can tell if different opinions are conflicting or not; however, this does not obviously translate into the formalism of belief functions. If we refine a bit the process, it appears that:

1. Several sources of information can agree or disagree on any phenomenon they have evidence on;
2. We call *degree of conflict among the sources* the level to which the sources disagree, yet no formal definition of such disagreement exists;
3. As the sources provide mass functions, a painless misnomer makes us talk about *degree of conflict among the mass functions*;
4. This degree of conflict is computed by applying various formulas to the mass functions.

Finally, the main difficulty is to define how agreement/disagreement of the sources translates into the result of a mathematical operation on mass functions, so that one can quantify it. During this "translation", distances are likely to be called for assistance. The reason is the following: In most applications, the level of conflict itself is of seldom interest, and the practitioner is more interested in the combination of the sources. This combination is somehow expressing a consensus among the sources. Naturally, one expects that consensus to be easier to find if the sources have similar opinions, while it is impossible to find it if the sources support completely opposite opinions. As the conflict is supposed to quantify this possibility to find a consensus, it makes intuitively sense to measure distances between the masses to combine.

3   Mathematical Discussion

At this point, one needs to check that the idea behind conflict measurement is compliant with the mathematical definition of a distance. Regarding *non-negativity* and *symmetry*, there should have very little problem: It is rather intuitive that the conflict is a non-negative quantity, and most of the works on the issue assume so. For instance, in [9], this assumption is explicitly included in our first axiom, referred to as *Extreme conflict value*; and in [17], one finds it in both the first axiom, simply called *non-negativity*, and in the fourth one, referred to as *normalization*, and which corresponds to our *Extreme conflict value* axiom. Similarly, it is also taken for granted that the conflict between m_1 and m_2 is the same as the one between m_2 and m_1. As such, both [17] and [9] propose an axiom named *symmetry*. However, the other properties (*subadditivity*, *binarity* and *separability*) do not directly fit, and they are separately addressed hereafter.

3.1   The Binarity Issue

First, let us consider *binarity*: So far, in most works devoted to conflict, it is assumed that $n > 2$ belief functions can generate some conflict, and that this latter can be measured, which strongly goes against the *binarity* property. Thus, if distances are involved in the process of conflict quantitation, a rigorous n-ary extension is required. The most natural way to define such extension is to rely on hypervolumes, i.e. a distance in the binary case, an era in the ternary case, a volume in the quaternary case, and so on. Naturally, this raises lots of questions:

- How to deal with hypervolume computation in case of belief functions presented by collinear/coplanar vectors? The problem is that the volume spanned by a set of non full rank vectors is nil.
- How to compare the conflict arisen among a set of n_1 belief functions, and the conflict arisen among another set of n_2 belief functions? In fact, volumes of different dimensionalities are not comparable.
- Which type of hypervolume to consider? The smallest encompassing hypersphere, the simplex spanned by the masses, etc.?

However, it has two major advantages: First, hypervolume computation being insensitive to the order of the vertices under consideration, it naturally fits with the n-ary generalization of the *symmetry* property discussed above. Second, it can rely on matrix algebra as a robust mathematical background, where most of the results are well documented: Indeed, determinant or eigenvalue computations relates to the geometry of the column vectors of a matrix. So far, such an algebraic vision is seldom considered, and only weak justifications appear in [15].

3.2   The Separability Issue

Behind *separability*, one questions the equivalence between the following two assertions: "These masses are non-conflicting" and "These masses are equal". To answer, one should question the implication of the first assertion by the second, and the reverse implication; that is: Is it possible to find separable mass functions with fully agreeing sources? and, is it possible to find fully disagreeing sources with equal evidence?

Separable Mass Functions with Agreeing Sources? Let us remark that in belief function theory, focal elements are most of the time interpreted as epistemic sets [3], i.e. imprecise descriptions of the reality: one assumes the truth is one and only one element amongst those composing the set[1]. Under such view, it is possible to have sources of information having different descriptions with a non-null intersection that they can agree on. The direct conclusion is that, contrarily to distances, conflict is quantity that does not fit with the separability property. Let us illustrate that with some examples:

Example 1 (Everyday life situation with an epistemic view). In this example, we do not assume any model based on belief functions. We simply consider two distinct sources of information. The first one supports an interval I_1 (for a range of acceptable values, a set of possible options, or whatever its meaning), while the second source support another interval I_2 included in I_1. In such a case, both sources can agree on I_2 (there is no conflict), while their opinions differ.

---

[1] To the best of my knowledge, no work proposes a new distance-based definition of conflict while explicitly assuming an ontic view.

Example 2 (Separable mass functions with fully agreeing sources). Assume that source S_1 provides a vacuous mass function m_1, and that source S_2 provides a non-vacuous consonant mass function m_2. One clearly has $m_1 \neq m_2$, and thus $d(m_1, m_2) > 0$ whatever d. However, S_1 and S_2 are not conflicting, as the evidence supported by m_1 is non-informative in an epistemic model.

It is also possible to define other similar examples by replacing m_2 by a consonant mass function having its focal elements included in those of m_1, while having $m_1 \neq m_2$. Whatever the example, the underlying idea is that a part of the distance between two separate mass functions can arise from their respective level of imprecision, and that this difference does not necessarily imply any conflicting views. This idea is implemented in the *Ignorance is bliss* axiom from [9] and in the *inclusion* axiom from [17]. However, these axioms are not here taken as the initial assumption to build these counter-examples on; I only rely on the weaker assumption that belief functions theory assumes an epistemic model. On the contrary, these axioms can be seen as a consequence of the epistemic modeling.

Disagreeing Sources with Equal Evidence? Let m_1 and m_2 be two mass functions such that $m_1 = m_2$, and thus $d(m_1, m_2) = 0$. Does this necessarily imply that the conflict between m_1 and m_2 is nil? This question should be sorted out with respect to the on-going discussions regarding the decomposition of conflict into its inner part and its outer part [7,20]. These works assume that the *global conflict* arising from m_1 and m_2 can be partly explained by the conflicts that are carried by m_1 on its own regardless m_2, and by m_2 on its own regardless m_1. As such the *outer conflict* is what remains from the global conflict once the *inner conflicts* have been subtracted. If $d(m_1, m_2) = 0$ implies a null (global) conflict, one has to assume that inner conflict does not exist, which so far contradicts with several state-of-the-art articles. An alternative is to assume that a distance-based measure of conflict only accounts for outer conflict. However, this line is also source of difficulties, as so far, no exact decomposition of the conflict into its outer and inner parts holds.

3.3   The Subadditivity Issue

Let us finally and rapidly turn to *subadditivity* (or *triangle ineqality*). Is there any reason to consider that the conflict between m_1 and m_2, plus the conflict between m_2 and m_3 should be greater than the conflict between m_1 and m_3? The following example provides a situation where this property is not desirable.

Example 3. Assume that m_1 and m_3 are consonant mass functions bearing on different opinions, and each being different from the vacuous one. Naturally, they have a non-null conflict. Now, let us assume m_2 is the vacuous mass: it is absolutely non-conflicting with either m_1 or m_3 so that the sum of these two conflicts is nil, leading to a situation where the triangle inequality does not hold.

Of course, this example relies on Example 2 and assumes an epistemic model. However, it makes sense: in everyday life, it is possible to consider two extreme positions that are in total conflict while an in-between position is hardly conflicting with both, as it supports an acceptable solution for everyone. In such case, the triangle inequality does clearly not hold.

3.4   To Conclude on the Distance Properties

Finally, amongst the five properties of metrics, two naturally fits to conflict definition (*symmetry* and *non-negativity*), one may accept some suitable generalization (*binarity*), and two are absolutely not compatible (*subadditivity* and *separability*) with an epistemic view of belief functions. At this point, we can argue that conflict and distances (or dissimilarities) are different notions which cannot be interchanged. Unfortunately, a lot of recent works assume it is possible to do so (see for example [18,22,19,15]), which is arguable. On the other hand, it is possible to agree on the mathematical differences between these notions, while proposing to build a sounded definition of conflict thanks to the involvement of an adapted metrics; most of the time, by coupling a distance measure to another index, such as in [16,17]. This second approach authorizes much more rigorous works. However, one needs to remain cautious regarding the semantic of such aggregation. For instance, what is the meaning of a multi-dimensional conflict [16], or of multiplying a distance by an inclusion measure [17]? This question is partly addressed in the next section.

4   Semantic Discussion

Now, I leave the axiomatic discussion to question how conflict and distance may interplay at a semantic level, i.e. at the moment when the practitioner involves belief functions to model a particular real life phenomenon. I will first push forward the line initiated in Section 3, by questioning the semantic of an aggregation function used to build a measure of conflict on the basis of, among others, a distance measure. Second, I will discuss the semantic of V, the normed vector space derived from $\mathcal{M}(\Omega)$. Finally, I will question the definition of a consensus between several sources when the conflict is geometrically defined.

4.1   Between Similarity and Agreement

Let us assume that a measure of conflict is defined thanks to an aggregation function which takes as input, among others, a distance measure. Let m_1 and m_2 be two mass functions, and $\mathbf{C}$ a conflict measure reading:

$$\mathbf{C}(m_1, m_2) = f\left(d\left(m_1, m_2\right), \mathbf{V}_1\left(m_1, m_2\right), \ldots, \mathbf{V}_n\left(m_1, m_2\right)\right)$$

where d is a distance over $\mathcal{M}(\Omega)$, f an aggregation function, and $\mathbf{V}_1, \ldots, \mathbf{V}_n$, $n \geq 1$ is a set of variables meaningfully describing some properties judged as interesting to quantify conflict. For instance:

- in [16], d is the Chebishev distance, f is a concatenation operator that builds a vector on the basis of a list of its coordinates, $n = 1$, and $\mathbf{V}_1\,(m_1, m_2)$ is the conflict mass.
- in [17], d is the Jousselme distance, f is a product, $n = 1$ and $\mathbf{V}_1\,(m_1, m_2)$ is an inclusion measure.
- one could also assume that a distance is involved to measure the outer conflict, and that this latter is complemented with another measure accounting for inner conflicts.

All these works assume that *similarity* and *agreement* are different notions, which is so far supported by Section 3. However, they make an additional assumption, which is that a distance can be combined with a finite set of other values, namely $\mathbf{V}_1\,(m_1, m_2), \ldots, \mathbf{V}_n\,(m_1, m_2)$ so that the resulting combination is a conflict measure that fairly describes the level of disagreement of the sources. So far, I do not have any support for this assumption, nor any argument against it. However, the assumption is often associated to a constructive approach I find prone to discussion: Generally, a measure of conflict of the form of $\mathbf{C}$ is built iteratively:

1. One starts from a first definition of conflict (either $\mathbf{V}_1\,(m_1, m_2)$ or $d\,(m_1, m_2)$ in the aforementioned examples);
2. One finds a counter-example on which this definition does not entirely capture what one expects as conflict;
3. One proposes a correction, generally by incorporating another variable, say $\mathbf{V}_i\,(m_1, m_2)$. At this point, if the resulting definition of conflict is not sounded, one goes back to the previous step.

During this process, one never has the confirmation that the collection $\{d\,(m_1, m_2)$, $\mathbf{V}_1\,(m_1, m_2), \ldots, \mathbf{V}_n\,(m_1, m_2)\}$ is complete: As long as no example puts it back into question, the definition is accepted; while, on the contrary, one should accept it only after proving its completeness. Practically, when discussing the separability issue in Section 3, I pointed out that some distance could arise from the different levels of imprecision between m_1 and m_2, without implying any conflict. A similar conclusion was drawn in [17], so that the proposed measure complements a distance by an inclusion measure. However, there is no evidence supporting that the resulting measure of conflict is complete.

4.2   Sensitivity to Permutations

The second issue to focus on is best illustrated by an example:

Example 4. Let $v_1 = (1, 0, 0)^\top$ and $v_2 = (0, 1, 0)^\top$ be two vectors of $\mathbb{R}^3$, and let $\sigma \in S_3$ be a permutation. As any permutation of the coordinates of a vector can be decomposed into a succession of cycles (which intuitively corresponds to rotations of the basis of $\mathbb{R}^3$), it is rather intuitive that most of the canonical distances (such as Minkowski distances) on $\mathbb{R}^3$ are insensitive to permutations: Practically, if d is such a distance, then $d(v_1, v_2) = d(\sigma(v_1), \sigma(v_2))$, $\forall \sigma \in S_3$.

However, if v_1 and v_2 are intepreted as mass functions (let us name them m_1 and m_2) over a binary frame the powerset of which reads $\{\{\omega_1\}, \{\omega_2\}, \{\omega_1, \omega_2\}\}$, things become different: m_1 and m_2 are naturally conflicting as they respectively fully support $\{\omega_1\}$ and $\{\omega_2\}$, however, if σ is the cycle $(2, 3)$, then $\sigma(m_1) = (1, 0, 0)^\top$ and $\sigma(m_2) = (0, 0, 1)^\top$ are not conflicting, as $\sigma(m_2)$ is vacuous.

The above example illustrates that, contrarily to a classical vector space such as $\mathbb{R}^n$, where the order of the coordinates of a vector are seldom important, $\mathcal{M}(\Omega)$ is rather sensitive to permutations. Naturally, this example also relies on the same tricks as Examples 2 and 3: one involves a vacuous mass function and one assumes it is not conflicting with any other consonant mass. However, this is mainly to keep the example both simple and catchy. What really matters here is much more general: as the semantic of each coordinate of a vector is not the same (some correspond to singleton focal elements, while others do not, respectively encoding precise knowledge, or not), any permutation of the vector space strongly modifies the semantic of the mass functions. However, several classical distances are unchanged by permutations. Thus, the sensitivity to permutation must be explicitly accounted for, if one expects a distance to be involved in a conflict definition. Jousselme's distance based on Jaccard's index, as well as other entropy-related distances, partially do, yet in different manners. However, other distances defined on $\mathcal{M}(\Omega)$ may not (including most of the canonical distances on a vector space).

4.3   Geometric Definition of Consensus

When combining belief functions, the resulting mass is supposed to reflect a consensus among the original sources. This consensus aims at being as compatible as possible with the pieces of evidences provided by the sources, while being specific enough (a vacuous mass is not a relevant consensus). Let us explore the consequences of that, in the case where conflict is reflected by distances. If the degree of disagreement between the sources if fairly captured by a distance measure, the consensus mass function is expected to have a minimal distance to all the original pieces of evidence. From a geometrical viewpoint, such a mass function is defined by the barycenter of the sources to combine. Thus, the merging of the pieces of information should not be conducted according to Dempster's rule, but according to a convex combination. Although in plain contradiction with the mainframe of belief function theory, the idea that a consensus is well-defined by a barycenter has already showed up in the literature: In [21], Assumption 1.1. reads that the pignistic transform should be invariant with respect to convex combination rather than with respect to Dempster's rule, such as advocated in [2]. In a slightly less related way, the pignistic transform is easily interpreted in terms of linear combination: It provides the barycenter of dominating probabilities [1], which can be interpreted as a geometric consensus between all the compliant probability distributions. However, by now, Dempster's rule is well established (it is seldom put into questions, such as in [11]), and such a change would have major impacts on the theory (far beyond the simple definition of conflict) and its consequences should be globally considered.

5   Conclusion

This article discusses the recent trend which focuses on using metrics to quantify the degree of conflict between belief functions. As I am sure it appeared through this discussion, I am not a supporter of this trend, and my views remain coherent with a previous article [9] I was a co-author of, where one has defined various axioms that we believe a sounded measure of conflict should meet. However, I understand that belief functions have rich and multiple semantics that may differ, and among which none is better than the others. As such, in this viewpoint, I considered the question through some constructive Cartesian skepticism: I tried to push as far as possible the line of mixing distances and conflict, with the hope that it would raise interesting questions.

As a result of the axiomatic discussion conducted in Section 3, it appears that the separability and subadditivity properties of distances contradict what can be expected from a conflict measure. It clearly indicates that, at a low mathematical level, the notions of conflict and of distance cannot be interchanged. However, at this point, it is impossible to reject another trend, which consists in elaborating a measure of conflict thanks to an aggregation function which takes into account, among others, a distance. This is why, in Section 4, I discuss the differences between distances and conflict at a semantic level, through different angles.

Finally, it appears that even if no blatant contradiction appears at this semantic level, several major issues remain, if one expects to build a complete vision-based definition of conflict:

1. Such as discussed in Section 3.1, a suitable n-ary $(n > 2)$ generalization of the distance is necessary. Moreover, this generalization should be insensitive to permutations, to fit with the symmetry property;
2. One only considers outer conflict (thus, a suitable separation of inner and outer conflict is mandatory), such as advocated in Section 3.2;
3. An exhaustive definition of all the differences between agreement and similarity must be given, so that the distance is aggregated to another set of measures accounting for these differences, such as it is outlined in Section 3.2 and detailed in Section 4.1;
4. The distance must be defined so that it has a semantic robust to permutations of the focal elements, in order to avoid situation such as illustrated in the Example 4 (Section 4.2);
5. The combination rule must be adapted to fit a barycentric vision of the consensus, such as described in Section 4.3.

Finally, most of these issues are real locks that can only be addressed in dedicated works. According to the amount of works focused on the definition of a geometric and distance-based vision of conflict, the subject is definitely an interesting question for the belief function community. However, its complete and rigorous definition still requires several issues (at least, the five aforementioned) to be solved beforehand. Should these issues be sorted out, it would be interesting to confront a distance-based conflict to pre-existing definitions.

References

1. Burger, T., Cuzzolin, F.: The barycenters of the k-additive dominating belief functions & the pignistic k-additive belief functions. In: Workshop on the Theory of Belief Functions (2010)
2. Cobb, B.R., Shenoy, P.P.: On the plausibility transformation method for translating belief function models to probability models. Int. J. Approx. Reasoning 41(3), 314–330 (2006)
3. Couso, I., Dubois, D.: Statistical reasoning with set-valued information: Ontic vs. epistemic views. Inter. J. Approx. Reasoning (2013)
4. Cuzzolin, F.: Geometry of dempster's rule of combination. IEEE Trans. Systems, Man, & Cyb. (B) 34(2), 961–977 (2004)
5. Cuzzolin, F.: Two new bayesian approximations of belief functions based on convex geometry. IEEE Trans. Systems, Man, & Cyb. (B) 37(4), 993–1008 (2007)
6. Cuzzolin, F.: A geometric approach to the theory of evidence. IEEE Trans. Systems, Man, and Cyb. 38(4), 522–534 (2008)
7. Daniel, M.: Conflicts within and between belief functions. In: IPMU, pp. 696–705 (2010)
8. Dempster, A.: Upper and lower probabilities induced by a multivalued mapping. Annals of Mathematical Statistics 38, 325–339 (1967)
9. Destercke, S., Burger, T.: Toward an axiomatic definition of conflict between belief functions. IEEE Trans. Systems, Man, & Cyb (B) 43(2), 585–596 (2013)
10. Geoarge, T., Pal, N.R.: Quantification of conflict in dempster-shafer framework: A new approach. Int. J. Gen. Sys. 24(4), 407–423 (1996)
11. Jøsang, A., Pope, S.: Dempster's rule as seen by little colored balls. Computational Intelligence 28(4), 453–474 (2012)
12. Jousselme, A.L., Grenier, D., Bossé, É.: A new distance between two bodies of evidence. Information Fusion 2(2), 91–101 (2001)
13. Jousselme, A.L., Maupin, P.: On some properties of distances in evidence theory. In: BELIEF, Brest, France (2010)
14. Jousselme, A.L., Maupin, P.: Distances in evidence theory: Comprehensive survey and generalizations. Int. J. Approx. Reasoning 53(2), 118 (2012)
15. Ke, X., Ma, L., Wang, Y.: A dissimilarity measure based on singular value and its application in incremental discounting. In: Information Fusion, pp. 1391–1397. IEEE (2013)
16. Liu, W.: Analyzing the degree of conflict among belief functions. Artificial Intelligence 170(11), 909–924 (2006)
17. Martin, A.: About conflict in the theory of belief functions. In: Denœux, T., Masson, M.-H. (eds.) Belief Functions: Theory & Appl. AISC, vol. 164, pp. 161–168. Springer, Heidelberg (2012)
18. Martin, A., Jousselme, A.L., Osswald, C.: Conflict measure for the discounting operation on belief functions. In: 11th International Conference on Information Fusion, pp. 1–8 (2008)
19. Sarabi-Jamab, A., Araabi, B.N., Augustin, T.: Information-based dissimilarity assessment in dempster-shafer theory. Knowledge-Based Sys. 54, 114–127 (2013)
20. Schubert, J.: The internal conflict of a belief function. In: Clarke, E., Kozen, D. (eds.) Logic of Programs 1983. LNCS, vol. 164, pp. 169–177. Springer, Heidelberg (1984)
21. Smets, P.: Decision making in the tbm: the necessity of the pignistic transformation. Int. J. Approx. Reasoning 38(2), 133–147 (2005)
22. Yang, J., Bai, B., Jiang, X., Liu, S., Huang, H.Z., He, L.P.: A novel method for measuring the dissimilarity degree between two pieces of evidence in dempster-shafer evidence theory. In: QR2MSE, pp. 894–899 (2013)

Fast Computation of L^p Norm-Based Specialization Distances between Bodies of Evidence

Mehena Loudahi, John Klein, Jean-Marc Vannobel, and Olivier Colot

Lille1 University, LAGIS UMR CNRS 8219,
avenue Carl Gauss, cité scientifique, 59650 Villeneuve d'Ascq, France
{john.klein,mehena.loudahi,jean-marc.vannobel,
olivier.colot}@univ-lille1.fr
http://www.lagis.cnrs.fr

Abstract. In a recent paper [12], we introduced a new family of evidential distances in the framework of belief functions. Using specialization matrices as a representation of bodies of evidence, an evidential distance can be obtained by computing the norm of the difference of these matrices. Any matrix norm can be thus used to define a full metric. In particular, it has been shown that the L^1 norm-based specialization distance has nice properties. This distance takes into account the structure of focal elements and has a consistent behavior with respect to the conjunctive combination rule. However, if the frame of discernment on which the problem is defined has n elements, then a specialization matrix size is $2^n \times 2^n$. The straightforward formula for computing a specialization distance involves a matrix product which can be consequently highly time consuming. In this article, several faster computation methods are provided for L^p norm-based specialization distances. These methods are proposed for special kinds of mass functions as well as for the general case.

Keywords: evidence theory, Dempster-Shafer theory, distances, metrics

1 Introduction

The belief function theory, or evidence theory [6,16], is a formal framework for reasoning under uncertainty. In the past decades, a growing interest has been shown toward determining meaningful dissimilarity measures between bodies of evidence. These measures are used in belief function approximation computation [1,4,5,2], in belief functions clustering [15,8], in evidential data classification [19], in evidential sensor reliability assessment [9,18] or in estimation of some parameters feeding refined belief function combinations [7,13] or update processes [11]. All (dis)similarity measures attempt to describe the degree of (non-)alikeness between belief functions in a meaningful way for the widest range of applications. Indeed, the choice of a particular measure is most of the time application-dependent.

F. Cuzzolin (Ed.): BELIEF 2014, LNAI 8764, pp. 422–431, 2014.
© Springer International Publishing Switzerland 2014

A thorough survey about dissimilarity measures in the evidence theory and their properties was presented by Jousselme and Maupin [10]. The authors also provided generalizations of some distances thereby introducing families of new measures.

We introduced in [12] a new family of evidential distances based on specialization matrices as a representation of bodies of evidence. In particular, the L^1 norm-based specialization distance has unprecedented properties as compared to state-of-the-art approaches. Unfortunately, a straightforward implementation of specialization distances requires a rather large computation time. In this work, we provide several faster computation methods for L^p norm-based specialization distances. These methods allow a computation at least as fast as for usual evidential metrics.

The rest of this paper is organized as follows. Section 2 provides the preliminaries of evidence theory. In section 3, faster computation methods for the L^p norm are proposed for special kinds of mass functions as well as for the general case. Finally, we conclude the paper in section 4.

2   Belief Function Framework: Notations and Definitions

In this section, mathematical notations for classical belief function concepts are given. The reader is expected to be familiar with belief function basics and consequently some definitions are not recalled. More material on belief functions basics is found in [12]. A greater stress is given to a reminder on matrix calculus as part of the belief function framework and on some specialization distances.

2.1   Belief Function Basics

For a given body of evidence Ev_i, the corresponding **mass function** representing this piece of evidence is denoted by m_i. These functions are set-functions with respect to a **frame of discernment** denoted by Ω. The power set 2^Ω is the set of all subsets of Ω and it is the domain of mass functions. For any $A \in 2^\Omega$, the **cardinality** of this set is denoted by $|A|$ and $|\Omega| = n$. The cardinality of 2^Ω is denoted by $N = 2^n$. Mass functions have $[0, 1]$ as codomain and they sum to one. A **focal element** of a mass function m_i is a set $A \subseteq \Omega$ such that $m_i(A) > 0$. A function having only one focal element A is called **categorical mass** function and denoted by m_A.

The most widely used way to combine pieces of evidence is to apply the **conjunctive combination rule** to their corresponding mass functions. This rule is denoted by $\bigcirc\!\!\!\cap$. For two given mass functions m_1 and m_2, their conjunctive combination is denoted by $m_{1\bigcirc\!\!\!\cap 2} = m_1 \bigcirc\!\!\!\cap m_2$. The conjunctive rule is a generalization of evidential conditioning (or Dempster's conditioning) which is itself a generalization of Bayesian conditioning. Indeed when mass functions are replaced with probability distributions, then Bayes' theorem is retrieved. An updated mass function given A is denoted by $m(.|A) = m \bigcirc\!\!\!\cap m_A$. The conjunctive rule can be applied if all sources of information providing pieces of evidence are fully reliable in the sense that the pieces of evidence they provide are true.

2.2   Belief Functions and Matrix Calculus

Mass functions can be viewed as vectors belonging to a vector space spanned by categorical mass functions. Since mass functions sum to one, the set of mass functions is the simplex of that vector space. In this paper, the following notations and conventions are used :

- Vectors are written in bold small letters and matrices in bold capital letters.
- Vectors are column vectors and their length is N. The ith element of a mass function vector $\mathbf{m}$ is such that $\mathbf{m}_i = m(A)$ with i the index of set A according to the binary order. The binary order [17] is a common way to index elements of 2^{Ω} without supposing any order on Ω.
- Matrices are square and their size is $N \times N$. A matrix can be represented by $\mathbf{X} = [X_{ij}]$, or alternatively by the notation $\mathbf{X} = [X(A, B)]$, $\forall A, B \in \Omega$. The row and column indexes i and j are those corresponding to the subsets A and B using the binary order.

Matrix calculus as part of the BFT is especially interesting when it comes to conjunctive combination computation. Indeed, from Smets [17], one has:

$$\mathbf{m}_{1 \cap 2} = \mathbf{M}^{-1} \text{diag}\left(\mathbf{M}\mathbf{m}_1\right) \mathbf{M}\mathbf{m}_2, \tag{1}$$

with diag the operator turning a vector into a diagonal matrix and $\mathbf{M}$ a matrix such that $M(A, B) = 1$ if $A \subseteq B$ and $M(A, B) = 0$ otherwise. Note that this matrix can be computed using n iterations of the following recurrence:

$$\mathbf{M}^{(i+1)} = \begin{bmatrix} 1 & 1 \\ 0 & 1 \end{bmatrix} \otimes \mathbf{M}^{(i)}, \tag{2}$$

with $\otimes$ the Kronecker matrix product and $\mathbf{M}^{(0)} = [1]$. Furthermore, the matrix $\mathbf{S}_1$ such that $\mathbf{S}_1\mathbf{m}_2 = \mathbf{m}_{1 \cap 2}$ is called the Dempsterian specialization matrix of m_1. This matrix thus writes:

$$\mathbf{S}_1 = \mathbf{M}^{-1} \text{diag}\left(\mathbf{M}\mathbf{m}_1\right) \mathbf{M}. \tag{3}$$

Each element of $\mathbf{S}_1$ represents actually the mass assigned to a set A after conditioning on B: $S_1(A, B) = m_1(A|B)$. In other words, $\mathbf{S}_1$ does not only represent the current state of belief depicted by m_1 but also all reachable states from m_1 through conditioning. From a geometric point of view [3], a specialization matrix contains the vertices the conditional subspace associated with the function m. Specialization matrices are consequently relevant candidates for assessing dissimilarities between bodies of evidence in consistence with evidential conditioning and the conjunctive combination rule.

2.3   Specialization Distances

The most natural way to design distances between specialization matrices is to rely on a given matrix norm $\| \cdot \|_x$. Indeed, suppose two bodies of evidence[1]

---

[1] For the sake of clarity, the distinction between a body of evidence and its corresponding mass function is omitted in equations.

represented respectively by m_1 and m_2, then the following function d_{Sx} is a normalized full metric:

$$d_{Sx}(m_1, m_2) = \frac{1}{\rho} \parallel \mathbf{S_1} - \mathbf{S_2} \parallel_x \tag{4}$$

with $\rho = \max_{m_i, m_j} \parallel \mathbf{S_i} - \mathbf{S_j} \parallel_x$ a normalization coefficient. Such distances are called **specialization distances**.

In this article, we focus on specialization distances relying on the L^p matrix norms. These distances are denoted by d_p. For these distances, the normalization coefficient is known in closed form: $\rho = (2\,(2^n - 1))^{\frac{1}{p}}$. Choosing L^p norm-based specialization distances is justified by the fact that, in particular, the distance d_1 has interesting properties [12]. It takes into account the interactions[2] between focal elements (structural property) and two mass functions are necessarily closer after conjunctive combination with addionnal evidence (conjunctive consistency property).

The straightforward computation of distances d_p is given by:

$$d_p(m_1, m_2) = \frac{1}{\rho} \parallel \mathbf{M}^{-1} \mathrm{diag}\left(\mathbf{M}\left(\mathbf{m}_1 - \mathbf{m}_2\right)\right) \mathbf{M} \parallel_p . \tag{5}$$

Unfortunately, equation (5) involves a matrix product. Its complexity is thus $O(N^3)$. Such a complexity can be prohibitive for many application contexts and appears to be greater than the complexity of other evidential distances. Consequently, faster ways to compute distances L^p are investigated in the next section.

3 Faster Computation of L^p Norm-Based Specialization Distances

In this section, new computation methods are introduced for L^p norm-based specialization distances. First, some results are given for special cases of mass functions and in the last subsection, an algorithm is provided for the general case.

3.1 Distances between Categorical Mass Functions

A fast way to compute L^p norm-based specialization distances between categorical mass functions is already given in [12]. Indeed, it is proved in this article that there exists an bijective link between the Hamming set distance and distances d_p restricted to categorical mass functions. More precisely, one has:

$$d_p\left(m_A, m_B\right) = \left(\frac{N - 2^{n - |A \Delta B|}}{N - 1}\right)^{\frac{1}{p}}, \tag{6}$$

---

[2] For instance, focal elements may have a non-empty intersection.

with Δ the set symmetric difference. The cardinality of the set symmetric difference is the Hamming set distance.

The interest of equation (6) is twofold: first the computation for such distances is now just $O\left(1\right)$, and second, it also sheds light on the fact that there is an order isomorphism between the Hamming set distance and the specialization distance. This latter property is extremely important for evidential distances as it proves that the distance abides by the structural principle stated in [10].

3.2   Distances between A Categorical Mass Function and any Mass Function

In this subsection, a broader case is investigated: computation of distances d_p between a categorical mass function and any mass function. We provide a result only for the L^1 norm-based specialization distance d_1:

Proposition 1. *Suppose m is a mass function on a frame Ω. Suppose $A \subseteq \Omega$ and m_A is its corresponding categorical mass function. The specialization matrix of m is denoted by $\mathbf{S}$ and that of m_A by $\mathbf{S_A}$. One has:*

$$d_1\left(m, m_A\right) = \frac{N - \| \mathbf{S} \circ \mathbf{S_A} \|_1}{N-1}, \tag{7}$$

$$= \frac{N - tr\left(\mathbf{S}\,{}^t\mathbf{S}_A\right)}{N-1}, \tag{8}$$

with $\circ$ the Hadamard matrix product[3], tr the matrix trace operator and ${}^t\mathbf{S}_A$ the transpose matrix of $\mathbf{S}_A$.

Proof. By definition of the L^1 norm, one has :

$$\| \mathbf{S} - \mathbf{S_A} \|_1 = \sum_{X,Y \subseteq \Omega} |S(X,Y) - S_A(X,Y)|.$$

It is known that $S_A(X,Y) = 1$ if $A \cap Y = X$ and $S_A(X,Y) = 0$ otherwise, which gives:

$$\| \mathbf{S} - \mathbf{S_A} \|_1 = \sum_{\substack{X,Y \subseteq \Omega \\ X = A \cap Y}} (1 - S(X,Y)) + \sum_{\substack{X,Y \subseteq \Omega \\ X \neq A \cap Y}} S(X,Y),$$

$$= \sum_{\substack{X,Y \subseteq \Omega \\ X = A \cap Y}} 1 + \sum_{\substack{X,Y \subseteq \Omega \\ X \neq A \cap Y}} S(X,Y) - \sum_{\substack{X,Y \subseteq \Omega \\ X = A \cap Y}} S(X,Y),$$

$$= \| \mathbf{S_A} \|_1 + \sum_{X,Y \subseteq \Omega} S(X,Y) - 2 \sum_{\substack{X,Y \subseteq \Omega \\ X = A \cap Y}} S(X,Y),$$

$$= \| \mathbf{S_A} \|_1 + \| \mathbf{S} \|_1 - 2 \| \mathbf{S} \circ \mathbf{S_A} \|_1 .$$

---

[3] The Hadamard matrix product is the entrywise product or Schur product. Let $\mathbf{X}$, $\mathbf{Y}$ and $\mathbf{Z}$ be three matrices such that $\mathbf{X} \circ \mathbf{Y} = \mathbf{Z}$, then we have $Z_{ij} = X_{ij}Y_{ij}$, $\forall i$ and j.

Since the L^1 norm of any specialization matrix is N, and remembering that $\rho = 2N - 2$ when $p = 1$, equation (7) is retrieved:

$$\| \mathbf{S} - \mathbf{S_A} \|_1 = 2N + 2 \| \mathbf{S} \circ \mathbf{S_A} \|_1,$$

$$\Leftrightarrow d_1 \left(m, m_A \right) = \frac{N - \| \mathbf{S} \circ \mathbf{S_A} \|_1}{N - 1}.$$

Equation (8) is obtained from equation (7) using a classical algebra result.   □

In terms of computation time, equation (7) should be preferred. Specialization matrices have 3^n non-null elements. The Hadamard product can be restricted to the entrywise product of these non-null elements. The complexity of equation (7) is thus:

$$O\left(3^n\right) = O\left(N^{\frac{\log(3)}{\log(2)}}\right),$$

$$\approx O\left(N^{1.58}\right).$$

3.3   Distances between any Mass Functions

We now address the d_p distance computation problem in the general case. An algorithm for optimizing this computation will be introduced. This algorithm relies on the following result:

Proposition 2. *Suppose m is a mass function on a frame Ω. Suppose $X \subseteq Y \subseteq \Omega$ and let $z \notin Y$. The following result holds:*

$$m\left(X|Y\right) = m\left(X|Y \cup \{z\}\right) + m\left(X \cup \{z\}\,|Y \cup \{z\}\right). \tag{9}$$

Proof. By definition of evidential conditioning, one has:

$$m\left(X|Y\right) = \sum_{\substack{A \subseteq \Omega \\ A \cap Y = X}} m(A) = \sum_{\substack{A \subseteq \Omega \\ A \cap Y = X, z \in A}} m(A) + \sum_{\substack{A \subseteq \Omega \\ A \cap Y = X, z \notin A}} m(A). \tag{10}$$

Let us deal with the first term in equation (10). We need to prove that $A \cap Y = X$ and $z \in A$ if and only if $A \cap (Y \cup \{z\}) = X \cup \{z\}$. Let us prove first that $A \cap Y = X$ and $z \in A$ implies $A \cap (Y \cup \{z\}) = X \cup \{z\}$. If $z \in A$ then

$$A \cap (Y \cup \{z\}) = (A \cap Y) \cup (A \cap \{z\}\,) = A \cap Y \cup \{z\}.$$

In addition if $A \cap Y = X$, we obtain:

$$A \cap (Y \cup \{z\}) = X \cup \{z\}.$$

Reciprocally, let us now prove that $A \cap (Y \cup \{z\}) = X \cup \{z\}$ implies $A \cap Y = X$ and $z \in A$. Suppose that $X \cup \{z\} = A \cap (Y \cup \{z\}) = (A \cap Y) \cup (A \cap \{z\}\,)$. Since $z \notin Y$, $z \notin A \cap Y$, hence $z \in A \cap \{z\}$, which implies $z \in A$.

In addition, we also have $X \cup \{z\} = (A \cap Y) \cup \{z\}$. Since $z \notin Y$, then $(A \cap Y) \cup \{z\} \setminus \{z\} = A \cap Y$. Again, since $z \notin Y$, then $z \notin X$ and therefore $X \cup \{z\} \setminus \{z\} = X = A \cap Y$. From the above reasoning, we deduce:

$$\sum_{\substack{A \subseteq \Omega \\ A \cap Y = X, z \in A}} m(A) = \sum_{\substack{A \subseteq \Omega \\ A \cap (Y \cup \{z\}) = X \cup \{z\}}} m(A) = m\left(X \cup \{z\} \mid Y \cup \{z\}\right).$$

Let us now deal with the remaining term in equation (10). We need to prove that $A \cap Y = X$ and $z \notin A$ if and only if $A \cap (Y \cup \{z\}) = X$. Let us prove first that $A \cap Y = X$ and $z \in A$ implies $A \cap (Y \cup \{z\}) = X$. Suppose $z \notin A$ and $A \cap Y = X$. One can write:

$$A \cap (Y \cup \{z\}) = (A \cap Y) \cup (A \cap \{z\}),$$
$$= A \cap Y \cup \emptyset,$$
$$= X. \tag{11}$$

Reciprocally, let us prove that $A \cap (Y \cup \{z\}) = X$ implies $A \cap Y = X$ and $z \notin A$. Suppose that $X = A \cap (Y \cup \{z\}) = (A \cap Y) \cup (A \cap \{z\})$. Since $z \notin Y$, then $z \notin X$. We thus have $z \notin A \cap \{z\}$, which implies $z \notin A$. In addition, this leads to $X = A \cap Y \cup \emptyset = A \cap Y$. From this reasoning, we deduce:

$$\sum_{\substack{A \subseteq \Omega \\ A \cap Y = X, z \notin A}} m(A) = \sum_{\substack{A \subseteq \Omega \\ A \cap (Y \cup \{z\}) = X}} m(A) = m\left(X \mid Y \cup \{z\}\right). \qquad \square$$

Proposition 2 is especially interesting when it comes to specialization matrix computation as it shows that any element of the matrix can be obtained by adding two other elements belonging to a right-hand column and lower lines. Since the last column vector is equal to $\mathbf{m}$, this matrix can be built incrementally starting from the column with index $N - 1$ down to the first column. In each column, we start with the lowest element up to the top one. This procedure is given by algorithm 1.

This fast specialization matrix computation algorithm can be directly used with $m_1 - m_2$ as entry in order to obtain the matrix difference $\mathbf{S_1} - \mathbf{S_2}$. This algorithm can also compute recursively distance d_p by updating its value each time a new element $S_1(X, Y) - S_2(X, Y)$ is obtained. Given the definition of matrix $\mathbf{M}$, there are 3^n loops in algorithm 1. Similarly to the previous subsection, the distance d_p computation complexity for any mass functions is thus $O\left(N^{1.58}\right)$. Figure 1 illustrates the computation time ease induced by algorithm 1 as compared to the computation time when using equation (5). These results were obtained using a laptop with an Intel® centrino2 2.53 GHz CPU and GNU Octave© programming environment. It can be seen that the log-ratio of computation times is linear with respect to n which is compliant with the claim that the complexity dropped from $O\left(N^3\right)$ to $O\left(N^{1.58}\right)$.

Concerning distance computation, it should also be noted that algorithm 1 does not only improve the time-complexity but also the memory occupation.

Algorithm 1. Fast computation of a specialization matrix **S**

entries : m, N, **M**.
S $\leftarrow$ **0**, the null matrix.
for $X \subseteq \Omega$ **do**
   $S(X, \Omega) \leftarrow m(X)$
end for
for $Y \subsetneq \Omega$ (following the decreasing binary order) **do**
   for $X \subseteq Y$ (following the decreasing binary order) **do**
      if $M(X, Y) > 0$ **then**
         choose $z \in \bar{Y}$.
         $S(X, Y) \leftarrow S(X, Y \cup \{z\}) + S(X \cup \{z\}, Y \cup \{z\})$.
      end if
   end for
end for
return **S**.
End

Indeed, it is unnecessary to store the whole matrix $\mathbf{S}_1 - \mathbf{S}_2$ when computing a specialization distance because some colums will never be used again and one can anticipate that.

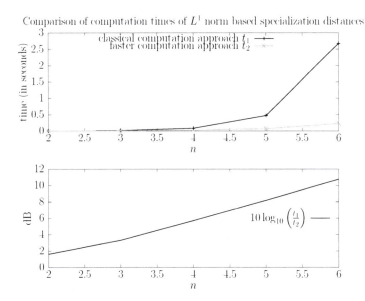

Fig. 1. Comparison of computation times using the classical approach (equation (5)) and using our faster approach (algorithm 1).

Most of state-of-the-art evidential metrics[4], such as Jousselme distance, resort to a product between a matrix and a mass function vector. Their complexity

---

[4] Perry and Stephanou [14] introduced a full metric with $O(N)$ complexity but it fails to grasp structural mass function aspects (see [10]).

is thus $O\left(N^2\right)$ (using naive programming). Consequently, we have succeeded in making the L^p norm-based specialization distances at least as attractive as other evidential metrics in terms of computation time.

4   Conclusion

In this article, several methods for a faster computation of L^p norm-based specialization distances are introduced. Initially, such distances are computed in $O\left(N^3\right)$ with N the size of the power set of the frame of discernment. We provide an algorithmic way to reduce this complexity to $O\left(N^{1.58}\right)$ in the general case. In case of categorical mass functions, the complexity is just $O\left(1\right)$.

Using these approaches, L^p norm-based specialization distances become usable tools for several potential applications. In particular, we plan to tackle mass function approximation problems using specialization distance minimization. The hope is that the one-of-a-kind properties of such distances will help resolving approximation problems more efficiently.

References

1. Bauer, M.: Approximation algorithms and decision making in the Dempster- Shafer theory of evidence — an empirical study. International Journal of Approximate Reasoning 17(2-3), 217–237 (1997)
2. Cuzzolin, F.: l_p consonant approximations of belief functions. IEEE Transactions on Fuzzy Systems 22(2), 420–436 (2014)
3. Cuzzolin, F.: Geometry of Dempster's rule of combination. IEEE Transactions on Systems, Man, and Cybernetics. Part B: Cybernetics 34(2), 961–977 (2004)
4. Cuzzolin, F.: Geometric conditioning of belief functions. In: Proceedings of BELIEF 2010, International Workshop on the Theory of Belief Functions, Brest, France, pp. 1–6 (2010)
5. Cuzzolin, F.: On consistent approximations of belief functions in the mass space. In: Liu, W. (ed.) ECSQARU 2011. LNCS, vol. 6717, pp. 287–298. Springer, Heidelberg (2011)
6. Dempster, A.: Upper and lower probabilities induced by a multiple valued mapping. Annals of Mathematical Satistics 38, 325–339 (1967)
7. Denœux, T.: Conjunctive and disjunctive combination of belief functions induced by nondistinct bodies of evidence. Artificial Intelligence 172, 234–264 (2008)
8. Denœux, T., Masson, M.H.: EVCLUS: Evidential clustering of proximity data. IEEE Transactions on Systems, Man and Cybernetics, Part B: Cybernetics 34(1), 95–109 (2004)
9. Elouedi, Z., Mellouli, K., Smets, P.: Assessing sensor reliability for multisensor data fusion within the transferable belief model. IEEE Transactions on Systems, Man, and Cybernetics. Part B: Cybernetics 34(1), 782–787 (2004)
10. Jousselme, A.-L., Maupin, P.: Distances in evidence theory: Comprehensive survey and generalizations. International Journal of Approximate Reasoning 53, 118–145 (2012)
11. Klein, J., Colot, O.: Automatic discounting rate computation using a dissent criterion. In: Proceedings of BELIEF 2010, International Workshop on the Theory of Belief Functions, Brest, France, pp. 1–6 (2010)

12. Loudahi, M., Klein, J., Vannobel, J.M., Colot, O.: New distances between bodies of evidence based on dempsterian specialization matrices and their consistency with the conjunctive combination rule. International Journal of Approximate Reasoning 55, 1093–1112 (2014)
13. Mercier, D., Quost, B., Denœux, T.: Refined modeling of sensor reliability in the belief function framework using contextual discounting. Information Fusion 9, 246–258 (2008)
14. Perry, W., Stephanou, H.: Belief function divergence as a classifier. In: Proceedings of the 1991 IEEE International Symposium on Intelligent Control, pp. 280–285 (August 1991)
15. Schubert, J.: Clustering decomposed belief functions using generalized weights of conflict. International Journal of Approximate Reasoning 48, 466–480 (2008)
16. Shafer, G.: A mathematical theory of evidence. Princeton University Press (1976)
17. Smets, P.: The application of the matrix calculus to belief functions. International Journal of Approximate Reasoning 31, 1–30 (2002)
18. Sunberg, Z., Rogers, J.: A belief function distance metric for orderable sets. Information Fusion 14, 361–373 (2013)
19. Zouhal, L.M., Denœux, T.: An evidence-theoretic k-nn rule with parameter optimisation. IEEE Transactions on Systems, Man and Cybernetics. Part C: Application and reviews 28(2), 263–271 (1998)

New Distance Measures of Evidence Based on Belief Intervals

Deqiang Han[1], Jean Dezert[2], and Yi Yang[3]

[1] Center for Information Engineering Science Research, Xi'an Jiaotong University, No. 28 West XianNing Road, Xi'an, China 710049
deqhan@gmail.com
[2] The French Aerospace Lab, Chemin de la Hunière, F-91761 Palaiseau, France
jean.dezert@onera.fr
[3] SKLSVMS, School of Aerospace, Xi'an Jiaotong University, No. 28 West XianNing Road, Xi'an, China 710049
jiafeiyy@mail.xjtu.edu.cn

Abstract. A distance or dissimilarity of evidence represents the degree of dissimilarity between bodies of evidence, which has been widely used in the applications based on belief functions theory. In this paper, new distance measures are proposed based on belief intervals $[Bel, Pl]$. For a basic belief assignment (BBA), the belief intervals of different focal elements are first calculated, respectively, which can be considered as interval numbers. Then, according to the distance of interval numbers, we can calculate the distance values between the corresponding belief intervals of the same focal elements in two given BBAs. Based on these distance values of belief intervals, new distance measures of evidence can be obtained using Euclidean and Chebyshev approaches, respectively. Some experiments and related analyses are provided to show the rationality and efficiency of the proposed measures.

Keywords: distance of evidence, dissimilarity, belief function theory, evidence theory.

1 Introduction

The theory of belief functions [1], also called Dempster-Shafer evidence theory (DST), proposes a mathematical model to represent sources of evidences and to deal with uncertainty reasoning. DST has been used with some success in different civilian and military applications, especially in information fusion, pattern recognition and decision making. However, some limitations and flaws have been put in light by different researchers, see for example [2,3], and references therein. With the development of DST, some refined or extended evidence theories have emerged, e.g., the transferable belief model (TBM) [4] and DSmT [5].

A distance or dissimilarity measure of evidence [6] can describe the degree of dissimilarity or similarity between bodies of evidence (BOEs), which has attracted more and more research interest recently and has been widely used in

F. Cuzzolin (Ed.): BELIEF 2014, LNAI 8764, pp. 432–441, 2014.

applications such as algorithm evaluation [7,8] or optimization, clustering analysis, etc. Among the different measures proposed in the literature, Jousselme's
distance of evidence [9] and Tessem's distance [10] (also called the betting commitment distance or the pignistic probability distance) are most frequently used.
The conflict coefficient in Dempster's rule can also be considered as a generalized
dissimilarity (not so strict). In our previous work [11], we have also proposed the
dissimilarity of evidence based on fuzzy sets theory. Most available definitions
on distance or dissimilarity measures of evidence can be found in an excellent
and detailed survey [6].

In this paper, we propose new ways to define distances of evidence. For each
piece of evidence, we calculate the belief interval of each focal element, respectively. Then, a basic belief assignment (BBA) is represented by a set of belief
intervals, which can also be considered as a set of interval numbers or data. For
two different BBAs, we calculate the distance between their corresponding focal
element's belief intervals using the distance of interval numbers [12]. Based on
the interval distance values corresponding to different focal elements, we propose
an Euclidean-family distance based on sum of squares, and a Chebyshev-family
distance based on the maximum selection, respectively. Actually, the distance
between BBAs is represented by the combination or selection of the distance
values between belief intervals corresponding to different focal elements. Some
experiments and related analyses are provided to show the effectiveness and
rationality of these new distances of evidence.

2   Basics of Belief Function Theory

In Dempster-Shafer evidence theory (DST) [1], the elements in frame of discernment (FOD) Θ are mutually exclusive and exhaustive. Define $m : 2^{\Theta} \to [0,1]$ as
a basic belief assignment (BBA, also called mass function) which satisfies:

$$\sum_{A \subseteq \Theta} m(A) = 1, \quad m(\emptyset) = 0 \tag{1}$$

When $m(A) > 0$, A is called a focal element. The belief function and plausibility
function are defined respectively as follows.

$$Bel(A) = \sum_{B \subseteq A} m(B); \quad Pl(A) = \sum_{A \cap B \neq \emptyset} m(B) \tag{2}$$

The belief interval $[Bel(A), Pl(A)]$ represents the imprecision or uncertainty degree of the proposition or focal element A.

Dempster's rule of combination is as follows. $\forall A \in 2^{\Theta}$:

$$m(A) = \begin{cases} 0, & \text{if} \quad A = \emptyset \\ \frac{\sum_{A_i \cap B_j = A} m_1(A_i) m_2(B_j)}{1-K}, & \text{if} \quad A \neq \emptyset \end{cases} \tag{3}$$

where

$$K = \sum_{A_i \cap B_j = \emptyset} m_1(A_i) m_2(B_j) \tag{4}$$

is the conflict coefficient representing the total degree of conflict between evidence sources. It is widely accepted that the combination should better not be
normalized. Many alternative rules were proposed to redistribute the conflict [5].

3 Traditional Distances of Evidence

A distance or dissimilarity between BBAs can represent the degree of dissimilarity between different BOEs. As we can find in [6], there are various types of distance or dissimilarity definitions in evidence theory. Some are defined by directly using the BBAs under the framework of geometrical interpretation of evidence theory [13]. Jousselme's distance d_J is a representative one [9].

1) Jousselme's Distance

$$d_J(m_1, m_2) = \sqrt{0.5 \cdot (m_1 - m_2)^T \mathbf{Jac}\,(m_1 - m_2)} \tag{5}$$

where the elements $Jac(A, B)$ of Jaccard's weighting matrix **Jac** are defined as

$$\mathbf{Jac}(A, B) = |A \cap B|/|A \cup B| \tag{6}$$

Jousselme's distance is in fact an L_2 Euclidean distance with weighting matrix **Jac**. It has been proved to be a strict distance metric in [14]; however, it might cause some unreasonable results in some cases as shown in Exmaples 2 and 3 listed in section 5 of this paper.

Some other distances are defined using a transformation of BBAs at first, e.g., Tessem's distance and the fuzzy membership function (FMF)-based dissimilarity.

2) Tessem's Betting Commitment Distance

The pignistic probability corresponding to a BBA $m(\cdot)$ is defined by [4]

$$\text{BetP}_m(A) = \sum_{B \subseteq \Theta} \frac{|A \cap B|}{|B|} m(B) \tag{7}$$

The betting commitment distance (or Tessem's distance) d_T is computed by [10]

$$d_T(m_1, m_2) = \max_{A \subseteq \Theta} \{|\text{BetP}_1(A) - \text{BetP}_2(A)|\} \tag{8}$$

d_T is a Chebyshev L_∞ alike distance. It is actually not a strict distance metric [15].

3) FMF-Based Dissimilarity

First transform BBAs $m_1(\cdot)$ and $m_2(\cdot)$ into FMFs: $\mu^{(1)}$ and $\mu^{(2)}$ as for $i = 1, 2$

$$\mu^{(i)} = \left[\mu^{(i)}(\theta_1), \mu^{(i)}(\theta_2), \cdots \mu^{(i)}(\theta_n)\right] = \left[Pl^{(i)}(\theta_1), Pl^{(i)}(\theta_2), \cdots, Pl^{(i)}(\theta_n)\right] \tag{9}$$

According to the dissimilarity definition between FMFs, d_F is defined as [11]

$$d_F(m_1, m_2) = 1 - \frac{\sum_{i=1}^{n} (\mu^{(1)}(\theta_i) \wedge \mu^{(2)}(\theta_i))}{\sum_{i=1}^{n} (\mu^{(1)}(\theta_i) \vee \mu^{(2)}(\theta_i))} \tag{10}$$

In (10), the operator $\wedge$ represents conjunction (min) and $\vee$ represents the disjunction (max). d_F in fact indirectly represents the dissimilarity between two BBAs using the dissimilarity between their corresponding FMFs.

Since the available definitions have some limitations, we attempt to propose new distances of evidence with desired properties, which are based on the distances between belief intervals as described in the next section.

4 Distance of Evidence Using Belief Intervals

Suppose that two BBAs $m_1(\cdot)$ and $m_2(\cdot)$ are defined on $\Theta = \{\theta_1, \theta_2, ..., \theta_n\}$. For each focal element $A_i \subseteq \Theta$ $(i = 1, ..., 2^n - 1)$, we can calculate belief intervals of A_i for $m_1(\cdot)$ and $m_2(\cdot)$, respectively, which are denoted by $[Bel_1(A_i), Pl_1(A_i)]$ and $[Bel_2(A_i), Pl_2(A_i)]$. A belief interval is nothing but a classical interval number included in $[0, 1]$. The strict distance between interval numbers $[a_1, b_1]$ and $[a_2, b_2]$ $(b_i \geq a_i, i = 1, 2)$ is defined[1] by [12]

$$d^I([a_1, b_1], [a_2, b_2]) = \sqrt{\left[\frac{a_1 + b_1}{2} - \frac{a_2 + b_2}{2}\right]^2 + \frac{1}{3}\left[\frac{b_1 - a_1}{2} - \frac{b_2 - a_2}{2}\right]^2} \tag{11}$$

Therefore, we can calculate the distance between $BI_1(A_i) : [Bel_1(A_i), Pl_1(A_i)]$ and $BI_2(A_i) : [Bel_2(A_i), Pl_2(A_i)]$ according to Eq. (11). $d^I(BI_1(A_i), BI_2(A_i))$ can be regarded as the dissimilarity between $m_1(\cdot)$ and $m_2(\cdot)$ when considering the focal element A_i. We can obtain totally $2^n - 1$ belief interval distance values for all $A_i \subseteq \Theta$. Using all the $2^n - 1$ distance values, we propose two different distances of evidence based on two commonly used distance types [6], i.e., the Euclidean family and the Chebyshev family.

1) Euclidean-family Belief Interval-Based Distance d_{BI}^E

$$d_{BI}^E(m_1, m_2) = \sqrt{N_c \cdot \sum_{i=1}^{2^n - 1} [d^I(BI_1(A_i), BI_2(A_i))]^2} \tag{12}$$

Here $N_c = 1/2^{n-1}$ is the normalization factor. Eq. (12) can be re-written as

$$d_{BI}^E(m_1, m_2) = \sqrt{N_c \cdot \mathbf{d}_I \cdot \mathbf{I}^{(2^n - 1)} \cdot \mathbf{d}_I^T} = \sqrt{N_c \cdot \mathbf{d}_I \cdot \mathbf{d}_I^T} \tag{13}$$

where T denotes transpose, $\mathbf{I}^{(2^n - 1)}$ is an identity matrix with rank $2^n - 1$, and $\mathbf{d}_I = [d^I(BI_1(A_1), BI_2(A_1)), \cdots, d^I(BI_1(A_{2^n - 1}), BI_2(A_{2^n - 1}))]$. The proof for the normalization factor N_c is as follows.

Proof. Suppose that the FOD is $\{\theta_1, \theta_2, ..., \theta_n\}$. $m_1(\cdot)$ and $m_2(\cdot)$ are two BOEs. The maximum distance value is reached when

$$m_1(\{\theta_i\}) = 1, m_2(\{\theta_j\}) = 1, \forall i \neq j. \tag{14}$$

When the focal element $|A| = 1$, there are only two belief intervals with distance value d^I of 1 (i.e., $d^I(BI_1(\theta_i), BI_2(\theta_i)) = 1$ and $d^I(BI_1(\theta_j), BI_2(\theta_j)) = 1$). The other values are 0.

When the focal element $|A| > 1$, d^I values of those focal elements including θ_i or θ_j (but not both including θ_i and θ_j) are 1. The other values are 0.

---

[1] It corresponds to Mallows' distance between two distributions when we assume that each interval is the support of a uniform distribution. It should be noted that there are also other types of distance between interval numbers [12]. We use the definition in (11), because it is a strict distance metric, which is very crucial for defining distances of evidence.

To be specific,

when $|A| = 2$, d^I values of $2 \times C_{n-2}^1$ focal elements are 1; [2]

when $|A| = 3$, d^I values of $2 \times C_{n-2}^2$ focal elements are 1;

$\vdots$

when $|A| = n - 1$, d^I values of $2 \times C_{n-2}^{n-2}$ focal elements are 1;

when $|A| = n$, the d^I value of unique focal element, i.e., total set (Θ) is 0.

So, the summation S_c of all the $(d^I)^2$ value is

$$\begin{aligned} S_c &= 2 \times 1 + 2 \times C_{n-2}^1 + 2 \times C_{n-2}^2 + \dots + 2 \times C_{n-2}^{n-2} + 0 \\ &= 2 \times (C_{n-2}^0 + C_{n-2}^1 + C_{n-2}^2 + \dots + C_{n-2}^{n-2}) \\ &= 2 \times 2^{n-2} \\ &= 2^{n-1} \end{aligned} \tag{15}$$

So, the normalization factor $N_c = 1/S_c = 1/2^{n-1}$ □

2) Chebyshev-family Belief Interval-based Distance d_{BI}^C

$$d_{BI}^C (m_1, m_2) = \max_{A_i \subseteq \Theta, i = 1, \dots, 2^n - 1} \left\{ d^I \left(BI_1(A_i), BI_2(A_i) \right) \right\} \tag{16}$$

Actually, we use the distance of belief intervals for focal elements instead of their mass assignments to define the distances of evidence when compared with the traditional definitions. A strict distance metric defined on the set ε $d : \varepsilon \times \varepsilon \to \Re$, $(x, y) \mapsto d(x, y)$ should satisfy that [9]

1) Nonnegativity: $d(x, y) \geq 0$;

2) Nondegeneracy: $d(x, y) = 0 \Leftrightarrow x = y$;

3) Symmetry: $d(x, y) = d(y, x)$;

4) Triangle inequality: $d(x, y) + d(y, z) \geq d(x, z), \forall z \in \varepsilon$.

It can be proved that our new definitions are strict distance metric. The proof is as follows.

Proof. d_{BI}^E and d_{BI}^C are defined over belief intervals. Given a BBA $(m(A_i), i = 1, \dots, 2^n - 1)$, we can generate a set of belief intervals $([Bel(A_i), Pl(A_i)])$. On the other hand, given a set of belief intervals $([Bel(A_i), Pl(A_i)])$, according to the Möbius transformation [1], we can generate a unique BBA $(m(A_i), i = 1, \dots, 2^n - 1)$ from $Pl(A_i), i = 1, \dots, 2^n - 1$ or $Bel(A_i), i = 1, \dots, 2^n - 1$. So, there is a one-to-one mapping between a set of belief intervals $([Bel(A_i), Pl(A_i)])$ and a BBA $(m(A_i), i = 1, \dots, 2^n - 1)$.

According to the Eq. (12-13, 16), it is easy to find that d_{BI}^E and d_{BI}^C satisfy nonnegativity, nondegeneracy and symmetry of are satisfied. Then we prove the property of triangle inequality of d_{BI}^E.

---

[2] Choose 1 element θ_k out of the $\Theta' = \Theta - \{\theta_i, \theta_j\}(|\Theta'| = n - 2)$. Then, together with θ_i and θ_j, respectively, to constitute focal element $\{\theta_k, \theta_i\}$ and $\{\theta_k, \theta_j\}$, respectively. So, the number of focal elements with d^I values of 1 is $2 \times C_{n-2}^1$ It is same way to obtain the values in other cases for $A > 1$.

Suppose that there are 3 BBAs $m_1(\cdot), m_2(\cdot), m_3(\cdot)$ defined over the same FOD with size of n. Because d^I defined in Eq. (11) is a strict distance metric [12], so, for each A_i ($i = 1, ..., s, s = 2^n - 1$) there exists
$$d_{BI}^E(m_1(A_i), m_2(A_i)) + d_{BI}^E(m_2(A_i), m_3(A_i)) \geq d_{BI}^E(m_1(A_i), m_3(A_i)).$$
Suppose that
$$d_{BI}^E(m_1(A_i), m_2(A_i)) = a_i; \quad d_{BI}^E(m_2(A_i), m_3(A_i)) = b_i;$$
$$d_{BI}^E(m_1(A_i), m_3(A_i)) = c_i.$$
There exists
$$\begin{aligned}
& a_i + b_i \geq c_i \\
\Rightarrow & (a_i + b_i)^2 \geq c_i^2 \\
\Rightarrow & a_i^2 + b_i^2 + 2a_i b_i \geq c_i^2 \\
\Rightarrow & \sum_{i=1}^{s} a_i^2 + \sum_{i=1}^{s} b_i^2 + 2\sum_{i=1}^{s} a_i b_i \geq \sum_{i=1}^{s} c_i^2
\end{aligned} \tag{17}$$

According to the famous Cauchy-Schwarz inequality, there exists
$$\sqrt{\sum_{i=1}^{s} a_i^2 \sum_{i=1}^{s} b_i^2} \geq \sum_{i=1}^{s} a_i b_i \tag{18}$$

So,
$$\begin{aligned}
& \sum_{i=1}^{s} a_i^2 + \sum_{i=1}^{s} b_i^2 + 2\sqrt{\sum_{i=1}^{s} a_i^2 \sum_{i=1}^{s} b_i^2} \geq \sum_{i=1}^{s} a_i^2 + \sum_{i=1}^{s} b_i^2 + 2\sum_{i=1}^{s} a_i b_i \geq \sum_{i=1}^{s} c_i^2 \\
\Rightarrow & \sum_{i=1}^{s} a_i^2 + \sum_{i=1}^{s} b_i^2 + 2\sqrt{\sum_{i=1}^{s} a_i^2 \sum_{i=1}^{s} b_i^2} \geq \sum_{i=1}^{s} c_i^2
\end{aligned} \tag{19}$$

Then we have
$$\begin{aligned}
& \sum_{i=1}^{s} a_i^2 + \sum_{i=1}^{s} b_i^2 + 2\sqrt{\sum_{i=1}^{s} a_i^2 \sum_{i=1}^{s} b_i^2} \\
& = \left(\sqrt{\sum_{i=1}^{s} a_i^2} + \sqrt{\sum_{i=1}^{s} b_i^2} \right)^2 \\
& = \left(d_{BI}^E(m_1, m_2) + d_{BI}^E(m_2, m_3) \right)^2 \\
\Rightarrow & \left(d_{BI}^E(m_1, m_2) + d_{BI}^E(m_2, m_3) \right)^2 \geq \left(d_{BI}^E(m_1, m_3) \right)^2 \\
\Rightarrow & d_{BI}^E(m_1, m_2) + d_{BI}^E(m_2, m_3) \geq d_{BI}^E(m_1, m_3)
\end{aligned} \tag{20}$$

So, the triangle inequality of d_{BI}^E is satisfied.

For d_{BI}^C, we have
$$\begin{aligned}
d_{BI}^C(m_1, m_2) + d_{BI}^C(m_2, m_3) & = \max_{i=1,...,s} a_i + \max_{i=1,...,s} b_i \\
d_{BI}^C(m_1, m_3) & = \max_{i=1,...,s} c_i = a_k + b_k, \quad k = \arg\max_{i=1,...,s} c_i
\end{aligned} \tag{21}$$

There exists
$$a_k + b_k \leq \max_{i=1,...,s} a_i + \max_{i=1,...,s} b_i = d_{BI}^C(m_1, m_2) + d_{BI}^C(m_2, m_3) \tag{22}$$

i.e., $d_{BI}^C(m_1, m_2) + d_{BI}^C(m_2, m_3) \geq d_{BI}^C(m_1, m_3)$. d_{BI}^C satisfies triangle inequality. In summary, d_{BI}^E and d_{BI}^C are strict distance metrics. □

5 Simulation Results

To verify the rationality of the proposed distances, numerical examples are provided. In each example, d_J, d_T, d_F, $d_C{}^3$, d_{BI}^E and d_{BI}^C are compared.

1) Example 1. The size of FOD is 3. We calculated the dissimilarities between $m_1(\cdot)$ and $m_i(\cdot)$, $i = 2, ..., 7$ as illustrated in Fig. 1. $m_1(\cdot)$ has relatively large mass assignment value for $\{\theta_2\}$. Therefore, intuitively, for $m_i(\cdot)$, $i = 2, ..., 7$ listed in Table 2, if the mass assignment for $\{\theta_2\}$ is relative large, the distance between $m_1(\cdot)$ and $m_i(\cdot)$ should be relatively small. As illustrated in Fig. 1, all the dissimilarities perform similarly in all seven cases, which show that they are all rational in this example. For m_5 and m_6, the mass of focal elements containing θ_2 (i.e., $\theta_1 \cup \theta_2$ and $\theta_2 \cup \theta_3$) is 0.8, it should be more rational if the distance values with respect to $m_5(\cdot)$ and $m_6(\cdot)$ decrease.

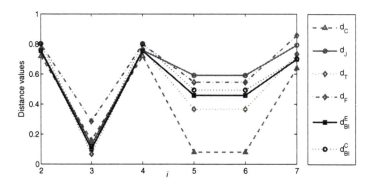

Fig. 1. Dissimilarities between m_1 and $m_i, i = 2, ..., 7$

2) Example 2 [16].

Let us define three BBAs on the FOD $\Theta = \{\theta_1, ..., \theta_n\}$ as follows:

$$m_1(\{\theta_1\}) = m_1(\{\theta_2\}) = \cdots = m_1(\{\theta_n\}) = 1/n;$$
$$m_2(\Theta) = 1;$$
$$m_3(\{\theta_k\}) = 1, \text{ for some } k \in \{1, ..., n\}.$$

---

^{3} d_C corresponds to the conflict coefficient K given by (4).

Table 1. BBA $m_1(\cdot)$

Focal element	θ_1	θ_2	θ_3	$\theta_1 \cup \theta_2$	$\theta_2 \cup \theta_3$	$\theta_1 \cup \theta_3$	$\theta_1 \cup \theta_2 \cup \theta_3$
Mass assignment	0.1	0.8	0.1	0	0	0	0

Table 2. BBAs $m_i(\cdot)$, $i = 2, \ldots, 7$

Focal el.\ BBAs	$m_2(\cdot)$	$m_3(\cdot)$	$m_4(\cdot)$	$m_5(\cdot)$	$m_6(\cdot)$	$m_7(\cdot)$
θ_1	0.8	0	0	0	0	0
θ_2	0	0.8	0	0	0	0
θ_3	0	0	0.8	0	0	0
$\theta_1 \cup \theta_2$	0	0	0	0.8	0	0
$\theta_2 \cup \theta_3$	0	0	0	0	0.8	0
$\theta_1 \cup \theta_3$	0	0	0	0	0	0.8
$\theta_1 \cup \theta_2 \cup \theta_3$	0.2	0.2	0.2	0.2	0.2	0.2

In this example, $m_3(\cdot)$ is absolutely confident in θ_k and it is significantly different from both $m_1(\cdot)$ and $m_2(\cdot)$. $m_1(\cdot)$ is rather different from $m_2(\cdot)$ even if they represent both two different uncertain sources. $m_2(\cdot)$ is actually a vacuous belief assignment representing the full ignorance. $m_1(\cdot)$ is much more specific than $m_2(\cdot)$ since it is a Bayesian belief assignment. As one sees in Fig 2, Jousselme's distance cannot discriminate well the difference between these two very different cases for dealing efficiently with the specificity of the information because $d_J(m_1, m_2) = d_J(m_1, m_3) = \sqrt{\frac{1}{2}(1 - \frac{1}{n})}$. For d_F, $d_F(m_1, m_2) = d_F(m_2, m_3)$. The discriminating ability is not so well. For Tessem's distance, one gets $d_T(m_1, m_2) = 0$ thus it cannot discriminate $m_1(\cdot)$ and $m_2(\cdot)$. d_C cannot discriminate $m_1(\cdot)$ and $m_2(\cdot)$, and also $m_2(\cdot)$ and $m_3(\cdot)$. For the new defined belief intervals-based distance of evidences can discriminate all the three BOE's pretty well as shown in Fig. 2.

3) Example 3 [16].

Let us define three BBAs on the FOD $\Theta = \{\theta_1, ..., \theta_n\}$ as follows:

$$m_1(\{\theta_1\}) = m_1(\{\theta_2\}) = m_1(\{\theta_3\}) = 1/3;$$
$$m_2(\{\theta_1\}) = m_2(\{\theta_2\}) = m_2(\{\theta_3\}) = 0.1, m_2(\Theta) = 0.7;$$
$$m_3(\{\theta_1\}) = m_3(\{\theta_2\}) = 0.1, m_2(\theta_3) = 0.8.$$

The values of the different dissimilarities between $m_1(\cdot)$ and $m_2(\cdot)$, and between $m_1(\cdot)$ and $m_3(\cdot)$ are given in Table 3.

Table 3. Example 3: Results based on different distances of evidence

Distance types	d_J	d_T	d_F	d_C	d_{BI}^E	d_{BI}^C
$d(m_1, m_2)$	0.4041	0	0.5833	0.2000	0.2858	0.2333
$d(m_1, m_3)$	0.4041	0.4667	0.6364	0.6667	0.4041	0.4667

$m_1(\cdot)$ and $m_2(\cdot)$ correspond to two very different situations in term of the specificity of their informational content. $m_3(\cdot)$ assigns its largest mass assignment to θ_3. Intuitively, it seems reasonable to consider that $m_1(\cdot)$ and $m_2(\cdot)$

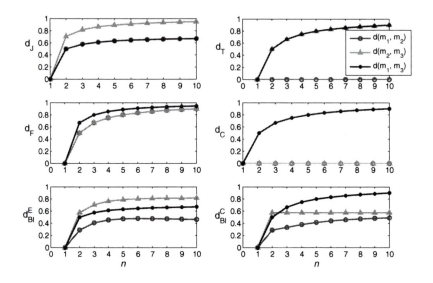

Fig. 2. Dissimilarities between $m_1(\cdot)$, $m_2(\cdot)$ and $m_3(\cdot)$ for Example 2

are closer than $m_1(\cdot)$ and $m_3(\cdot)$ since $m_1(\cdot)$ and $m_2(\cdot)$ yield the same indeterminate choice in decision-making because of the ambiguity in choice among the singletons in the FOD. Using Jousselme's distance, one obtains $d_J(m_1, m_2) = d_J(m_1, m_3) = 0.4041$ which is not very satisfactory for such a case. Based on the results of Table 3, one sees that when using d_T, d_F, d_{BI}^E and d_{BI}^C, one gets $d(m_1, m_2) < d(m_1, m_3)$ which is more reasonable. However, for Tessem's distance, one gets $d_T(m_1, m_2) = 0$ which is not rational (intuitively acceptable) or at least very questionable.

According to the above simple examples, we can see that the new defined belief intervals-based distances present an acceptable behavior with respect to other classical distances presented in this paper.

6   Conclusions

In this paper, two novel distances of evidence are proposed based on the distances between belief intervals. It is experimentally shown that our proposed distances can well describe the degree of dissimilarity between different BOEs. In future work, besides the simple examples in this paper, we will try to use a general formal property to show that our measures can satisfy a reasonable set of properties. Furthermore, we will use these new distances in different applications, like data clustering, target recognition, etc, to evaluate how they perform with respect to classical distances used so far.

Acknowledgement. This work was supported by the Grant for State Key Program for Basic Research of China (973) No. 2013CB329405, National Natural Science Foundation (No. 61104214, No. 61203222), Specialized Research Fund for the Doctoral Program of Higher Education (20120201120036), Shaanxi Province Science and Technology Research and Development Program (2013KJXX-46), and Fundamental Research Funds for the Central Universities.

References

1. Shafer, G.: A Mathematical Theory of Evidence. Princeton University Press, Princeton (1976)
2. Zadeh, L.A.: A Simple View of the Dempster-Shafer Theory of Evidence and Its Implication for the Rule of Combination. AI Magazine 7, 85–90 (1986)
3. Dezert, J., Tchamova, A.: On the Validity of Dempster's Fusion Rule and Its Interpretation as a Generalization of Bayesian Fusion Rule. Int. J. of Intelligent Systems 29, 223–252 (2014)
4. Smets, P., Kennes, R.: The Transferable Belief Model. Artificial Intelligence 66, 191–234 (1994)
5. Smarandache, F., Dezert, J. (eds.): Applications and Advances of DSmT for Information Fusion, vol. III. American Research Press, Rehoboth (2009)
6. Jousselme, A.-L., Maupin, P.: Distances in Evidence Theory: Comprehensive Survey and Generalizations. Int. J. of Approximate Reasoning 5, 118–145 (2012)
7. Cuzzolin, F.: Lp Consonant Approximations of Belief Functions. IEEE Trans. on Fuzzy Systems 22, 420–436 (2014)
8. Cuzzolin, F.: Two New Bayesian Approximations of Belief Functions Based on Convex Geometry. IEEE Trans. on SMC - part B 37, 993–1008 (2007)
9. Jousselme, A.-L., Grenier, D., Bossé, E.: A New Distance between Two Bodies of Evidence. Information Fusion 2, 91–101 (2001)
10. Tessem, B.: Approximations for Efficient Computation in the Theory of Evidence. Artificial Intelligence 61, 315–329 (1993)
11. Han, D.Q., Dezert, J., Han, C.Z., et al.: New Dissimilarity Measures in Evidence Theory. In: Proc. of the 14th Int. Conf. on Information Fusion, Chicago, USA, pp. 483–489 (2011)
12. Irpino, A., Verde, R.: Dynamic Clustering of Interval Data Using a Wasserstein-based Distance. Pattern Recognition Letters 29, 1648–1658 (2008)
13. Cuzzolin, F.: A Geometric Approach to the Theory of Evidence. IEEE Trans. on SMC - Part C 38, 522–534 (2008)
14. Bouchard, M., Jousselme, A.-L., Doré, P.-E.: A Proof for the Positive Definiteness of the Jaccard Index Matrix. Int. J. of Approximate Reasoning 54, 615–626 (2013)
15. Han, D.Q., Deng, Y., Han, C.Z., et al.: Some Notes on Betting Commitment Distance in Evidence Theory. Science China - Information Sciences 55, 558–565 (2012)
16. Liu, Z.G., Dezert, J., Pan, Q.: A New Measure of Dissimilarity between Two Basic Belief Assignments (2010),
http://hal.archives-ouvertes.fr/docs/00/48/80/45/PDF/
DissimilarityV8.pdf

Author Index